Lecture Notes in Computer Science 1070
Edited by G. Goos, J. Hartmanis and J. van Leeuwen

Springer
Berlin
Heidelberg
New York
Barcelona
Budapest
Hong Kong
London
Milan
Paris
Santa Clara
Singapore
Tokyo

Ueli Maurer (Ed.)

Advances in Cryptology – EUROCRYPT '96

International Conference on the Theory
and Application of Cryptographic Techniques
Saragossa, Spain, May 12-16, 1996
Proceedings

Springer

Volume Editor

Ueli Maurer
Swiss Federal Institute of Technology (ETH)
Department of Computer Science
CH-8092 Zürich, Switzerland

Cataloging-in-Publication data applied for

Die Deutsche Bibliothek - CIP-Einheitsaufnahme

Advances in cryptology : proceedings / EUROCRYPT '96, International Conference on the Theory and Application of Cryptographic Techniques, Saragossa, Spain, May 12 - 16, 1996. Ueli Maurer (ed.). - Berlin ; Heidelberg ; New York ; Barcelona ; Budapest ; Hong Kong ; London ; Milan ; Paris ; Santa Clara ; Singapore ; Tokyo : Springer, 1996
(Lecture notes in computer science ; Vol. 1070)
ISBN 3-540-61186-X
NE: Maurer, Ueli [Hrsg.]; EUROCRYPT <14, 1996, Zaragoza>; GT

CR Subject Classification (1991): E.3-4, G.2.1, D.4.6,F.2.1-2, C.2, J.1

1991 Mathematics Subject Classification: 94A60,11T71, 11Yxx, 68P20, 68Q20, 68Q25

ISBN 3-540-61186-X Springer-Verlag Berlin Heidelberg New York

Typesetting: Camera-ready by author
SPIN 10512863 06/3142 – 5 4 3 2 1 0 Printed on acid-free paper

PREFACE

The EUROCRYPT '96 conference was sponsored by the International Association for Cryptologic Research (IACR)[1], in cooperation with the University of Saragossa. It took place at the Palacio de Congresos in Saragossa, Spain, during May 12–16, 1996. This was the fifteenth annual EUROCRYPT conference (this name has been used since the third conference held in 1984), each of which has been held in a different city in Europe. For the second time, proceedings were available at the conference. José Pastor Franco, the General Chair, was responsible for local organization and registration. His contribution to the success of the conference is gratefully acknowledged.

The Program Committee considered 126 submitted papers and selected 34 for presentation. Each paper was sent to all members of the Program Committee and was assigned to at least three of them for careful evaluation. There were also two invited talks. James L. Massey, this year's IACR Distinguished Lecturer, gave a lecture entitled "The difficulty with difficulty". Massey is the third to receive this honor, the first two being Gustavus Simmons and Adi Shamir. Shafi Goldwasser gave an invited talk entitled "Multi party secure protocols: past and present".

These proceedings contain revised versions of the 34 contributed talks. While the papers were carefully selected, they have not been refereed like submissions to a refereed journal. The authors bear full responsibility for the contents of their papers. Some authors may write final versions of their papers for publication in a refereed journal.

I am very grateful to the members of the Program Committee for generously spending much of their time on the difficult task of selecting the papers to be presented at the conference. Following recent tradition, the submissions were anonymous. Each committee member could be an author of at most one accepted paper.

The help of the following referees and external experts in evaluating various papers is gratefully acknowledged: Philippe Béguin, Matt Blaze, Daniel Bleichenbacher, Bert den Boer, Antoon Bosselaers, Jørgen Brandt, Gilles Brassard, Christian Cachin, Jan Camenisch, Ran Canetti, Florent Chabaud, Ronald Cramer, Scott Decatur, Markus Dichtl, Marten van Dijk, Jan-Hendrik Evertse, Joan Feigenbaum, Eiichiro Fujisaki, Rosario Gennaro, Jean Geordiades, Jeroen van de Graaf, Louis Granboulan, Shai Halevi, Erwin Hess, Martin Hirt, Nobuyuki Imoto, David-Olivier Jaquet-Chiffelle, Stasio Jarecki, Mike Just, Gregory Kabatianski, Volker Kessler, Lars Knudsen, Jack Lacy, Françoise Levy-dit-Vehel, Mitsuru Matsui, Willi Meier, J. Merkle, Kazuo Ohta, Torben Pedersen, David Pointcheval, Mike Reiter, Vincent Rijmen, Kazue Sako, Berry Schoenmakers,

[1] The main purpose of the IACR is to sponsor two annual conferences: CRYPTO, every summer at the University of California, Santa Barbara (UCSB), and EUROCRYPT, every spring in a different European country. The IACR also publishes the Journal of Cryptology.

Peter Schweitzer, J. P. Seifert, Peter Shor, Markus Stadler, Jacques Stern, Ramarathnam Venkatesan, Stefan Wolf, Aaron Wyner, and Hirosuke Yamamoto. I apologize for possible omissions.

Special thanks go to Martin Hirt for his help with the organization of the committee's work and with the preparation of the proceedings. Martin Burkart provided help with software for automatically handling correspondence with authors. Don Coppersmith, Louis Guillou, Kevin McCurley, and Jean-Jacques Quisquater gave advice for the organization of the committee's work. Louis provided LaTeX files for preparing parts of these proceedings.

Finally, I would like to thank all who have submitted papers to EUROCRYPT '96 and to the authors of accepted papers for their cooperation.

March 1996 Ueli Maurer

EUROCRYPT '96

Saragossa, Spain
May 12–16, 1996

Sponsored by the

International Association for Cryptologic Research (IACR)

in cooperation with the

University of Saragossa, Spain

General Chairman

Jose Pastor Franco, University of Saragossa, Spain

Program Chairman

Ueli Maurer, ETH Zürich, Switzerland

Program Committee

Stefan Brands	CWI, The Netherlands
Claude Crépeau	University of Montréal, Canada
Ivan Damgård	Aarhus University, Denmark
Josep Domingo	Universitat Rovira i Virgili, Spain
Walter Fumy	Siemens, Germany
Jovan Dj. Golić	QUT, Australia
Arjen K. Lenstra	Bellcore, USA
David Naccache	Gemplus, France
Andrew M. Odlyzko	AT&T Bell Labs., USA
Tatsuaki Okamoto	NIT Labs., Japan
Jean-Marc Piveteau	UBILAB, Switzerland
Bart Preneel	K. U. Leuven, Belgium
Ronald Rivest	MIT, USA
Claus P. Schnorr	University of Frankfurt, Germany
Othmar Staffelbach	Federal Cryptology Section, Switzerland
Serge Vaudenay	ENS, France

CONTENTS

Cryptanalysis I

Low-exponent RSA with related messages 1

Don Coppersmith (IBM T. J. Watson, USA), Matthew Franklin (AT&T Research, USA), Jacques Patarin (CP8 Transac, France), Michael Reiter (AT&T Research, USA)

Generating ElGamal signatures without knowing the secret key 10

Daniel Bleichenbacher (ETH Zürich, Switzerland)

On the security of two MAC algorithms 19

Bart Preneel (K. U. Leuven, Belgium), Paul C. van Oorschot (Bell-Northern Research, Canada)

Public Key Cryptosystems

Hidden fields equations (HFE) and isomorphisms of polynomials (IP): two new families of asymmetric algorithms 33

Jacques Patarin (CP8 Transac, France)

A public key cryptosystem based on elliptic curves over $\mathbb{Z}/n\mathbb{Z}$ equivalent to factoring 49

Bernd Meyer (Universität des Saarlandes, Germany), Volker Müller (University of Waterloo, Canada)

Public key encryption and signature schemes based on polynominals over $\mathbb{Z}_n$ 60

Jörg Schwenk (Deutsche Telekom AG, Germany), Jörg Eisfeld (University of Giessen, Germany)

New Schemes and Protocols

Multi-authority secret-ballot elections with linear work 72

Ronald Cramer (CWI, The Netherlands), Matthew Franklin (AT&T Bell Labs., USA), Berry Schoenmakers (DigiCash, The Netherlands), Moti Yung (IBM T. J. Watson, USA)

Asymmetric fingerprinting 84
Birgit Pfitzmann, Matthias Schunter (University of Hildesheim, Germany)

Multi-Party Computation

Homomorphisms of secret sharing schemes: a tool for verifiable signature sharing 96
Mike Burmester (Royal Holloway, England)

Efficient multiplicative sharing schemes 107
Simon R. Blackburn, Mike Burmester (Royal Holloway, England), Yvo Desmedt (University of Wisconsin, USA), Peter R. Wild (Royal Holloway, England)

Equivocable oblivious transfer 119
Donald Beaver (Transarc, USA)

Proofs of Knowledge

Short discreet proofs 131
Joan Boyar (Odense University, Denmark), René Peralta (JAIST, Japan)

Designated verifier proofs and their applications 143
Markus Jakobsson (UC San Diego, USA), Kazue Sako (NEC, Japan), Russell Impagliazzo (UC San Diego, USA)

Number Theory and Algorithms

Finding a small root of a univariate modular equation 155
Don Coppersmith (IBM T. J. Watson, USA)

New modular multiplication algorithms for fast modular exponentiation 166
Seong-Min Hong, Sang-Yeop Oh, Hyunsoo Yoon (KAIST, Korea)

Finding a small root of a bivariate integer equation; factoring with high bits known 178
Don Coppersmith (IBM T. J. Watson, USA)

Secret Sharing

Publicly verifiable secret sharing 190
Markus Stadler (ETH Zürich, Switzerland)

Optimum secret sharing scheme secure against cheating 200
Wakaha Ogata (Himeji Institute of Technology, Japan), Kaoru Kurosawa (Tokyo Institute of Technology, Japan)

Cryptanalysis II

The security of the Gabidulin public key cryptosystem 212
Keith Gibson (Birkbeck College, England)

Non-linear approximations in linear cryptanalysis 224
Lars R. Knudsen (K. U. Leuven, Belgium), Matthew J. B. Robshaw (RSA Laboratories, USA)

On the difficulty of software key escrow 237
Lars R. Knudsen (K. U. Leuven, Belgium), Torben P. Pedersen (Cryptomathic, Denmark)

Pseudorandomness

An efficient pseudo-random generator provably as secure as syndrome decoding 245
Jean-Bernard Fischer (Thomson, France), Jacques Stern (ENS, France)

On the existence of secure feedback registers 256
Andrew Klapper (University of Kentucky, USA)

Cryptographic Functions

Fast low order approximation of cryptographic functions 268
Jovan Dj. Golić (QUT, Australia)

Construction of t-resilient functions over a finite alphabet 283
Paul Camion, Anne Canteaut (INRIA, France)

Auto-correlations and new bounds on the nonlinearity of Boolean functions 294
Xian-Mo Zhang (University of Wollongong, Australia), Yuliang Zheng (Monash University, Australia)

Foiling birthday attacks in length-doubling transformations 307
William Aiello, Ramarathnam Venkatesan (Bellcore, USA)

Key Management and Identification Schemes

Session key distribution using smart cards 321
Victor Shoup, Avi Rubin (Bellcore, USA)

On Diffie-Hellman key agreement with short exponents 332
Paul C. van Oorschot, Michael J. Wiener (Bell-Northern Research, Canada)

On the security of a practical identification scheme 344
Victor Shoup (Bellcore, USA)

Digital Signature Schemes

Robust threshold DSS signatures 354
Rosario Gennaro, Stanislaw Jarecki (MIT, USA), Hugo Krawczyk (IBM T. J. Watson, USA), Tal Rabin (MIT, USA)

New convertible undeniable signature schemes 372
Ivan Damgård (Aarhus University, Denmark), Torben P. Pedersen (Cryptomathic, Denmark)

Security proofs for signature schemes 387
David Pointcheval, Jacques Stern (ENS, France)

The exact security of digital signatures — how to sign with RSA and Rabin 399
Mihir Bellare (UC San Diego, USA), Phillip Rogaway (UC Davis, USA)

Author Index 417

Low-Exponent RSA with Related Messages

Don Coppersmith* Matthew Franklin** Jacques Patarin*** Michael Reiter†

Abstract. In this paper we present a new class of attacks against RSA with low encrypting exponent. The attacks enable the recovery of plaintext messages from their ciphertexts and a known polynomial relationship among the messages, provided that the ciphertexts were created using the same RSA public key with low encrypting exponent.

1 Introduction

In this paper we present a new class of attacks against RSA [8] with low encrypting exponent. The attacks enable the recovery of plaintext messages from their ciphertexts and a known polynomial relationship among the messages, provided that the ciphertexts were created using the same RSA public key with low encrypting exponent. Our attacks differ from the low-exponent attacks described by Moore [6] and Hastad [5] and the common modulus attack identified by Simmons [10], which pertain only to ciphertexts encrypted under *different* public keys.

Given encryptions of k messages under the same RSA public key with exponent e, together with knowledge of a polynomial relation of degree δ among the messages, the goal of the attacks is to recover all messages. Our results were influenced by an attack presented by Franklin and Reiter [4] for the case $k = 2$, $e = 3$, $\delta = 1$. Starting with this case, we generalize the exponent e in Section 2, the degree δ in Section 3, and the number of messages k in Section 4. Implications of the attack are considered in Section 5.

2 Generalizing the exponent e

Suppose we have two messages m_1 and m_2 related by a known affine relation

$$m_2 = \alpha m_1 + \beta.$$

Suppose further that the messages are encrypted under RSA with an exponent of 3 using a single public modulus N.

$$c_i = m_i^3 \bmod N, \quad i = 1, 2$$

* IBM Research, Yorktown Heights, NY, USA; copper@watson.ibm.com
** AT&T Research, Murray Hill, NJ, USA; franklin@research.att.com
*** CP8 Transac, Louveciennes, France; patarin@hades.inria.fr
† AT&T Research, Murray Hill, NJ, USA; reiter@research.att.com

Ueli Maurer (Ed.): EUROCRYPT '96 Proceedings, LNCS 1070

Then from

$$c_1, c_2, \alpha, \beta, N$$

we can calculate the secret messages m_i algebraically as follows:

$$\frac{\beta(c_2 + 2\alpha^3 c_1 - \beta^3)}{\alpha(c_2 - \alpha^3 c_1 + 2\beta^3)} = \frac{3\alpha^3\beta m_1^3 + 3\alpha^2\beta^2 m_1^2 + 3\alpha\beta^3 m_1}{3\alpha^3\beta m_1^2 + 3\alpha^2\beta^2 m_1 + 3\alpha\beta^3} = m_1 \bmod N.$$

The algebra is more transparent if we assume (without loss of generality) that $\alpha = \beta = 1$.

$$\frac{(m+1)^3 + 2m^3 - 1}{(m+1)^3 - m^3 + 2} = \frac{3m^3 + 3m^2 + 3m}{3m^2 + 3m + 3} = m \bmod N. \tag{1}$$

So if the RSA exponent is $e = 3$ and we have $k = 2$ messages, satisfying a known polynomial relation of degree $\delta = 1$, we can recover the messages m_i algebraically from the ciphertexts and the coefficients of the polynomial relation.

When $e = 5$, setting $c_1 = m^5 \bmod N$ and $c_2 = (m+1)^5 \bmod N$, we can find

$$P(m) = c_2^3 - 3c_1c_2^2 + 3c_1^2c_2 - c_1^3 + 37c_2^2 + 176c_1c_2 + 37c_1^2 + 73c_2 - 73c_1 + 14$$
$$mP(m) = 2c_2^3 - 1c_1c_2^2 - 4c_1^2c_2 + 3c_1^3 + 14c_2^2 - 88c_1c_2 - 51c_1^2 - 9c_2 + 64c_1 - 7$$
$$m = \frac{mP(m)}{P(m)}$$

For an arbitrary exponent e in the case of $k = 2$ messages subject to a linear relation, it will always be possible to write down an equation analogous to (1). Specifically, there will exist polynomials $P(m)$ and $Q(m)$ such that each can be expressed as rational polynomials in m^e and $(m+1)^e$, and such that $Q(m) = mP(m)$. Already for $e = 5$, however, this is fairly complicated. As e grows, this explicit expression of m as a ratio of two polynomials in c_1 and c_2 requires $\Theta(e^2)$ coefficients, and it is not immediately obvious how to calculate these coefficients efficiently.

Fortunately there is an easier method. Let z denote the unknown message m. Then z satisfies the following two polynomial relations:

$$z^5 - c_1 = 0 \bmod N$$
$$(z+1)^5 - c_2 = 0 \bmod N.$$

where the c_i are treated as known constants. Apply the Euclidean algorithm to find the greatest common divisor of these two univariate polynomials over the ring $\mathbf{Z}/N$:

$$\gcd(z^5 - c_1, (z+1)^5 - c_2) \in \mathbf{Z}/N[z].$$

This should yield the linear polynomial $z - m$ (except possibly in rare cases[1]).

[1] We do not fully understand the cases $m = (1 - \omega^j)/(\omega - 1) \in \mathbf{Z}/p, 2 \le j \le e-1$, where p is a prime factor of N and ω is a primitive eth root of 1 in some extension of $\mathbf{Z}/p$. This condition seems to imply that $e|p-1$, in contradiction to the RSA requirement $\gcd(e, p-1) = 1$, but work needs to be done to verify this. Other than these at most $(e-1)(e-2)$ possible exceptions, the gcd will in fact be linear.

The attack applies for any value of e, but is limited by the cost of computing the gcd of two polynomials of degree e. A straightforward implementation of Euclid's algorithm takes $O(e^2)$ operations in the ring $\mathbf{Z}/N$. More sophisticated techniques can be used to compute the gcd in $O(e \log^2 e)$ time [12]. Using these methods, the attack may be practical for all exponents of length up to around 32 bits. For example, the attack will be very efficient against $e = 2^{16}+1$, a popular choice in many applications.

3 Generalizing the degree δ of the polynomial

One generalization is immediate. Suppose we have two messages m_1, m_2 satisfying a known polynomial relation of the form

$$m_2 = p(m_1), \qquad \deg(p) = \delta,$$

and we know p and the two ciphertexts c_i. Then as before, the two equations

$$\begin{aligned} z^e - c_1 &= 0 \bmod N \\ (p(z))^e - c_2 &= 0 \bmod N \end{aligned}$$

are both satisfied by $z = m_1 \bmod N$ so that

$$\gcd(z^e - c_1, (p(z))^e - c_2) \in \mathbf{Z}/N[z]$$

will be divisible by $z - m_1$, and except in rare cases we will have

$$\gcd(z^e - c_1, (p(z))^e - c_2) = z - m_1.$$

(One of the exceptional cases, in which this procedure fails, is when $p(z)$ is of the form $p(z) = z^h q(z^e)$, because then the ciphertext c_2 is easily derived from the ciphertext c_1, namely

$$c_2 = c_1^h (q(c_1))^e,$$

and we gain no new information.)

What if m_1 and m_2 satisfy an *implicit* polynomial relation?

$$p(m_1, m_2) = 0 \bmod N$$

In this case we have three polynomials relating two unknowns mod$N$:

$$\begin{aligned} P_1 &= p(m_1, m_2) &&= 0 \bmod N \\ P_2 &= m_1^e - c_1 &&= 0 \bmod N \\ P_3 &= m_2^e - c_2 &&= 0 \bmod N \end{aligned}$$

Now we need another algebraic tool: the resultant. The resultant of two multivariate polynomials, with respect to one of their variables x, is a third multivariate polynomial, in all the variables except the special variable x. For any setting of all the variables (including x) for which the two input polynomials are simultaneously 0, the resultant is also 0. This gives us a means of eliminating x from a system of equations.

In the example above, substitute x and y for the unknowns m_1 and m_2, respectively. We can take the resultant of $P_1(x,y)$ and $P_2(x)$ with respect to the variable x, over the ring $\mathbf{Z}/N$. This will yield a polynomial P_4 in y, whose degree is at most δe (the product of the total degrees of the original polynomials). Then we can take the gcd of this new polynomial P_4 with P_3 (as univariate polynomials in y over $\mathbf{Z}/N$) to yield (hopefully) the linear polynomial $y - m_2$. Substitute this value of m_2 which we have discovered, back into P_1, to find a polynomial in x alone, which we can combine with P_2 by the gcd to find the correct value of $x = m_1$. The complexity of this attack is dominated by the computation of the resultant, i.e., the determinant of a $(\delta + e) \times (\delta + e)$ matrix whose elements are univariate polynomials of degree δ. This can naively be done in $O((\delta + e)^3 \delta^2)$ operations.

The two operations, resultant and gcd, can be combined under the general heading of "Groebner basis." Indeed, fixing the coefficients of p and the ciphertexts c_i as constants, and computing the Groebner basis of $P_1(x,y), P_2(x), P_3(y)$, as polynomials over $\mathbf{Z}/N$, will generally produce the result $[(x - m_1), (y - m_2)]$. In this paper, however, we work explicitly with the resultant and gcd, in order to better estimate the complexity of the attacks.

4 Generalizing the number of messages k

4.1 Arbitrary polynomial relationship among messages

Suppose we have k messages $m_1, \ldots, m_k$, related by a polynomial $p(m_1, \ldots, m_k)$, and that we know the ciphertexts $c_i = m_i^e \bmod N$ and the coefficients of the polynomial p. As before, substitute variables x_i for the unknown messages m_i, and obtain the $k+1$ polynomials

$$\begin{aligned}
P_0(x_1, \ldots, x_k) &= p(x_1, \ldots, x_k) &&= 0 \bmod N \\
P_1(x_1) &= \quad x_1^e - c_1 &&= 0 \bmod N \\
P_2(x_2) &= \quad x_2^e - c_2 &&= 0 \bmod N \\
&\ldots \\
P_i(x_i) &= \quad x_i^e - c_i &&= 0 \bmod N \\
&\ldots \\
P_k(x_k) &= \quad x_k^e - c_k &&= 0 \bmod N
\end{aligned}$$

which must be simultaneously satisfied. We can just compute

$$\text{Groebner}([P_0, P_1, \ldots, P_k])$$

and generally obtain the answer

$$[x_1 - m_1, \ldots, x_k - m_k].$$

Or, more explicitly, we can set

$$Q_0(x_1, \ldots, x_k) = P_0$$

and iteratively evaluate

$$Q_i(x_{i+1}, \ldots, x_k) = \text{Resultant}_{x_i}(Q_{i-1}, P_i)$$

until we find

$$Q_{k-1}(x_k).$$

Then evaluating

$$\gcd(Q_{k-1}(x_k), P_k(x_k))$$

we hope to find the linear polynomial $(x_k - m_k)$, from which we discover m_k. Finally, repeatedly back substitute:

$$\gcd(P_i(x_i), Q_{i-1}(x_i, m_{i+1}, m_{i+2}, \ldots, m_k)) = (x_i - m_i),$$

as i goes from $k-1$ to 1, to find all the messages m_i.

The complexity of this general attack is dominated by the computation of the resultants $Q_1, \ldots, Q_{k-1}$. Each Q_i is a polynomial of total degree $e^i\delta$, in $k-i$ variables. The number of monomial terms in each Q_i is potentially as large as $\Theta(\delta^{k/2}e^{k^2/4})$. Thus, this attack may require $\delta^{\Theta(k)}e^{\Theta(k^2)}$ operations over $\mathbf{Z}/N$.

4.2 A special case: linearly related messages

As will be seen in Section 5.2, a special case of interest is that in which $P_0 = p$ is linear, say

$$p(x_1, \ldots, x_k) = x_1 + x_2 + \ldots + x_k - w$$

with w some known constant. The special form of p allows us to make the computations more efficient. In addition, the success of the attack differs depending on whether w is zero or nonzero.

Inhomogeneous case. In the inhomogeneous case $w \neq 0$, the attack proceeds as follows. Introduce unknowns

$$y_i = x_1 + x_2 + \ldots + x_i = w - x_k - x_{k-1} - \ldots - x_{i+1}$$

satisfying

$$y_{i-1} = y_i - x_i$$
$$y_{i+1} = y_i + x_{i+1}$$

Set $h = \lfloor k/2 \rfloor$. Introduce polynomials:

$$R_1(y_1) = P_1(y_1)$$
$$R_i(y_i) = \text{Resultant}_{x_i}(R_{i-1}(y_i - x_i), P_i(x_i)), \quad i = 1, 2, \ldots, h$$
$$S_{k-1}(y_{k-1}) = P_k(w - y_{k-1})$$
$$S_i(y_i) = \text{Resultant}_{x_i}(S_{i+1}(y_i + x_{i+1}), P_{i+1}(x_{i+1})), \quad i = k-2, k-3, \ldots, h$$

Both $R_h(y_h)$ and $S_h(y_h)$ are univariate polynomials in y_h. Their gcd will hopefully be the linear polynomial

$$y_h - (m_1 + m_2 + \ldots + m_h)$$

and we can proceed from there by divide-and-conquer.

A shortcut to computing each $R_i(y_i)$ is to evaluate $R_{i-1}(y_i - x_i)$ by Horner's rule, replacing each occurrence of x_i^e by c_i. The complexity of the attack is dominated by the complexity of computing $\gcd(R_h(y_h), S_h(y_h))$. This is $O(e^{k/2}k^2)$ since the degrees of R_h and S_h are both $\Theta(e^{k/2})$.

Homogeneous case. A difficulty arises in the homogeneous case $w = 0$. Because P_0 is homogeneous, and all the other polynomials are of the form $x^e - c$, given any solution $(x_1, x_2, \ldots, x_k)$ and any eth root of unity ϕ, the tuple $(\phi x_1, \phi x_2, \ldots, \phi x_k)$ is also a solution of all the P_i. Thus the attacker cannot solve for the individual x_i; the most it can hope for is to be able to solve for all homogeneous polynomials of degree e in the x_i. In particular, when the attacker attempts to compute y_h, the gcd yields at best something like

$$y_h^e - (m_1 + m_2 + \ldots + m_h)^e$$

rather than the desired linear polynomial. This is an inherent difficulty in our approach, and has a bearing on the application described in Section 5.2.

However, there are occasions when the attack succeeds even in the homogeneous case. For example, suppose

$$\begin{aligned} m_1 &= (m + \lambda_1 \beta) \bmod N \\ m_2 &= (m + \lambda_2 \beta) \bmod N \\ m_3 &= (m + \lambda_3 \beta) \bmod N \end{aligned}$$

where $\lambda_1, \lambda_2, \lambda_3$ are known, while m, β are unknown, and $e = 3$. Further suppose that β is known to satisfy $\beta^3 < N$. This is a homogeneous case, because the three plaintexts are known to satisfy the linear relation

$$(\lambda_3 - \lambda_2)m_1 + (\lambda_1 - \lambda_3)m_2 + (\lambda_2 - \lambda_1)m_3 = 0 \bmod N.$$

From the three ciphertexts $c_i = m_i^3 \bmod N$ and the three coefficients $\lambda_1, \lambda_2, \lambda_3$, it is possible to solve for $B = \beta^3 \bmod N$: e.g., $B - \beta^3 = \gcd(f, g)$, where

$$\begin{aligned} f &= \mathrm{Resultant}_m((m + \lambda_1 \beta)^3 - c_1, (m + \lambda_2 \beta)^3 - c_2) \\ g &= \mathrm{Resultant}_m((m + \lambda_1 \beta)^3 - c_1, (m + \lambda_3 \beta)^3 - c_3) \end{aligned}$$

Then β can be recovered by computing the real cube root of B (i.e., without modular reduction), from which m can be recovered using previous techniques.

5 Implications

Due to the widespread popularity of RSA with low encrypting exponent, our attacks potentially have implications to the security of a wide range of current and future cryptographic protocols. In this section we show how our attacks reveal vulnerabilities in two protocols.

5.1 The TMN protocol

In [13], Tatebayashi, Matsuzaki and Newman proposed a key distribution protocol. In this protocol, a passive eavesdropper sees $r_1^e \bmod N$, $r_2^e \bmod N$, and $r_1 + r_2 \bmod N$ exchanged among the protocol participants, where $e = 3$ and r_1, r_2 are randomly generated values. The techniques of the previous sections enable a passive eavesdropper to learn the shared session key r_2 distributed in the protocol.

Simmons [11] previously found an *active* attack on this scheme (requiring two conspirators), for which three counter measures were suggested in [13]. The first two countermeasures—incorporating structure into r_1 and r_2, and prepending timestamps to r_1 and r_2—do not prevent our passive attack. The third, which assumes a shared secret key between the server and each party, appears to withstand our attack. Park et. al. [7] exploited the use of $e = 3$ in TMN to show that after the same two parties exchange a session key three times, each has enough information to impersonate the other in future protocol executions. In contrast, our attack enables any eavesdropper to recover the session key exchanged in any run of the protocol. Nevertheless, our attack does not immediately apply to the fix proposed in [7].

5.2 Verifiable signature sharing

In [3], Franklin and Reiter presented a scheme to efficiently share an RSA signature of a known message among $n \geq 5t + 1$ servers so that the servers could verify the signature relation, despite the malicious misbehavior of up to t of the servers. As part of this protocol, the holder of the signature shares the signature using Shamir's secret sharing scheme [9], i.e., by choosing at random a univariate polynomial

$$B(x) = \sum_{j=0}^{t} b_j x^j$$

over $\mathbf{Z}/N$ such that b_0 is the secret signature, and privately sending the share $B(i)$ to the i-th server for $1 \leq i \leq n$. The intention is to ensure that a subset of $t+1$ servers can use their shares to recover B (by Lagrange interpolation), but to prevent t or fewer malicious servers from doing so. However, the holder of the signature also publishes the RSA encryption of each share under the same RSA public key with exponent $e = 3$, i.e., $\{B(i)^e \bmod N\}_{1 \leq i \leq n}$.

The techniques of this paper enable one server S_{i_0}, knowing its share $B(i_0)$ and the ciphertexts $B(i_1)^e \bmod N, \ldots, B(i_k)^e \bmod N$ of at least $k = t+1$ other shares (i.e., $i_0 \neq i_j$ for any $1 \leq j \leq k$), to compute the secret polynomial B. Specifically, because the shares $B(i_0), \ldots, B(i_k)$ are linear combinations of the unknowns b_j with known coefficients, S_{i_0} can compute a linear relation that holds among the shares:

$$\sum_{j=0}^{k} p_j B(i_j) = 0 \bmod N. \tag{2}$$

Since server S_{i_0} knows $p_0 B(i_0)$, which is nonzero with high probability, it can learn an inhomogeneous linear relation among the other k terms $\{p_j B(i_j)\}_{1 \leq j \leq k}$:

$$\sum_{j=1}^{k} p_j B(i_j) = -p_0 B(i_0) \bmod N.$$

Using this information, and the easily computable ciphertext $p_j^e B(i_j)^e \bmod N$ of each term, it can use the techniques described before to recover each term $p_j B(i_j)$ and hence $B(i_j)$. Using Lagrange interpolation, it can then recover the secret polynomial B and the signature b_0.

It is interesting to note that this attack fails for a passive eavesdropper that is not one of the n servers. Such an eavesdropper sees only the published RSA encryptions of each share, i.e., $\{B(i)^e \bmod N\}_{1 \leq i \leq n}$. The eavesdropper can again find a linear equation of the form (2) among any $k+1$ of the shares. However, since this equation is homogeneous, it can recover only homogeneous polynomials of degree e in the terms $p_j B(i_j)$ (see Section 4.2).

6 Conclusion

We have identified a new class attacks against RSA with low encrypting exponent, which exploit known polynomial relationships among the encrypted messages. This can lead to weaknesses in protocols for which such relationships can be inferred. When the relationships are essential to the correctness of a protocol, as in the case of Section 5.2, the only repair seems to be increasing the size of the encrypting exponent. If the polynomial relationships are not essential, then another repair might be to transform the plaintexts so that those relationships no longer hold. Possible transformations are applying a public permutation, such as DES with a fixed key, or padding the plaintext with random bits (though this may not always suffice; see [2]). Such transformations are discussed, e.g., in [1].

References

1. M. Bellare and P. Rogaway. Optimal asymmetric encryption. In *Advances in Cryptology—EUROCRYPT '94* (Lecture Notes in Computer Science 950), A. De Santis, Ed. 1995, pp. 92–111, Springer-Verlag.
2. D. Coppersmith. Finding a small root of a univariate modular equation. In *Advances in Cryptology—EUROCRYPT '96*, U. Maurer, Ed. 1996, Springer-Verlag.

3. M. K. Franklin and M. K. Reiter. Verifiable signature sharing. In *Advances in Cryptology—EUROCRYPT '95* (Lecture Notes in Computer Science 921), L. C. Guillou and J. Quisquater, Eds. 1995, pp. 50–63, Springer-Verlag.
4. M. K. Franklin and M. K. Reiter. A linear protocol failure for RSA with exponent three. Presented at the CRYPTO '95 Rump Session, Aug. 1995.
5. J. Hastad. Solving simultaneous modular equations of low degree. *SIAM Journal of Computing* 17:336–341, 1988.
6. J. H. Moore. Protocol failures in cryptosystems. *Proceedings of the IEEE* 76(5), May 1988.
7. C. Park, K. Kurosawa, T. Okamoto, and S. Tsujii. On key distribution and authentication in mobile radio networks. In *Advances in Cryptology—EUROCRYPT '93* (Lecture Notes in Computer Science 765), T. Helleseth, Ed. 1994, pp. 461–465, Springer-Verlag.
8. R. L. Rivest, A. Shamir and L. Adleman. A method for obtaining digital signatures and public-key cryptosystems. *Communications of the ACM* 21(2):120–126, Feb. 1978.
9. A. Shamir. How to share a secret. *Communications of the ACM* 22(11):612–613, Nov. 1979.
10. G. Simmons. A "weak" privacy protocol using the RSA cryptoalgorithm. *Cryptologia* 7:180–182, 1983.
11. G. Simmons. Proof of soundness (integrity) of cryptographic protocols. *Journal of Cryptology* 7:69–77, 1994.
12. V. Strassen. The computational complexity of continued fractions. *SIAM Journal of Computing* 12(1):1–27, 1983.
13. M. Tatebayashi and N. Matsuzakai and D. B. Newman. Key distribution protocol for digital mobile communication systems. In *Advances in Cryptology—CRYPTO '89* (Lecture Notes in Computer Science 435), G. Brassard, Ed. 1990, pp. 324–333, Springer-Verlag.

Generating ElGamal Signatures Without Knowing the Secret Key

Daniel Bleichenbacher

ETH Zürich
Institute for Theoretical Computer Science
CH-8092 Zürich, Switzerland
email: bleichen@inf.ethz.ch

Abstract. We present a new method to forge ElGamal signatures if the public parameters of the system are not chosen properly. Since the secret key is hereby not found this attack shows that forging ElGamal signatures is sometimes easier than the underlying discrete logarithm problem.

1 Introduction

ElGamal's digital signature scheme [4] relies on the difficulty of computing discrete logarithm in the multiplicative group $\mathbb{F}_p^*$ and can therefore be broken if the computation of discrete logarithms is feasible. However, the converse has never been proved. In this paper we show that it is sometimes possible to forge signatures without breaking the underlying discrete logarithm problem. This shows that the ElGamal signature scheme and some variants of the scheme must be used very carefully.

The paper is organized as follows. Section 2 describes the ElGamal signature scheme. In Section 3 we present a method to forge signatures if some additional information on the generator is known. We show that signatures can be forged if the generator α is smooth and divides $p-1$. Hence for example $\alpha = 2$ is a totally insecure choice. In Section 4 we discuss the case where the public parameters are not chosen by the user itself. The authority that chooses these parameters may generate some trapdoor information, which will allow it to sign arbitrary messages for any user. Section 5 contains a brief description of some possible countermeasures. In Section 6 we discuss a variant of the ElGamal scheme over $\mathbb{Z}/n\mathbb{Z}$ with $n = pq$, which was believed to be as hard as factoring and computing discrete logarithms. However, the factorization of n can often be derived from known signatures. Moreover, we show that in this case computation in only one of the groups $\mathbb{F}_p^*$ or $\mathbb{F}_q^*$ is sufficient to forge signatures. Again it is not necessary to discover the complete secret key of a user to generate signatures.

Ueli Maurer (Ed.): EUROCRYPT '96 Proceedings, LNCS 1070

2 ElGamal's signature scheme

ElGamal's signature scheme can be described as follows.

Public parameters. Let p be a large prime and α a generator of the multiplicative group $\mathbb{F}_p^*$.

Secret key and public key. Every user A chooses a secret key $x_A \in \{0, \ldots, p-2\}$ and publishes $y_A \equiv \alpha^{x_A} \pmod{p}$ as his public key.

Computation of a signature. Let $0 \leq h < p-1$. To compute a signature on h user A proceeds as follows. First he chooses a random value $k \in \{0, \ldots, p-2\}$ relatively prime to $p-1$ and computes $1 \leq r < p$ and s by

$$\begin{aligned} r &\equiv \alpha^k \pmod{p} \\ \text{and} \quad s &\equiv (h - x_A r)k^{-1} \pmod{p-1}. \end{aligned}$$

The pair (r, s) is a valid signature on h.

Verification of a signature. Any user knowing the public key y_A can verify the signature by checking that $1 \leq r < p$ and the following equation are satisfied.

$$\alpha^h \equiv r^s y_A^r \pmod{p}$$

The ElGamal signature scheme can be broken when discrete logarithms in $\mathbb{F}_p^*$ can be computed. The prime p must therefore be chosen large enough to prevent the computation of discrete logarithms by the number field sieve [6] and $p-1$ must contain at least one large prime factor to disable the algorithm of Pohlig and Hellman [13]. The value h that occurs in the signature is normally not equal to the message to sign, it is rather the result of a collision free hash function applied to the message. This avoids the existential attack described in [4]. It is important that the verifier checks whether $1 \leq r < p$ is satisfied. If he would accept signatures where r is larger than p then any signature (r, s) on h could be used to generate a signature (r_2, s_2) on an arbitrary hash value h_2 by setting $u \equiv h_2 h^{-1} \pmod{p-1}$. This implies

$$\alpha^{h_2} \equiv \alpha^{hu} \equiv (y_A)^{ru} r^{su} \pmod{p}.$$

Now (r_2, s_2) can be found by setting $s_2 \equiv su \pmod{p-1}$ and by computing r_2 satisfying $r_2 \equiv ru \pmod{p-1}$ and $r_2 \equiv r \pmod{p}$ by using the Chinese Remainder Theorem. This kind of attack will for example be used in Section 6.

3 Weak generators

The security of the ElGamal signature scheme depends heavily on the parameters p and α. The following theorem shows that ElGamal signatures can be generated when some additional information on the generator α is available.

Theorem 1. *Let $p-1 = bw$ where b is smooth and let y_A be the public key of user A. If a generator $\beta = cw$ with $0 < c < b$ and an integer t are known such that $\beta^t \equiv \alpha \pmod{p}$ then a valid ElGamal signature (r, s) on a given h can be found.*

Proof. First we show that the equation

$$\alpha^{wz} \equiv (y_A)^w \pmod{p}$$

can be solved for z. It follows from $p-1 = bw$ that the subgroup H generated by α^w has order b. Since b is smooth it is possible to compute discrete logarithms in H by using the algorithm of Pohlig and Hellman [13], so that z can be found. Now let

$$\begin{aligned} r &= \beta \\ s &\equiv t(h - cwz) \pmod{p-1}. \end{aligned}$$

Then (r, s) is a valid signature on h since

$$\begin{aligned} r^s (y_A)^r &\equiv (\beta^t)^{(h-cwz)} (y_A)^{cw} \\ &\equiv \alpha^{h-cwz} \alpha^{cwz} \equiv \alpha^h \pmod{p}. \quad \square \end{aligned}$$

Corollary 2. *If α is smooth and divides $p-1$ then it is possible to generate a valid ElGamal signature on an arbitrary value h.*

Proof. Let $\beta = (p-1)/\alpha$ and $t = (p-3)/2$. Then $\beta^t \equiv (-1)\beta^{-1} \equiv \alpha \pmod{p}$. Thus it follows by Theorem 1 that signatures for all h can be forged. □

Thus if the generator α is chosen badly then signatures on every given message can be found without knowing the secret key. Choosing $\alpha = 2$ is exceptionally bad since it allows to forge signatures independently of the choice of p. Such small generators are sometimes chosen in order to get an efficient exponentiation.

It should be noted that this attack succeeds because of the special choice of r, which reduces the discrete logarithm problem in $\mathbb{F}_p^*$ to the discrete logarithm problem in a subgroup of $\mathbb{F}_p^*$ with smooth order. Another attack that is based on the fact that discrete logarithms in small subgroups are computable has been described recently by Menezes Qu and Vanstone [11]. (Their attack shows that authenticity is not guaranteed in a few Diffie-Hellman based key agreement protocols.)

4 Constructing a trapdoor

The public parameters p and α may be fixed so that every user in the system uses the same group and generator. Such a convention is attractive because it allows the use of shorter public keys. Additionally, signatures can be computed and verified much faster by using precomputed exponents [2]. However, the authority choosing the prime p and the generator α for a signature system may additionally generate some trapdoor information that can be used to forge arbitrary messages later.

One way to generate a prime p such that $\mathbb{F}_p^*$ has a trapdoor has been pointed out in [1, p.50]. The prime p can be generated together with a polynomial that is highly suitable for the number field sieve. The authority will then be able to compute discrete logarithms faster than a user who does not know the trapdoor [5]. However, this gives only a moderate advantage and can be avoided by chosing the prime p sufficiently large. Moreover, such primes can be recognized fairly easily [14].

Here we present another way to generate a trapdoor. An authority that can choose the public parameters p and α can generate these parameters such that it additionally knows secret values β and t satisfying the constraints of Theorem 1. We illustrate this possibility by giving two different methods to generate the trapdoor. The first method shows how a generator α and the trapdoor information can be generated given a fixed prime p. The second method shows how a prime p and the trapdoor information can be generated given a fixed small generator α. There is no guarantee that these methods succeed. However, the probability of success is sufficiently high to threaten the security of the system.

Method A. Let $p-1 = bw$ with b smooth. If b is not too small then we can find α, β and t in the following way. We choose $c \in \{1, \ldots, b-1\}$ randomly until $\beta = cw$ is a generator of $\mathbb{F}_p^*$. Finally we chose t with $\gcd(t, p-1) = 1$ and compute $\alpha = \beta^t$.

This attack is practical when a generator $\beta = cw$ of $\mathbb{F}_p^*$ can be found in reasonable time. When b is too small then no generator of the form cw may exist. However, the number of generators of $\mathbb{F}_p^*$ is $\varphi(p-1)$. Since $n/\varphi(n) = O(\ln\ln(n))$ (see for example [7]) we expect to find a generator after $O(\ln\ln(p))$ trials.

When t is chosen uniformly from the set of all $1 \le t < p-1$ that are relatively prime to $p-1$ then $\alpha = \beta^t$ is a random generator of $\mathbb{F}_p^*$. Thus it is impossible to detect the trapdoor as long as no false signature has been published. However, the trapdoor can be reconstructed from a given false signature (β, s) on h since $\alpha^h \equiv y_A^\beta \beta^s \pmod{p}$ implies $h \equiv ts \pmod{w}$. In order to find t it is then sufficient to compute $\log_\alpha(\beta) \pmod{b}$ and this can be done efficiently as b is smooth.

Method B. When the generator α is fixed then p, β and t can be generated as follows. First three positive integers u, v, c are selected such that v is odd and $c^v\alpha^u$ has approximately the size of the prime to construct. Next the smooth divisors of $c^v\alpha^u - 1$ are computed. This can be done easily using for example trial division or Pollard-rho factorization since only the small prime factors of

$c^v\alpha^u - 1$ are wanted. If there exists a smooth divisor $d > c$ of $c^v\alpha^u - 1$ such that $p = c^v\alpha^u - d^v$ is prime, $\frac{p-1}{2} - u$ is relatively prime to $p-1$ and α is a generator of $\mathbb{F}_p^*$ then it is possible to construct a trapdoor as follows.

$$\beta = c\frac{p-1}{d}$$
$$t \equiv v(\frac{p-1}{2} - u)^{-1} \pmod{p-1}$$

It follows from $d|(c^v a^u - 1)$ that d divides $p-1$. Thus β satisfies the precondition of Theorem 1. Because of $\alpha^u c^v \equiv d^v \pmod{p}$ we have $\alpha^{-u} \equiv (cd^{-1})^v \pmod{p}$ and therefore $\beta^v \equiv (-cd^{-1})^v \equiv (-1)\alpha^{-u} \equiv \alpha^{(p-1)/2-u} \pmod{p}$. Hence $\beta^t \equiv \alpha \pmod{p}$. It follows that Theorem 1 can be applied.

A heuristic analysis shows that the runtime of this method depends on the size of c and should find a trapdoor after trying $O((\ln p)(\ln\ln p)^2)$ values for p of An example for such a trapdoor, which has been generated in less than a day on a SPARC IPC, is given by the values $\alpha = 5, u = 227, v = 1, c = 1629$ and $d = 2^2 \cdot 7 \cdot 23 \cdot 47 \cdot 78541 \cdot 3489781$.

5 Countermeasures

The attacks shown in Section 3 and 4 can be avoided if signatures (r, s) are considered to be valid only if — additionally to the other conditions — r is not divisible by a large prime divisor q of $p-1$. This condition should always be checked by the verifier. Moreover, an authorized signer will almost always generate a valid signature since it is very unlikely that he randomly generates an r that is divisible by q. Such a condition has been included in the digital signature standard (DSS) [12]. Hence the DSS is not susceptible to the attacks presented in this paper.

Alternatively trapdoors may be avoided if the authority that is choosing the public parameters p and α is forced to use an algorithm like the one proposed by NIST for the generation of p in DSS. The values produced by this algorithm allow to verify publicly that the parameters have indeed been generated by the algorithm. This would make it very hard for a dishonest authority to create a trapdoor. The two methods to generate trapdoors shown in Section 4 indicate that both p and α must be generated with this algorithm if no other steps to prevent the attacks are taken.

Yet another possibility to avoid the attacks might be to modify the equations for signature generation and verification (see for example [9] for an overview of ElGamal variants). Such a variant must be chosen carefully since other problems may arise. For example if a signature on h is computed by $r \equiv \alpha^k \pmod{p}$ and $s \equiv x_A + hkr \pmod{p-1}$ and therefore verified by $\alpha^s \equiv y_A r^{hr} \pmod{p}$ then a chosen message attack is possible if the signer can be forced to sign a message h where $\gcd(p-1, h)$ is large. Any such signature leaks information about the secret key x_A since $s \equiv x_A + hkr \pmod{p-1}$ implies $s \equiv x_A \pmod{\gcd(p-1, h)}$. A special case of this attack has been discussed in [9].

6 An ElGamal scheme over $\mathbb{Z}/n\mathbb{Z}$

In [15] Saryazdi has proposed a variant of the ElGamal signature system using $(\mathbb{Z}/n\mathbb{Z})^*$ where n is the product of two large primes p and q. The author hopes that the security of the proposed signature system relies on the factoring problem and the discrete logarithm problem. Moreover, the existential attack shown in [4] seems not possible in that scheme, because this attack requires that the order of the group $(\mathbb{Z}/n\mathbb{Z})^*$ is known. However, Horster et al. observed in [10] that the signatures leak information that can be used to factor the modulus. Even though their attack does not work as described it is possible to modify the attack in such a way that it works for Saryazdi's scheme as well as the improved scheme proposed in [10]. Moreover, we show that computing discrete logarithms in only one of the two groups $\mathbb{F}_p^*$ or $\mathbb{F}_q^*$ is sufficient to break the scheme.

Description of the scheme. In Saryazdi's variation of the ElGamal signature scheme every user A chooses two large primes p and q and computes $n = pq$. Then she tries to find an integer $\alpha \in (\mathbb{Z}/n\mathbb{Z})^*$ with order $\lambda(n)$. Furthermore he chooses a random element x_A and computes $y_A = \alpha^{x_A} \pmod{n}$. p, q and x_A are kept secret whereas n, α and y are published as A's public key. To sign $h \in \mathbb{Z}/n\mathbb{Z}$ user A chooses a random number $k \in (\mathbb{Z}/n\mathbb{Z})^*$ and computes

$$r \equiv \alpha^k \pmod{n} \tag{1}$$
$$s \equiv (h - x_A r)k^{-1} \pmod{\varphi(n)} \tag{2}$$

Then (r, s) is the signature on h where h is either the message or the hash value of a message. A verifyer accepts a signature (r, s) on h if $1 \leq r < n$ and

$$\alpha^h \equiv (y_A)^r r^s \pmod{n}.$$

This scheme does not allow a modulus n that is common to all users, since every user has to know $\varphi(n)$ in order to be able to compute signatures.

Description of the attack. Assume that t is a small prime that divides $p-1$ but not $q-1$. Assume further that $(r_i, s_i) : 1 \leq i \leq d$ are known signatures on h_i such that t divides s_i and such that the system

$$\sum_{i=1}^{d} c_i h_i \equiv 0 \pmod{t} \tag{3}$$

$$\text{and} \quad \sum_{i=1}^{d} c_i r_i \equiv 0 \pmod{t} \tag{4}$$

has a nontrivial solution (i.e. $c_i \not\equiv 0 \pmod{t}$ for at least one i) in the coefficients c_i. Such a solution to (3) and (4) can always be found when at least 3 signatures with $t|s_i$ are known. If we set $B := \sum_{i=1}^{d} c_i h_i$ and $C := \sum_{i=1}^{d} c_i r_i$ then we have

$$\alpha^B \equiv (y_A)^C \prod_{i=1}^{d} r_i^{c_i s_i} \pmod{n}. \tag{5}$$

Since t divides all exponents in (5) we can compute the gcd of n and

$$\alpha^{B/t} - (y_A)^{C/t} \prod_{i=1}^{d} r_i^{c_i s_i/t}.$$

This will factor n if exactly one of the following two equations are satisfied.

$$\alpha^{B/t} \equiv (y_A)^{C/t} \prod_{i=1}^{d} r_i^{c_i s_i/t} \pmod{p} \tag{6}$$

$$\alpha^{B/t} \equiv (y_A)^{C/t} \prod_{i=1}^{d} r_i^{c_i s_i/t} \pmod{q} \tag{7}$$

Since t is relatively prime to $q-1$ it follows from (5) that (7) is satisfied. Since α is a generator modulo p it follows that (6) is satisfied if and only if

$$B/t \equiv x_A(C/t) + \sum_{i=1}^{d} k_i c_i (s_i/t) \pmod{p-1}$$

or equivalently

$$B \equiv x_A C + \sum_{i=1}^{d} k_i c_i s_i \pmod{t(p-1)} \tag{8}$$

is satisfied. From (2) follows only $B \equiv x_A C + \sum_{i=1}^{d} k_i c_i s_i \pmod{\varphi(n)}$. Let t^z be the maximal power of t dividing $\varphi(n)$. It follows that t^z divides $p-1$ and hence t^{z+1} divides $t(p-1)$. Thus we expect that (8) is only satisfied with probability about $1/t$.

It should be noted that an attacker does not know which primes t may be successful since he does not know p and q and can generally not determine whether a given t divides $p-1$ but not $q-1$. But this is not a big problem because an attacker can simply try all small primes t that are a divisor of some s_i's.

If the factorization of n can be discovered then signatures can be found if computing discrete logarithms in $\mathbb{F}_p^*$ but not necessarily in $\mathbb{F}_q^*$ is feasible, provided that p is not much smaller than q. This can be done as follows.

We may assume that the attacker knows a valid signature (r, s) on h. This may be a previously given signature or one that was generated using the existential forgery described in [4]. If he wants to generate a signature on h' then he uses the Chinese Remainder Theorem to compute $0 \le r' < q(q-1)$ such that

$$r' \equiv r h^{-1} h' \pmod{q-1}$$
$$r' \equiv r \pmod{q}$$

If p is not much smaller than q then he will find an $r' < n$ in reasonable time. If we set $s_q \equiv s h^{-1} h' \pmod{q-1}$ then we have

$$\alpha^{h'} \equiv (y_A)^{r'} r'^{s_q} \pmod{q}$$

Assuming that the discrete logarithm in $\mathbb{F}_p^*$ is feasible it is possible to solve

$$h' \equiv \log_\alpha(y_A)r' + \log_\alpha(r')s_p \pmod{p-1}$$

for s_p if $\log_\alpha(r')$ is relatively prime to $p-1$. If additionally the system

$$s' \equiv s_p \pmod{p-1}$$
$$s' \equiv s_q \pmod{q-1}$$

is solvable then (r', s') is a valid signature on h'.

Remarks. If t divides both $p-1$ and $q-1$ then it follows from (2) that

$$B \equiv x_A C + \sum_{i=1}^{d} k_i c_i s_i \pmod{\varphi(n)}$$

is satisfied. This implies that (8) and the analogous equation modulo $q-1$ are satisfied. The attack does therefore not work when t divides $p-1$ and $q-1$. The attack described in [10] considers the case $t = 2$ only and does not work therefore. However, it would work when equation (2) is reduced modulo $\lambda(n)$ instead of $\varphi(n)$ provided that the maximal powers of 2 in $p-1$ and $q-1$ are not the same. The authors of [10] propose that only signatures (r, s) where s is odd are allowed. This proposal does not prevent the attack described here since s can still be divisible by a small prime divisor t.

Another consequence of the note above is that the attack does not work when the smooth parts of $p-1$ and $q-1$ are equal. Thus the attack presented here can be avoided by choosing $p-1$ and $q-1$ such that $(p-1)/2$ and $(q-1)/2$ are prime, since then no small prime t exists dividing $p-1$ but not $q-1$. Some of the extensions proposed in [10] seem to avoid the attack presented here too. Other variants of ElGamal based on the discrete logarithm problem and the factoring problem that are more practical than Saryazdi's scheme have been proposed by Brickell and McCurley [3] and Harn [8].

7 Conclusion

The results presented in this paper show that ElGamal signatures can be forged in some cases without knowing the secret key. The attacks presented can be avoided by restricting the values of signatures that are considered to be valid. The ElGamal digital signature scheme has therefore not been broken but it has been shown that the system must be used very carefully.

Acknowledgments

I'm grateful to Ueli Maurer, Markus Stadler, Holger Petersen Markus Michels and some members of the EUROCRYPT program committee for their comments and suggestions.

References

1. T. Beth, M. Frisch, and G.J. Simmons (eds). *Public-key Cryptography, State of the Art and Future Directions*, volume 578 of *Lecture Notes in Computer Science.* Springer-Verlag, Berlin, 1992.
2. E. F. Brickell, D. M. Gordon, K. S. McCurley, and D. B. Wilson. Fast exponentiation with precomputation. *Advances in Cryptology - EUROCRYPT '92*, volume 658 of *Lecture Notes in Computer Science*, pages 200–207, 1993.
3. E. F. Brickell and K. S. McCurley. An interactive identification scheme based on discrete logarithms and factoring. *Journal of Cryptology*, 5(1):29–39, 1992.
4. T. El Gamal. A public key cryptosystem and a signature scheme based on discrete logarithms. *Advances in Cryptology: Proceedings of CRYPTO '84*, volume 196 of *Lecture Notes in Computer Science*, pages 10–18. Springer-Verlag, 1985.
5. D. M. Gordon. Designing and detecting trapdoors for discrete log cryptosystems. *Advances in Cryptology– CRYPTO '92*, volume 740 of *Lecture Notes in Computer Science*, pages 66–75. Springer-Verlag, 1992.
6. D. M. Gordon. Discrete logarithms in GF(p) using the number field sieve. *SIAM J. Disc. Math.*, 6(1):124–138, February 1993.
7. G. H. Hardy and E. M. Wright. *An introduction to the theory of numbers.* Clarendon Press, Oxford, 5th edition, 1979.
8. L. Harn. Public-key cryptosystem design based on factoring and discrete logarithm. *IEE Proc. Comput. Digit. Tech.*, 141(3):193–195, 1994.
9. P. Horster, M. Michels, and H. Petersen. Generalized ElGamal signatures for one message block. Technical Report TR-94-3, University of Technology Chemnitz-Zwickau, May 1994.
10. P. Horster, M. Michels, and H. Petersen. Meta-ElGamal signature schemes using a composite module. Technical Report TR-94-16-E, University of Technology Chemnitz-Zwickau, November 1994.
11. A. Menezes, M. Qu, and S. Vanstone. Key agreement and the need for authentication. PKS, November 1995.
12. National Institute of Standards and Technology (NIST). *FIPS Publication 186: Digital Signature Standard*, May 19, 1994.
13. S. C. Pohlig and M. E. Hellman. An improved algorithm for computing logarithms over $GF(p)$ and its cryptographic significance. *IEEE Trans. Inform. Theory*, IT-24:106–110, January 1978.
14. R. A. Rueppel, A. K. Lenstra, M. E. Smid, K. S. McCurley, Y. Desmedt, A. Odlyzko, and P. Landrock. Panel discussion: Trapdoor primes and moduli. *Advances in Cryptology — EUROCRYPT '92*, volume 658 of *Lecture Notes in Computer Science*, pages 194–199. Springer-Verlag, 1993.
15. S. Saryazdi. An extension to ElGamal public key cryptosystem with a new signature scheme. *Communication, Control, and Signal Processing*, pages 195–198. Elsevier, 1990.

On the Security of Two MAC Algorithms

Bart Preneel[1]* Paul C. van Oorschot[2]

[1] Katholieke Universiteit Leuven, Dept. Electrical Engineering-ESAT
Kardinaal Mercierlaan 94, B–3001 Heverlee, Belgium
bart.preneel@esat.kuleuven.ac.be

[2] Bell-Northern Research, Box 3511 Station C
Ottawa, Ontario K1Y 4H7, Canada
paulv@bnr.ca

Abstract. The security of two message authentication code (MAC) algorithms is considered: the MD5-based envelope method (RFC 1828), and the banking standard MAA (ISO 8731–2). Customization of a general MAC forgery attack allows improvements in both cases. For the envelope method, the forgery attack is extended to allow key recovery; for example, a 128-bit key can be recovered using 2^{67} known text-MAC pairs and time plus 2^{13} chosen texts. For MAA, internal collisions are found with fewer and shorter messages than previously by exploiting the algorithm's internal structure; consequently, the number of chosen texts (each 256 Kbyte long) for a forgery can be reduced by two orders of magnitude, e.g. from 2^{24} to 2^{17}. This attack can be extended to one requiring only short messages (2^{24} messages shorter than 1 Kbyte) to circumvent the special MAA mode for long messages. Moreover, certain internal collisions allow key recovery, and weak keys for MAA are identified.

1 Introduction

Message authentication code (MAC) algorithms are symmetric-key techniques which provide data origin authentication and data integrity. They have received widespread use in many practical applications, e.g. banking [9]. The primary MAC algorithms used historically have been CBC-MAC and MAA. CBC-MAC [10, 11] is derived from the cipher-block chaining (CBC) mode of block ciphers such as DES; some theoretical support for this method has been given [1]. The Message Authenticator Algorithm (MAA) is an ISO standard [10] which dates back to 1984 [7]. The so-called envelope-based MACs of Tsudik [18] and others have also received recent attention (see e.g. Kaliski and Robshaw [12]). Recently several new practical MAC algorithms were proposed: XOR-MAC by Bellare et al. [2], HMAC by Bellare et al. [4], MDx-MAC by Preneel and van Oorschot [14], and the bucket-hashing MAC of Rogaway [16].

* N.F.W.O. postdoctoral researcher, sponsored by the National Fund for Scientific Research (Belgium).

Ueli Maurer (Ed.): EUROCRYPT '96 Proceedings, LNCS 1070

Envelope-based MACs offer speed and simplicity. The basic technique involves using a secret key as part of the input to an unkeyed hash function. The envelope method of RFC 1828 [12, 17], arising from the IPSEC working group of the Internet Engineering Task Force (IETF), prepends and appends a secret key K to the message input: $\mathrm{MAC}(x) = h(K\|p\|x\|K)$. Here $\|$ denotes concatenation, and p denotes some padding bits. This construction was supported by a security proof under assumptions regarding the pseudo-randomness of MD5 [3]. An alternative HMAC [4], involving two invocations of $h(\cdot)$, is defined as $\mathrm{MAC}(x) = h(K\|p_1\|h(K\|p_2\|x))$, where p_1 and p_2 are strings of padding bits which pad K out to a full block; a version without padding was proposed earlier in [12]. The security of HMAC can be proven based on the assumptions that $h(\cdot)$ is collision resistant for a random and secret IV, and that the complete output of the compression function is hard to predict when its first input is random and secret.

Recent systematic analysis of MACs includes a new general attack by Preneel and van Oorschot [14] which applies to all iterated MACs. It involves a birthday attack using known text-MAC pairs, after which additional chosen text-MAC pairs (e.g. a single text for the most common version of CBC-MAC) allows MAC forgery. Overall this requires about $2^{n/2}$ known text-MAC pairs, where n is the bitlength of the internal memory (chaining variable) of the MAC algorithm.

The current paper adapts and refines this attack schema specifically for the envelope method (e.g. RFC 1828) and for MAA, yielding significant improvements and new results in each case. The sequel is organized as follows. §2 reviews definitions and the general attack on iterated MACs. §3 presents a new key recovery attack on the envelope method, while §4 gives an optimized forgery attack plus a new key recovery attack on MAA. §5 concludes the paper.

2 Background Definitions and Review

A hash function h map bitstrings of arbitrary finite length into strings of fixed length (say m bits). An *unkeyed hash function* does not involve secret parameters. Such a function is said to be *one-way* if it is both *preimage-resistant* (it is computationally infeasible to find any input which hashes to any pre-specified output); and *second-preimage resistant* (it is computationally infeasible to find any second input which has the same output as any specified input). Ideally, finding a preimage or second preimage requires about 2^m operations. A one-way hash function is said to be *collision resistant* if it is furthermore computationally infeasible to find a collision (i.e. two distinct inputs that hash to the same result). For ideal such functions, no collisions may be found more efficiently than by a birthday-like attack of about $2^{m/2}$ operations.

A *keyed* hash function h has a secret k-bit key K as a secondary input; when used for message authentication, such a function is called a message authentication code (MAC). Computing $h_K(x)$ (denoted simply $h(x)$ when K is understood) must be easy, given h, K, and an input x. An adversary able, without initial knowledge of K, to find a corresponding MAC for any single message, is said to be capable of *existential forgery*. An adversary able to determine the MAC for a message of his choice is said to be capable of *selective forgery*. Ideally, existential forgery is computationally infeasible; a less demanding requirement is that only selective forgery is so. Practical attacks often require that a forgery is *verifiable*, i.e. that the forged MAC is known to be correct (e.g. before attempting to use it to advantage) with probability near 1. A *key recovery* attack is more devastating than forgery – here an adversary is able to recover K itself, and thus carry out arbitrary selective forgeries. Ideally, any attack allowing key recovery requires about 2^k operations. Verification of such an attack requires k/m text-MAC pairs.

In a *chosen-text attack*, an adversary may request and receive MACs corresponding to a number of messages of his choice, before completing his (forgery or key recovery) attack. For forgery, the forged MAC must be on a message different than any for which a MAC was previously obtained. In an *adaptive* chosen-text attack, requests may depend on the outcome of previous requests.

Iterative hash functions and MACs h process inputs in successive fixed-size b-bit blocks. A message or text input x is divided into blocks x_1 through x_t, the last of which is padded appropriately if required for completeness. h involves a *compression function* f and an n-bit $(n \geq m)$ *chaining variable* H_i between stage $i-1$ and stage i: $H_0 = IV$; $H_i = f(H_{i-1}, x_i), 1 \leq i \leq t$; $h(x) = H_t$.

MACs often involve an output transformation g applied to H_t, yielding a MAC result $h(x) = g(H_t)$. The secret key may be employed in the IV, in f, and/or in g. For an input pair (x, x') with $h(x) = g(H_t)$ and $h(x') = g(H'_t)$, a collision $h(x) = h(x')$ is an *internal* collision if $H_t = H'_t$, and an *external* collision if $H_t \neq H'_t$ but $g(H_t) = g(H'_t)$.

A general forgery attack [14] is applicable to all iterated MACs. Its feasibility depends on the bitsizes n of the chaining variable and m of the hash-result, and the number s of common trailing blocks of the known texts $(s \geq 0)$. The basic version is a known-text attack; if the message length is an input to the output transformation, all messages must have equal length. Two results are cited for convenience.

Lemma 1 [14]. *An internal collision for an iterated MAC allows a verifiable MAC forgery, through a chosen-text attack requiring a single chosen text.* ∎

This follows since for an internal collision (x, x'), $h(x \,\|\, y) = h(x' \,\|\, y)$ for any single block y; thus a requested MAC on the chosen text $x \,\|\, y$ provides a forged MAC (the same) for $x' \,\|\, y$. The general forgery attack (Proposition 2) depends on the nature of the compression function f. In MAA and in envelope methods based on MD5 [15], the compression function f is considered to behave as a random mapping for fixed x_i. The parameters of the original attack [14] may be improved slightly, as stated in Proposition 2.

Proposition 2. *Let h be an iterated MAC with n-bit chaining variable, m-bit result, a compression function f which behaves like a random function (for fixed x_i), and output transformation g. An internal collision for h can be found using u known text-MAC pairs, where each text has the same substring of $s \geq 0$ trailing* *blocks, and v chosen texts. The expected values for u and v are:* $u = \sqrt{2/(s+1)} \cdot 2^{n/2}$; $v = 0$ *if g is a permutation or* $s + 1 \geq 2^{n-m+6}$, *and otherwise*

$$v \approx 2\left(\frac{2^{n-m}}{s+1} \cdot \left(1 - \frac{1}{e}\right) + \left\lceil \frac{n - m - \log_2(s+1)}{m-1} \right\rceil + 1\right) . \qquad (1)$$

■

3 New Key Recovery Attack on the Envelope Method

The *envelope method* as proposed by Tsudik [18] consists of respectively prepending and appending secret keys K_1 and K_2 to the message input: $\mathrm{MAC}(x) = h(K_1\|x\|K_2)$. An Internet proposed standard recommended by the IP Security (IPSEC) working group for authentication of IP datagrams, namely RFC 1828 [17], specifies a variant of this using MD5 and a single key K: $\mathrm{MAC}(x) = h(K\|p\|x\|K)$. Here p denotes some padding bits chosen such that $K\|p$ fills the first block, and allows for a security proof assuming pseudo-randomness of MD5 [3]. RFC 1828 allows a variable length key, and mandates support for bitlengths up to 128 bits. An important consideration motivating use of envelope MACs is that they require minimal implementation and deployment effort: code for the underlying unkeyed hash function can be used without modification.

A divide and conquer key recovery attack on the envelope method with distinct keys $K_1 \neq K_2$ was given by Preneel and van Oorschot [14]. Rather than an exhaustive search over $k_1 + k_2$ bits (where $k_i = |K_i|$ and $k_1 = n$ is the bitlength of the chaining variable), first K_1 and then K_2 are found. For an MD5-based MAC, the attack uses Proposition 2 with about 2^{64} known text-MAC pairs (assume $s = 0$ for simplicity) to find an internal collision. An off-line exhaustive search involving 2^{k_1} operations results in a small set of possible keys K_1 from which the correct key can be determined with a few chosen texts, reducing security to an appended secret key alone. K_2 is then determined by off-line exhaustive search. $K_1 \neq K_2$ thus offers substantially less additional security than one would hope, relative to k_1 bits of security for $K_1 = K_2$, although the former nonetheless requires an extremely large number of known text-MAC pairs. In any case, for $k_1 = 128$, a search requiring 2^{k_1} operations is completely infeasible.

We describe now a new divide and conquer key recovery attack. It applies to the method of RFC 1828 (also proposed in [12]), and exploits the padding procedure of MD5, which was not designed to conceal secret keys. This attack again requires a very large number of known text-MAC pairs (variable depending on choices made, but on the order of 2^{64}); however, the work complexity for key recovery is decreased dramatically from previous numbers (from 2^{128} to 2^{66}).

The new key recovery attack is applicable to the basic envelope method including the MD5-based RFC 1828 (IPSEC) variant and other hash functions using MD5-like padding. It can also recover the trail key of the variation with distinct keys. First recall the padding procedure for MD5 for a message input y of bitlength $b = |y|$. A single '1' bit is appended to y, followed by z '0' bits ($0 \leq z \leq 511$), where z is chosen to make the sum of b and the bitlength of the padding equal 448 mod 512. The 64-bit integer representation of b is then appended to complete the last block. For the special case of the IPSEC envelope method with a 128-bit key, the data, after padding, processed by the compression function of MD5 has the form: $K\|p\|x\|K\|1000\ldots000\|b$. Here x is the message on which a MAC is desired, $y = K\|p\|x\|K$, and $b = 512 + 128 + |x|$. Defining $r = |x| \bmod 512$,

$$z = \begin{cases} 319 - r & \text{if } \quad 0 \le r \le 319 \\ 831 - r & \text{if } 320 \le r \le 511 \end{cases}$$

If $z \in [0, 319]$, the key K will lie completely in the last block, and the number of message bits in the last block is r. For $z \in [320, 446]$, $z - 319$ bits of the key K will be in the second last block, with the remaining key bits in the last block. For $z \in [447, 511]$, K falls completely in the second last block. In the latter two cases, there will be r message bits in the second last block (see Figure 1).

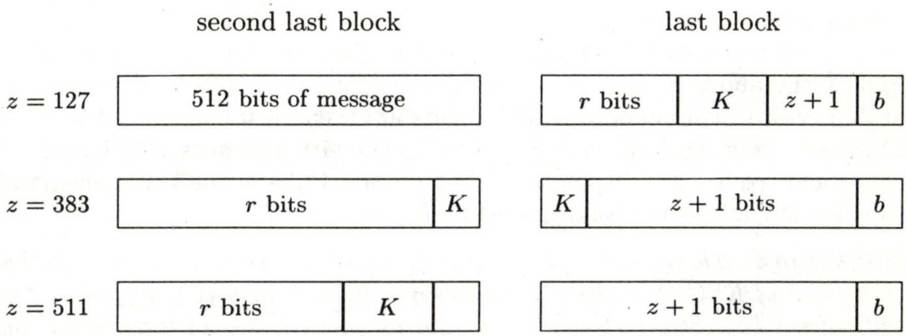

Fig. 1. Message, key, padding, and length fields in final blocks of envelope method.

Define an internal collision as a pair of inputs (x, x') which produce the same MAC output, and for which the internal chaining variables collide just before the block containing the key (or any partial key). Since such a collision is detectable only through a collision for the MAC, all blocks following the internal collision must be identical in the two members of the colliding input pair. Therefore the attack of Proposition 2 requires the lengths of all the messages to be equal, and the last r message bits (which are either in the last or in the second last block) to be the same. If $r = 0$ (i.e. $|x| = 0 \bmod 512$), there is no condition on the last message bits.

Consider the case $r = 511$ (i.e. $z = 320$). There is a single key bit in the second last block. Therefore 511 message bits in the second last block must be identical to allow for identification of an internal collision. However, if we simply guess that key bit, the unknown key is restricted to the last block, and collisions after the second last block are again internal collisions (or *almost internal* collisions). A first observation is that this reduces the constraint on the message. A more significant consequence is that by using the attack of Lemma 1, one can actually verify the guess for that key bit. This leads to a powerful divide and conquer attack for extracting the key, which may be illustrated as follows.

Let x be a 480-bit message. Then r=480, z=351, and the first block contains the padded key K. The second block contains 480 message bits and 32 key bits. The last block contains the 96 remaining key bits, a '1' bit followed by 351 '0' bits, and the 64-bit length field b=1120 (i.e. $512 + 128 + 480$). If the MACs for about $2^{64.5}$ such messages x are known, one may expect (by Proposition 2 with n=128=m, s=0) about two collisions: one after the second block (an almost internal collision), and one after the last block (an external collision). Denote the almost internal colliding pair (x, x'). Construct 2^{32} message pairs of the form $(x\|k_i\|y,\ x'\|k_i\|y)$, where k_i is 32 bits and ranges over all 2^{32} possible values, and y is now an arbitrary block. Request the 2^{33} corresponding MACs. When k_i takes on the value of the correct partial key, the two MACs agree; moreover, with probability $\approx 1 - 1/2^{96}$, no other pairs of MACs will be equal. This reveals 32 key bits. For the external collision, with overwhelming probability none of the pairs gives the same MAC.

It is easy to extend the attack to find further key bits. One possibility is to repeat the above procedure using messages of length 448 bits, yielding the next 32 key bits. The remaining 64 key bits are then most efficiently found (off-line) exhaustively. Alternatively, one could begin with messages of bitlength 448, which would require 2^{66} chosen texts, but reveal 64 bits of the key immediately. This reasoning allows the following general result:

Proposition 3. *There exists a key recovery attack on one-key envelope methods such as that of RFC 1828, which requires* $q = \lceil 64/t \rceil$ *steps* ($1 \le t \le 64$) *to find 64 bits of the key. Step i* ($1 \le i \le q$) *requires* $\sqrt{2} \cdot 2^{64}$ *known texts of bitlength* $c_i \cdot 512 - t \cdot i$ *for some fixed* $c_i > 1$, *and* 2^{t+2} *chosen texts.* ∎

Table 1 summarizes the complexity to find 64 key bits in t-bit slices, for different values of t. If a 128-bit key is used with the remaining bits found by exhaustive search, the overall time complexity is on the order of the number of known texts. The attack is easily modified for keys exceeding 128 bits; e.g. recovering a 256-bit key in three 64-bit slices requires about 2^{66} known text-MAC pairs and the same order of chosen texts. Thus relative to this attack, this MAC design makes very poor use of key bits beyond 128. For context, recall that linear cryptanalysis of DES [13], viewed as a tremendous breakthrough, requires 2^{43} known texts against a 56-bit key, while differential cryptanalysis requires 2^{47} chosen texts [5]. The above key recovery attack, relative to its larger 128-bit key, requires substantially fewer known texts (and time); this indicates that the general construction fails to make good use of key bits.

The above attack requires that $|x| \mod 512 \in [448, 511]$, because the number of bits of K in the penultimate block must be between 1 and 64 (the attack becomes less feasible if more than 64 bits need be guessed); and that the known texts have the same number of blocks, because the value of b must be the same for the two messages forming the internal collision. However, if a set of about 2^{73} "short" (say ten or fewer blocks) known messages is available, we expect to find

Table 1. Complexity of key recovery attack on envelope method (128-bit key)

t	# known texts	# chosen texts
4	$2^{68.5}$	2^{10}
8	$2^{67.5}$	2^{13}
16	$2^{66.5}$	2^{20}
32	$2^{65.5}$	2^{35}
64	$2^{64.5}$	2^{66}

among those a sufficient number of messages suitable for the attack (without fixing t in advance); the attack will still require a much smaller number (less than 2^{20}) of chosen texts to identify the key bits.

The attack relies on the key being split across blocks. While it is not practical, vulnerability to it represents a certificational weakness, and indicating an architectural flaw. One concludes it is more secure to isolate the entire trailing key in a separate block (together with the message length and possibly a pseudo-random string). However, this requires changing the padding procedure for MD5, contravening an original motivating factor – being able to call the underlying hash function directly. Nonetheless, customized MACs (as suggested in [12, 14]) appear to offer a more secure alternative to constructions relying directly on unkeyed hash functions. Note also that no one has yet evaluated functions such as MD5 with respect to pseudo-randomness properties (especially if only part of the input is replaced by a secret key).

4 New Forgery and Key Recovery Attacks on MAA

In this section, a preliminary description of MAA is followed by a discussion of how the basic attack of Proposition 2 may be customized for MAA, and optimized using special messages. An extension of these to the special mode of MAA for long messages is then presented, followed by a new key recovery attack.

4.1 Description of MAA

Designed by Davies, MAA was presented at Crypto'84 [7, 8] and is in the ISO 8731-2 banking standard [10]. On PCs and workstations it runs only 40% slower than MD5. The algorithm consists of three parts. The *prelude* is a key expansion from 64 bits (two 32-bit words) to 192 bits (six 32-bit words). From the first key word are derived the parameters $H1_0$, V, S; from the second, the parameters $H2_0$, W, T. The prelude, which needs only be executed during installation of a new key, also eliminates "weaker bytes" $\mathtt{00_x}$ or $\mathtt{FF_x}$ in keys and parameters. The two words of the chaining variable $(H1_i, H2_i)$ are initialized with $(H1_0, H2_0)$. The *main loop* mixes the chaining variable with message word x_i $(0 \leq i \leq t-1)$

and key dependent parameters V and W. It consists of two inter-dependent parallel branches with logical operations, addition modulo 2^{32} ($\boxplus$), and multiplication modulo $2^{32}-1$ ($\otimes_1$) and modulo $2^{32}-2$ ($\otimes_2$); due to the peculiar definition (see [10]), the result may actually be equal to $2^{32}-1$ respectively $2^{32}-2$. In the *coda*, S and T are introduced as message blocks to be processed as per the main loop. The 32-bit MAC result is computed using addition mod 2: $H_{t+2} = H1_{t+2} \oplus H2_{t+2}$.

A single iteration of the main loop can be described as follows:

Step 1: $V := \text{rol}(V)$; $K_i := V \oplus W$; % rol denotes 1 bit cyclic shift left

Step 2: $t_1 := H1_{i-1} \oplus x_i$; $t_2 := H2_{i-1} \oplus x_i$;

$H1_i := t_1 \otimes_1 (((K_i \boxplus t_2) \vee A) \wedge C)$; $H2_i := t_2 \otimes_2 (((K_i \boxplus t_1) \vee B) \wedge D)$;

Here $A = \texttt{02040801}_\mathbf{x}$, $B = \texttt{00804021}_\mathbf{x}$, $C = \texttt{BFEF7FDF}_\mathbf{x}$, and $D = \texttt{7DFEFBFF}_\mathbf{x}$. These constants fix 8 bits of the second factor (four to 0, and four to 1). The output transformation g consists of the coda iterations (where the key-dependent S and T play the role of x_i) and final XORing as noted above.

4.2 Basic MAC Forgery on MAA

The basic attack of Proposition 2 can be applied to MAA with parameters $n = 64$, $m = 32$. However, an internal collision (i.e. a collision for $H1$ and $H2$) yields an external collision only if V is in the same position (the number of bits over which V is rotated effectively adds 5 bits to the 64-bit MAA internal memory). This effect can be countered by using messages of the same length modulo 32, or messages for which the common trailing blocks start at the same position modulo 32. Note however that this is not strictly necessary: if the number of known texts given by Proposition 2 is multiplied by about 32, the condition on the length can be omitted. A second observation is that the output transformation consists of two iterations, providing two ways to obtain an external collision; we expect two additional external collisions after processing S and T (for $2^{32.5}$ messages), which accounts for (an expected) four additional chosen texts to eliminate them. A third observation is that in the second chain, the modulus $(2^{32}-2)$ is even, while the second multiplier is odd (the least significant bit of D is 1). This implies that the least significant bit of $H2_i$, denoted $\text{LSB}(H2_i)$, is equal to the $\text{LSB}(H2_{i-1} \oplus x_i)$. Consequently, $\text{LSB}(H2_t) = LSB(H2_0) \oplus \bigoplus_{i=1}^{t} \text{LSB}(x_i)$, and the 64-bit internal memory can be reduced to 63 bits by making the second term of the right hand side a constant. This assumes that the attacker can choose texts for which the value of this sum is constant.

Table 2 gives the parameters of the attack for various values s. Here $n = 63$, $m = 32$, and the last column counts the total number of bytes of the known and chosen texts. Increasing s allows a reduction in the number of known and chosen texts (the 'known' messages begin to resemble 'chosen' messages), but increases the total number of bytes which must be processed with the known key. This situation can be improved (as subsequently explained) by selecting messages with a special structure. Since fast MAA implementations process 3–4 Megabytes per second, processing 2^{32} bytes requires about 20 minutes.

Table 2. Parameters for basic forgery attack on MAA

# com. blocks s	# known texts u	length (bytes) $4(s+1)$	# chosen texts $v+1$	length (bytes) $4(s+2)$	total size (bytes)
0	2^{32}	≥ 4	$2^{31.3}$	≥ 8	$2^{35.2}$
$2^8 - 1$	2^{28}	$\geq 2^{10}$	$2^{23.3}$	$\geq 2^{10} + 4$	$2^{38.1}$
$2^{16} - 1$	2^{24}	$\geq 2^{18}$	$2^{15.3}$	$\geq 2^{18} + 4$	$2^{42.0}$
$2^{32} - 1$	2^{16}	$\geq 2^{34}$	4	$\geq 2^{34} + 4$	$2^{50.0}$

4.3 Optimized MAC Forgery using Special Messages

As noted by the designer of MAA, $2^{32} - 1$ has several small prime factors (in fact $2^{32} - 1 = 3 \cdot 5 \cdot 17 \cdot 257 \cdot 65537$), and if one of these appears in $H1_i$, it might remain there due to multiplicative properties. The fact that x_i is added in every iteration should destroy this property; however if all x_i's for $i \geq i_0$ are chosen equal to 0, such a factor would remain nonetheless. If p is a prime factor of $2^{32} - 1$, the probability that i is the smallest index for which $H1_{i_0+i}$ is divisible by p is given by $\frac{1}{p}(1 - \frac{1}{p})^i$, a geometric distribution with expected value $i = p-1$ for success (note this assumes that the $H1_i$'s are uniformly distributed; this assumption has been confirmed by some computer experiments). Thus, after about 2^{16} iterations (each with $x_i = 0$), $H1_i$ will be divisible by all its prime factors and thus equal to $\texttt{FFFFFFFF}_\mathbf{x}$ (and not $\texttt{00000000}_\mathbf{x}$, due to the special definition of $\otimes_1$). It is easy to prove the following:

Lemma 4. *Let p be a prime divisor of $2^{32} - 1$. If $i = \alpha(p-1)$ zero blocks are inserted, starting with x_{i_0}, the probability that p divides $H1_{i_0+i}$ is $1 - e^{-\alpha}$.* ∎

Once $H1_i$ is constant, finding a collision for $H2_i$ yields an internal collision. Consider the second chain. For $H1_i = \texttt{FFFFFFFF}_\mathbf{x}$ and $x_i = \texttt{00000000}_\mathbf{x}$, $H2_i = H2_{i-1} \otimes_2 U_i$, where $U_i = ((\texttt{FFFFFFFF}_\mathbf{x} \boxplus K_i) \vee B) \wedge D$. Note the value of U_i depends only on i mod 32. To make this equation independent of i, first define $\tilde{U} = \prod_{i=0}^{31} U_i$ (with multiplication mod $2^{32} - 2$). Then note $H2_{i+32} = H2_{i-1} \otimes_2 \tilde{U}$. Since $LSB(D) = 1$, and $2^{31} - 1$ is a Mersenne prime, all U_i's are elements of the cyclic subgroup (of order $2^{31} - 1$) of $\mathbb{Z}_{2^{32}-2}$. This implies that the same holds for $\tilde{U}$, and thus by Fermat's (little) theorem we have that $\tilde{U}^{2^{31}-2} \bmod (2^{32}-2) = 1$. This may be used directly in a forgery attack as follows. A message ending with 2^{16} zero blocks (denoted $X \| 0^{2^{16}}$; here 0^i denotes i blocks of 32 zero-bits) has high probability of having $H1_i = \texttt{FFFFFFFF}_\mathbf{x}$. If the MAC for such a message is requested, with high probability $X \| 0^{2^{16}} \| 0^{32 \cdot (2^{31}-2)}$ will have the same MAC. This existential forgery, while not likely of practical use (the message ends in about 2^{38} zero bytes), illustrates a certificational weakness of MAA.

Proposition 5. *An existential forgery on MAA is possible which requires a single chosen text of about 2^{18} bytes to forge the MAC for a text of length about 2^{38} bytes.* ∎

The above assumptions are however worst case (for the attacker): for certain values of V and W, the U_i's will have a shorter period. This leads to the definition of weak keys for MAA. A first type of weak keys are external keys which result in an internal key V of rotational period < 32. For such keys, rotating V over 2, 4, 8, or 16 positions will yield V again (there are no keys V of period 1 since the all zero and all one values are eliminated). There are respectively 2, 14, 254, and 64 516 values of V for which this holds.[1] One can find by exhaustive examination which values of the first 32-bit word of the input key yield such values of V. Therefore the number of weak keys is independent of the second input key word, and thus 2^{32} times larger. If V has period r, the forgery above requires $r \cdot (2^{31} - 2)$ zero blocks. Verifying the forgery allows an attacker to obtain information on V, which is undesirable since it leaks partial key bits. It is relatively easy (§4.5) to detect whether a key is weak, leading to a key recovery attack on these keys. *These observations suggest that the fact that V depends on only 32 bits of the input key is a design weakness in MAA.*

A second class of weak keys are keys for which $\tilde{U}$ has small order. The order of $\tilde{U}$ must divide D, where D is the order of $\mathbb{Z}_M^*$ for $M = 2^{32} - 2$; in some cases the order of $\tilde{U}$ is considerably smaller than D. More specifically, $D = \phi(M) = \phi(2) \cdot \phi(2^{31} - 1) = 2^{31} - 2 = 2 \cdot 3^2 \cdot 7 \cdot 11 \cdot 31 \cdot 151 \cdot 331$, where $\phi()$ is Euler's totient function. For each divisor d of D, the number of elements of order exactly d is $\phi(d)$, and the total number of elements whose order divides d is exactly d. For example, from $d = D/331 = 6\,487\,866$, it follows that 1 key in 331 will yield a forgery after appending about $6\,487\,866 \cdot 32 \cdot 4 = 2^{29.6}$ zero bytes.

It is possible to obtain an internal collision using shorter messages (cf. Table 2) by exploiting the properties of zero blocks presented in Lemma 4. This requires chosen texts rather than known texts. As discussed above, for a text with a sufficiently large number of trailing zero blocks, $H1_t$ becomes constant (i.e. $\mathtt{FFFFFFFF_x}$) with high probability; if about $\sqrt{2} \cdot 2^{16}$ such texts are available, one expects by the birthday paradox to find two texts with colliding values for $H2_t$ as well. The third observation of §4.2 implies that 2^{16} such texts will suffice if the sum of the least significant bits of the message blocks is kept constant. We will assume that this condition is satisfied. Note that the attack can be extended easily to the case where the zero blocks are followed by some arbitrary common trailing blocks.

The exact number of chosen texts for this improved variant can be computed as follows. Lemma 4 (with $p = 2^{16} + 1$) implies that among $r = 2^{16}/(1 - e^{-\alpha})$ messages each containing $\alpha 2^{16}$ trailing zero blocks for some α, we expect to find about 2^{16} messages for which the first chaining variable $H1_t$ becomes equal to $\mathtt{FFFFFFFF_x}$ (for simplicity it is assumed that $\alpha \geq 1/32$, since otherwise the second prime factor ($p = 257$) has to be taken into account in the calculation). By the birthday paradox, the expected number of collisions for the second chaining variable $H2_t$, which corresponds to a (complete) internal collision is then equal to $(2^{16})^2/2^{32} = 1$. The expected number of external collisions is equal to $r^2/2^{33} = 1/(2(1 - e^{-\alpha})^2)$; these collisions can be eliminated by simulating (see [14]) the

[1] Recall that bytes equal to $\mathtt{00_x}$ or $\mathtt{FF_x}$ are eliminated from V in the prelude.

attack of Lemma 1. Two additional chosen texts are sufficient to identify an external collision with high probability; the expected value is about $2(1-1/e)$ as will be shown in the full paper. The total number of blocks in the chosen texts is then approximately

$$2^{32}\frac{\alpha}{(1-e^{-\alpha})}+2^{16}\left(1-e^{-1}\right)\frac{\alpha}{(1-e^{-\alpha})^2}\,. \qquad (2)$$

If $\alpha \to 0$, the first term approaches 2^{32}, but the second term increases quickly. The sum is minimized for $\alpha \approx 1/228$ (but this violates the constraint on α), and for $\alpha > 1/228$ it increases monotonically with α. The number of blocks is thus minimized for $\alpha = 1/32$ (for this value the first term in equation (2) dominates and is approximately equal to $2^{32} + 2^{26}$), while the number of chosen texts can be reduced by increasing α.

It is possible to use even shorter messages, but then we assume that $H1_t$ has become with high probability a multiple of $(2^{32}-1)/65\,537 = 65\,535 = \mathtt{FFFF_x}$. A complete internal collision requires then a collision in a set of size about 2^{47}, which implies that more chosen messages are needed. In this case α must exceed 1/4 to avoid interference of the second prime factor (257).

An overview of the trade-offs is given in Table 3. These trade-offs are more realistic (cf. Table 2) with respect to the total number of bytes; this number increases only slightly while reducing the number of chosen texts. However, chosen texts are more difficult to obtain than known texts.

Table 3. Parameters for improved forgery attack on MAA. Attacks with < 256 zero blocks avoid the 'long message mode' (see §4.4).

	α	# 0 blocks	# chosen texts	total size (bytes)
$H1_t$ = $\mathtt{FFFFFFFF_x}$	1/32	2 048	$2^{21.0}$	$2^{34.0}$
	1/4	16 384	$2^{18.2}$	$2^{34.2}$
	1/2	32 768	$2^{17.3}$	$2^{34.3}$
	1	65 636	$2^{16.7}$	$2^{34.7}$
	2	131 072	$2^{16.2}$	$2^{35.2}$
$H1_t$ = multiple of $\mathtt{FFFF_x}$	1/4	64	$2^{26.2}$	$2^{34.3}$
	1/2	128	$2^{25.3}$	$2^{34.4}$
	1	256	$2^{24.7}$	$2^{34.7}$
	2	512	$2^{24.2}$	$2^{35.2}$

4.4 Long Message MAC Forgery on MAA

For a fixed key and message block x_i, the compression function of MAA is not a permutation. This causes the "loss of memory" problem, as was pointed out by Block [6], and mentioned by Davies [7]. If a large number of variations of the first blocks are chosen, all 2^n states will be reached at some point. However, if the next message blocks are kept constant, it can be shown that the fraction of states $y[i]$ at stage i can be approximated by $2/(i + \frac{1}{3}\ln i + \frac{9}{5})$, for $i \geq 1$. To control this effect, ISO 8731 [10] limits the size of the messages to $4 \cdot 10^6$ bytes ($\approx$ 3.8 Megabytes). Also, the standard defines a special mode for messages longer than 1024 bytes (256 blocks). In this mode, MAA is applied to the first 1024 bytes, and the corresponding 4-byte MAC is concatenated to the next 1024 bytes of the message to form the new input of MAA. This procedure is repeated with the next 1024-byte block, until the end of the message is reached. This may be interpreted as the definition of a "meta" compression function based on MAA which compresses 1028 bytes to 4 bytes. This thwarts attacks using more than 256 zero blocks, including the forgery attack of Proposition 5 which requires a single chosen text.

However, it follows from Table 3 that the attack with zero blocks can be done with about $2^{24.7}$ messages of about 1000 bytes, independent of the special mode. Ironically the basic attack (using Proposition 2) of §4.2 works even slightly better with the special mode: in the case that $s \geq 256$, an additional non-bijective mapping exists, resulting in an additional opportunity for an internal collision. Consequently s may be replaced by $s + \lfloor s/256 \rfloor$.

4.5 Key Recovery Attack on MAA

A key recovery attack on a MAC is considerably more serious than a forgery, as key recovery allows MAC forgery on arbitrary messages and without additional work, whereas forgeries are often existential only (and then of questionable practical use) and often chosen texts are required for each additional forged MAC. Under certain circumstances an internal collision for MAA allows key recovery.

A first case is when we have a weak key for which the period of $V < 32$ (see §4.3). One can verify the period of V by simulating the attack of Lemma 1, using two sets of $2^{17.3}$ chosen texts containing 131 072 trailing zero blocks each. In one set all messages have length 0 mod 32; in the other all have length 16 mod 32. One expects 9 internal collisions between messages of these two sets and 6 external collisions, but these cannot yet be distinguished from each other. The simulated attack of Lemma 1 then (with high probability) filters the external collisions. If V has period < 32, this attack will work for all the internal collisions, and it will fail otherwise. The key recovery attack will fail if there are no internal collisions; since the number of internal collisions is Poisson distributed, the probability of this event, for 9 internal collisions as above, is $e^{-9} \approx 0.01\%$. In this way it is evident if V belongs to this special set of 2^{48} keys. If so, finding the key then requires an exhaustive search over only 2^{48} keys (rather than 2^{64}). This attack has success probability 2^{-16} (since 2^{48} of 2^{64} keys are weak). Note that in this case the long message mode can be thwarted by using two sets of $2^{25.8}$ messages with about 256 trailing zero blocks; this will yield about 9 internal collisions, and about $2^{19.6}$ external collisions. The rest of the attack is similar; the second step requires slightly more work. We partially summarize these observations as follows.

Proposition 6. *For MAA, one can detect, using 2^{27} chosen messages of about 1 Kbyte each, whether a key belongs to a subclass of 2^{48} weak keys.* ∎

A second attack is based on an internal collision which is created by the message only, i.e. the chaining variables that enter the round are identical. This can be achieved by trying all 2^{32} possible values for the first message block, or similarly by doing this for the first block after a number of common leading blocks. The expected number of internal collisions is then Poisson distributed with $\lambda = 1/2$, with the probability that there are two internal collisions is given by $e^{-1/2}/4 = 0.152$. The unknowns affecting the internal collision are the parameters $(H1_0, V)$, and $(H2_0, W)$; see §4.1. A single internal collision ($H1_1 = H1'_1$, $H2_1 = H2'_1$) gives 64 bits of information about these parameters. Therefore two internal collisions yield enough information to find a solution.

We have developed an algorithm which can then solve for the 64 bits of the key inputs (via the 128 bits of the unknown parameters), starting from the least significant bit (to control the propagation of the carries). Also, the algorithm exploits the fact that $(H1_0, V)$ and $(H2_0, W)$ depend on different halves of the input key. A preliminary estimate is that the key can be recovered in at most 2^{50} operations (cf. 2^{64} for exhaustive key search). The expected number of chosen texts required is about 2^{35} to guarantee a high success probability. More details will be provided in the full paper.

5 Concluding Remarks

Two improved variations of a general MAC forgery attack have been presented, tailored for specific algorithms. For both the envelope method as discussed herein and the MAA, the forgery attack may be adapted to allow key recovery. In addition the internal structure of MAA may be exploited to reduce the total number of bytes of known text-MAC pairs required for the attack. An important conclusion is that the standard padding of a hash function should be modified when it is transformed into a MAC. This should not be surprising, since unkeyed hash functions are not typically designed for use as MACs.

Acknowledgements

We would like to thank Vincent Rijmen for help on the MAA attack.

References

1. M. Bellare, J. Kilian, P. Rogaway, "The security of cipher block chaining," *Proc. Crypto'94, LNCS 839*, Springer-Verlag, 1994, pp. 341–358.

2. M. Bellare, R. Guérin, P. Rogaway, "XOR MACs: new methods for message authentication using block ciphers," *Proc. Crypto'95, LNCS 963*, Springer-Verlag, 1995, pp. 15–28.
3. M. Bellare, R. Canetti, H. Krawczyk, "How to key Merkle–Cascaded pseudorandomness and its concrete security", 10 November 1995, http:// www.research.ibm.com/security/.
4. M. Bellare, R. Canetti, H. Krawczyk, "Keying hash functions for message authentication," 25 January 1996, http:// www.research.ibm.com/security/.
5. E. Biham, A. Shamir, *Differential Cryptanalysis of the Data Encryption Standard,* Springer-Verlag, 1993.
6. H. Block, "File authentication: A rule for constructing algorithms," *SÄKdata Report,* October 12, 1983.
7. D. Davies, "A message authenticator algorithm suitable for a mainframe computer," *Proc. Crypto'84, LNCS 196*, Springer-Verlag, 1985, pp. 393–400.
8. D. Davies, D.O. Clayden, "The message authenticator algorithm (MAA) and its implementation," *NPL Report DITC 109/88*, Feb. 1988.
9. D. Davies, W. Price, *Security for Computer Networks*, 2nd ed., Wiley, 1989.
10. ISO 8731:1987, *Banking – approved algorithms for message authentication, Part 1, DEA,* IS 8731-1, *Part 2, Message Authentication Algorithm (MAA),* IS 8731-2.
11. ISO/IEC 9797:1993, *Information technology – Data cryptographic techniques – Data integrity mechanisms using a cryptographic check function employing a block cipher algorithm.*
12. B. Kaliski, M. Robshaw, "Message authentication with MD5," *CryptoBytes (RSA Laboratories Technical Newsletter)*, Vol. 1, No. 1, Spring 1995, pp. 5–8.
13. M. Matsui, "The first experimental cryptanalysis of the Data Encryption Standard," *Proc. Crypto'94, LNCS 839*, Springer-Verlag, 1994, pp. 1–11.
14. B. Preneel, P.C. van Oorschot, "MDx-MAC and building fast MACs from hash functions", *Proc. Crypto'95, LNCS 963*, Springer-Verlag, 1995, pp. 1–14.
15. R.L. Rivest, "The MD5 message-digest algorithm," *Request for Comments (RFC) 1321*, Internet Activities Board, Internet Privacy Task Force, April 1992.
16. P. Rogaway, "Bucket hashing and its application to fast message authentication", *Proc. Crypto'95, LNCS 963*, Springer-Verlag, 1995, pp. 29–42.
17. P. Metzger, W. Simpson, "IP Authentication using Keyed MD5", Internet Request for Comments 1828, August 1995.
18. G. Tsudik, "Message authentication with one-way hash functions," *ACM Computer Communications Review*, Vol. 22, No. 5, 1992, pp. 29–38.

Hidden Fields Equations (HFE) and Isomorphisms of Polynomials (IP): Two New Families of Asymmetric Algorithms

Jacques PATARIN

CP8 Transac,
68 route de Versailles, BP 45,
78431 Louveciennes Cedex, France

Abstract. In [6] T. Matsumoto and H. Imai described a new asymmetric algorithm based on multivariate polynomials of degree two over a finite field, which was subsequently broken in [9]. Here we present two new families of Asymmetric Algorithms that so far have resisted all attacks, if properly used: Hidden Field Equations (HFE) and Isomorphism of Polynomials (IP). These algorithms can be seen as two candidate ways to repair the Matsumoto-Imai Algorithm. HFE can be used to do signatures, encryption or authentication in an asymmetric way, with very short signatures and short encryptions of short messages. IP can be used for signatures and for zero knowledge authentication.
An extended version of this paper can be obtained from the author. Another way to repair the Matsumoto-Imai Algorithm will be presented in [10].

1 Introduction

Currently the security of most algorithms that we know in Asymmetric Cryptography for encryption or signatures relies on the unproved intractability of the integer factorization or discrete log problem. One of the challenges of Asymmetric Cryptography is to find new and efficient algorithms for encryption or signatures that do not depend on these two closely related problems. For authentication the situation is much better, due to the algorithms presented for example in [12] and [13].

In this paper we propose two new classes of Asymmetric Algorithms whose security does not depend on factoring or discrete logs: Hidden Field Equations (HFE) and Isomorphism of Polynomials (IP). Furthermore HFE also address two other problems facing Asymmetric Cryptography: generating very short asymmetric signatures, and generating short encryptions of short messages. Both HFE and IP are based on a scheme described by T. Matsumoto and H. Imai (cf. [6]). In [9] an efficient attack against this scheme was presented. Unfortunately, we are not able to prove the security of HFE or IP either, but so far they have resisted all attacks, including the one from [9]. Moreover IP-based authentications can be proved to be zero-knowledge.

Ueli Maurer (Ed.): EUROCRYPT '96 Proceedings, LNCS 1070

2 Preliminaries

Throughout this paper we use the following notation. We denote by $\mathbf{F}_q$ a finite field of cardinality q and characteristic p, for some prime p and prime power $q = p^m$. let $\mathbf{F}_{q^n}$ be an extension of degree n of $\mathbf{F}_q$. Let

$$f(x) = \sum_{i,j} \beta_{ij} x^{q^{\theta_{ij}} + q^{\varphi_{ij}}} + \sum_k \alpha_k x^{q^{\xi_k}} + \mu \in \mathbf{F}_{q^n}[x]$$

be a polynomial in x over $\mathbf{F}_{q^n}$ of degree d, for integers $\theta_{ij}, \varphi_{ij}, \xi_k \geq 0$.

Since $\mathbf{F}_{q^n}$ is isomorphic to $\mathbf{F}_q[x]/(g(x))$, if $g(x) \in \mathbf{F}_q[x]$ is irreducible of degree n, elements of $\mathbf{F}_{q^n}$ may be represented as n-tuples over $\mathbf{F}_q$, and f may be represented as a polynomial in n variables $x_1, x_2, \ldots, x_n$ over $\mathbf{F}_q$:

$$f(x_1, \ldots, x_n) = (p_1(x_1, \ldots, x_n), \ldots, p_n(x_1, x_2, \ldots, x_n)) \in \mathbf{F}_q[x_1, \ldots, x_n],$$

with $p_i(x_1, \ldots, x_n) \in \mathbf{F}_q[x_1, \ldots, x_n]$, for $i = 1, 2, \ldots, n$. The p_i are quadratic polynomials due to the choice of f and the fact that $x \mapsto x^q$ is a linear function of $\mathbf{F}_{q^n} \to \mathbf{F}_{q^n}$.

Note that f may be a permutation of $\mathbf{F}_{q^n}$, in which case each $a \in \mathbf{F}_{q^n}$ gives rise to precisely one solution $x \in \mathbf{F}_{q^n}$ to the equation $f(x) = a$. If f consists of more than one monomial in x, however, it seems to be difficult to choose f such that it is a permutation (cf. [5: Chapter 7] or [8]). Obviously, for any $a \in \mathbf{F}_{q^n}$ there are at most d solutions to $f(x) = a$, and often there are only a few. It is well known that solutions to $f(x) = a$ can be found in deterministic time polynomial in p, m, n, and d, and in expected time polynomial in $\log p$, m, n, and d, cf. [1: 17-26], [5: Chapter 4], [14], [15]. Some run times can be found in [7].

3 Hidden Field Equations for Encryption

In this paragraph we will describe a first version of HFE for encryption (i.e. the version with the easiest description).

We assume that the message M is represented as an n-tuple x over $\mathbf{F}_q$, where $\mathbf{F}_q$ as above is publicly known. (Thus, if $p = 2$, each message can be represented by nm bits.) Moreover, we assume that some redundancy has been included in the representation of each message, in such a way that the redundancy depends in a non-linear way on M. A nice way to do this is to make use of an error correcting code. If $p = 2$ we could also obtain x by concatenating the binary representation of M and the first 64 bits of $h(M)$, where h is a hash function such as MD5 or SHA, as long as the resulting x has at most nm bits.

Let s and t be two affine bijections $(\mathbf{F}_q)^n \to (\mathbf{F}_q)^n$, where $(\mathbf{F}_q)^n$ is regarded as an n-dimensional vector space over $\mathbf{F}_q$. Both s and t can be represented as n-tuples of polynomials in n variables over $\mathbf{F}_q$ of total degree 1. Using the function f from Section 2 and some representation of $\mathbf{F}_{q^n}$ over $\mathbf{F}_q$ as in Section 2, the function $(\mathbf{F}_q)^n \to (\mathbf{F}_q)^n$ that assigns $t(f(s(x)))$ to $x \in (\mathbf{F}_q)^n$ can be written as

$$t(f(s(x_1, \ldots, x_n))) = (p_1(x_1, \ldots, x_n), \ldots, p_n(x_1, x_2, \ldots, x_n)) \in \mathbf{F}_q[x_1, \ldots, x_n],$$

with $p_i(x_1, \ldots, x_n) \in \mathbf{F}_q[x_1, \ldots, x_n]$, for $i = 1, 2, \ldots, n$. The p_i are quadratic polynomials due to the choices of s, t, and f. Furthermore, given s, t, f and the way $\mathbf{F}_{q^n}$ is represented over $\mathbf{F}_q$, the polynomials p_i can efficiently be computed. The converse, however, seems to be hard, if s, t, and f are properly chosen. This leads to the following public key encryption scheme, which we call 'Hidden Field Equations' (HFE).

Secret key. A function f as in Section 2, two affine bijections s and t as above, and some way of representing $\mathbf{F}_{q^n}$ over $\mathbf{F}_q$. The latter may or may not be secret since changing the representation is equivalent to changing s or t; therefore, we may assume some fixed (and public) way of representing $\mathbf{F}_{q^n}$.

Public key. Polynomials p_i for $i = 1, 2, \ldots, n$ as above, computed using the secret key f, s, t. Furthermore, $\mathbf{F}_q$, the extension degree n and the way to add redundancy to a message are public.

Encryption. To encrypt the n-tuple $x = (x_1, \ldots, x_n) \in (\mathbf{F}_q)^n$ (representing the message M plus redundancy), compute the ciphertext

$$y = (p_1(x_1, \ldots, x_n), \ldots, p_n(x_1, x_2, \ldots, x_n)).$$

Decryption. To decrypt the ciphertext y, first find all solutions z to the equation $f(z) = t^{-1}(y)$ (cf. Section 2), next compute all $s^{-1}(z)$'s, and finally use the redundancy to find M from these.

Security considerations. We conclude this section with a few remarks concerning the security of HFE. We have restricted ourselves to the case where the characteristic p is equal to 2, even though HFE works for any small prime value p (unlike the Matsumoto-Imai scheme from [6], which only works for $p = 2$).

1. To avoid exhaustive search attacks we recommend that the message M consists of at least 64 bits and of at least 128 bits including redundancy.

2. In order to avoid the "affine multiple attack" that is described in the next section, we recommend to choose f of degree at least 17, but small enough to make decryption efficient. For computational examples of this attack we refer to the next section. Furthermore, to foil this attack it is necessary (but not sufficient) that f consists of at least two monomials in x: HFE with one monomial is equivalent to a Matsumoto-Imai algorithm, and can be attacked as described in [9]. We have done some Toy simulations of the vulnerability of HFE to the attack from [9] for $n = 13$. Though our tests enabled us to identify weak keys, they did not lead to a method to break HFE for well chosen keys. Details can be found in the extended version of this paper.

3. Some authentication algorithms (such as [12] or [13]) are proved to be as secure as a NP hard problem. (This is a very nice result of security but of course

this is not a proof of absolute security: a problem can be NP hard but easy in average, or easy with bad parameters, or difficult only with very large parameters). Can we also hope to prove that HFE is as secure as a NP hard problem? No: from a generalisation of a theorem given by G. Brassard in [2] we can prove that to recover a cleartext from an encrypted HFE Text is never an NP hard problem (if NP $\neq$ co NP). However this is not really a flaw of HFE but a property of almost all asymmetric encryption algorithms.

Idea of the proof. Let F be an asymmetric encryption algorithm with a secret key K and a public key k such that when the secret key K is given and when a value y is given it is always very easy to see if there is or not a cleartext x such that $y = F_k(x)$, i.e. such that y is the encryption of x by the algorithm F with the public key k. HFE, as all efficient encryption algorithms (such as RSA) has of course this property. Now let us consider the problem: "Is there an x such that $y = F_k(x)$?", where y is a given value. Then if the answer is "yes" x is a certificate that indeed the answer is "yes", i.e. it is easy to verify that the answer is "yes" if such an x is given (K is also another certificate). Moreover if the answer is "no" K is a certificate that indeed the answer is "no". So this problem is in NP $\cap co$ NP. But (if NP $\neq co$ NP) there is no NP hard problem in NP $\cap co$ NP. Similarly if from the secret key K we can compute easilly all the x such that $y = F_k(x)$, then the problem: "Is there an x such that $y = F_k(x)$ and $a \leq x \leq b$?", where a and b are two integers, is also in NP $\cap co$ NP.So to recover a cleartext x from its corresponding cyphertext y can not be a NP hard problem. This shows that there is little hope to design any practical asymmetric encryption algorithm with a security proved to be based on a NP hard problem. It is also instructive to see that RSA may (or may not) be as secrure as the factorisation problem because the factorisation problem is in $NP \cap co\ NP$ (so is not a NP hard problem).

This result could suggest that when we have introduce a trapdoor in HFE, in order to have a cryptosystem usefull for encryption, we may have weaken the problem. This results shows also that the problem on with the security of HFE relies is not clearly shown (it can not be the general NP hard problem of solving randomly selected system of multivariate quadratic equations over $GF(2)$). However to recover a cleartext from its HFE ciphertext is still expected to be exponentally difficult when the HFE parameters are properly chosen.

4 The affine multiple attack

Introduction The "affine multiple attack" of the basic HFE that we will consider in this paragraph is a generalization of the main attack of [9] of the Matsumoto-Imai Algorithm. It is the only attack that we know against the basic HFE that can sometimes be much better than "quasi" exhaustive search on the cleartext (i.e. exhaustive search on most of the cleartext).

Principle of the attack Let f be a polynomial used in the basic HFE algorithm. By using a general algorithm (see for example [1] p. 25) we know that there are always some affine (in x) multiple $A(x, y)$ of the polynomial $f(x) - y$. (This means that $x \mapsto A(x, y)$ is an affine function and that each solution x of $f(x) = y$ is also a solution of $A(x, y) = 0$). For example in characteristic 2 the polynomial $A(x, y)$ will have only $1, x, x^2, x^4, x^8 \ldots, x^{2^j}, \ldots$ as monomials in x.

From now on we will assume for simplicity that the characteristic is 2.

Moreover, sometimes for such an affine multiple $A(x, y)$ all the exponents in y have small Hamming Weight in base 2. If this occurs, then the polynomial f will be a weak key for HFE.

More precisely if all the exponents in y have a Hamming Weight $\leq k$, then there will be an attack with a Gaussian reduction on $0(n^{1+k})$ terms (more precisely with about $\sum_{i=1}^{k} n^{1+i}/i!$ terms because we have about $n^{1+i}/i!$ terms of total degree i in the y_j variables, $1 \leq i \leq k$) where n is the number of bits of the message. This attack will work exactly as the attack of [9] for the Matsumoto-Imai Algorithm. The Gaussian reduction needed may be easier than a general Gaussian reduction but the complexity will be at worst in $0(n^{3k+3})$ and at least in $0(n^{1+k})$. Gaussian reductions with N terms are asymptotically in N^{ω} with $\omega < 2.376$ (cf. [3]). Moreover we can choose some x but not some y, so in the equations on which we need to do a Gaussian reduction we will have at least $O(n^{1+2k})$ unpredictible values. So it seems that more precisely the Gaussian reduction needed will be at most in $O(n^{(1+k)\omega})$ and at least in $O(n^{1+2k})$.

Example 1. Let $f(x) = x^{1+2^\theta}$. So $x^{1+2^\theta} = y$.

Then $x^{2^{2\theta}}.y = x.y^{2^\theta}$. So $A(x, y) = x^{2^{2\theta}}y + xy^{2^\theta}$ is an affine multiple of $f(x) + y$, and here all the exponents in y have a Hamming Weight ≤ 1. This leads to the attack with a Gaussian reduction on $0(n^2)$ terms described in [9].

Example 2. Let $f(x) = x^5 + x^3 + x = y$.

Then it is possible to prove that $y^3.x + (y^2 + 1)x^4 + x^{16} = 0$.

Here all the exponents in y have a Hamming Weight ≤ 2. So this leads to an attack of the HFE algorithm with a Gaussian reduction on $0(n^3)$ terms if this polynomial f is used. So this polynomial should not be used (it's a weak polynomial).

Example 3. Let $f(x) = x^9 + x^6 + x^5 + x^3 + x = y$.

Then the affine multiple $A(x,y)$ of $f(x)$ of degree 2^8 in x found by AXIOM is:

$$\begin{aligned}
&(y^{27}+y^{24}+y^{23}+y^{20}+y^{19}+y^{11}+y^{8}+y^{7}+y^{4}+y^{3})x\\
&+(y^{27}+y^{25}+y^{21}+y^{20}+y^{15}+y^{9}+y^{7}+y^{5}+y^{4}+y^{3})x^2\\
&+(y^{28}+y^{26}+y^{25}+y^{20}+y^{18}+y^{16}+y^{14}+y^{9}+y^{8}+y^{6}+y^{4}+1)x^4\\
&+(y^{22}+y^{21}+y^{18}+y^{16}+y^{15}+y^{14}+y^{13}+y^{10}+y^{8}+y^{7})x^8\\
&+(y^{25}+y^{22}+y^{21}+y^{19}+y^{17}+y^{12}+y^{11}+y^{6}+y^{5})x^{16}\\
&+(y^{23}+y^{20}+y^{19}+y^{18}+y^{17}+y^{16}+y^{15}+y^{14}+y^{13}+y^{11}+y^{10}+y^{9}+y^{8}+y^{6}+y^{5})x^{32}\\
&+(y^{18}+y^{17}+y^{14}+y^{11}+y^{10}+y^{9}+y^{6}+y^{3})x^{64}\\
&+(y^{13}+y^{11}+y^{5}+y^{4}+y^{3})x^{128}\\
&+x^{256}.
\end{aligned}$$

In $A(x,y)$ the largest Hamming Weight of the exponents in y is 4.
So this leads to an attack with a Gaussian reduction on $0(n^5)$ terms if this polynomial is used. This attack will need a lot of power but may be feasible. (For example if $n=64$ it will need Gaussian reduction on 2^{25} variables ($\simeq n^5/4!$) and if $n=128$ it will need Gaussian reduction on 2^{30} variables...). So we do not recommend to use this function f.

Example 4. Let $f(x)=x^{12}+x^8+x^4+x^3+x^2+x=y$.
Then one of the affine multiple of $f(x)$ found by axiom is:

$$\begin{aligned}
&x^{256}+(y^{16}+y)x^{64}+(y^8+y^5+y^2)x^{16}+(y^3+1)x^4\\
&+yx+y^{16}+y^8+y^5+y^3+y^2=0.
\end{aligned}$$

Here all the exponents in y have a Hamming Weight ≤ 2.
So this polynomial f should not be used for HFE.
Since the degree of f was not so small (it was 12), and since f had a lot of monomials (6), this example shows that the affine multiple attack has to be taken seriously: it is not always obvious whether it works or not.

Example 5. Let $f(x)=x^{17}+x^9+x^4+x^3+x^2+x=y$.
With AXIOM, we have computed the least affine multiple $A(x,y)$ of $f(x)+y$ (it took us two days on a workstation).
In $A(x,y)$ all the exponents in y are ≤ 3840, and the exponent with the largest Hamming Weight as a Hamming Weight of 11.
So this affine multiple leads to an attack of HFE with this polynomial f with a Gaussian reduction on $0(n^{12})$ terms, where $n\geq 64$. (For $n=128$ it will need Gaussian reduction on 2^{58} terms because $2^{58}\simeq n^{12}/11!$).
Since this attack is completely impracticable, this polynomial f resists to the "affine multiple attack" and may be a strong polynomial for HFE.

Example 6. Let $f(x)=x^{17}+x^{16}+x^5+x=y$.
With AXIOM (also after two days of computations) we have computed the least affine multiple $A(x,y)$ of $f(x)+y$. In $A(x,y)$ the exponents with the largest Hamming Weight have a Hamming Weight also of 11.
So this function may also be a strong polynomial for HFE.

Note: What is nice with this function is that this function is not only quadratic over $\mathbf{F}_2$ but also quadratic over $\mathbf{F}_4$. (So the public computations will be easier with this function).

Asymptotic complexity For large d, and for most of the polynomials f of degree d, the complexity of the affine multiple attack of the basic HFE with this polynomial f is expected to be in $0(n^{0(d)})$.
So, if $d = 0(n)$ the complexity of the attack is expected to be exponential in n. Moreover, $d = 0(\ln n)$ is expected to be sufficient to avoid all polynomial attacks.

Conclusion The affine multiple attack is very efficient for some very special polynomials. However when the degree of f is ≥ 17 and when f is well chosen, this attack is expected to fail completely.

Note For easier computations, we have chosen in all the examples the constant terms in the monomials of f equal to 0 or 1.
Of course this is not an obligation and any elements of the extension field can be chosen.

5 HFE variations

HFE plus and minus some p_i equations. The polynomials $(p_1, \ldots, p_n)$ of the HFE Algorithm of paragraph 3 gives y from x. Since there is some redundancy in x it may be possible to recover x from y without some of these polynomials. For example when p_{n-1} and p_n are omitted it may still be possible to recover x from y: we will just compute the 2^{2m} possibilities and find the good x thanks to the redundancy in x. When m is very small, for example when $m = 1$ or 2 this is clearly feasible.
So we can imagine that just $p_1, \ldots p_{n-2}$ are public.

Note. This idea of ommiting some polynomial p_i can also be done in the original Matsumoto-Imai scheme (instead of HFE). However this is not recommended: in the extended version of this paper we give some ideas for the cryptanalysis of such a scheme.

HFE with multivariate field equations for encryption. Here the idea is to change the description of the function f given in paragraph 2. We can notice that what we need for f is that:
1. In a basis, f is a multivariate quadratic function.
2. For any value a, it is easy to find all the x so that $f(x) = a$.
3. f is a function with inputs and outputs with at least 64 bits (the reason for this is that we can not have small "branches" in the algorithm: we will give more details about this in the next paragraph).
The solution given in paragraph 2 was to choose for f a polynomial in only one variable x over $\mathbf{F}_{q^n}$ so that, in a basis, f is a multivariate quadratic function.

In the extended version of this paper we present some different candidates for f: polynomials in two variables x_1 and x_2, or more. An efficient algorithm of resolution of $f(x) = a$ (for example with Gröbner basis or with something else) will be hidden by the two affine functions s and t.

HFE with more than one branch. In the original Matsumoto-Imai Algorithm [6] the values are split in different branchs after the first affine transformation s. We could also imagine to do this in a HFE scheme. However, in the extended version of this paper we show that if the branchs are small then it is always easy to attack the scheme by detecting and isolating the small branchs. So we do not recommend to use more than one branch.

HRE: Hidden Rings Equations. In paragraph 2 we said that the field $\mathbf{F}_{q^n}$ is typically $\mathbf{F}_q[x]/(g(x))$, where $g(x) \in \mathbf{F}_q[x]$ is irreductible of degree n.
If $g(x)$ is not irreductible, then $\mathbf{F}_q[x]/(g(x))$ will then not be a finite field, but a finite ring. In such a space the resolution of $f(x) = y$, where f is a univariate polynomial is still feasible. For example the linearized polynomial algorithm still works. So we can design an asymetric scheme in such a space exactly as HFE in the finite field $\mathbf{F}_{q^n}$.

HFE with public polynomials of degree ≥ 3. Of course we can also choose for f a polynomial with some exponents in x of Hamming Weight still small but ≥ 3. A very important subcase, from a practical point of view, if when this function is $f(x) = x^{1+q^\theta+q^\varphi}$, i.e. with only one monomial and Hamming Weight 3. The study of these functions is one of the main subject of [10].

Concatenation of two basic HFE or HRE for fast decryptions. Let x be the cleartext. Let $y_1 = HFE_1(x)$ be the encryption of x with a first HFE encryption with secret affine functions s_1 and t_1. Let $y_2 = HFE_2(x)$ be the encryption of x with another HFE, such that HFE_1 and HFE_2 have different polynomials f_1 and f_2 and independent secret affine functions t_1 and t_2, but the same extension field $\mathbf{F}_{q^n}$, and the same secret affines functions $s_1 = s_2$. Then let $y_1||y_2$ be the encryption of x, where $||$ is the concatenation function.
The main advantage of this scheme is that decryption with the secret keys may be very fast, as we will see now. From y_1 and y_2, $f_1(a)$ and $f_2(a)$ will be obtained, and then $GCD(f_1(a), f_2(a))$ will be computed. Then from this GCD the value of a will be obtained with one of the classical algorithm of resolution of equation. Then $x = s_1^{-1}(a)$ will be obtained.
In average the time of computation of $GCD(f_1(a), f_2(a))$ is expected to be dominant. This time is $\leq 0(d^2n^2)$, where $d = \sup(d_1, d_2)$. So if d_1 and d_2 are not too large decryption will really be very fast (and much faster than in the basic HFE).
For example the complexity of decryption may be $\leq 0(n \ln^3 n)$ for well chosen f_1 and f_2 with degree $(f_1) \leq 0(\ln n)$ and degree $(f_2) \leq 0(\ln n)$.
However it is not recommended generally in cryptography to encrypt the same message twice by two different encryptions. Moreover this is generally particulary

not recommended when the two encryptions are not independents. So if this variation is really used we recommend to be extra-careful in the choice of the polynomials f_1 and f_2. For example not only f_1 and f_2 should avoid the "Affine multiple attack", but also $f_1 + f_2$.

6 HFE in signature or Authentication

All encryption algorithm can also be use as an authentication algorithm: the verifier will encrypt a challenge and ask for the cleartext. So HFE can be use for authentications. Moreover HFE can also be slightly modified in order to give asymmetric signatures. We will now give two examples of such transformations. In the first example the signatures will have 160 bits, and in the second example the signature will have about 128 bits. However in these examples the time needed to compute a signature is not constant: some messages may be much easier to sign than some others.

Example 1

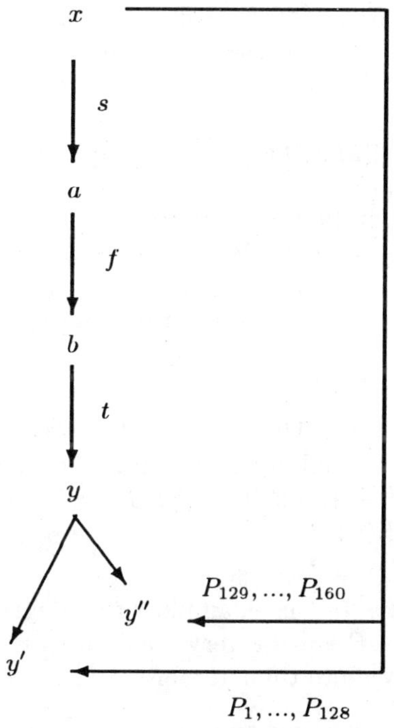

Fig. 1. Example 1 of HFE in signature. x : the signature (160 bits). y' : the hash to sign (128 bits). $P_1, \ldots, P_{128}$ are public. $P_{129}, \ldots, P_{160}$ are secrets.

Let us consider an HFE algorithm, as described in the next paragraphs, with x and y of about 128+32=160 bits.
Let $p_1, \ldots, p_n$ be the n public polynomials that give y from x, with $n = 160$ and $\mathbf{F}_q = \mathbf{F}_2$ for example.
If only p_1 to p_{128} of these polynomials are public (the over are secret), then the polynomials $p_1, \ldots p_{128}$, give a value z of 128 bits from a value x of 160 bits.
In our algorithm here z is the hash of a message to sign and x will be the signature of z. When z is given, then with the secret polynomials p_{129} to p_{160} and the other secret values we will be able to find a value x so that from this x, the polynomials $p_1, \ldots, p_{128}$ will give exactly the value z.
For this we will padd z with 32 extra bits and try to find an x with a decryption of the HFE algorithm. If it fails we try with another padding until we succeed.
In figure 1 we illustrate such a use of HFE in signature.

Example 2

Computation of the signature In this example 2 to sign a message M there will be three steps.

Step 1. We generate a small integer R with no block of numbers with 10000 in its expression in base 2 (for example $R = 0$ to start).
Step 2. We compute $h(R||10000||M)$ where h is a public collision free hash function with an output of 128 bits (for example h is the MD5 algorithm).
Step 3. We consider an HFE algorithm (as in paragraph 3) with values x and y of 128 bits.
If we take $y = h(R||10000||M)$, then we can (with the secret key) try to find a cleartext x so that $HFE(x) = y$.
If we succeed, then $R||x$ will be the signature of M.
If we do not succeed (because since HFE is not a permutation some value y have no corresponding x) then we try again at Step 1 with another R (for example with the new R equal to the old $R + 1$ if this new R has no block of 10000 in base 2).

Verification of a signature The message M and a signature $R||x$ of M is given. First, we separate R and x (since x has a fix length of 128 bits this is easy). Then we compute $h(R||10000||M)$ and $HFE(x)$ and the signature is valid if $h(R||10000||M) = HFE(x)$.

Length of the signature In this example 2 the length of the signature is not fixed. However in average R will be very small so that the signature $R||x$ will have in average just a few more than 128 bits.

Note. Of course the pattern 10000 is just an example and another pattern P can be chosen. More precisely the property that we want is that from $R||P||M$ we can recover R and M when we know that R do not have the pattern P. (So the pattern will have at least one 1 and one 0).

7 The Isomorphism of Polynomials (IP) authentication and signature scheme

7.1 Introduction

We will now present a new authentication scheme called "Isomorphism of Polynomials" (IP).
IP authentications have a few nice properties:
- It is proved zero-knowledge.
- We know exactly the problem on which the security of the scheme relies.
- The scheme is very symmetric, and the design of the scheme is very similar to the well known "Graph Isomorphism Authentication scheme" (cf. [11] p. 88-89 for example).
- No hash functions are needed.
- IP illustrates the fact that if in HFE the function f is public the HFE scheme may be still secure.

However if all these nice properties show that IP is a scheme of theoretical interest IP may not be as practical in Authentication as the schemes of [12] or [13] or as HFE. (Essentially because of the large number of bits to exchange or because of the lenght of the public key). Moreover HFE can be used for authentication, signatures, or encryption, and IP is just for authentication or signatures.

7.2 The Isomorphism of Polynomials Problem with two secrets s and t

Let u and n be two integers. Let $\mathbf{F}_q$ be a finite field.
Let A be a public set of u quadratic equations with n variables $x_1, \ldots, x_n$ over the field $\mathbf{F}_q$. We can write all these equations like this:

$$y_k = \sum_i \sum_j \gamma_{ijk} x_i x_j + \sum_i \mu_{ik} x_i + \delta_k, \quad \text{for } k = 1, \ldots u \tag{1}$$

Now let s be a bijective and affine transformation of the variables x_i, $1 \leq i \leq n$, and let t be a bijective and affine transformation of the variables y_k, $1 \leq k \leq u$. Let $s(x_1, \ldots, x_n) = (x'_1, \ldots, x'_n)$, and $t(y_1, \ldots, y_u) = (y'_1, \ldots, y'_u)$.
From (1) we will obtain k equations that gives the y'_k values from the x'_i values like this:

$$y'_k = \sum_i \sum_j \gamma'_{ijk} x'_i x'_j + \sum_i \mu'_{ik} x'_i + \delta'_k, \quad \text{for } k = 1, \ldots u. \tag{2}$$

Let B be the set of these u equations. We will say that A and B are "isomorphic", i.e. there is a double bijective and affine transformation that gives B from A. And we will say that (s, t) is an "isomorphism" from A to B. The "Isomorphism of Polynomials Problem" is this problem: when A and B are two public sets of u quadratic equations, and if A and B are isomorphic, find an isomorphism (s, t) from A to B.

Example. If $u = n$ no polynomial algorithms to solve this problem are known. If such an algorithm were found then it would give us a way to find the keys of the Matsumoto-Imai algorithm (and not only a way to decrypt most of the messages). So it would give us a new, and more powerful, attack on the Matsumoto-Imai Algorithm. Moreover if such an algorithm were found then in HFE it would be essential for security to keep f secret. On the contrary as long as no such algorithm is found HFE may be still secure if f is public.

Note. We could think to proceed like this in order to find s and t: to introduce the matrix of s and t values and to formaly identify the equations (1) and (2). However we will obtain like this some equations of total degree three in the values of s and t and the general problem of solving equations of degree $\geq$ two in a finite field is NP hard. So this idea does not work.

7.3 The IP authentication scheme with two secrets s and t

Public: Two isomorphic sets A and B of u quadratic equations with n variables over a field $\mathbf{F}_q$.
Secret: An isomorphism (s, t) from A to B.

Notations The equations of A are the equations (1) of paragraph 7.2, they give the y_k values from x_i values, and the equations of B are the equations (2) of paragraph 7.2, they give the y'_k values from the x'_i values.
Let us assume that Alice knows the secret (s, t) and that Alice wants to convince Bob of this knowledge, without revealing her secret. Alice and Bob will follow this protocol:

Step 1. Alice randomly computes a set C of equations isomorphic to A.
For this, she randomly computes an affine bijection s' of the values $x_i, 1 \leq i \leq n$, and an affine bijection t' of the variables $y_k, 1 \leq k \leq u$.
The u equations of C are u equations like this:

$$y''_k = \sum_i \sum_j \gamma''_{ijk} x''_i x''_j + \sum_i \mu''_{ik} x''_i + \delta''_k, \quad \text{for } k = 1, \dots u. \tag{3}$$

- s gives the transformation $x \to x'$.
- t gives the transformation $y \to y'$.
- s' gives the transformation $x \to x''$.
- t' gives the transformation $y \to y''$.

Step 2. Alice gives the set C of equations (3) to Bob.
Step 3. Bob asks Alice either to

(a) Prove that A and C are isomorphic.
(b) Prove that B and C are isomorphic.

Moreover Bob choose to ask (a) or (b) randomly with the same probability 1/2.

Step 4. Alice complies.

If Bob ask (a), then she reveals s' and t'.

If Bob ask (b), then she reveals $s' \circ s^{-1}$ and $t' \circ t^{-1}$ (i.e. the transformations $x' \to x''$ and $y' \to y''$).

It is easy to prove that this protocol is zero-knowledge and that if somebody doesn't know an isomorphism (s, t) from A to B the probability to successfully pass the protocol is at most 1/2.
So if Alice and Bob repeat steps (1) to (4) N times, the probability of success will be at most $1/2^N$.

7.4 Parameters

Analogous to the problem of finding the secret affine transformations s and t of HFE when f is public or of the Matsumoto-Imai Algorithm, we could have $u = n = 64$ or 128 and $\mathbf{F}_q = \mathbf{F}_2$ for example in a IP authentication scheme. However more practical values may be sufficient for security.
In the extended version of this paper we give some comments about more practical values.

7.5 The IP problem with one secret s

Let n be an integer. Let $\mathbf{F}_q$ be a finite field. Let A be one public cubic equation with n variables $x_1, \ldots, x_n$ over the field $\mathbf{F}_q$. (Here in A we have only one equation, but of degree 3 and not 2). We can write this equation (A) like this:

$$\sum\sum\sum \gamma_{ijk} x_i x_j x_k + \sum\sum \mu_{ij} x_i x_j + \sum \alpha_i x_i + \delta_0 = 0. \qquad (A).$$

Now let s be a bijective and affine transformation of the variables $x_i, 1 \leq i \leq n$.
Let $s(x_1, \ldots, x_n) = (x'_1, \ldots, x'_n)$.
From (A) we will obtain one equation (B) in x'_i like this:

$$\sum\sum\sum \gamma'_{ijk} x'_i x'_j x'_k + \sum\sum \mu'_{ij} x'_i x'_j + \sum \alpha'_i x'_i + \delta_0 = 0 \qquad (B).$$

We will say that (A) and (B) are "isomorphic", i.e. there is a bijective and affine transformation that gives B from A. And we will say that s is an "isomorphism" from A to B. The "Isomorphism of Polynomials Problem" is now this problem: when A and B are two public sets of such equations, and if A and B are isomorphic, find an isomorphism s from A to B.

Note. For equations of total degree ≥ 3, we know no polynomial algorithm to solve this IP problems. However for equations of total degree 2 there is a polynomial algorithm to solve the problem, because there is a "canonical" representation of each quadratic equations over a finite field (cf. [5], chapter 6 for example). If (A) and (B) are isomorphic, then the two canonical representations of (A) and (B) will be easilly found, will be the same, and this will give the isomorphism from (A) to (B). This is the reason why we have chosen equations of degree ≥ 3.

7.6 The IP authentication scheme with one secret s

The IP problem with one secret s can easilly be use to design an authentication scheme in the same way we used the IP problem with two secrets s and t (more details are given in the extended version of this paper).

7.7 Less computations with larger public keys

Instead of only two public isomorphic equations (A) and (B), less us now assume that we have k public isomorphic equations $(P_1), (P_2), \dots (P_k)$.
We denote by $x_i^{(1)}$ the variables of $(P_1), \dots$ and by $x_i^{(k)}$ the variables of (P_k). And we denote by s_j the secret affine transformation from $x^{(1)}$ to $x^{(j)}$, $2 \le j \le k$. (So all the k equations are isomorphic to (P_1), so each couple of these equations are isomorphic).
Of course we can assume if we want that all the secret affine transformations $s_j, 2 \le j \le k$, are computed from one small secret K, for example K is a secret DES key and the matrix of the s_j are obtained by some computations of DES_K. So the public key is larger, since we have k equations (P_j), but the secret key can be still small.
The authentication now proceed like this:

Step 1. Alice randomly computes, as usual, one equation C isomorphic to P_1.
Step 2. Alice gives this equation C to Bob.
Step 3. Bob randomly chose a value u, $1 \le u \le k$, and ask Alice to prove that C and P_u are isomorphic.
Step 4. Alice complies.

It is still easy to prove that this protocol is zero-knowledge and that if somebody doesn't know any isomorphism s from one (P_i) to one (P_j), $i \neq j$, then the probability to successfully pass the protocol is at most $1/k$.
So if Alice and Bob repeat steps (1) to (4) N times, the probability of success will be at most $1/(k^N)$.

7.8 IP for asymmetric signatures

The Fiat-Shamir authentication scheme and the Guillou-Quisquater authentication scheme can be transformed in signature scheme by using a now classical transformation by introducing hash function. This transformation works also very well here for the IP algorithm.
Let M be the message to sign. The signature algorithm is this one:

Step 1. Alice randomly computes λ equations C_i isomorphic to P_1.
Step 2. Alice computes hash $(M||C_1||\dots C_\lambda)$, where $||$ is the concatenation function, and hash a public hash function sufficiently large such that the first bits of output can give λ values $e_1, \dots, e_\lambda$, where each e_i is a value between 1 and k.

Step 3. Alice computes the λ isomorphisms $t_i, 1 \leq i \leq \lambda$, such that each t_i is an isomorphism from C_i to P_{e_i}.

The signature on M by Alice is then (T, E) where T is the vector $(t_1, t_2, \ldots t_\lambda)$ and E is the vector $(e_1, e_2, \ldots e_\lambda)$.

To verify this signature, Bob proceeds like this:
Step 1. Bob computes $C_1, \ldots, C_\lambda$ such that $t_i, 1 \leq i \leq \lambda$ is an isomorphism from C_i to P_{e_i}.
Step 2. Bob checks that the first bits of hash $(M||C_1|| \ldots C_\lambda)$ are the entries e_i of E.

7.9 Numerical examples of IP signatures with one secret s

In signature we must have $k^\lambda \geq 2^{64}$ for security.
It is not clear what value of n should be taken, but we suggest $n \geq 16$ if $K = \mathbf{F}_2$. With $K = \mathbf{F}_2, n = 16, \lambda = 16$ and $k = 16$ then the lenght of the public key is 1120 bytes and the lenght of the signature is about 4128 bits. With $K = \mathbf{F}_2, n = 16, \lambda = 4$ and $k = 2^{16}$ then the lenght of the public key is $k.16.15.14/3!$ bits $=$ 4,4 Mo. This is huge but can be store in a hard disc of a Personal computer, and the lenght of the signature is $\simeq 4.(16 + 16.16) = 1088$ bits.

8 Conclusion

We have designed two new classes of Algorithms: HFE and IP. These algorithms are based on multivariate polynomials over a finite field of total degree two. One interesting point of HFE is that these algorithms can lead to very short asymmetric signatures (128 bits for example). Similarly they can encrypt messages by blocks whith very short blocks (128 bits blocks for example).
Another interesting point of these algorithms is that their security do not depend on factorisation or discret log, and very few algorithms for encryption or signatures in asymmetric cryptography are known that do no rely on these problems.
However a lot of problems are still open, for example:
Are these algorithms really secure ?
Is it possible to design strong HFE, with public polynomials of degree two and a secret function f with two or more monomials, that are also permutations ?
Is it possible to solve a general system of multivariate quadratic equations over $GF(2)$ much more quickly than with a quasi exhaustive search ?

Acknowledgments

I want to thank Isabelle Guerrin-Lassous for doing the simulations of paragraph 3.2. I want also to thank Daniel Augot for doing the simulations of paragraph 4. However Daniel Augot told me that he does not want to endorse the security of HFE... Finally I want to thank Arjen Lenstra for all the time he has spend to improve the redaction of this paper.

References

1. F. BLAKE, X. GAO, R. MULLIN, S. VANSTONE and T. YAGHOOBIAN, *"Application of Finite Fields"*, Kluwer Academic Publishers.
2. G. BRASSARD, *"A note on the complexity of cryptography"*, IEEE Tran. Inform. Theory, Vol. IT-25, pp. 232-233, 1979.
3. D. COPPERSMITH and S. WINOGRAD, *"Matrix Multiplication via Arithmetic Progressions"*, J. Symbolic Computation, 1990, Vol. 9, pp. 251-280.
4. M. GAREY, D. JOHNSON, *"Computers and intractability, A Guide to the Theory of NP-Completeness"*, FREEMAN.
5. R. LIDL, H. NIEDERREITER, *"Finite Fields"*, Encyclopedia of Mathematics and its applications, Volume 20, Cambridge University Press.
6. T. MATSUMOTO and H. IMAI, *"Public Quadratic Polynomial-tuples for efficient signature-verification and message-encryption"*, EUROCRYPT'88, Springer Verlag 1988, pp. 419-453.
7. A. MENEZES, P. VAN OORSCHOT ans S. VANSTONE, *"Some computational aspects of root finding in $GF(q^m)$"*, in Symbolic and Algebraic Computation, Lecture Notes in Computer Science, 358 (1989), pp. 259-270.
8. Gary L. MULLEN, *"Permutation Polynomials over Finite Fields"*, in "Finite Fields, Coding Theory, and Advances in Communications and Computing", Dekker, Volume 141, 1993, pp. 131-152.
9. J. PATARIN, *"Cryptanalysis of the Matsumoto and Imai Public Key Scheme of Eurocrypt'88"*, CRYPTO'95, pp. 248-261.
10. J. PATARIN, *"Asymmetric Cryptography with a Hidden Monomial"*, available but not yet published paper.
11. B. SCHNEIER, *"Applied Cryptography"*, John Wiley and Sons, first edition.
12. A. SHAMIR, *"An efficient Identification Scheme Based on Permuted Kernels"*, CRYPTO'89, pp. 606-609.
13. J. STERN, *"A new identification scheme based on syndrome decoding"*, CRYPTO'93, pp. 13-21.
14. P. VAN OORSCHOT and S. VANSTONE, *"A geometric approach to root finding in $GF(q^m)$"*, IEEE Trans. Info. Th., 35 (1989), pp. 444-453.
15. J. VON ZUR GATHEN and V. SHOUP, *"Computing Frobenius maps and factoring polynomials"*, Proc. 24th Annual ACM Symp. Theory of Comput., ACM Press, 1992.

A Public Key Cryptosystem Based on Elliptic Curves over $\mathbb{Z}/n\mathbb{Z}$ Equivalent to Factoring

Bernd Meyer[1]* and Volker Müller[2]

[1] Universität des Saarlandes
Fachbereich Informatik
Postfach 15 11 50
66041 Saarbrücken
Germany
Email: bmeyer@cs.uni-sb.de

[2] Department of Combinatorics & Optimization
University of Waterloo
Waterloo, Ontario
Canada N2L 3G1
Email: vmueller@crypto2.uwaterloo.ca

Abstract Elliptic curves over the ring $\mathbb{Z}/n\mathbb{Z}$ where n is the product of two large primes have first been proposed for public key cryptosystems in [4]. The security of this system is based on the integer factorization problem, but it is unknown whether breaking the system is equivalent to factoring. In this paper, we present a variant of this cryptosystem for which breaking the system is equivalent to factoring the modulus n. Moreover, we extend the ideas to get a signature scheme based on elliptic curves over $\mathbb{Z}/n\mathbb{Z}$.

1 Introduction

In recent years, elliptic curves over finite fields have gained a lot of attention. The use of elliptic curves over finite fields in public key cryptography was suggested by Koblitz [3] and Miller [7]. The security of these cryptosystems is based on the difficulty of the discrete logarithm problem in the group of points on an elliptic curve. Later Vanstone et. al. proposed to use elliptic curves over the ring $\mathbb{Z}/n\mathbb{Z}$, where n is the product of two large prime numbers [4]. The security of their public key cryptosystem is based on the factorization problem for n, but it is not known whether decryption is equivalent to factoring n. They use elliptic curves of special form such that the factorization of n directly gives the order of the group $E(\mathbb{Z}/n\mathbb{Z})$. The knowledge of the group order is important in the decryption procedure. A detailed description of all these systems can be found in [6].

* Author was supported by the Deutsche Forschungsgemeinschaft

Ueli Maurer (Ed.): EUROCRYPT '96 Proceedings, LNCS 1070

On the other hand, there exist several RSA-variants equivalent to factoring, see for example [10]. We use similar ideas to develop a new public key cryptosystem based on elliptic curves over the ring $\mathbb{Z}/n\mathbb{Z}$. For the new cryptosystem, decryption is equivalent to factoring n. Moreover, we discuss a generalization of our ideas to get a public key signature scheme using elliptic curves over $\mathbb{Z}/n\mathbb{Z}$.

The remainder of the paper is organized as follows. Section 2 gives a short introduction to elliptic curves over $\mathbb{Z}/n\mathbb{Z}$. In Sections 3 and 4, we describe the cryptosystem and the signature scheme. Section 5 describes some algorithms needed in the decryption part and proves the security of the system. Finally, Section 6 makes some concluding remarks.

2 Elliptic Curves over $\mathbb{Z}/n\mathbb{Z}$

In this section we will introduce basic facts about elliptic curves over the ring $\mathbb{Z}/n\mathbb{Z}$, where n is a square free rational integer not divisible by 2 and 3. A detailed description of the theory of elliptic curves can be found in [9].

Definition 1. Let $n \in \mathbb{N}$ be not divisible by 2 and 3. The projective plane $\mathcal{P}^2(\mathbb{Z}/n\mathbb{Z})$ is the set of all triples $(x, y, z) \in (\mathbb{Z}/n\mathbb{Z})^3 - \{(0,0,0)\}$ modulo the equivalence relation

$$(x, y, z) \sim (x', y', z') \Leftrightarrow \exists \lambda \in (\mathbb{Z}/n\mathbb{Z})^* \text{ with } x = \lambda x', y = \lambda y', z = \lambda z' .$$

Let $a, b \in \mathbb{Z}/n\mathbb{Z}$ with $4a^3 + 27b^2 \in (\mathbb{Z}/n\mathbb{Z})^*$. Then the set of points on the elliptic curve $E = (a, b)$ over $\mathbb{Z}/n\mathbb{Z}$ is defined as

$$E(\mathbb{Z}/n\mathbb{Z}) = \left\{(x : y : z) \in \mathcal{P}^2(\mathbb{Z}/n\mathbb{Z}) \mid y^2 z \equiv x^3 + axz^2 + bz^3 \bmod n\right\} .$$

The point $(0 : 1 : 0)$ is called *point at infinity*.

Let the prime factorization of n be given as

$$n = \prod_{i=1}^{k} p_i$$

where p_i are distinct prime numbers greater than 3. Using the Chinese Remainder Theorem it is easy to show that there is a bijection

$$E(\mathbb{Z}/n\mathbb{Z}) \cong E(\mathbb{Z}/p_1\mathbb{Z}) \times \ldots \times E(\mathbb{Z}/p_k\mathbb{Z}) . \quad (1)$$

This bijection maps a point $(x : y : z) \in E(\mathbb{Z}/n\mathbb{Z})$ to a tuple of points

$$\Big((x \bmod p_1 : y \bmod p_1 : z \bmod p_1), \ldots, (x \bmod p_k : y \bmod p_k : z \bmod p_k)\Big) .$$

Note that $(x \bmod p_i : y \bmod p_i : z \bmod p_i)$ indeed is a point on $E(\mathbb{Z}/p_i\mathbb{Z})$ for all $1 \leq i \leq k$. It is well known that the set $E(\mathbb{Z}/p\mathbb{Z})$ (where p is a prime greater 3) has the structure of an abelian (usually additively written) group, where

$(0:1:0)$ is the zero element (see [9]). Using the bijection (1), we can define an addition on $E(\mathbb{Z}/n\mathbb{Z})$, such that $E(\mathbb{Z}/n\mathbb{Z})$ also forms an abelian group.

Usually, one has a slightly different notation for points on elliptic curves. Assume that the z-coordinate of the point $(x:y:z) \in E(\mathbb{Z}/n\mathbb{Z})$ is coprime to n. Then there exists a triple $(\tilde{x}, \tilde{y}, 1)$ in the set $(x:y:z)$. Such a point can be represented as a pair $(\tilde{x}, \tilde{y})$. On the other hand, points which can not be represented in this way directly lead to a factorization of n. It seems to be very unlikely to find such points, because the factorization problem is expected to be hard. Therefore we will represent points as a pair of a x- and y-coordinate.

With this representation, we can use exactly the same formulas for addition in $E(\mathbb{Z}/n\mathbb{Z})$ as given in [9] for fields. But note that there is a tiny probability that these formulas fail (which is equivalent to finding a factor of n). We will only describe the formulas for doubling points.

Let $E = (a, b) \in (\mathbb{Z}/n\mathbb{Z})^2$ be an elliptic curve and $P = (x, y) \in E(\mathbb{Z}/n\mathbb{Z})$ be a point with order greater two. Then we can double P, i.e. we can compute the point $2 \cdot P = (X, Y)$, using the formulas

$$\lambda = (3x^2 + a) \cdot (2y)^{-1} ,$$

$$X = -2x + \lambda^2 , \tag{2}$$

$$Y = -y + \lambda (x - X) . \tag{3}$$

3 The Public Key Cryptosystem

In this section we will describe the new public key cryptosystem based on elliptic curves over $\mathbb{Z}/n\mathbb{Z}$. The security of this system is based on the integer factorization problem, as will be shown later.

Assume that n is the product of two large primes p, q, where $p, q \equiv 11 \bmod 12$. As remarked in [10], each square in $(\mathbb{Z}/n\mathbb{Z})^*$ has exactly four square roots of whom exactly one is itself a square (especially, n is a Blum integer). Moreover, for every element in $(\mathbb{Z}/n\mathbb{Z})^*$ there exists exactly one cube root. We can classify the square roots of a square κ even further: exactly two square roots of κ have Jacobi symbol $+1$ (so called type I roots), the two others have Jacobi symbol -1 (type II roots). If a is a type I root of a square κ (resp. type II root), then $-a$ is the other type I root (resp. type II root). Moreover we can distinguish between a and $-a$: consider elements in $(\mathbb{Z}/n\mathbb{Z})^*$ as numbers in the set $\{1, \ldots, n-1\}$. Then exactly one of the two elements a and $-a$ is an even number (note that n is an odd number). For $a \in (\mathbb{Z}/n\mathbb{Z})^*$, we define $\text{lsb}(a)$ to be the least significant bit of the "number" a. Thus, given a square $\kappa \in (\mathbb{Z}/n\mathbb{Z})^*$, we can identify each square root of κ with the help of two bits, the type and the least significant bit.

The keys of the cryptosystem are then given in the following way: The public key of Bob is the modulus n. The two prime factors p and q of n form the private key of Bob and are kept secret.

Assume that Alice wants to send a "message" m to Bob, where $0 < m < n$ (in the following we always assume that text messages are transformed into numbers in some publicly known way). She encrypts this message m with the help of Bob's public key in the following way:

Encryption procedure:

(1) choose $\lambda \in \mathbb{Z}/n\mathbb{Z} - \{0\}$ at random.
(2) set $P = (m^2, \lambda m^3)$.
(3) set $a = \lambda^3$ and compute $b = (\lambda^2 - 1) m^6 - a m^2$.
(4) **if** $(\gcd(4a^3 + 27b^2, n) > 1)$ **then**
(5) **return** (protocol error: $4a^3+27b^2 \equiv 0 \bmod n$ or factor of n found)
(6) **fi**
(7) send $E = (a, b)$, $x(2 \cdot P), \text{type}(y(2 \cdot P))$ and $\text{lsb}(y(2 \cdot P))$ to Bob.

Note that the computation of the gcd in step (4) can be omitted, if one accepts that the probability of "guessing" a factor of a large integer n is extremely small. Then the encryption procedure can be done with only a few multiplications and one inversion modulo n (in the doubling part of P).

Assume that Bob receives an encrypted message E, x_Q, t, l, where $E = (a, b)$ is an elliptic curve over $\mathbb{Z}/n\mathbb{Z}$, $x_Q \in \mathbb{Z}/n\mathbb{Z}$ and t, l are two bits. He can decrypt this message using the following decryption procedure:

Decryption procedure:

(1) compute the square root y_Q of $x_Q^3 + a\, x_Q + b$ with type t and lsb l.
(2) set $Q = (x_Q, y_Q)$.
(3) compute all points $P_i \in E(\mathbb{Z}/n\mathbb{Z})$, $1 \le i \le s$, such that $2 \cdot P_i = Q$.
(4) compute set $I = \{1 \le i \le s;\ a^2 = y(P_i)^6\, x(P_i)^{-9}\}$.
(5) **if** $(\#I > 1)$ **then**
(6) **return** (protocol error: more than one solution)
(7) **else**
(8) **return** $(m = y(P_I)^3\, x(P_I)^{-4}\, a^{-1})$

Note that in step (8) the index set I must have only one element, such that the notation P_I denotes the point P with the index given in I. The correctness of the decryption algorithm follows directly since the "correct plain text point" P satisfies both tests in step (3) and (4).

The coefficient a of the elliptic curve E determines λ exactly. However, the determination of λ given only the ciphertext is supposed to be difficult if the factorization of n is unknown. If an intruder would know λ, then the cryptosystem would be equivalent to the cryptosystem of Williams [10], as was pointed out to us by M. Joye and J.-J. Quisquater [1].

In the following theorem, we will consider the case that the index set has more than one element.

Theorem 2. *The probability that the index set I in step (4) of the decryption procedure has more than one element and we cannot factor the modulus n is at most* $118^2/(n-1)$.

Proof. We have shown that the input to the decryption procedure uniquely determines the point Q on the elliptic curve E. By construction, there is a point P on E ("the embedded message") which satisfies the conditions in step (3) and (4) of the decryption procedure. Then we can express the coefficients of E and $x(Q)$ as rational functions in $x(P)$ and λ (in the following we will consider the coefficients of all polynomials as rational functions in λ and $x(P)$). In Lemma 3 we will show that there exists a degree 4-polynomial $f(X) \in (\mathbb{Z}/n\mathbb{Z})(\lambda, x(P))[X]$ such that x-coordinates of points passing test (3) are zeros of f. Passing step (4) means that x-coordinates of such points have to be zeros of a degree 9-polynomial $g(X)$.

Assume that there exists a point P_2 different from P which passes both tests. Then $x(P_2)$ has to be a zero of the remainder $k(X)$ of $g(X)/(X - x(P))$ and $f(X)/(X - x(P))$, which is a degree 2-polynomial (or we find a non trivial factor of n). On the other hand, we know that P_2 is the sum of P and a two-torsion point $(r, 0) \in E(\mathbb{Z}/n\mathbb{Z})$. We express the x-coordinate of P_2 as a rational function in $x(P)$ and r and substitute this expression into $k(X)$. Using the fact that $r^3 + a\,r + b \equiv 0 \bmod n$, we obtain an equation in $x(P)$ and λ which must be zero. This equation has "degree" 118 in λ. Therefore, for given and fixed $x(P)$, there exist at most 118^2 different values for λ such that this equation vanishes modulo n. Since we choose λ at random in step (1) of the encryption procedure, the probability of choosing a "bad" λ is at most $118^2/(n-1)$. □

Since the modulus n has to be a number difficult to factor (i.e. it should be sufficiently large), Theorem 2 shows that the error probability for the decryption procedure is very small.

We have not yet mentioned how to solve the so called *square root problem in* $E(\mathbb{Z}/n\mathbb{Z})$ in step (3). We will explain an algorithm for doing this in Section 5. In addition, we will give an upper bound for the running time of the encryption and decryption procedure in Theorem 5. In the following section we will explain how the idea of using square roots of points on elliptic curves over $\mathbb{Z}/n\mathbb{Z}$ can be used to construct a public key signature scheme.

4 A Signature Scheme

In this section we extend the ideas given in the last section to describe a public key signature scheme. Assume that the public key and private key of Bob are chosen as in the last section, i.e. Bob's public key is an integer n which is the product of two primes $p, q \equiv 11 \bmod 12$ and his secret key is the knowledge of the two prime factors p, q of n. We assume that some publicly known cryptographic hash function is used to compute fingerprints for messages.

Signing a message m:

(1)	compute a fingerprint $0 \leq m' < n$ for the message m using a cryptographic hash function.
(2)	find $\lambda, \zeta \in (\mathbb{Z}/n\mathbb{Z}^*)$ such that for the elliptic curve $E = (\lambda^3, .)$ we get $x(2 \cdot (\zeta^2, \lambda\zeta^3)) = m'$ and $y(2 \cdot (\zeta^2, \lambda\zeta^3))$ has type I.
(3)	**return** (Signature for m' is (ζ, λ))

Note that the formulas for doubling a point do not depend on the coefficient b of the given elliptic curve. As will be shown in the next section, the problem in step (2) can be solved by finding a root of a polynomial in the two variables λ and ζ. Since the factorization of n is known to Bob, he solves this problem modulo p (resp. q) and uses the Chinese Remainder Theorem to compute the values for λ, ζ modulo n. The checking of a signature is then obvious:

Checking a signature:

(1)	set $a = \lambda^3$ and $P = (\zeta^2, \lambda\zeta^3)$.
(2)	compute $Q = 2 \cdot P$ on $E = (a, (\lambda^2 - 1)\zeta^6 - a\zeta^2)$.
(3)	check whether $x(Q) = m'$ and $y(Q)$ has type I.
(4)	check whether m' is a correct fingerprint for m.
(5)	**if** (all tests are successful) **then**
(6)	**return** (accept the signature.)
(7)	**else**
(8)	**return** (reject the signature.)

It should be mentioned that Bob should be very careful in signing arbitrary messages. As will be shown in Theorem 6, this signature scheme is very vulnerable to a chosen plaintext attack where a hash value m' is given to Bob for signing.

In the next section, we will consider the square root problems for various situations. The interesting cases are elliptic curves over prime fields and over $\mathbb{Z}/n\mathbb{Z}$, where the factorization of n is either known or unknown. We will show that the ability of signing arbitrary messages is equivalent to knowing the factorization of n.

5 The Square Root Problem in $E(\mathbb{Z}/n\mathbb{Z})$

In this section, we will consider the missing parts in the decryption algorithm. Obviously, decryption can be done if we can invert the operation of doubling a point. Therefore we study the so called *square root problem*, which has the following form:

Given a point $Q \in E(\mathbb{Z}/n\mathbb{Z})$. Compute all points $P \in E(\mathbb{Z}/n\mathbb{Z})$ with

$$2 \cdot P = Q \ .$$

Such points P will be called *square roots* of Q. Note that the notation "square root" is used to show the analogy to the corresponding problem for the ring $(\mathbb{Z}/n\mathbb{Z})^*$. In the following subsection, we describe a solution to this problem if n is a prime number.

5.1 Computing Square Roots in $E(\mathbb{Z}/p\mathbb{Z})$

Let E be an elliptic curve defined over a prime field $\mathbb{Z}/p\mathbb{Z}$, where p is a prime number greater than 3 and let Q be any point on E for which we want to solve the square root problem. First note that the existence of a square root is not necessarily assured. In contrary, there exist points Q such that there is no square root of Q. An easy example for such a situation occurs, if E is a cyclic group of even order and Q is a generator of $E(\mathbb{Z}/p\mathbb{Z})$. Nevertheless there is an algorithm for solving this existence problem and the square root problem for Q. The algorithm is based on the following lemma:

Lemma 3. *Let $E = (a, b) \in (\mathbb{Z}/p\mathbb{Z})^2$ be an elliptic curve over $\mathbb{Z}/p\mathbb{Z}$ and $Q = (x_Q, y_Q) \in E(\mathbb{Z}/p\mathbb{Z})$, $Q \neq \mathcal{O}$. If $P \in E(\mathbb{Z}/p\mathbb{Z})$ is a square root of Q, then the x-coordinate of P is a root (in $\mathbb{Z}/p\mathbb{Z}$) of the polynomial $f(X, a, b, x_Q) \in (\mathbb{Z}/p\mathbb{Z})[X]$, where*

$$f(X, a, b, x_Q) = X^4 - 4\,x_Q\,X^3 - 2\,a\,X^2 - (4\,a\,x_Q + 8\,b)\,X + a^2 - 4\,b\,x_Q \ .$$

Proof. Using the doubling formula (2), we can compute the x-coordinate of $2 \cdot (X, Y)$ for an arbitrary point (X, Y) of order greater 2 as

$$-2 \cdot X \quad + \quad \left(\frac{3\,X^2 + a}{2\,Y}\right)^2 \ .$$

Equalizing this with the x-coordinate of Q and using simple transformations, we obtain the result of the lemma. □

This lemma is the basis for the following algorithm which solves the square root problem in $\mathbb{Z}/p\mathbb{Z}$. First we check whether the polynomial given in the lemma has a root in $\mathbb{Z}/p\mathbb{Z}$. If there is no root, then there cannot exist a square root of Q and we exit. Otherwise we compute all roots in $\mathbb{Z}/p\mathbb{Z}$ of the polynomial $f(X, a, b, x_Q)$, where a, b, x_Q are given as input. One should observe that not every root $x_P \in \mathbb{Z}/p\mathbb{Z}$ of $f(X, a, b, x_Q)$ is actually a x-coordinate of a square root of Q. It might be that $x_P^3 + a x_P + b$ is not a square in $\mathbb{Z}/p\mathbb{Z}$ and that x_P is a x-coordinate of a point in the quadratic extension of $\mathbb{Z}/p\mathbb{Z}$. In our context, we are only interested in square roots defined over the prime field such that the second step of an algorithm has to check whether a root x_P actually is the x-coordinate of a point defined over $\mathbb{Z}/p\mathbb{Z}$. In addition, the x-coordinate of a point does not specify the point exactly, since P and $-P$ have the same x-coordinate. Therefore we have to check whether $2 \cdot P = Q$ or whether $2 \cdot (-P) = Q$. These observations lead to the following Algorithm 4 which solves the square root problem for prime fields $\mathbb{Z}/p\mathbb{Z}$.

Algorithm 4.

INPUT: *Elliptic curve* $E = (a, b) \in (\mathbb{Z}/p\mathbb{Z})^2$, $Q \in E(\mathbb{Z}/p\mathbb{Z})$.
OUTPUT: *Set* S *of all square roots of* Q *in* $E(\mathbb{Z}/p\mathbb{Z})$.

(1) $S = \emptyset$.
(2) *compute all roots of the polynomial* $f(X, a, b, x(Q))$ *in* $\mathbb{Z}/p\mathbb{Z}$.
(3) **for** *(all roots* x_P *computed in step (2))* **do**
(4) **if** *(*$x_P^3 + a\,x_P + b$ *is a square in* $\mathbb{Z}/p\mathbb{Z}$*)* **then**
(5) *compute a square root* y_P *of* $x_P^3 + a\,x_P + b \bmod p$.
(6) *check whether* $2 \cdot (x_P, y_P) = Q$ *or* $2 \cdot (x_P, -y_P) = Q$*, add a found square root to* S.
(7) **fi**
(8) **od**
(9) **return** *(S)*

All steps of Algorithm 4 can be done using a factorization routine for polynomials over $\mathbb{Z}/p\mathbb{Z}$. There exists a probabilistic algorithm which computes all roots of a fixed degree polynomial modulo a prime p in expected time $O(\log(p)^3)$ (for a detailed treatment of polynomial factorization see e.g. [8]). Thus the expected running time of Algorithm 4 is $O(\log(p)^3)$.

5.2 Computing Square Roots in $E(\mathbb{Z}/n\mathbb{Z})$

Next we discuss the square root problem for elliptic curves over a ring $\mathbb{Z}/n\mathbb{Z}$ where n is a composite number. We distinguish two situations:

Factorization of n Known Let us first consider the problem when the factorization of n is known, e.g.

$$n = \prod_{i=1}^{k} p_i$$

and $p_i \in \mathbb{P}_{>3}$. Using the isomorphism map (1) defined in Section 2, the square root problem in $E(\mathbb{Z}/n\mathbb{Z})$ can be reduced to the solution of k many square root problems in $E(\mathbb{Z}/p_i\mathbb{Z})$, $1 \le i \le k$.

Assume that we want to compute all square roots of a point $Q \in E(\mathbb{Z}/n\mathbb{Z})$. For all prime factors p_i of n we proceed in the following way: first reduce the x-

and y-coordinate of Q modulo p_i and obtain $Q_{p_i} \in E(\mathbb{Z}/p_i\mathbb{Z})$. Then we compute all square roots of the reduced point Q_{p_i} in $E(\mathbb{Z}/p_i\mathbb{Z})$ with Algorithm 4. If there exists no square root of Q_{p_i}, we have proven that there cannot exist a square root of Q in $E(\mathbb{Z}/n\mathbb{Z})$ and we return. Otherwise we know sets S_i of all square roots of Q_{p_i} for all $1 \leq i \leq k$. Since the map (1) is an isomorphism, we can compute all square roots of Q in $E(\mathbb{Z}/n\mathbb{Z})$ by using the Chinese Remainder Theorem for all elements of $S = S_1 \times \ldots \times S_k$. Clearly, this shows that the number of square roots of Q in $E(\mathbb{Z}/n\mathbb{Z})$ is exactly the product of the cardinalities of the sets $S_i, 1 \leq i \leq k$. Obviously, two square roots can only differ by a point of order 2. It is well known (see [9]) that there are at most 4 points of exponent 2 in $E(\mathbb{Z}/p_i\mathbb{Z})$ such that $\#S_i \leq 4$. Therefore the square root problem with given factorization of the modulus n can be solved in probabilistic time $O(4^k \log(n)^3)$, where k is the number of prime factors of the modulus n.

It is well known that the extended euclidean algorithm for computing inverses in $(\mathbb{Z}/n\mathbb{Z})^*$ needs time $O(\log(n)^2)$. Using these observations in the special situation of the cryptosystem presented in Section 3, we can derive the following running time result.

Theorem 5. *The encryption procedure takes time $O(\log(n)^2)$, decryption can be done in probabilistic time $O(\log(n)^3)$.*

Factorization of n Unknown The security of the cryptosystem presented in Section 3 is based on the intractability of solving the square root problem in $E(\mathbb{Z}/n\mathbb{Z})$ when the factorization of n is not known. In this section we will show that the existence of an algorithm for decrypting encrypted messages without knowledge of the factorization of the modulus n would induce a probabilistic polynomial time algorithm for factoring n.

Theorem 6. *Assume there is an oracle which can decrypt encrypted messages. Then there exists a probabilistic polynomial time algorithm for factoring n.*

Proof. We use the help of the oracle to compute two square roots of different type in $(\mathbb{Z}/n\mathbb{Z})^*$. This will give us a non trivial factor of n. We proceed as follows:

1. choose elements $\kappa, \lambda \in (\mathbb{Z}/n\mathbb{Z})^*$ at random.
2. compute $a = \lambda^3$ and $b = (\lambda^2 - 1)\,\kappa^6 - a\,\kappa^2$.
3. compute $x_Q = \left((9 - 8\,\lambda^2)\,\kappa^8 + 6\,\kappa^4\lambda^3 + \lambda^6\right)\left(4\,\lambda^2\kappa^6\right)^{-1}$ and
$$t = \text{type}\Big(2\,\lambda\,\left((36\,\lambda^2 - 27 - 8\,\lambda^4)\,\kappa^{12} + (12\,\lambda^2 - 27)\,\lambda^3\kappa^8 - 9\,\kappa^4\lambda^6 - \lambda^9\right)\Big)\,.$$
4. If $\text{type}(\kappa) = t$, then call the oracle with input $E = (a, b)$, x_Q, type II and arbitrary lsb; otherwise use the input $E = (a, b)$, x_Q, type I, arbitrary lsb. The oracle outputs a message m.
5. compute a non trivial divisor of n as $\gcd(\kappa - m, n)$.

We have to show the correctness of this procedure. Assume that $m \in (\mathbb{Z}/n\mathbb{Z})^*$ such that $m^2 = \kappa^2$ and set $P = (m^2, \lambda m^3)$. Then P is a point on the elliptic curve $E = (a, b)$ computed in step 2. We compute the x-coordinate of $2 \cdot P$ as

$$x(2 \cdot P) \quad = \quad \frac{(9 - 8\lambda^2)\, m^8 + 6\, m^4 \lambda^3 + \lambda^6}{4\, \lambda^2 m^6} \; .$$

Since $\kappa^2 = m^2$, the value x_Q computed in step 3 is equal to $x(2 \cdot P)$. If we compute the Jacobi symbol of $y(2 \cdot P)$ over n, we obtain

$$\left(\frac{m}{n}\right) \left(\frac{2\lambda\, \left((36\lambda^2 - 27 - 8\lambda^4)\, m^{12} + (12\lambda^2 - 27)\, \lambda^3 m^8 - 9\, m^4 \lambda^6 - \lambda^9\right)}{n}\right) .$$

Therefore the choice of the type in step 4 of the above procedure guarantees that the oracle indeed "computes" a message m whose type is different from type(κ). Hence, we know two square roots of κ^2 of different types (namely κ and m), which surely factors n and we are done. □

This theorem shows that the ability to decrypt an arbitrary message without knowing the factorization of the public key n is equivalent to factoring n. Since the factorization problem for integers is believed to be hard, it should not be possible to decrypt arbitrary messages without the secret key. Exactly the same arguments as given in the proof of Theorem 6 can be used to show that the ability of signing arbitrary messages is equivalent to factoring n.

In the last section of this paper, we will discuss some practical aspects of the described cryptosystem.

6 Advantages and Disadvantages

The cryptosystem presented in this paper is a generalization of the system presented in [4]. Using small "encryption exponents" as 2 in our system has the advantage of speeding up the encryption process. On the other hand, our decryption process seems to be a bit more difficult than the decryption process of [4], but usage of known root formulas for polynomials of degree 4 might speed up our decryption procedure. Therefore, a comparison of the two systems can only be done by actually implementing and comparing the two systems in practice. An implementation of our system will probably be done in future.

One disadvantage versus [4] is obviously the fact that for the system of this paper one has to develop different code for encryption and decryption, whereas in [4] en- and decryption can be done by a fast exponentiation.

A disadvantage of all cryptosystems equivalent to factoring is the fact, that such systems are vulnerable to chosen ciphertext attacks. This was already mentioned in the paper of Williams [10]. A chosen ciphertext attack can simulate the proof of Theorem 6 and so factor the public key n. There is no way to come around this problem.

Another attack on elliptic curve cryptosystems is the so called low exponent attack (see [5]). This attack shows that one should not send the same message to more than 11 people. If an eavesdropper knows the 11 encrypted messages, he can find the original message in polynomial time. This attack is very similar to the low exponent attack on RSA. One referee proposed to append a few bits (for example the user name) to a message before encrypting and sending it. At the moment, we do not know whether this proposal will make the low exponent attack useless. This question has to be examined by further research.

Acknowledgment: We are very grateful to Marc Joye and Jean-Jacques Quisquater who pointed out to us the equivalence of an earlier version of the cryptosystem of this paper to the cryptosystem of Williams. (See [2, 10].) In this earlier version, the parameter λ in step (2) of the encryption procedure was a fixed square root of 2 which was part of Bob's public key.

References

1. M. Joye, J.-J. Quisquater: *Personal communication*
2. M. Joye, J.-J. Quisquater: *Note on the public-key cryptosystem of Meyer and Müller*, Technical Report CG-1996/2, Université catholique de Louvain
3. N. Koblitz: *Elliptic curve cryptosystems*, Mathematics of Computation, **48** (1987), 203–209
4. K. Koyama, U. Maurer, T. Okamoto, S. Vanstone: *New Public-Key Schemes Based on Elliptic Curves over the Ring* $\mathbb{Z}_n$, Advances in Cryptology: Proceedings of Crypto '91, Lecture Notes in Computer Science, **576** (1991), Springer-Verlag, 252–266
5. K. Kurosawa, K. Okada, S. Tsujii: *Low exponent attack against elliptic curve RSA*, Advances in Cryptology–ASIACRYPT '94, Lecture Notes in Computer Science, **917** (1995), Springer-Verlag, 376–383
6. A. Menezes: *Elliptic Curve Public Key Cryptosystems*, Kluwer Academic Publishers (1993)
7. V. Miller: *Uses of elliptic curves in cryptography*, Advances in Cryptology: Proceedings of Crypto '85, Lecture Notes in Computer Science, **218** (1986), Springer-Verlag, 417–426
8. V. Shoup: *A New Polynomial Factorization Algorithm and its Implementation*, Preprint, (1995)
9. J. H. Silverman: *The Arithmetic of Elliptic Curves*, Graduate Texts in Mathematics, **106**, Springer-Verlag, (1986)
10. H.C. Williams: *A modification of the RSA public-key encryption procedure*, IEEE Transactions on Information Theory, **IT-26**, No. 6, (1980), 726–729

Public Key Encryption and Signature Schemes Based on Polynomials over $\mathbb{Z}_n$

Jörg Schwenk[1] and Jörg Eisfeld[2]

[1] Deutsche Telekom AG, Forschungszentrum, Am Kavalleriesand 3, D-64295 Darmstadt, Germany, schwenk@fz.telekom.de

[2] Justus-Liebig-Universität Gießen, Mathematisches Institut, Arndtstr. 2, D-35392 Gießen, Germany, joerg.eisfeld@math.uni-giessen.de

Abstract. The problem of computing roots of a polynomial over the ring $\mathbb{Z}_n$ is equivalent to factoring n. Starting from this intractable problem we construct a public key encryption scheme where the message blocks are encrypted as roots of a polynomial over $\mathbb{Z}_n$ and a signature scheme where the signature belonging to a message is a (set of) root(s) of a polynomial having the message blocks as coefficients. These schemes can be considered as extensions of Rabin's encryption and signature scheme. However, our signature scheme has some new properties: a short signature can be generated for a long message without using a hash function, and the security features of the scheme can be chosen either to be similar to those of the RSA scheme or to be equivalent to those of Rabin's scheme.

1 Introduction

In this paper we investigate an intractable problem related to the problem of factoring. This problem can be stated as follows:

Root Finding Problem (RFP): *Compute one (all) root(s) of a polynomial $f(x)$ over the ring $\mathbb{Z}_n$ where $n = pq$ is the product of two large primes.*

For randomly chosen polynomials the RFP is equivalent to the problem of factoring n whenever $f(x)$ has at least two different roots. If $f(x)$ has exactly one root, the root finding problem seems to be related to the problem of decrypting an RSA ciphertext. Section 2 summarizes some mathematical results on the RFP.

In Sect. 3 we present a public key encryption scheme the security of which is based on the difficulty of the root finding problem: A message is divided into blocks and a certain redundancy is added to these blocks. The result of this operation is interpreted as an integer less or equal to n. These numbers $z_1, \ldots, z_k$ are then encrypted as roots of the polynomial $f(x) := (x - z_1) \cdots (x - z_k) \bmod n$. The public key used for this operation is the modulus n. Decryption can be done by using the private key (p, q) to compute roots of the polynomials $f(x) \bmod p$ and $f(x) \bmod q$ in the corresponding finite fields, e.g. with the algorithm described by Ben-Or in [BO81], and by combining these results via the Chinese

Ueli Maurer (Ed.): EUROCRYPT '96 Proceedings, LNCS 1070

remainder theorem. The chosen redundancy scheme will then help to find the k correct roots out of the k^2 solutions.

In Sect. 4 a signature scheme is described where the roles of coefficients and roots are interchanged: The blocks of the message are interpreted as coefficients of a polynomial. The signature z of the message is a root of this polynomial. However, since not all the polynomials in $\mathbb{Z}_n[x]$ have a root, some randomization must be used in order to generate a signature, e.g. by choosing the coefficient of x^0 randomly. The feasability of the signature scheme is guaranteed by Thm. 3. This theorem and the corollaries following it give the number of polynomials in $\mathbb{Z}_n[x]$ which have at least one root (at least two roots, resp.).

The encryption and signature scheme presented in this paper are extensions of ideas of Rabin [Rab80], but due to the more general setting they are more flexible. By choosing a randomized polynomial with the appropriate number of roots, the security features of our signature scheme can be chosen either to be equivalent to those of Rabin's scheme or to be similar to those of the RSA scheme.

Furthermore, our signature scheme has the property that we can generate short signatures for long messages without using a hash function. As far as the authors know no other signature scheme with this property exists.

2 Some Properties of Polynomials over $\mathbb{Z}_n$

The root finding problem is a new intractable problem based on the problem of factoring integers. Other well-known problems based on factoring are the problems of computing square roots of quadratic residues and breaking the RSA public key cryptosystem. In this paper, n always denotes an integer that is the product of two large primes p and q: $n = pq$.

Finding a root of a randomly chosen polynomial $f \in \mathbb{Z}_n[x]$ is equivalent to factoring n if $f(x)$ has at least two different roots. This will be proved in Thm. 2. If $f(x)$ has only one root over $\mathbb{Z}_n$, then the root-finding problem includes the problem of decrypting an RSA ciphertext as a special case: To decrypt $c = m^e$, we have to find the unique root of the polynomial $x^e - c \in \mathbb{Z}_n[x]$.

If we know the factorization (p, q) of n, the problem of finding a root of a polynomial $f \in \mathbb{Z}_n[x]$ can be reduced to the (easy) problem of computing roots in the finite fields GF(p) and GF(q) [BO81]. The results can be combined to construct solutions of the root-finding problem by using the extended Euclidean algorithm and the Chinese remainder theorem. Details of this construction can be found in the appendix.

In order to get a better understanding of the structure of the set of roots of a polynomial defined over $\mathbb{Z}_n$, and in order to be able to prove Thm. 2 given below, we need the following definitions.

Definition 1. Let $f(x)$ be a polynomial over $\mathbb{Z}_n$.
(1) Two roots z_1 and z_2 of $f(x)$ are said to be *in the same row* (resp. *in the same column*) if they are equivalent modulo q (resp. modulo p).

(2) A set $\{z_1, \ldots, z_t\}$ of roots of $f \in \mathbb{Z}_n[x]$ is called a *partial transversal* if no two of its elements are in the same row or column. A *transversal* is a maximal partial transversal.

The following examples illustrate the concepts of transversal and being in a row or column.

Example 1. (1) The set $\{u_1, \ldots, u_t\}$ is a transversal of the set of roots of $g(x) := (x - u_1)(x - u_2)\cdots(x - u_t) \bmod n$ if the u_i are such that $(u_i)_p \neq (u_j)_p$ and $(u_i)_q \neq (u_j)_q$ for $i \neq j$.
(2) In the picture given below the set of roots of the polynomial $g(x) = (x-1)(x-2)(x-3) \pmod{15}$ is given. It has six transversals $\{1,2,3\}$, $\{6,7,8\}$, $\{11,12,13\}$, $\{1,12,8\}$, $\{6,2,13\}$ and $\{11,7,3\}$.

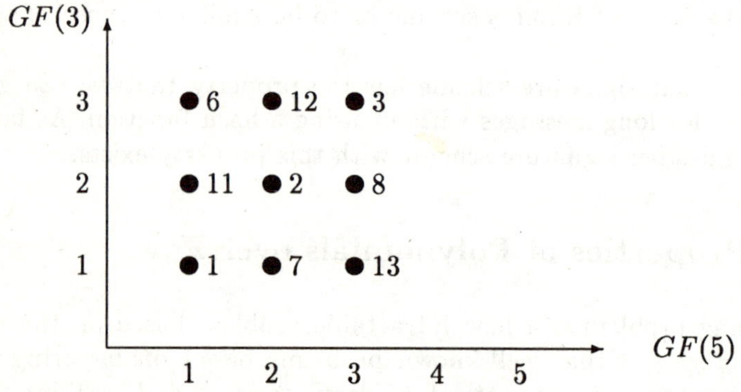

The proofs of the following theorems can be found in the appendix.

Theorem 2. *The problem of computing roots of polynomials over $\mathbb{Z}_n$ which have at least two different roots is equivalent to the the problem of factoring n.*

If we choose a polynomial $f(x)$ at random, e.g. by choosing its coefficients at random, we cannot be sure if this polynomial has a root or not. E.g. if $f(x)$ is irreducible either over GF(p) or over GF(q), then $f(x)$ has no roots modulo n. The following theorem gives the percentage of polynomials of degree k which have exactly m roots over the finite field GF(p).

Theorem 3. *The fraction of polynomials of degree d over* GF(q) *which have exactly m roots converges for $q \to \infty$ to $\frac{1}{m!} \cdot \sum_{i=0}^{d-m} (-1)^i \cdot \frac{1}{i!}$. By increasing $d - m$ this number converges very quickly to $\frac{1}{m!} \cdot e^{-1}$.*

The following corollaries guarantee that the generation of signatures in the signature scheme described in Sect. 4 is feasible. They give the probability that a randomly chosen polynomial will have al least one root (at least two roots, resp.).

Corollary 4. *(1) The fraction of polynomials of degree d over* GF(q) *which have no roots converges for* $q \to \infty$ *to* $\sum_{i=0}^{d}(-1)^i \cdot \frac{1}{i!}$. *By increasing d this number converges very quickly to* $e^{-1} \approx 0.36788$.
(2) The fraction of polynomials of degree d over GF(q) *that have at most one root converges for* $q \to \infty$ *to* $2\left(\sum_{i=0}^{d}(-1)^i \cdot \frac{1}{i!}\right) - (-1)^d \cdot \frac{1}{d!}$. *By increasing d, this number converges very quickly to* $2e^{-1} \approx 0.73576$.

Corollary 5. *(1) For large d and q the fraction of polynomials of degree d over* GF(q) *that have at least one root (at least two roots, resp.) can be approximated by* $1 - e^{-1}$ *(*$1 - 2e^{-1}$*, resp.).*
(2) For large d and n the fraction of polynomials of degree d over $\mathbb{Z}_n$ *that have at least one root can be approximated by* $(1 - e^{-1})^2$.
(3) For large d and n the fraction of polynomials of degree d over $\mathbb{Z}_n$ *that have at least two roots can be approximated by* $1 - 2e^{-1}$.

3 Encrypting a Message as Roots of a Polynomial

In the preceding section we have established an intractable problem: computing roots of a polynomial defined over $\mathbb{Z}_n$. It is quite natural to use this problem to encrypt data, in the same way as Rabin used the problem of computing square roots for his encryption system [Rab80].

The public key of this encryption scheme is the modulus n, the private key is the factorization (p, q) of n.

Encryption function E(m)

1. Split the message m into blocks $m = \overline{m_1}||\ldots||\overline{m_k}$.
2. Add some redundany to these blocks to make them recognizable and to order them. Let $m_1, \ldots, m_k$ denote the result of this operation.
3. Interpret $m_1, \ldots, m_k$ as numbers less or equal to n.
4. Compute $f(x) := (x - m_1) \cdots (x - m_k) \bmod n = x^k + a_{k-1}x^{k-1} + \cdots + a_1 x + a_0$.
5. Transmit the ciphertext $c = E(m) := (a_{k-1}, \ldots, a_1, a_0)$.

The necessity of the second step, making the numbers *recognizable*, will become clear when we look at the decryption function.

Decryption function D(c)

1. Reconstruct the polynomial $f(x) = x^k + a_{k-1}x^{k-1} + \cdots + a_1 x + a_0$ from the ciphertext $c := (a_{k-1}, \ldots, a_1, a_0)$.
2. Compute the roots $v_1, \ldots, v_k$ of $f_p(x) := f(x) \bmod p$ over GF(p) and $w_1, \ldots, w_k$ of $f_q(x) := f(x) \bmod q$ over GF(q).
3. The extended Euclidean algorithm yields $1 = \lambda p + \mu q$. Use this equation in the Chinese remainder theorem to compute the k^2 roots $z_{ij} = w_i \lambda p + v_j \mu q \bmod n$ of $f(x)$ in $\mathbb{Z}_n$.
4. With high probability, exactly k of these roots will fit into the given redundancy scheme. Arranging these roots in the right order and removing the redundancy will give the original message $m := D(c)$.

Security of the encryption scheme

Public Key property. Computing a root of a polynomial over $\mathbb{Z}_n$ is equivalent to factoring n by Thm. 2. But we cannot apply Thm. 2 directly since we are not dealing with random polynomials, but only with a certain subset of $R[x] \subseteq \mathbb{Z}_n[x]$. It consists of those polynomials which have at least one transversal satisfying the redundancy scheme.

However, if the redundancy scheme is weak in the sense that this subset is large, we could use an oracle that outputs a root which fits into this redundancy scheme exactly like the more general oracle in the proof of Thm. 2. This would just increase the number of trials by a factor of $\frac{n^d}{|R_d[x]|}$, where $R_d[x]$ consists of the polynomials of degree d from $R[x]$.

There is a clear relation between the strength of the redundancy scheme and our ability to prove equivalence to the factoring problem. But if we choose the redundancy scheme too weak, the second plaintext attack described below can break the system completely.

It should be clear that is not possible to break the system (i.e. to factor the public key n) by simply choosing some message blocks $m_1, \ldots, m_k$ and the trying to use these roots and the corresponding polynomial $f(x)$ to factor n, because with overwhelming probability the numbers $m_1, \ldots, m_k$ will form a transversal (cf. proof of Thm. 2).

Second plaintext attack. If an attacker chooses the message blocks $m_1, \ldots, m_k$ and then manages to make the owner of the private key decrypt the ciphertext c for him, the redundancy scheme must be strong enough to prevent this attack. I.e. regardless how the attacker chooses $m_1, \ldots, m_k$, the probability that there is a root different from $m_1, \ldots, m_k$ satisfying the redundancy scheme is negligible.

GCD attack. If two messages m, m' are encrypted with the same public key n, and if these messages have one message block m_i in common, then it may be possible to recover m_i by calculating the greatest common divisor of the corresponding polynomials f and f'. However, this does not mean that the system is broken. Observe that information which is common in many messages can not be considered to be very confidential (e.g. the name of the owner of the public key).

4 Signing a Message by Computing a Root

A less obvious application of polynomials over $\mathbb{Z}_n$ is the signature scheme described in this section. We get a signature scheme based on the RFP if we interchange the roles of coefficients and roots in the encryption scheme of the last section. In this scheme, blocks of a message are interpreted as coefficients of a polynomial. The signature of this message consists of one or more roots of this polynomial; in case of two or more roots, these roots must of course be part of a transversal.

Signature function Sig(m)

1. Divide the message m into blocks $a_{k-1}, \ldots, a_1$.
2. Interpret these blocks as numbers less or equal to n.
3. Choose a random number $\overline{a_0} \leq n$. Add some redundancy to this number and use the result a_0 as the coefficient of x^0.
4. Compute one or more roots $r_1, \ldots, r_t$ $(1 \leq t \leq k)$ which are part of one transversal of the polynomial $f(x) := x^k + a_{k-1}x^{k-1} + \cdots + a_1x + a_0 \bmod n$. If $f(x)$ has no roots or doesn't have enough roots, then repeat step (3).
5. Add the signature $s = Sig(m) = (a_0, r_1, \ldots, r_t)$ to the message m.

If we add at least two roots from a transversal, then the problem of breaking this signature scheme is equivalent to the problem of factoring.

Verification function Ver(m,s)

1. Reconstruct the polynomial $f(x) := x^k + a_{k-1}x^{k-1} + \cdots + a_1x + a_0$ from m and $s = (a_0, r_1, \ldots, r_t)$.
2. For $i = 1, \ldots, t$ compute $f(r_i) \bmod n$ and check whether all these values equal 0. If this is the case, the signature is accepted, otherwise rejected.

The signature can be made much shorter than the message to be signed: it is sufficient to use one root r, and the random part of the coefficient a_0 can be made as short as it is possible without allowing for an exhaustive search attack. E.g., this means if factoring of 768 Bit numbers is considered to be intractable, a short signature could consist of $768 + 64$ Bit, for messages of arbitrary length. *To produce such a short signature, no hash function is necessary.*

Choosing a_0 at random is not the only way to make the signature scheme work. It is only necessary to use some randomization for generating messages, but there are various other possibilities for doing this, e.g. choosing some bits of each coefficient at random. However, this randomization has to be integrated in the signature function in such a way that the attacks described below will not work.

Security of the signature scheme

Any direct attack on the signature scheme, i.e. trying to directly compute a signature for a given message m, is in difficulty either equivalent to factoring n or related to the security of the RSA signature scheme If the polynomial $f(x)$ has at least two different roots, Thm. 2 applies and guarantees the equivalence with the factoring problem. If $f(x)$ has only one root, our scheme includes the computation of a RSA signature as a special case: the RSA signature of m is the unique root of $x^e - m \pmod{n}$.

We can now state a number of possible attacks on our scheme and how they can be made impossible. In describing the security features of our signature scheme we make use of the classification of attacks and features given in [GMR88].

Existential forgery by multiplication with a linear polynomial. It is possible to get a valid pair (m, s) by first choosing a message $\widehat{m}$, computing the corresponding polynomial $\widehat{f}(x)$ of degree $k-1$ and multiplying this polynomial by $x-r$: $f(x) := \widehat{f}(x)(x-r) \bmod n$. Then the coefficients $(a_{k-1}, \ldots, a_1)$ of $f(x)$ form the message m, and (a_0, r) is a valid signature for this message. However, if we proceed in this way, it is difficult to determine $\widehat{m}$ and r in such a way that the resulting message m makes any sense: If we could fix the message (m, a_0) in advance and then determine $\widehat{m}$ and r, this would give an algorithm for solving the root finding problem.

It should be noted that a similar attack works for the RSA signature scheme: Choose a number r and compute $r^e \bmod n$. Then $(m, s) := (r^e, r)$ is a valid message-signature pair.

Universal forgery by choosing a pair $(\mathbf{a_0}, \mathbf{s})$. If we want to sign a message $(a_{k-1}, \ldots, a_1)$, we may simply use the polynomial $g(x) := x^k + a_{k-1}x^{k-1} + \cdots + a_1 x$ to compute a_0 from s. Choose r randomly and let $s := r$ and $a_0 := -g(r)$. Then the polynomial $f(x) = g(x) + a_0 = g(x) - g(r)$ has $s = r$ as a root.

To make this attack impossible it is necessary to guarantee that the root r is calculated from the whole set of coefficients including a_0. This can be achieved by e.g. requiring that the coefficient a_0 fits into a given redundancy scheme, or by computing a_0 from the other coefficients.

Total breakability by a directed Chosen Message Attack. An attacker may choose the message $(a_{k-1}, \ldots, a_1)$ and a coefficient $\widehat{a_0}$ in such a way that he knows one root of the corresponding polynomial. He may then try to make the owner of the private key sign the message with the given $\widehat{a_0}$ in order to get a different root in the same row or column.

To avoid this attack, it must be guaranteed that the coefficient a_0 (or any other probabilistic element of the scheme) is choosen by the signer of the message only. In this case the probability that $a_0 = \widehat{a_0}$ is negligible.

Another method to make such an attack impossible is to require that the coefficient a_0 is chosen in such a way that the polynomial $f(x)$ has exactly one root over $\mathbb{Z}_n$. The fraction of polynomials with this property is large enough to guarantee the feasability of this approach (cf. Cor. 5).

Redundancy Schemes

During our previous discussions, we used the term "redundancy scheme" in a very broad sense. A redundancy scheme in this sense could consist of fixing some of the bits of the a_i, or of applying an error correcting code or a cryptographic hash function on the $\overline{a_i}$. There may be some applications where some redundancy scheme is already given, e.g. an error correcting code is needed for the reliable transmission of the coefficients. The only requirement on the redundancy scheme used is that the number of bits which will be determined through this scheme is large enough to prevent an exhaustive search attack; this number may e.g. range from 64 to 128 bits.

5 Performance

The most time consuming task in the two schemes presented is to compute roots of polynomials defined over GF(p)[x]. A fast probabilistic polynomial time algorithm for computing roots of polynomials of degree d in GF(p) was proposed by Rabin [Rab80a]. The investigation of its complexity was later refined by Ben-Or [BO81]: he proved that Rabin's algorithm needs only $O\left(d(\log d)^2 \log^2 d \log p\right)$ arithmetical operations in GF(p) to compute all the roots of a polynomial of degree d.

When using Rabin's algorithm to compute roots of a polynomial in a finite field, in the worst case the same number of arithmetical operations is needed for computing only one root or all the roots. So the complexity for decryption of a ciphertext and for the computation of a signature only differ by a constant factor, namely the expected number of times one has to choose a random $\overline{a_0}$ to be able to compute a signature.

The following table gives a comparison of the performance of our schemes with the RSA variant where the public exponent is always chosen to be equal to 3. The advantages of our scheme are more obvious if compared to the normal RSA scheme.

	Polynomial Schemes	RSA (d blocks) with $e = 3$
Encryption	$O(d)$	$O(d)$
Decryption	$O\left(d(\log d)^2 \log^2 d \log p\right)$	$O(d \log n)$
Generationof a signature	$O\left(d(\log d)^2 \log^2 d \log p\right)$	$O(d \log n)$
Verification of a signature	$O(d)$	$O(d)$

6 Open Problems

An interesting open problem is to investigate in more detail the difficulty of computing the unique root of a polynomial that has only one root. This could throw some light on the famous open question about the security of the RSA scheme in relation to the difficulty of factoring integers.

The following variant of our schemes has been proposed by one of the referees: Take $f(x) := a_k x^k + \ldots + a_1 x + a_0 \bmod n$ as Alice's public key, and let (p, q) be her private key. Then a message m can be encrypted as the polynomial $c(x) := f(x) - f(m)$, where m is a root of $c(x)$. The message m could be signed by computing a root of either $c(x)$ or of $\bar{c}(x) := f(x) - m$. The properties of the polynomial $c(x)$ have to be investigated. This approch has as disadvantage the length of the ciphertext to be transmitted, but may be useful as a signature scheme.

7 Acknowledgements

The authors thank A. Beutelspacher for valuable comments on the schemes proposed above, and A. Scheerhorn for performing some important statistical tests with the computer algebra system AXIOM which prepared the grounds for Thm. 3. We also thank the referees for their comments on a previous version of the paper, which helped to improve the quality of this paper.

References

[BO81] M. Ben-Or, *Probabilistic Algorithms in Finite Fields.* Proc. IEEE FOCS 1981, pp. 394-398.

[FN93] A. Fiat and M. Naor, *Broadcast Encryption.* Pre-Proceedings of CRYPTO '93, 39.1-39.10.

[GMR88] S. Goldwasser, S. Micali and R. L. Rivest, A Digital Signature Scheme Secure Against Adaptive Chosen-Message Attacks. SIAM J. Comput. Vol. 17 No. 2 (1988), pp. 281-308.

[Rab80] M. O. Rabin, *Digital Signatures and Public-Key Functions as Intractable as Factorization.* MIT/LCS/TR-212, Jan 1979. Cited after B. Schneier.

[Rab80a] M. O. Rabin, *Probabilistic Algorithms in Finite Fields.* SIAM J. Comput. 9(1980), pp. 273-280.

[Sha93] A. Shamir, *On the Generation of Multivariate Polynomials which are Hard to Factor.* Preprint.

[Sch93] B. Schneier, *Applied Cryptography.* Wiley 1993.

8 Appendix: Proofs of the Theorems in Section 2

For any $a, p \in \mathbb{Z}$ let a_p denote $a \bmod p$. If p and q are different primes, the extended Euclidean algorithm computes integers λ and μ such that

$$1 = \lambda p + \mu q.$$

This equation is used in the Chinese remainder theorem to construct a solution,

$$a = a_q \lambda p + a_p \mu q,$$

which is unique in $\mathbb{Z}_n$, of the system of congruences

$$a \equiv a_p \pmod p \qquad \text{and} \qquad a \equiv a_q \pmod q.$$

Lemma 6. *The integer a is a root of the polynomial $f \in \mathbb{Z}_n[x]$ $(n = pq)$ if and only if $f(a_p) \equiv 0 \pmod p$ and $f(a_q) \equiv 0 \pmod q$.*

Proof. Reducing modulo p (modulo q) is a ring homomorphism from $\mathbb{Z}_{pq}$ to $\mathbb{Z}_p$ ($\mathbb{Z}_q$), so it is clear that from $f(a) \equiv 0 \pmod n$ the two reduced equations follow.
On the other hand, $f(a) \equiv f(a_p) \equiv 0 \pmod p$ and $f(a) \equiv f(a_q) \equiv 0 \pmod q$, which gives $f(a) \equiv 0 \pmod n$. □

Lemma 7. *(1) The map* $\mathrm{GF}(p) \times \mathrm{GF}(q) \to \mathbb{Z}_{pq}$ *given by* $(a_p, a_q) \mapsto a \equiv a_q\lambda p + a_p\mu q \pmod{n}$ *is a ring isomorphism.*
(2) If

$$a \equiv a_q\lambda p + a_p\mu q \pmod{n} \quad \textit{and} \quad b \equiv b_q\lambda p + b_p\mu q \pmod{n}$$

are roots of $f \in \mathbb{Z}_n[x]$, *then*

$$c \equiv a_q\lambda p + b_p\mu q \pmod{n} \quad \textit{and} \quad d \equiv b_q\lambda p + a_p\mu q \pmod{n}$$

are also roots of f.
(3) If k_p *and* k_q *are the numbers of roots of* $f(x)$ *in* $\mathrm{GF}(p)$ *and* $\mathrm{GF}(q)$ *resp., then* k_pk_q *is the number of roots of* $f \in \mathbb{Z}_n[x]$. *In particular, the number of roots of* $f(x) \pmod{n}$ *is at most* $(\deg f)^2$.

Proof. (1) The solution given by the Chinese remainder theorem is unique in $\mathbb{Z}_n$.
(2) We have $f(c) \equiv f(a_q) \equiv f(a) \equiv 0 \pmod{q}$ and $f(c) \equiv f(b_p) \equiv f(b) \equiv 0 \pmod{p}$. Combining this we get $f(c) \equiv 0 \pmod{n}$, and the same argument applies to d.
(3) This follows from (1), Lemma 1 and the fact that in the fields $\mathrm{GF}(p)$ and $\mathrm{GF}(q)$ the polynomial f has at most $\deg f$ roots. □

If we know the factorization of n, we can compute all roots of $f(x)$ mod n: There are probabilistic polynomial time algorithms for computing roots of polynomials of degree d [BO81] that need $O\left(d(\log d)^2 \log^2 d \log p\right)$ arithmetical operations in $\mathrm{GF}(p)$, and from the two lemmas above we get all the roots in $\mathbb{Z}_n$.

Lemma 8. *Let* $g(x) := (x-u_1)\cdots(x-u_t)h(x)$ *a polynomial from* $\mathbb{Z}_n[x]$, *where* $\{u_1, \ldots, u_t\}$ *is a transversal of the set of roots of* $g(x)$.
(1) If we know two roots of $g(x)$ *that are in the same row or in the same column, then we can easily compute the factorization of* n.
(2) If $\{z_1, \ldots, z_t\}$ *is a transversal different from* $\{u_1, \ldots, u_t\}$, *then* $g(x) \equiv (x-z_1)\cdots(x-z_t)h(x) \pmod{n}$.

Proof. (1) Let z_i and z_j be in the same row, i. e. $(z_i)_q = (z_j)_q$. Then $q = \gcd(n, z_i - z_j)$.
(2) We have $(x-u_1)\cdots(x-u_t) \cdot h(x) \equiv (x-(u_1)_p)\cdots(x-(u_t)_p) \cdot h(x) \equiv (x-(z_1)_p)\cdots(x-(z_t)_p) \cdot h(x) \equiv (x-z_1)\cdots(x-z_t) \cdot h(x) \equiv g(x) \pmod{p}$. A similar equation holds for q, so the statement is proved. □

Proof of Theorem 2. If we know the factorization of n, we can compute the roots of $f(x)$ in the finite fields $\mathrm{GF}(p)$ and $\mathrm{GF}(q)$ in polynomial time [BO81] and combine the results via Lemma 1 and 2.

Now lets assume that we have an oracle that, when fed with a polynomial $f(x) \in \mathbb{Z}_n[x]$, which has at least two different roots, outputs one root of this polynomial. We can use this oracle to factor n in the following way.

First we choose $a, b \in \mathbb{Z}_n$ and $g(x) \in \mathbb{Z}_n[x]$ at random. Then we compute

$$f(x) := (x-a)(x-b)g(x)$$

and ask the oracle about a root of $f(x)$. Let the oracle's answer be c. If c is different from a and b and lies in the same row or column than a or b, we can factor n. If not, we repeat this process again.

Now let d be the minimal degree of a polynomial for which the oracle works. In this case we may choose as $g(x)$ a random polynomial of degree $d-2$. Then $f(x)$ has at most d^2 roots. The probability that n can be factored by applying the process described above once is larger or equal to

$$\frac{4d-6}{d^2} = \text{const.},$$

so by repeating the process roughly $\lceil \frac{d^2}{4d-6} \rceil$ times n will be factored. □

This result is a generalization of the problem of computing square roots in $\mathbb{Z}_n$. In [Sha93] Shamir generalized this problem in terms of factorizations of polynomials: If one can factor the polynomial $x^2 - a \equiv (x-b)(x-c) \in \mathbb{Z}_n[x]$, then b and $c = -b$ are square roots of a. To factor n, one has to find two different factorizations of this form.

Proof of Theorem 3. For fixed d and q, we may represent the number of polynomials from $\mathrm{GF}(q)[x]$ of degree d that have no root over $\mathrm{GF}(q)$ as a polynomial from $\mathbb{R}[x]$ of degree d in the variable q. Since we are only interested in asymptotic results, we consider only the coefficient of q^d.

The number of polynomials of degree d having a multiple root in $\mathrm{GF}(q)$ can be expressed as a real polynomial of degree $d-1$. Therefore in our analysis we can ignore all effects coming from multiple roots, and we may assume that all the roots of the polynomials we are considering are different.

Now let d be fixed. Let the number of monic polynomials of degree d over $\mathrm{GF}(q)$ which have exactly m roots be asymptotically equal to

$$A_m(q) = a_m q^d = \frac{c_{d-m}}{m!} q^d.$$

(The right hand side term being the definition of c_m.)

We now count the (k+1)-tuples $(f_1, f_2, \ldots, f_k, g)$, where the f_i are monic linear polynomials and g is a monic polynomial of degree $d-k$ over $\mathrm{GF}(q)$. The number of these tuples equals $q^k \cdot q^{d-k} = q^d$.

We can also count differently: If we associate to each tuple $(f_1, f_2, \ldots, f_k, g)$ the polynomial $f_1 f_2 \cdots f_k g$, then each polynomial with exactly $m \geq k$ (different) roots occurs exactly $\binom{m}{m-k} \cdot k!$ times. (Here we ignore multiple roots.)

Together we get

$$q^d = \sum_{m=k}^{d} \binom{m}{m-k} \cdot k! \cdot A_m(q).$$

Division by q^d gives:

$$1 = \sum_{m=k}^{d} \frac{m!}{(m-k)!} \cdot a_m = \sum_{m=k}^{d} \frac{c_{d-m}}{(m-k)!}.$$

With $j = d - k$ and $i = d - m$ it follows that

$$c_j = 1 - \sum_{i=0}^{j-1} \frac{c_i}{(j-i)!}.$$

This is a recursion formula for c_j. With induction we get:

$$c_k = \sum_{i=0}^{k} (-1)^i \cdot \frac{1}{i!}.$$

(It is sufficient to show that $\sum_{k=0}^{m} \left(\sum_{i=0}^{k} (-1)^i \cdot \frac{1}{i!} \right) \cdot \frac{1}{(m-k)!} = 1$. With the substitution $j = m - k + i$ this is equivalent to $\sum_{j=0}^{m} \left(\sum_{i=0}^{j} \frac{(-1)^i}{i!(j-i)!} \right) = 1$, which holds in view of the binomial theorem.)

Now we can calculate asymptotically the number of polynomials of degree d over GF(q) which have no roots:

$$A_0(q) = c_d \cdot q^d = \sum_{i=0}^{d} (-1)^i \cdot \frac{1}{i!} \cdot q^d.$$

□

Proof of Corollary 5. Part (1) is an immediate consequence of Cor. 4.

(2) Note that the mapping $\phi : \mathbb{Z}_n[x] \to \mathbb{Z}_p[x] \times \mathbb{Z}_q[x]$ defined by $\phi(f) := (f \bmod p, f \bmod q)$ is a bijection by the Chinese remainder theorem. The polynomial $f \in \mathbb{Z}_n[x]$ has at least one root if and only if both $f \bmod p$ and $f \bmod q$ have at least one root. Hence (2) follows from (1).

(3) A polynomial $f \in \mathbb{Z}_n[x]$ has exactly one root if and only if both $f \bmod p$ and $f \bmod q$ have exactly one root. Hence the fraction of polynomials with this property is approximately equal to $(e^{-1})^2$, and so the fraction of polynomials with at least two roots can be approximated by $(1-e^{-1})^2 - e^{-2} = 1 - 2e^{-1}$. □

Multi-Authority Secret-Ballot Elections with Linear Work

Ronald Cramer*
Matthew Franklin**
Berry Schoenmakers***
Moti Yung†

Abstract. We present new cryptographic protocols for multi-authority secret ballot elections that guarantee privacy, robustness, and universal verifiability. Application of some novel techniques, in particular the construction of witness hiding/indistinguishable protocols from Cramer, Damgård and Schoenmakers, and the verifiable secret sharing scheme of Pedersen, reduce the work required by the voter or an authority to a linear number of cryptographic operations in the population size (compared to quadratic in previous schemes). Thus we get significantly closer to a practical election scheme.

1 Introduction

An electronic voting scheme is viewed as a set of protocols that allow a collection of voters to cast their votes, while enabling a collection of authorities to collect the votes, compute the final tally, and communicate the final tally that is checked by talliers. In the cryptographic literature on voting schemes, three important requirements are identified:

Universal Verifiability ensures that any party, including a passive observer, can convince herself that the election is fair, i.e., that the published final tally is computed fairly from the ballots that were correctly cast.

Privacy ensures that an individual vote will be kept secret from any (reasonably sized) coalition of parties that does not include the voter herself.

Robustness ensures that the system can recover from the faulty behavior of any (reasonably sized) coalition of parties.

The main contribution of this paper is to present an **efficient** voting scheme that satisfies universal verifiability, privacy and robustness. Central to our methods is the application of witness indistinguishable protocols from [CDS94] to

* CWI, P.O. Box 94079, 1090 GB Amsterdam, The Netherlands. cramer@cwi.nl

** AT&T Bell Labs., 600 Mountain Ave., Murray Hill, NJ 07974, USA. franklin@big.att.com

*** DigiCash bv, Kruislaan 419, 1098 VA Amsterdam, The Netherlands. Work done while at CWI. berry@digicash.com

† IBM T.J. Watson Research Center, P.O. Box 218, Yorktown Heights, NY 10598, USA. moti@watson.ibm.com

Ueli Maurer (Ed.): EUROCRYPT '96 Proceedings, LNCS 1070

achieve greater simplicity and efficiency than previous voting schemes. The efficiency of our schemes can be summarized as follows, when there are n authorities, m voters, and security parameter k. The total amount of communication will be $O(kmn)$ bits (posted to a "bulletin board"), while the required effort (in elementary operations) for any authority and any voter will be $O(km)$ and $O(kn)$ operations, respectively. For any threshold $t \leq n$, privacy will be assured against coalitions that include at most $t-1$ authorities, and robustness against coalitions that includes at most $n-t$ authorities.

A fourth property recently stated is that of ***vote-duplication***, i.e., one voter copying the vote of another voter without knowing the actual vote (see [SK95, Gen95]). There are various efficient ways to incorporate this property in the schemes we present. We will include a straightforward solution.

1.1 Overview of the Approach

The parties in a voting scheme are modelled as probabilistic polynomial time processes. Two means of communication are typically assumed to be available for these parties:

A **bulletin board**, which is a broadcast channel with memory that can be observed and read by all parties. Each party controls her own section of the board in the sense that she can post messages exclusively to her own section, but not to the extent that she can erase or overwrite previously posted messages.

Private channels to support private communication between voters and authorities. For this task any secure public-key encryption scheme is suitable, possibly using the bulletin board to post the corresponding encryptions.

The parties of the voting scheme perform the following steps to execute an election. To cast a vote, each voter constructs a ballot as an encryption of the desired vote, and posts the ballot to the bulletin board. At this point, a proof of validity is also required that convinces all parties that the posted encryption contains a valid vote, without revealing it. The authorities, however, are able to decrypt the ballots (because of extra information received from the voter through a private channel). In the end, the final tally is published together with some auxiliary information to enable universal verifiability: any interested party (a tallier) may "accumulate" the encrypted votes and check the final tally, by holding it against this accumulation and the auxiliary information.

More technically, universal verifiability is achieved by requiring the encryption function to be suitably homomorphic. At the same time a different security property of the encryption function, which is similar to the binding property of commitment schemes, ensures that the authority (assume momentarily to be a single entity) cannot accumulate the individual votes in any other way than the voters actually voted. Such homomorphic encryption schemes are available under a wide variety of common cryptographic assumptions.

Central to our results is the way we achieve an efficient proof of validity for ballots. The proof of validity shows to any interested party that a ballot actually represents a vote, e.g., that it either represents a yes or a no, and nothing else.

To maintain privacy for the voters, the general idea is to use some sort of zero-knowledge proof. The problem is however that zero-knowledge proofs usually require a large number of repetitions before the desired level of confidence is achieved. The efficiency of these proofs to a great extent influences the efficiency of the whole scheme, both in terms of computational effort and in terms of the required bandwidth for each voter.

Our contribution now is twofold. We use a particular efficient homomorphic encryption scheme, based on the discrete logarithm problem (although, as we show, it can be based on other cryptographic assumptions as well). Moreover, by applying results from [CDS94], the proof of validity is a simple three-move protocol which is *witness indistinguishable* (in fact, witness hiding as well), instead of zero-knowledge as in previous schemes. This leads to a significant reduction of the effort required by the voter, from quadratic in the security parameter to linear, while still hiding the vote.

Clearly, in the scenario above, the authority learns individual votes. This situation is alleviated by having multiple authorities instead of one. The encrypted vote is distributed over the authorities such that fewer than some number of authorities remain ignorant about individual votes. To make sure that the authorities are convinced that the posted shares actually represent the vote cast, verifiable secret sharing is employed. Here, we apply Pedersen's scheme [Ped92], as it fits with the other primitives remarkably well. It is also by this method that robustness is achieved in the sense that only a subset (of a size larger than a certain threshold) of the authorities is required to participate throughout the execution of the scheme in order to compute the final tally.

1.2 Related Work

The type of voting schemes considered in this paper was first introduced and implemented in [CF85, BY86, Ben87b]. In these schemes, privacy and robustness are achieved by distributing the ballots over a number of tallying authorities, while still achieving universal verifiability. This contrasts with other approaches in which the ballots are submitted anonymously to guarantee privacy for the individual voters. Such schemes rely on the use of anonymous channels [Cha81], or even some form of blind signatures as in privacy-protecting payment systems (see, e.g., [Che94]) to achieve privacy. For these approaches it seems difficult however to attain all desired properties, and still achieve high performance and provable security.

The voting schemes of [CF85, BY86, Ben87b] rely on an r-th residuosity assumption. In [SK94] it is shown that such schemes can also be based on a discrete logarithm assumption (without fully addressing robustness, though), and how this leads to considerable efficiency improvements. In the present paper we will also address various number-theoretic assumptions.

As with our result, the efficiency improvement in [SK94] is mainly due to an improved zero-knowledge protocol to show validity of ballots. As noted by Benaloh, such *cryptographic capsules* [Ben87a, Ben87b] are at the heart of the problem of electronic elections and also useful for other applications. We note that the technique of [CDS94] can also be used to obtain efficient solutions for group signatures (see [CDS94, CP95]).

2 Cryptographic Primitives

2.1 The Discrete Logarithm Problem

Let $\mathcal{G} = \{\mathcal{G}_k\}$ be a family of groups of prime order such that the group operations can be performed efficiently, group elements can be efficiently sampled with uniform distribution and group membership as well as equality of group elements can be efficiently tested. Let *Gen* be a probabilistic polynomial time generator that on input 1^k outputs a description of a group $G \in \mathcal{G}_k$ (including the group order), and two random elements g, h from G. We say that the discrete logarithm problem for $\mathcal{G}$ is intractable (over *Gen*) if there is no probabilistic polynomial time algorithm that on input of G, g and h as output by $Gen(1^k)$ can compute $\log_g h$ with non-negligible probability in k.

Each family $\mathcal{G}$ for which it is reasonable to assume the intractability of the discrete logarithm problem is suitable for our purpose of constructing efficient and secure homomorphic encryption schemes with corresponding proofs of validity. A well-known family, however, is obtained by choosing large primes p and q at random such that $q \mid p-1$; then G is the unique subgroup of order q in $\mathbb{Z}_p^*$. The discrete logarithm problem for elliptic curves over finite fields is also a candidate for implementation.

2.2 Homomorphic Encryption with Efficient Proof of Validity

Let $\mathcal{G}$ be a family of groups of prime order, and generator *Gen* as above. Assume that the discrete logarithm problem for $\mathcal{G}$ is intractable. The encryption scheme below is obtained as an extension of Pedersen's commitment scheme [Ped92] with an efficient proof of validity.

Initialization: The participants, or a designated subset of them, run $Gen(1^k)$ and obtain a group G_q of prime order q, and random group elements g and h. One way to do this honestly, is that the participants agree on a program for *Gen* first. Then they each run separately $Gen(1^k)$ where the coinflips needed are selected mutually at random, either by observing a common source of physical randomness, or by executing some well-known cryptographic protocol suitable for this purpose.

Encryption: A participant encrypts $v \in \mathbb{Z}_q$ by choosing $\alpha \in \mathbb{Z}_q$ at random, and computing

$$B \leftarrow g^{\alpha} h^{v}.$$

Opening: A participant can later open B by revealing both v and α. A verifying party then checks whether $B = g^{\alpha} h^{v}$, and accepts v as the encrypted value.

Voter ($v = 1$)	Voter ($v = -1$)		Verifier
$\alpha, r_1, d_1, w_2 \in_R \mathbb{Z}_q$	$\alpha, r_2, d_2, w_1 \in_R \mathbb{Z}_q$		
$B \leftarrow g^\alpha h$	$B \leftarrow g^\alpha / h$		
$a_1 \leftarrow g^{r_1}(Bh)^{-d_1}$	$a_1 \leftarrow g^{w_1}$		
$a_2 \leftarrow g^{w_2}$	$a_2 \leftarrow g^{r_2}(B/h)^{-d_2}$		
		$\xrightarrow{B, a_1, a_2}$	
			$c \in_R \mathbb{Z}_q$
		$\xleftarrow{c}$	
$d_2 \leftarrow c - d_1$	$d_1 \leftarrow c - d_2$		
$r_2 \leftarrow w_2 + \alpha d_2$	$r_1 \leftarrow w_1 + \alpha d_1$		
		$\xrightarrow{d_1, d_2, r_1, r_2}$	
			$d_1 + d_2 \stackrel{?}{=} c$
			$g^{r_1} \stackrel{?}{=} a_1(Bh)^{d_1}$
			$g^{r_2} \stackrel{?}{=} a_2(B/h)^{d_2}$

Fig. 1. Encryption and Proof of Validity of Ballot B

Homomorphic Property: Encryption is homomorphic in the sense that, if B_1 and B_2 are encryptions of v_1 and v_2, respectively, then $B_1 B_2$ is an encryption of $v_1 + v_2 \bmod q$. In general, an encryption of any linear combination of v_1 and v_2 can be obtained from B_1 and B_2; in particular, the sign of v_1 can be flipped by computing B_1^{-1}. Note also that, e.g., $B_1 h$ encrypts $v_1 + 1 \bmod q$.

Proof of Validity: In our voting scheme to follow, it will be the case that a voter posts an encryption of a value $v \in \{1, -1\}$. To demonstrate that the encrypted value is indeed in $\{1, -1\}$, without revealing it, the voter and the verifier execute the efficient *proof of validity* of Figure 1. This proof requires only a very small number of modular exponentiations.

Theorem 1 *Under the discrete logarithm assumption, the encryption scheme is binding in the sense that it is infeasible to open a given encryption in two different ways. Furthermore, the proof of validity is a convincing argument that a given encryption is indeed an encryption of a value from the set $\{1, -1\}$, thereby not releasing any information about the actual value.*

Proof If any party is able to open an encryption B in two different ways, i.e., to present values α, v, α', v' such that $B = g^\alpha h^v = g^{\alpha'} h^{v'}$ with $\alpha \neq \alpha'$ and $v \neq v'$, it follows that $\log_g h = \frac{\alpha - \alpha'}{v' - v}$, which contradicts the discrete logarithm assumption. Furthermore, by the results of [CDS94], the protocol in Figure 1 is a witness indistinguishable proof of knowledge that the voter knows $\log_g Bh$ or $\log_g B/h$; here, Schnorr's identification protocol [Sch91] is used as the basic protocol in the construction of [CDS94]. Thus the verifier learns that the voter knows α and $v \in \{1, -1\}$ such that $B = g^\alpha h^v$, without obtaining any information about the actual value of v. □

Note that it even follows that the proof of validity is witness hiding.

Jumping ahead a little bit, envision that a voter posts an encryption of his vote and that all other participants must verify its validity. As depicted in Figure 1, a source of randomness is required in the program for the verifier. For this purpose, one can use some unpredictable physical source of randomness [CF85], or agree on mutually random bits by cryptographic means. A more practical way, however, making the protocol *non-interactive*, is to apply the well-known Fiat-Shamir heuristic [FS87]. Their idea is to compute the challenge in a three-move identification scheme as a hash value of the message to be signed and the first message of the prover. So, let $\mathcal{H}$ be a suitable strong cryptographic hash function (thought of as a random oracle). In the non-interactive version of our proof of validity, the challenge c is computed as $c = \mathcal{H}(B, a_1, a_2)$. The set of values d_1, d_2, r_1 and r_2 is denoted proof(B). Given the values in proof(B), any participant can check the validity of B by verifying that $d_1 + d_2 = \mathcal{H}(B, g^{r_1}(Bh)^{-d_1}, g^{r_2}(B/h)^{-d_2})$.

2.3 Verifiable Secret Sharing

To achieve robustness efficiently, non-interactive verifiable secret sharing is employed. We use the scheme of Pedersen [Ped92], as it is based on discrete logarithms as well and fits nicely with our encryption scheme. Being information theoretically secure, this scheme also contributes to privacy in our multiple authority scenario.

3 Secret Ballot Election Scheme

We now present our main result, a secret ballot election scheme satisfying privacy, universal verifiability and robustness. The participants in the election scheme are n authorities $A_1, \ldots, A_n$ and m voters $V_1, \ldots, V_m$. Privacy and robustness are as follows. No collusion of fewer than t authorities can reveal an individual vote, while the election will be successful when at least t authorities operate properly $(1 \leq t \leq n)$. At the same time we incorporate a simple mechanism to postpone the decision on what to vote until the preparation of the election has been completed. In this way several elections can be prepared beforehand at the beginning of the year, say, and casting a vote in an election then boils down to publishing essentially one bit of information.

Informally the scheme works as follows. Each voter V_i prepares a vote by randomly selecting a number b_i in $\{1, -1\}$. The voter first encrypts b_i by computing $B_i = g^{\alpha_i} h^{b_i}$, where $\alpha_i \in \mathbb{Z}_q$ is chosen randomly, and posts B_i to the bulletin board. Subsequently, b_i is considered as a secret which is to be shared among the authorities. We employ a verifiable secret sharing scheme to prevent voters from disrupting elections by sending false shares to authorities. The efficient scheme by Pedersen [Ped92] is a perfect candidate as it applies exactly to the discrete log setting we are considering. The idea is thus to let the voter act as the dealer in Pedersen's scheme, sending a verifiable share of the secret b_i to each authority using the proper private channels. The voter also posts proof(B_i) to the bulletin board to prove that B_i indeed encrypts a value in $\{1, -1\}$. Later, voter V_i may then cast a vote $v_i \in \{1, -1\}$ by publishing the value $s_i = b_i v_i$. In the end, the aggregate value $T = \sum_{i=1}^{m} v_i$ reduced modulo q such that $-q/2 < T < q/2$ represents the total number of yes-votes minus the total number of no-votes, hence the total number of yes-votes is $(m+T)/2$. For these numbers to be correct the obvious requirement is that $m < q/2$.

We assume that the group G_q and the members g and h are generated as described in Section 2. In particular, it then follows that $\log_g h$ is not known to any participant.

Ballot Construction

Each voter V_i prepares a masked vote $b_i \in \{1, -1\}$ in the following way.

1. The voter chooses b_i randomly from $\{1, -1\}$, and computes the ballot $B_i = g^{\alpha_i} h^{b_i}$, where α_i is randomly chosen from $\mathbb{Z}_q$. The voter also computes proof(B_i). Finally, the voter determines polynomials G_i and H_i,

$$G_i(x) = \alpha_i + \alpha_{i1} x + \cdots + \alpha_{i,t-1} x^{t-1}$$
$$H_i(x) = b_i + \beta_{i1} x + \cdots + \beta_{i,t-1} x^{t-1},$$

   where the coefficients α_{il}, β_{il}, $1 \le l < t$, are chosen at random from $\mathbb{Z}_q$. Also, for these coefficients the voter computes the commitments $B_{il} = g^{\alpha_{il}} h^{\beta_{il}}$.
2. The voter posts B_i, proof(B_i), $B_{i1}, \ldots, B_{i,t-1}$ to the bulletin board.
3. All participants verify whether ballot B_i is correctly formed by checking proof(B_i).[5]
4. The voter sends the respective shares $(a_{ij}, b_{ij}) = (G_i(j), H_i(j))$ to authority A_j, using a private channel.
5. Each authority checks the received share (a_{ij}, b_{ij}) by verifying that

$$g^{a_{ij}} h^{b_{ij}} = B_i \prod_{l=1}^{t-1} B_{il}^{j^l}.$$

Vote Casting

To cast a vote, V_i simply posts $s_i \in \{1, -1\}$ such that $v_i = b_i s_i$ represents the desired vote.

---

[5] To prevent vote duplication, a bit string specific to voter V_i is also included in the input to the hash function $\mathcal{H}$ in proof(B_i). In case the proof of validity is done interactively, as depicted in Figure 1, this bit string could be incorporated in the challenge.

Tallying

1. Each authority A_j posts the sum $S_j = \sum_{i=1}^{m} a_{ij}s_i$ and the sub-tally $T_j = \sum_{i=1}^{m} b_{ij}s_i$.
2. Each tallier checks the share (S_j, T_j) posted by authority A_j by verifying that
$$g^{S_j}h^{T_j} = \prod_{i=1}^{m}\left(B_i\prod_{l=1}^{t-1}B_{il}^{j^l}\right)^{s_i}.$$
3. From t pairs (j, T_j) that correspond to authorities for which the shares (S_j, T_j) are correct, each tallier can compute the final tally T from the formula:
$$T = \sum_{j\in A} T_j \prod_{l\in A\setminus\{j\}} \frac{l}{l-j},$$
where A denotes a set of t correct authorities.

We assume (w.l.o.g.) that in a successful election the shares of every voter have been accepted by all authorities. That is, all verifications by the authorities in the last step of the ballot construction are successful. In case an authority receives a share that does not pass this step, the authority may post the share so that anybody can verify that the share is not correct and that it corresponds to the posted encryption of step 4 of the ballot construction.

Theorem 2 *Under the discrete logarithm assumption, our secret-ballot election scheme satisfies universal verifiability, robustness and privacy.*

Proof To prove universal verifiability first note that only correct ballots are counted on account of Theorem 1. Further, to prove that the final tally is correct, we reason as follows for each correct authority A_j. Let $G(x) = \sum_{i=1}^{m} s_i G_i(x)$ and $H(x) = \sum_{i=1}^{m} s_i H_i(x)$. By the binding property[6] of the encryptions B_i (see Section 2), we have:

$$\begin{aligned} g^{G(j)}h^{H(j)} &= g^{\sum_{i=1}^{m} s_i G_i(j)}h^{\sum_{i=1}^{m} s_i H_i(j)} \\ &= g^{\sum_{i=1}^{m} s_i a_{ij}}h^{\sum_{i=1}^{m} s_i b_{ij}} \\ &= \prod_{i=1}^{m}(g^{a_{ij}}h^{b_{ij}})^{s_i} \\ &= \prod_{i=1}^{m}(B_i\prod_{l=1}^{t-1}B_{il}^{j^l})^{s_i}. \end{aligned}$$

By the assumption that the verification in step 2 of the tallying protocol holds for (S_j, T_j), we thus have $g^{G(j)}h^{H(j)} = g^{S_j}h^{T_j}$, which implies $S_j = G(j)$ and $T_j = H(j)$ under the discrete logarithm assumption. As a consequence, the final tally T is indeed equal to $H(0)$ and thus represents the result of the election

[6] The description of our scheme above assumes that the hash function in the Fiat-Shamir style proof(B_i), behaves like a random-oracle. Instead of using this technique, the participants can get the necessary random bits as explained in Section 2, thus also removing the need for this extra assumption.

if the verification in step 2 of the tallying holds for at least t authorities. This deals with universal verifiability and robustness. The privacy property can easily be proved from the fact that the secret sharing scheme used and the proofs of validity (see Section 2) are information-theoretically secure. □

Thus, fewer than t authorities do not obtain any information about individual votes, other than what can be derived from the final tally (and accounting for votes that have been revealed by individual voters).

To summarize the *performance* of our scheme, we note the following. The hard operations are the modular exponentiations with full exponents (i.e., exponents of expected size $|q|$). Counting these operations, we see that the work for each voter is $O(1)$ for the construction of the ballot (including the proof of validity) plus $O(t)$ for the commitments for the verifiable secret sharing scheme. Each authority has to do $O(m)$ work to check all the shares. So active participants do linear work. Finally, verification of the election (done only by interested talliers) requires $O(m)$ work to check the ballots plus $O(t \log^2 t)$ multiplications to check the shares of the final tally. Note that the parties' work can all be done either before or after the casting of the votes. The actual election simply consists of every voter posting essentially one bit of information to the bulletin board. This represents essentially an improvement of two orders of magnitude over the best schemes known so far (assuming $k = 100$), and enables much of the work required to be done off-line.

4 Extensions

The ballots B we have worked with so far are basically of the form $B = g^\alpha h^b$, where b represents the (masked) vote. There are numerous ways to extend this form, which will be elaborated upon in forthcoming work. We sketch some of the ideas in this section.

Parallel elections Several elections may be held at the same time by running several instances of the scheme from Section 3 in parallel. A possibly more efficient approach to perform K elections in parallel is to use ballots B of the form $B = g^\alpha h_1^{v_1} \cdots h_K^{v_K}$, where each v_l denotes the intended vote for the l-th election. The scheme of Section 3 can be carried over easily to this setting by observing that the immediate generalization of Okamoto's variation of Schnorr's scheme [Oka93] can be used to prove knowledge of either $\log_{g,h_1,\ldots,h_{l-1},h_{l+1},\ldots,h_K} Bh_l$ or $\log_{g,h_1,\ldots,h_{l-1},h_{l+1},\ldots,h_K} B/h_l$, for each $l = 1, \ldots, K$. Again the technique from [CDS94] can be applied to hide which of the two is known.

Multiway Elections In a multiway election each voter has to choose between a number of options. That is, if there are K options, the voter has to say yes to one of them and no to all of the others. (See also [BY86].) This is achieved efficiently through ballots of the same form as in a parallel election, with the additional requirement that $\sum_{l=1}^{K} v_l = 1$, if yes and no are represented by 1 and 0 respectively.

An even more efficient way is to take $B = g^\alpha h^{M^l}$ to represent option l, where M is larger than the number of voters. The voter then proves knowledge of at least one of $\log_g B/h, \log_g B/(h^M), \ldots, \log_g B/(h^{M^K})$, without revealing which. Note, however, that the number of options K is now bounded by approximately $\log_M q$.

Batched Elections A drawback of the above solutions for parallel and multi-way elections is that there is no mechanism to perform masked votes. An interesting extension therefore is to consider *batched* elections, where the same ballot is used several times. So, with a ballot of the form $B_i = g^{\alpha_i} h_1^{b_{i1}} \cdots h_K^{b_{iK}}$, a voter can later post the numbers s_{il} such that $v_{il} = b_{il} s_{il}$ represents the intended vote for the lth election, for $l = 1, \ldots, K$. Although this reveals the sums $\sum_i \alpha_i s_{il}$, $\sum_i b_{i1} s_{il}$, …, $\sum_i b_{iK} s_{il}$, for $l = 1, \ldots, K$, this is not a problem if the number of voters is sufficiently large. (Note that $\sum_i b_{il} s_{il}$ is the result of the l-th election.)

Integer Votes Instead of requiring that votes are in $\{0, 1\}$ say, it is a natural extension to consider votes in $\{0, \ldots, N-1\}$ for some integer N. This can be achieved directly by using 1-out-of-N proofs (see [CDS94]). Also, using the above approach for parallel elections, the bits b_i can be assigned weights like 2^{i-1}, and then we get integer votes with $N = 2^K$.

5 Alternative Number Theoretic Assumptions

Under the RSA assumption and the factoring assumption we obtain voting schemes that are comparable in performance and functionality. Note, however, that the initialization of these schemes is more complicated than the initialization of the discrete log based schemes, if it is required that the modulus is generated by multiple parties.

Under the RSA assumption, we have the following scheme. We assume that a modulus N, which is the product of two large distinct primes, a prime v, with $\gcd(v, \phi(N)) = 1$, and an element h of $\mathbb{Z}_N^*$ are available to all parties. The RSA assumption then roughly states that it is infeasible to compute $h^{1/v} \bmod N$. For this setting we have the following efficient commitment scheme. To commit to a value $m \in \mathbb{Z}_v$, the committer chooses $\alpha \in_R \mathbb{Z}_N^*$, and reveals $B = \alpha^v h^m$. The commitment is opened by revealing α and m.

In this setting we may directly apply the technique of [CDS94] to Guillou-Quisquater's identification protocol [GQ88] to construct proofs of validity for ballots of the form $B_i = \alpha_i^v h^{b_i}$. To extend this to a solution with multiple authorities, as in Section 3, we run into a problem as we have no matching verifiably secret sharing scheme. However, an efficient solution for the n-out-of-n case is possible. The idea is simply that the voter chooses shares $a_{ij} \in_R \mathbb{Z}_N^*$, for $j = 1, \ldots, n$, and $b_{ij} \in_R \mathbb{Z}_v$, for $j = 2, \ldots, n$, and sets $\alpha_i = \prod_{j=1}^n a_{ij}$ and $b_{i1} = b_i - \sum_{j=2}^n b_{ij}$. The ballot is then computed as $B_i = \alpha_i^v h^{b_i}$ with $\alpha_i = (\prod_{j=1}^n a_{ij}) h^{(\sum_{j=1}^n b_{ij}) \operatorname{div} v}$. The protocols of Section 3 are translated accordingly.

Similarly for the factoring assumption, these ideas apply to such encryption functions as $\alpha^2 4^b \bmod N$, where N is the product of two primes $p \equiv 3 \pmod 8$ and $q \equiv 7 \pmod 8$.

6 Conclusion

We have presented election schemes of provable security and practical efficiency. The computational and communication complexity are essentially linear, instead of quadratic as for previous schemes. Even with a large number of authorities like $n = 10$, a voter need not communicate more than approximately 10.000 bits of information to submit a vote, assuming that $|p| = 512$ bits and $|q| = 160$ bits for our discrete log scheme. (Note that the actual ballot plus its proof of validity require only 1152 bits.) Compare this, for instance, to [SK94] with in the order of a million bits per vote for the same level of security.

A property of voting schemes, recently identified, that we did not consider in the present paper is that of *non-coercibility* [BT94]. Non-coercibility ensures that no voter will obtain, as a result of an execution of the voting scheme, a receipt that can prove how she voted. The intention of this property is to prevent vote-buying and other tactics of voter persuasion. It is possible (and is part of work in progress) that extensions of our ideas can give a scheme which incorporate non-coercibility while maintaining universal verifiability, privacy, robustness, and efficiency.

References

[Ben87a] J. Benaloh. Cryptographic capsules: A disjunctive primitive for interactive protocols. In *Advances in Cryptology—CRYPTO '86*, volume 263 of *Lecture Notes in Computer Science*, pages 213–222, Berlin, 1987. Springer-Verlag.

[Ben87b] J. Benaloh. *Verifiable Secret-Ballot Elections.* PhD thesis, Yale University, Department of Computer Science Department, New Haven, CT, September 1987.

[BT94] J. Benaloh and D. Tuinstra. Receipt-free secret-ballot elections. In *Proc. 26th Symposium on Theory of Computing (STOC '94)*, pages 544–553, New York, 1994. A.C.M.

[BY86] J. Benaloh and M. Yung. Distributing the power of a government to enhance the privacy of voters. In *Proc. 5th ACM Symposium on Principles of Distributed Computing (PODC '86)*, pages 52–62, New York, 1986. A.C.M.

[CDS94] R. Cramer, I. Damgård, and B. Schoenmakers. Proofs of partial knowledge and simplified design of witness hiding protocols. In *Advances in Cryptology—CRYPTO '94*, volume 839 of *Lecture Notes in Computer Science*, pages 174–187, Berlin, 1994. Springer-Verlag.

[CF85] J. Cohen and M. Fischer. A robust and verifiable cryptographically secure election scheme. In *Proc. 26th IEEE Symposium on Foundations of Computer Science (FOCS '85)*, pages 372–382. IEEE Computer Society, 1985.

[Cha81] D. Chaum. Untraceable electronic mail, return addresses, and digital pseudonyms. *Communications of the ACM*, 24(2):84–88, 1981.

[Che94] L. Chen. *Witness Hiding Proofs and Applications.* PhD thesis, Aarhus University, Computer Science Department, Aarhus, Denmark, August 1994.

[CP95] L. Chen and T. P. Pedersen. New group signature schemes. In *Advances in Cryptology—EUROCRYPT '94*, volume 950 of *Lecture Notes in Computer Science*, pages 171–181, Berlin, 1995. Springer-Verlag.

[FS87] A. Fiat and A. Shamir. How to prove yourself: Practical solutions to identification and signature problems. In *Advances in Cryptology—CRYPTO '86*, volume 263 of *Lecture Notes in Computer Science*, pages 186–194, New York, 1987. Springer-Verlag.

[Gen95] R. Gennaro. Achieving independence efficiently and securely. In *Proc. 14th ACM Symposium on Principles of Distributed Computing (PODC '95)*, New York, 1995. A.C.M.

[GQ88] L. C. Guillou and J.-J. Quisquater. A practical zero-knowledge protocol fitted to security microprocessor minimizing both transmission and memory. In *Advances in Cryptology—EUROCRYPT '88*, volume 330 of *Lecture Notes in Computer Science*, pages 123–128, Berlin, 1988. Springer-Verlag.

[Oka93] T. Okamoto. Provably secure and practical identification schemes and corresponding signature schemes. In *Advances in Cryptology—CRYPTO '92*, volume 740 of *Lecture Notes in Computer Science*, pages 31–53, Berlin, 1993. Springer-Verlag.

[Ped92] T. P. Pedersen. Non-interactive and information-theoretic secure verifiable secret sharing. In *Advances in Cryptology—CRYPTO '91*, volume 576 of *Lecture Notes in Computer Science*, pages 129–140, Berlin, 1992. Springer-Verlag.

[Sch91] C. P. Schnorr. Efficient signature generation by smart cards. *Journal of Cryptology*, 4(3):161–174, 1991.

[SK94] K. Sako and J. Kilian. Secure voting using partially compatible homomorphisms. In *Advances in Cryptology—CRYPTO '94*, volume 839 of *Lecture Notes in Computer Science*, pages 411–424, Berlin, 1994. Springer-Verlag.

[SK95] K. Sako and J. Kilian. Receipt-free mix-type voting scheme—a practical solution to the implementation of a voting booth. In *Advances in Cryptology—EUROCRYPT '95*, volume 921 of *Lecture Notes in Computer Science*, pages 393–403, Berlin, 1995. Springer-Verlag.

Asymmetric Fingerprinting

(Extended Abstract)

Birgit Pfitzmann*, Matthias Schunter†

Universität Hildesheim, Institut für Informatik
D-31141 Hildesheim, Germany

Abstract. Fingerprinting schemes deter people from illegal copying of digital data by enabling the merchant of the data to identify the original buyer of a copy that was redistributed illegally. All known fingerprinting schemes are symmetric in the following sense: Both the buyer and the merchant know the fingerprinted copy. Thus, when the merchant finds this copy somewhere, there is no proof that it was the buyer who put it there, and not the merchant.

We introduce asymmetric fingerprinting, where only the buyer knows the fingerprinted copy, and the merchant, upon finding it somewhere, can find out and prove to third parties whose copy it was. We present a detailed definition of this concept and constructions. The first construction is based on a quite general symmetric fingerprinting scheme and general cryptographic primitives; it is provably secure if all these underlying schemes are. We also present more specific and more efficient constructions.

1 Introduction

Where information is sold, the merchants want to ensure that it is not redistributed illegally on a large scale. Thus copyright protection of digital data has recently found increased attention given the widespread feeling that electronic marketplaces, mainly on the World Wide Web, may soon be reality. In particular, images and text are now considered in addition to software, where the problem has been relevant much longer. There are two basic approaches to copyright protection. One is based on tamper-resistant modules in the buyers' machines that prevent copying at least of the internal representation of the data. However, this approach is limited, as experiences with software have shown. The second approach, fingerprinting, does not rely on special hardware. Thus it cannot prevent copying, but it deters people from illegal copying by allowing a redistributed copy to be traced back to its original owner.

1.1 Fingerprinting

Fingerprinting software, images, or other data means introducing some errors into each copy sold that make this copy unique, as fingerprints make people unique. These intentional errors are called *marks*, and all the marks in one copy are *the fingerprint*. Once an illegal copy turns up, the merchant can see from the fingerprint which of the original copies was illegally redistributed. Usually, the following informal requirements are posed on such a scheme:

---

* pfitzb@informatik.uni-hildesheim.de

† schunter@acm.org

Ueli Maurer (Ed.): EUROCRYPT '96 Proceedings, LNCS 1070

- The data must tolerate the errors: On the one hand, the marks must not decrease the usefulness of the copy to the buyer. On the other hand, the buyer should not be able to derive from redundancy in the data where the marks are.
- Collusion-tolerance: Even if dishonest buyers have up to a certain number of copies, they should not be able to find all the marks by comparing the copies. In particular, the fingerprints must have a common intersection.
- Tolerance of additional errors: If a dishonest buyer adds some noise to the copy, the fingerprint should still be recognizable, unless there is so much noise that the copy as such is useless. In other words, the fingerprints should tolerate a greater level of noise than the data. In particular, this should hold for lossy data compression.

For previous literature on fingerprinting, see, e.g., [W83, BMP86, C95, BS95]. Related problems are treated in [CFN94] for Pay-TV, in [BLM94, CMP95] for data that are not digital, but on paper, and in [MQ95, Section V], where a so-called watermark that proves the identity of the merchant is desired. Examples of cryptographic work on software copyright protection with special hardware are [G87, O90].

1.2 Asymmetric Fingerprinting

In all the previous fingerprinting schemes, two parties know the data with the fingerprint: the buyer of the original copy and the merchant. Thus, if another copy with this fingerprint turns up, one cannot really assign responsibility to one of them: The copy might just as well have been redistributed by a dishonest employee of the merchant as by the buyer, or the merchant as such may want to gain money by wrongly claiming that there are illegal copies around. In other words, the merchant does not obtain means to prove to a third party that the buyer redistributed the copy.

This is as with symmetric message authentication codes: As two people know the same secret key, no non-repudiation is offered. In contrast, only one person can make a digital signature (at least if we neglect problems with hardware protection and key distribution), and thus a signed message can really be used to hold someone responsible. We want to achieve similar security for fingerprinting.

Thus our goal is to construct fingerprinting schemes that are asymmetric in the following sense: After a sale, *only* the buyer knows the data with the fingerprint. However, if the merchant later finds this copy somewhere, he can identify the buyer and prove to third parties that this buyer bought this copy.

2 The Model

To make our goals and assumptions precise, we give a formal definition of asymmetric fingerprinting. We first define the components of such a scheme and then the security requirements.

2.1 Algorithms and Parameters

A fingerprinting scheme works for a specific space of data to be sold. We call it *Pic_Space*, because in the examples and illustrations, we mostly consider pictures. As the original data the merchant sells have to remain secret, and the buyers may have some a priori knowledge about it, we have to assume that *Pic_Space* is equipped with an arbitrary probability distribution. One buyer, identified by a public key that is constant over some time, may buy several data from the same merchant. We use an input parameter *text* to the fingerprinting protocol to distinguish these sales. In practice, *text* would typically identify the contract referring to this sale. This is particularly important if different data are sold with different licensing terms.

Definition 1. An asymmetric fingerprinting scheme consists of four protocols, *key_gen*, *fing*, *identify*, and *dispute*. All algorithms in these protocols have a security parameter, k, as a common input, and are probabilistic polynomial-time in k. Furthermore, the scheme contains *Pic_Space*, the space of data to be sold, with a given probability distribution, and *Text_Space*; both are subsets of $\{0, 1\}^*$. For simplicity, we have omitted in the notation that *Pic_Space* and *Text_Space* may depend on k. Moreover, there may be a parameter N denoting the maximum number of times the merchant can sell the same data. The protocols have the following parameters:

- For *key_gen*, the key generation protocol, we only define the simplest case: The buyer generates a pair of values (sk_B, pk_B), which we call a secret and a public key, and broadcasts pk_B reliably to all merchants and third parties, e.g., via certification authorities.
- *fing*, the fingerprinting protocol, is a 2-party protocol between a merchant, M, and a buyer, B; see Figure 1. The merchant inputs the data to be sold, *Pic*, the identity of the buyer, represented by the buyer's public key, pk_B, and a string $text \in Text\_Space$. Moreover, his algorithm may depend on the history, represented by $Record\_list_{Pic}$, a list of records from previous sales of the same data. The buyer inputs *text* and her secret key, sk_B. The main output to the buyer are the data Pic_{bought} with a small error. The buyer may also obtain a record, $record_B$, to be stored for future disputes. Instead, she may obtain a specific output *failed*, which means that the protocol failed. The output for the merchant is a record of the sale, $record_M$, or *failed*.

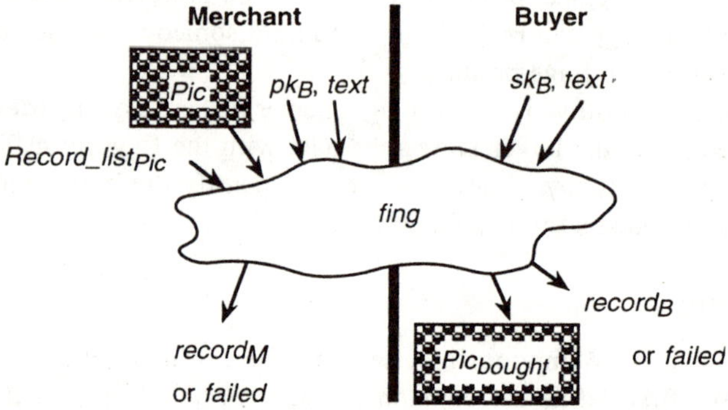

Fig. 1. Parameters of asymmetric fingerprinting

- *identify* is an algorithm the merchant executes to identify the original buyer of a certain copy, see Figure 2. The inputs are the data with a small error, Pic_{found}, the data the merchant sold, *Pic*, and a list $Record\_list_{Pic}$ of all the records of sales of these data. The output is either *failed* or the identity of a buyer, represented by pk_B and *text*, and a string *proof*.

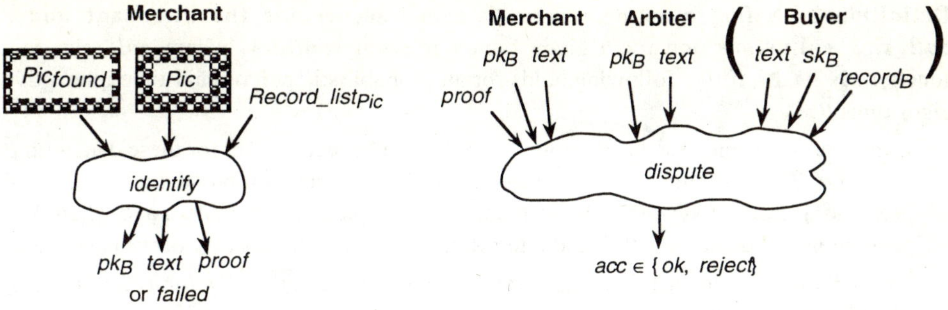

Fig. 2. Parameters in the identification of the original owner and the subsequent dispute

- *dispute* is a 2- or 3-party protocol between the merchant, an arbitrary third party that we briefly call *arbiter*, and possibly the accused buyer. The merchant and the arbiter input pk_B and *text*. The merchant additionally inputs *proof*. If the accused buyer takes part, she inputs *text*, her secret key, sk_B, and $record_B$, the record from the purchase with *text*. The output is a Boolean value *acc* for the arbiter, where $acc = ok$ means that the arbiter finds the buyer guilty or, more precisely, that the arbiter accepts that the merchant has found the data bought by the accused buyer with *text*. ♦

2.2 Security

There are three types of requirements on an asymmetric fingerprinting scheme: First, it should be effective in the sense that buyers obtain useful data as long as nobody cheats. Secondly, merchants want to be protected from cheating buyers: If an illegal copy turns up, they want some buyer to be identified and found guilty as responsible for it. Thirdly, buyers want to be protected from cheating merchants and other buyers: If they do not redistribute their copies illegally, they should not be falsely found guilty.

The notion of "useful data" that the buyer is supposed to obtain depends on the type of data to be fingerprinted. Thus we assume an arbitrary given relation $similar_1$, where $similar_1(Pic, Pic_{bought})$ means that Pic_{bought} is good enough as a replacement for *Pic*. For instance, with pictures, $similar_1$ will typically mean $Pic_{bought} = Pic \oplus \varepsilon_{bought}$ with an error vector of small Hamming weight. With programs, it may mean semantic equivalence. Similarly, we assume an arbitrary given relation $similar_2$ where $similar_2(Pic, Pic_{found})$ means that an illegal copy Pic_{found} is still so close to *Pic* that the merchant wants to identify the original buyer.

The protection of the merchant usually only works for collusions of a certain maximum size, just as with symmetric fingerprinting. In contrast, we guarantee the protection of a buyer even if any number of others collude against her, because falsely being found guilty of fraud would be a completely unacceptable consequence of the use of fingerprinting.

Now we are ready for the formal definitions.

Definition 2. A fingerprinting scheme is called **effective** for a certain given binary relation $similar_1$ on *Pic_Space* iff the following holds: If both parties execute *fing* honestly for any $Pic \in Pic\_Space$ and $text \in Text\_Space$, after correct key generation and any intermediate history, the protocol succeeds and the buyer obtains a close enough variant Pic_{bought} of *Pic*, i.e., $similar_1(Pic, Pic_{bought})$ holds. ♦

Definition 3. A fingerprinting scheme is called **secure for the merchant under *coll_size* collusions** and for a given binary relation $similar_2$, where *coll_size* is a function: $\mathbb{N} \to \mathbb{N}$, iff the following holds for all probabilistic polynomial-time interactive algorithms $\tilde{B}$:

- If the merchant selects data *Pic* from *Pic_Space* and executes *fing* for these data with $\tilde{B}$ at most *coll_size*(k) times, where $\tilde{B}$ can choose the merchant's input *text* arbitrarily and pk_B among a set of keys that the merchant has accepted as distributed, and where key generation and disputes with $\tilde{B}$ and interactions with other buyers may occur in between,
- and if $\tilde{B}$ then outputs data Pic_{found} similar to *Pic*, i.e., such that $similar_2(Pic, Pic_{found})$ holds,
- then *identify*, on input Pic_{found}, *Pic*, and the current list of records, outputs a triple (pk_B, *text*, *proof*), where pk_B is one of the previous inputs to *fing*, such that
- when *dispute* is executed with these parameters (input by the merchant and the arbiter), and in the 3-party-case with $\tilde{B}$, the arbiter's output will be *ok*, except with negligible probability.

The probability is over all the random choices of all the participants. ♦

Definition 4. A fingerprinting scheme is called **secure for the buyer** iff the following holds: No probabilistic polynomial-time algorithm $\tilde{M}$

- carrying out *fing* with B arbitrarily often (after B has generated a key pair and distributed pk_B), where $\tilde{M}$ can choose the buyer's input *text* arbitrarily for the same or different data, and possibly carrying out some disputes in between,
- and obtaining the outputs Pic_{bought} from some of these executions, which $\tilde{M}$ may choose adaptively by inputting the corresponding *text*,
- can compute parameters *text* and *proof*, where *text* is not among those for which $\tilde{M}$ obtained Pic_{bought} in the previous step,
- and then execute *dispute* with an arbiter that has the inputs pk_B and *text* such that the arbiter's output is *ok*, except with negligible probability.

The probability is over all the random choices of all the participants. ♦

We could distinguish whether parallel or only sequential executions of *fing* and other protocols are allowed in both definitions. Furthermore, we can make several additional requirements that are useful at least in some applications, e.g., protecting merchants from making wrong accusations and making disputable whether a merchant delivered the promised information.

3 A General Construction

Our first construction relies on a quite general given symmetric fingerprinting scheme and some further general cryptographic primitives and is provably secure if all these primitives are secure. The buyer need not participate in disputes, nor store records. More efficient, less general constructions are shown in later sections. By an arbitrary symmetric fingerprinting scheme, we mean one according to the following very general definition:

Definition 5 (Sketch). A symmetric fingerprinting scheme consists of two algorithms, *fing* and *identify*, a data space, *Pic_Space*, with a given probability distribution, and an identity space, *Id_Space*. Both algorithms are assumed to be executed by the merchant. Their parameters are shown in Figure 3.

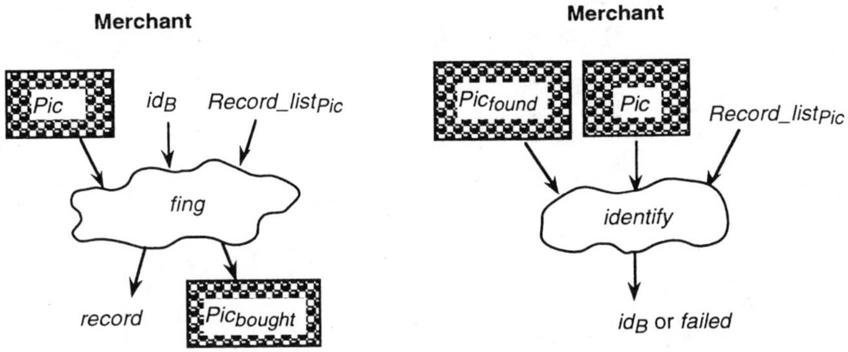

Fig. 3. Symmetric fingerprinting, general model

We require that such a scheme is **effective** for a relation $similar_1$ and **secure under *coll_size* collusions** for a relation $similar_2$; these definitions are similar to Definition 2 and 3. ♦

Definition 6. The **restrictions** we have to make on the symmetric fingerprinting scheme for Construction 1 are:

a) Memory-less. The algorithm *fing* does not produce records depending on id_B. Thus the whole content of $Record\_list_{Pic}$ can be derived from *Pic* and the merchant's string of random bits. For explicitness, we denote it by $Record_{Pic}$. In practice, $Record_{Pic}$ will typically be the secret tuple of mark positions used with *Pic*.

b) Sufficiently large identity space. *Id_Space* is simply $\{0, 1\}^{id\_len(k)}$ for some function *id_len* of the security parameter *k*, and large enough to serve as the preimage of a one-way function. In theory, $id\_len(k) \geq k^{\varepsilon}$ for some $\varepsilon > 0$ suffices. In practice, symmetric fingerprinting schemes typically do not have a parameter *k* for cryptographic security; their parameters are *id_len* and *coll_size*, and then the minimum size *L* of elements of *Pic_Space* is derived. Then we need that *L* is polynomial in *id_len*. This is the case, e.g., in the explicit examples in [C95] and the main scheme in [BS95]. ♦

In the following construction, we use a general 2-party protocol for secure evaluation of an arbitrary function; see, e.g., [Y86, CDG88, GMW87]. We do not particularly require either party to be unconditionally secure, nor do we require gradual release of a secret.

Construction 1. Let a symmetric fingerprinting scheme with the above restrictions, a general 2-party protocol, a signature scheme with algorithms *sign* and *verify*, and a one-way function *f* be given. In the notation, we distinguish the given symmetric scheme and the asymmetric scheme to be constructed by indices *sym* or *asym*, respectively.

$\boldsymbol{key\_gen_{asym}}$ is the key generation of the given signature scheme.

$\boldsymbol{fing_{asym}}$. For the first buyer, the merchant selects $Record_{Pic,sym}$ based on *Pic* and stores it as a part of $Record\_list_{Pic,asym}$. Any buyer first chooses an identity $id_{sym} \in Id\_Space_{sym}$

randomly. Then the buyer and the merchant execute a 2-party protocol for secure evaluation of the function shown in Figure 4. The merchant obtains his output first.

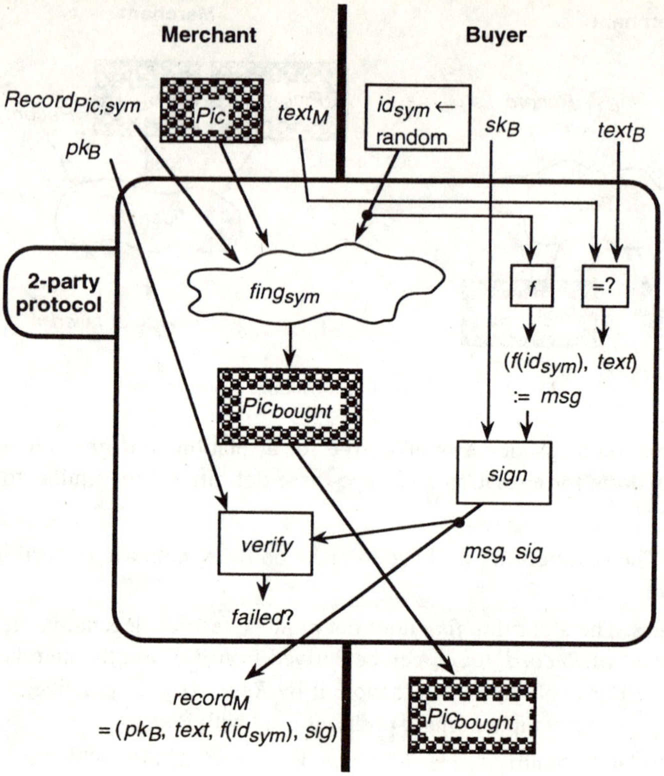

Fig. 4. General construction of asymmetric fingerprinting from a symmetric scheme

identify*$_{asym}$*, on input Pic_{found}, Pic, and $Record\_list_{Pic,asym}$, works as follows:

1. It executes $identify_{sym}(Pic_{found}, Pic, Record_{Pic,sym})$. If the output is *failed*, it stops. Otherwise, one obtains a value id^*_{sym}.
2. It computes $f(id^*_{sym})$ and searches for a record with $f(id_{sym}) = f(id^*_{sym})$.
3. If such a record is found, the output consists of the values pk_B and *text* from this record and $proof := (id^*_{sym}, sig)$.

dispute. The arbiter, which has the input $(pk_B, text)$ and obtains a value *proof* from the merchant, verifies that *proof* is of the form (id_{sym}, sig) and that *sig* is a valid signature with respect to pk_B on $msg = (f(id_{sym}), text)$. ♦

Theorem 1. Assume that all the underlying primitives in Construction 1 are secure, and in particular, that the 2-party protocol is secure in the sense that it can be used in the place of an oracle computing the same function. Then Construction 1 is a secure asymmetric fingerprinting scheme with the same function *coll_size* and the same relations $similar_1$, $similar_2$ as the given symmetric scheme. ♦

All the proof sketches had to be omitted in this extended abstract.

Note that with some unsolved problems about definitions of secure computation, see [B91, MR91], our requirement on the 2-party protocol, or at least on its proof, is quite strong, even though we do not require simultaneous outputs; to our knowledge no such proof has been fully carried out. Nevertheless, it is what such protocols are intuitively intended for and thus supposed to achieve.

4 More Specific Construction

We now derive more efficient asymmetric fingerprinting schemes from a more specific class of symmetric fingerprinting schemes. This class can be seen as typical for black-and-white pictures, except that we still make the restrictions from Definition 6.

Definition 7. The **restricted symmetric fingerprinting for black-and-white pictures** is based on two algorithms, *place_marks* and *code*:

- *place_marks* is a probabilistic algorithm that, on input a picture *Pic*, selects a tuple *marks* = $(mark_1, \ldots, mark_l)$ of suitable positions for marks. Each mark is a subset of all the pixel positions of *Pic*, say $\{1, \ldots, L\}$, and will be used to encode one bit. Any pair of two marks is disjoint.
- *code*: *Id_Space* $\rightarrow \{0, 1\}^l$ is a deterministic algorithm. Its purpose is to encode the original identities such that certain collusions cannot simply find all the marks by comparing their versions of a picture.

$fing_{sym}$ is constructed from these components as follows: For the first buyer, the merchant selects *marks* with *place_marks*(*Pic*) and stores it once and for all as $Record_{Pic}$. The picture Pic_{bought} for an individual buyer, id_B, is $Pic \oplus \varepsilon$ with

$$\varepsilon(pixel) = 1 \Leftrightarrow pixel \in mark_i \text{ for some } i \text{ with } code(id_B)(i) = 1.$$

$identify_{sym}$ has the inputs Pic_{found}, *Pic*, and *marks*.

Id_Space must be $\{0, 1\}^{id\_len(k)}$ with sufficiently large *id_len*, where in theory, $id\_len(k) \geq k^{\varepsilon}$ is again sufficient, and the use in practice can be seen in Construction 2 below. ♦

For instance, in [C95], the marks are essentially small squares, chosen according to characteristics of *Pic*, and encoding a "1" means making the square slightly darker. For black-and-white pictures, this means changing certain pixels in the square from "0" to "1". The set of these pixels within one square, which is fixed given *Pic*, is a mark.

The following construction relies on a homomorphic bit commitment scheme, see [BCC88]. For brevity, we restrict ourselves to the quadratic residuosity scheme: One party chooses a Blum integer $n = pq$, i.e., p and q are primes with $p \equiv q \equiv 3 \bmod 4$. Commitments to 0 are quadratic residues, commitments to 1 are quadratic non-residues with Jacobi symbol +1. The party who has chosen n can decode all commitments. Even the other party can encode 0 as x^2 and 1 as $-x^2$ with random x. $BC(s)$ for a string s means the concatenation of commitments to the bits of s.

Furthermore, as we still have an abstract mapping *code* in the symmetric scheme, we need an abstract zero-knowledge proof system, but for a much smaller problem than the 2-party protocol was needed in Construction 1. An example instantiation is shown below.

Construction 2 (BC Fingerprinting). Let a symmetric fingerprinting scheme according to Definition 7, the quadratic residue bit commitment scheme, and a zero-knowledge proof system be given. Then an asymmetric fingerprinting scheme is defined as follows: We split *id_len*(k) into a field of length $len_1 = \lceil \log_2(N) \rceil$ and the rest of length len_2, which is still at least of some order k^{ε}.

***key_gen**$_{asym}$* is the key generation of the given signature scheme.

***fing**$_{asym}$*. For the first buyer, the merchant executes *place_marks*(*Pic*) and stores the result *marks* as a part of *Record_list*$_{Pic,asym}$. Moreover, he initializes a len_1-bit counter *seq_no* with zero. Then, for any buyer:

1. The merchant sends the current value of *seq_no* to the buyer and increments *seq_no*.
2. The buyer chooses an instance n_B of the bit commitment scheme. She gives the merchant a zero-knowledge proof that n_B is at least a generalized Blum integer, i.e., of the form $p^r q^s$ with p, q as above and r, s odd [GP88].
3. The buyer chooses a value *id_proof* $\in \{0, 1\}^{len_2}$ randomly and sets id_{sym} := (*seq_no*, *id_proof*) $\in$ *Id_Space*$_{sym}$. She encodes id_{sym} according to the symmetric fingerprinting scheme and commits to the result, i.e., she computes $com := BC(code(id_{sym}))$. She sends *msg* := (*com*, *text*) and a signature *sig* on *msg* to the merchant.
4. The buyer proves in zero-knowledge that she knows a value id_{sym} whose first part is *seq_no*, and such that *com* is a commitment on $code(id_{sym})$.
5. The merchant verifies *sig*. Then he encodes the whole picture as *BC*(*Pic*) and multiplies the obtained commitments into the picture at the mark positions. Thus, for $i = 1, \ldots, l$, he multiplies all the commitments to pixels in $mark_i$ by $com_i = BC(code(id_{sym})(i))$. He sends the result, which will be $BC(Pic_{bought})$, to the buyer.
6. The buyer decrypts Pic_{bought}.

The merchant stores $record_M$ = (*seq_no*, pk_B, *text*, *msg*, *sig*). The buyer's $record_B$ consists of *text*, *seq_no*, id_{sym}, and the strings needed to open the commitments in *com*.

***identify**$_{asym}$*. On input Pic_{found}, *Pic*, and *Record_list*$_{Pic,asym}$, first execute $identify_{sym}(Pic_{found}, Pic, marks)$. If this is successful, verify that the output is a pair id_{sym} = (*seq_no*, *id_proof*) where *seq_no* occurs in some record $record_M$. If yes, retrieve $record_M$ = (*seq_no*, pk_B, *text*, *msg*, *sig*) and output pk_B, *text*, and *proof* = (id_{sym}, *msg*, *sig*).

***dispute**$_{asym}$*

1. On input (pk_B, *text*), and upon receiving *proof* = (id_{sym}, *msg*, *sig*) from the merchant, the arbiter verifies that *sig* is a valid signature on *msg* with respect to pk_B and that the second component of *msg* is *text*. If not, it stops with the output *reject*. Otherwise, it retrieves *com* from *msg*.
2. The arbiter now has to verify that $code(id_{sym})$ is the content of the commitments *com*. As it cannot do this alone, it asks the buyer to prove her innocence. She gives the arbiter a zero-knowledge proof that the content of at least one commitment in *com* is not the corresponding bit of $code(id_{sym})$. If the buyer succeeds in this, the arbiter outputs *reject*, otherwise *ok*.

◆

Theorem 2. If all the underlying primitives are secure, Construction 2 is a secure asymmetric fingerprinting scheme with the same function *coll_size* and the same relations $similar_1$, $similar_2$ as the given symmetric scheme. ♦

For specific symmetric fingerprinting schemes, we need efficient zero-knowledge proof systems for Step 4 of $fing_{asym}$ in Construction 2. We show this for a small example from [BS95].

Example. Consider $code = \Gamma_0$ from [BS95, Section 4]: For m identities, $code(id)$ is the id-th row of the following table, where the length of each block is a certain parameter d related to our k.

11...1	11...1	•••	11...1
00...0	11...1		⋮
⋮		⋱	⋮
			11...1
00...0	•••		00...0

To gain efficiency, we do not let the buyer commit to a complete codeword. First, she only needs to commit to one bit per block, and the merchant can replicate it d times. Secondly, the first len_1 bits of id_{sym} have to be a specific value *seq_no*. Thus the buyer's codeword is one of a contiguous set of rows. All these rows start with a certain number of zeros and end with a certain number of ones. Only certain $x = 2^{len_2}$ values in the middle are not fixed and have to be hidden in commitments. Thus the buyer commits to some word $w = w_0 w_1 \ldots w_{x-1}$. She must prove in zero-knowledge that she knows w, and that it consists of a string of none or more zeros, followed by a string of none or more ones. The following steps are repeated k times:

- The buyer makes x+1 random commitments to 0, followed by x commitments to 1, and rotates them randomly, say, by $r \in_R \{0, \ldots, 2x\}$ steps. She sends the result, *circle*, to the merchant.
- The merchant has two choices:
    - The buyer must either open *circle* to show that it was constructed correctly.
    - Or she must prove that she can map w into *circle*. This means that she sends the index $r^* \in \{0, \ldots, 2x\}$ where w starts, and shows that w_i equals the content of $circle_{(r^*+i) \bmod (2x+1)}$ for $i = 0, \ldots, x-1$. Equality is shown by opening the product of the two commitments to reveal zero. Furthermore she proves that w does not consist of ones followed by zeros by opening $circle_{(r^*-1) \bmod (2x+1)}$, the commitment immediately before w in the circle, to reveal zero. ♦

5 Using Higher Residues

We can user higher residues to improve the efficiency of Construction 2. Let r be a fairly small prime, say, k^*+1 bits long, where k^* might be 10, and $n = pq$ such that r divides $\varphi(n)$ and r^2 does not. We can commit to a value from $\{0, 1, \ldots, r-1\}$ using the r residue classes modulo the subgroup of r-th powers within $\mathbb{Z}_n^*$, if we believe that distinguishing these classes is hard [CF85]. These commitments are homomorphic with respect to addition modulo r. We denote them by *HRC*. More details, in particular about efficient en- and decoding, can be found in [B87].

We want to improve efficiency by a factor of k^* by using these commitments on k^*-bit blocks of *Pic*. This may seem impossible at first sight, because we have to execute bitwise exor on the hidden values, not addition modulo r. However, let $HRC(Pic^*)$ be the commitment to a block of *Pic*, and let Pic_j^* be the pixel that serves as the coefficient of 2^j when Pic^* is interpreted as a binary number. Assume that this pixel lies in $mark_i$, and let b be the bit of $code(id_{sym})$ encoded in this mark. The buyer sends $HRC(b)$. The merchant shifts the hidden bit to the correct position by computing $HRC(b)^{2^j} = HRC(b\,2^j)$. Now we exploit that the merchant knows Pic_j^*: If $Pic_j^* = 0$, he computes $HRC(Pic^*) \bullet HRC(b\,2^j) = HRC((Pic^* + b\,2^j) \bmod r)$, and if $Pic_j^* = 1$, he computes $HRC(Pic^*)/HRC(b\,2^j) = HRC((Pic^* - b\,2^j) \bmod r)$. No carry occurs in this addition or subtraction, and in particular no modular reduction, and thus these operations are the desired exors.

With a similar trick, higher residues can be used to encode operations on grayscale pictures efficiently.

6 Conclusion

We have introduced the notion of asymmetric fingerprinting, which gives copyright protection by identification after the fact the kind of security that asymmetric cryptography can offer. In particular, it offers non-repudiation, i.e., there is proof that one particular person was responsible for an action.

We presented constructions that show that this notion can be realized. The most efficient ones of these are not bad in the context of secure computation, i.e., there are no high-degree polynomials if the underlying code is simple enough, but obviously the message expansion is still prohibitive for any large-scale use, because data to be fingerprinted is typically large, and even symmetric fingerprinting only works well on large data.

However, we think that the problem has enough structure to give reason to hope that constructions without significant message expansions can be found in the future, in particular, by extending the ideas of Section 5.

Acknowledgments

We thank Andreas Pfitzmann and Michael Waidner for helpful discussions.

References

[B87] Josh Cohen Benaloh: *Verifiable Secret-Ballot Elections*; Dissertation, Yale University, September 1987.

[B91] Donald Beaver: *Secure Multiparty Protocols and Zero Knowledge Proof Systems Tolerating a Faulty Minority*; Journal of Cryptology 4/2 (1991) 75-122.

[BCC88] Gilles Brassard, David Chaum, Claude Crépeau: *Minimum Disclosure Proofs of Knowledge*; Journal of Computer and System Sciences 37 (1988) 156-189.

[BLM94] J. Brassil, S. Low, N. Maxemchuk, L. O'Gorman: *Electronic Marking and Identification Techniques to Discourage Document Copying*; Proceedings IEEE INFOCOM 94, Toronto, June 12-16, 1994, 1278-1287.

[BMP86] G. R. Blakley, C. Meadows, G. B. Purdy: *Fingerprinting Long Forgiving Messages*; Crypto '85, LNCS 218, Springer-Verlag, Berlin 1986, 180-189.

[BS95] Dan Boneh, James Shaw: *Collusion-Secure Fingerprinting for Digital Data*; Crypto '95, LNCS 963, Springer-Verlag, Berlin 1995, 452-465.

[C95] Germano Caronni: *Assuring Ownership Rights for Digital Images*; Proceedings VIS '95; Vieweg, Wiesbaden 1995, 251-263.

[CDG88] David Chaum, Ivan B. Damgård, Jeroen van de Graaf: *Multiparty computations ensuring privacy of each party's input and correctness of the result*; Crypto '87, LNCS 293, Springer-Verlag, Berlin 1988, 87-119.

[CF85] Josh D. Cohen, Michael J. Fischer: *A robust and verifiable cryptographically secure election scheme*; 26th FOCS, 1985, 372-382.

[CFN94] Benny Chor, Amos Fiat, Moni Naor: *Tracing traitors*; Crypto '94, LNCS 839, Springer-Verlag, Berlin 1994, 257-270.

[CMP95] Abhijit K. Choudhury, Nicholas F. Maxemchuk, Sanjoy Paul, Henning G. Schulzrinne: *Copyright Protection for Electronic Publishing Over Computer Networks*; IEEE Network 9/3 (1995) 12-20.

[G87] Oded Goldreich: *Towards a Theory of Software Protection and Simulation by Oblivious RAMs*; 19th STOC, 1987, 182-194.

[GMW87] Oded Goldreich, Silvio Micali, Avi Wigderson: *How to play any mental game – or – a completeness theorem for protocols with honest majority*; 19th STOC, 1987, 218-229.

[GP88] Jeroen van de Graaf, René Peralta: *A simple and secure way to show the validity of your public key*; Crypto '87, LNCS 293, Springer-Verlag, Berlin 1988, 128-134.

[MQ95] Benoit M. Macq, Jean-Jacques Quisquater: *Cryptology for Digital TV Broadcasting*; Proceedings of the IEEE 83/6 (1995) 944-957.

[MR91] Silvio Micali, Phillip Rogaway: *Secure Computation (Chapters 1-3)*; Laboratory for Computer Science, MIT; distributed at Crypto '91.

[O90] Rafail Ostrovsky: *An efficient software protection scheme*; Crypto '89, LNCS 435, Springer-Verlag, Heidelberg 1990, 610-611.

[W83] Neal R. Wagner: *Fingerprinting*; IEEE Symposium on Security and Privacy, Oakland, 1983, 18-22.

[Y86] Andrew Chi-Chih Yao: *How to Generate and Exchange Secrets*; 27th FOCS, 1986, 162-167.

Homomorphisms of Secret Sharing Schemes: A Tool for Verifiable Signature Sharing

Mike Burmester

Information Security Group, Department of Mathematics
Royal Holloway - University of London, Egham, Surrey TW20 OEX, U.K.
m.burmester@vms.rhbnc.ac.uk.

Abstract. Franklin and Reiter introduced at Eurocrypt '95 verifiable signature sharing, a primitive for a fault tolerant distribution of signature verification. They proposed various practical protocols. For RSA signatures with exponent $e = 3$ and n processors their protocol allows for up to $(n-1)/5$ faulty processors (in general $(n-1)/(2+e)$).
We consider a new unifying approach which uses homomorphisms of secret sharing schemes, and present a verifiable signature sharing scheme for which as many as $(n-1)/3$ processors can be faulty (for any value of e), and for which the number of interactions is reduced.

1 Introduction

Verifiable signature sharing schemes enable the holder of a signed document (who may not be the original signer) to distribute the signature among a set of proxies in such a way that each proxy can verify whether a valid signature can be reconstructed later, even if some of the proxies (but not too many) are malicious or if the original signer is malicious. The signature itself is not revealed until later when it is reconstructed. Verifiable signature sharing is related to the distributed verification of undeniable signatures [18] and to threshold signatures schemes [8]. However there are fundamental differences. With the distributed verification of undeniable signatures, the signed document is public and secret information for the signature is shared. With threshold signatures the power to sign (not to verify) is shared. Such schemes enable any sufficiently large set of shareholders to construct the signature of any document, without any further interaction with the signer.

Verifiable signature sharing has many applications. It can be used to escrow digital cash, by verifiably sharing the signature of a bank for a banknote. Another application is the secure distribution of financial services such as auction bidding [11].

At Eurocrypt '95 Franklin and Reiter presented practical verifiable signature sharing protocols for several signature schemes, including RSA (exponentiation) based signatures with small exponents[1] e and El Gamal based signatures [10]. In this paper we introduce a new approach based on homomorphisms of secret

[1] At the Rump session of Crypto '95 the authors pointed out that their scheme for RSA with $e = 3$ was flawed, and that various repairs were considered [12].

Ueli Maurer (Ed.): EUROCRYPT '96 Proceedings, LNCS 1070

sharing schemes to describe verifiable signature sharing. We use this to extend the Franklin Reiter protocol for El Gamal signatures to a more general setting, and obtain an optimal[2] verifiable signature sharing scheme. Our construction is natural and simplifies significantly the protocol for RSA based signatures in [10].

2 Definitions and notation

Let $A = \{1, \ldots, n\}$ be a set of proxies, K a set of secrets, $S_1, \ldots, S_n$ sets of shares, and $V = S_1 \times \cdots \times S_n$ the set of n-tuples of elements from S_i.

Definition 1. [3, 19] A (t, n)-*threshold scheme* consists of a pair of algorithms, a sharing algorithm $\mathcal{S}$ and a reconstruction algorithm $\mathcal{R}$. $\mathcal{S}$ is probabilistic and takes as input a secret $k \in K$. It generates an element $c = (s_1, \ldots, s_n) \in V$ according to a distribution depending on k, and distributes the share s_i to proxy $i \in A$. $\mathcal{R}$ is deterministic. It takes as input an element $c \in V$ with up to $n - t$ erasures and will output the secret k, if c is an output of $\mathcal{S}$ when k is input. A (t, n)-threshold scheme is *perfect* if $\text{Prob}(k \mid s_{i_1}, \ldots, s_{i_{t-1}}) = \text{Prob}(k)$, for all distributions on $k \in K$, all $\{i_1, \ldots, i_{t-1}\} \subset A$, and all subsets of shares $(s_{i_1}, \ldots, s_{i_{t-1}})$ output by $\mathcal{S}$ on input k.

Notation. We write $\mathcal{S}(k) = (s_1, \ldots, s_n)$ if (the probabilistic algorithm) $\mathcal{S}$ outputs $(s_1, \ldots, s_n)$ on input k, and $\mathcal{R}(s_1, \ldots, s_n) = k$ if $\mathcal{R}$ outputs k on input $(s_1, \ldots, s_n)$. If $B = \{i_1, \ldots, i_r\} \subset A$ and $c = (s_1, \ldots, s_n) \in V$, then $c_B = (s_{i_1}, \ldots, s_{i_r})$. We write $\mathcal{S}_B(k) = (s_{i_1}, \ldots, s_{i_r})$. If $r \geq t$ then $\mathcal{R}_B(s_{i_1}, \ldots, s_{i_r}) = k$. Finally we denote by $\{\mathcal{S}(k)\}$ the set of all $c \in V$ output by $\mathcal{S}$ on input k.

We shall assume that the scheme $(\mathcal{S}, \mathcal{R})$ belongs to a family $\{(\mathcal{S}_x, \mathcal{R}_x)\}$ indexed by a parameter $x \in J$, $J \subset \{0, 1\}^*$, but for simplicity of notation, when there is no ambiguity, we do not refer explicitly to x and just consider single schemes rather than families. The proxies are polynomially bounded in $|x|$, the binary length of x. A threshold scheme is *polynomial-time* if for any set B of $r \geq t$ proxies, $\mathcal{R}_B$ runs in polynomial-time in r and $|x|$. Algorithm $\mathcal{S}$ is not necessarily polynomial-time (in $|x|$ and n).

Definition 2. A threshold scheme is *perfectly zero-knowledge* if for any set B' of $t - 1$ or less proxies, the view of B' (*i.e.* their shares and public information) can be simulated perfectly in expected polynomial-time bounded by $t|x|^c$, c constant. A threshold scheme is *perfectly minimal-knowledge* if given any $k \in K$ by an oracle, the view of any $r \geq t$ proxies can be simulated perfectly in expected polynomial-time bounded by $r|x|^c$, c constant. For a formal definition the reader is referred to [15, 13, 8].

Zero-knowledge guarantees that no knowledge at all leaks. Minimal knowledge guarantees that no more than what follows from the joint knowledge of the proxies leaks.

[2] The optimality is with respect to the number of faulty processors T. In the information theoretic model the bound is $T < n/3$ [2, 4]; in the computational model it is $T < n/2$ [14].

Remark. A threshold scheme which is perfectly zero-knowledge is also perfect.

Remark. If a (t,n)-threshold scheme is perfect and if $(s_{i_1}, \ldots s_{i_{t-1}})$ are shares of a set B' of $t-1$ proxies, then for any $k \in K$: $(s_{i_1}, \ldots, s_{i_{t-1}}) \in \{\mathcal{S}_{B'}(k)\}$.

Definition 3. A (t,n)-threshold scheme is an *erasure* scheme if for any $k \in K$, the shares $(s_{i_1}, \ldots, s_{i_{t-1}}) \in \{\mathcal{S}_{B'}(k)\}$ of any $t-1$ proxies B' have a *unique* extension $(s_1, \ldots, s_n) \in \{\mathcal{S}(k)\}$. An erasure scheme is *polynomial-time* if this extension can be computed in $t\,\mathrm{poly}(|x|)$ time.

Remark. With an erasure scheme, a share-assignment $(s_1, \ldots, s_n) \in \{\mathcal{S}(k)\}$ can be reconstructed if $n-t+1$ shares are erased, given k.

Definition 4. [5], [8, p. 676] A (t,n)-threshold scheme for which the set of secrets is a group $K(*)$ is *multiplicative* if for any set of t proxies $B = \{i_1, \ldots, i_t\}$ there are selection functions $f_{j,B} : S_j \to K$, $j \in B$, and a public ordering of $\{i_1, \ldots, i_t\}$ such that,

$$k = f_{i_1,B}(s_{i_1}) * \cdots * f_{i_t,B}(s_{i_t}), \tag{1}$$

for all $k \in K$ and shares $(s_{i_1}, \ldots, s_{i_t})$ output by $\mathcal{S}$ on input k. A multiplicative scheme is *polynomial-time* if the operation "$*$" and its inverse are polynomial-time in $|x|$, and if all selection functions are polynomial-time in $|x|$.

Definition 5. Let $\sigma = (\mathcal{S}, \mathcal{R})$ and $\sigma' = (\mathcal{S}', \mathcal{R}')$ be (t,n)-threshold schemes with secret sets K, K' and share sets S_i, S_i', $i = 1, \ldots, n$, respectively, and let $h_0 : K \to K'$, $h_i : S_i \to S_i'$, $i = 1, \ldots, n$, be mappings. The mapping $h = (h_0, h_1, \ldots h_n)$ is a *homomorphism of σ to σ'* if the following conditions hold. For any $k \in K$, if $\mathcal{S}(k) = (s_1, \ldots, s_n)$,

- $(h_1(s_1), \ldots, h_n(s_n)) \in \{\mathcal{S}'(h_0(k))\}$
- $h_0(\mathcal{R}(s_1, \ldots, s_n)) = \mathcal{R}'(h_1(s_1), \ldots, h_n(s_n))$. (2)

That is, the mapping h commutes with the sharing and reconstruction operators.

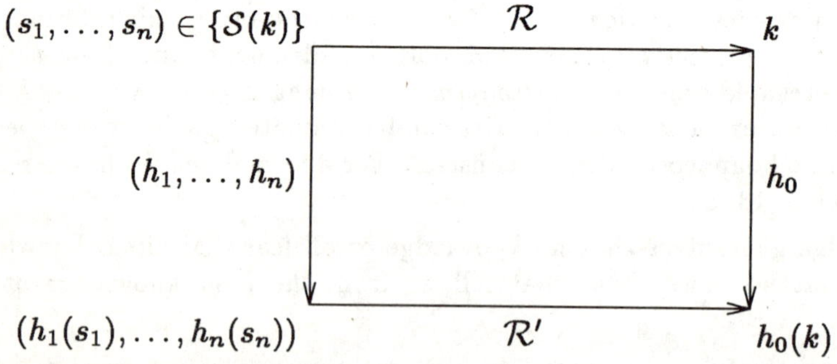

Fig. 1. The commutative diagram of a homomorphism $h : \sigma \to \sigma'$.

A homomorphism h is *polynomial-time* if the mappings $h_i, i = 0, 1, \ldots, n$, are polynomial-time in $|x|$.

Notation. If $B = \{i_1, \ldots, i_r\}$ then $h_B(s_{i_1}, \ldots, s_{i_r}) = (h_{i_1}(s_{i_1}), \ldots, h_{i_r}(s_{i_r}))$.

A homomorphism $h : \sigma \to \sigma'$ induces in a natural way a threshold scheme $h(\sigma) = (\mathcal{S}^*, \mathcal{R}^*)$ with secret set $K^* = h_0(K) \subset K'$, share sets $S_i^* = h_i(S_i) \subset S'$, and $V^* = S_1^* \times \cdots \times S_n^* \subset V'$. $\mathcal{S}^*$ on input $k^* \in K^*$ outputs $(s_1^*, \ldots, s_n^*) \in V^*$ where $s_1^* = h_1(s_1), \ldots, s_n^* = h_n(s_n)$, with the distribution induced by $(s_1, \ldots, s_n) \in \{\mathcal{S}(k)\}$ where $h_0(k) = k^*$. $\mathcal{R}^*$ on input $(s_1^*, \ldots, s_n^*) \in V^*$ with $s_1^* = h_1(s_1), \ldots, s_n^* = h_n(s_n)$ and $k = \mathcal{R}(s_1, \ldots, s_n)$, outputs $k^* = h_0(k)$. We call this, the scheme *induced* by the homomorhism h.

Remark. One should distinguish between homomorphisms of threshold schemes, as introduced here, and homomorphic threshold schemes [1]. With the former no algebraic structure is imposed on the set of secrets or on the shares. However, if "$*$" is a binary operation on the set of secrets K and "$\cdot$" a binary operation on the sets of shares S_i, with $\mathcal{R}(s_1, \ldots, s_n) * \mathcal{R}(s_1', \ldots, s_n') = \mathcal{R}((s_1 \cdot s_1'), \ldots, (s_n \cdot s_n'))$ for all $(s_1, \ldots, s_n)$, $(s_1', \ldots, s_n')$ output by $\mathcal{S}$, as in [1], then a homomorphism $h : \sigma \times \sigma \to \sigma$ is defined in a natural way, with $h_0(k, k') = k * k'$ and $h_i(s_i, s_i') = s_i \cdot s_i'$. So the notion of homomorphisms of sharing schemes is an extension of homomorphic sharing schemes.

Remark. Homomorphisms are an important structure preserving mechanism in algebra. As we shall see they also play an important role in the analysis of cryptographic primitives, by linking verifiable signature sharing to secret sharing.

3 Verifiable signature sharing based on homomorphisms of secret sharing schemes

The scheme we describe is based on a homomorphism $h = (h_0, h_1, \ldots, h_n)$ of the (t, n)-threshold schemes σ, σ', and uses the induced threshold scheme $h(\sigma)$. The secrets in K are the signatures $sgn(m)$ and the elements in $K^* = h_0(K)$ are the (hashed/processed) messages m. We take $\sigma = (\mathcal{S}, \mathcal{R})$, $h(\sigma) = (\mathcal{S}^*, \mathcal{R}^*)$ and $T = t - 1$. Our scheme consists of a pair of protocols: a sharing protocol and a reconstruction protocol. In the sharing protocol a dealer D runs $\mathcal{S}$ on input $sgn(m)$. The dealer gives privately to each of n proxies a share s_i of $sgn(m)$, and sends by reliable broadcast to all proxies the message M and the shares $h_j(s_j)$, $j = 1, \ldots, T$, in $h(\sigma)$. At the end of this protocol the proxies either accept or reject. In the reconstruction protocol a reconstructor R computes $sgn(m)$ by majority vote. The scheme is described schematically in Fig 2. In the upper part we use the zero-knowledge scheme $\sigma = (\mathcal{S}, \mathcal{R})$ and the shares s_i are kept secret. In the lower part we use the erasure scheme $h(\sigma) = (\mathcal{R}^*, \mathcal{S}^*)$ and the shares $h_i(s_i)$ are in the clear. The homomorphism h links the parts. The path $\mathcal{S}(sgn(m)) \to \mathcal{S}^*(m)$ is used for verification: proxy i checks that the map $h_i(s_i)$ of his share s_i is the appropriate component of $(h_1(s_1), \ldots, h_n(s_n))$, which he gets by extending $(h_1(s_1), \ldots, h_T(s_T))$ using the message m. The commutativity of the diagram guarantees correctness.

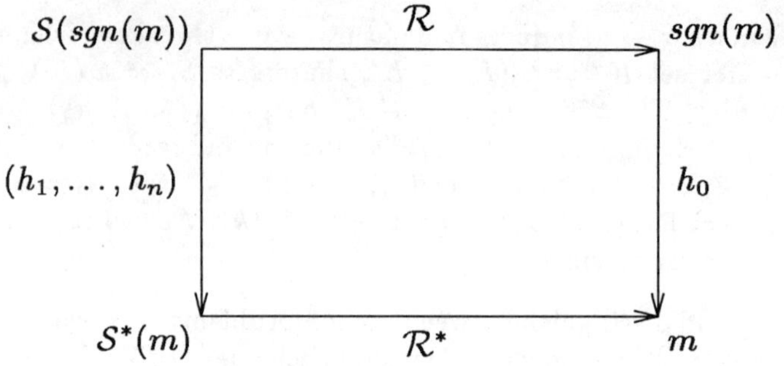

Fig. 2. A diagram for verifiable signature sharing.

We now describe our scheme in detail.

4 A Verifiable Signature Sharing scheme

Sharing Protocol

Step 1 The dealer D uses algorithm $\mathcal{S}$ of σ to get shares $s_1, \ldots, s_n$ of the signature $sgn(m)$.

a. $D \rightarrow P_i$ privately: the share s_i, $i = 1, \ldots, n$.

b. $D \rightarrow P_1, \ldots, P_n$ by reliable broadcast: the message M, and the shares $h_1(s_1), \ldots, h_T(s_T)$ in $h(\sigma)$, or something equivalent[3].

Step 2 Let the broadcast values in Step 1b be $M, u_1, \ldots, u_T$. Each proxy P_i computes $m = hash(M)$ and makes the following reliable broadcasts to all proxies:

a. COMPLAIN if the share $s_i \notin S_i$, or if the share $h_i(s_i)$ is not the i-th component of the extension $(u_1, \ldots, u_n) \in \{\mathcal{S}^*(m)\}$ of $(u_1, \ldots, u_T)$.

b. ALLOW otherwise.

Step 3 Without further communication, each proxy ACCEPTS if (REJECTS otherwise):

a. At most T proxies COMPLAINed (Nonsensical responses are counted as COMPLAINs).

b. $(u_1, \ldots, u_T) \in \{\mathcal{S}^*_{\{1,\ldots,T\}}(m)\}$.

Reconstruction Protocol

Step 1 Each proxy P_i sends to the reconstructor R the following information:

a. The shares s_i sent in Step 1a of the Sharing Protocol.

b. The values $M, u_1, \ldots, u_T$ broadcast in Step 1b of the Sharing Protocol.

[3] For example a polynomial-time invertible bijection of these, as in [10].

Step 2 Without further communication:

a. The reconstructor R finds $\bar{M}, \bar{u}_1, \ldots, \bar{u}_T$ by majority vote on the lists received in Step 1b (of this protocol).

b. R discards every share s_i received in Step 1a (of this protocol) that is inconsistent with $\bar{M}, \bar{u}_1, \ldots, \bar{u}_T$, in $h(\sigma)$, *i.e.*, for which the share $s_i \notin S_i$, or the share $h_i(s_i)$ is not the i-th component of the extension $(\bar{u}_1, \ldots, \bar{u}_n) \in \{\mathcal{S}^*(\bar{m})\}$ of $(\bar{u}_1, \ldots, \bar{u}_T)$.

c. Let $B = \{i_1, \ldots, i_r\}$ be the set of proxies with the remaining shares. R computes $\mathcal{R}_B(s_{i_1}, \ldots, s_{i_r})$ and outputs this as its signature.

We shall prove that this protocol achieves a slightly stronger goal than in [10].

Definition 6. A verifiable signature sharing scheme is T-resilient if the following conditions hold.
(*i*) (*Completeness*) If the dealer is honest and at most T proxies are faulty then honest proxies accept, and the reconstruction is successful.
(*ii*) (*Soundness*) If at most T proxies are faulty and an honest proxy accepts, then every proxy accepts and the reconstruction is successful.
(*iii*) (*Secrecy*) Anything that can be computed by an adversary who, (a) controls up to T faulty proxies who have participated in earlier sharing protocols with an honest dealer and (b) has access to the view of the reconstructor in earlier reconstructions, can also be computed by the adversary without participating in any of these protocols.

Remark. Secrecy is based on the simulation of the view of the adversary. To simulate the shares of faulty (dishonest) proxies in the sharing protocols, σ must be zero-knowledge. To simulate the (uncorrupted) shares of the honest proxies revealed in the reconstruction protocols, $h(\sigma)$ must be minimal knowledge.

Remark. Our definition of secrecy is stronger than that in [10], since we allow the adversary to access earlier reconstruction protocols. We feel that this is an essential security requirement for verifiable signature sharing. Although the schemes proposed in [10] satisfy the stronger secrecy requirement, their model overlooked this aspect.

Remark. If h_0 is a one-way function then this scheme can also be used as a verifiable secret sharing scheme with heuristic security. The security is only heuristic because with one-way functions there is no guarantee that the input will not leak.

Theorem 7. *Suppose that σ, σ' are polynomial-time (t, n)-threshold schemes with $t = T + 1$ and $T \leq (n-1)/3$. The protocol above is a T-resilient verifiable signature sharing scheme if $h : \sigma \to \sigma'$ is a polynomial-time homomorphism and if the following conditions hold:*

1. *All the mappings h_i, $i = 0, 1, \ldots, n$, are injections.*
2. *σ is a perfectly zero-knowledge polynomial-time erasure scheme, and membership in S_i for all i can be checked in polynomial-time.*

3. σ' is a polynomial-time erasure scheme, and membership in $\{\mathcal{S}^*_{\{1,\ldots,T\}}(m)\}$ can be checked in polynomial-time.

To prove this theorem we need the following results.

Lemma 8. *Let σ, σ' be polynomial-time threshold schemes with σ perfectly zero-knowledge, σ' a polynomial-time erasure scheme, and $h : \sigma \to \sigma'$ a polynomial-time homomorphism. Then $h(\sigma)$ is perfectly minimal-knowledge.*

Proof. Since h is a homomorphism, $h(\sigma)$ is a perfectly zero-knowledge erasure scheme (it is not necessary that $h(\sigma) = \sigma'$). We describe an expected polynomial-time simulator M^* which given any $k^* \in K^*$ simulates shares of any set of t proxies $B = \{i_1, \ldots, i_{t-1}, i_t\}$ in $h(\sigma)$. Now σ is perfectly zero-knowledge, so there is a simulator M which simulates the shares in σ of the set of $t-1$ proxies $B' = \{i_1, \ldots, i_{t-1}\}$. To simulate the shares of B in $h(\sigma)$, M^* first simulates the shares of B' using M, to get $(s_{i_1}, \ldots, s_{i_{t-1}})$ with a distribution identical to the real one. Then M^* computes $(h_{i_1}(s_{i_1}), \ldots, h_{i_{t-1}}(s_{i_{t-1}}))$. Because $h(\sigma)$ is an erasure scheme, given any $k^* \in K^*$, M^* can compute its unique extension $c^*_B \in \{\mathcal{S}^*_B(k^*)\}$ (perfect zero-knowledge guarantees that $c^*_{B'}$ belongs to $\{\mathcal{S}^*_{B'}(k^*)\}$ – *cf.* the Remarks after Definition 2). Finally M^* outputs c^*_B as the simulated shares for B.

Corollary 9. *If the conditions in the Lemma are satisfied and h_0 is a one-way function then each h_i, $i = 1, \ldots, n$, is one-way.*

Proof. Suppose that it is easy to invert h_j. Let $B = \{i_1, \ldots, i_t\}$ be a set of t distinct proxies with $j = i_t$ and let $B' = \{i_1, \ldots, i_{t-1}\}$. We describe a polynomial-time algorithm $\mathcal{A}$ which inverts h_0, that is, given $k^* \in K^*$ computes a $k \in K$ with $h_0(k) = k^*$. As in Lemma 8, $\mathcal{A}$ chooses shares $s_{i_1}, \ldots, s_{i_{t-1}}$ for B' and computes $h_{i_1}(s_{i_1}), \ldots, h_{i_{t-1}}(s_{i_{t-1}})$ and their unique extension c^*. Then $\mathcal{A}$ inverts the j-th component $s^*_j \in h_j(S_j)$ of c^* to get an $s_j \in S_j$ such that $h_j(s_j) = s^*_j$, and computes $k = \mathcal{R}_B(s_{i_1}, \ldots, s_{i_{t-1}}, s_j)$. Since h is a homomorphism, $h_0(k) = k^*$.

Corollary 10. *A polynomial-time threshold scheme which is a perfectly zero-knowledge polynomial-time erasure scheme is perfectly minimal knowledge.*

Proof. Take $\sigma = \sigma'$ and h the identity homomorphism in Lemma 8.

Proof of the theorem:
Completeness: This follows directly from the fact that h is a homomorphism.
Soundness: If one honest proxy accepts then all honest proxies accept. We must show that in this case the reconstruction is successful. First observe that $h(\sigma)$ is a polynomial-time erasure scheme. So $(u_1, \ldots, u_T)$ has a unique extension $c^* = (s^*_1, \ldots, s^*_n)$ in $h(\sigma)$ with $\mathcal{R}(c^*) = m$, which can be computed in polynomial-time. Allowing for up to T COMPLAINs and up to T faulty proxies we see that at most $2T$ of the components of c^* are in error in the majority vote count. Since $n - 2T \geq T + 1 = t$, there is a set $B = \{i_1, \ldots, i_r\}$ of $r \geq t$ proxies with shares $(h_{i_1}(s_{i_1}), \ldots, h_{i_r}(s_{i_r})) \in \{\mathcal{S}^*_B(m)\}$. We are assuming that the mappings h_i are injections. It follows that $(s_{i_1}, \ldots, s_{i_r}) \in \{\mathcal{S}_B(k)\}$. Because h is a homomorphism and h_0 is injective, $k = sgn(m)$.

Secrecy: We have to simulate, essentially, tuples $(h_{\{1,\ldots,T\}}(c_{\{1,\ldots,T\}}), c_{B'})$, with $|B'| \leq T$, for the sharing protocol, and tuples $(h(c), c, sgn(m))$ with up to T corrupted entries in c for the reconstruction protocol. Since the sharing algorithm $\mathcal{S}$ distributes shares independently for each run of the verifiable signature sharing scheme (the dealer is honest), it is sufficient to simulate one run. Furthermore we only need to simulate the uncorrupted parts. Now σ is zero-knowledge, so $c_{B'}$ can be simulated. Therefore given the unsigned (hashed/processed) message m, $(h_{\{1,\ldots,T\}}(c_{\{1,\ldots,T\}}), c_{B'})$ can be simulated, because $h(\sigma)$ is a polynomial-time erasure scheme. For the reconstruction protocol we have to simulate the uncorrupted parts of $(h(c), c, sgn(m))$. In this case the simulator is also given the signature $sgn(m)$. By Corollary 10, σ is minimal-knowledge, so c can be simulated. Then $h(c)$ can be simulated, since h is polynomial-time. □

Remark. For this scheme $T \leq (n-1)/3$. The upper (exclusive) bound for the number faulty processors in a fault tolerant distributed computation in the information theoretic model is $n/3$ [2, 4]. So the scheme is optimal in this respect.

5 Applications

5.1 A Verifiable Signature Sharing scheme based on the Desmedt-Frankel zero-knowledge RSA threshold scheme

Take σ to be the zero-knowledge RSA threshold scheme in [8] with $\sigma' = \sigma$. This scheme is homomorphic (*cf.* the Remark after Definition 5) and uses polynomial interpolation for the reconstruction of the secret. In this case however the coefficients of the polynomials are not taken from a field but from a ring extension $Z[u]$ of the integers. We briefly explain this scheme.

Let N be a composite number, n be polynomially bounded in $|N|$, q a prime with $q \geq n+1$, and $Z[u] = Z[x]/((x^q-1)/(x-1))$ be the ring of all polynomial expressions in u with integer coefficients taken modulo the cyclotomic polynomial $(u^q-1)/(u-1)$. The set of secrets K and the share sets S_i, $i = 1, \ldots, n$, have a group structure. K is the multiplicative group $Z_N^*(\cdot)$ and S_i is the $Z[u]$-module $M = Z[u] \otimes_Z Z_N^*$, the tensor product [17] of $Z[u](+)$ and $Z_N^*(\cdot)$. It is easy to see that $M \cong (Z_N^*)^{q-1} = Z_N^* \times \cdots \times Z_N^*$. Each shareholder is given a share $s_i \in S_i$, and a set of $r \geq t$ shareholders $B = \{i_1, \ldots, i_r\}$ reconstructs the secret by using

$$\mathcal{R}_B(s_{i_1}, \ldots, s_{i_r}) = \mathrm{proj}_1\left(\textstyle\sum_{i \in B} y_{i,B} \cdot s_i\right),$$

where proj_1 is the projection of the elements of $(Z_N^*)^{q-1}$ onto their first coordinate in Z_N^*, the sum is the internal module operation, the product is the external module operation, and the $y_{i,B}$ are the Lagrange interpolation coefficients,

$$y_{i,B} = \textstyle\prod_{j \in B, j \neq i} (0 - u^j)/(u^i - u^j),$$

which are invertible elements in $Z[u]$ [8].

For our application, $h_0 : Z_N^* \to Z_N^* : x \to x^e \bmod N$, where $\gcd(e, \phi(N)) = 1$, and $h_i : (Z_N^*)^{q-1} \to (Z_N^*)^{q-1} : (x_1, \ldots, x_{q-1}) \to (x_1^e, \ldots, x_{q-1}^e)$, $i = 1, \ldots, n$. Clearly h is injective. Also $h_i(s) = e \cdot s$, $s \in (Z_N^*)^{q-1}$, using the external module operation. Furthermore the mappings h_i commute with proj_1 and the module operations (*i.e.* h is a morphism), since

$$\text{proj}_1(h_i(s_i)) = \text{proj}_1(e \cdot s_i) = h_0(\text{proj}_1(s_i)), \text{ and}$$
$$\textstyle\sum_i y_i \cdot h_i(s_i) = \sum_i y_i \cdot (e \cdot s_i) = e \cdot (\sum_i y_i \cdot s_i) = h_j \left(\sum_i y_i \cdot s_i\right),$$

for all $s_i \in (Z_N^*)^{q-1}$, $y_i \in Z[u]$. It follows that conditions (2) in Section 2 hold, and that h is a homomorphism of σ onto σ. It is easy to prove that all the other conditions of Theorem 7 are satisfied. In particular σ is an erasure scheme. Also $\{\mathcal{S}_{\{1,\ldots,T\}}(k)\} = (Z_N^*)^T$, so that one only has to check membership in each of the components Z_N^*, to check membership in $\{\mathcal{S}_{\{1,\ldots,T\}}(k)\}$. Thus we have a T-resilient verifiable signature sharing scheme.

5.2 A Verifiable Signature Sharing scheme based on the Desmedt-DiCrescenzo-Burmester zero-knowledge threshold scheme

Take σ to be the perfect zero-knowledge threshold scheme in [5] with $\sigma' = \sigma$. This scheme is multiplicative and the set of secrets $K(*)$ can be any group (not necessarily abelian). The shares are sets of sub-shares which are tuples (list_a, k_a). A set B of t distinct proxies can recompute the secret k by taking the product of appropriate k_a's whose selection depends on B, and is determined by the lists list_a. The lists define selection functions $f_{j,B}(s_j)$, $j \in B$, which are such that equation (1) in Section 2 holds. The functions $f_{j,B}$ commute with any homomorphism of the multiplicative group $K(*)$. We take h_0 to be a one-way injective group homomorphism of a polynomial-time group $K(*)$ (for which the operation "$*$" and its inverse are polynomial-time). As in the previous case we use h_0 to define injections h_i on the shares s_i (for which each (list_a, k_a) is mapped to $(\text{list}_a, h_0(k_a))$). Then conditions (2) hold, as can easily be checked, and we get a homomorphism from σ to σ. It is easy to check that σ is an erasure scheme when $t = 2$. All conditions of Theorem 7 are then satisfied. So we get a 1-resilient verifiable signature scheme. In this case the size of the shares is reduced, roughly, from $n \log N$ to $(\log n)(\log N)$.

6 Conclusion

We have shown that by using homomorphisms of secret sharing schemes we can get RSA based verifiable signature sharing schemes which are optimal with respect to the number of faulty processors. Our approach is natural, uses existing secret sharing schemes, and simplifies significantly the RSA based protocol of Franklin and Reiter [10].

Acknowledgements

The author discussed the topic of this paper with Yvo Desmedt during Eurocrypt '95, who independently made the observation that a generalization of Pedersen's undeniable signatures could be used with the Desmedt-Frankel zero-knowledge threshold scheme to improve the Franklin-Reiter scheme.

The author wishes to thank Yvo Desmedt, Simon Blackburn and Peter Wild for many useful discussions.

References

1. J.C. Benaloh: Secret sharing homomorphisms: Keeping shares of a secret secret. In: A. Odlyzko (ed.): Advances in Cryptology, Proc. of Crypto '86. Lecture Notes in Computer Science 263, Berlin: Springer 1987, pp. 251–260
2. M. Ben-Or, S. Goldwasser, A. Wigderson: Completeness theorems for non-cryptographic fault-tolerant distributed computation. Proceedings of the twentieth annual ACM Symp. Theory of Computing, STOC, 1988, pp. 1–10
3. G. R. Blakley: Safeguarding cryptographic keys. In: Proc. Nat. Computer Conf. AFIPS Conf. Proc., 48, 1979, pp. 313–317
4. D. Chaum, C. Crépeau and I. Damgård: Multiparty unconditionally secure protocols. Proceedings of the twentieth annual ACM Symp. Theory of Computing, STOC, 1988, pp. 11–19
5. Y. Desmedt, G. Di Crescenzo, and M. Burmester: Multiplicative non-abelian sharing schemes and their application to threshold cryptography. In: J. Pieprzyk, R. Safavi-Naini (eds.): Advances in Cryptology – Asiacrypt '94. Lecture Notes in Computer Science 917. Berlin: Springer 1995, pp. 21–32
6. A. De Santis, Y. Desmedt, Y. Frankel, and M. Yung: How to share a function securely. In: Proceedings of the twenty-sixth annual ACM Symp. Theory of Computing (STOC), 1994, pp. 522–533. Full paper in preparation.
7. Y. G. Desmedt: Threshold cryptography. European Trans. on Telecommunications, 5(4), pp. 449–457 (1994)
8. Y.G. Desmedt, Y. Frankel: Homomorphic zero-knowledge threshold schemes over any finite abelian group. SIAM Journal on Discrete Mathematics, 7(4), 667–679, (1994)
9. M. De Soete, J-J. Quisquater, and K. Vedder: A signature with shared verification scheme. In: G. Brassard (ed.): Advances in Cryptology – Crypto '89. Lecture Notes in Computer Science 435. Berlin: Springer 1990, pp. 253–262
10. M. K. Franklin and M. K. Reiter: Verifiable signature sharing. In: L.C. Guillou, J.J. Quisquater (eds.): Advances in Cryptology – Eurocrypt '95. Lecture Notes in Computer Science 921. Berlin: Springer 1995, pp. 50–63
11. M. K. Franklin and M. K. Reiter: The design and implementation of a secure auction service. IEEE Symposium on Security and Privacy. Oakland CA, 1995
12. M. K. Franklin and M. K. Reiter: A linear protocol failure for RSA with exponent three. Presented at the Rump session of Crypto '95, Santa Barbara, California, USA, August 27-31, 1995.
13. Z. Galil, S. Haber, and M. Yung: Minimum-knowledge interactive proofs for decision problems. Siam J. Comput., 18(4), 711–739 (1989)

14. O. Goldreich, S. Micali and A. Wigderson: How to play any mental game. Proceedings of the Nineteenth annual ACM Symp. Theory of Computing, STOC, 1987, pp. 218–229
15. S. Goldwasser, S. Micali, and C. Rackoff: The knowledge complexity of interactive proof systems. Siam J. Comput., 18(1), 186–208 (1989)
16. L. Harn: Digital signature with (t, n) shared verification based on discrete logarithms. Electronics Letters, 29(24), 2094–2095 (1993)
17. N. Jacobson: Basic Algebra I. W. H. Freeman and Company, New York (1985)
18. T. P. Pedersen: Distributed provers with applications to undeniable signatures. In: D.W. Davies (ed.): Advances in Cryptology – Eurocrypt '91. Lecture Notes in Computer Science 547, Berlin: Springer 1991, pp. 221–242
19. A. Shamir: How to share a secret. Commun. ACM, 22, 612–613 (1979)

Efficient Multiplicative Sharing Schemes

Simon R. Blackburn[⋆] [⋆⋆], Mike Burmester[⋆], Yvo Desmedt[⋆⋆⋆] and Peter R. Wild[⋆]

Abstract. Multiplicative threshold schemes are useful tools in threshold cryptography. For example, such schemes can be used with a wide variety of practical homomorphic cryptosystems (such as the RSA, the El Gamal and elliptic curve systems) for threshold decryption, signatures, or proofs. The paper describes a new recursive construction for multiplicative threshold schemes which makes it possible to extend the number of users of such schemes for a relatively small expansion of the share size. We discuss certain properties of the schemes, such as the information rate and zero knowledge aspects.
The paper extends the Karnin–Greene–Hellman bound on the parameters of ideal secret sharing schemes to schemes which are not necessarily ideal and then uses this as a yardstick to compare the performance of currently known multiplicative sharing schemes.

1 Introduction

Secret sharing — the process of distributing a secret key amongst several participants so that only certain subsets of these participants can recover any information about the key — has been intensively studied since its invention by Blakley [2] and Shamir [13] in the late 1970's. The more specific notion of homomorphic secret sharing was introduced by Benaloh [1] in the context of creating secret ballot election schemes and can be used to achieve secret sharing without a mutually trusted authority. In such schemes, binary operations are defined on the set of keys and the set of shares in such a way that the process of a collection of participants pooling their shares to recompute the key may be regarded as a homomorphism from the set of n-tuples of shares to the set of keys. This paper is concerned with the design of sharing schemes which possess a close analogue of the homomorphic property known as the multiplicative property. In multiplicative sharing schemes there is a multiplication defined on the set K of all possible keys such that the recomputation of the key can be achieved by multiplying together appropriate elements of K derived from some of the participants' shares (see Section 2 for a formal definition). Any ideal homomorphic sharing

⋆ Department of Mathematics, Royal Holloway, University of London, Egham, Surrey TW20 0EX, United Kingdom. E-mail addresses: s.blackburn@vms.rhbnc.ac.uk, m.burmester@vms.rhbnc.ac.uk, p.wild@vms.rhbnc.ac.uk.

⋆⋆ This author is supported by an E.P.S.R.C. Advanced Fellowship.

⋆⋆⋆ Dept. EE & CS, Univ. of Wisconsin – Milwaukee, P.O. Box 784, WI 53201 Milwaukee, U.S.A. Email address: desmedt@cs.uwm.edu. This author was supported by N.S.F. NCR-9508528 and the E.P.S.R.C.

Ueli Maurer (Ed.): EUROCRYPT '96 Proceedings, LNCS 1070

scheme automatically satisfies the multiplicative property [7, 8]. Such schemes have played a crucial role in threshold cryptography and function sharing — see for example [3, 6, 4]. Threshold cryptography refers to the study of schemes which share the ability to compute a cryptographic function analogously to the way threshold secret sharing schemes share a secret. One application, for example, allows shareholders to co-sign messages non-interactively. In the process of co-signing, users divulge only enough information to allow the co-signature of a particular message and nothing more — for example, no information about their secret shares is revealed. This property is achieved by requiring that the secret sharing scheme has such properties as being zero-knowledge (the computational equivalent of perfect sharing).

In applications where K can be regarded as the additive group of a finite field, multiplicative and homomorphic zero-knowledge threshold schemes exist that are ideal [13] (i.e. the size of the shares is the same as the size of the key). But in many applications K cannot be regarded in this way (for example in the context of RSA based threshold schemes) and known multiplicative and homomorphic zero-knowledge threshold schemes have a large share expansion (the reciprocal of the information rate). Indeed in the Desmedt–Frankel zero-knowledge t out of n threshold scheme [7], which is multiplicative and homomorphic, the shares are roughly n times larger than the key. Although the scheme in [4] has only a $\log_2 n$ expansion of the shares when $t = 2$, its performance when t is only moderately larger is poor.

The goal of this paper is to present multiplicative zero-knowledge threshold schemes for which the share expansion is substantially better than for competing schemes. The schemes we present are also homomorphic if the group K is abelian. We also consider an inequality of Karnin, Greene and Hellman [12] which bounds the number n of participants of an ideal t out of n secret sharing scheme in terms of t and the size q of the set of shares. We extend their bound to the case when the scheme is not necessarily ideal.

The paper is organised as follows. Section 2 contains some basic definitions and introduces the notation that we use in the remainder of the paper. In Section 3 we extend the Karnin–Greene–Hellman bound from the situation of ideal threshold schemes to the general case. The result will be used in Section 5 to prove that if t and the order of K are held constant, our threshold schemes are asymptotically optimal as $n \to \infty$. All our schemes are recursive in nature (cf. [4]) — we construct a t out of n scheme by using several copies of a t out of ℓ scheme for some $\ell < n$. This recursive construction is given in Section 4. An analysis of the share expansion of the schemes, the zero-knowledge properties, and a discussion of the performance of the schemes can be found respectively in Sections 5, 6 and 7.

2 Definitions and Notation

Informally, a perfect t out of n threshold scheme is a scheme in which a collection of n users (called participants) are each given a share (which may, for example, be a finite string or an element of a finite field). The shares are chosen such that any t of the participants can pool their shares to compute some secret piece of information (called the key) and such that the knowledge of at most $t-1$ of the shares gives absolutely no information about the key.

We define our notation as follows. Let P be a set of n participants which we identify with the set $\{1, 2, \ldots, n\}$. Let K be a finite set whose elements we call keys and suppose that K has two or more elements (to avoid trivialities). Let S be a finite set of order q whose elements we call shares[4]. Finally, let V be the set of all n-tuples of elements from S, where each n-tuple is indexed by the elements of P.

Definition 1. A t out of n threshold scheme consists of two algorithms. The *distribution algorithm* $\mathcal{D}$ is a probabilistic algorithm which takes as input an element $k \in K$. It randomly generates an element $(s_1, s_2, \ldots, s_n) \in V$ according to some distribution depending on k. The algorithm then distributes share s_i to participant i. The *reconstruction algorithm* $\mathcal{R}$ is an algorithm which takes as input an element $(s_1, s_2, \ldots, s_n) \in V$ with up to $n-t$ erasures (i.e. up to $n-t$ of the components $s_1, \ldots, s_n$ have been omitted). It outputs a key $k \in K$. The pair $(\mathcal{D}, \mathcal{R})$ is a *perfect* t *out of* n *threshold scheme* if the following two conditions are satisfied.

1. Any t participants may use algorithm $\mathcal{R}$ to reconstruct the key. More formally, if $c \in V$ is a possible output from algorithm $\mathcal{D}$ when $k \in K$ is input, then algorithm $\mathcal{R}$ outputs k when the element c with up to $n-t$ erasures is input.
2. No information is revealed about the key k by knowing up to $t-1$ of the participants' shares. More formally, suppose that X is a random variable taking values in K according to some distribution. Let Y_i (where $i \in P$) be random variables taking values in S defined by the distribution on the set of shares given to participant i when algorithm $\mathcal{D}$ is run on input X. Then the variable X is independent of the joint distribution of the variables $Y_{i_1}, \ldots, Y_{i_{t-1}}$ for all $i_1, \ldots, i_{t-1} \in P$.

We remark that, since S and K are finite, Condition 2 is equivalent to Equation (2) in the paper of Karnin, Green and Hellman [12]. All schemes that we consider are perfect, that is, satisfy Condition 2 above, so from now on we drop this term and just refer to t out of n threshold schemes.

In this paper we concentrate on multiplicative threshold schemes [4].

Definition 2. Let $(\mathcal{D}, \mathcal{R})$ be a t out of n threshold scheme for which the key space K is a finite group[5] with respect to the operation "$*$". The scheme $(\mathcal{D}, \mathcal{R})$

[4] In this paper we assume, for simplicity, that all participants receive shares taken from the same set S. The results of the paper easily extend to the situation where the share sets associated with each participant are allowed to differ.

[5] The definitions and results in this paper can easily be extended to the case when K is a finite quasigroup.

is *multiplicative* over $(K, *)$ if for all sets $B = \{i_1, i_2, \ldots, i_t\}$ of t distinct participants there exists a family $f_{i_1,B}, f_{i_2,B}, \ldots, f_{i_t,B}$ of functions from S to K and a public ordering $i_1, i_2, \ldots, i_t$ of the elements of B with the following property. For all keys $k \in K$ and shares $s_{i_1}, s_{i_2}, \ldots, s_{i_t}$ that have been distributed to B by algorithm $\mathcal{D}$ on input k, we may express k in the form:

$$k = f_{i_1,B}(s_{i_1}) * f_{i_2,B}(s_{i_2}) * \cdots * f_{i_t,B}(s_{i_t}). \qquad (1)$$

Note that multiplicative schemes only impose a group structure on the set of keys K — no group structure on the set of shares S is assumed. This is in contrast to the notion of homomorphic schemes [1].

2.1 An Example

We illustrate the concept of a multiplicative threshold scheme and its use in threshold cryptography with the following example. Let q be a prime and let $K = (\mathbb{F}_q, +)$ be the additive group of the field $\mathbb{F}_q$ of q elements. The Shamir threshold scheme [13] over $\mathbb{F}_q$ is a multiplicative scheme over K. Indeed, in the Shamir t out of n threshold scheme, Lagrange interpolation allows the secret $k \in K$ to be written as

$$k = e_{i_1,B}s_{i_1} + e_{i_2,B}s_{i_2} + \ldots + e_{i_t,B}s_{i_t}$$

where B is a set of t participants $\{i_1, i_2, \ldots, i_t\}$ who hold shares $s_{i_1}, s_{i_2}, \ldots, s_{i_t}$, and $e_{i_1,B}, e_{i_2,B}, \ldots, e_{i_t,B}$ are elements of $\mathbb{F}_q$ which may be calculated from public information about the subset B. Thus, in this case, $f_{i_j,B}(s_{i_j}) = e_{i_j,B}s_{i_j}$ for $j = 1, \ldots, t$.

This multiplicative scheme may be used to provide threshold decryption in the El Gamal public key cryptosystem as follows (see [5]).

Let p be a prime and let q be a prime divisor of $p-1$. Let g be an element of $\mathbb{F}_p$ of multiplicative order q. Let $k \in K$ and put $y = g^k$. The value y is the public key (corresponding to secret key k) used to encrypt messages so that only a threshold of t participants holding shares of k can decrypt the corresponding cryptograms.

To encrypt a message block $m \in \mathbb{F}_p$, a value r is chosen at random in K and cryptogram (R, c) is formed, where $R = g^r$ and $c = zm$ with $z = y^r$. A set B of t participants $i_1, i_2, \ldots, i_t$ decrypt (R, c) as follows. Individually, using their secret shares, they calculate $z_{i_j} = R^{e_{i_j,B}s_{i_j}}$ for $j = 1, \ldots, t$. Provided q is large, these values $z_{i_1}, z_{i_2}, \ldots, z_{i_t}$ may be made public without compromising $s_{i_1}, s_{i_2}, \ldots, s_{i_t}$. From these values, $z = z_{i_1}z_{i_2}\cdots z_{i_t}$ may be calculated and $m = cz^{-1}$ recovered. Thus the cryptogram is decrypted (by a threshold of participants) while the secret key k and shares $s_{i_1}, s_{i_2}, \ldots, s_{i_t}$ remain secret.

Schemes which are multiplicative over the group of units of the integers modulo n can be used in conjunction with RSA to achieve threshold decryption and signature schemes (see [7] for a description of suitable schemes). Note that the Shamir scheme can no longer be used in this situation because there is no natural way of regarding the group of units of the integers modulo n as a field.

Schemes which are multiplicative over a non-abelian group are useful in zero-knowledge proofs which utilise joint knowledge of a graph isomorphism (see [4]). Multiplicative schemes are especially useful in this last situation, as suitable homomorphic schemes do not always exist [9].

Because of the above applications, it is desirable to construct multiplicative threshold schemes for a wide range of groups. Note that, for such schemes to be practical, a multiplicative scheme should be computationally feasible. Moreover, one must take care that the computational information required to carry out the multiplicative scheme efficiently does not compromise any public key system used as part of the application. For example, the factorisation of n should not be required in RSA based schemes. Thus one should check in any given situation whether the use of a given multiplicative scheme is appropriate. Such issues motivate the study of zero-knowledge techniques, see Section 6.

3 Extending the Karnin–Greene–Hellman bound

Karnin, Greene and Hellman established [12, Theorem 5] that for an ideal t out of n threshold scheme where the set of shares has order q, the inequality $n \leq q + t - 2$ always holds, provided that $t \geq 2$. They used a correspondence between ideal schemes and Maximum Distance Separable codes together with a bound on the lengths of such codes due to Singleton [14]. The aim of the present section is to show that this bound holds for schemes which are not necessarily ideal — our method of proof is of necessity quite different.

Theorem 3. *Let $t \geq 2$ and suppose there exists a perfect t out of n threshold scheme where the shares are taken from a set of order q. Then*

$$n \leq q + t - 2. \tag{2}$$

Proof: We may realise a 2 out of $n - (t - 2)$ threshold scheme using a t out of n scheme by making public the shares of a fixed set of $t - 2$ participants in the t out of n scheme. Thus the existence of a t out of n scheme implies the existence of a 2 out of $n - (t - 2)$ scheme. So in order to prove (2), it suffices to show that for a 2 out of n threshold scheme with shares taken from a set of order q, we have

$$n \leq q. \tag{3}$$

Suppose, for a contradiction, that there exists a 2 out of n threshold scheme $(\mathcal{D}, \mathcal{R})$ with a share set of order q and such that $n \geq q + 1$. Recall that the algorithm $\mathcal{D}$ proceeds by generating an element $c \in V$ and distributing the ith component of c to participant i. For $k \in K$, define C_k to be the set of all $c \in V$ generated by algorithm $\mathcal{D}$ with positive probability when k is given as input. If $k, k' \in K$ are distinct keys and $c \in C_k, c' \in C_{k'}$, then c and c' can agree in at most one component, because two components uniquely determine the key in a 2 out of n threshold scheme.

Let X be a random variable taking values uniformly in the set of keys K. Let Y be the random variable taking values in V formed by applying algorithm $\mathcal{D}$

to X, and for all $i \in \{1, \ldots n\}$ let Y_i be its ith component. For $k \in K$, define Y^k to be the random variable taking values in $C_k \subseteq V$ with probability distribution equal to the distribution of elements $c \in V$ generated by algorithm $\mathcal{D}$ when the key k is input, and for all $i \in \{1, \ldots, n\}$ let Y_i^k be the ith component of Y^k. Since Y_i and X are independent, we may note that $Prob(Y_i^k = s) = Prob(Y_i = s \mid X = k) = Prob(Y_i = s)$. So $Prob(Y_i^k = s) = Prob(Y_i^{k'} = s)$ for all $s \in S$ and all $k, k' \in K$. Let $k, k' \in K$ be distinct keys. Define $\delta : S \times S \to \mathbb{Z}$ by

$$\delta(s, s') = \begin{cases} 1 \text{ if } s = s' \text{ and} \\ 0 \text{ if } s \neq s'. \end{cases}$$

Let $Z_i^{k,k'}$ be a random variable defined by $Z_i^{k,k'} = \delta(Y_i^k, Y_i^{k'})$. Let E denote the expected value function. Since our scheme is perfect, we find

$$E(Z_i^{k,k'}) = Prob(Y_i^k = Y_i^{k'}) = \sum_{s \in S} Prob(Y_i^k = s) \cdot Prob(Y_i^{k'} = s)$$
$$= \sum_{s \in S} \left(Prob(Y_i^k = s)\right)^2 \geq \frac{1}{q} .$$

So

$$E(\sum_{i=1}^{q+1} Z_i^{k,k'}) = \sum_{i=1}^{q+1} E(Z_i^{k,k'}) \geq \frac{q+1}{q} > 1.$$

This implies that there exist $c \in C_k$ and $c' \in C_{k'}$ such that c and c' agree in more than one component (indeed, they agree in more than one of their first $q+1$ components). This is the contradiction that we have been seeking, so the inequality (3), and therefore the inequality (2), follow. □

4 A Recursive Construction

We describe a method for constructing a t out of ℓ^d threshold scheme whenever ℓ is a prime power such that

$$\ell \geq \binom{t}{2}(d-1) \tag{4}$$

by using a t out of ℓ threshold scheme. The t out of ℓ^d scheme is multiplicative provided that the t out of ℓ scheme is.

Let $(\mathcal{D}, \mathcal{R})$ be a t out of ℓ threshold scheme, where ℓ is a prime power. Let S be the set of shares of the scheme $(\mathcal{D}, \mathcal{R})$ and identify the set P of participants of the scheme with the finite field $\mathbb{F}_\ell$ of order ℓ. Suppose that d is a positive integer such that $\ell \geq \binom{t}{2}(d-1)$ and set $b = \binom{t}{2}(d-1)$. We define a t out of ℓ^d threshold scheme $(\mathcal{D}', \mathcal{R}')$ as follows.

The shares of our new scheme will be taken from the set $S' = S^{b+1}$, the set of all $(b+1)$-tuples of shares from $(\mathcal{D}, \mathcal{R})$. We identify the set P' of participants in our new scheme with the set of polynomials of degree less than d with coefficients in $\mathbb{F}_\ell$. If $f(X) = \sum_{i=0}^{d-1} a_i X^i \in P'$, then define $f(\infty) = a_{d-1}$. Let $\alpha_1, \alpha_2, \ldots, \alpha_b$ be distinct elements of $\mathbb{F}_\ell$ and let $\alpha_0 = \infty$.

We define the distribution algorithm $\mathcal{D}'$ as follows. On being given $k \in K$, algorithm $\mathcal{D}'$ executes algorithm $\mathcal{D}$ a total of $b+1$ times, to produce elements $c^0, c^1, c^2, \ldots, c^b \in S^\ell$. The random input used by $\mathcal{D}$ in each execution should be independent of the random inputs used by previous executions. For each $j \in \{0, \ldots, b\}$, we may write $c^j = (c^j_\alpha)_{\alpha \in \mathbb{F}_\ell}$ for some elements $c^j_\alpha \in S$. The algorithm then distributes the share $c'_f \in S'$ to $f \in P'$ where c'_f is defined by

$$c'_f = (c^0_{f(\infty)}, c^1_{f(\alpha_1)}, c^2_{f(\alpha_2)}, \ldots, c^b_{f(\alpha_b)}).$$

We define the reconstruction algorithm $\mathcal{R}'$ as follows. Let $f_1, f_2, \ldots, f_t$ be distinct participants. The algorithm $\mathcal{R}'$ must recompute the key $k \in K$ given the shares $c'_{f_1}, c'_{f_2}, \ldots, c'_{f_t}$. The algorithm $\mathcal{R}'$ begins by trying to find an integer $i \in \{0, 1, \ldots, b\}$ such that the elements $f_1(\alpha_i), f_2(\alpha_i), \ldots, f_t(\alpha_i)$ are distinct. Such an integer i always exists, by the following argument. Consider the polynomial h defined by

$$h = \prod_{1 \le u < v \le t} (f_u - f_v).$$

Then h is a nonzero polynomial of degree at most b. We consider two cases separately.

Firstly, suppose that $\deg h \le b-1$. Since h can have at most $\deg h$ roots, there exists an integer $i \in \{1, 2, \ldots, b\}$ such that $h(\alpha_i) \ne 0$. But for any $\alpha \in \mathbb{F}_\ell$, $h(\alpha) = 0$ if and only if $f_u(\alpha) = f_v(\alpha)$ for some distinct $u, v \in \{1, 2, \ldots, t\}$. So the values $f_1(\alpha_i), f_2(\alpha_i), \ldots, f_t(\alpha_i)$ are distinct, as required.

We now consider the case when $\deg h = b$. This condition implies that $\deg(f_u - f_v) = d-1$ for all u and v such that $1 \le u < v \le t$. But $\deg(f_u - f_v) = d-1$ if and only if $f_u(\infty) \ne f_v(\infty)$. So the elements $f_1(\infty), f_2(\infty), \ldots, f_t(\infty)$ are distinct and we may take $i = 0$.

The algorithm $\mathcal{R}'$ now extracts the ith component from each of the shares $c'_{f_1}, \ldots, c'_{f_t}$ to obtain the set $c^i_{f_1(\alpha_i)}, \ldots, c^i_{f_t(\alpha_i)}$. Now $f_1(\alpha_i), f_2(\alpha_i), \ldots, f_t(\alpha_i)$ are distinct elements of P, so the algorithm $\mathcal{R}'$ possesses t distinct components of the element $c^i \in S^l$ and can use algorithm $\mathcal{R}$ to reconstruct the key $k \in K$.

Theorem 4. *The scheme $(\mathcal{D}', \mathcal{R}')$ is a perfect t out of ℓ^d threshold scheme, provided that $(\mathcal{D}, \mathcal{R})$ is a perfect t out of ℓ threshold scheme. The scheme $(\mathcal{D}', \mathcal{R}')$ is also multiplicative or homomorphic, provided that this is also true of the scheme $(\mathcal{D}, \mathcal{R})$.*

The argument above shows that algorithm $\mathcal{R}'$ reconstructs the key from t distinct shares, so any t participants can recover the key. Furthermore, any $t-1$ participants possess at most $t-1$ components of each of the elements $c^0, c^1, c^2, \ldots, c^b$, so are unable to deduce any information about the key k. It is also clear that the scheme $(\mathcal{D}', \mathcal{R}')$ is multiplicative if $(\mathcal{D}, \mathcal{R})$ is, for in this case the algorithm $\mathcal{R}'$ uses the multiplicative algorithm $\mathcal{R}$ in its final step. A similar remark holds for the homomorphic property.

4.1 Geometric interpretation

For the reader familiar with normal rational curves the following provides a geometrical description of our construction. (The construction above was originally found by using this geometrical approach and so we include this interpretation in the hope that it might prove a fruitful perspective in future. However, readers unfamiliar with finite geometry may skip this subsection without prejudicing their understanding of the remainder of the paper).

We identify the participants of the threshold scheme $(\mathcal{D}', \mathcal{R}')$ with the points of the affine geometry $\mathrm{AG}(d, \ell)$ of dimension d over $\mathbb{F}_\ell$. The coordinates of a point correspond to the coefficients of a polynomial of degree at most $d-1$. A parallel class of this geometry consists of ℓ mutually disjoint hyperplanes. We identify these hyperplanes with the participants of the threshold scheme $(\mathcal{D}, \mathcal{R})$. The $b+1$ executions of $(\mathcal{D}, \mathcal{R})$ correspond to $b+1$ parallel classes. Points in the same hyperplane of a given parallel class are given the share for that hyperplane in the corresponding execution of $(\mathcal{D}, \mathcal{R})$ to obtain their share (a $(b+1)$-tuple) in $(\mathcal{D}', \mathcal{R}')$.

The property required of the $b+1$ parallel classes is that any t points should belong to distinct hyperplanes of some parallel class. If this is the case then these t participants can use their shares of the corresponding execution of $(\mathcal{D}, \mathcal{R})$ to reconstruct the key. There is a correspondence between the parallel classes of $\mathrm{AG}(d, \ell)$ and the hyperplanes of the projective space $\mathrm{PG}(d-1, \ell)$ that is the hyperplane at infinity of $\mathrm{AG}(d, \ell)$. Two points belong to different hyperplanes of a parallel class if and only if the line joining them does not meet $\mathrm{PG}(d-1, \ell)$ in a point of the hyperplane corresponding to the parallel class. Our objective is achieved if the $b+1$ hyperplanes in $\mathrm{PG}(d-1, \ell)$ are chosen on a dual normal rational curve.

Any d hyperplanes of a dual normal rational curve in $\mathrm{PG}(d-1, \ell)$ are independent so that any point of $\mathrm{PG}(d-1, \ell)$ is on at most $d-1$ hyperplanes belonging to the curve. For any t points of $\mathrm{AG}(d, \ell)$ the $\binom{t}{2}$ lines joining two of them meet $\mathrm{PG}(d-1, \ell)$ in points belonging to at most $\binom{t}{2}(d-1)$ hyperplanes of the dual normal rational curve. Thus if $b = \binom{t}{2}(d-1)$ there exists at least one of the $b+1$ parallel classes with the property that the t points belong to distinct hyperplanes of this class. Since a dual normal rational curve consists of $\ell + 1$ hyperplanes we obtain the condition $\ell \geq \binom{t}{2}(d-1)$.

5 Share expansion

Let $(\mathcal{D}, \mathcal{R})$ be a threshold scheme with share set S of order q and a key set K of order m. We define the *share expansion* E of the scheme by $E = (\log q)/(\log m)$. (Thus the share expansion of a scheme is just the reciprocal of its information rate). The share expansion of a scheme is a measure of its inefficiency. For all perfect schemes, the share expansion is at least 1 and it is desirable to construct schemes whose expansion is as close to 1 as possible. Define $s_K(t, n)$ to be the smallest share expansion of a t out of n threshold scheme which is multiplicative over K. Theorem 3 gives the following corollary.

Corollary 5. *Let K be a group of order m. For all integers t and n such that $2 \le t \le n$,*

$$s_K(t, n) \ge (\log(n - (t - 2)))/\log m.$$

Proof: If the set S of shares has order q, then Theorem 1 states that $n - (t-2) \le q$. So the share expansion $(\log q)/(\log m)$ of any t out of n scheme which is multiplicative over K is at least $(\log(n - (t - 2)))/(\log m)$. □

On the other hand, the construction of the previous section shows that

$$s_K(t, \ell^d) \le (\tbinom{t}{2}(d - 1) + 1)s_K(t, \ell)$$

whenever ℓ is a prime power such that $\ell \ge \binom{t}{2}(d-1)$. By using this construction repeatedly, one can show that we may realise a scheme with a share expansion of $O((\log n)^{1+\epsilon})$ as $n \to \infty$ for fixed t and for any $\epsilon > 0$. Comparing this expansion with the bound in the corollary above, we see that this scheme seems to be good when n is large compared with t.

5.1 An Explicit Construction

Analysing the behaviour of our recursive construction when we allow t to vary as well as n is a delicate matter. In general, when the recursive construction is being used several times in order to achieve a scheme with desired parameters t and n, it is better to use the recursive construction a small number of times with values for d as large as possible. In this subsection, we use our recursive construction to produce an explicit t out of n scheme for any values of t and n in the case when K is abelian. Although the explicit scheme will not use our recursive construction in an optimal way, the resulting bound on the achievable share expansion for a multiplicative t out of n scheme will be useful in the next section.

Let t and n be arbitrary integers such that $2 < t \le n$ and let K be an abelian group. We construct a t out of n threshold scheme as follows. We choose a positive constant a. Let ℓ be the first prime power such that $\ell \ge \binom{t}{2}^{1+a}$. We produce a multiplicative t out of ℓ scheme by using a construction of Desmedt and Frankel [7]. This scheme has a share expansion of less than 2ℓ. We then apply our recursive construction with $d = \lceil \ell/\binom{t}{2} \rceil$ a total of m times where $m = \lfloor \log_d \log_\ell n \rfloor + 1$. Note that we can do this since $\ell \ge \binom{t}{2}(d-1)$. At the end of this process, we have a t out of N scheme where $N = \ell^{d^m} \ge n$. By removing the $N - n$ surplus participants, we have constructed a t out of n scheme which is multiplicative over the abelian group K. One can calculate that the share expansion of this scheme is at most

$$2\ell\left\{\binom{t}{2}d\right\}^m < 16\binom{t}{2}^{2+2a}\left\{\frac{\log n}{(1+a)\log\binom{t}{2}}\right\}^{1+\frac{1}{a}}. \qquad (5)$$

When $t = 2$, one may use the same methods to produce a scheme with share expansion at most $4\log n$.

6 Zero Knowledge

In many threshold cryptosystems it is important that the amount of knowledge that participants obtain (individually or jointly in groups) from their shares and any public information is no more than is strictly necessary. The study of zero-knowledge threshold schemes [7] addresses this issue. In this section we analyse our scheme from a computational complexity point of view in order to study its zero-knowledge aspects. For this purpose, we implicitly assume that we are studying a family of schemes indexed by some parameter x taken from a set of finite binary strings — this allows us to talk meaningfully about such notions as polynomial time. For reasons of space, we do not explicitly refer to this parameter (e.g. we use the term 'scheme' for a family of schemes) except when discussing the computational complexity of our algorithms. We assume the computational power of the participants in P is polynomially bounded in $|x|$, the binary length of x, and for a t out of n threshold scheme to be *multiplicative* we require in addition to (1) that a polynomial time (in $|x|$) algorithm exists to compute the operations of the group K and a polynomial time (in $|x|$) algorithm exists that can compute the image of any element of the set of shares S under any one of the family of mappings $\{f_{i,B} : S \to K \mid i \in B\}$. We must also take into account the fact that the distribution algorithm $\mathcal{D}$, given the key, may have to distribute shares to a possibly superpolynomial number of participants, and that in the reconstruction algorithm $\mathcal{R}$ the power of many participants may be combined. For this reason we allow $\mathcal{D}$ (when given k) to run in expected polynomial time in $max\{|x|, n\}$ and $\mathcal{R}$ to run in polynomial time in $max\{|x|, t, |n|\}$.

A t out of n threshold scheme is *perfectly zero-knowledge* if the shares of any $t-1$ or less participants can be simulated perfectly in expected polynomial time bounded by $(t-1)|x|^c$ where c is some constant. Informally, this condition says that $t-1$ participants learn nothing new from their shares and any publicly available information. A t out of n threshold scheme is *perfectly minimal-knowledge* if, given any key $k \in K$, the shares of any $m \geq t$ participants can be simulated perfectly in expected polynomial time bounded by $m|x|^c$, where c is some constant. Informally, this condition says that t or more participants learn no more than is strictly necessary from their shares and any publicly available information. Similar definitions can be formulated for statistical and computational analogues of perfect zero- and minimal-knowledge. For the formal definitions and a more rigourous approach, the reader is referred to [7, 10, 11].

Theorem 6. *Let $(\mathcal{D}, \mathcal{R})$ be a multiplicative t out of ℓ threshold scheme over the group K and let d be polynomially bounded in $|x|$ with $\ell \geq \binom{t}{2}(d-1)$. Then the scheme $(\mathcal{D}', \mathcal{R}')$ constructed in Section 4 is a multiplicative t out of ℓ^d threshold scheme. If, furthermore, t is polynomially bounded in $|x|$ and $(\mathcal{D}, \mathcal{R})$ is perfectly zero-knowledge or minimal-knowledge, then so is $(\mathcal{D}', \mathcal{R}')$. Similar statements can be made for the statistical and computational analogues of perfect zero- and minimal-knowledge.*

Sketch Proof: We use the same notation as in Section 4. First observe that algorithm $\mathcal{R}'$ can certainly find an integer i such that $1 \leq i \leq b$ with the property that all the field elements $f_1(\alpha_i), f_2(\alpha_i), \ldots, f_t(\alpha_i)$ are distinct, since d is polynomially bounded. It follows that $(\mathcal{D}', \mathcal{R}')$ is a threshold scheme.

Next suppose that t is polynomially bounded, that $(\mathcal{D}, \mathcal{R})$ is zero-knowledge and that $f_1, f_2, \ldots, f_{t-1}$ are $t-1$ participants in $(\mathcal{D}', \mathcal{R}')$. The simulator for $(\mathcal{D}', \mathcal{R}')$ runs the simulator for $(\mathcal{D}, \mathcal{R})$ as a black box $b+1$ times, independently. For $i \in \{0, 1, \ldots, b\}$, define $B_i = \{f_1(\alpha_i), f_2(\alpha_i), \ldots, f_{t-1}(\alpha_i)\} \subseteq \mathbb{F}_\ell$, which we regard as a set of participants in $(\mathcal{D}, \mathcal{R})$. For each i, let $\hat{c}^i_{B_i}$ be the vector $(\hat{c}^i_{f_1(\alpha_i)}, \hat{c}^i_{f_2(\alpha_i)}, \ldots, \hat{c}^i_{f_{t-1}(\alpha_i)})$ of simulated shares and let $\hat{c}'_{f_j}$ be defined by $\hat{c}'_{f_j} = (\hat{c}^0_{f_j(\infty)}, \hat{c}^1_{f_j(\alpha_1)}, \ldots, \hat{c}^b_{f_j(\alpha_b)})$, for $1 \leq j \leq t-1$. The components of the shares $\hat{c}'_{f_j}$ are independent and simulate those of the shares c'_{f_j} for the participants $f_1, f_2, \ldots, f_{t-1}$ in $(\mathcal{D}', \mathcal{R}')$, which are also independent. So $\hat{c}'_{f_1}, \ldots, \hat{c}'_{f_{t-1}}$ simulates the shares of $f_1, \ldots, f_{t-1}$. Hence the threshold scheme $(\mathcal{D}', \mathcal{R}')$ is zero-knowledge. The proof for minimal-knowledge is similar and is omitted. □

Corollary 7. *If K is abelian and both t and $\log_2 n$ are polynomially bounded in $|x|$ with $t \geq 2$ then there exists a multiplicative and homomorphic zero- and minimal-knowledge t out of n threshold cryptosystem.*

Proof: The constructions of Subsection 5.1 (with a any positive constant) have share expansion at most $ct^{4+4a}(\log_2 n)^{1+1/a}$, for some constant c. □

If $n = \Theta(2^{|x|})$, but t is polynomially bounded in $|x|$, then the scheme in [7, pp. 673–674] is not zero-knowledge, but Corollary 7 shows that ours is.

7 Discussion

We have presented a recursive construction of threshold schemes that has several useful properties, the property that it preserves the homomorphic and multiplicative nature of the underlying scheme being amongst the most important. The explicit scheme in Subsection 5.1 implies the following.

Corollary 8. *For all constants b such that $0 < b \leq 1/4$, if $t = O(n^{1/4-b})$ then the shares are asymptotically shorter than in the zero-knowledge sharing scheme in [7, pp. 673–674], which has share expansion $\Theta(n)$.*

Proof: If we set $a = 4b$, then the result follows by the proof of Corollary 7. □

It is also obvious that the explicit scheme in Subsection 5.1 is substantially better than the scheme in [7, pp. 673–674] when $t = O((\log_2 n)^b)$ for any constant b — in this case our share expansion is only $O((\log_2 n)^{b'})$ for some constant b'.

When $t > 2$ and n is large compared to t, the recursive construction given in this paper is considerably more efficient than the scheme presented in [4]. In particular, when ϵ is any positive constant, t is constant and $n \to \infty$, the scheme presented here has share expansion of the order of $(\log n)^{1+\epsilon}$ whereas the scheme in [4] has share expansion of at least $c(\log n)^{t-1}$ for some constant c.

Our construction can be combined with existing threshold cryptosystems such as the ones in [3, 4] to make them more efficient (with shorter shares and hence faster computation), whilst maintaining their security.

We conclude by observing that although we were able to prove that our scheme is asymptotically optimal when the order of K and t are constant, the discovery of good bounds on the share expansion of multiplicative or homomorphic zero-knowledge threshold schemes for all parameters K, t and n (and the construction of schemes which meet these bounds) is still an open problem.

References

1. J.C. Benaloh: Secret sharing homomorphisms: Keeping shares of a secret secret. In: A. Odlyzko (ed.): Advances in Cryptology – Crypto '86, Proceedings. Lecture Notes in Computer Science 263. Berlin: Springer 1987, pp. 251–260
2. G.R. Blakley: Safeguarding cryptographic keys. In: Proc. Nat. Computer Conf. AFIPS Conf. Proc., 48, 1979, pp. 313–317
3. A. De Santis, Y. Desmedt, Y. Frankel, and M. Yung: How to share a function securely. In: Proceedings of the twenty-sixth annual ACM Symp. Theory of Computing (STOC), IEEE Press 1994, pp. 522–533. Full paper in preparation (available from authors when completed)
4. Y. Desmedt, G. Di Crescenzo, and M. Burmester: Multiplicative non-abelian sharing schemes and their application to threshold cryptography. In: J. Pieprzyk, R. Safavi-Naini (eds.): Advances in Cryptology – Asiacrypt '94, Proceedings. Lecture Notes in Computer Science 917. Berlin: Springer 1995, pp. 21–32
5. Y. Desmedt and Y. Frankel: Threshold cryptosystems. In: G. Brassard (ed.): Advances in Cryptology – Crypto '89, Proceedings. Lecture Notes in Computer Science 435. Berlin: Springer 1990, pp. 307-315
6. Y. Desmedt and Y. Frankel. Shared generation of authenticators and signatures. In: J. Feigenbaum (ed.): Advances in Cryptology – Crypto '91, Proceedings. Lecture Notes in Computer Science 576. Berlin: Springer 1992, pp 457–469
7. Y. Desmedt and Y. Frankel: Homomorphic zero-knowledge threshold schemes over any finite abelian group. SIAM Journal on Discrete Mathematics, 7(4), 667–679 (1994)
8. Y. Frankel and Y. Desmedt. Classification of ideal homomorphic threshold schemes over finite Abelian groups. In: R.A. Rueppel (ed.): Advances in Cryptology – Eurocrypt '92, Proceedings. Lecture Notes in Computer Science 658. Berlin: Springer 1993, pp 25–34
9. Y. Frankel, Y. Desmedt and M. Burmester. Non-existence of homomorphic general sharing schemes for some key spaces. In: E.F. Brickell (ed.): Advances in Cryptology – Crypto '92, Proceedings. Lecture Notes in Computer Science 740. Berlin: Springer 1993, pp 549–557
10. Z. Galil, S. Haber, and M. Yung: Minimum-knowledge interactive proofs for decision problems. SIAM J. Comput., 18(4), 711–739 (1989)
11. S. Goldwasser, S. Micali, and C. Rackoff: The knowledge complexity of interactive proof systems. SIAM J. Comput., 18(1), 186–208 (1989)
12. E.D. Karnin, J.W. Greene, and M. Hellman: On secret sharing systems. IEEE Trans. Inform. Theory, 29(1), 35–41 (1983)
13. A.Shamir: How to share a secret. Commun. ACM, 22, 612–613 (1979)
14. R.C. Singleton: Maximal distance q-nary codes. IEEE Trans. Inform. Theory, IT-10, 116–118 (1964)

Equivocable Oblivious Transfer

Donald Beaver*

Transarc Corporation

Abstract. We analyze and enhance Oblivious Transfer (OT) protocols to accommodate security against adaptive attacks. Previous analysis has been static in nature, treating the security of Alice and the security of Bob as separate cases, determined in advance. It remains unclear whether existing protocols are provably secure against adaptive attacks, but we provide enhancements to make them provably secure against attacks by *adaptive* 1*-adversaries*, who can choose *at any time* whether to corrupt Alice or Bob. We determine circumstances under which OT can be executed "in the open," without encrypting the messages, thereby giving simple alternatives to encrypting an entire interaction. We isolate *equivocation* properties that provide enough flexibility for a simulator to handle adaptive attacks. These properties also provide a means for classifying OT protocols and understanding the subtle demands of security against adaptive adversaries, as well as designing protocols that can be *proven* secure against adaptive attacks.

1 Introduction

Oblivious Transfer is one of the most broadly-applicable tools available for building secure interactive protocols. Its applicability is matched only by its simplicity: Alice must send a bit b to Bob without knowing whether it arrives, but with the assurance that it arrives with precisely 50-50 probability [Rab81]. A variety of implementations with varying efficiency and security have been offered, along with (occasional) proofs of security when Alice is bad or Bob is bad [Rab81, EGL82, BCR86a, BCR86b, BM89, KMO89, HL90, Boe91, B92]. Yet security in the most natural adversarial situation – namely in which neither Alice nor Bob need be bad at the outset, yet one *or both* can be corrupted *at any time* – does not follow from existing two-case analyses.

It seems intuitively clear, however, that an eavesdropper Eve overhearing the conversation between A and B should gain no knowledge. If Eve learned anything about whether b arrived, then so could Alice. If Eve learned anything about b, then so could Bob – and thus Alice could infer that Bob did gain information about b.

The "flaw" in this reasoning is that it presupposes that Alice is faulty (perhaps only overly curious) or that Bob is faulty, but does not address other goals that Eve may have. For example, both A and B may be honest, and Eve may

* Transarc Corp., 707 Grant St., Pittsburgh, PA 15219; (412) 338-4365; `beaver@transarc.com`; `http://www.transarc.com/~beaver`.

Ueli Maurer (Ed.): EUROCRYPT '96 Proceedings, LNCS 1070

be using the overheard conversation to decide whom to corrupt. Eve might wish to corrupt Bob only if he has a good chance of receiving b in that particular conversation. If she does corrupt Bob, Eve is indeed (unlike Alice) entitled to learn whether he received b and to learn b if so.

Of course, it may be possible to address each such motive with a plausible argument against insecurity, but we cannot be sure of listing all of Eve's ulterior motives. The situtation calls for a proper simulation result.

Simulation Results. Building a simulator $\mathcal{S}(A)$ for faulty Alice, and a second $\mathcal{S}(B)$ for faulty Bob, is a straightforward if tedious task for most secure OT protocols (sometimes with suitable modifications, such as the inclusion of zero-knowledge proofs of knowledge).

But attacks by adaptive adversaries are another thing. Based on the information it receives from an *ideal* OT channel, a simulator $\mathcal{S}$ should be able to provide Eve with an appropriate view of the corresponding messages between Alice and Bob, even before any corruptions are made. Should Eve decide to corrupt Alice, $\mathcal{S}$ is entitled to learn b (and if not too late, to decide what value to send), but $\mathcal{S}$ must then augment Eve's current view with a facsimile of Alice's internal history (random tapes, keys, *etc.*). This newly-gained history should look realistic to Eve, given the view she has already seen. The same should hold with respect to Bob, should Eve decide to corrupt him.

Furthermore, the case in which Eve ultimately corrupts *both* Alice and Bob should not be treated as moot. If the OT is part of a larger network protocol, it is certainly plausible that two arbitrary parties may be attacked. A proof of security for the larger protocol should not collapse when a module is "overrun." Only when attacks are *static* – namely when Eve decides *in advance* whom to corrupt – is such analysis indeed moot.

When Alice is corrupt, and Eve bases a decision whether to corrupt Bob based on subsequent interactions, the static analysis is insufficient. In particular, we must demand that $\mathcal{S}$ be able to augment Eve's view of Alice's history with a newly-created view of Bob's past history, should Eve decide to corrupt Bob also. A similar task is required when Bob is initially corrupt and Alice is later compromised.

Insufficiency of Current Work. In stark contrast to what intuition suggests, many if not all "secure" implementations of OT fail these requirements. In many cases, merely overhearing the conversation itself is enough to fix a particular value of b, even though it may be unknown. In other words, $\mathcal{S}$ cannot patch a current simulated view to be consistent with $\bar{b}$ having been sent. Brassard, Chaum and Crépeau's *chameleon blobs* [BCC88] are an appropriate but insufficient idea.[2]

[2] The chameleon property is generally sufficient against *static* adveraries, which is the scenario implicitly considered in [BCC88]. Also, they address commitment, which has weaker objectives than OT.

In other cases, the arrival of b is absolutely fixed by the conversation, so that even though nothing can be inferred (computationally), $\mathcal{S}$ cannot later pretend that b arrived when it didn't (or vice versa).

As a consequence, $\mathcal{S}$ may be able to construct reasonable facsimiles of views, but when a new party is corrupted, $\mathcal{S}$ has no freedom to pretend either a 0 or 1 was sent, or to pretend b arrived or didn't. Such inflexibility precludes a proper simulator-based proof of security against *adaptive* attacks.

Equivocation. Essentially, a simulator must be able to create equivocable views. We say an implementation of OT is **content-equivocable** if views can be generated (whether or not B is already corrupt) so that if Alice is suddenly corrupted, the views can be made consistent with Alice having sent either 0 or 1. We call it **result-equivocable** if a simulator can expand a view consistently to include either "received" or "failed to receive" when Bob is suddenly corrupted.

We discuss several OT implementations and show that these properties vary among them. It should be noted that the "chameleon" property of [BCC88] is distinct: the chameleon property requires that *Bob* be able to open a commitment to 0 or 1, but strictly speaking, an *eavesdropper* may be unable to do so without Bob's private knowledge. Moreover, Bob (*a.k.a.* the simulator augmenting Bob's view) may not be able to open bits of 0 or to 1 if the rest of Alice's information is newly compromised.

Weaker forms of equivocation are also helpful under certain circumstances. We say an implementation of OT is **weakly content-equivocable** if an already-corrupt Bob can make it consistent with either 0 or 1 whenever he has failed to receive b, even if Alice is also subsequently corrupted.[3] Likewise, we say the protocol is **weakly result-equivocable** if an already-corrupt Alice can fill in the view to make it consistent with reception or failure, even if Bob is also subsequently compromised.

Enclosure. If openly transmitting the messages of an OT protocol raises problems, the simple answer *seems* to be to enclose the conversation with an appropriate encryption scheme. An adversary would have to corrupt either Alice or Bob just to gain any meaningful knowledge about the conversation. While this does not quite reduce the adaptive analysis to the static case, it will work in certain cases, namely if the enclosed OT protocol is *weakly* equivocable (both by content and by result). It does not work for many commonly-known OT protocols.

Moreover, using an encryption scheme presents something of a chicken-and-egg dilemma. The encryption scheme itself must be secure against adaptive attacks. Such encryptions can be found in the work of Beaver and Haber [BH92], in the ingenious but impractical very recent scheme by Canetti, Feige, Goldreich and Naor [CFGN96], and most recently in an efficient scheme by Beaver [B96]. Unless erasing is permitted, the weakest assumptions (one-way trapdoor permutations) require third parties to assist in the encryption. Stronger assumptions,

[3] This is nearly the same as the "chameleon" property. It differs in requiring consistency *even* if Alice is then corrupted.

such as RSA or Diffie-Hellman [RSA78, DH76], require no third-party assistance [CFGN96, B96].

Efficiency. The expense of involving third parties for every message bit and the danger of attempting to erase bits completely lead us to seek to minimize the use of such techniques. We show that it is not necessary to protect the entire conversation but that encrypting one or two extra bits suffices. We also show that encrypting one bit securely against *adaptive* attacks is *necessary.*

Contributions. In summary, we provide the following observations and technologies regarding OT:

- Static analysis of security does not show security against adaptive attacks.
- Static security plus encryption is not sufficient to protect OT against adaptive attacks.
- Certain equivocability properties plus encryption do suffice to provide provable security against fully adaptive attacks.
- Equivocability varies among proposed OT schemes (including a new scheme discussed within), but most can be enhanced for security against adaptive 1-adversaries;
- Encrypting two extra bits is a sufficient alternative to encrypting the conversation; encrypting one bit is necessary.

2 Background

Attacks: Static or Adaptive. An adversary is a probabilistic poly-time TM (PPTM) that issues two sorts of messages: "*corrupt* i," "*send* m from i to j." It receives two sorts of responses: "*view of* i," "*receive* m from j to i." Whether its send/receive message is honored depends on whether it has issued a request to corrupt i.

A **static t-adversary** is an adversary who issues up to t *corrupt* requests before the protocol starts. An **adaptive t-adversary** may issue up to t such requests at any time.

OT specification. The **specification protocol for OT** is a three-party protocol consisting of $\hat{A}$, $\hat{B}$, and incorruptible party OT. $\hat{A}$ has input b, which it is instructed to send to OT. OT flips a coin, $?b$, and sends $(?b, ?b \wedge b)$ to $\hat{B}$.[4] The communication channels between $\hat{A}$ and OT and between OT and $\hat{B}$ are absolutely private.

Simulation-based security. The definition of simulator-based static security is the standard approach: find an appropriate simulator for the case in which Alice is bad, and another simulator for when Bob is bad. We focus on the adaptive case.

[4] Thus, $(0, 0)$ means "failed," while $(1, b)$ means "received b."

In the adaptive case, there is a single simulator, $\mathcal{S}$, who receives requests from and delivers responses to the attacker, $\texttt{Adv}$, creating an environment for $\texttt{Adv}$ as though $\texttt{Adv}$ were attacking a given implementation. $\mathcal{S}$ is itself an attacker acting within the specification protocol for OT, which is run with $\hat{A}$ on input b. When $\texttt{Adv}$ corrupts player i, $\mathcal{S}$ issues a corruption request and is given $\hat{i}$'s information.[5] $\mathcal{S}$ responds to $\texttt{Adv}$ with a facsimile of the "*view of i*" response that $\texttt{Adv}$ expects. $\mathcal{S}$ receives all of $\texttt{Adv}$'s "*send m*" requests and provides $\texttt{Adv}$ with facsimiles of "*receive m*" responses. Finally, $\texttt{Adv}$ (or $\mathcal{S}$ on $\texttt{Adv}$'s behalf) writes its output, $y_{\texttt{Adv}}$.

Let $\texttt{Adv}$, with auxiliary input $x_{\texttt{Adv}}$, attack a given OT implementation $\texttt{OT}$ in which Alice holds input b. The execution induces a distribution $(A(b), B, \texttt{Adv}(x_{\texttt{Adv}}))$ on output triples, $(y_A, y_B, y_{\texttt{Adv}})$.

Let $\mathcal{S}(\texttt{Adv}(x_{\texttt{Adv}}))$ attack the OT specification. The execution induces a distribution $(\hat{A}(b), \hat{B}, \mathcal{S}(\texttt{Adv}(x_{\texttt{Adv}})))$ on output triples, $(y_{\hat{A}}, y_{\hat{B}}, y_{S})$.

An extra, "security parameter" k may be included. This provides a sequence of distributions on output triples in each scenario. Let $\approx$ denote *computational indistinguishability*, a notion whose formal definition is omitted for reasons of space (*cf.* [GMR89]).

The implementation $\mathcal{OT}$ is **secure against adaptive t-adversaries** if, for any adaptive t-adversary $\texttt{Adv}$, there is a PPTM simulator $\mathcal{S}$ such that for any b, $(A(b), B, \texttt{Adv}(x_{\texttt{Adv}})) \approx (\hat{A}(b), \hat{B}, \mathcal{S}(\texttt{Adv}(x_{\texttt{Adv}})))$. In other words, the simulator maps attacks on the implementation to equivalent attacks on the specification.

Encryption. The **specification protocol for secure channels** is a two-party protocol consisting of $\hat{S}$, $\hat{R}$, in which $\hat{S}$ produces a bit m which is transferred securely to $\hat{R}$. An eavesdropper knows only that a bit was sent, or that one or the other party decided to abort. An **encryption scheme secure against adaptive t-adversaries** is a (two-party) protocol such that, for any adaptive t-adversary $\texttt{Adv}$, there is a PPTM simulator $\mathcal{S}$ such that for any m, $(S(m), R, \texttt{Adv}(x_{\texttt{Adv}})) \approx (\hat{S}(m), \hat{R}, \mathcal{S}(\texttt{Adv}(x_{\texttt{Adv}})))$.[6] We generally assume that the implementation network provides authenticated, service-undeniable, point-to-point connections. The traffic over the lines is public, however.

OT Variants. We also consider two variants on OT: one-out-of-two OT ($\frac{1}{2}$OT), in which Alice holds (b_0, b_1) and Bob receives (c, b_c) for a random c unknown to Alice [EGL82]; and chosen one-out-of-two OT ($\binom{2}{1}$OT), in which Alice holds (b_0, b_1) and Bob receives b_c for a c of his choice, but unknown to Alice.

3 Equivocation

As described above, content-equivocation involves the simulator adjusting or augmenting a view to be consistent with sending either $b = 0$ or $b = 1$. This

---

5 $\hat{i}$ is a player in the specification protocol and is unaware of messages being passed in a given implementation. In particular, $\hat{A}$ knows only its input b (and its message to OT), and $\hat{B}$ knows only its message from OT.

6 A multiparty implementation is also possible; the formalities are similar.

may be necessary when $\mathcal{S}$ did not corrupt $\hat{A}$ before it started to create views for `Adv`, and thus did not know the bit b sent by $\hat{A}$ to OT in the specification protocol. If or when `Adv` corrupts Alice, $\mathcal{S}$ does obtain b (perhaps already sent to OT, perhaps not) and must bend its views so that the up-until-now honest Alice appears to have used b as its input.

Likewise, result-equivocation involves the simulator augmenting a view to be consistent with having received b or failed to receive b, depending on what $\hat{B}$ may actually have received in the specification protocol.

3.1 Various Implementations

We characterize several implementations according to whether they are content-equivocable (C.E.) or result-equivocable (R.E.). This list is not meant to be exhaustive.

Often, such implementations omit certain requirements such as Alice proving in zero-knowledge that she knows the effective bit b she is sending. Without such ZK proofs of knowledge (ZKPK's), some protocols can be broken (*cf.* [B92]). For the purposes of this paper, we assume that such ZKPK's are included, and postpone an analysis of the equivocability of the ZKPK's themselves.

Rabin. Rabin proposed an implementation based on the intractability of factoring [Rab81]. Let $E_{p,q}(x,r)$ be a probabilistic encryption of x with decryption key (p,q). For example, $E_{p,q}(b,r) = (-1)^b r^2 \pmod n$; then the quadratic residuosity of $E_{p,q}(b,r)$ can be determined when p and q are known. (This requires the stronger QRA assumption: determining Quadratic Residuosity is intractable [GM84].)

1. $A \rightarrow B$: $n = pq$ and $E_{p,q}(b,r)$, for a random $r \pmod n$.
2. $B \rightarrow A$: $z = x^2 \pmod n$, for a random $x \pmod n$.
3. $A \rightarrow B$: $w = \sqrt{z} \pmod n$, chosen at random from the four square roots $\{\pm x, \pm y\}$ of z.
4. B: if $w = \pm x$, output $(0,0)$; else factor n, decrypt b, and output $(1,b)$.

This protocol is neither C.E. nor weakly C.E., because $E_{p,q}(b,r)$ fixes the value of b. It is, however, R.E., since simulator $\mathcal{S}$ can pretend that Bob internally generated $\pm x$ whenever $\hat{B}$ obtained $?b = 0$ ("failed") in the specification, or pretend that Bob held $\pm y$ whenever $\hat{B}$ obtained $?b = 1$ ("received") in the specification.

Den Boer. In Den Boer's method [Boe91], based on the QRA, Bob generates $n = pq$. Alice sends a couple of residues, which with probability 1/2 have the same quadratic residuosity (also equal to b), and with probability 1/2 have different quadratic residuosity (hence Bob learns nothing). Let $Q_n(x) = 0$ if x is a quadratic residue mod n, else let $Q_n(x) = 1$.

1. $B \rightarrow A$: $n = pq$ and a for a random $a \pmod n$.

2a. A: choose random bits c, d, and random $r \pmod n$. Set $x_0 = (-1)^b r^2 \pmod n$, $x_1 = (-1)^c a x_0^{-1} \pmod n$.

2b. $A \to B$: $(x_d, x_{\overline{d}})$.[7]

3. B: receive (y_0, y_1). If $Q_n(y_0) = Q_n(y_1)$, then output $(1, Q_n(y_0))$ ["received $Q_n(y_0)$"]. Else output $(0,0)$.

This protocol is neither R.E. nor weakly R.E., because the quadratic residuosities of (y_0, y_1) are fixed, once seen. Thus, if they are $(0,0)$ or $(1,1)$, then $\mathcal{S}$ cannot pretend that Bob failed to receive the bit. If one witnesses the conversation between honest players, then it will be impossible to change the bit sent when it is forced to arrive, so the protocol is not C.E.. On the other hand, the protocol is weakly C.E., because, having seen that Bob failed to receive the bit, $\mathcal{S}$ can swap the roles of x_0 and x_1, thereby choosing between Alice's having sent $Q_n(x_0)$ or $Q_n(x_1)$ (which is $1 \oplus Q_n(x_0)$). This choice is perfectly acceptable even when Alice is subsequently corrupted.

Novel. In this method, bearing similarity to Den Boer's OT protocol and the commitment schemes of Brassard, Chaum and Crépeau [BCC88], Alice sends b over a channel that, with 50-50 probability, delivers nothing but quadratic residues.

1. $B \to A$: $n = pq$ and a for a random $a \pmod{n}$.[8]

2a. A: choose random bit c, and random $r \pmod{n}$. Set $s = (-1)^c a \pmod{n}$ and $x = s^b r^2 \pmod{n}$.

2b. $A \to B$: (x, c).[9]

3. B: receive (x, c). If $c \neq Q_n(a)$, then output $(1, Q_n(x))$. Else output $(0,0)$.

Note that when s is a quadratic residue ($c = Q_n(a)$), no information is transmitted. Otherwise, the residuosity of $x = s^b$ determines b. This protocol is neither R.E. nor weakly R.E., because the quadratic residuosity of a and the value of c, once seen, determine whether the bit arrives. If one witnesses the conversation between honest players, then it will be impossible to change the bit sent in those cases that it is forced to arrive, so the protocol is not C.E.. On the other hand, the protocol is weakly C.E., as can be seen by applying the arguments of [BCC88] for their commitment scheme. If $\mathcal{S}$ wishes to reveal a fake b it initially used to construct a view, it can use the original fake r. If $\mathcal{S}$ wishes to patch $b = 0$ to pretend that $b = 1$ was sent, it replaces r with $r/\sqrt{s}$, so that the already-seen value of x, namely $s^0 r^2 \equiv s^1 (r/\sqrt{s})^2$, remains unchanged. Similarly, to patch $b = 1$ to $b = 0$, $\mathcal{S}$ replaces r with $r\sqrt{s}$. These arguments make it evident that the weak-C.E. property is comparable to the chameleon property of [BCC88].

Even-Goldreich-Lempel. Two different implementations of $\frac{1}{2}$OT were given by [EGL82]. In the earlier version, a protocol that assumes Bob does not cheat was given. Because the later version contains an apparently more robust but subtly

---

[7] Alice must also give a ZKPK that she knows the effective b she is sending, else the protocol is breakable [B92]. We have also slightly modified the protocol to send x_i's in random order.

[8] Along with ZKPK of p, q.

[9] Along with ZKPK of effective b.

breakable protocol, we focus on the simpler approach. The simpler approach permits Bob to gain both bits (b_0, b_1) if he departs from the protocol. Canetti, Feige, Goldreich and Naor, however, have applied this otherwise undesirably vulnerable method to provide an remarkable solution to adaptively-secure encryption [CFGN96]. Thus, the properties of the EGL protocol are of interest.

Let $f(x)$ be a trapdoor one-way permutation, and let Alice hold the trapdoor. Let $B_f(x)$ give a hard bit of x with respect to f. Recall that Alice has input bits b_0, b_1. Bob will receive either b_0 or b_1 along one of two channels. One channel is masked by a bit that Bob knows, the other by a hard bit.

1a. B: choose random bit c and random strings x_0, x_1. If $c = 0$, set $(y_0, y_1) = (f(x_0), x_1)$, set $(y_0, y_1) = (x_0, f(x_1))$.
1b. $B \rightarrow A$: (y_0, y_1).
2a. A: choose random bit d. Set $z_0 = B(f^{-1}(y_d)) \oplus b_0$, $z_1 = B(f^{-1}(y_{\overline{d}})) \oplus b_1$.
2b. $A \rightarrow B$: (z_0, z_1, d).
3. B: receive (z_0, z_1, d). Set $e = c \oplus d$, $\beta = z_e \oplus B(x_c)$. Output $(e, \beta) =$ "received bit e with value β."

Clearly, malicious Bob can send $(f(x_0), f(x_1))$ and always receive both bits without detection. Let us consider whether views can be generated even when Alice and Bob are honest but curious. $\mathcal{S}$ cheats by indeed using $(f(X_0), f(X_1))$ for random strings X_0,X_1. This permits $\mathcal{S}$ to use $(x_0 = X_0, x_1 = f(X_1))$ or $(x_0 = f(X_0), x_1 = X_1)$ when it reveals Bob's internal history. Such a simulation is *perfectly* indistinguishable from actual histories. This flexibility allows $\mathcal{S}$ to reverse c at the last minute. Since c determines which bit arrives, the protocol is R.E..

On the other hand, (y_0, y_1) determines the hard bits used as masks in step 3, and this cannot be reversed once Bob or an outsider has seen those messages. Thus the protocol is not weakly C.E..

Bellare-Micali. Unlike the previous protocols, this implementation of $\binom{2}{1}$OT seeks to use the intractability of discrete logarithm for protection [BM89]. Although it has subtle correlation problems if used to send more than one message, its use of an alternate intractability assumption makes it of interest. Let p be a prime, g be a primitive element mod p, and let C be a public value mod p whose discrete logarithm is unknown.

1a. A: choose random bit i and random $x \pmod p$. If $c = 0$, set $(\beta_0, \beta_1) = (g^x, Cg^{-x})$, else set $(\beta_0, \beta_1) = (Cg^{-x}, g^x)$.
1b. $A \rightarrow B$: (β_0, β_1).[10]
2a. A: choose random $y_0, y_1 \pmod{p-1}$. Set $\alpha_0 = g^{y_0}$, $\alpha_1 = g^{y_1}$. Set $\gamma_0 = \beta_0^{y_0}$, $\gamma_1 = \beta_1^{y_1}$. Set $r_0 = b_0 \oplus \gamma_0$, $r_1 = b_1 \oplus \gamma_1$,
2b. $A \rightarrow B$: $(\alpha_0, \alpha_1, r_0, r_1)$.
3. B: receive $(\alpha_0, \alpha_1, r_0, r_1)$. Set $\gamma_i = \alpha_i^x$. Set $b_i = \gamma_i \oplus r_i$.

[10] Verified by comparing to public C generated by third-party.

With simple modifications, this is easily converted to $\frac{1}{2}$OT or OT. The protocol is neither R.E. nor C.E.. Notice that witnessing (β_0, β_1) fixes x. Simple algebra shows that it is impossible to find an x and $\hat{x}$ such that $(\beta_0, \beta_1) = (g^x, Cg^{-x})$ and $(\beta_0, \beta_1) = (Cg^{-\hat{x}}, g^{\hat{x}})$, unless $C = 1$ (which defeats the protocol). Thus, once an eavesdropper or Bob sees (β_0, β_1), the values of x and c are determined. The α_0, α_1 values determine y_0, y_1 and therefore also determine the masks γ_0, γ_1; thus the simulator cannot get away with changing the bits b_0, b_1.

Summary. Altogether, we observe the following variability among several proposed implementations of OT:

Protocol	Result Eq.(str/wk)	Content Eq. (str/wk)	Comment
Rabin	+/+	−/−	factoring
Den Boer	−/−	−/+	QRA
Novel	−/−	−/+	QRA
EGL-1	+/+	−/−	weak adversary model
BM	−/−	−/−	discrete log

Although the Rabin and EGL implementations are quite different in robustness, they share the same equivocation characteristics.

3.2 General Reductions

We note that reductions among variants of OT can preserve equivocability:

Theorem 1. *The following are equivalent: (1) there exists a result-equivocable implementation of* OT*; (2) there exists a result-equivocable implementation of* $\frac{1}{2}$OT*; (3) there exists a result-equivocable implementation of* $\binom{2}{1}$ *OT.*

Proof. Crépeau's reductions suffice [C87]. Consider (1) ⇒ (2). Say that Alice transmits $15k$ random bits $\{r_1, \ldots, r_{15k}\}$, and Bob receives those with indices in $R \subseteq \{1, \ldots, 15k\}$. With probability $\geq 1 - 2^{-k}$, Bob can choose a random subset $U_0 \subseteq R$ of size $5k$; Bob also chooses $U_1 \subseteq \overline{R}$. Then Bob knows $\beta_0 = \oplus_{i \in U_0} r_i$ but with probability $\geq 1 - 2^{-k}$ he cannot determine $\beta_1 = \oplus_{i \in U_1} r_i$. By sending (U_0, U_1) to Alice in random order, a half-obscured pair of channels is created; Alice sends (b_0, b_1) along them in random order. For our purposes, it suffices to note that a simulator can reverse the roles of U_0 and U_1 at will, since the underlying OT is result-equivocable. Thus the identity of the arriving bit in the higher-level $\frac{1}{2}$OT protocol can be reversed. Showing (1) ⇒ (3) is similar, and the reverse directions are trivial. □

Theorem 2. *The following are equivalent: (1) there exists a content-equivocable implementation of* OT*; (2) there exists a content-equivocable implementation of* $\frac{1}{2}$OT*; (3) there exists a content-equivocable implementation of* $\binom{2}{1}$ *OT.*

Proof. Similar to 1. □

4 Enclosure

Given an OT implementation `OT` and an encryption scheme $\mathcal{E}$, let ENCLOSE(`OT`,$\mathcal{E}$) be the protocol that requires each message in `OT` to be encrypted with $\mathcal{E}$.

Theorem 3. *Let $\mathcal{E}$ be an encryption scheme secure against adaptive 2-adversaries. If* `OT` *is secure against static 1-adversaries, then* ENCLOSE*(*`OT`*,$\mathcal{E}$)* **is secure** *against adaptive 1-adversaries, but it is* **not necessarily secure** *against adaptive 2-adversaries.*

Proof. Let `Adv` be an adaptive 1-adversary. If `Adv` corrupts Alice, then the encrypted messages can be opened to any values, hence $\mathcal{S}$ runs a "static" simulator for Alice, extracts a view up to the moment of corruption, and equivocates the ciphertexts seen by `Adv` to be consistent with encrypting that view. `Adv` has used up its corruptions, hence we needn't worry about ever adjusting the view. A similar analysis holds for Bob.

For the adaptive 2-adversary case, note that even if the messages are encrypted, `Adv` can corrupt Bob to see them in the clear. Rabin's OT protocol does not permit b to be changed after corrupt Bob has seen the conversation and failed to receive b. Upon corrupting Alice, the simulator has at best a 50-50 chance of filling in the view to be consistent with the value b that $\mathcal{S}$ learns by corrupting $\hat{A}$ in the specification protocol. □

With enclosure, the weak equivocation properties suffice, however. (Notice that Rabin's OT failed above because it is not content-equivocable.)

Theorem 4. *Let $\mathcal{E}$ be an encryption scheme secure against adaptive 2-adversaries. If* `OT` *is secure against static 1-adversaries and both weakly content- and weakly result- equivocable, then* ENCLOSE*(*`OT`*,$\mathcal{E}$) is secure against adaptive 2-adversaries.*

Proof. Let `Adv` be an adaptive 2-adversary. As before, when `Adv` makes its first request to corrupt Alice or Bob, $\mathcal{S}$ corrupts $\hat{A}$ or $\hat{B}$ in the specification protocol and calls on the static simulator to generate an appropriate view, then equivocates the ciphertexts `Adv` has seen, to make them consistent with the view.

Now, say Alice is corrupted first. If `Adv` requests to corrupt Bob, $\mathcal{S}$ corrupts $\hat{B}$, determines the bit reception pattern (if the specification protocol is that far along), and based on the result-equivocability property, extends the view to appear as though Bob received the same pattern. If Bob is corrupted first, then upon later corruption of Alice, $\mathcal{S}$ discovers b by corrupting $\hat{A}$ and uses content-equivocability to extend the view to appear as though Alice had been using b all along. □

5 Efficient Enclosure

It turns out that many OT protocols can be made provably robust against 1-adaptive attacks without taking the drastic measure of encrypting the entire conversation.

Theorem 5. *Let $\mathcal{E}$ be an encryption scheme secure against adaptive 1-adversaries. The Rabin, Den Boer, and Novel protocols can be made secure against adaptive 1-adversaries by encrypting at most 2 additional bits while running the rest of the protocol in the open.*

Proof. In each protocol, Alice applies a random bit r instead of b, and she also sends $\mathcal{E}(r \oplus b)$. The Rabin protocol needs no further modification.

The Den Boer protocol is further modified as follows. In step 2b, Alice sends x_d instead of $(x_d, x_{\overline{d}})$, and Bob receives it as y_0. Alice sends $\mathcal{E}(c)$, Bob calculates $y_1 = x_{\overline{d}} = (-1)^c a y_0^{-1}$, and the protocol continues as written. The Novel protocol is further modified as follows. In step 2b, Alice sends $(x, \mathcal{E}(c))$ instead of (x, c). Simulation details are omitted for space. □

Necessity of Encrypting $\Omega(1)$ Bits. Let OT be an implementation of OT secure against adaptive 1-adversaries. By treating OT as a noisy channel, Alice can transmit N bits to Bob using $O(N)$ invocations of OT, in the limit. Because OT is secure, an adversary must corrupt either Alice or Bob to gain any knowledge about the bit stream. Because OT is secure against adaptive 1-adversaries, the bit stream can be equivocated when Alice or Bob is corrupted, to match any desired sequence.

Thus the existence of an OT protocol secure against adaptive 1-adversaries implies the existence of a communication scheme secure against adaptive 1-adversaries.

6 Conclusions

Our results advance toward the 2-adversary case by improving security from static to adaptive 1-adversaries and providing the analytical support to develop stronger methods.

Two intriguing open problems are raised. First, is it possible to combine two protocols with different properties to give a protocol with the combination of those properties? For example, is it possible to combine a weakly R.E. protocol (such as Rabin) with a weakly C.E. protocol (such as Den Boer or Novel) to obtain a hybrid protocol that is weakly R.E. and weakly C.E.?

Second, does there exist an OT protocol that is secure against adaptive 2-adversaries, but which does not require erasing [BH92] or the impractical overhead (numerous third-party assistance and/or $\Omega(k)$ repeated encryptions per bit sent) of [CFGN96]?

A positive answer to the first would enable a positive answer to the second, using results [B96] obtained after the submission of this article. The proofs behind theorems 4 and 5 generalize to show that, if an implementation $\binom{2}{1}$OT of $\binom{2}{1}$OT is secure against static 1-adversaries and both weakly content- and weakly result- equivocable, then $\binom{2}{1}$OT can be made secure against adaptive 2-adversaries by encrypting 3 bits while running the rest of the protocol in the open. The simple and efficient two-party, adaptively-secure encryption scheme of [B96] provides the means to encrypt the additional 3 bits at minimal cost.

References

[B92] D. Beaver. "How to Break a 'Secure' Oblivious Transfer Protocol." *Advances in Cryptology - Eurocrypt '92 Proceedings,* Springer-Verlag LNCS 658, 1993, 285–296.

[B96] D. Beaver. "Adaptively Secure Encryption." Penn State Univ. Tech Report PSU-CSE-96-031, February 7, 1996.

[BH92] D. Beaver, S. Haber. "Cryptographic Protocols Provably Secure Against Dynamic Adversaries." *Advances in Cryptology - Eurocrypt '92 Proceedings,* Springer-Verlag LNCS 658, 1993, 307–323.

[BM89] M. Bellare, S. Micali. "Non-Interactive Oblivious Transfer and Applications." *Advances in Cryptology - Crypto '89 Proceedings,* Springer-Verlag LNCS 435, 1990, 547–557.

[BCR86a] G. Brassard, C. Crépeau, J. Robert. "All or Nothing Disclosure of Secrets." *Advances in Cryptology - Crypto '86 Proceedings,* Springer-Verlag LNCS 263, 1987, 234–238.

[BCR86b] G. Brassard, C. Crépeau, J. Robert. "Information Theoretic Reductions among Disclosure Problems." *Proceedings of the* 27th *FOCS,* IEEE, 1986, 168–173.

[BCC88] G. Brassard, D. Chaum, C. Crépeau. "Minimum Disclosure Proofs of Knowledge." *J. Comput. Systems Sci.* **37**, 1988, 156–189.

[CFGN96] R. Canetti, U. Feige, O. Goldreich, M. Naor. "Adaptively Secure Multiparty Computation." To appear, *Proceedings of the* 28th *STOC,* ACM, 1996.

[C87] C. Crépeau. "Equivalence Between Two Flavours of Oblivious Transfers." *Advances in Cryptology - Crypto '87 Proceedings,* Springer-Verlag LNCS 293, 1988, 350–354.

[Boe91] B. den Boer. "Oblivious Transfer Protecting Secrecy." *Advances in Cryptology - Eurocrypt '91 Proceedings,* Springer-Verlag LNCS 547, 1991, 31–45.

[DH76] W. Diffie, M. Hellman. "New Directions in Cryptography." *IEEE Transactions on Information Theory* **IT-22**, November 1976, 644–654.

[EGL82] S. Even, O. Goldreich, A. Lempel. "A Randomized Protocol for Signing Contracts." *Comm. of the ACM* **28**:6, 1985, 637–647. (Early version: *Proceedings of Crypto 1982,* Springer-Verlag, 1983, 205–210.)

[GM84] S. Goldwasser, S. Micali. "Probabilistic Encryption." *J. Comput. Systems Sci.* **28**, 1984, 270–299.

[GMR89] S. Goldwasser, S. Micali, C. Rackoff. "The Knowledge Complexity of Interactive Proof Systems." *SIAM J. on Computing* **18**:1, 1989, 186–208.

[HL90] L. Harn, H. Lin. "Noninteractive Oblivious Transfer." *Electronics Letters* **26**:10, May 1990, 635–636.

[KMO89] J. Kilian, S. Micali, R. Ostrovsky. "Minimum Resource Zero-Knowledge Proofs." *Proceedings of the* 30th *FOCS,* IEEE, 1989, 1989, 474–479.

[Rab81] M.O. Rabin. "How to Exchange Secrets by Oblivious Transfer." TR-81, Harvard, 1981.

[RSA78] R. Rivest, A. Shamir, L. Adleman. "A Method for Obtaining Digital Signatures and Public Key Cryptosystems." *Communications of the ACM* **21**:2, 1978, 120–126.

Short Discreet Proofs

Joan Boyar[1] René Peralta [*2]

[1] Department of Mathematics and Computer Science, Odense University, Campusvej 55, 5230 Odense M, Denmark (joan@imada.ou.dk)

[2] Japan Advanced Institute of Science and Technology, School of Information Science, Asahidai 15, Tatsunokuchi, Nomi, Ishikawa 923-12, Japan (peralta@cs.uwm.edu)

Abstract. We show how to produce short proofs of theorems such that a distrusting Verifier can be convinced that the theorem is true yet obtains no information about the proof itself. The proofs are non-interactive provided that the quadratic residuosity bit commitment scheme is available to the Prover and Verifier. For typical applications, the proofs are short enough to fit on a floppy disk.

1 Introduction

The main goal of this work is to show how to produce short proofs of theorems such that a distrusting Verifier can be convinced that the theorem is true yet obtains no information about the proof itself. The paper makes use of what we have called "set certification", which consists of proving that a vector of bit commitments encodes a vector of bits in a given set without revealing the bit-vector itself. We have high hopes for what useful results this technique might eventually yield. Since our shortest proofs don't exactly fit any of the published categories of zero-knowledge proofs, we have named them "discreet proofs". As an example of the power of these techniques, we show discreet proofs of knowledge of RSA and DES keys which fit on a floppy disk.

We assume that a bit commitment scheme (blobs scheme) is available as a primitive. The blobs scheme used should satisfy certain properties described in [6, 4, 5]. In addition, they must allow *non-interactive processing* of XOR gates (see [5, 3]). As a concrete example, we choose the following bit commitment scheme, which is based on the "Quadratic Residuosity Assumption" (QRA).

Definition 1. A "Blum integer" is a composite integer $N = P^r Q^s$, with P and Q primes such that $P \equiv Q \equiv 3 \ (mod\ 4)$ and r and s are odd.

* Supported in part by NSF Grant CCR-9207204. This author is currently on sabbatical leave from the University of Wisconsin at Milwaukee.

Ueli Maurer (Ed.): EUROCRYPT '96 Proceedings, LNCS 1070

Definition 2. (Brassard–Crépeau [7]) Let N be a fixed Blum integer produced by the Prover. "QR–blobs" are constructed as follows: the Prover selects a random $x \in Z_N^*$. To commit to a 0 the Prover sends $x^2 \bmod N$. To commit to a 1 the Prover sends $-x^2 \bmod N$.

Notation: If $x = (x_1, \ldots, x_n)$ is a vector of blobs, then $\hat{x}$ will denote the vector in GF_2^n encoded by x. Sometimes we will use $\hat{x}$ before x has been defined. In this case, x will denote any sequence of blobs which encodes $\hat{x}$.

We start by assuming that the Prover-Verifier pair has access to a common source of randomness. Our results here give non-interactive zero-knowledge proofs, in the shared random string model proposed by Blum, Feldman and Micali [1], of length $O(m \log m)$. [3] for the satisfiability of a circuit of size of size m, assuming that the security parameter is $1/m^{O(m)}$. This asymptotic complexity has also been obtained by Damgård [8], who also assumes the QRA, and impressively by Kilian and Petrank [11], who base their results on much more general assumptions. The advantage to our non-interactive proofs is in the constant factors, which are of course of practical interest. Our system beats Damgård's by a factor of about 7.5, and Petrank's and Kilian's by a very large factor.

As a next step towards our efficient discreet proofs, we allow the Prover and Verifier to engage in more than one round in which they *sequentially* query the randomness source. That is, during any round they do not have access to the random bits of the following rounds. We later remove these assumptions by simulating the randomness source. The resulting proof is efficient and non-interactive, but no longer zero-knowledge.

2 Constructible and Certifiable Sets

We start by looking at what can be done without recourse to shared randomness.

Definition 3. A subset S of GF_2^n is said to be *constructible* if it is possible for the Prover to construct, for any chosen $\hat{b} \in S$, a vector $b = (b_1, \ldots, b_n)$ of blobs, along with a proof that $\hat{b}$ belongs to S. The proof must not reveal any information about which element of S is $\hat{b}$. The proof must be non-interactive (hence we simply call it a *certificate*) and must be constructible without using the shared random string.

[3] This is not counting the necessary precomputation for establishing a blob encryption system. An efficient interactive protocol for showing that N is a Blum integer can be found in [16] A non-interactive zero-knowledge proof that N is a Blum integer can be found in [13].

For example, the existence of blob encryption schemes implies that the set $S = \{0,1\}$ is (trivially) constructible. If the blob encryption scheme allows non-interactive processing of XOR gates then the sets $E = \{00, 11\}$ and $D = \{01, 10\}$ are also constructible. Given QR-blobs $b = (b_1, b_2)$, a proof that $\hat{b} \in E$ is simply a square root of $b_1 b_2$ mod N. A proof that $\hat{b} \in D$ is a square root of $-b_1 b_2$ mod N. For details and security proofs related to this scheme see [5].

Definition 4. A subset S of GF_2^n is said to be *certifiable* if, given any vector $b = (b_1, \ldots, b_n)$ of blobs such that $\hat{b} \in S$, the Prover can construct a proof that $\hat{b}$ belongs to S. The proof must not reveal any information about which element of S is $\hat{b}$. The proof must be non-interactive and must not use the shared random string.

The difference between certifiable and constructible sets is that, with a certifiable set, the Prover has not created the blobs herself; this gives her less freedom in producing the proof.

Note that a set which is certifiable is also constructible. Also note that the sets E and D are certifiable when QR-blobs are used. Whenever E is certifiable, it will follow that any set which is constructible is also certifiable. To see this, suppose $x = (x_1, \ldots, x_n)$ is given, and that the Prover wants to certify that $\hat{x}$ belongs to a constructible set S. To do this, the Prover simply constructs $y = (y_1, \ldots, y_n)$ such that $\hat{x} = \hat{y}$ along with a proof that $\hat{y}$ is in S. Then the Prover certifies that $\hat{x}_i \hat{y}_i \in E$ for each i. Thus, *if QR blobs are used, then certifiable sets and constructible sets are the same.*

Lemma 5. *If QR blobs are used, then any subspace S of GF_2^n is certifiable and constructible.*

Proof. Note that S must be the image of GF_2^n under multiplication by an $n \times n$ matrix M over GF_2. To certify a vector $x = (x_1, \ldots, x_n)$ of blobs, the Prover constructs blobs $y = (y_1, \ldots, y_n)$ such that $M\hat{y} = \hat{x}$. Then the Verifier and Prover can non-interactively compute blobs $v = (v_1, \ldots, v_n)$ such that $\hat{v} = M\hat{y}$ (see [3] for more details). The Prover then gives certificates that $\hat{v}_i \hat{x}_i \in E$ for each i. □

By a *linear map* from GF_2^m to GF_2^n we mean a function $f(x) = Mx + b$, where M is an $n \times m$ matrix over GF_2 and $b \in GF_2^n$. Sets of the form $f(S)$ where S is a subspace of GF_2^m will be called *cosets* (each such set is a coset of the subspace $\{v \mid v = Mx; x \in S\}$). The proof of the following lemma is analogous to the proof of Lemma 5. The details are left to the reader.

Lemma 6. *If QR blobs are used, then cosets are certifiable and constructible.*

If, for example, the set $\overline{\wedge} = \{001, 011, 101, 110\}$, which contains the rows of a truth table for a NAND gate, was certifiable, it would follow that a non-interactive zero-knowledge proof for circuit satisfiability is possible without using the shared random string. Unfortunately we have not been able to construct certificates for $\overline{\wedge}$. It may well be that, if we restrict ourselves to QR blobs, then cosets are the only certifiable sets. Other blob encryption schemes can be constructed for which sets corresponding to truth tables of various boolean functions are certifiable. But we have not been able to construct a blob encryption scheme such that a logically complete set of boolean functions is certifiable.

The next best thing to constructible/certifiable sets are sets which can be constructed/certified using the shared random string. Then the proofs that the vector defined belongs to the set would be probabilistic. Thus there would be some chance that the vector in question does not belong to the set, but that probability would be small compared to some specified security parameter.

Definition 7. A subset S of GF_2^n is said to be *probabilistically constructible* if it is possible for the Prover to construct, for any chosen $\hat{b} \in S$, a vector $b = (b_1, \ldots, b_n)$ of blobs, along with a probabilistic proof that $\hat{b}$ belongs to S. The proof must not reveal any information about which element of S is $\hat{b}$.

Definition 8. A subset S of GF_2^n is said to be *probabilistically certifiable* if, given any vector $b = (b_1, \ldots, b_n)$ of blobs such that $\hat{b} \in S$, the Prover can construct a probabilistic proof that $\hat{b}$ belongs to S. The proof must not reveal any information about which element of S is $\hat{b}$.

Both the previous constructions may use the shared random string, and the Verifier must accept an exponentially small probability that $\hat{b} \notin S$. We will show that the set $\overline{\wedge}$ is probabilistically certifiable. This will be used in designing non-interactive zero-knowledge proofs for circuit satisfiability, using a shared random string. It is convenient to first show that two other sets, T and U, defined below, are probabilistically certifiable.

2.1 The Set $T = \{01, 10, 11\}$

Using QR blobs, the shared random string determines, by standard techniques, a sequence $x = (x_1, \ldots, x_n)$ of randomly distributed blobs. This can be done by dividing the bits of the random string into substrings of the appropriate length k for the blobs. The substrings are interpreted as integers. The resulting integers which have Jacobi symbol $+1$ are used directly. Those with Jacobi symbol -1 are multiplied by a fixed number β with Jacobi symbol -1 (if N is constructed such that it is congruent to 5 modulo 8 then $\beta = 2$ will do). This construction requires nk shared random bits.

The number of blobs n will be specified later; it will be a function of the size of the circuit and a security parameter for the proof. With probability $1-2^{-n}$ the vector $\hat{x}$ is not the zero-vector. If the Prover chooses a random $\hat{y} \notin \{0, \hat{x}\}$ and lets $\hat{z} = \hat{x} \oplus \hat{y}$, then the set $A = \{0, \hat{x}, \hat{y}, \hat{z}\}$ is a subspace of GF_2^n. Suppose the Prover writes down two randomly chosen non-zero vectors $\hat{u}, \hat{v}$ from the set A. Note that these two vectors completely define A, since A must equal $\{0, \hat{u}, \hat{v}, \hat{u} \oplus \hat{v}\}$. If the Verifier can be convinced that $\hat{x}$ belongs to A, then this is a probabilistic proof that $\hat{x}$ is one of the three given non-zero bit vectors.

Note that A must be the kernel of a linear homomorphism $f(t) = Mt$ where M is an $(n-2) \times n$ matrix. The matrix M is easily computable non-interactively from u and v. The blob-vector z, corresponding to $M\hat{x}$ can be computed non-interactively ($z_i = \prod_{m_{i,j}=1} x_j \mod N$, where $m_{i,j}$ is the i,j-th entry in M). Now, if $M\hat{x} = 0$, then it follows that $\hat{x} \in A$. Thus, if the Prover opens all the blobs in Mx, and they are all zero, then the Verifier is convinced that x encodes one of three given non-zero bit vectors $\{\hat{x}, \hat{y}, \hat{z}\}$.

For any vector $v \in GF_2^n$, let $v^{(i)}$ denote the ith bit of v. With probability larger than $1 - 3(1/2)^n$, there exist i, j such that $\{\hat{x}^{(i)}\hat{x}^{(j)}, \hat{y}^{(i)}\hat{y}^{(j)}, \hat{z}^{(i)}\hat{z}^{(j)}\} = \{01, 10, 11\}$. To see this, note that there are $4^n - 3 \cdot 2^n + 2$ possible $\hat{x}, \hat{y}$ pairs for which $\hat{x}^{(i)}\hat{y}^{(i)}$ takes at least two values from $\{01, 10, 11\}$ as i ranges from 1 to n (the third value, $\hat{z}^{(i)}$, is determined by the equation $\hat{z} = \hat{x} \oplus \hat{y}$). In the unlikely event that $\hat{x}$ is not the zero-vector yet the $\hat{x}^{(i)}\hat{y}^{(i)}$ do not take at least two values from $\{01, 10, 11\}$, the Prover simply generates another y.

Since the set $\{\hat{x}, \hat{y}, \hat{z}\}$ is known to both Prover and Verifier, both may find a pair (i, j) with the required property.[4] Then the two blobs x_i, x_j encode an element in $T = \{01, 10, 11\}$. The Verifier has no information about which element of T it is. This construction fails only when $\hat{x} = 0$. The probability of this is $1 - (1/2)^n$.

Thus we have shown how the Prover can construct two blobs which commit to a random element of the set $T = \{01, 10, 11\}$. To actually choose which two bits to commit to, the Prover can use the transformation $f(a, b) = (a \oplus b, a)$. Figure 1 shows the effect of this linear transformation.

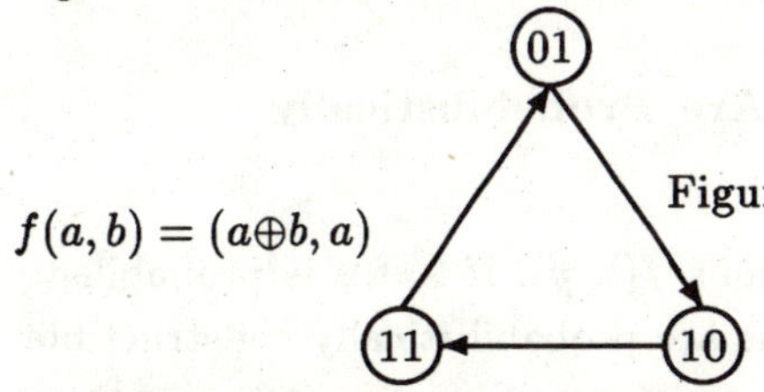

Figure 1: Going from random commitments to chosen commitments in the set T.

[4] Since typically many such pairs (i, j) will exist, some way of choosing one must be specified, e.g. choose (i, j) which minimizes $ni + j$.

To convert from a *random* member of T to a *chosen* member of T, the Prover sends two bits. The two bits tell the Verifier to advance 0, 1, or 2 positions in the diagram. i.e. the bits tell the Verifier how many times to apply the linear transformation f.

Thus we have proven

Lemma 9. *If QR blobs are used, then the set* $T = \{01, 10, 11\}$ *is probabilistically constructible using* n *random blobs with probability of failure bounded above by* $(1/2)^n$. *The certificate consists of* $n-2$ *numbers modulo* N, *two* n*-bit vectors, and two bits.*

As mentioned before, this also implies that the set T is probabilistically certifiable. But we will not make use of this result in this paper. From here on we concentrate on the techniques and cost of probabilistically constructing sets related to boolean functions. Later we also introduce techniques for reducing the amortized cost of certifying many pairs of blobs as belonging to the set T.

2.2 The Set $U = \{0111, 1011, 1101, 1110\}$

If we generate bits $ab \in T$ and $cd \in T$, then $abcd$ may take any value in

$$\{0101, 0110, 0111, 1001, 1010, 1011, 1101, 1110, 1111\}.$$

The set U may be formed by considering only the strings with odd parity. Thus the set U is probabilistically constructible as follows. Construct blobs x, y along with a proof that $\hat{x}\hat{y} \in T$. Do the same for blobs z, w. Now prove that $\hat{x} \oplus \hat{y} \oplus \hat{z} \oplus \hat{w} = 1$ by displaying a square root of $-xyzw$ modulo N. This construction guarantees that $\hat{x}\hat{y}\hat{z}\hat{w} \in U$ and, by Lemma 9, fails with probability no more than $2(1/2)^n$. Thus we have proven

Lemma 10. *If QR blobs are used, then the set* $U = \{0111, 1011, 1101, 1110\}$ *is probabilistically constructible using* $2n$ *random blobs with probability of failure bounded above by* $2(1/2)^n$. *The certificate consists of* $2n-3$ *numbers modulo* N, *four* n*-bit vectors, and four bits.*

2.3 All Two-input Boolean Gates Are Probabilistically Constructible Using QR Blobs

There are sixteen two-input boolean functions $f(x, y)$. If NAND is probabilistically constructible then all sixteen functions are probabilistically constructible. Since it will be more efficient to directly construct gates in a circuit (i.e. without simulating the gates using NAND gates), we show how to probabilistically construct the four most common gates whose truth tables do not form cosets. To do this, use the technique of the previous section to construct blobs (a, b, c, d) which commit to a four-bit string in the set U. The following linear transformations map (a, b, c, d) to sets corresponding to boolean gates:

- $\bigwedge = \{000, 010, 100, 111\}$: $(a \oplus c, a \oplus b, b \oplus c \oplus d)$;
- $\bigvee = \{000, 011, 101, 111\}$: $(a \oplus c, a \oplus b, d)$;
- $\overline{\bigwedge} = \{001, 011, 101, 110\}$: $(a \oplus c, a \oplus b, a)$;
- $\overline{\bigvee} = \{001, 010, 100, 110\}$: $(a \oplus c, a \oplus b, a \oplus b \oplus c)$.

We leave it to the reader to verify that the image of U under each of these transformations is precisely the set of rows of the truth tables for the corresponding boolean function.

There are four more functions whose truth tables do not form cosets ($x \vee \overline{y}; \overline{x} \vee y; x \wedge \overline{y}; \overline{x} \wedge y$). We leave it to the reader to verify that appropriate transformations exist which map U to the truth tables of each of these functions. The following lemma summarizes these observations:

Lemma 11. *If QR blobs are used, then each of the subsets of GF_2^3 corresponding to the rows of the truth tables of two-input boolean functions, can be (probabilistically) constructed. For those functions which form cosets, the certificate is constructible without using the shared random strings and with zero probability of failure. For those functions which do not form cosets, the certificate is constructible using $2n$ random blobs for a probability of failure bounded above by $2(1/2)^n$. The certificate consists of $2n-3$ numbers modulo N, four n-bit vectors, and four bits.*

3 A Non-interactive Zero-knowledge Proof of Circuit Satisfiability

Let C be a circuit with m boolean gates. For simplicity we assume that all gates have 1 or 2 inputs. We assume that QR blobs are available as a primitive. That is, we will not be concerned about any precomputation necessary to establish a blob encryption system between Prover and Verifier.

Prover's algorithm.

0. The Prover commits to the values of all inputs to the circuit.
1. Use the techniques of section 2.3 to probabilistically construct commitments to the inputs and output of each non-coset gate.
2. Use the techniques of section 6 to compute the values of the outputs of coset gates.
3. For each blob x which is the output of some gate and corresponds to an input blob y of a non-coset gate, certify that $\hat{x} = \hat{y}$.

4. Open the blob corresponding to the circuit's output showing it encodes 1.

Verifier's algorithm.

1. Check each gate certification provided by the Prover in step 1 of the proof.
2. Perform step 2 of the Prover's construction just as the Prover does.
3. Verify each certification of step 3 in the proof.

The above protocol can be proven to be non-interactive zero-knowledge in the shared random string model. In the proof, the Simulator produces a shared random tape with commitments to zeros where it needs to cheat and produce something not in T. After doing that, it can get a commitment to the pair 00, claim that the pair is in T, get whatever it wants in U, and then whatever it wants for the gate for which it is cheating.

The protocol above can be extended in the obvious way to circuits with more than one output bit. In addition, although binary gates are enough to build a circuit to compute any boolean function, using gates with more than two inputs will usually reduce the number of gates in the circuit. This, in turn, will usually make the proof shorter. For example, a three-input MAJORITY gate can be simulated by 5 binary gates. However, the cost of probabilistically constructing such a gate is the same as that of probabilistically constructing a single AND gate. Here is how:

$M = \{0000, 0010, 0100, 0111, 1000, 1011, 1101, 1111\}$ is the set that must be constructed. Recall the set U from section 2.2. The set $V = \{abcde \mid abcd \in U; e \in GF_2\}$ is clearly constructible at the same cost as constructing an element from U. Now note that the transformation $abcde \rightarrow (a \oplus c \oplus e, a \oplus b \oplus e, e, b \oplus c \oplus d \oplus e)$ maps V onto M.

Note that step 3 of both the Verifier's and the Prover's algorithm is simply to check that $\hat{x} \oplus \hat{y}$ is the zero vector for many pairs x, y. In sections 4 and 5 we will introduce techniques that allow the Prover to simply skip step 3 and the Verifier to exchange step 3 by a probabilistic constant-cost test. An analogous modification to step 1 will drastically reduce the length of the proof.

4 A Two-round Discreet Proof of Circuit Satisfiability

In lemma 11, we show that constructing input-output blobs for any boolean gate (with probability of error less than $2(1/2)^n$) can be done by opening about $2n$ blobs and sending about $4n$ bits. The purpose of opening the $2n$ blobs is to show that they are all 0. Step 3 of the Prover's and Verifier's algorithm also amounts to showing that a number of blobs are 0. Rather than opening these blobs the Prover can *probabilistically* show that all blobs are 0 as follows: If not all blobs are 0, then the exclusive-or of a random subset of the blobs is 1 with probability

1/2. Thus the Verifier can be convinced that all blobs are 0, with confidence level $1-(1/2)^n$, by the Prover opening n non-interactively computed blobs. However, one more query to the randomness source is needed to select n random subsets of the blobs (alternatively, the Verifier could select the random subsets). Thus, if we allow two rounds in our proof, then the Prover need only send about $4n$ m bits plus n blob openings to prove circuit satisfiability with exponentially small probability of getting away with a false proof.[5] This is an extremely short zero-knowledge proof. In the next section we see how these observations allow us to construct practical non-interactive proofs. We also postpone, until section 5.1, the discussion of the actual error probability as a function of n and m.

5 How to Construct Non-interactive Discreet Proofs by Simulating the Randomness Source

It is a standard technique in cryptographic protocol design to substitute a random "challenge string" by a string constructed deterministically but in such a way that the Prover has no control. For example, Fiat-Shamir's scheme [10], Schnorr's scheme [15], and the DSA all use a one-way hash function to construct a "challenge" to the Prover, hence eliminating the need for interaction.

The proofs described in this work consist of rounds where Prover and Verifier first obtain a random string from a trusted source and then the Prover sends a message to the Verifier. We can replace the random string by the output of a cryptographically secure pseudo-random number generator. For the first round we seed the generator with the description of the circuit. For the following rounds[6] we seed the generator with the Prover's message in the previous round. The generator must be run in the forward direction (so that both the Prover and the Verifier can compute the output without interaction). Note that the simulation of the randomness source converts the two-round protocol into a one-round (i.e. non-interactive) proof. Note also that the random strings are not part of the proof. Considering the security parameter a constant (or even $1/m^{O(m)}$), the simulation yields a non-interactive proof of size $O(m \log m)$ bits (see section 5.1 for the explanation of the $\log(m)$ factor). The theoretical justification is, of course, not as clean as that for non-interactive zero-knowledge proofs as introduced by Blum et. al. (see [2, 9]). However, our proofs are short enough to be used in practice (e.g. they will typically fit on a floppy disk). A more precise analysis of the length and the error probability follows.

---

[5] The error probability is slightly more than $1-(1/2)^n$. We will be more precise about this in section 5.

[6] We simulate only two rounds in this paper, but the technique is applicable to any number of rounds.

There is a temptation to apply our methods to earlier interactive zero-knowledge proofs for circuit satisfiability (such as [7] [5],[3]) in order to obtain even more efficient non-interactive proofs. This fails because in those protocols, the Verifier's challenges are too short when the security parameter is $1/m^{O(m)}$. This means that while producing the non-interactive proof, a cheating Prover can simply try random values until it finds one that satisfies all the challenges.

5.1 Performance

Until now we have been assuming the worse case scenario: that all gates in the circuit are non-coset gates. This is clearly unrealistic. Therefore we introduce a new parameter θ to denote the number of non-coset gates of the circuit (The tired reader may choose to think of the circuit as containing only AND, XOR, and NOT gates. In this case θ is just the number of AND gates).

Recall that k is the size of the Blum integer N. The length of the proof is essentially $n(4\theta + k)$ where n is a security parameter which determines the probability that the Prover can get away with a false proof.

There are two events which *might* allow the Prover to cheat:[7]

1. In the process of constructing the commitments to a gate, a vector $\hat{x}$ derived from the random source is the zero vector.
2. In the final step of the proof not all blobs are 0, yet the exclusive-or of the n random subsets of the blobs are all 0.

A moment's thought will convince the reader that the probability of the first of these events dominates for moderately large values of θ. Therefore we concentrate on this event only. There are 4θ vectors to worry about. The probability that at least one of these vectors is 0 is $1-(1-(1/2)^n)^{4\theta}$. Letting $n = \log_2(\theta)+r$, we have that $1-(1-(1/2)^n)^{4\theta} \longrightarrow 2^{2-r}$.

In practice, we can take $r = 50$. The convergence is fast. Thus the length of the proof, in bits, is

$$(4\theta + k)(\log_2(\theta) + 50) = 200\,\theta + 4\theta\log_2(\theta) + k\log_2(\theta) + 50\,k. \qquad (I)$$

Recent developments in factorization suggest we best take $k = 1024$ (two succinct and up-to-date discussions on the status of factorization algorithms and their implementations are contained in [12, 14]). Nevertheless, the term $200\,\theta$ dominates this expression for practical applications.

[7] In practice even if one of these events occur, the Prover is unlikely to be able to cheat.

6 Length of Discreet Proofs For RSA and DES

The aim of this section is to show that our proofs are short enough to be used in practice for commonly used cryptographic functions. No attempt at circuit optimization has been done. That is the subject of work in progress. We note that the construction of circuits which minimize the number of non-coset gates is a new problem. Until now, circuit designers would have had no reason to consider such a problem.

Suppose we want to prove to the world that we know a DES key K such that $\text{DES}_K(X) = Y$ for public X and Y. The techniques introduced in this paper involve constructing a circuit for DES where the unknown input is the key K. The circuit must be constructed so as to minimize the number of AND gates. In DES, AND gates are only needed for indexing into the S-boxes. A straightforward construction, without exploiting any structure in the S-boxes (there shouldn't be any ☺), yields a circuit with 57 AND gates per S-box. There are 8 S-boxes and each is used 16 times. Therefore the number of AND gates in our circuit is 7296. This is the value of θ defined in the previous section. Equation (I) then yields approximately 240 kilobytes.

Let us now consider proving to the world that we know and RSA decryption key d. Since knowing d is poly-time equivalent to knowing the factorization of N, we can prove this fact instead. Therefore all we need is a circuit which multiplies two inputs P and Q, verifies that the product is equal to a hard-wired N, and verifies that P is not 1 or N.

Assume N is of length 2 d bits. Standard techniques yield a circuit of size about $d^{1.6}$. For $d = 512$, equation (I) yields approximately 700 kilobytes.

References

1. Blum, M., Feldman, P., Micali, S.: Non-interactive zero-knowledge and its applications. In Proceedings of the 20th ACM Symposium on Theory of Computing (1988) pp. 103-112.
2. Blum, De Santis, Micali, Persiano: Non-interactive zero-knowledge. SIAM Journal on Computing **20** (1991) 1084–1118.
3. Boyar, J., Brassard, G., Peralta, R.: Subquadratic zero-knowledge. In Proceedings of the 32th IEEE Symposium on Foundations of Computer Science (1991) pp. 69–78 (to appear in JACM).
4. Boyar, J., Krentel, M., Kurtz, S.: A discrete logarithm implementation of zero-knowledge blobs. Journal of Cryptology **2** (1990) 63–76.
5. Boyar, J., Lund, C., Peralta, R.: On the communication complexity of zero-knowledge proofs. Journal of Cryptology **6** (1993) 65–85.

6. Brassard, G., Chaum, D., Crépeau, C.: Minimum disclosure proofs of knowledge. Journal of Computer and System Sciences **37** (1988) 156–189.
7. Brassard, G., Crépeau, C.: Zero-knowledge simulation of boolean circuits. In Advances in Cryptology - Proceedings of CRYPTO 86 (1987) vol. 263 of Lecture Notes in Computer Science, Springer-Verlag pp. 223–233.
8. Damgård, I.: Non-interactive circuit based proofs and non-interactive perfect zero-knowledge with preprocessing. In Advances in Cryptology - Proceedings of EUROCRYPT 92 (1993) vol. 658 of Lecture Notes in Computer Science, Springer-Verlag pp. 341–355.
9. Feige, U., Lapidot, D., Shamir, A.: Multiple non-interactive zero-knowledge proofs based on a single random string. In Proceedings of the 31th IEEE Symposium on Foundations of Computer Science (1990) pp. 308–317.
10. Fiat, A., Shamir, A.: How to prove yourself: practical solutions to identification and signature problems. In Advances in Cryptology - Proceedings of CRYPTO 86 (1987) vol. 263 of Lecture Notes in Computer Science, Springer-Verlag pp. 186–194.
11. Kilian, J., Petrank, E.: An efficient non-interactive zero-knowledge proof ystem for NP with general assumptions. Technical Report No. TR95-038, Electronic Colloquium in Computational Complexity (ECCC), July 1995.
12. Lenstra, A. K.: Factoring integers using the web and number field sieve. In Proceedings of JAIST International Forum on Multimedia and Information Security (1995) Japan Advanced Institute of Science and Technology pp. 93–113.
13. De Santis, A., Di Crescenzo, G., Persiano, G.: Secret sharing and perfect zero knowledge. In Advances in Cryptology - Proceedings of CRYPTO 93 (1993) vol. 773 of Lecture Notes in Computer Science, Springer-Verlag pp. 73–84.
14. Odlyzko, A.: The future of integer factorization. In Proceedings of JAIST International Forum on Multimedia and Information Security (1995) Japan Advanced Institute of Science and Technology pp. 139–151.
15. Schnorr, C.: Efficient signature generation for smart cards. Journal of Cryptology **4** (1991) 161–174.
16. van de Graaf, J., Peralta, R.: A simple and secure way to show the validity of your public key. In Advances in Cryptology - Proceedings of CRYPTO 87 (1988) vol. 293 of Lecture Notes in Computer Science, Springer-Verlag pp. 128–134.

Designated Verifier Proofs and Their Applications

Markus Jakobsson[1] *, Kazue Sako[2], and Russell Impagliazzo[1]**

[1] Department of Computer Science and Engineering,
University of California, San Diego, La Jolla, CA 92093.
Email: {markus,russell}@cs.ucsd.edu.
[2] NEC Corporation, 4-1-1 Miyazaki Miyamae, Kawasaki 216, JAPAN
Email: sako@sbl.cl.nec.co.jp.

Abstract. For many proofs of knowledge it is important that only *the verifier designated by the confirmer* can obtain any conviction of the correctness of the proof. A good example of such a situation is for undeniable signatures, where the confirmer of a signature wants to make sure that only the intended verifier(s) in fact can be convinced about the validity or invalidity of the signature.
Generally, authentication of messages and off-the-record messages are in conflict with each other. We show how, using designation of verifiers, these notions can be combined, allowing authenticated but private conversations to take place. Our solution guarantees that *only* the specified verifier can be convinced by the proof, even if he shares all his secret information with entities that want to get convinced.
Our solution is based on *trap-door commitments* [4], allowing the designated verifier to open up commitments in any way he wants. We demonstrate how a trap-door commitment scheme can be used to construct designated verifier proofs, both interactive and non-interactive. We examplify the verifier designation method for the confirmation protocol for undeniable signatures.

1 Introduction

Background. When undeniable signatures [5] were introduced, the following scenario served as a motivation: A software vendor puts digital signatures on its products to allow it to authenticate them as correct, free of viruses, etc, but only wants paying customers to be able to verify the validity of these signatures. One property of undeniable signatures is that their validity or invalidity cannot be verified without interaction with a prover. This in itself, however, only allows the prover to decide *when* a signature is verified, and not *by whom* (or even by

* Research supported by NSF YI Award CCR-92-570979, Sloan Research Fellowship BR-3311, and The Royal Swedish Academy of Sciences.
** Research supported by NSF YI Award CCR-92-570979 and Sloan Research Fellowship BR-3311.

Ueli Maurer (Ed.): EUROCRYPT '96 Proceedings, LNCS 1070

how many), because of blackmailing [11, 22] and mafia[3] attacks [10]. In order to avoid these types of attacks, in both of which the conviction is transferred to one or several hidden co-verifiers, the prover must be able to designate *who* will be convinced by a proof.

Another situation where it is important for the prover to designate who can be convinced by the validity of a proof is when a voting center wants only a voter himself to be convinced that the vote he cast was counted. Here, it is important for the voter Bob to be convinced by the proof, but we want to prevent an armed coercer, Cindy, to be able to force Bob to prove to her how he voted. Other methods – not clearly stating designation of verifiers – of avoiding such attacks in order to obtain receipt-free electronic voting schemes were studied in [3, 34].

RESULTS. This paper suggests a solution, *designation of verifiers*, that resolves the conflict between authenticity and privacy, and dodges the described attacks by limiting who can be convinced by a proof. We say that we *designate a verifier* in a proof when we acertain that nobody but this participant can be convinced by the proof. The intuition behind the solution can be described in one sentence: *Instead of proving Θ, Alice will prove the statement "Either Θ is true, or I am Bob."* Bob will certainly trust that Θ is true upon seeing such a proof[4], but if Bob diverts the proof to Cindy, Cindy will have no reason at all to believe that Θ is true, as Bob is fully capable of proving himself to be Bob. We show how, with only small changes in the confirmation protocol for undeniable signatures, the confirmer can designate verifiers. Also we demonstrate that we can have designated verifier non-interactive undeniable signatures, which combines desireable properties of ordinary signatures and undeniable signatures.

In order to solve the problem, we will use trap-door commitment schemes, also known as chameleon commitment schemes, introduced by Brassard, Chaum and Crépeau [4]. Assume the trap-door information is known to Bob only. If Alice uses the scheme to commit to a value, Bob will trust her commitment as Alice cannot find collisions, but if the proof is diverted to Cindy by Bob, Cindy has no reason to trust the commitment, as Bob can decommit as he wishes. It is important to point out that the verifier designation holds even if the designated verifier chooses to reveal secret information to cooperating co-verifiers, since Bob can *still* find collisions after revealing secret information.

RELATED WORK. A large variety of digital signature schemes (e.g., [12, 23, 33]) has been introduced, in which the validity of the signatures is publicly verifiable. On the other hand, there also are more authentication-like schemes, such as schemes built on zero-knowledge protocols, e.g., the Feige Fiat Shamir identification protocol [16], where the authenticity of a message cannot be verified by *anyone* once the interactive verification session is terminated. In between

---

3 Also known as the man-in-the-middle attack.

4 Technically, this is not a *proof* of Θ, but an argument, as a powerful prover could cheat by calculating the verifier's secret key from his or her public key.

these two schemes are undeniable signatures [5], which can be freely distributed and verified any number of times, but only with the cooperation of a confirmer. However, several cooperating verifiers can each be convinced about the validity of the signature in these interactive protocols, as is shown in [11, 22]. (Here, the verifiers jointly set the challenge in a way so that none of them can determine the outcome.) This attack shows that designation of messages is a necessary tool for authentication of private messages. A well-known method of doing this is for the sender of a message to encrypt it using a secret key that only he and the receiver knows, but this only applies to plain messages and not to proofs. Still, it is a form of verifier designation, as it allows the receiver of a message to simulate identical transcripts, thereby making it impossible to prove that the transcript indeed originated with the claimed sender.

In [13], Dolev, Dwork and Naor presented a solution, non-malleable cryptography, avoiding some mafia-attacks. In their scenario, researcher A has proven that $P \neq NP$, and wants to convince researcher B about this in a zero-knowledge fashion, but without allowing this person to convince researcher C and claim credit for the discovery himself. However, researcher C *will* be convinced that the statement proven is true, although she will know that A, not B, is the prover. Thus, conviction is transferable, but credits not. However, in the cases we presented, where the sender *does not* want the conversation to be possible to trace back to him or her, this is not sufficient. If a *designated verifier proof* is used, it will be impossible for a third party to be convinced about the validity of a proof sent from A to B. This holds *even if B should cooperate with C.*

OUTLINE. We start by explaining our model in Section 2, followed by definitions and examples in Section 3. We examplify our method in Section 4 by showing how to designate verifiers in the verification protocol for undeniable signatures. A designated verifier proof can be made heuristically non-interacative, and we give examples and applications for this in Section 5. In Section 6, we show how the result can be extended to multiple designated verifiers. We discuss practical issues in Section 7, and an alternative (and stronger) definition of designated verifier in the Appendix.

2 Approach and Model

APPROACH. Alice wants to prove to Bob – but only to him – that the statement Θ is true. Let Φ_{Bob} be the statement "I know Bob's secret key." Using the methods soon to be introduced, Alice will prove $\Theta \vee \Phi_{Bob}$ to Bob, who will be convinced that Θ is true (or that his secret key has been compromised.) Given that Bob knows his secret key, Cindy will not be convinced that Θ is true after seeing a proof of $\Theta \vee \Phi_{Bob}$, which holds even if Bob cooperates with her and shares secret information with her. This is so since Bob can produce such a proof himself, independently of whether Θ is true or not.

PARTICIPANTS. All participants are assumed to be polynomial-time limited. Partipants must only be able to be convinced by a proof designated to them if they are able to simulate transcripts of the same distribution themselves, i.e., they have to know their secret key. (We discuss methods to ensure this in section 7.)

THREAT MODEL. It is important to remember that we want to reach our goal of designating who will be convinced by a proof for pragmatic reasons, in order for the use of authentication of data not to be possible to abuse with a purpose of damaging the interests of the legal participants *in the real, physical world.* Should an attacker be in total control of Bob's physical and mental self, then we mean that the attacker has already achieved his goal. Also, in a sense, the attacker has *become* Bob. We therefore mean that it is realistic assumption to make that the verifier has *not* totally lost control of his ability to access his data, perform calculations and freely communicate.

This, in particular, excludes two possible attacks:

1. *The Suicide Attack*
   Bob kills all his aliases, provides the attacker, Cindy, with his secret data, and then self-destructs. (This effectively transfers the notion of "being Bob" from Bob to Cindy.)
2. *The Demon Attack*
   Cindy locks Bob (and all his aliases) up, preventing him from communicating with anybody but her, and forces him to perform certain calculations and prove them correct. (This corresponds to taking total command of somebody's mental functions.)

TRUST MODEL. Let us call a person who wants to act as a verifier in a proof, but is not designated by the prover, a *hidden verifier.* We assume that a hidden verifier, Cindy, will not trust the designated verifier, Bob, that he did not produce the transcript for the proof of $\Theta \vee \Phi_{Bob}$, where Φ_{Bob} is a proof of knowledge of Bob's secret key, or she could just as well take his word for that Θ is true in the first place, without seeing a proof of it.
In Appendix A, we introduce a weaker trust model and a correspondingly stronger notion of designated verifier, *strong designated verifier*, in which Cindy trusts Bob to be perfectly honest, i.e., never to engage in a protocol that is not part of the system. (Here, trying to convince Cindy that $\Theta \vee \Phi_{Bob}$ is true is *not* one of the prescribed protocols.) However, Cindy can try to trick Bob to convince her by interacting in "legal" protocols. The reason why this is a *weaker* trust model and a stronger security notion is that a protocol that is *designated verifier* is not necessarily *strong designated verifier*, whereas the converse holds.

3 Definitions

In this section, we give informal and intuitive definitions.

Definition 1 Designated Verifier.
Let (P_A, P_B) be a protocol for Alice to prove the truth of the statement θ to Bob.

We say that Bob is a *designated verifier* [5] if the following is true: For any protocol (P_A, P'_B, P_C) involving Alice, Bob, and Cindy, in which Bob proves the truth of ϑ to Cindy, there is another protocol (P''_B, P_C) such that Bob can perform the calculations of P''_B, and Cindy cannot distinguish transcripts of (P_A, P'_B, P_C) from those of (P''_B, P_C).

Definition 2 Trap-Door Commitment. (also see [4])
Let c be a function with input (y_i, w, r), where y_i is the public key of the user who will be able to invert c. Here, the secret key corresponding to y_i is x_i, $w \in W$ is the value committed to and r a random string. We say that c is a *trap-door commitment scheme* if and only if

1. no polynomial-time machine can, given y_i, find a collision (w_1, r_1), (w_2, r_2) such that $c(y_i, w_1, r_1) = c(y_i, w_2, r_2)$
2. no polynomial-time machine can, given y_i and $c(y_i, w, r)$, output w.
3. there is a polynomial-time machine that given any quadruple (x_i, w_1, r_1, w_2) in the set of possible quadruples finds r_2 such that $c(y_i, w_1, r_1) = c(y_i, w_2, r_2)$ for the public key y_i corresponding to the secret key x_i.

Let us give two examples of trap-door schemes:

Example Trap-door commitment scheme 1. [4]
Secret key of the receiver: $x_B \in_u Z_q$.
Public key of the receiver: $y_B = g^{x_B} \bmod p$. Here, $p = q * k + 1$ for two primes p, q and $k \in Z$; g is a generator of the subgroup G_q of Z_p^*, of order q.
Value to commit to: $w \in Z_q$.
Commitment: Alice selects $r \in_u Z_q$. The commitment is $c = g^w {y_B}^r \bmod p$.
Decommitment: Alice sends Bob (w, r).

Example Trap-door commitment scheme 2. [8]
Secret decryption scheme of the receiver: $D_B(.)$
Public encryption scheme of the receiver: $E_B(.)$
Value to commit to: $w \in Range(E_B)$.
Commitment: Alice will uniformly at random select $r \in Range(E_B)$. She calculates a commitment $c = E_B(w) \oplus E_B(r)$, where $\oplus$ is a combiner such as XOR.
Decommitment: Alice sends Bob (w, r).

Scheme 2 is a trap-door commitment scheme if arbitrary collisions (w_1, r_1), (w_2, r_2) such that $E_B(w_1) \oplus E_B(r_1) = E_B(w_2) \oplus E_B(r_2)$ can be found if and only if $D_B(.)$ is known. The use of e.g. RSA [33] seems plausible.

4 Interactive Designated Verifier Proof of Undeniable Signatures

We show how to change the normal verification protocol for undeniable signatures to make it designated verifier. We will base our scheme on the confirmation

[5] Occasionally, we will also refer to the (prover's part of the) corresponding protocol as designated verifier.

scheme for undeniable signatures[6][6]. We use denotation similar to that in the original scheme: We will let p be a large prime, g a generator of G_q, participant i's secret key is x_i and his public key is $y_i = g^{x_i} \bmod p$. If m is a message, participant i's signature on m will be $s = m^{x_i} \bmod p$.

The following scheme is the confirmation scheme for undeniable signatures, given in [6]:

1. Bob uniformly at random selects two numbers a and b from Z_q and calculates $v = m^a g^b \bmod p$. Bob sends Alice v.
2. Alice calculates $w = v^{x_A} \bmod p$. She calculates a commitment c to w and sends c to Bob.
3. Bob sends (m, s, a, b) to Alice, who verifies that v is of the right form.
4. Alice decommits to c by sending w, and any possible random string r used for the commitment to Bob. Bob verifies that $w = s^a {y_A}^b \bmod p$ and that the commitment c was correctly formed.

Making it Designated Verifier: The above scheme can be made designated verifier by letting c be a trap-door commitment scheme, using the public key of the designated verifier.

5 Non-interactive Designated Verifier Proofs and Their Applications

In this section we present a *non-interactive* designated verifier proof of an undeniable signature. Such a scheme bridges the gap between publicly verifiable digital signatures and undeniable signatures, in that it limits who can verify it *without help from the prover*, but does not necessitate interaction. Still, and in contrast to publicly verifiable signatures that are made designated verifier, they can be used for contracts, etc., as their validity can be verified when the prover agrees to this. We believe that this property makes them a very useful tool in balancing the need for privacy against that of authenticity.

First, we discuss a general method to transform ordinary three-move zero-knowledge protocols to non-interactive designated verifier proofs. Then, we examplify this method by showing a non-interactive undeniable signature verification scheme with designation of verifiers. Our technique can be used to obtain non-interactive, non-transitive signatures [28].

Non-Interactive Designated Verifier Proofs

An ordinary three-move zero-knowledge protocol can be described as a commit - challenge - response protocol. The Fiat-Shamir technique [18] is a famous trick for making such a protocol non-interactive, while preserving the security of the protocol in a practical manner [17]. By generating challenges from a hashed value

[6] We show the "folklore generalization" of this scheme, in which the commitment scheme is not specified.

of multiple commitments, the three moves can be collapsed into one single move. However, this resulting transcript is in itself a transitive proof whose correctness can be verified by anyone.

In order to construct a designated verifier proof, we modify the scheme and use a trap-door commitment in the commitment stage. It becomes a designated verifier proof, as Bob, the designated verifier, can always use his trap-door to simulate a transcript for any statements. Cindy cannot distinguish a valid proof of a true statement from an invalid proof forged by Bob.

A Non-interactive Undeniable Signature Scheme

We use the same denotation as in section 4, where the confirmation scheme consists of a three-move zero-knowledge protocol for proving that Alice's public key y_A and the signature s have a common exponent x_A with respect to a public generator g and the message m [7]. This is a corresponding non-interactive designated verifier proof:

Constructing a proof:
The prover, Alice, selects $w, r, t \in_u Z_q$ and calculates

$$\begin{cases} c = g^w {y_B}^r \bmod p \\ G = g^t \bmod p \\ M = m^t \bmod p \\ h = hash_q(c, G, M) \\ d = t + x_A(h + w) \bmod q \end{cases}$$

where $hash_q$ gives you a hashed value in Z_q. The prover sends (w, r, G, M, d) to the verifier, Bob.

Verifying a proof:
The designated verifier can verify a proof by calculating

$$\begin{cases} c = g^w {y_B}^r \bmod p \\ h = hash_q(c, G, M). \end{cases}$$

and verifying that

$$\begin{cases} G\, {y_A}^{h+w} = g^d \bmod p \\ M\, s^{h+w} = m^d \bmod p. \end{cases}$$

Simulating transcripts:
The designated verifier can simulate correct transcripts by selecting $d, \alpha, \beta \in_u Z_q$ and calculate

$$\begin{cases} c = g^\alpha \bmod p \\ G = g^d {y_A}^{-\beta} \bmod p \\ M = m^d s^{-\beta} \bmod p \\ h = hash_q(c, G, M) \\ w = \beta - h \bmod q \\ r = (\alpha - w){x_B}^{-1} \bmod q. \end{cases}$$

[7] A disavowal scheme can also be described as a series of 3-move protocols[9] which can be merged in a non-interactive designated verifier proof.

6 Extension to Multiple Designated Verifiers

If Alice in a proof of knowledge wants to convince a set of n verifiers, $\{\text{Bob}_i\}_{i=1}^n$, but only these, the trivial approach is for Alice to convince each individual verifier, Bob_i, in an individual proof.

A more appealing approach is the following solution: We will use exactly the same protocol as for only one designated verifier, but let c be a function that is one-way to each coalition of less than n of the designated verifiers, but invertible if they all cooperate. This can easily be done by letting the secret key corresponding to the public key used be distributed among all the n designated verifiers so that they all need to cooperate to calculate it. It is, however, not necessary for the designated verifiers to share a secret in advance. For example, using the DL-based commitment scheme (trap-door commitment scheme number one,) the following modified commitment scheme can be used to extend to multiple verifiers, Bob_1 to Bob_n:

Trapdoor commitment scheme 1, modified for multiple verifiers:
Individual secret keys of the receivers: $\{x_{B_i}\}_{i=1}^n$, $x_{B_i} \in_u Z_q$.
Shared secret key of the receivers: $x_B = \sum_{i=1}^n x_{B_i} \bmod q$.
Individual public keys of the receivers: $\{y_{B_i}\}_{i=1}^n$, $y_{B_i} \in Z_p$.
Shared public key of the receivers: $y_B = \prod_{i=1}^n y_{B_i} \bmod p$.
Value to commit to: $w \in Z_q$.
Commitment: *Alice selects* $r \in_u Z_q$. *The commitment is* $c = g^w {y_B}^r \bmod p$.
Decommitment: *Alice sends all the Bobs* (w, r).

Conviction. Each designated verifier would be convinced by the proof as long as he knows that his share of the secret key has not been compromised. However, no "outsider", Cindy, would be able to receive conviction, as the set of designated verifiers, $\{\text{Bob}\}_{i=1}^n$, could have cooperated to cheat her. This they can do without revealing their personal shares of the secret key to each other.

7 Practical Issues

In order to assure that a designated verifier who can be convinced by a proof indeed also is able to simulate identically distributed transcripts, we have to require that he can only be convinced of a proof designated to him if he knows his secret key.

Depending on the situation, different relationships between logical and computational entities will have to be enforced. Sometimes, it is sufficient to define a logical entity as the set of computational entities who must cooperate in order to output the secret key corresponding to the public key of the logical entity and not enforce any particular relationship. One example where this may be sufficient is for a company being the logical entity and its employees being the computational entities. It is in the best interest of the company not to allow a competitor to be part of the set of computational entities, as this makes the company rely on its competitor for signing, decryption, etc. However, this way of defining logical entities is not appropriate in all settings. We can find an example of such a setting in the motivation for undeniable signatures: A software company will prove validity of signatures, and thereby virus freeness of the corresponding programs, but only to clients who buy this service. Here, the company wants to make sure that it is not possible for several computational entities to be one logical entity, thereby letting them all be convinced by one proof of validity.

We see that it is of interest that Bob cannot convince Cindy that he does not know his own secret key, or she *would* trust that Θ is true upon seeing a proof of $\Theta \vee \Phi_{Bob}$. Bob can convince her that he does not know his secret key in one of two ways:

1. Bob shows Cindy a preimage over a one-way function of his public key, other than his secret key. If Cindy believes that Bob cannot calculate a triple (public key, secret key, other preimage), then she believes that Bob does not know his secret key, and consequently, cannot prove Φ_{Bob}.
2. Bob and Cindy secret shares his secret key, which they generated together, and Cindy has not released her share of it to Bob. Here, Cindy and Bob has to collude before the proof session started in order for Cindy to be convinced by the proof of Θ.

We suggest two alternative approaches for ensuring that Bob cannot transfer the conviction using the former technique:

1. Before the proof of knowledge of $\Theta \vee \Phi_{Bob}$ from Alice to Bob, Bob has to prove knowledge of Φ_{Bob} to Alice.
2. When proving $\Theta \vee \Phi_{Bob}$, Alice probablistically encrypts the transcripts she sends (or parts thereof) using an encryption function for which decryption abilities enables arbitrary collision finding for the trap-door commitment scheme used. This is easily done for our second example of trap-door commitment schemes.

In order to avoid the second "attack", the sharing of the secret key, we suggest two possible approaches:

1. When Bob is registering his public key to have it certified, he has to prove knowledge of his secret key to the Certification Agency, in a setting where he can *only* communicate with the CA (e.g., a smart-card setting.)
2. When registering his public key, Bob presents his secret key to the CA, who then has to be trusted to neither divulge it to someone else nor to prove knowledge of it.

In an implementation, a combination of the above approaches has to be taken to ensure that the receiver of a readable[8] proof indeed knows his secret key, and that the prover is convinced of this.

[8] Referring to the possible use of probabilistic encryption.

8 Conclusion

We have presented a method to designate verifiers, allowing authentication to be combined with privacy (in the sense that the authentication cannot be forwarded to a non-designated party.) We have shown how the verification protocol for undeniable signatures can be made designated verifier, and have demonstrated both an interactive and a non-interactive version. We have discussed how the results can be extended to multiple designated verifiers, and briefly treated practical issues.

Acknowledgements

The first author wishes to thank Mihir Bellare, David Chaum, Giovanni Di Crescenzo, Niels Ferguson and Moti Yung for interesting and helpful comments. Special thanks to Ivan Damgård for valuable comments and important guidance during the preparation of the final version. Finally, we wish to thank the anonymous referees for important feedback.

References

1. M. Bellare, S. Goldwasser, "New Paradigms for Digital Signatures and Message Authentication Based on Non-Interactive Zero Knowledge Proofs," Crypto '89, pp. 194-211.
2. M. Bellare, S. Micali, "How to Sign Given Any Trapdoor Function," 20th Annual STOC, 1988, pp. 32-42.
3. J.C. Benaloh, D. Tuinstra, "Receipt-Free Secret-Ballot Elections," 26th Annual STOC, 1994, pp. 544-553.
4. G. Brassard, D. Chaum, C. Crépeau, "Minimum Disclosure Proofs of Knowledge," Journal of Computer and System Sciences, Vol. 37, No. 2, Oct. 1988, pp. 156-189
5. D. Chaum, H. van Antwerpen, "Undeniable Signatures," Crypto '89, pp. 212-216
6. D. Chaum, "Zero-Knowledge Undeniable Signatures," Eurocrypt '90, pp. 458-464
7. D. Chaum, E. van Heijst, B. Pfitzmann, "Cryptographically Strong Undeniable Signatures, Unconditionally Secure for the Signer," Crypto '91, pp. 470-484
8. D. Chaum, personal communication
9. I. Damgård, personal communication
10. Y. Desmedt, C. Goutier, S. Bengio, "Special Uses and Abuses of the Fiat-Shamir Passport Protocol," Crypto '87, pp. 21-39
11. Y. Desmedt, M. Yung, "Weaknesses with Undeniable Signature Schemes," Eurocrypt '91, pp. 205-220
12. W. Diffie, M.E. Hellman, "New Directions in Cryptography," IEEE Transactions on Information Theory, v. IT-22, n. 6, Nov 1976, pp. 644-654
13. D. Dolev, C. Dwork, M. Naor, "Non-Malleable Cryptography," 23rd Annual STOC, 1991, pp. 542-552
14. T. ElGamal, "A public key cryptosystem and a signature scheme based on discrete logarithm," IEEE IT 31 (1985), pp. 469-472
15. S. Even, O. Goldreich, S. Micali, "On-Line/Off-Line Digital Signatures," Crypto '89, pp. 263-275

16. U. Feige, A. Fiat, A. Shamir, "Zero Knowledge Proofs of Identity," Proceedings of the 19th annual ACM Symposium on Theory of Computing, pp. 210-217
17. U. Feige, A. Shamir, "Witness Indistinguishable and Witness Hiding Protocols," 22nd Annual STOC, 1990, p. 416–426.
18. A. Fiat, A. Shamir, "How to prove yourself; practical solution to identification and signature problems," Crypto '86, pp. 186-194
19. Z. Galil, S. Haber, M. Yung, "Symmetric Public-Key Cryptosystems", submitted to J. of Cryptology
20. S. Goldwasser, S. Micali, "Probabilistic Encryption & How To Play Mental Poker Keeping Secret All Partial Information," Proceedings of the 18th ACM Symposium on the Theory of Computing, 1982, pp. 270-299
21. O. Goldreich, S. Micali, A. Widgerson, "Proofs that Yield Nothing but their Validity or All Languages in NP Have Zero-Knowledge Proof Systems," Journal of the ACM, vol. 38, n. 1, 1991, pp. 691-729
22. M. Jakobsson, "Blackmailing using Undeniable Signatures", Eurocrypt '94, pp. 425-427
23. R.C. Merkle, "Secure Communication over Insecure Channels," Communications of the ACM, v. 21, n. 4, 1978, pp. 294-299
24. R. Merkle, "A Certified Digital Signature," Crypto '89, pp. 218-238
25. S. Micali, A. Shamir, "An Improvement of the Fiat-Shamir Identification and Signature Scheme," Crypto '88, pp. 244-247
26. M. Naor, M. Yung, "Universal One-Way Hash Functions and their Cryptographic Application," 21st Annual STOC, 1989, pp. 33-43
27. T. Okamoto, K. Ohta, "Divertible Zero-Knowledge Interactive Proofs and Commutative Random Self-Reducibility," Eurocrypt '89, pp. 134-149
28. T.Okamoto, K. Ohta, "How to Utilize Randomness of Zero-Knowledge Proofs," Crypto '90, pp 456–475.
29. H. Ong, C. P. Schnorr, "Fast signature generation with a Fiat-Shamir like scheme," Eurocrypt 90, pp. 432-440
30. T. Pedersen, "Distributed Provers with Applications to Undeniable Signatures," Eurocrypt '91, pp. 221-238
31. J.-J. Quisquater, L.S. Guillou, "A practical zero-knowledge protocol fitted to security microprocessor minimizing both transmission and memory," Eurocrypt '88, pp. 123-128
32. C. Rackoff, D. Simon, "Non-Interactive Zero-Knowledge Proof of Knowledge and Chosen Ciphertext Attack", Crypto '91, pp. 433-444
33. R. Rivest, A. Shamir, L. Adleman, "A Method for Obtaining Digital Signatures and Public-Key Cryptosystems," Communications of the ACM, v. 21, n. 2, Feb 1978, pp. 120-126
34. K. Sako, J. Kilian, "Receipt-Free Mix-Type Voting Scheme," Eurocrypt'95, pp 393-403.
35. A. Yao, "Protocols for Secure Computations," Proceedings of the 23rd FOCS, 1982, pp. 160-164

Appendix: Strong Designated Verifier

Previously, we have assumed that Cindy, the third party, will not be convinced that Θ holds after seeing a proof of $\Theta \vee \Phi_{Bob}$, as she knows that Bob could have produced such a transcript himself, Φ_{Bob} being the proof of knowledge of Bob's secret key. Let us now assume that it is widely believed that Bob would not engage in such "transcript forgery," being the thoroughly pure and honest person he is, and will only engage in the prescribed protocols of the system. Under such circumstances, Cindy would, indeed, be convinced that Θ is true after seeing a proof of $\Theta \vee \Phi_{Bob}$. If we want this not to be possible, we need a stronger notion of what it means to be a designated verifier:

Definition 3 Strong Designated Verifier.
Let (P_A, P_B) be a protocol for Alice to prove the truth of the statement θ to Bob. We say that Bob is a *strong designated verifier* if the following is true: For any protocol (P_A, P_B, P_D, P_C) involving Alice, Bob, Dave and Cindy, in which Dave proves the truth of ϑ to Cindy, there is another protocol (P'_D, P_C) such that Dave can perform the calculations of P'_D, and Cindy cannot distinguish transcripts of (P_A, P_B, P_D, P_C) from those of (P'_D, P_C).

This definition captures the fact that Bob is honest (i.e., he engages only in the protocol P_B, where this may be a concatenation of any polynomial number of "legal" protocols.) In order to make protocols strong designated verifier, transcripts can be probabilistically encrypted using the public key of the intended verifier. No "pure and honest" participant will be agree to decrypt ciphertexts of this particular type. Thus, since Dave will not be able to present the decrypted transcripts to Cindy, and Cindy cannot (due to the probabilistic encryption) distinguish encrypted transcripts from random strings of the same length and distribution (which is sampleable,) Dave will be able to produce transcripts (P_B, P'_D, P_C) that Cindy cannot distinguish from transcripts of (P_A, P_B, P_D, P_C).

Finding a Small Root of a Univariate Modular Equation

Don Coppersmith

IBM Research
T.J. Watson Research Center
Yorktown Heights, NY 10598, USA

Abstract. We show how to solve a polynomial equation (mod N) of degree k in a single variable x, as long as there is a solution smaller than $N^{1/k}$. We give two applications to RSA encryption with exponent 3. First, knowledge of all the ciphertext and 2/3 of the plaintext bits for a single message reveals that message. Second, if messages are padded with truly random padding and then encrypted with an exponent 3, then two encryptions of the same message (with different padding) will reveal the message, as long as the padding is less than 1/9 of the length of N. With several encryptions, another technique can (heuristically) tolerate padding up to about 1/6 of the length of N.

1 Introduction

Let N be a large composite integer of unknown factorization. Let

$$p(x) = x^k + a_{k-1}x^{k-1} + \ldots + a_2x^2 + a_1x + a_0$$

be an integer polynomial of degree k in a single variable x, which we may assume to be monic. Suppose there is an integer solution x_0 to

$$p(x_0) = 0 \pmod{N}$$

satisfying

$$|x_0| < N^{1/k} \ .$$

We show how to find such a solution x_0, using lattice basis reduction techniques, in time polynomial in $\log N$ and k.

An immediate application is to RSA encryption of stereotyped messages with small exponents. If we know the high order $\frac{2}{3}\log_2(N)$ bits B of a plaintext, and the ciphertext c resulting from RSA encryption with exponent 3, then we can recover the unknown bits x_0 of the plaintext by solving the equation $p(x) = (B+x)^3 - c = 0 \pmod{N}$.

Another important application is to RSA encryption with small exponents and random padding. Suppose a message m is padded with a random value t before encryption with a small exponent such as $e = 3$, so that the ciphertext is

$$c = (m+t)^3 \pmod{N} \ .$$

Ueli Maurer (Ed.): EUROCRYPT '96 Proceedings, LNCS 1070

Suppose it happens that a single message is encrypted twice, using different values of the random padding:

$$c_1 = (m + t_1)^3 \pmod N ,$$

$$c_2 = (m + t_2)^3 \pmod N .$$

From these two ciphertexts we can recover an equation of degree 9 in the quantity $t_2 - t_1$ (using the resultant), and if t_1 and t_2 are small – less than 1/9 of the length of N – then we can solve that equation for $t_2 - t_1$. Then, using techniques developed by Franklin and Reiter [2], we recover the original message $m + t_1$.

This can be viewed as a warning that, when using RSA with small exponents, the use of random padding might not be helpful and might even be dangerous.

2 Solving a univariate polynomial

We show first how to find solutions x_0 to $p(x) = 0 \pmod N$ satisfying the tighter restriction $|x_0| < \frac{1}{2}N^{(1/k)-\epsilon}$ in time polynomial in $\log N$, k and $1/\epsilon$. Then by setting $\epsilon = 1/\log N$ and exhaustively searching the few unknown high bits of x_0 we can extend the range to $|x_0| < N^{1/k}$.

Begin by selecting an integer $h \geq \max\{7/k,\ (k + \epsilon k - 1)/(\epsilon k^2)\} \approx 1/(k\epsilon)$ so that

$$h - 1 \geq (hk - 1)\left(\frac{1}{k} - \epsilon\right) \text{ and } hk \geq 7 .$$

For each pair of integers i, j satisfying $0 \leq i < k$, $1 \leq j < h$, we set

$$q_{ij}(x) = x^i p(x)^j$$

and remark that, for the desired solution x_0, we know

$$q_{ij}(x_0) = 0 \pmod{N^j} .$$

Indeed, setting

$$y_0 = \frac{p(x_0)}{N}$$

and noting that y_0 is an integer, we see that

$$q_{ij}(x_0) = x_0^i y_0^j N^j .$$

We build a rational matrix M of size $(2hk - k) \times (2hk - k)$, using the coefficients of the polynomials $q_{ij}(x)$, in such a way that an integer linear combination of the rows of M corresponding to powers of x_0 will give a vector with relatively small Euclidean norm. Further, all such short vectors will satisfy a certain linear relation which we will discover by lattice basis reduction techniques [3]; this relation will translate to a polynomial relation on x_0 over $\mathbb{Z}$ (not mod N), which we can solve over $\mathbb{Z}$ to discover x_0.

The matrix M is broken into blocks. The upper right block, of size $(hk) \times (hk - k)$, has rows indexed by the integer g with $0 \leq g < hk$, and columns indexed by $\gamma(i,j) = hk + i + (j-1)k$ with $0 \le i < k$ and $1 \le j < h$, so that $hk \le \gamma(i,j) < 2hk - k$. The entry at $[g, \gamma(i,j)]$ is the coefficient of x^g in the polynomial $q_{ij}(x)$.

The lower right $(hk-k) \times (hk-k)$ block is a diagonal matrix, with the value N^j in each column $\gamma(i,j)$.

The upper left $(hk) \times (hk)$ block is a diagonal matrix, whose value in row g is a rational approximation to $X^{-g}/\sqrt{hk}$, where $X = \frac{1}{2}N^{(1/k)-\epsilon}$ is an upper bound to the solutions $|x_0|$ of interest.

The lower left $(hk-k) \times (hk)$ block is zero.

We illustrate the matrix M in the case $h = 3$, $k = 2$. (For this illustration we ignore the condition $hk \ge 7$.) Assume that $p(x) = x^2 + ax + b$ and $p(x)^2 = x^4 + cx^3 + dx^2 + ex + f$. For simplicity we write δ instead of $1/\sqrt{hk}$.

$$M = \begin{bmatrix} \delta & 0 & 0 & 0 & 0 & 0 & b & 0 & f & 0 \\ 0 & \delta X^{-1} & 0 & 0 & 0 & 0 & a & b & e & f \\ 0 & 0 & \delta X^{-2} & 0 & 0 & 0 & 1 & a & d & e \\ 0 & 0 & 0 & \delta X^{-3} & 0 & 0 & 0 & 1 & c & d \\ 0 & 0 & 0 & 0 & \delta X^{-4} & 0 & 0 & 0 & 1 & c \\ 0 & 0 & 0 & 0 & 0 & \delta X^{-5} & 0 & 0 & 0 & 1 \\ 0 & 0 & 0 & 0 & 0 & 0 & N & 0 & 0 & 0 \\ 0 & 0 & 0 & 0 & 0 & 0 & 0 & N & 0 & 0 \\ 0 & 0 & 0 & 0 & 0 & 0 & 0 & 0 & N^2 & 0 \\ 0 & 0 & 0 & 0 & 0 & 0 & 0 & 0 & 0 & N^2 \end{bmatrix}$$

We will need to estimate $\det(M)$, which is easy because M is upper triangular. Its determinant is

$$\det(M) = N^{kh(h-1)/2} X^{-(hk)(hk-1)/2} / \sqrt{hk}^{hk} = \left(N^{h-1} X^{-(hk-1)} (hk)^{-1}\right)^{hk/2} .$$

Because $hk \ge 7$, a calculation shows that $hk < 2^{(hk-1)/2}$. This implies

$$\det(M) > \left(N^{h-1} X^{-(hk-1)} 2^{-(hk-1)/2}\right)^{hk/2} .$$

Then from our choice of X we calculate

$$\det(M) > \left(N^{(h-1)-(hk-1)(\frac{1}{k}-\epsilon)} 2^{+(hk-1)/2}\right)^{hk/2} ,$$

and the condition $h - 1 \ge (hk-1)\left(\frac{1}{k} - \epsilon\right)$ gives

$$\det(M) > 2^{(hk)(hk-1)/4} .$$

We will do lattice basis reduction on the rows of M to find an expression for those integer linear combinations of rows of M with small Euclidean norm ("short" vectors).

One such short vector is related to the unknown solution x_0. Consider a row vector $\mathbf{r}$ whose left-hand elements are powers of the unknown x_0:

$$r_g = x_0^g$$

and whose right-hand elements are the negatives of powers of x_0 and y_0:

$$r_{\gamma(i,j)} = -x_0^i y_0^j$$

$$\mathbf{r} = (1, x_0, x_0^2, \ldots, x_0^{hk-1}, -y_0, -x_0 y_0, \ldots, -x_0^{k-1} y_0, -y_0^2, -x_0 y_0^2, \ldots, -x_0^{k-1} y_0^{h-1}) \ .$$

The product $\mathrm{s} = \mathbf{r}M$ is a row vector with left-hand elements given by

$$s_g = (x_0/X)^g / \sqrt{hk}$$

and right-hand elements by

$$s_{\gamma(i,j)} = q_{ij}(x_0) - x_0^i y_0^j N^j = 0 \ .$$

The Euclidean norm of s is estimated by:

$$|\mathrm{s}| = \left[\sum_g s_g{}^2\right]^{1/2} < \left[\sum_g (1/\sqrt{hk})^2\right]^{1/2} = 1 \ .$$

Because $p(x)$ and hence $q_{ij}(x)$ are monic polynomials, the submatrix of M formed by rows k through $hk-1$ and the right-hand $hk-k$ columns is an upper triangular matrix with 1 on the diagonal. This implies that we can do elementary row operations on M to produce a block matrix $\tilde{M}$ whose lower right $(hk-k) \times (hk-k)$ block is the identity matrix and whose upper right $(hk) \times (hk-k)$ block is zero. The upper left $(hk) \times (hk)$ block $\hat{M}$ satisfies $\det(\hat{M}) = \det(M) > 2^{(hk)(hk-1)/4}$.

We now restrict our attention to the upper hk rows of $\tilde{M}$, or equivalently on $\hat{M}$: the lattice elements represented by vectors whose right-hand side is 0.

Let $n = hk = \dim(\hat{M})$. Perform lattice basis reduction on $\hat{M}$, using the procedure in [3]. Let $\mathbf{b}_1, \mathbf{b}_2, \ldots, \mathbf{b}_n$ be the resulting row basis of $\hat{M}$, and let $\mathbf{b}_n^*$ denote the component of $\mathbf{b}_n$ orthogonal to the span of $\mathbf{b}_1, \mathbf{b}_2, \ldots, \mathbf{b}_{n-1}$. From the discussion in [3] we know that the last basis element $\mathbf{b}_n$ satisfies

$$|\mathbf{b}_n^*| \geq \{\det(\hat{M})\}^{1/n} 2^{-(n-1)/4} > 1 \ ,$$

the latter estimate coming from our lower bound on $\det(\hat{M})$.

The Euclidean norm of any element $\sum c_i \mathbf{b}_i$ of the lattice of $\hat{M}$ is at least $|c_n| \times |\mathbf{b}_n^*| > |c_n|$. So any lattice element with norm less than 1 must have $c_n = 0$; it lies in the subspace spanned by $\mathbf{b}_1, \mathbf{b}_2, \ldots, \mathbf{b}_{n-1}$. In particular, s is such a lattice element: it has norm less than 1, and it lies in the lattice of $\hat{M}$ because its right-hand entries are 0.

In terms of the original matrix M, let an arbitrary short lattice element (with 0 in the right-hand side and length less than 1) be given by

$$(d_0, d_1, \ldots, d_{hk-1}, e_{\gamma(0,1)}, \ldots, e_{\gamma(k-1,h-1)})M \ .$$

Because these short rows span a vector space of dimension at most $n-1 = hk-1$, simple linear algebra can produce a collection of integers $f_0, f_1, \ldots, f_{hk-1}$ (not all zero) satisfying

$$\sum_g f_g d_g = 0$$

for each short row; this equation holds over $\mathbb{Z}$. (Notice that the $e_{\gamma(i,j)}$ are not involved.)

Our unknown solution row $\mathbf{s} = \mathbf{r}M$ is such a short row, with $d_g = r_g = x_0^g$. So it must be true that

$$\sum_g f_g d_g = \sum_g f_g x_0^g = 0 \ .$$

This is a polynomial equation in x_0 which holds in $\mathbb{Z}$, not just mod N. We can solve this for x_0 in polynomial time, using known techniques for solving univariate polynomial equations over $\mathbb{Z}$. Thus we have produced the desired solution x_0.

Theorem 1. *Let $p(x)$ be a monic integer polynomial of degree k, N a positive integer of unknown factorization, and $\epsilon > 0$. In time polynomial in $\log N$, k and $1/\epsilon$, we can find all integer solutions x_0 to $p(x_0) = 0 \pmod N$ with $|x_0| < \frac{1}{2}N^{(1/k)-\epsilon}$.*

Proof. The lattice basis reduction algorithm from [3] operates in time polynomial in the dimension and the logarithms of the numerators and denominators of the matrix entries; the dimension is polynomial in k and $1/\epsilon$, and the numbers of bits in the matrix entries are polynomial in $\log N$, k and $1/\epsilon$. □

Corollary 2. *Let $p(x)$ be a monic integer polynomial of degree k and N a positive integer of unknown factorization. In time polynomial in $\log N$ and k, we can find all integer solutions x_0 to $p(x_0) = 0 \pmod N$ with $|x_0| < N^{1/k}$.*

Proof. Set $\epsilon = 1/\log_2 N$ and do exhaustive search on $O(1)$ unknown high order bits of x. □

Remark: We have not attempted to find the shortest vector(s) of the lattice, but rather to confine all sufficiently short vectors to a subspace. This appears to be a novel use of lattice basis reduction techniques. It is fortunate, because our desired vector need not be the shortest one. The technique allows us to claim that we will always find the solution, not just with high probability.

Remark: If there are several short solutions x_0, this procedure will find all of them simultaneously.

2.1 Comparison to Previous Work

Vallée et al. [4] apply an LLL-based solution to solving $p(y) = 0 \pmod N$, but require $y < N^{2/[k(k+1)]}$ where $k = \deg(p)$. Our methods are similar to theirs, except that they use only one polynomial $q_{01}(y) = p(y)$ where we use several.

Considering our requirement that $\det(M) > 2^{(hk)(hk-1)/4}$: Each equation $q_{ij}(x) = 0 \pmod{N^j}$ gives a factor of N^j to $\det(M)$, while each unknown x^g costs a factor of about X^{-g}. We must balance the two contributions in order to achieve $\det(M) > 2^{(hk)(hkj-1)/4}$. In the present paper we are able to amortize the cost of the variables over several equations, and this yields the improvement in the bound from $N^{2/[k(k+1)]}$ to $N^{1/k}$.

Another difference is that, because of our technique of confining all small lattice elements to a subspace, we always find the solution if it exists, while Vallée et al., searching for the smallest lattice elements themselves, will succeed with high probability but not always.

3 Extension to Multivariate Polynomials

We encountered some technical difficulties trying to extend this procedure to multivariate polynomials. The guarantee breaks down at a crucial step, so this extension is heuristic. Our sketch is brief because this is irrelevant to the present application.

If we are given a polynomial $p(x_1, \ldots, x_m) \pmod N$ of total degree k, and we know there is a solution $x_i = y_i$ with $|y_i| < N^{\alpha_i}$, we hope to find this solution as long as $\sum \alpha_i < (1/k) - \epsilon$.

Define

$$z = p(y_1, \ldots, y_m)/N$$
$$q_{i_1 \ldots i_m j}(x_1, \ldots, x_m) = x_1^{i_1} \cdots x_m^{i_m} p(x_1, \ldots, x_m)^j \quad ,$$

and notice that $q_{i_1 \ldots i_m j}(y_1, \ldots, y_m)$ is divisible by N^j. Set a limit T and develop the modular equations $q_{i_1 \ldots i_m j}(y_1, \ldots, y_m) = 0 \pmod{N^j}$ for all nonnegative integer indices $(i_1, \ldots, i_m, j)$ with $i_m < k$ and $i_1 + i_2 + \ldots + i_m + kj \le T$.

Build the matrix M analogous to that of Section 2. The vector $\mathbf{r}$ contains all monomials of total degree at most T, so the sum of the total degrees of these monomials is $m \binom{T+m}{m+1}$, and the sum of the degrees in each $x_i, i = 1, 2, \ldots, m-1$, is $\binom{T+m}{m+1}$. These appear as negative exponents of α_i in the diagonal entries of the upper left block of M.

The powers of N appearing in the lower right of M (the moduli) add to

$$\frac{1}{k}\binom{T+m}{m+1} - O(\binom{T+m}{m})$$

(asymptotically for large T). With the requirement $\sum \alpha_i < (1/k) - \epsilon$, we will have $\det(M) > 1$.

The vector $\mathbf{s}$ will be shorter than 1, so it will be among the shorter vectors in the lattice. By the methods of Section 2 we can get at least one polynomial equation satisfied by the y_i over $\mathbb{Z}$. But to solve for y_i over $\mathbb{Z}$ we would need m independent equations. We might or might not get the required equations; if we get m equations, they might not be independent. So the procedure might work or might fail in a particular application. Much work needs to be done in this area.

4 RSA with Stereotyped Messages

An easy application is to RSA encryption with low exponent where most of the message is fixed or "stereotyped".

Suppose we use an RSA exponent of 3 to encrypt a plaintext consisting of two pieces:

(1) A known piece $B = 2^k b$, such as the ASCII representation of "May 14, 1996. The secret key for the day is "

(2) An unknown piece m, such as "Squeamish Ossifrage".

If we know B and the ciphertext $c = (B+m)^3 \pmod{N}$, then we can recover m as long as $|m| < N^{1/3}$. Here $p(m) = (B+m)^3 - c = 0 \pmod{N}$.

This is obvious when $B = 0$, but the present paper makes it possible for nonzero B as well.

5 Application to RSA with Random Padding

The present work was motivated by the following result of Franklin and Reiter [2]; see also [1]. Suppose two messages m and m' satisfy a *known* affine relation, say

$$m' = m + t$$

with t known. Suppose we know the RSA-encryptions of the two messages with an exponent of 3:

$$\begin{aligned} c &= m^3 && \pmod{N} \\ c' &= (m')^3 = m^3 + 3m^2t + 3mt^2 + t^3 && \pmod{N} \end{aligned}$$

Then we can recover m from c, c', t and N:

$$m = \frac{t(c' + 2c - t^3)}{c' - c + 2t^3} = \frac{t(3m^3 + 3m^2t + 3mt^2)}{3m^2t + 3mt^2 + 3t^3} \pmod{N}$$

What if we do not know the exact relation between m and m', but we do know that t is small, say

$$\begin{aligned} m' &= m + t \\ |t| &< N^{1/9} \end{aligned}$$

Can we still find m?

One can imagine a protocol in which messages M are subjected to random padding before being RSA-encrypted with an exponent of 3. Perhaps M is left-shifted by k bits, and a random k-bit quantity T is added, to form a plaintext m; the ciphertext c is then the cube of $m \pmod{N}$:

$$c = m^3 = (2^k M + T)^3 \pmod{N}$$

Now suppose the same message is encrypted twice, but with a different random pad each time. Let the second random pad be $T' = T + t$ so that the second plaintext is $m' = m + t$. Then we see the two ciphertexts

$$\begin{aligned} c &= m^3 = (2^k M + T)^3 && \pmod{N} \\ c' &= (m')^3 = (2^k M + T')^3 = (m+t)^3 && \pmod{N} \end{aligned}$$

Can we recover t and m?

We can eliminate m from the two equations above by taking their resultant:

$$\text{Resultant}_m(m^3 - c, (m+t)^3 - c') =$$
$$= t^9 + (3c - 3c')t^6 + (3c^2 + 21cc' + 3(c')^2)t^3 + (c - c')^3 = 0 \pmod N$$

This is a univariate polynomial in t of degree 9 (mod N). If $|t| < N^{1/9}$, we can apply the present work to recover t. We can then apply Franklin and Reiter's result to recover m, and strip off the padding to get M.

This works just as well if the padding goes in the high order bits, or in the middle; just divide each ciphertext by the appropriate power of 2, in order to divide each plaintext by another power of 2, to move the random bits to the low order bits.

The warning is clear: If the message is subject to random padding of length less than 1/9 the length of N, and then encrypted with an exponent of 3, multiple encryptions of the same message will reveal the message.

Notice that for a 1024-bit RSA key, this attack tolerates 100 bits of padding fairly easily.

Some possible steps to avoid this attack:

(1) Spread the random padding into several blocks (not one contiguous block). Then the present attack needs to be modified, and apparently will tolerate only a smaller total amount of padding. The padding could be two small blocks t and u, positioned so that the encryption is $c = (2^\ell t + 2^k m + u)^3 \pmod N$. Two encryptions of the same message would yield a resultant which is a single equation in two small integer variables t and u. The generalized attack of Section 3 might work, provided that $|t|$ and $|u|$ are subject to bounds T and U with $TU < N^{1/9}$. The computation is more complicated and results are not guaranteed.

(2) Spread the padding throughout the message: two bits out of each eight-bit byte, for example. This seems to be a much more effective defense against the present attack.

(3) Increase the amount of padding. This decreases efficiency; also if the padding is less than 1/6 the length of N, the alternate solution shown in Section 6 might still recover the message if multiple encryptions have been done.

(4) Make the "random" padding depend on the message deterministically. For example we could subject the message to a hashing function, and append that hash value as the random padding. Then two encryptions would be identical, because the random padding would be identical. A possible weakness still exists: suppose a time-stamp is included in each message, and this time-stamp occupies the low order bits, next to the padding. Then two plaintexts for the same message (with different time stamps) will differ in the time-stamp and (possibly) the pad; just let t combine these two fields and proceed as before.

(5) Use larger exponents for RSA encryption. If the exponent is e, the attack apparently tolerates random padding of length up to $1/e^2$ times the length of N. So already for $e = 7$ the attack is useless: on a 1024-bit RSA key with $e = 7$, the attack would tolerate only 21 bits of padding, and this would be better treated by exhaustion.

6 Another Solution for Multiple Encryptions

If instead of two encryptions of the same message we have several, say $k+1$, then we can mount other attacks which might tolerate larger fields of random padding. We sketch here an attack which (heuristically) seems to tolerate random padding up to α times the length of N where

$$\alpha < \frac{k-2}{6k-3} < \frac{1}{6} \ .$$

We begin with

$$\begin{aligned} A_0 &= m^3 && \pmod N \\ A_i &= (m+t_i)^3 && \pmod N \\ c_i = A_i - A_0 &= 3m^2t_i + 3mt_i^2 + t_i^3 && \pmod N \end{aligned}$$

where we know A_0, A_i, c_i and N, but not m or t_i. We assume the padding is small:

$$|t_i| \le \frac{1}{2}N^\alpha.$$

For indices $i < j < \ell$ define $d_{ij} = t_it_j(t_i - t_j)$ and $e_{ij\ell} = -t_it_jt_\ell(t_i - t_j)(t_j - t_\ell)(t_\ell - t_i)$. The $C(k,2) = \binom{k}{2}$ linearly independent quantities d_{ij} each satisfy $|d_{ij}| < N^{3\alpha}$, and the $C(k,3)$ linearly independent quantities $e_{ij\ell}$ each satisfy $|e_{ij\ell}| < N^{6\alpha}$. One can check the following identity:

$$d_{ij}c_\ell + d_{j\ell}c_i - d_{i\ell}c_j = e_{ij\ell} \pmod N \ .$$

This suggests lattice basis reduction on the row basis of the following matrix. M is a square upper triangular integer matrix of dimension $(C(k,2)+C(k,3))$. Its upper left $C(k,2) \times C(k,2)$ block is the identity times an integer approximation to $N^{3\alpha}$. Its lower left $C(k,3) \times C(k,2)$ block is 0. Its lower right $C(k,3) \times C(k,3)$ block is N times the identity. Its upper right $C(k,2) \times C(k,3)$ block has rows indexed by pairs of indices $(i,j), i<j$, and columns indexed by triples of indices $(i,j,\ell), i<j<\ell$. Column (i,j,ℓ) has three nonzero entries: c_ℓ at row (i,j), c_i at row (j,ℓ), and $-c_j$ at row (i,ℓ).

We illustrate the matrix M for the case $k=4$. The first $C(k,2) = 6$ rows are indexed by (1,2), (1,3), (1,4), (2,3), (2,4) and (3,4). The last $C(k,3) = 4$ columns are indexed by (1,2,3), (1,2,4), (1,3,4) and (2,3,4).

$$M = \begin{bmatrix} N^{3\alpha} & 0 & 0 & 0 & 0 & 0 & c_3 & c_4 & 0 & 0 \\ 0 & N^{3\alpha} & 0 & 0 & 0 & 0 & -c_2 & 0 & c_4 & 0 \\ 0 & 0 & N^{3\alpha} & 0 & 0 & 0 & 0 & -c_2 & -c_3 & 0 \\ 0 & 0 & 0 & N^{3\alpha} & 0 & 0 & c_1 & 0 & 0 & c_4 \\ 0 & 0 & 0 & 0 & N^{3\alpha} & 0 & 0 & c_1 & 0 & -c_3 \\ 0 & 0 & 0 & 0 & 0 & N^{3\alpha} & 0 & 0 & c_1 & c_2 \\ 0 & 0 & 0 & 0 & 0 & 0 & N & 0 & 0 & 0 \\ 0 & 0 & 0 & 0 & 0 & 0 & 0 & N & 0 & 0 \\ 0 & 0 & 0 & 0 & 0 & 0 & 0 & 0 & N & 0 \\ 0 & 0 & 0 & 0 & 0 & 0 & 0 & 0 & 0 & N \end{bmatrix}$$

Consider the integer row vector $\mathbf{r}$ whose first $C(k,2)$ entries are d_{ij}, and whose last $C(k,3)$ entries are the integers $(e_{ij\ell} - (d_{ij}c_\ell + d_{j\ell}c_i - d_{i\ell}c_j))/N$. The product $\mathbf{r}M = \mathrm{s}$ has left-hand elements $d_{ij}N^{3\alpha}$ and right-hand elements $e_{ij\ell}$; all its entries are bounded by $N^{6\alpha}$. We hope that lattice basis reduction will find this row.

The determinant of M is $N^{3\alpha C(k,2)+C(k,3)}$. Because of our choice of α, this is larger than $(N^{6\alpha})^{C(k,2)+C(k,3)}$. So s is among the shorter elements of the lattice generated by the rows of M.

The difficulty in finding s depends on its rank among the short elements. If $|t_i|$ are much smaller than N^α then we can hope that s is the shortest lattice element, and that lattice basis reduction methods can recover it efficiently. We do not here supply efficiency estimates or probabilities of success; we treat this as a heuristic attack.

Assuming that we can actually find s, we will be able to recover the values t_i by taking *g.c.d.* of elements of $\mathbf{r} = \mathrm{s}M^{-1}$:

$$\begin{aligned} g.c.d.\{d_{1,2}, d_{1,3}, \ldots, d_{1,k}\} &= g.c.d.\{t_1t_2(t_1-t_2), t_1t_3(t_1-t_3), \ldots, t_1t_k(t_1-t_k)\} \\ &= t_1 \times g.c.d.\{t_2(t_1-t_2), t_3(t_1-t_3), \ldots, t_k(t_1-t_k)\} \ , \end{aligned}$$

and hopefully the latter *g.c.d.* will be small enough to discover by exhaustive search. Having found t_i, we can recover m by Franklin and Reiter's technique.

If we have 14 encryptions of the same message ($k = 13$), then we can tolerate a random padding of about 150 bits in a 1024-bit RSA message.

7 Conclusions and Open Problems

We have shown how to solve a univariate polynomial equation (mod N) of degree k if there is a solution smaller than $N^{1/k}$. We have applied this to stereotyped RSA messages with small encryption exponent. We have also applied it to the case of RSA encryption with exponent 3 with random padding of less than 1/9 (resp. 1/6) of the length of N, to recover a message which has been enciphered twice (resp. several times) with different random padding each time.

We warn against RSA encryption with exponent 3 and with random padding of such length, in the case where a protocol allows a message to be enciphered several times with different values of the padding.

An important open problem is to find conditions under which the multivariate case works. In particular, how effectively does it work for the case of two messages with random padding in two blocks?

8 Acknowledgments

The author gratefully acknowledges several enlightening discussions with Andrew Odlyzko and Jean-Jacques Quisquater. Matt Franklin and Mike Reiter's Crypto 95 rump session paper and subsequent discussions were most useful. Jacques Patarin was independently working on the idea of unknown offsets in the RSA setting. The Eurocrypt program committee supplied us with missing references to existing literature.

References

1. D. Coppersmith, M. Franklin, J. Patarin and M. Reiter, "Low Exponent RSA with Related Messages," Proceedings of Eurocrypt 96.
2. M. Franklin and M. Reiter, "A Linear Protocol Failure for RSA with Exponent Three," presented at the rump session, Crypto 95, but not in the proceedings.
3. A. K. Lenstra, H. W. Lenstra and L. Lovasz, "Factoring Polynomials with Integer Coefficients," Matematische Annalen **261** (1982), 513–534.
4. B. Vallée, M. Girault and P. Toffin, "How to Guess ℓ-th Roots Modulo n by Reducing Lattice Bases," Proceedings of AAECC–6, Springer LNCS **357** (1988) 427–442.

New Modular Multiplication Algorithms for Fast Modular Exponentiation

Seong-Min Hong, Sang-Yeop Oh, Hyunsoo Yoon

Department of Computer Science and Center for AI Research
Korea Advanced Institute of Science and Technology(KAIST)
Taejeon, 305-701, KOREA
E-mail: {smhong,hyoon}@camars.kaist.ac.kr

Abstract. A modular exponentiation is one of the most important operations in public-key cryptography. However, it takes much time because the modular exponentiation deals with very large operands as 512-bit integers. The modular exponentiation is composed of repetition of modular multiplications. Therefore, we can reduce the execution time of it by reducing the execution time of each modular multiplication. In this paper, we propose two fast modular multiplication algorithms. One is for modular multiplications between different integers, and the other is for modular squarings. These proposed algorithms require single-precision multiplications fewer than those of Montgomery modular multiplication algorithms by 1/2 and 1/3 times, respectively. Implementing on PC, proposed algorithms reduce execution times by 50% and 30% compared with Montgomery algorithms, respectively.

1 Introduction

Since Diffie and Hellman had proposed public-key cryptography in 1976, many public-key cryptosystems have been developed[8, 9]. Many of them require modular exponentiations[10, 8, 11]. Therefore, a modular exponentiation becomes one of the most important operations. However, it takes much time because the modular exponentiation deals with very large operands as 512-bit integers. Therefore, many researchers have studied for the speedup of the modular exponentiation[1, 14, 18, 6, 7].

A modular exponentiation is composed of repetition of modular multiplications. Therefore, there are two possible methods to reduce the execution time of the modular exponentiation. One is to reduce the number of modular multiplications, and the other is to reduce the execution time of each modular multiplication.

Again, the latter is classified into two classes. One is the approach of considering a modular reduction apart from a multiple-precision multiplication[2, 17, 12, 13]. The other is the approach of considering together them as one operation[16, 15, 18]. Algorithms which will be proposed in this paper are included in the latter class.

It is the small-window method that can find the shortest addition-chain among systematically analyzable algorithms. Modular multiplications can be

Ueli Maurer (Ed.): EUROCRYPT '96 Proceedings, LNCS 1070

classified into two species when we execute a modular exponentiation with the small-window method. Ones are modular multiplications of two different integers, and the others are modular squarings. In this paper, we propose two algorithms. One is for fast modular multiplications of two different integers. It is the algorithm expanded from the Kawamura's[15]. The other is for fast modular squarings. It executes a modular squaring fast by altering the sequence of calculation. The former shows good performance for modular multiplications of two different integers, but it can not be applicable to modular squarings. Therefore, we can execute a modular exponentiation fast with both the former and the latter.

This paper is organized as follows. In Section 2, we explain briefly the process of modular exponentiation using the small-window method. In Section 3, we explain the basic method for modular multiplications and propose two modular multiplication algorithms. In Section 4, we analyze performances of proposed algorithms and compare them to that of Montgomery algorithm. In Section 5, performances of proposed algorithms implemented on a PC are presented, followed by discussions. Finally, we conclude in Section 6.

2 The Procedure of A Modular Exponentiation

The modular exponentiation used in public-key cryptosystems like RSA is defined as follows.

Definition 1. $C = M^E \bmod N \quad (b^{k-1} \leq E < N < b^k, 0 \leq M < N)$.

In the above definition, M means a message, and E means a public-key. It is desirable to obtain a sequence of modular multiplications for the fast execution of the modular exponentiation in advance, because E is known previously. An addition-chain is used to represent the sequence, which is defined as follows.

Definition 2. An *addition-chain* of length l for an integer n is a sequence of integers $a_0, a_1, ..., a_l$ satisfying

1. $a_0 = 1$, $a_l = n$.
2. $a_i = a_j + a_k$, *where* $0 \leq j \leq k < i \leq l$.

We can enumerate the sequence of modular multiplications for a modular exponentiation according to Definition 1 and Definition 2.

$$\begin{aligned}
C_0 &= M^{a_0} \bmod N \quad = M, \\
C_1 &= M^{a_1} \bmod N, \\
C_2 &= M^{a_2} \bmod N, \\
&\vdots \\
C_{l-1} &= M^{a_{l-1}} \bmod N, \\
C_l &= M^{a_l} \bmod N \quad = M^E \bmod N (= C).
\end{aligned} \tag{1}$$

Each step of Equation (1) is connected with previous steps by the following relation.

$$C_i = (C_j \times C_k) \bmod N, \\ where \;\; 0 \le j \le k < i \le l. \tag{2}$$

As we can see in Equations (1) and (2), the shorter the addition-chain is the shorter the execution time of the modular exponentiation is. Many researchers have proposed addition-chain algorithms[1, 2, 3, 4, 5, 6, 7]. Among these algorithms, the Bos-Coster's heuristic algorithm[1] shows the best performance. However, the gap between the small-window method[2] and the Bos-Coster's algorithm is very small and the latter is more complex. Modular multiplication algorithms which will be proposed later in this paper are applicable to both algorithms. Therefore, we suppose that the small-window method is used to execute a modular exponentiation for the sake of convenient explanation.

A modular exponentiation is executed by the repetition of following two kinds of operations according to the above supposition, where w means the window size in the small-window method.

$$C_i = C_{i-1} \times C_\alpha \bmod N, \;\; where \;\; 0 < i \le l, \; 0 \le \alpha < 2^{w-1}. \tag{3}$$

$$C_i = C_{i-1}^2 \bmod N, \;\; where \;\; 0 < i \le l. \tag{4}$$

3 Algorithms

In this section, we explain the basic method for modular multiplications and propose two modular multiplication algorithms. We call Equation (3) a *window modular multiplication* and Equation (4) a *modular squaring*.

3.1 Basic Method

The basic method for a modular multiplication is as follows. A multiple-precision multiplication and a modular reduction are separate tasks. The former is executed first and the latter is executed secondly. The result of the multiplication is the input of the modular reduction. Equation (3) and Equation (4) are calculated by Equation (5) and Equation (6), respectively.

$$\begin{aligned} C_i &= C_{i-1} \times M^\alpha \bmod N \\ &= (C_{i-1} \times (M^\alpha \bmod N)) \bmod N \\ &= (C_{i-1} \times T[\alpha]) \bmod N, \\ &\quad where \;\; T[\alpha] = M^\alpha \bmod N, 0 \le \alpha < 2^{w-1}. \end{aligned} \tag{5}$$

$$\begin{aligned} C_i &= C_{i-1}^2 \bmod N \\ &= (C_{i-1}^2) \bmod N. \end{aligned} \tag{6}$$

3.2 Proposed Algorithms

In this section, we propose two modular multiplication algorithms. One is for the window modular multiplication and the other is for the modular squaring. We express a multiple-precision integer C_{i-1} as follows:

$$C_{i-1} = \sum_{j=0}^{k-1} c_j b^j. \tag{7}$$

Note that we write C_{i-1} as C for the sake of simplicity in this section.

Window Modular Multiplication. A feature of the small-window method is that one of two operands in the window modular multiplication is restricted in narrow limits. As we suppose that the small-window method is used to decide the sequence of modular multiplications, Equation (3) can be expanded to Equation (8).

$$\begin{aligned} C_i &= C \times M^\alpha \bmod N \\ &= (\textstyle\sum_{j=0}^{k-1} c_j b^j) \times M^\alpha \bmod N \\ &= (\textstyle\sum_{j=0}^{k-1} c_j \times (b^j \times M^\alpha \bmod N)) \bmod N \\ &= (\textstyle\sum_{j=0}^{k-1} c_j \times T[\alpha][j]) \bmod N, \\ &\quad \textit{where } T[\alpha][j] = b^j \times M^\alpha \bmod N \textit{ and } 0 \le \alpha < 2^{w-1}. \end{aligned} \tag{8}$$

On executing a modular exponentiation with the small-window method, M^α and N can be considered constant numbers. Therefore, $b^j \times M^\alpha \bmod N$ can be calculated in advance. The table T in Equation (8) can be calculated by the following equation.

$$\begin{aligned} T[\alpha][0] &= M^\alpha \bmod N, \\ T[\alpha][j] &= (T[\alpha][j-1] \times b) \bmod N, \\ &\quad \textit{where } 0 \le \alpha < 2^{w-1} \textit{ and } 0 < j \le k-1. \end{aligned} \tag{9}$$

Modular Squaring. It is required to execute more modular squarings than window modular multiplications in order to execute a modular exponentiation. However, the algorithm explained in the previous section can not be applicable to modular squarings, because C_{i-1} in Equation (6) is not known in advance. Therefore, we need a fast modular squaring algorithm.

In this section, we propose a fast modular squaring algorithm. It uses the fact that modular reductions can be executed fast for small operands. Equation (4) can be expanded as follows.

$$\begin{aligned} C_i &= C^2 \bmod N \\ &= (c_{k-1}b^{k-1} + c_{k-2}b^{k-2} + \cdots + c_1 b^1 + c_0)^2 \bmod N \\ &= ((\cdots(c_{k-1}b + c_{k-2})b + \cdots + c_1)b + c_0)^2 \bmod N \\ &= (C^{(1)}b + c_0)^2 \bmod N \\ &= ((C^{(1)})^2 b^2 + 2c_0 C^{(1)} b + c_0^2) \bmod N \\ &= (((C^{(1)})^2 \bmod N) b^2 + 2c_0 C^{(1)} b + c_0^2) \bmod N, \\ &\quad \textit{where } C^{(1)} = (\cdots(c_{k-1}b + c_{k-2})b + \cdots + c_2)b + c_1. \end{aligned} \tag{10}$$

Looking at the first and the last term among all of right terms in the above equation, $C^2 \bmod N$ and $(C^{(1)})^2 \bmod N$ are included, respectively. They have the same form as each other. Therefore, we can compute Equation (10) recursively. In addition to it, $C^{(1)}$ in Equation (10) is the value which is shifted to the right by one digit from C. If we repeat the recursive function call $\frac{k}{2}$ times, the final value is as follows:

$$C^{(\frac{k}{2})} = \sum_{j=0}^{\frac{k}{2}-1} c_{j+\frac{k}{2}} b^j. \tag{11}$$

Because $C^{(\frac{k}{2})}$ is a $\frac{k}{2}$-digit integer, the result of squaring is a k-digit integer at most, and $(C^{(\frac{k}{2})})^2 \bmod N$ can be calculated by only one subtraction or no operation except for a squaring. Therefore, we can consider Equation (11) basis of recursive calls and get the result of a modular squaring by repeating the following equation $\frac{k}{2}$ times.

$$\begin{aligned} &(C^{(j-1)})^2 \bmod N \\ &= (((C^{(j)})^2 \bmod N)b^2 + 2c_0 C^{(j)} b + c_0^2) \bmod N, \\ &\textit{where } 1 \le j \le \tfrac{k}{2} \textit{ and } C^{(0)} = C. \end{aligned} \tag{12}$$

The only term to be reduced by modulus N is $((C^{(j)})^2 \bmod N)b^2$ when we calculate Equation (12). Because $(C^{(j)})^2 \bmod N$ is the value calculated in the previous step, $((C^{(j)})^2 \bmod N)b^2 \bmod N$ can be calculated by shifting $(C^{(j)})^2 \bmod N$ to the left by two digits and by executing a simple modular reduction to the result of shifting. This procedure can be processed using only subtractions, and is appeared in the following equation.

$$\begin{aligned} &(((C^{(j)})^2 \bmod N)b^2) \bmod N \\ &= (((((C^{(j)})^2 \bmod N) \log s - T[m_0]) \log s - T[m_1]) \cdots) \log s - T[m_{t-1}], \\ &\textit{where } T[m_x] = m_x \times N,\ 0 \le m_x < s,\ 0 \le x < t,\ t = \tfrac{2 \log b}{\log s}. \end{aligned} \tag{13}$$

In the above equation, t must be as small as possible because it means the number of shifts and subtractions. However, b is determined by the system on which the algorithm is implemented, and s is limited by the memory capacity. The reasonable value of b and s are 2^{16} and 2^8 on current 32-bit computer systems, respectively. Note that m_x can be determined easily using backward pointer array, which can be made during the table construction.

4 Time Complexity

In this section, we compute time complexities of algorithms proposed in this paper and compare them with those of existing algorithms. The metric of the time complexity is the number of single-precision multiplications required for the execution of the corresponding algorithm.

4.1 Basic Method

The number of single-precision multiplications required to multiply two large integers which is represented like Equation (7) is k^2. All of existing modular reduction algorithms require $k(k+c)$ single-precision multiplications, where c is the constant according to the algorithm used. Therefore, the number of single-precision multiplications required to execute a modular multiplication by the basic method is as follows:

$$2k^2 + ck.$$

The value of c is '1' if the used algorithm is the Montgomery's which is the best modular reduction algorithm[12, 18, 14].

4.2 Proposed Algorithms

Window Modular Multiplication. It is not required to execute any explicit modular reduction to calculate Equation (3) using Equation (8). Only a few additional operations are required to reduce an intermediate result into a k-digit integer.

First, k single-precision multiplications are required to multiply each digit and the residue equivalent to it. The residue is $T[\alpha][j]$ in Equation (8). Because an integer has k digits, the number of single-precision multiplications required is k^2 totally. The intermediate result is larger than N. However, we can get the final result with no single-precision multiplication using the table explained in Section 3.2, because the difference is very small. Therefore, the number of single-precision multiplications required to calculate Equation (8) is as follows:

$$k^2. \tag{14}$$

Next, we consider single-precision multiplications required to construct the table explained in Section 3.2. Seeing Equation (9), there is no additional operation required to calculate $T[\alpha][0]$s, because they are values that are calculated in the previous step. Each of the next operations needs one shift to the left and one modular reduction. The integer to be reduced by modulus N has $k+1$ digits at most. Therefore, the modular reduction can be executed by k single-precision multiplications. The number of single-precision multiplications required to construct the table is as follows:

$$2^{w-1} \times k(k-1). \tag{15}$$

In the above equation, w means the window size. If we use the table explained in Section 3.2, all table entries can be calculated with no single-precision multiplication.

Modular Squaring. We count the number of single-precision multiplications required to execute a modular squaring by the proposed algorithm. First, $\frac{k^2+2k}{8}$ single-precision multiplications are required to calculate Equation (11). Second, we count the number of single-precision multiplications required to execute Equation (12). The first term in the right side of the equation needs no single-precision multiplication, as we can see in Equation (13). The second term requires $\frac{3k^2-2k}{8}(=\sum_{j=\frac{k}{2}}^{k-1} j)$ single-precision multiplications during all recursive function calls. The third term requires $k/2$ single-precision multiplications because it requires one for each recursive call. Therefore, the number of single-precision multiplications required to execute Equation (4) by the proposed algorithm is as follows:

$$\frac{k^2+k}{2}. \tag{16}$$

The table T in Equation (13) can be constructed without any single-precision multiplication.

4.3 Comparison

We have computed time complexities of proposed algorithms and the basic method so far. However, there are many existing algorithms for modular multiplications other than the basic method[15, 13, 18, 7, 16]. Some are algorithms using pre-computation table and others are algorithms which regard a multiple-precision multiplication and a modular reduction as one operation. We briefly examine them.

An efficient algorithm was proposed when a modular exponentiation was executed using the binary method[2] as an addition-chain algorithm in [7] and [15]. However, it is not good for a modular exponentiation because the binary method is very inefficient. Findlay et. al. proposed an algorithm using partial modular reductions based on sums of residues in [13]. However, the number of single-precision multiplications required for partial modular reductions is k^2. Furthermore, a few additional operations are required because it is not the final result. Therefore, the number of single-precision multiplications required for this algorithm is much the same as that of the basic method. Morita et. al. proposed a new modular multiplication algorithm in [16]. However, it reduces only the required available memory for the computation but not the number of single-precision multiplications.

As we look at in the above paragraph, existing algorithms using a pre-computation table or combining a multiple-precision multiplication and a modular reduction into a single operation are not much different from the basic method in regard to the number of single-precision multiplications. The best modular reduction algorithm known to us is the Montgomery algorithm[14]. Therefore, we compare our algorithms with the basic method which uses the Montgomery reduction algorithm.

Time complexities of proposed algorithms and those of Montgomery algorithms are compared in Table 1 and Figure 1. The time required for table construction in proposed algorithms and the time required for pre-/post-calculation in Montgomery algorithms are excluded, because many modular multiplications are required to execute a modular exponentiation. The number of single-precision multiplications required to execute an ordinary multiple-precision multiplication is recorded together, for reference. The ordinary multiple-precision multiplication means one which needs not modular reduction. s in Table 1 is the same as that in Equation (13).

Table 1. *The time complexity and the memory requirement of each algorithm. NOSPM means the number of single-precision multiplications. The metric of memory requirement is the number of operands.*

Algorithm		NOSPM	Memory Requirement
Window Modular Multiplication	Montgomery	$2k^2 + k$	2^{w-1}
	Proposed	k^2	$k \times 2^{w-1}$
Ordinary Multiplication		k^2	2^{w-1}
Modular Squaring	Montgomery	$\frac{3}{2}(k^2 + k)$	0
	Proposed	$\frac{1}{2}(k^2 + k)$	$k \times s$
Ordinary Squaring		$\frac{1}{2}(k^2 + k)$	0

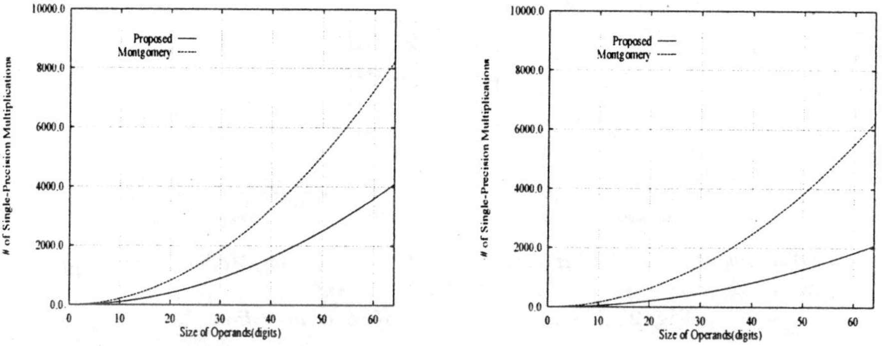

(a) *Window Modular Multiplication* (b) *Modular Squaring*

Fig. 1. *The time complexity of each algorithm*

As we can see in Table 1 and Figure 1, numbers of single-precision multiplications required for proposed algorithms are the same as those required for ordinary multiple-precision multiplications. That is, explicit modular multiplications are not required for proposed algorithms. The proposed window modular multiplication algorithm removes them by pre-calculations and the proposed modular squaring algorithm removes them by pre-calculations and subtractions.

5 Implementation and Discussion

We implemented proposed algorithms and the Montgomery algorithm. The system on which we implemented is a PC with Pentium-90 microprocessor. We implemented them in C language, and compiled with Watcom C(version 10.0) compiler. A digit is 16-bit($b = 2^{16}$). Results are appeared in Table 2.

Table 2. *The execution time of each algorithm*

Algorithm		Time of Execution(msec.)			
		256-bit	512-bit	768-bit	1024-bit
Window Modular Multiplication	Montgomery	0.137	0.544	1.16	2.07
	Proposed	0.0604	0.220	0.489	0.868
Modular Squaring	Montgomery	0.121	0.445	0.917	1.65
	Proposed	0.0851	0.297	0.698	1.22

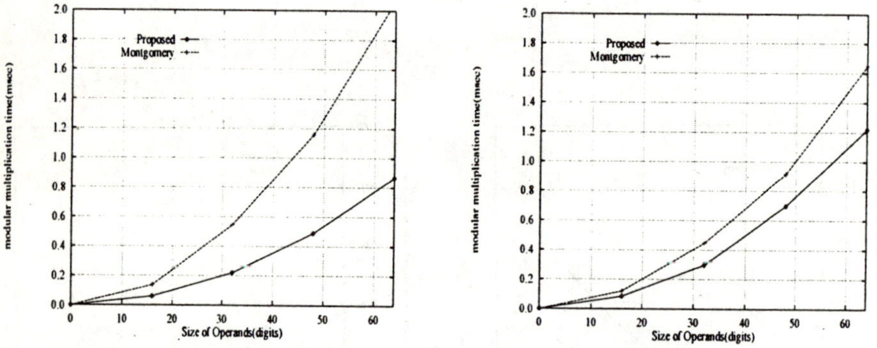

(a) *Window Modular Multiplication* (b) *Modular Squaring*

Fig. 2. *The execution time of each algorithm*

According to Table 1, proposed algorithms are faster than Montgomery algorithms by two and three times, respectively. As we can see in Table 2 and Figure 2(a), the real execution time agrees with Table 1 and Figure 1(a) in the case of window modular multiplications. However, it is not in the case of modular squarings. The reason is that we count only the number of single-precision multiplications in Table 1. While it is a fact that a multiplication takes much time than an addition in general purpose processors, as the proposed modular squaring algorithm uses many additions we must consider the number of single-precision additions, also. Time complexities are appeared in consideration of the number of single-precision additions in Table 3. r is the constant required to represent the time complexity as the number of single-precision multiplications. It is defined as follows and determined by the system on which the corresponding algorithm is implemented.

Definition 3. $r = \dfrac{\text{the time required for a single-precision addition}}{\text{the time required for a single-precision multiplication}}$

Table 3. *The time complexity in consideration of single-precision additions. NOSPM means the number of single-precision multiplications.*

Algorithm		NOSPM
Window Modular Multiplication	Montgomery	$2k^2 + k + r \times (2k^2)$
	Proposed	$k^2 + r \times (k^2 + 3(k+1))$
Modular Squaring	Montgomery	$\frac{3}{2}(k^2 + k) + r \times (\frac{3}{2}k^2 + k)$
	Proposed	$\frac{1}{2}(k^2 + k) + r \times \frac{5}{2}(k^2 + k)$

Figure 3 is the graph to represent changes of expected performance ratios of proposed algorithms to Montgomery algorithms according to r when the value of k is 32. The expected performance ratio is defined as follows.

Definition 4. The *expected performance ratio* of the proposed algorithm to Montgomery algorithm

$$= \frac{\text{NOSPM required to execute Montgomery algorithm}}{\text{NOSPM required to execute the proposed algorithm}}$$

NOSPM has the same meaning as that used in Table 3.

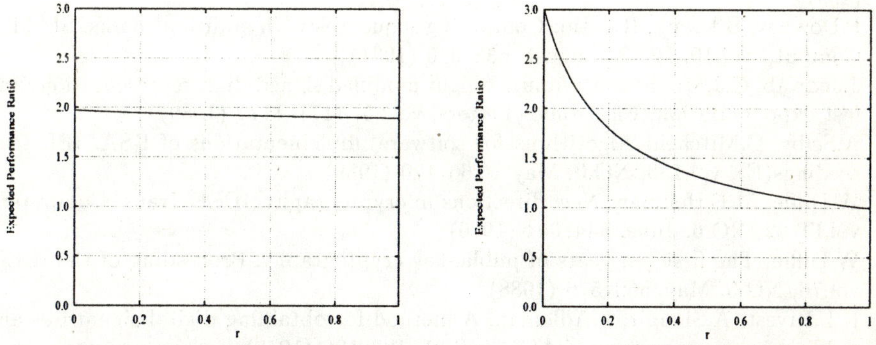

(a) *Window Modular Multiplication* (b) *Modular Squaring*

Fig. 3. *Change of the expected performance ratio according to r*

As we can see in Figure 3(a), the performance ratio of the proposed window modular multiplication algorithm to the Montgomery algorithm is little changed although the r is largely changed. This means that the proposed window modular multiplication algorithm is faster than the Montgomery algorithm by two times in almost systems. However, the performance ratio in Figure 3(b) is largely changed according to r. That is, the performance of the proposed modular squaring algorithm is largely dependent on the system on which the algorithm is implemented. For example, as the value of r is about 0.37 in the case of Pentium PC, the proposed modular squaring algorithm is faster than the Montgomery algorithm by 30% on it.

6 Conclusion

We proposed two algorithms to execute modular multiplications fast. One is the window modular multiplication algorithm and it uses the feature of the addition-chain found with the small-window method. The other is the modular squaring algorithm and it uses the fact that a modular reduction can be executed easily for an integer which is not much larger than a modulus. Proposed algorithms require single-precision multiplications 1/2 and 1/3 times of that required for Montgomery algorithms, respectively. Implementing on PC, proposed algorithms reduce execution times by 50% and 30% compared with Montgomery algorithms, respectively.

References

1. J.Bos, M.Coster: Addition chain heuristics. Crypto'89, 400–407 (1989)
2. D.E.Knuth: The art of computer programming Vol.2. Addison–Wesley,Inc. (1981)
3. M.J.Coster: Some algorithms on addition chains and their complexity. CWI Report CS–R9024 (1990)
4. Y.Yacobi: Exponentiating faster with addition chains. Eurocrypt'90, 222–229 (1991)
5. P.Downey, B.Leong, R.Sethi: Computing sequences with addition chains. SIAM J. Comput., vol.10, NO.3, August, 638–646 (1981)
6. J.Jedwab, C.J.Mitchell: Minimum weight modified signed-digit representations and fast exponentiation. Electronics Letters, vol.25, 1171–1172 (1989)
7. A.Selby, C.Mitcheil: Algorithms for software implementations of RSA. IEE Proceedings(E), vol.136, NO.3, May", 166–170 (1989)
8. W.Diffie, M.E.Hellman: New directions in cryptography. IEEE Trans. Computers, vol.IT-22, NO.6, June, 644–654 (1976)
9. W.Diffie: The first ten years of public-key cryptography. Proceeding of the IEEE, vol.76, NO.5, May, 560–576 (1988)
10. R.L.Rivest, A.Shamir, L.Adleman: A method for obtaining digital signatures and public key cryptosystems. CACM, vol.21, 120–126 (1978)
11. T.ElGmal: A public-key cryptosystem and a signature scheme based on discrete logarithms. IEEE Transactions on Information Theory, vol.IT-31, NO.4, 469–472 (1985)

12. P.L.Montgomery: Modular multiplication without trial division. Mathematics of Computation, vol.44, 519–521 (1985)
13. P.Findlay, B.Johnson: Modular exponentiation using recursive sums of residues. Crypto'89, 371–386 (1990)
14. A.Bosselaers, R.Govaerts, J.Vandewalle: Comparison of three modular reduction functions. Crypto'93, 175–186 (1994)
15. S.Kawamura, K.Takabayashi, A.Shimbo: A fast modular exponentiation algorithm. IEICE Transactions., vol.E-74, NO.8, August, 2136–2142 (1991)
16. H.Morita, C.Yang: A modular-multiplication algorithm using lookahead determination. IEICE Trans. Fundamentals, vol.E76-A, NO.1, January, 70–77 (1993)
17. P.Barrett: Implementing the Rivest Shamir and Adleman public key encryption algorithm on a standard digital signal processor. Crypto'86, 311–323 (1987)
18. S.R.Dusse, B.S.Kaliski: A cryptographic library for the motorola DSP56000. Eurocrypt'90, 230–244 (1991)

Finding a Small Root of a Bivariate Integer Equation; Factoring with High Bits Known

Don Coppersmith

IBM Research
T.J. Watson Research Center
Yorktown Heights, NY 10598, USA

Abstract. We present a method to solve integer polynomial equations in two variables, provided that the solution is suitably bounded. As an application, we show how to find the factors of $N = PQ$ if we are given the high order $((1/4)\log_2 N)$ bits of P. This compares with Rivest and Shamir's requirement of $((1/3)\log_2 N)$ bits.

1 Introduction

We present a method to solve a polynomial equation $p(x, y) = 0$ over $\mathbb{Z}$, provided that the solution is suitably bounded: $|x| < X$ and $|y| < Y$, with X, Y depending on the coefficients and degree of p.

Our algorithm uses lattice basis methods [2]. It is similar in spirit to [1], which solved equations in one variable in ($\mathbb{Z}$ mod N), but the present algorithm requires a different analysis.

We require bounds X and Y on the absolute values of x and y in our solution. Suppose $p(x, y)$ has degree δ in each variable, and $p(x, y) = \sum_{ij} p_{ij} x^i y^j$. Define $D = \max_{ij} |p_{ij}| X^i Y^j$ as the largest possible term in $p(x, y)$ in the region of interest. Then we will find a bounded solution (x, y) (if it exists) provided that

$$XY < D^{2/(3\delta)} .$$

For fixed degree δ, the algorithm runs in time polynomial in $(\log D)$.

Similar methods can be applied to the multivariate case but are not assured of success; the proof breaks down at a critical point.

Our immediate application, and the framework in which the algorithm is described, is the problem of factoring an integer when we know the high order bits of its factors. If we know $N = PQ$ and we know the high order $\left(\frac{1}{4}\log_2 N\right)$ bits of P, then by solving the equation $(P_0 + x)(Q_0 + y) - N = 0$ over a suitable range of x and y we can find the factorization of N. By comparison, Rivest and Shamir [5] need about $\left(\frac{1}{3}\log_2 N\right)$ bits of P. This has applications to some RSA-based cryptographic schemes; see for example [7].

We give here a sketch of our algorithm. Define integer variables r_{gh} representing $x^g y^h$. Form the lattice of those values of $\{r_{gh}\}$ satisfying several polynomial relations $q_{ij}(x, y) = x^i y^j p(x, y) = 0$ under this interpretation. Claim that the lattice element $\mathbf{s}$ corresponding to our desired solution is relatively short (less

Ueli Maurer (Ed.): EUROCRYPT '96 Proceedings, LNCS 1070

than the nth root of the determinant of a certain matrix). The expression of $\mathbf{s}$ in terms of a reduced basis of our lattice cannot involve the longest basis element (because $\mathbf{s}$ is short), so $\mathbf{s}$ is confined to the hyperplane spanned by the other basis elements. This gives a linear equation on $\{r_{gh} = x^g y^h\}$, which we interpret as a polynomial equation on x and y. We combine this with $p(x, y) = 0$ and solve for x_0 and y_0.

The remainder of the paper is organized as follows. In Section 2 the algorithm is developed, concentrating on the concrete case where $p(x, y)$ has degree 1 in each variable. Section 3 gives a brief discussion of linear lattice methods as applied to the nonlinear problem of solving polynomials. In Section 4 we extend the algorithm to other bivariate polynomials, and discuss the dependence on the size parameter D and degree δ of the polynomial p. We comment on possible extensions to three or more variables in Section 5. In Sections 6 and 7 we compare the current algorithm with previous ones. An application to Vanstone and Zuccherato's RSA variant is given in Section 8. The appendix proves a technical result on Toeplitz matrices.

2 Factoring with high order bits known

We present the algorithm in terms of the problem of factoring an integer when we know the high-order bits of one of the factors.

Suppose we know $N = PQ$, and suppose that for some $\epsilon > 0$ we know the high order $(\frac{1}{4} + \epsilon)(\log_2 N)$ bits of P. (We will dispense with the ϵ later.) By division we know the high order bits of Q as well.

$$\begin{aligned}
P &= P_0 + x_0 \\
Q &= Q_0 + y_0 \\
|x_0| &< X = P_0/N^{(1/4)+\epsilon} \\
|y_0| &< Y = Q_0/N^{(1/4)+\epsilon} \\
p(x, y) &= (P_0 + x)(Q_0 + y) - N \\
&= (P_0Q_0 - N) + Q_0x + P_0y + xy \\
p(x_0, y_0) &= PQ - N = 0
\end{aligned}$$

Here P_0 and Q_0 are known, while x_0 and y_0 are unknown, and x and y are dummy variables. $p(x, y)$ is an irreducible polynomial with integer coefficients, and its coefficients share no common factor.

We will relate the bounds X and Y to the quantity

$$D = \max\{|P_0Q_0 - N|, Q_0X, P_0Y, XY\} .$$

This is the largest possible size of an individual term of $p(x, y)$ with bounded x and y. For our methods to work, we will require $(XY)^{3/2} < D$. In the case of a more general polynomial $p(x, y) = \sum_{ij} p_{ij} x^i y^j$, of degree δ separately in each variable, we would define

$$D = \max_{ij}\{|p_{ij}|X^i Y^j\}$$

and demand $(XY)^{3\delta/2} < D$. (The definitions of X, Y, D appear circular, but it's all right; the condition is equivalent to existence of indices $i, j \leq \delta$ such that $X^{(3\delta/2)-i}Y^{(3\delta/2)-j} < |p_{ij}|$, and the exponents $(3\delta/2) - i$ and $(3\delta/2) - j$ are strictly positive.)

We are trying to find a bounded pair of integers (x_0, y_0) solving $p(x_0, y_0) = 0$. We begin by selecting an integer $k > 1/(4\epsilon)$. For each pair of integers (i, j) with $0 \leq i < k$ and $0 \leq j < k$, form the polynomial $q_{ij}(x, y) = x^i y^j p(x, y)$. Obviously $q_{ij}(x_0, y_0) = 0$.

Form a matrix M_1 with $(k+1)^2$ rows, indexed by $\gamma(g, h) = (k+1)g + h$ with $0 \leq g, h < k+1$. M_1 has $(k+1)^2 + k^2$ columns, the left-hand columns indexed by $\gamma(g, h)$, and the right-hand columns indexed by $\beta(i, j) = (k+1)^2 + ki + j$ with $0 \leq i, j < k$. The left-hand block is a diagonal matrix whose $(\gamma(g, h), \gamma(g, h))$ entry is given by $X^{-g}Y^{-h}$. The $(\gamma(g, h), \beta(i, j))$ entry of the right-hand block is the coefficient of $x^g y^h$ in the polynomial $q_{ij}(x, y)$.

An explanation of M_1 is in order. The $\gamma(g, h)$ row corresponds to an integer unknown r_{gh} which represents $x_0^g y_0^h$. In the left-hand block, the diagonal entry $X^{-g}Y^{-h}$ will be used to bound $|r_{gh}|$ by approximately $X^g Y^h$. We will be concentrating on the sublattice in which the right-hand columns are zero; a zero in column $\beta(i, j)$ will correspond to the condition $q_{ij}(x_0, y_0) = 0$.

Perform elementary row operations on M_1 to produce a matrix M_2 whose right-hand block has the $k^2 \times k^2$ identity matrix on the bottom and the $(2k + 1) \times k^2$ zero matrix on the top. We can do this because the coefficient of xy in p is 1, so that the right-hand block of M_1 contains an upper triangular matrix with 1 on the diagonal. (For a more general polynomial $p(x, y)$, we require that the coefficients of p share no nontrivial common factor; in other words, $p(x, y)$ does not factor as $k \times u(x, y)$ over $\mathbb{Z}$.)

The lattice formed by these top $2k + 1$ rows of M_2 is the sublattice of the original lattice gotten by forcing to 0 all the right-hand columns. Call it M_3.

Consider the $(k+1)^2$-long row vector $\mathbf{r}$ whose $\gamma(g, h)$ entry is $x_0^g y_0^h$. The row vector $\mathbf{s}$ of length $(k + 1)^2 + k^2$ given by $\mathbf{s} = \mathbf{r}M_1$ satisfies

$$\begin{aligned} s_{\gamma(g,h)} &= (x_0/X)^g (y_0/Y)^h \\ |s_{\gamma(g,h)}| &\leq 1 \\ s_{\beta(i,j)} &= q_{ij}(x_0, y_0) = 0 \\ |\mathbf{s}| &< k + 1 \end{aligned}$$

Because its right-hand side is 0, $\mathbf{s}$ is one of the vectors in the lattice spanned by the rows of M_3. We will show that it is a "relatively short" vector in the lattice, which will enable us to confine it to a hyperplane, thus producing a linear equation relating its coefficients. This will translate directly to a polynomial equation on x_0 and y_0: $u(x_0, y_0) = 0$, where $u(x, y)$ is not a multiple of $p(x, y)$. We can then take the resultant of $u(x, y)$ with $p(x, y)$ to find a single polynomial equation $v(x) = 0$ satisfied by x_0, and solve this equation over $\mathbb{Z}$ to find x_0.

We proceed to estimate the sizes of the vectors in row lattice spanned by M_3, by estimating the determinant of a square submatrix of M_3. Define the diagonal matrix W of dimension $(k + 1)^2 \times (k + 1)^2$, with $(\gamma(g, h), \gamma(g, h))$ entry given by X^gY^h. In the matrix WM_1, the left-hand block is the identity. In the $\beta(i,j)$ column of the right-hand side of WM_1, the largest element has absolute value X^iY^jD. That is, the element at $(\gamma(g,h),\beta(i,j))$ is

$$X^gY^hp_{g-i,h-j} = X^{i+a}Y^{j+b}p_{ab} = X^iY^j(X^aY^bp_{ab})$$

where $a = g - i$ and $b = h - j$. Further, the right-hand columns are "nearly orthogonal", because they are part of a Toeplitz array. (A formal statement and proof appear in the appendix.) Associated with this near orthogonality, there is a specific set of k^2 columns in the left-hand block. Whenever we delete these k^2 columns from a rectangular matrix M, we denote the resulting square matrix as $\hat{M}$. Deleting these columns from WM_1 leaves a matrix $W\hat{M}_1$ whose determinant satisfies

$$\begin{aligned}|\det(W\hat{M}_1)| &= \Omega(\textstyle\prod_{ij}(X^iY^jD)) \\ &= \Omega((XY)^{k^2(k-1)/2}D^{k^2}) \ ,\end{aligned}$$

the constant implicit in Ω depending on k and the pattern of nonzero coefficients in the polynomial $p(x,y)$, as shown in the appendix. For the polynomial in our example, the constant is 1 (see appendix) so we drop the "Ω":

$$|\det(W\hat{M}_1)| = (XY)^{k^2(k-1)/2}D^{k^2} \ .$$

Since

$$\det(W) = \prod_{gh}(X^gY^h) = (XY)^{(k+1)^2k/2} \ ,$$

we can calculate

$$\begin{aligned}|\det(\hat{M}_1)| &= |\det(W\hat{M}_1)|/\det(W) \geq D^{k^2}(XY)^{\{k^2(k-1)/2\}-\{(k+1)^2k/2\}} \\ &= D^{k^2}(XY)^{-k(3k+1)/2} = \left(D^k(XY)^{-(3k+1)/2}\right)^k \ .\end{aligned}$$

Remark. Here is where we will use the fact that $(XY)^{3/2} < D$; in this example, it happens to be a consequence of the knowledge of $(\frac{1}{4}+\epsilon)(\log_2 N)$ bits.

From

$$\begin{aligned}D &\geq |P_0Y| &&= P_0Q_0/N^{1/4+\epsilon} \\ XY &= (P_0/N^{1/4+\epsilon})(Q_0/N^{1/4+\epsilon}) &&= P_0Q_0/N^{1/2+2\epsilon}\end{aligned}$$

we see

$$D^k(XY)^{-(3k+1)/2} \geq (P_0Q_0)^{-(k+1)/2}N^{(k/2)+(1/4)+(2k+1)\epsilon} \ .$$

Because $P_0Q_0 = N(1+o(N^{-1/4}))$ we can replace P_0Q_0 by N and incur negligible error:

$$D^k(XY)^{-(3k+1)/2} \geq N^{(-1/4)+(2k+1)\epsilon}(1+o(kN^{-1/4})) \ .$$

Recall $k > 1/(4\epsilon)$. Then

$$D^k(XY)^{-(3k+1)/2} > N^{(+1/4)+\epsilon}(1+o(kN^{-1/4})) > N^{1/4} \ ,$$

$$|\det(\hat{M}_1)| > N^{k/4} \gg 1 \ .$$

The same estimate applies to $|\det(\hat{M}_2)|$ because $\hat{M}_2$ was gotten from M_1 by elementary row operations. Also, because the lower right $k^2 \times k^2$ submatrix of $\hat{M}_2$ is the identity and the upper right submatrix is zero, the same estimate applies to the determinant of the upper left $(2k+1) \times (2k+1)$ submatrix of $\hat{M}_2$, namely the left-hand $(2k+1)\times(2k+1)$ square submatrix of M_3. For the following discussion, we call that square submatrix L and its dimension $n = 2k+1$. So $|\det(L)| > N^{k/4}$.

We apply lattice basis reduction to the row basis of L, as prescribed in [2], to produce a reduced basis $\mathbf{b}_1, \mathbf{b}_2, \ldots, \mathbf{b}_n$. From the discussion in [2], the last element $\mathbf{b}_n$ of this reduced basis satisfies

$$|\mathbf{b}_n^*| \geq |\det(L)|^{1/n} 2^{-(n-1)/4} ,$$

where $\mathbf{b}_n^*$ denotes the component of $\mathbf{b}_n$ orthogonal to the subspace spanned by the vectors $\mathbf{b}_1, \ldots, \mathbf{b}_{n-1}$. As long as

$$k < \frac{1}{4} \log_2 N - 2 \log_2 \log_2 N - \Omega(1) ,$$

we will have that $|\mathbf{b}_n^*| > |\mathbf{s}|$:

$$\begin{aligned}|\mathbf{b}_n^*| &\geq |\det(L)|^{1/n} 2^{-(n-1)/4} > N^{(k/4)(1/(2k+1))} 2^{-2k/4} \\ &\approx N^{(1/8)-(1/(16k))} 2^{-k/2} > k+1 > |\mathbf{s}| .\end{aligned}$$

Assume this inequality holds. For any row vector $\mathbf{t}$ in the lattice spanned by L, if $\mathbf{t}$ is not in the lattice spanned by $\mathbf{b}_1, \ldots, \mathbf{b}_{n-1}$, then its expression as an integer combination of the $\mathbf{b}_i$ involves $\mathbf{b}_n$ nontrivially. Thus we have $|\mathbf{t}| \geq |\mathbf{b}_n^*| > k+1 > |\mathbf{s}|$. Looked at the other way, for any $\mathbf{t}$ in the lattice spanned by L, if $|\mathbf{t}| \leq |\mathbf{s}|$, then $\mathbf{t}$ is in the lattice spanned by $\mathbf{b}_1, \ldots, \mathbf{b}_{n-1}$.

Consider $\mathbf{s}$ itself. The $n = 2k+1$ entries of $\mathbf{s}$ corresponding to those columns in the left-hand side that remain when we transform M to $\hat{M}$, form a row vector $\hat{\mathbf{s}}$ in the lattice spanned by L (since the right-hand elements of $\mathbf{s}$ are 0). Also, $|\hat{\mathbf{s}}| \leq |\mathbf{s}|$. Thus $\hat{\mathbf{s}}$ is in the lattice spanned by $\mathbf{b}_1, \ldots, \mathbf{b}_{n-1}$.

Membership in this subspace gives us a linear relation on the coefficients $r_{gh} = x_0^g y_0^h$ expressing $\mathbf{s}$ as a linear combination of the rows of M_1. This relation is linearly independent of the k^2 relations given by the polynomials $q_{ij}(x,y)$ which determined that $\mathbf{s}$ had right-hand side 0 and thus was in the lattice of M_3 to start with. So this relation translates to a polynomial relation $u(x_0, y_0) = 0$ where $u(x,y)$ is not a polynomial multiple of $p(x,y)$.

Take the resultant of $p(x,y)$ and $u(x,y)$ with respect to y. Because $p(x,y)$ is irreducible and $u(x,y)$ is not a polynomial multiple of $p(x,y)$, we have that $\text{Resultant}_y(p(x,y), u(x,y)) = v(x)$ is a nontrivial integer polynomial $v(x)$ in one variable x satisfied by x_0: $v(x_0) = 0$. Since $u(x,y)$ has degree at most k in each variable and $p(x,y)$ has degree 1 in each variable, $v(x)$ has degree at most $2k$. Solve $v(x) = 0$ over $\mathbb{Z}$ to find a small number of candidates for x_0, namely those integer solutions satisfying the bound $|x_0| < X$.

Each candidate value of x_0 can be substituted into p to get an equation $p(x_0, y) = 0$ which we can solve for y over $\mathbb{Z}$, and select those integer solutions satisfying the bound $|y_0| < Y$.

Thus we have proven:

Theorem 1. *If we know an integer* $N = PQ$ *and we know the high order* $(1/4+\epsilon)(\log_2 N)$ *bits of* P*, with* $\epsilon > 2/(\log_2 N)$*, then in time polynomial in* $\log N$ *and* $1/\epsilon$ *we can discover* P *and* Q*.*

Proof. The condition on ϵ insures that k can be chosen to satisfy

$$\frac{1}{4\epsilon} < k < \frac{\log_2 N}{4} - O(\log\log N) \ .$$

The complexity is due to invocation of lattice basis reduction on a matrix of size $2k+1 \approx 1/(2\epsilon)$, whose elements are integers with bit length bounded by a polynomial in $\log N$. (We have to transform our rational matrices to integer matrices by multiplying by some integer.) □

Corollary 2. *If we know an integer* $N = PQ$ *and we know the high order* $(1/4)(\log_2 N)$ *bits of* P*, then in time polynomial in* $\log N$ *we can discover* P *and* Q*.*

Proof. Set $\epsilon = 4/\log_2 N$ and do exhaustive search on $O(1)$ unknown high order bits of x_0 (or middle bits of P). □

3 Discussion on lattice methods

The lattice basis reduction method is inherently linear. If we want to relate several unknowns by a polynomial equation $p(x,y) = \sum_{gh} p_{gh} x^g y^h = 0$, one natural approach is to replace each monomial $x^g y^h$ by a new independent variable r_{gh}, and let p become a linear relation among several independent bounded variables: $\sum_{gh} p_{gh} r_{gh} = 0$, $|r_{gh}| \leq X^g Y^h = R_{gh}$. In order to get results, we would need the desired vector to be among the shortest of the lattice; we would need its length to be smaller than the root of the determinant of the appropriate square matrix. This requirement translates to (approximately) $\prod R_{gh} \leq D$, and this would imply severe restrictions on X and Y, namely $(XY)^{(\delta+1)^2\delta/2} \leq D$, where $p(x,y)$ has degree δ in each variable. This is essentially the technique used by [6] in the modular setting.

In the present paper we have extended this approach by using several polynomials q_{ij} but reusing the same independent bounded variables r_{gh}. We are able to amortize the cost of the several variables over several equations. This accounts for the success of the present method in increasing the feasible sizes of X and Y. Specifically, each unknown r_{gh} contributes a factor of $X^{-g}Y^{-h}$ to $\det(\hat{M}_1)$, while each equation $q_{ij}(x,y) = 0$ contributes a factor of $X^i Y^j D$. In order for our techniques to work, we require $\det(\hat{M}_1) \gg 1$, which yields a bound on X and Y in terms of D. Because we have several polynomial equations, each contributing positively to the determinant, this bound is relatively mild; we can tolerate larger ranges X, Y on our variables (in terms of D) than with other methods, namely $(XY)^{3\delta/2} < D$, as we will see in the next section.

4 Other bivariate polynomials

Similar techniques can be applied successfully to other polynomial equations besides the given $p(x,y)=0$. They are not guaranteed for polynomials of more than two variables; see Section 5.

Even in the case of two variables, the present technique is sensitive to the form of the polynomial $p(x,y)$. For an arbitrary quadratic polynomial we could not tolerate ranges X, Y for the unknowns x, y quite as large as we did here. In the case that we used for our example, although $p(x,y)$ has degree two, it does not have terms involving x^2 or y^2, only xy.

We sketch here how the bounds X and Y depend on D and the form of p. When we estimated $|\det(\hat{M}_1)|$ by dividing the estimate of $|\det(W\hat{M}_1)|$ by $\det(W)$, there was considerable cancellation in the powers of X and Y. The term $|\det(W\hat{M}_1)|$ had a factor X^iY^jD for each pair (i,j) with $0 \le i,j < k$; these pairs represented the monomials x^iy^j by which $p(x,y)$ was multiplied. The term $\det(W)$ had a factor X^gY^h for each pair (g,h) with $0 \le g,h < k+1$; these pairs represented the monomials x^gy^h appearing in these products $x^iy^jp(x,y)$. The range on g exceeds the range on i by 1 because p has degree 1 in x. If p had an x^2 term, we would have needed to enlarge the range of g. The powers of X and Y appearing in the ratio $|\det(W\hat{M}_1)|/\det(W)$ arise from the pairs (g,h) outside the range of (i,j), namely

$$\{(g,h)|g=k, 0 \le h < k\} \cup \{(g,h)|h=k, 0 \le g \le k\} .$$

The inclusion of an x^2 term would have enlarged that region by another layer. This would have led directly to a stricter requirement on the sizes of X and Y.

If our polynomial $p(x,y)$ has degree δ in x and τ in y, then we can tolerate ranges X and Y satisfying

$$X^{\delta+(\tau/2)}Y^{\tau+(\delta/2)} < D$$

by using polynomials $q_{ij}(x,y)$ in the range $0 \le i,j < k$. More generally, for any positive value of the parameter α we can tolerate X and Y with

$$X^{\delta+(\alpha\tau/2)}Y^{\tau+(\delta/(2\alpha))} < D$$

by allowing $0 \le i < k\alpha$ and $0 \le j < k$.

If $p(x,y)$ has total degree δ then we can tolerate about

$$D > (XY)^{\delta}$$

by allowing pairs (i,j) with $i \ge 0$, $j \ge 0$, and $i+j < k$. This is better than the previous approach if p is a general bivariate polynomial of total degree δ, but worse if (like the current example) it is really of degree $\delta/2$ separately in each variable.

We summarize these results:

Theorem 3. *Let* $p(x,y) = \sum_{ij} p_{ij} x^i y^j$ *be a bivariate polynomial over* $\mathbb{Z}$ *of degree* δ *in* x *and* τ *in* y. *Assume* p *is irreducible over* $\mathbb{Z}$. *Let* X *and* Y *be bounds on desired solutions* $|x_0|$ *and* $|y_0|$. *Define* $D = \max_{ij} |p_{ij}| X^i Y^j$. *Choose* $\alpha > 0$. *Assume*

$$X^{\delta+(\alpha\tau/2)} Y^{\tau+(\delta/(2\alpha))} < D \times 2^{-3(\delta^2+\tau^2)-2} .$$

In time polynomial in δ, τ *and* $\log_2 D$, *our algorithm will produce all integer pairs* (x_0, y_0) *with* $|x_0| < X$, $|y_0| < Y$, *and* $p(x_0, y_0) = 0$.

Let $p(x,y)$ *be as before, but with total degree* δ. *Assume*

$$(XY)^\delta < D \times 2^{-6\delta^2-2} .$$

In time polynomial in δ *and* $\log_2 D$, *our algorithm will produce all integer pairs* (x_0, y_0) *with* $|x_0| < X$, $|y_0| < Y$, *and* $p(x_0, y_0) = 0$.

Proof. The proof will be given in the full paper, but is quite similar to that of Theorem 1 and Corollary 2. □

5 More variables

Suppose we have a polynomial $p(x,y,z)$ in three variables. We can mimic the present approach. If the ranges X, Y, Z are small enough, we will end up with a polynomial relation $u(x,y,z)$, not a multiple of p, satisfied by (x_0, y_0, z_0). Then the resultant of p and u with respect to z will give a polynomial $v(x,y)$ in two variables. We can then try to solve v by the current methods. But the degree of v will be quite high, so that the ranges X and Y which can be tolerated will be quite small. This approach will be unsatisfactory in general.

We still have a heuristic procedure which *might* work for a given multivariate polynomial. We are guaranteed to find a space of codimension 1 (a hyperplane) containing all the short vectors of the lattice M_3. But we might easily find a space of larger codimension. (There is a good possibility that for many basis vectors $\mathbf{b}_i$, the orthogonal component $|\mathbf{b}_i^*|$ exceeds our known upper bound on $|\mathbf{s}|$, and each one increases the codimension of the space which contains all the short vectors.) We develop several polynomial equations $u_i(x,y,z)$ satisfying $u_i(x_0, y_0, z_0) = 0$; the number of such equations is equal to the codimension of this space. We can then take resultants and gcd's of the various u_i and p and hope to produce a single polynomial equation in a single variable $v(x_0) = 0$, which we solve over $\mathbb{Z}$. This is only a heuristic approach, which might or might not work for a given polynomial p. (Even if we can generate several equations, they may not be independent.)

There must be limits to the success of this approach in general. Manders and Adleman [3] show that finding suitably bounded solutions to $p_N(x,y,z) = x^2 - yN - z = 0$ is NP-hard. Nonetheless the approach might work for a particular polynomial, and it is worth trying.

6 Comparison with the univariate modular algorithm

In a companion paper [1], the author applies a very similar algorithm for the solution of a univariate modular polynomial.

Two differences between the algorithms are worth noticing. In the modular case, the size X of the acceptable solutions x_0 was related to the modulus N. In the present integer case, there is no such natural measure as N, and we needed to develop a bound in terms of D.

A second difference is that in the modular case, we were able to define polynomials $q_{ij}(x) = x^i p(x)^j$ and assert that $q_{ij}(x_0) = 0 \pmod{N^j}$; the extra information ($\bmod N^j$ versus $\bmod N$) improved our bound on X from $N^{1/(2\delta-1)}$ to $N^{1/\delta}$. In the present integer case, using the polynomial equations $q_{ijk}(x,y) = x^i y^j p(x,y)^k = 0$ would not help, because (for the appropriate ranges of indices i, j, k) the integer linear combinations of the polynomials q_{ij} are exactly the same as those of the polynomials q_{ijk}. For example, with the given $p(x,y)$, $\delta = 1$, and setting $k = 4$, the integer linear combinations of

$$q_{ij}(x,y) = x^i y^j p(x,y), \quad 0 \le i,j < 4$$

are the same as the integer linear combinations of

$$p, xp, x^2p, x^3p, yp, y^2p, y^3p, p^2, xp^2, x^2p^2, yp^2, y^2p^2, p^3, xp^3, yp^3, p^4 \quad ,$$

so that we end up defining the same matrix M_1 (up to elementary column operations). (If p is not monic, we appear to gain something from the high coefficient of p, but we actually lose a corresponding amount in the proof, so that using powers of p still neither helps nor hurts us.) This much is also true in the modular case; however, there we gain the extra advantage of working $\bmod N^j$ as opposed to working $\bmod N$, and here in the integer case we can derive no such advantage.

7 Comparison with previous work

Rivest and Shamir [5] solve the problem of factorization if given $(\log_2 N)/3$ bits rather than $(\log_2 N)/4$ bits as we do. They too use lattice methods, but only one polynomial $q_{00}(x,y) = p(x,y)$.

Vallée et al. [6] employ a method similar to [5] in the case of modular polynomials, again using only one polynomial.

Maurer [4] uses a different approach, related to factoring algorithms based on smooth integers, to ask $(\epsilon \log_2 N)$ yes/no oracle questions and determine the factorization of N with failure probability $O\left(N^{-\epsilon/2}\right)$.

8 Application to RSA variant

Vanstone and Zuccherato [7] propose an identity-based variant of RSA in which the user's modulus N is related to his identity. For example, the high order bits of N may be the user's name encoded in ASCII.

Unfortunately, the modulus N is generated in such a way that somewhat more than the high order $((1/4)\log_2 N)$ bits of P are revealed to the public. This enables the present attack to discover the factorization of each modulus and break the scheme.

9 Acknowledgements

Matt Franklin and Mike Reiter's Crypto 95 rump session talk opened this whole line of investigation; subsequent discussions were also useful. The author gratefully acknowledges enlightening discussions with Andrew Odlyzko. Barry Trager helped the experimental effort by coding up in Axiom an implementation of the Lenstra Lenstra Lovasz lattice basis reduction algorithm. The Eurocrypt program committee made suggestions which improved the presentation of the paper.

References

1. D. Coppersmith, "Finding a Small Root of a Univariate Modular Equation," Proceedings of Eurocrypt 96.
2. A. K. Lenstra, H. W. Lenstra and L. Lovasz, "Factoring Polynomials with Integer Coefficients," Matematische Annalen **261** (1982), 513–534.
3. K. Manders and L. Adleman, "NP-complete decision problems for binary quadratics," *J. Comput. System Sci.* **16**, 168-184.
4. U. M. Maurer, "Factoring with an Oracle," Advances in Cryptology – EUROCRYPT '92, Springer LNCS **658** (1993) 429–436.
5. R. L. Rivest and A. Shamir, "Efficient factoring based on partial information," Advances in Cryptology – EUROCRYPT '85, Springer LNCS **219** (1986) 31–34.
6. B. Vallée, M. Girault and P. Toffin, "How to Guess ℓ-th Roots Modulo n by Reducing Lattice Bases," Proceedings of AAECC-6, Springer LNCS **357** (1988) 427–442.
7. S. A. Vanstone and R. J. Zuccherato, "Short RSA Keys and Their Generation," Journal of Cryptology **8** number 2 (Spring 1995) 101–114.

10 Appendix

In this appendix we give a proof of the technical result needed in Section 2: that several columns of the matrix WM_1 are "nearly orthogonal". A modification of this proof would apply to any Toeplitz matrix.

We develop the corresponding result for a general bivariate polynomial. Let M_4 be the right-hand block of WM_1. Let $p(x,y)$ have degree δ in each variable separately. Define indexing functions γ and μ for M_4: The rows of M_4 are indexed by $\gamma(g,h) = (k+\delta)g+h$ for $0 \leq g,h < k+\delta$, and the columns by $\mu(i,j) = ki+j$ for $0 \leq i,j < k$. Define $\tilde{p}(x,y) = p(Xx, Yy)$, so that $\tilde{p}_{ab} = X^a Y^b p_{ab}$ and $\max_{ab} |p_{ab}| = D$.

Lemma 4. *There is a $k^2 \times k^2$ submatrix of M_4 whose determinant has absolute value at least*

$$D^{k^2} 2^{-6k^2\delta^2 - 2k^2} .$$

If the largest coefficient of $\tilde{p}$ is one of $\tilde{p}_{00}$, $\tilde{p}_{0\delta}$, $\tilde{p}_{\delta 0}$ or $\tilde{p}_{\delta\delta}$, then the absolute value of the determinant is exactly D^{k^2}.

Proof. Select indices (a, b) so that $D = |\tilde{p}_{ab}|$ is the largest coefficient of $\tilde{p}$. Select indices (c, d) to maximize the quantity

$$8^{(c-a)^2+(d-b)^2} |\tilde{p}_{cd}| \; .$$

Select the rows

$$\gamma(c+i, d+j), 0 \leq i, j < k$$

of M_4 to create the desired submatrix $\tilde{M}$. The rows and columns of $\tilde{M}$ are indexed by $\mu(i,j) = ki + j$. The matrix element $\tilde{M}_{\mu(g,h),\mu(i,j)}$ is the coefficient of $x^{c+g} y^{d+h}$ in $x^i y^j \tilde{p}(x, y)$, namely

$$\tilde{M}_{\mu(g,h),\mu(i,j)} = \tilde{p}_{g-i+c,h-j+d}$$

Multiply the $\mu(g, h)$ row of $\tilde{M}$ by $8^{2(c-a)g+2(d-b)h}$, and multiply the $\mu(i, j)$ column by $8^{-2(c-a)i-2(d-b)j}$, to create a new matrix M' with the same determinant. Its typical element is

$$M'_{\mu(g,h),\mu(i,j)} = \tilde{p}_{g-i+c,h-j+d} 8^{2(c-a)(g-i)+2(d-b)(h-j)} .$$

From maximality of (c, d) we find

$$|\tilde{p}_{g-i+c,h-j+d}| 8^{(g-i+c-a)^2+(h-j+d-b)^2} \leq |\tilde{p}_{cd}| 8^{(c-a)^2+(d-b)^2} ,$$

from which

$$|\tilde{p}_{g-i+c,h-j+d}| 8^{2(g-i)(c-a)+2(h-j)(d-b)} \leq |\tilde{p}_{cd}| 8^{-(g-i)^2-(h-j)^2} .$$

Thus each diagonal entry of M' is $\tilde{p}_{cd}$, and each off-diagonal entry is bounded in absolute value by $|\tilde{p}_{cd}| 8^{-(g-i)^2-(h-j)^2}$. This implies that M' is diagonally dominant, because the absolute values of the off-diagonal entries in its $\mu(i, j)$ row sum to at most

$$\begin{aligned} &|\tilde{p}_{cd}| \times \textstyle\sum_{(g,h)\neq(i,j)} 8^{-(g-i)^2-(h-j)^2} = |\tilde{p}_{cd}| \times \textstyle\sum_{(a,b)\neq(0,0)} 8^{-a^2-b^2} \\ &= |\tilde{p}_{cd}| \times \left[-1 + \textstyle\sum_{(a,b)} 8^{-a^2-b^2}\right] = |\tilde{p}_{cd}| \times \left[-1 + (\textstyle\sum_a 8^{-a^2})^2\right] < \tfrac{3}{4} |\tilde{p}_{cd}| \end{aligned}$$

Each eigenvalue of M' is within $\frac{3}{4}|\tilde{p}_{cd}|$ of $\tilde{p}_{cd}$, and so exceeds $\frac{1}{4}|\tilde{p}_{cd}|$ in absolute value. By choice of (c, d) we know

$$8^{(c-a)^2+(d-b)^2} |\tilde{p}_{cd}| \geq 8^0 |\tilde{p}_{ab}| = D$$

$$|\tilde{p}_{cd}| \geq 8^{-2\delta^2} D$$

$$|\det(M')| \geq \left(\frac{1}{4}|\tilde{p}_{cd}|\right)^{k^2} \geq \left(\frac{1}{4}8^{-2\delta^2}D\right)^{k^2} = D^{k^2}2^{-6k^2\delta^2-2k^2}.$$

For the second claim of the lemma: If the largest coefficient of $\tilde{p}$ is either $\tilde{p}_{00}$ or $\tilde{p}_{\delta\delta}$, set $(c,d) = (a,b)$ and notice that $\tilde{M}$ is an (upper or lower) triangular matrix whose diagonal entries have absolute value D. If the largest coefficient is either $\tilde{p}_{0\delta}$ or $\tilde{p}_{\delta 0}$, redefine the indexing function on columns as $\mu(i,j) = ki+(k-1-j)$ so that again $\tilde{M}$ is a triangular matrix whose diagonal entries have absolute value D. Similar results hold if (a,b) is any corner of the Newton polygon associated with $\tilde{p}$.

For the particular case $p(x,y) = (P_0+x)(Q_0+y) - N$, we have $\delta = 1$, and the only non-zero coefficients of $\tilde{p}$ are $\tilde{p}_{00}$, $\tilde{p}_{0\delta}$, $\tilde{p}_{\delta 0}$ and $\tilde{p}_{\delta\delta}$; thus the second claim must hold. □

The lemma gives a $k^2 \times k^2$ submatrix $\tilde{M}$ of M_4, where M_4 is the right-hand $(k+\delta)^2 \times k^2$ block of WM_1. To apply the lemma, we need to find k^2 column indices in the left-hand block of WM_1 whose deletion leaves a $(k+\delta)^2 \times (k+\delta)^2$ submatrix $\widehat{WM_1}$ of WM_1 with $|\det(\widehat{WM_1})| = |\det(\tilde{M})|$. We simply delete those columns whose indices match those of the k^2 rows accepted in $\tilde{M}$. Recall that the left-hand side of WM_1 is the identity matrix, so each remaining left-hand column has a single 1 among the 0's, and expansion by minors gives $|\det(\widehat{WM_1})| = |\det(\tilde{M})|$ as desired.

Publicly Verifiable Secret Sharing

Markus Stadler *

Institute for Theoretical Computer Science
ETH Zurich
CH-8092 Zurich, Switzerland
Email: stadler@inf.ethz.ch

Abstract. A secret sharing scheme allows to share a secret among several participants such that only certain groups of them can recover it. Verifiable secret sharing has been proposed to achieve security against cheating participants. Its first realization had the special property that everybody, not only the participants, can verify that the shares are correctly distributed. We will call such schemes publicly verifiable secret sharing schemes, we discuss new applications to escrow cryptosystems and to payment systems with revocable anonymity, and we present two new realizations based on ElGamal's cryptosystem.

1 Introduction

A *secret sharing* scheme [20, 2] allows to split a secret into different pieces, called shares, which are given to the participants, such that only certain groups of them can recover the secret. The first secret sharing schemes have been threshold schemes, where only groups of more than a certain number of participants can recover the secret.

Verifiable secret sharing (VSS) is a cryptographic primitive proposed in [7] to achieve security against cheating participants. A verification protocol allows the honest participants to ensure that they can recover a unique secret. VSS plays an important role in the design of protocols for secure multi-party computation (see e.g. [1]). The first realization of VSS, presented in [7], has the very special property that not only the participants, but everybody is able to verify that the shares have been correctly distributed. We will call such schemes *publicly verifiable secret sharing (PVSS)* schemes. Apart from the applications for "ordinary" VSS, PVSS can be used for new escrow-cryptosystems, and for the realization of digital payment systems with revocable anonymity.

The main technical results of this paper are two new PVSS schemes which can also be used with general (monotone) access structures. Both schemes are based on ElGamal's cryptosystem [9]. Furthermore, the security of the first scheme can be proved to be equivalent to some well-known cryptographic problems.

* Supported by the Swiss Federal Commission for the Advancement of Scientific Research (KWF) and by the Union Bank of Switzerland.

Ueli Maurer (Ed.): EUROCRYPT '96 Proceedings, LNCS 1070

2 Publicly Verifiable Secret Sharing and Applications

2.1 An Informal Model of PVSS

In the sequel we give a informal description of secret sharing, verifiable secret sharing, and publicly verifiable secret sharing. It is not our goal to present a precise mathematical definition, but to illustrate the basic properties of the schemes and to point out the difference between ordinary and publicly verifiable secret sharing.

A secret sharing scheme consists of a *dealer*, n participants $P_1, \ldots, P_n$, and an access structure $\mathcal{A} \subseteq 2^{\{1,\ldots,n\}}$. The access structure is monotone, which means that if $A \in \mathcal{A}$ and $A \subseteq B$ then $B \in \mathcal{A}$. For instance, in a threshold secret sharing scheme with threshold k the access structure is defined as $\mathcal{A} = \{A \in 2^{\{1,\ldots,n\}} \mid |A| \geq k\}$, which means that any coalition of at least k participants can recover the secret.

To share a secret s among the participants, the dealer runs an algorithm *Share*

$$\mathit{Share}(s) = (s_1, \ldots, s_n)$$

to compute the shares. The dealer then sends each share s_i secretly to P_i, $i = 1, \ldots, n$. If a group of participants wants to recover the secret, they run an algorithm *Recover*, which has the property that

$$\forall A \in \mathcal{A}: \quad \mathit{Recover}(\{s_i | i \in A\}) = s \ ,$$

and that for all $A \notin \mathcal{A}$ it is computationally infeasible to calculate s from $\{s_i | i \in A\}$. Thus, only those coalitions of participants defined by the access structure $\mathcal{A}$ are able to recover the secret s. A secret sharing scheme is called *perfect* if for all $A \notin \mathcal{A}$ the shares $\{s_i | i \in A\}$ give no Shannon information about the secret.

One problem of such secret sharing schemes is that they are not secure against cheating participants who send false shares when the secret is to be recovered. Another problem is that a cheating dealer could distribute false shares, so that different groups of participants recover different secrets. Such problems arise in protocols for secure multi-party computations (see e.g. [1]), and can be solved with verifiable secret sharing (VSS) schemes [7].

A VSS scheme is a secret sharing scheme with an additional, possibly interactive algorithm *Verify* which allows the participants to verify the validity of their shares:

$$\exists u \; \forall A \in \mathcal{A}: \quad (\forall i \in A: \mathit{Verify}(s_i) = 1) \quad \Rightarrow \quad \mathit{Recover}(\{s_i | i \in A\}) = u,$$
$$\textit{and } u = s \textit{ if the dealer was honest.}$$

In other words, all groups of participants recover the same value if their shares are valid, and this unique value is the secret if the dealer was honest. A VSS scheme is called non-interactive, if the algorithm *Verify* requires no interaction between the participants [11].

But even with a non-interactive VSS scheme, the participants can verify the validity of only their own shares, but they cannot know whether other participants (with whom they might be able to recover the secret) have also received valid shares. This problem can be solved with publicly verifiable secret sharing (PVSS). In a PVSS scheme a public encryption function E_i is assigned to each participant P_i, such that only he knows the corresponding decryption function D_i. The dealer now uses the public encryption functions to distribute the shares by calculating

$$S_i = E_i(s_i), \quad i = 1, \ldots, n$$

and publishing the encrypted shares S_i. To verify the validity of all the encrypted shares, there is an algorithm *PubVerify* with the property that

$$\exists u \; \forall A \in 2^{\{1,\ldots,n\}} : \\ (\mathit{PubVerify}(\{S_i | i \in A\}) = 1) \;\Rightarrow\; \mathit{Recover}(\{D_i(S_i) | i \in A\}) = u$$

and $u = s$ if the dealer was honest. In other words: If a set of encrypted shares is "good" according to *PubVerify*, then the honest participants can decrypt them and recover the secret. Note that *PubVerify* can be executed even if the participants have not received their shares so far. To run *PubVerify* it may be necessary to communicate with the dealer (but not with any participant). A PVSS scheme is called non-interactive if *PubVerify* requires no interaction with the dealer at all.

Theoretically, PVSS could be realized using techniques of [4] to prove (or to argue about) the satisfiability of a circuit, but this would be very inefficient. We will present more practical solutions for sharing discrete logarithms and for sharing *e-th* roots in Sections 3 and 4, respectively. Both schemes are based on ElGamal's cryptosystem [9].

2.2 Applications of PVSS

Apart from the applications of ordinary secret sharing and of VSS, there are two interesting problems for which PVSS can be used. One of those is software key escrow, such as Micali's fair cryptosystems [16]. The basic idea of fair cryptosystems is that any user shares his secret key among several trustworthy (from the user's point of view) escrow agents by means of a VSS scheme. Each escrow agent can verify that he obtained a correct share of the secret key. However, one problem of such fair cryptosystems is that the recipient of an encrypted message decides on the set of trustworthy escrow agent, although the sender of the message might trusts a different set of agents. Furthermore, the set of escrow agents can only be changed by changing the key. A better solution for this problem would be to have the sender provide information for the escrow agents to decrypt the message. Such a system could be realized using a non-interactive PVSS scheme with an access structure that allows the recipient as well as a the escrow agents to recover (i.e. decrypt) the message. Since the encrypted shares can be publicly verified, everybody, e.g. any network provider, can verify that the message could be recovered by a legitimate subset of escrow agents.

Another application of PVSS is the design of electronic cash systems providing revocable anonymity [5, 21, 15, 6]. Payments made with such systems are (usually) not traceable to the payer, but if the anonymity of the scheme is abused for criminal activities, the payer's identity can be recovered with the help of so-called trustees or judges. PVSS could be used to verifiably encrypt tracing-information for the trustees in a transaction without compromising the anonymity of that transaction.

3 PVSS for Sharing Discrete Logarithms

We will first describe two well-known methods for verifiably sharing discrete logarithms. The verification for both schemes consists of checking whether the secret share is the discrete logarithm of a publicly known element. Therefore, these schemes can be extended to PVSS schemes by means of an encryption scheme that allows to verify that a cipher-text contains the discrete logarithm of a given value. Let us first briefly describe the number-theoretical setting.

3.1 Double Exponentiation and Double Discrete Logarithms

Let p be a large prime so that $q = (p-1)/2$ is also prime[1], and let $h \in \mathbb{Z}_p^*$ be an element of order q. Let further G be a group of order p, and let g be a generator of G so that computing discrete logarithms to the base g is difficult.

Our scheme will make use of double exponentiation. By double exponentiation with bases g and h we mean the function

$$\mathbb{Z}_q \to G : x \mapsto g^{(h^x)} .$$

By the double discrete logarithm of $y \in G$ to the bases g and h we mean the unique $x \in \mathbb{Z}_q$ with

$$y = g^{(h^x)}$$

if such an x exists.

3.2 Verifiable Sharing of Discrete Logarithms

Let $s \in \mathbb{Z}_p$ be the secret value and let $S = g^s$ be publicly known. There are different ways to verifiably share this secret. We first present a solution for general monotone access structures, and then briefly describe a threshold scheme [11, 18].

Let $\mathcal{A}$ be a monotone access structure. For each $A = \{j_1, \ldots, j_k\} \in \mathcal{A}$, the dealer proceeds as follows: He computes the secret shares

$$s_{Ai} = \begin{cases} \text{randomly chosen in } \mathbb{Z}_p \text{ for } i = j_1, \ldots, j_{k-1} \\ s - \sum_{\ell=1}^{k-1} s_{Aj_\ell} \pmod{p} \text{ for } i = j_k \end{cases}$$

[1] This property is necessary in order to prove the security of the scheme.

and secretly sends s_{Ai} to the participant P_i. The values $S_{Ai} = g^{s_{Ai}}$ are published so that everybody can verify that

$$\forall A \in \mathcal{A} : \prod_{i \in A} S_{Ai} = S.$$

The participant P_i can verify his share by checking whether s_{Ai} is the discrete logarithm of S_{Ai}. Note that this construction is quite unpractical for large access-structures.

To share s in a threshold-scheme with threshold k, a publicly-known element $x_i \in \mathbb{Z}_p$, $x_i \neq 0$ is assigned to each participant P_i. The dealer chooses random elements $f_j \in \mathbb{Z}_p$, $j = 1, \ldots, k-1$, and publishes the values $S = g^s$ and $F_j = g^{f_j}$, $j = 1, \ldots, k-1$. Then he secretly sends to each P_i the share

$$s_i = s + \sum_{j=1}^{k-1} f_j x_i^j \pmod{p}$$

Any group of at least k participants can now compute s using Lagrange's interpolation formula. To verify a share s_i, the participant P_i can compute

$$S_i = S \cdot \prod_{j=1}^{k-1} F_j^{(x_i^j)}$$

and check whether $S_i = g^{s_i}$. See [11, 18] for further details.

To make these schemes publicly verifiable, we need a public-key encryption scheme that allows to verifiably encrypt the discrete logarithm of a publicly known element. In other words, given a cipher-text W and a group element S, it should be possible to convince everybody that the recipient obtains $\log_g S$ by decrypting W.

3.3 Verifiable Encryption of Discrete Logarithms

Our encryption scheme is identical to ElGamal's public key system [9], which is a variation of the Diffie-Hellman key-exchange protocol [8].

First, each participant randomly chooses a secret key $z \in \mathbb{Z}_q$ and publishes his public-key $y = h^z \pmod{p}$. To encrypt a message $m \in \mathbb{Z}_p^*$ with the public-key y, the dealer randomly chooses $\alpha \in \mathbb{Z}_q$ and calculates the pair

$$(h^\alpha, m^{-1} \cdot y^\alpha) \pmod{p}.$$

The cipher-text (A, B) can be decrypted by the recipient by calculating

$$m = A^z / B \pmod{p}.$$

Let us now describe a protocol for verifying that a pair (A, B) encrypts the discrete logarithm of a public element $V = g^v$ of the group G. It is based on the fact that if (A, B) is equal to $(h^\alpha, v^{-1} \cdot y^\alpha) \pmod{p}$ for any $\alpha \in \mathbb{Z}_q$ then

$$V^B = g^{vB} = g^{(y^\alpha)}.$$

The prover (who will be the dealer in the secret sharing scheme) now proves to the verifier that the discrete logarithm of A to the base h is identical to the double discrete logarithm of V^B to the bases g and y.

Prover		**Verifier**
repeat K times:		
$w \in_R \mathbb{Z}_q$ $t_h = h^w \pmod p$ $t_g = g^{(y^w)}$	$\xrightarrow{t_h,\, t_g}$	
		$c \in_R \{0,1\}$
	$\xleftarrow{c}$	
$r = w - c \cdot \alpha \pmod q$	$\xrightarrow{r}$	
		$t_h \stackrel{?}{=} h^r A^c \pmod p$
		$t_g \stackrel{?}{=} \begin{cases} g^{(y^r)} & \text{if } c = 0 \\ V^{(B \cdot y^r)} & \text{if } c = 1 \end{cases}$

With the techniques of [12] for converting an identification scheme into a signature scheme, combined with ideas from [19], we can construct a non-interactive "proof": Let $\mathcal{H}_\ell : \{0,1\}^* \to \{0,1\}^\ell$ be a cryptographically strong hash-function ($\ell \approx 100$). For $i = 1 \ldots \ell$, the prover chooses $w_i \in_R \mathbb{Z}_q$ and calculates $t_{hi} = h^{w_i} \pmod p$, and $t_{gi} = g^{(y^{w_i})}$. Then he computes the ℓ-tuple

$$R = (r_1, \ldots, r_\ell) = (w_1 - c_1\alpha \pmod q), \ldots, w_\ell - c_\ell\alpha \pmod q))$$

where c_i denotes the i-th bit of

$$c = \mathcal{H}_\ell(V||A||B||t_{h1}||t_{g1}|| \ldots ||t_{h\ell}||t_{g\ell}) \qquad (*)$$

The non-interactive proof consists of R and c. A verifier computes $t_{hi} = h^{r_i} A^{c_i} \pmod p$ and $t_{gi} = (g^{1-c_i} V^{c_i B})^{(y^{r_i})}$ for $i = 1 \ldots \ell$, and checks whether (*) holds.

3.4 Analysis

There are two points to consider when discussing the security of the scheme. First, even if we assume that computing discrete logarithms and breaking ElGamal's public-key system is hard, we have to check whether computing v from both $V = g^v$ and the cipher-text (A, B), is also hard. Second, we have to make sure that the dealer cannot cheat in the verification protocol and that no "useful" information about v is given away. We can prove the following two propositions.

Proposition 1. *Under the assumption that computing discrete logarithms in G is infeasible, and that breaking the ElGamal cryptosystem is hard, computing v from g^v and $(h^\alpha, v^{-1}y^\alpha)$ is at least as hard as solving the Decision-Diffie-Hellman problem to the base h in $\mathbb{Z}_p^*$.*[2]

Sketch of Proof: Note that it is possible to decide whether the encrypted logarithm v is a quadratic residue in $\mathbb{Z}_p^*$, because the base h (and the public key y) is a quadratic residue, but that it remains difficult to break ElGamal's cryptosystem, i.e. to completely recover the encrypted message.

Assume that there is an efficient algorithm $\mathcal{P}$ that computes v on input $(g^v,\ h^z,\ h^\alpha,\ v^{-1}h^{\alpha z})$ with a non-negligible probability ε over all $v \in \mathbb{Z}_q^*$, and $z, \alpha \in \mathbb{Z}_q^*$. We show how to use $\mathcal{P}$ to decide whether a given triple (A, B, C) of elements in $\langle h \rangle$, is a Diffie-Hellman triple, i.e. whether $C = h^{\log_h A \cdot \log_h B} \pmod p$.

First, we need a method to randomize (A, B, C). Therefore, we choose $\rho \in \mathbb{Z}_q^*$, and $\sigma, \tau \in \mathbb{Z}_q$ at random and calculate $(\bar{A}, \bar{B}, \bar{C}) = (A^\rho h^\sigma, Bh^\tau, C^\rho A^{\rho\tau} B^\sigma h^{\sigma\tau})$. Since q, the order of h in $\mathbb{Z}_p^*$, is prime, it can easily be shown that the triple $(\bar{A}, \bar{B}, \bar{C})$ is a random Diffie-Hellman triple if (A, B, C) is a Diffie-Hellman triple, and a random non-Diffie-Hellman triple, otherwise.

Now, we randomly choose $v \in \mathbb{Z}_q^*$ and run $\mathcal{P}$ on input $(g^v, \bar{A}, \bar{B}, v^{-1}\bar{C})$. The probability that $\mathcal{P}$ returns v depends on whether (A, B, C) is a Diffie-Hellman triple or not:

- If (A, B, C) is a Diffie-Hellman triple then $\mathcal{P}$ returns v with probability ε.
- If (A, B, C) is not a Diffie-Hellman triple then the probability that $\mathcal{P}$ returns v is negligible. Let us assume on the contrary that $\mathcal{P}$ returns v with a non-negligible probability γ. Then the discrete logarithm of any $Y \in G$ can be computed by repeatedly running $\mathcal{P}$ on input $(Yg^\rho, h^\sigma, h^\tau, t)$ with $\rho \in_R \mathbb{Z}_p$, $\sigma, \tau \in_R \mathbb{Z}_q$, and $t \in_R \mathbb{Z}_p^*$ until $\mathcal{P}$ returns $\rho + \log_g Y \pmod p$. Because the probability that $t/(\rho + \log_g Y) \pmod p \in \langle h \rangle$ is approximately $1/2$, the expected number of repetitions is $2/\gamma$.

After sufficiently many repetitions, a decision on whether (A, B, C) is a Diffie-Hellman triple can be made with arbitrarily small probability of error.

Proposition 2. *The prover in the interactive protocol in Section 3.3 can successfully cheat with a probability of at most 2^{-K}. The protocol is perfectly zero-knowledge.*

Sketch of Proof: It can easily be seen that if in one round both challenges, $c = 0$ and $c = 1$, can correctly be answered then the claim holds, i.e. the logarithm of A to base h is equal to the double logarithm of V^B to the bases g and h. So if the claim does not hold, i.e.the two logarithms are different, a cheating prover can prepare t_g and t_h for only one challenge and will therefore be caught at cheating with probability $1/2$ in this round.

Zero-knowledgeness can be shown using standard techniques for constructing a simulator. □

[2] See [3] for a discussion of the Decision-Diffie-Hellman problem.

4 PVSS for Sharing e-th Roots

Methods similar to those presented in the previous Section can be used to share an e-*th* root of an element in a group $\mathbb{Z}_n^*$, where the factorization of n is unknown. For example, n and e could be the public parameters of a Fiat-Shamir [10] or a Guillou-Quisquater [14] signature scheme. A verifiable sharing scheme with general access-structure can be constructed in a similar way as described in Section 3.2; for the construction of a threshold scheme see [11]. What remains to show is an encryption scheme that allows to efficiently prove that a cipher-text contains the e-*th* root of a given element.

4.1 Verifiable Encryption of e-th Roots

Let $g \in \mathbb{Z}_n^*$ be a public value of large order. Each participant randomly chooses a secret key $z \in \mathbb{Z}_n$ and computes the corresponding public key $y = g^z \pmod{n}$.

A sender can now encrypt a value $m \in \mathbb{Z}_n^*$ by randomly choosing $\alpha \in \mathbb{Z}_n$ and calculating

$$A = g^\alpha \pmod{n}, \text{ and } B = m \cdot y^\alpha \pmod{n}.$$

The recipient can easily obtain the e-*th* root of M by calculating

$$m = B/A^z \pmod{n}.$$

With the following interactive protocol the sender can prove that the pair (A, B) encrypts the e-*th* root of $M = m^e \pmod{n}$ $(\epsilon > 0)$.

Prover		**Verifier**
repeat K times:		
$w \in_R \{0, \ldots, \lceil 2^\ell n^{1+\epsilon} \rceil\}$		
$t_g = g^w \pmod{n}$		
$t_y = y^{ew} \pmod{n}$	$\xrightarrow{t_g,\ t_y}$	
		$c \in_R \{0, \ldots, 2^\ell - 1\}$
	$\xleftarrow{c}$	
$r = w - c \cdot \alpha$		
(calculation in $\mathbb{Z}$)		
	$\xrightarrow{r}$	
		$t_g \stackrel{?}{=} g^r A^c \pmod{n}$
		$t_y \stackrel{?}{=} y^{er} (B^e/M)^c \pmod{n}$

For a non-interactive proof we need a cryptographically strong hash-function $\mathcal{H}_\ell : \{0,1\}^* \to \{0,1\}^\ell$. The sender chooses a random $w \in \{0, \ldots, \lceil 2^\ell n^{1+\epsilon} \rceil\}$ and computes $t_g = g^w \pmod{n}$, $t_y = y^{ew} \pmod{n}$, $c = \mathcal{H}(M||A||B||t_g||t_y)$, and $r = w - c \cdot \alpha$. The resulting proof is (r, c); verification is straightforward. If M

and the cipher-text (A, B) are included, the whole share has a length of only $2\ell + (4 + \epsilon) \cdot \log_2 n$ bits. For a "practical" scheme we recommend to choose $n > 2^{750}$, $\ell > 80$ and $\epsilon \approx \frac{1}{5}$.

4.2 Analysis

As in Section 3.4, we have to consider the security of the encryption scheme and the security of the verification protocol. Unfortunately, a statement similar to proposition 1 is difficult to prove. This is mainly because the order of g is not prime and therefore a good randomization of non-Diffie-Hellman triples is not possible anymore. If we required that the order of g is prime, then the security of the scheme could only be proved (in the manner of proposition 1) for messages m that belong to the subgroup generated by g.

For the security of the verification protocol, we can prove the following proposition:

Proposition 3. *The prover in the interactive protocol in Section 4.1 can successfully cheat with a probability of at most $2^{-K\ell}$. The protocol is statistically zero-knowledge if $\ell = \mathcal{O}(\log \log n)$.*

Sketch of Proof: The first claim can be proved in a similar manner as for proposition 2. For proving zero-knowledgeness we construct a simulator that first randomly chooses $r \in \{0, \ldots, \lceil 2^\ell n^{1+\epsilon} \rceil\}$, guesses $c \in \{0, \ldots, 2^\ell - 1\}$, computes t_g and t_y, and then checks whether c was correctly guessed or not (according to the verifier's strategy). For $\ell = \mathcal{O}(\log \log n)$ this simulator runs in expected polynomial time. It remains to show that the output of the simulator and the output of the protocol are statistically indistinguishable (see [13] for definition). □

Acknowledgments

Many thanks to U. Maurer, D. Bleichenbacher, C. Cachin, J. Camenisch, and the anonymous referees for their useful comments.

References

1. M. Ben-Or, S. Goldwasser, and A. Wigderson. Completeness theorems for non-cryptographic fault-tolerant distributed computation. In *20th Annual Symposium on the Theory of Computing (STOC)*, pages 1–10, 1988.
2. B. Blakley. Safeguarding cryptographic keys. In *Proceedings of the National Computer Conference 1979*, volume 48 of *American Federation of Information Processing Societies Proceedings*, pages 313–317, 1979.
3. S Brands. An efficient off-line electronic cash system based on the representation problem. Technical Report CS-R9323, CWI, Amsterdam, 1993.
4. G. Brassard, D. Chaum, and C. Crépeau. Minimum disclosure proofs of knowledge. *Journal of Computer and System Sciences*, 37(2):156–189, Oct. 1988.

5. E. Brickell, P. Gemmell, and D. Kravitz. Trustee-based tracing extensions to anonymous cash and the making of anonymous change. In *Proceedings of the Sixth Annual ACM-SIAM Symposium on Discrete Algorithms*, pages 457–466. ACM, 1995.
6. J. Camenisch, J.-M. Piveteau, and M. Stadler. An Efficient Fair Payment System. To appear in *Proc. 3rd ACM Conference on Computer and Communications Security*, 1996.
7. B. Chor, S. Goldwasser, S. Micali, and B. Awerbuch. Verifiable secret sharing and achieving simultaneity in the presence of faults. In *Proceedings of the 26th IEEE Symposium on the Foundations of Computer Science (FOCS)*, pages 383–395, 1985.
8. W. Diffie and M. Hellman. New directions in cryptography. *IEEE Transactions on Information Theory*, IT-22(6):644–654, November 1976.
9. T. ElGamal. A public key cryptosystem and a signature scheme based on discrete logarithms. *IEEE Transactions on Information Theory*, IT-31(4):469–472, July 1985.
10. U. Feige, A. Fiat, and A. Shamir. Zero-knowledge proofs of identity. *Journal of Cryptology*, 1:77–94, 1988.
11. P. Feldman. A practical scheme for non-interactive verifiable secret sharing. In *Proceedings of the 28th IEEE Symposium on Foundations of Computer Science (FOCS)*, pages 427–437, 1987.
12. A. Fiat and A. Shamir. How to prove yourself: Practical solution to identification and signature problems. In *Advances in Cryptology – CRYPTO '86*, volume 263 of *Lecture Notes in Computer Science*, pages 186–194. Springer-Verlag, 1987.
13. S. Goldwasser, S. Micali, and C. Rackoff. The knowledge complexity of interactive proof-systems. In *Proc. 17th ACM Symposium on Theory of Computing (STOC)*, pages 291–304, 1985.
14. L. Guillou and J.-J. Quisquater. A practical zero-knowledge protocol fitted to security microprocessor minimizing both transmission and memory. In *Advances in Cryptology – EUROCRYPT '88*, volume 330 of *Lecture Notes in Computer Science*, pages 123–128. Springer-Verlag, 1988.
15. M. Jakobsson and M. Yung. Revokable and Versatile Electronic Money. To appear in *Proc. 3rd ACM Conference on Computer and Communications Security*, 1996.
16. S. Micali. Fair cryptosystems. Technical Report TR-579.b, MIT, November 1993.
17. NIST. Clipper chip technology, 30 April 1993.
18. T. Pedersen. Distributed provers with applications to undeniable signatures. In *Advances in Cryptology – EUROCRYPT '91*, volume 547 of *Lecture Notes in Computer Science*, pages 221–242. Springer-Verlag, 1992.
19. C. Schnorr. Efficient identification and signature for smart cards. In *Advances in Cryptology – CRYPTO '89*, volume 435 of *Lecture Notes in Computer Science*, pages 239–252. Springer-Verlag, 1990.
20. A. Shamir. How to share a secret. *Communications of the ACM*, 22(11):612–613, 1979.
21. M. Stadler, J.-M. Piveteau, and J. Camenisch. Fair blind signatures. In *Advances in Cryptology – EUROCRYPT '95*, volume 921 of *Lecture Notes in Computer Science*, pages 209–219. Springer-Verlag, 1995.

Optimum Secret Sharing Scheme Secure against Cheating

Wakaha Ogata[1] and Kaoru Kurosawa[2]

[1] Himeji Institute of Technology, 2167 Shosha, Himeji-shi, Hyogo 671–22, Japan
wakaha@comp.eng.himeji-tech.ac.jp
[2] Tokyo Institute of Technology, 2–12–1 O-okayama, Meguro-ku, Tokyo 152, Japan
kurosawa@ss.titech.ac.jp

Abstract. Tompa and Woll considered a problem of cheaters in (k, n) threshold secret sharing schemes. We first derive a tight lower bound on the size of shares $|\mathcal{V}_i|$ for this problem: $|\mathcal{V}_i| \geq (|\mathcal{S}| - 1)/\delta + 1$, where $\mathcal{V}_i$ denotes the set of shares of participant P_i, $\mathcal{S}$ denotes the set of secrets, and δ denotes the cheating probability. We next present an optimum scheme which meets the equality of our bound by using "difference sets."

1 Introduction

(k, n) threshold secret sharing schemes [2, 3] have been studied extensively so far because of their wide applications in fields, like key management and secure computation. In such a scheme, a dealer D distributes a secret s to n participants $P_1, \ldots, P_n$ in such a way that any k or more participants can recover the secret s but any $k - 1$ or fewer participants have no information on s. A piece of information given to P_i is called a share and is denoted by v_i. An important issue in secret sharing schemes is the size of shares $|\mathcal{V}_i|$, where $\mathcal{V}_i \triangleq \{v_i \mid \Pr(v_i) > 0\}$, because the security of a system will decrease if $|\mathcal{V}_i|$ increases. Let $\mathcal{S} \triangleq \{s \mid \Pr(s) > 0\}$. Then it is known that

$$|\mathcal{V}_i| \geq |\mathcal{S}|$$

in any (k, n) threshold scheme [4].

Tompa and Woll [1] considered the following scenario. Suppose that $k - 1$ participants $P_1, \ldots, P_{k-1}$ want to cheat a k-th participant P_k by opening forged shares $v'_1, \ldots, v'_{k-1}$. They succeed if the secret s' reconstructed from $v'_1, \ldots, v'_{k-1}$ and v_k is different from the original secret s. Tompa and Woll showed that Shamir's scheme [2] is insecure against this attack in that even a single participant can, with high probability, deceive $k - 1$ honest participants. They showed a scheme secure against this problem, but $|\mathcal{V}_i|$ in their scheme is very large:

$$|\mathcal{V}_i| = ((|\mathcal{S}| - 1)(k - 1)/\epsilon + k)^2 \tag{1}$$

where ϵ denotes the cheating probability. Carpentieri, De Santis, and Vaccaro [5] recently showed the following lower bound on $|\mathcal{V}_i|$ for this problem:

$$|\mathcal{V}_i| \geq |\mathcal{S}|/\epsilon. \tag{2}$$

Ueli Maurer (Ed.): EUROCRYPT '96 Proceedings, LNCS 1070

Now, we see that there is a big gap between eq. (1) and (2). Both of them can be improved. Furthermore, in the derivation of eq. (2) it is assumed that $k-1$ cheaters $P_1, \ldots, P_{k-1}$ somehow know the secret s before they cheat P_k. (We call this the CDV assumption.)

In this paper we first derive a tight lower bound on $|\mathcal{V}_i|$ for this problem by using a probabilistic method. In deriving our bound, we do not use the CDV assumption. That is, it is assumed that $k-1$ cheaters have no information on s (according to the definition of (k,n) threshold secret sharing schemes). Let δ be the probability that $P_1, \ldots, P_{k-1}$ can cheat P_k. Then our bound is

$$|\mathcal{V}_i| \geq (|\mathcal{S}|-1)/\delta + 1. \tag{3}$$

We then present an optimum scheme which meets the equality of our bound by using "difference sets." A planar difference set modulo $N = l(l-1)+1$ is a set of l numbers $B = \{d_0, d_1, \ldots, d_{l-1}\}$ with the property that the $l(l-1)$ differences $d_i - d_j$ ($d_i \neq d_j$), when reduced modulo N, are exactly the numbers $1, 2, \ldots, N-1$ in some order [6]. It is known that there exists a planar difference set if l is a prime power [6]. Our optimum scheme is then characterized as follows. If there exists a planar difference set modulo $N = l(l-1)+1$ such that N is a prime, then there exists a (k,n) threshold secret sharing scheme which meets the equality of our bound eq. (3) such that $|\mathcal{S}| = l, \delta = 1/l, n < N$.

Furthermore, this result is generalized as follows. Let $(\Gamma, +)$ be a group of order N and let $B = \{d_0, d_1, \ldots, d_{l-1}\}$ be a subset of Γ. Then B is called a (N, l, λ) difference set [7] if each nonzero element x of Γ appears λ times as a difference $d_i - d_j$ ($d_i \neq d_j$). Our generalized scheme is then given as follows. There exists a (k,n) threshold secret sharing scheme which meets the equality of our bound eq. (3) such that $|\mathcal{S}| = l, \delta = \lambda/l, n < N$ if there exists a (N, l, λ) difference set B in $(GF(N), +)$. It is known that there exists a (N, l, λ) difference set B in $(GF(N), +)$ such that $N = 4t-1, l = 2t-1, \lambda = t-1$ [7].

Finally, for the model with the CDV assumption, we show a lower bound on $|\mathcal{V}_i|$ more tight than eq. (2) by using the same technique we use to derive eq. (3). Our bound for the model with the CDV assumption is

$$|\mathcal{V}_i| \geq (|\mathcal{S}|-1)/\epsilon^2 + 1.$$

A slightly different problem has been studied by other researchers. McElice and Sarwate [8] showed that in Shamir's (k,n) threshold scheme, any group of $k+2e$ participants which includes at most e cheaters can always identify cheaters and correctly calculate the secret. (More than k participants are required though.) The problem of identifying cheaters has also been studied [9, 10, 11, 12]. Those schemes, however, require $|\mathcal{V}_i|$ much bigger than the bound given in eq. (3). On the other hand, in this paper, we are interested only in detecting the fact of cheating.

2 Preliminaries

2.1 Definition of cheating

D denotes a probabilistic Turing machine called a dealer, S denotes a random variable distributed over a finite set $\mathcal{S}$, and $s \in \mathcal{S}$ is called a secret. On input $s \in \mathcal{S}$, D outputs $(v_1, \ldots, v_n)$ randomly. For $1 \leq i \leq n$, each participant P_i holds v_i as his share. V_i denotes the random variable induced by v_i. Let $\mathcal{V}_i \triangleq \{v_i \mid \Pr(V_i = v_i) > 0\}$.

Definition 1. We say that (D, S) is a (k, n) threshold secret sharing scheme if the following two requirements hold: For any $\{i_1, \ldots, i_j\} \subseteq \{1, \ldots, n\}$ and $(v_{i_1}, \ldots, v_{i_j})$ such that $\Pr(V_{i_1} = v_{i_1}, \ldots, V_{i_j} = v_{i_j}) > 0$,
(A1) if $j \geq k$, there exists a unique $s \in \mathcal{S}$ such that

$$\Pr(S = s \mid V_{i_1} = v_{i_1}, \ldots, V_{i_j} = v_{i_j}) = 1,$$

(A2) if $j < k$, for each $s \in \mathcal{S}$,

$$\Pr(S = s \mid V_{i_1} = v_{i_1}, \ldots, V_{i_j} = v_{i_j}) = \Pr(S = s).$$

Definition 2. For $w \in \mathcal{V}_{i_1} \times \cdots \times \mathcal{V}_{i_k}$,

$$Sec_{(i_1,\ldots,i_k)}(w) \triangleq \begin{cases} s & \text{if } \exists s \in S \text{ such that } \Pr(S = s \mid V_{i_1} \cdots V_{i_k} = w) = 1, \\ \perp & \text{otherwise.} \end{cases}$$

($(i_1, \ldots, i_k)$ will be omitted.)

Definition 3. Suppose that $k-1$ cheaters $P_{i_1}, \ldots, P_{i_{k-1}}$ have $b = (v_{i_1}, \ldots, v_{i_{k-1}})$ as their shares. We say that the cheaters can cheat P_{i_k} by opening $b' = (v'_{i_1}, \ldots, v'_{i_{k-1}})$ if $Sec(b', v_{i_k}) \neq Sec(b, v_{i_k})$ and $Sec(b', v_{i_k}) \in \mathcal{S}$, where v_{i_k} denotes the share of P_{i_k}.

2.2 Known bound on $|\mathcal{V}_i|$ under the CDV assumption

Carpentieri, De Santis, and Vaccaro [5] showed the following lower bound on $|\mathcal{V}_i|$ by using entropy. In deriving that bound they assumed that $k-1$ cheaters $P_{i_1}, \ldots, P_{i_{k-1}}$ shomehow know the secret s before they cheat P_k, although, in the definition of (k, n) threshold secret sharing schemes, $k-1$ cheaters have no information on s. (We call this the CDV assumption.) Let $b = (v_{i_1}, \ldots, v_{i_{k-1}})$ denote the shares of the cheaters, and let $b' = (v'_{i_1}, \ldots, v'_{i_{k-1}})$ denote the forged shares that the cheaters open to cheat P_{i_k}. Carpentieri et al. defined the average cheating probability as follows:

$$P'(Cheat \mid V_{i_1}, \ldots, V_{i_{k-1}}, S) \triangleq E[\max_{b'} \Pr(P_{i_k} \text{ is cheated by } b' \mid P_{i_1} \cdots P_{i_{k-1}} \text{ have } b. \text{ They also know } s)], \quad (4)$$

Definition 4. [5] A (k,n) threshold secret sharing scheme is called a (k,n,ϵ) robust secret sharing scheme if $P'(Cheat \mid V_{i_1},\ldots,V_{i_{k-1}},S) \le \epsilon$ for any $\{i_1,\ldots,i_{k-1}\} \subseteq \{1,\ldots,n\}$.

Proposition 5. *[5] In a (k,n,ϵ) robust secret sharing scheme, if the secret is uniformly chosen, then $|\mathcal{V}_i| \ge |\mathcal{S}|/\epsilon$.*

3 New Lower Bound on $|\mathcal{V}_i|$

3.1 Definition of secure secret sharing

In this section we derive a tight lower bound on $|\mathcal{V}_i|$ by using a probabilistic method. In deriving this bound we do not make the CDV assumption (see subsection 2.2). That is, it is assumed that, according to the definition of (k,n) threshold secret sharing schemes, $k-1$ cheaters have no information on s. Suppose that $P_{i_1},\ldots,P_{i_{k-1}}$ are cheaters. Let $b=(v_{i_1},\ldots,v_{i_{k-1}})$ denote the shares of the cheaters, and let $b'=(v'_{i_1},\ldots,v'_{i_{k-1}})$ denote the forged shares that the cheaters open to cheat P_{i_k}. Since the cheaters have no information on s, we define the average cheating probability as follows:

$$P(Cheat \mid V_{i_1},\ldots,V_{i_{k-1}}) \\ \triangleq E[\max_{b'} \Pr(P_{i_k} \text{ is cheated by } b' \mid P_{i_1}\cdots P_{i_{k-1}} \text{ have } b)], \qquad (5)$$

(S and s in eq. (4) are absent from eq. (5).)

Definition 6. A (k,n) threshold secret sharing scheme is called a (k,n,δ) secure secret sharing scheme if $P(Cheat \mid V_{i_1},\ldots,V_{i_{k-1}}) \le \delta$ for any $\{i_1,\ldots,i_{k-1}\} \subseteq \{1,\ldots,n\}$.

3.2 New lower bound on $|\mathcal{V}_i|$

In the distribution phase, suppose that cheaters $P_{i_1},\ldots,P_{i_{k-1}}$ have $b=(v_{i_1},\ldots,v_{i_{k-1}})$ as their shares of a secret s and P_{i_k} has x as his share. That is, $Sec(b,x)=s$. In the reconstruction phase, if P_{i_1} opens $v'_{i_1}(\ne v_{i_1})$ such that $Sec(v'_{i_1},v_{i_2},\ldots,v_{i_{k-1}},x)=s'$ and $s'\ne s$, then P_{i_k} is cheated. Now, let

$$Y(x,s) \triangleq \{v'_{i_1} \in \mathcal{V}_{i_1} \mid Sec(v'_{i_1},v_{i_2},\ldots,v_{i_{k-1}},x) = s' \in \mathcal{S}, s' \ne s\}$$

For fixed x and s, $Y(x,s)$ denotes the set of forged shares of P_{i_1} which can cheat P_{i_k}. (However, the cheaters do not know x nor s.) Let

$$W(s) \triangleq \{x \in \mathcal{V}_{i_k} \mid Sec(b,x) = s\}.$$

$W(s)$ denotes the set of possible shares of P_{i_k} for a fixed s.

Lemma 7. *For $\forall s \in \mathcal{S}, \forall x \in W(s)$,*

$$|Y(x,s)| \ge |\mathcal{S}| - 1.$$

Proof. Since k participants can recover the secret uniquely, for $\forall s', s''(s' \neq s'')$,

$$\{v'_{i_1} \in \mathcal{V}_{i_1} \mid Sec(v'_{i_1}, v_{i_2}, \ldots, v_{i_{k-1}}, x) = s'\}$$
$$\cap \{v'_{i_1} \in \mathcal{V}_{i_1} \mid Sec(v'_{i_1}, v_{i_2}, \ldots, v_{i_{k-1}}, x) = s''\} = \emptyset.$$

From (A2) of Def.1, for any $s' \in \mathcal{S}$, there exists at least one v'_{k_1} such that

$$Sec(v'_{i_1}, v_{i_2}, \ldots, v_{i_{k-1}}, x) = s'.$$

Therefore, from the definition of $Y(x, s)$,

$$\begin{aligned} |Y(x,s)| &= |\bigcup_{s' \in \mathcal{S}, s' \neq s} \{v'_{i_1} \in \mathcal{V}_{i_1} \mid Sec(v'_{i_1}, v_{i_2}, \ldots, v_{i_{k-1}}, x) = s'\}| \\ &= \sum_{s' \in \mathcal{S}, s' \neq s} |\{v'_{i_1} \in \mathcal{V}_{i_1} \mid Sec(v'_{i_1}, v_{i_2}, \ldots, v_{i_{k-1}}, x) = s'\}| \\ &\geq \sum_{s' \in \mathcal{S}, s' \neq s} 1 \\ &= |\mathcal{S}| - 1. \end{aligned}$$

□

Now our lower bound on $|\mathcal{V}_i|$ is given as follows. The following bound holds for any distribution on S.

Theorem 8. *In a (k, n, δ) secure secret sharing scheme,*

$$|\mathcal{V}_i| \geq \frac{|\mathcal{S}| - 1}{\delta} + 1. \tag{6}$$

Proof. Consider cheaters $P_{i_1}, \ldots, P_{i_{k-1}}$ such that only P_{i_1} opens a forged share $v'_{i_1}(\neq v_{i_1})$. The other $P_{i_2}, \ldots, P_{i_{k-1}}$ open their shares honestly. For these specific cheaters,

$$\max_{b'} \Pr(P_{i_k} \text{ is cheated by } b' \mid P_{i_1} \cdots P_{i_{k-1}} \text{ have } b)$$

$$\geq \max_{v'_{i_1}} \Pr(P_{i_k} \text{ is cheated by } v'_{i_1} \mid P_{i_1} \cdots P_{i_{k-1}} \text{ have } b) \tag{7}$$

Now, we randomize v'_{i_1} in order to compute the right-hand side. Consider P_{i_1} who opens $v'_{i_1}(\neq v_{i_1})$ randomly. More precisely,

$$\Pr(P_{i_1} \text{ opens } v'_{i_1}) = \begin{cases} 1/(|\mathcal{V}_{i_1}| - 1) & \text{if } v'_{i_1} \neq v_{i_1} \\ 0 & \text{if } v'_{i_1} = v_{i_1}. \end{cases}$$

For this probabilistic P_{i_1}, let's compute

$$E[\Pr(P_{i_k} \text{ is cheated by } v'_{i_1} \mid P_{i_1} \cdots P_{i_{k-1}} \text{ have } b)],$$

where E is taken over v'_{i_1} and Pr() is taken over s and x. Then from lemma 7,

$$\begin{aligned}
&E_{v'_{i_1}}[\Pr_{s,x\in W(s)}(P_{i_k} \text{ is cheated by } v'_{i_1} \mid P_{i_1}\cdots P_{i_{k-1}} \text{ have } b)] \\
&= E_{s,x\in W(s)}[\Pr_{v'_{i_1}}(P_{i_k} \text{ is cheated by } v'_{i_1} \mid P_{i_1}\cdots P_{i_{k-1}} \text{ have } b)] \\
&= E_{s,x\in W(s)}[|Y(x,s)|/(|\mathcal{V}_{i_1}|-1)] \\
&\geq (|\mathcal{S}|-1)/(|\mathcal{V}_{i_1}|-1).
\end{aligned}$$

Therefore

$$\begin{aligned}
&\max_{v'_{i_1}} \Pr(P_{i_k} \text{ is cheated by } v'_{i_1} \mid P_{i_1}\cdots P_{i_{k-1}} \text{ have } b) \\
&\geq E_{v'_{i_1}}[\Pr(P_{i_k} \text{ is cheated by } v'_{i_1} \mid P_{i_1}\cdots P_{i_{k-1}} \text{ have } b)] \\
&\geq (|\mathcal{S}|-1)/(|\mathcal{V}_{i_1}|-1).
\end{aligned}$$

Hence, from eq. (7),

$$\max_{b'} \Pr(P_{i_k} \text{ is cheated by } b' \mid P_{i_1}\cdots P_{i_{k-1}} \text{ have } b) \geq (|\mathcal{S}|-1)/(|\mathcal{V}_{i_1}|-1).$$

$$E_b[\max_{b'} \Pr(P_{i_k} \text{ is cheated by } b' \mid P_{i_1}\cdots P_{i_{k-1}} \text{ have } b)] \geq (|\mathcal{S}|-1)/(|\mathcal{V}_{i_1}|-1).$$

Consequently, in a (k,n,δ) secure secret sharing scheme,

$$\delta \geq P(Cheat \mid V_{i_1},\ldots,V_{i_{k-1}}) \geq (|\mathcal{S}|-1)/(|\mathcal{V}_{i_1}|-1).$$

Therefore, $|\mathcal{V}_{i_1}| \geq (|\mathcal{S}|-1)/\delta + 1$. □

4 Optimum (k,n,δ) Secure Scheme

In this section, we show an optimum scheme which meets the equality of Theorem 8 by using "difference sets."

4.1 Difference set

Definition 9. [6] A *planar difference set* modulo $N = l(l-1)+1$ is a set of l numbers $B = \{d_0, d_1, \ldots, d_{l-1}\}$ with the property that the $l(l-1)$ differences $d_i - d_j$ $(d_i \neq d_j)$, when reduced modulo N, are exactly the numbers $1, 2, \ldots, N-1$ in some order.

Example 1. [6] $\{d_0 = 0, d_1 = 1, d_2 = 3\}$ is a planar difference set modulo 7 with $l = 3$. Indeed, the differences modulo 7 are

$$1-0=1,\ 3-0=3,\ 3-1=2,\ 0-1=6,\ 0-3=4,\ 1-3=5.$$

Proposition 10. *[6] In a projective plane $PG(2,q)$, a line has $l = q+1$ points $\alpha^{d_0}, \ldots, \alpha^{d_{l-1}}$, where q is a prime power. Then $\{d_0, \ldots, d_{l-1}\}$ is a planar difference set modulo q^2+q+1.*

Definition 9 is generalized as follows.

Definition 11. [7] Let $(\Gamma, +)$ be a group of order N. B is called a (N, l, λ)-difference set if it satisfies

- $B \subset \Gamma$ and $|B| = l$,
- the list of differences $d - d' \neq 0$, where $d, d' \in B$, contains each nonzero element of Γ precisely λ times.

Proposition 12. *[7] There exists a (N, l, λ) difference set B in $(GF(N), +)$ such that $N = 4t - 1, l = 2t - 1, \lambda = t - 1$, where t is a positive integer.*

Example 2. [7] $B = \{1, 3, 4, 5, 9\}$ is a $(11, 5, 2)$-difference set in $(GF(11), +)$.

4.2 Optimum scheme based on planar difference set

In this subsection we show that if there exists a planar difference set modulo $N = l(l-1)+1$ such that N is a prime, then there exists a (k, n, δ) secure secret sharing scheme which meets the equality of our bound eq. (6) such that $|\mathcal{S}| = l, \delta = 1/l, n < N$.

Let $B = \{d_0, \ldots, d_{l-1}\}$ be a planar difference set modulo $N = l(l-1)+1$ such that N is a prime. We show a (k, n, δ) secure secret sharing scheme such that $\mathcal{S} = B$. Assume that S is uniformly distributed over $\mathcal{S}$. In what follows, all operations are done over $GF(N)$.

Distribution phase. For a secret $d_s \in \mathcal{S}(= B)$, the dealer D chooses a random polynomial $f(x)$ of degree $k-1$ over $GF(N)$ such that $f(0) = d_s$. The share of P_i is given as $v_i = f(i)$. Note that

$$\forall i, \quad |\mathcal{V}_i| = N = l(l-1)+1. \tag{8}$$

Reconstruction phase. Suppose that $P_{i_1}, \ldots, P_{i_k}$ open $\tilde{v}_{i_1}, \ldots, \tilde{v}_{i_k}$. Each participant computes $\tilde{d}_s = \sum_{j=1}^{k} c_j \tilde{v}_{i_j}$, where $c_j = \prod_{l \neq j} (-i_l)/(i_j - i_l)$ for $1 \leq j \leq k$. If $\tilde{d}_s \in B$, they accept $\tilde{d}_s$ as the secret. Otherwise, they output $\perp$. Note that, for any k honest shares $v_{i_1} = f(i_1), \ldots, v_{i_k} = f(i_k)$,

$$d_s = \textstyle\sum_{j=1}^{k} c_j v_{i_j} \tag{9}$$

from Laglange formula [13].

Proposition 13 (Lagrange formula). *[13] Let $h(x)$ be a polynomial over $GF(N)$ such that $\deg h(x) = k - 1$. For any distinct $i_1, \ldots, i_k$,*

$$h(0) = \sum_{j=1}^{k} c_j h(i_j), \ \textit{where}\ c_j = \prod_{l \neq j} (-i_l)/(i_j - i_l)$$

Lemma 14. *The proposed scheme is a (k, n) threshold secret sharing scheme.*

Proof. (A1) of Defnition 1 is satisfied from eq. (9). Next,

$$\begin{aligned}&\Pr(S = d_s \mid V_{i_1} = v_{i_1}, \ldots, V_{i_{k-1}} = v_{i_{k-1}}) \\ &= \frac{\Pr(S = d_s)\Pr(V_{i_1} = v_{i_1}, \ldots, V_{i_{k-1}} = v_{i_{k-1}} \mid S = d_s)}{\Pr(V_{i_1} = v_{i_1}, \ldots, V_{i_{k-1}} = v_{i_{k-1}})}.\end{aligned}$$

For each $d_s \in \mathcal{S}$, $f(x)$ is randomly chosen and $\deg f(x) = k-1$. Therefore $V_{i_1} \cdots V_{i_{k-1}}$ is random for each $d_s \in \mathcal{S}$. Hence

$$\Pr(V_{i_1} = v_{i_1}, \ldots, V_{i_{k-1}} = v_{i_{k-1}} \mid S = d_s) = \Pr(V_{i_1} = v_{i_1}, \ldots, V_{i_{k-1}} = v_{i_{k-1}}).$$

Consequently,

$$\Pr(S = d_s \mid V_{i_1} = v_{i_1}, \ldots, V_{i_{k-1}} = v_{i_{k-1}}) = \Pr(S = d_s).$$

Thus (A2) of Defnition 1 is also satisfied. □

Lemma 15. *The proposed scheme is a (k, n, δ) secure secret sharing scheme such that $|\mathcal{S}| = l, \delta = 1/l$ and $n < N$. Furthermore, the equality of eq. (6) is satisfied.*

Proof. Suppose that cheaters $P_{i_1}, \ldots, P_{i_{k-1}}$ have $b = (v_{i_1}, \ldots, v_{i_{k-1}})$. Let the share of P_{i_k} be $x \in \{0, 1, \ldots, N-1\}$. Then, from eq. (9),

$$Sec(b, x) = \sum_{j=1}^{k-1} c_j v_{i_j} + c_k x = d_s \in B(= \mathcal{S}). \tag{10}$$

Define

$$T \triangleq \{x \mid Sec(b, x) \in B\}.$$

For any fixed b, eq. (10) defines a bijection τ from B to T such that $\tau(d_s) = x \in T$ because $c_k \neq 0$. Since d_s is uniformly distributed over B, x is uniformly distributed over T. (Remember that S is uniformly distributed over $\mathcal{S}$.) Therefore for any fixed b and b',

$$\Pr(P_{i_k} \text{ is cheated by } b' \mid P_{i_1} \cdots P_{i_{k-1}} \text{ have } b) = |\tilde{\mathcal{V}}_{i_k}(b \to b')|/|T|, \tag{11}$$

where

$$\tilde{\mathcal{V}}_{i_k}(b \to b') = \{x \mid Sec(b, x) \in B, Sec(b', x) \in B \text{ and } Sec(b, x) \neq Sec(b', x)\}.$$

Since τ is a bijection,

$$|T| = |B| = l. \tag{12}$$

Now let's compute $|\tilde{\mathcal{V}}_{i_k}(b \to b')|$. Fix $b = (v_{i_1}, \ldots, v_{i_{k-1}})$ and $b' = (v'_{i_1}, \ldots, v'_{i_{k-1}})$ arbitrarily. Define

$$a \triangleq \sum_{j=1}^{k-1} c_j v_{i_j}, \quad a' \triangleq \sum_{j=1}^{k-1} c_j v'_{i_j}.$$

From eq. (10) and since τ is a bijection,

$$\begin{aligned}|\tilde{\mathcal{V}}_{i_k}(b \to b')| &= |\{x \mid a + c_k x \in B, a' + c_k x \in B \text{ and } a + c_k x \neq a' + c_k x\}| \\ &= |\{d \mid d \in B, d - (a - a') \in B \text{ and } a - a' \neq 0\}|\end{aligned}$$

Note that $a - a'$ is a constant for fixed b and b'. On the other hand, from Definition 9, for $\forall e \neq 0$,

$$\begin{aligned}|\{(d, d') \mid d \in B, d' \in B, d - d' = e\}| = 1 \\ |\{d \mid d \in B, d - e \in B\}| = 1\end{aligned}$$

since $d' = d - e$. So we obtain

$$|\tilde{\mathcal{V}}_{i_k}(b \to b')| \;=\; 1 \tag{13}$$

for b and b' such that $a - a' \neq 0$. If $a - a' = 0$, then $|\tilde{\mathcal{V}}_{i_k}(b \to b')| = 0$ because no d (or no x) satisfies $a - a' \neq 0$. Therefore, from eq. (11),(12) and (13),

$$\max_{b'} \Pr(P_{i_k} \text{ is cheated by } b' \mid P_{i_1} \cdots P_{i_{k-1}} \text{ have } b) = 1/l.$$

Consequently, from eq. (5),

$$P(Cheat \mid V_{i_1}, \ldots, V_{i_{k-1}}) \;=\; 1/l.$$

Thus this scheme is a (k, n, δ) secure scheme such that $\delta = 1/l$. It is clear that $|\mathcal{S}| = |B| = l$. Finally, from eq. (8), $\forall j, |\mathcal{V}_j| = N = (l-1)l + 1 = (|\mathcal{S}| - 1)/\delta + 1$. Hence, this scheme meets the equality of eq. (6). □

Now the following theorem is obtained from lemma 14 and 15.

Theorem 16. *If there exists a planar difference set modulo $N = l(l-1) + 1$ such that N is a prime, then there exists a (k, n, δ) secure secret sharing scheme which meets the equality of our bound eq. (6) such that $|\mathcal{S}| = l, \delta = 1/l, n < N$.*

From proposition 10, we obtain the following corollary.

Corollary 17. *Let q be a prime power such that $q^2 + q + 1$ is a prime. Then, there exists a (k, n, δ) secure secret sharing scheme which meets the equality of eq. (6) such that $|\mathcal{S}| = q + 1, \delta = 1/(q + 1)$ and $n < q^2 + q + 1$.*

Remark. Instead of publicizing a planar difference set B itself, it is enough to publicize two points α^0 and α^1 of $PG(2, |\mathcal{S}| - 1)$. According to Proposition 10, B can be obtained from (α^0, α^1).

4.3 Optimum scheme based on a (N, l, λ) difference set

Theorem 16 is generalized as follows.

Theorem 18. *If there exists a (N, l, λ) difference set B in $(GF(N), +)$, then there exists a (k, n, δ) secure secret sharing scheme which meets the equality of our bound eq. (6) such that $|\mathcal{S}| = l, \delta = \lambda/l, n < N$.*

The following corollary is obtained from proposition 12.

Corollary 19. *For a positive integer t such that $4t-1$ is a prime power, there exists a (k, n, δ) secure secret sharing scheme which meets the equality of our bound eq. (6) such that $|\mathcal{S}| = 2t-1, \delta = (t-1)/(2t-1), n < 4t-1$.*

5 Tighter Bound on $|\mathcal{V}_i|$ under the CDV Assumption

In this section, we use the same technique used in subseection 3.2 and, under the CDV assumption, show a lower bound on $|\mathcal{V}_i|$ that is more tight than proposition 5. (The CDV assumption is that $k-1$ cheaters $P_1, \ldots, P_{k-1}$ somehow know the secret s.)

In the distribution phase, suppose that cheaters $P_{i_1}, \ldots, P_{i_{k-1}}$ have $b = (v_{i_1}, \ldots, v_{i_{k-1}})$ as their shares of a secret s and P_{i_k} has x as his share. That is, $Sec(b, x) = s$. Fix s and b. Let

$$Y'(x) \triangleq \{v'_{i_1} \in \mathcal{V}_{i_1} \mid Sec(v'_{i_1}, v_{i_2}, \ldots, v_{i_{k-1}}, x) = s' \in \mathcal{S}, s' \neq s\}$$
$$W' \triangleq \{x \in \mathcal{V}_{i_k} \mid Sec(b, x) = s\}.$$

In the reconstruction phase, if P_{i_1} opens $v'_{i_1} \in Y'(x)$, then P_{i_k} is cheated. W' denotes the set of possible shares of P_{i_k}.

Lemma 20. *For fixed s and b such that* $\Pr(V_{i_1} \cdots V_{i_{k-1}} = b, S = s) > 0$,

$$|W'| \geq 1/\epsilon. \tag{14}$$

Proof. Consider cheaters $P_{i_1}, \ldots, P_{i_{k-1}}$ such that only P_{i_1} opens a forged share $v'_{i_1} (\neq v_{i_1})$. The other $P_{i_2}, \ldots, P_{i_{k-1}}$ open their shares honestly. The way that P_{i_1} opens v'_{i_1} is as follows. First, P_{i_1} chooses $\hat{x} \in W'$ such that

$$\Pr(V_{i_k} = \hat{x} \mid V_{i_1} \cdots V_{i_{k-1}} = b, S = s) = \max_{x \in W'} \Pr(V_{i_k} = x \mid V_{i_1} \cdots V_{i_{k-1}} = b, S = s).$$

Then, P_{i_1} opens $v'_{i_1} \in Y'(\hat{x})$ arbitrarily. In this case, P_{i_k} is cheated if his share is $\hat{x}$. For these specific cheaters, in eq. (4),

$$\begin{aligned}
&\max_{b'} \Pr(P_{i_k} \text{ is cheated by } b' \mid P_{i_1} \cdots P_{i_{k-1}} \text{ have } b. \text{ They also know } s) \\
&\geq \Pr(P_{i_k} \text{ is cheated by } v'_{i_1} \mid P_{i_1} \cdots P_{i_{k-1}} \text{ have } b. \text{ They also know } s) \\
&\geq \Pr(V_{i_k} = \hat{x} \mid V_{i_1} \cdots V_{i_{k-1}} = b, S = s)
\end{aligned}$$

$$
\begin{aligned}
&= \max_{x \in W'} \Pr(V_{i_k} = x \mid V_{i_1} \cdots V_{i_{k-1}} = b, S = s) \\
&\geq |W'|^{-1} \sum_{x \in W'} \Pr(V_{i_k} = x \mid V_{i_1} \cdots V_{i_{k-1}} = b, S = s) \\
&\geq |W'|^{-1}.
\end{aligned}
$$

Since the scheme is ϵ-robust, $\epsilon \geq E[|W'|^{-1}] = |W'|^{-1}$. Therefore, we obtain eq. (14). □

Lemma 21. *For* $\forall x \in W'$, $|Y'(x)| \geq (|\mathcal{S}| - 1)/\epsilon$.

Proof. From lemma 20, $|\{y \in \mathcal{V}_{i_1} \mid Sec(y, v_2, \ldots, v_{k-1}, x) = s'\}| \geq 1/\epsilon$. Therefore,

$$
\begin{aligned}
|Y'(x)| &= |\bigcup_{s' \in \mathcal{S}, s' \neq s} \{y \in \mathcal{V}_{i_1} \mid Sec(v'_{i_1}, v_{i_2}, \ldots, v_{i_{k-1}}, x) = s'\}| \\
&= \sum_{s' \in \mathcal{S}, s' \neq s} |\{y \in \mathcal{V}_{i_1} \mid Sec(y, v_2, \ldots, v_{k-1}, x) = s'\}| \\
&\geq \sum_{s' \in \mathcal{S}, s' \neq s} 1/\epsilon \\
&= (|\mathcal{S}| - 1)/\epsilon.
\end{aligned}
$$

□

Now, our lower bound on $|\mathcal{V}_i|$ is as follows.

Theorem 22. *In a* (k, n, ϵ) *robust secret sharing scheme,*

$$|\mathcal{V}_i| \geq \frac{|\mathcal{S}| - 1}{\epsilon^2} + 1. \tag{15}$$

Proof. Consider a probabilistic P_{i_1} such as shown in the proof of Theorem 8. For such P_{i_1}, let's compute

$$E[\Pr(P_{i_k} \text{ is cheated by } v'_{i_1} \mid P_{i_1} \cdots P_{i_{k-1}} \text{ have } b \text{ and they know } s],$$

where E is taken over v'_{i_1} and Pr() is taken over $x \in W'$. Then from lemma 21,

$$
\begin{aligned}
&E_{v'_{i_1}}[\Pr_{x \in W'}(P_{i_k} \text{ is cheated by } v'_{i_1} \mid P_{i_1} \cdots P_{i_{k-1}} \text{ have } b \text{ and they know } s] \\
&= E_{x \in W'}[\Pr_{v'_{i_1}}(P_{i_k} \text{ is cheated by } v'_{i_1} \mid P_{i_1} \cdots P_{i_{k-1}} \text{ have } b \text{ and they know } s] \\
&= E_{x \in W'}[|Y'(x)|/(|\mathcal{V}_{i_1}| - 1)] \\
&\geq (|\mathcal{S}| - 1)/\epsilon(|\mathcal{V}_{i_1}| - 1).
\end{aligned}
$$

Therefore

$$
\begin{aligned}
&\max_{v'_{i_1}} \Pr(P_{i_k} \text{ is cheated by } v'_{i_1} \mid P_{i_1} \cdots P_{i_{k-1}} \text{ have } b \text{ and they know } s) \\
&\geq E_{v'_{i_1}}[\Pr(P_{i_k} \text{ is cheated by } v'_{i_1} \mid P_{i_1} \cdots P_{i_{k-1}} \text{ have } b \text{ and they know } s)] \\
&\geq (|\mathcal{S}| - 1)/\epsilon(|\mathcal{V}_{i_1}| - 1).
\end{aligned}
$$

Hence

$$\max_{b'} \Pr(P_{i_k} \text{ is cheated by } b' \mid P_{i_1} \cdots P_{i_{k-1}} \text{ have } b \text{ and they know } s)$$
$$\geq (|\mathcal{S}| - 1)/\epsilon(|\mathcal{V}_{i_1}| - 1).$$

Consequently, in a (k, n, ϵ) robust secret sharing scheme,

$$\epsilon \geq E[\max_{b'} \Pr(P_{i_k} \text{ is cheated by } b' \mid P_{i_1} \cdots P_{i_{k-1}} \text{ have } b. \text{ They also know } s)]$$
$$\geq (|\mathcal{S}| - 1)/\epsilon(|\mathcal{V}_{i_1}| - 1).$$

Then, eq. (15) is obtained. □

References

1. M. Tompa and H. Woll. "How to share a secret with cheaters". In *Journal of Cryptology, vol.1*, pages 133–138, 1988.
2. A. Shamir. "How to Share a Secret". In *Communications of the ACM, vol.22, no.11*, pages 612–613, 1979.
3. G.R. Blakely. "Safeguarding cryptographic keys". In *Proc. of the AFIPS 1979 National Computer Conference, vol.48*, pages 313–317, 1979.
4. E.D. Karnin, J.W.Green, and M.E. Hellman. "On secret sharing systems". In *IEEE Trans. IT-29, No.1*, pages 35–41, 1982.
5. M. Carpentieri, A. De Santis, and U. Vaccaro. "Size of Shares and Probability of Cheating in Threshold Schemes". In *Proc. of Eurocrypto'93, Lecture Notes in Computer Science, LNCS 765, Springer Verlag*, pages 118–125, 1993.
6. F.J. MacWilliams and N.J.A. Sloane. "The theory of error-correcting codes". In *North-Holland*, pages 397–398, 1981.
7. T.Beth,T, D.Jungnickel and H.Lenz. "Design Theory". In *Cambridge University Press*, pages 260–264, 1993.
8. R.J. McEliece and D.V. Sarwate. "On sharing secrets and Reed-Solomon codes". In *Comm.ACM, 24*, pages 583–584, 1981.
9. T. Rabin and M. Ben-Or. "Verifiable secret sharing and multiparty protocols with honest majority". In *Proc. 21st ACM Symposium on Theory of Computing*, pages 73–85, 1989.
10. E.F. Brickell and D.R. Stinson. "The Detection of Cheaters in Threshold Schemes". In *SIAM J. DISC. MATH, Vol.4, No.4*, pages 502–510, 1991.
11. M. Carpentieri. "A perfect threshold secrety sahring scheme to identify cheaters". In *Designs, Codes and Cryptography, vol.5, no.3*, pages 183–187, 1995.
12. K. Kurosawa, S. Obana, and W. Ogata. "t-cheater identifiable (k,n) threshold secret sharing schemes". In *Proc. of Crypt'95, Lecture Notes in Computer Science, LNCS 963, Springer Verlag*, pages 410–423, 1995.
13. D.R. Stinson. "Cryptography: Theory and Practice". In *CRC Press*, pages 330–331, 1995.

The Security of the Gabidulin Public Key Cryptosystem

Keith Gibson

Department of Computer Science, Birkbeck College, Malet Street, London WC1E 7HX, England.
Email: jkg@uk.ac.bbk.dcs

Abstract. The Gabidulin Public Key Cryptosystem (PKC), like the well known McEliece PKC, is based on error correcting codes, and was introduced as an alternative to the McEliece system with the claim that much smaller codes could be used, resulting in a more practical system. In this paper an attack on the Gabidulin PKC is given which breaks it for codes of the size envisaged, destroying much of its advantage over the McEliece system. The attack succeeds in polynomial time for Gabidulin's choice of one of his system parameters, but it does show how to choose this parameter more appropriately. It consists of a reduction of the decryption problem for the Gabidulin PKC to consideration of a search problem that is easier to describe, and which with luck should be easier to analyse. It therefore provides a possible starting point for a proof that decryption for the Gabidulin PKC is an NP-complete problem.

1 Introduction

1.1 Algebraic Coded Public Key Cryptosystems

An Algebraic Coded Public Key Cryptosystem (PKC) is based on a family F of linear block error correcting codes with a fast decoding algorithm whose operation for each member of F requires knowledge of a key for that member. An instance I of the PKC uses a member C of F with key K. The public key for I is any generator matrix G for C, and the secret key is K. Four Algebraic Coded PKC's have been proposed:

1. McEliece[10] (1978), using Goppa codes,
2. Niederreiter[11] (1986), using generalised Reed-Solomon (GRS) codes,
3. Gabidulin[4] (1991) and [6] (1993), using Gabidulin codes,
4. Sidelnikov[12] (1994), using Reed-Muller codes.

The Neiderreiter system was broken by Sidelnikov and Shestakov[13] in 1992, though a modification suggested by Gabidulin[6] remains unbroken. The Sidelnikov system is too recent to have been evaluated. The McEliece system remains unbroken, — the statement by Sidelnikov and Shestakov that because Goppa codes are subfield codes of GRS codes their methods can easily be adapted to break the McEliece system is just wishful thinking. The McEliece system is probably the hardest of the four systems to break precisely because it uses subfield

Ueli Maurer (Ed,): EUROCRYPT '96 Proceedings, LNCS 1070

codes. An analysis of the 1991 version of the Gabidulin system has been given by the author in [7]. It is to the modified 1993 version that this paper is addressed.

1.2 The search for an NP-secure PKC

Unlike the RSA system, Algebraic Coded PKC's suffer from message expansion. The encrypted message is longer than the original, usually about twice as long, which means the sender's key cannot be kept secret, so that they cannot be used for signature schemes. They also tend to have large public keys. However the RSA system is unlikely to be NP-secure[1].

There is no known PKC for which decryption is an NP-complete problem, and it is an open question whether such a PKC exists. If one does exist it is possible that an Algebraic Coded PKC might provide an example. Although such an example would not necessarily be practically secure, since NP-complete problems are notorious for being almost always easy, there is some evidence[9] that NP-security, once obtained, can be amplified to the required cryptographic security.

1.3 Gabidulin codes and the Gabidulin PKC

Definition 1. Let x be any q-vector over $GF(2^m)$. The $p \times q$ **Gabidulin matrix** with generating vector x is the matrix whose first row is x, and whose i th row is the square of the $i-1$ th row, $i = 2 \ldots p$, powers of vectors being taken co-ordinatewise.

Let g be an m-vector over $GF(2^m)$ whose coordinates are linearly independent over $GF(2)$, and let G be the $k \times m$ Gabidulin matrix with generating vector g. The **Gabidulin code** C with generating vector g has generator matrix G, and corrects $e = (m-k)$ div 2 errors. Gabidulin in [3] and [5] gives fast decoding algorithms for C for which g acts as a key. Errors for Gabidulin codes are not counted using the usual Hamming metric, but with the rank metric induced by the rank norm $|v|$ of a vector v over $GF(2^m)$, which is defined to be the number of coordinates of v that are linearly independent over $GF(2)$. The associated rank norm $|D|$ of a matrix D over $GF(2^m)$ is the number of linearly independent columns of D over $GF(2)$. It can be shown that $|vD| \leq t$, with equality for some v, if and only if $|D| = t$.

An instance of the Gabidulin PKC using the code C is constructed by choosing a random $k \times k$ non-singular **scramble matrix** S over $GF(2^m)$, and a random $k \times m$ **distortion matrix** D over $GF(2^m)$ with rank norm $t < e$. The public key is then $Z = S(G + D)$, and the secret key is the triple (g, D, S).

The code C' with generator matrix Z corrects at least $e-t$ errors. Encryption of an information vector v is performed by encoding v with Z and adding $e - t$ random errors to obtain a received word r' of C'. It is easy to show that a decoder for C with key g, together with knowledge of D and Z, can be used to recover v from r'.

The distortion matrix D is needed because it is easy to show that if D is known then a secret key can quickly be determined. The McEliece PKC does not need a distortion matrix, but one can be used for the Niederreiter PKC, and that was Gabidulin's modification to this system referred to earlier.

The distortion matrix D can be written in the form $D = AB$, where B is a $t \times m$ binary matrix of rank t, and A is a $k \times t$ matrix over $GF(2^m)$ which has t linearly independent columns over $GF(2)$, but whose rank s over $GF(2^m)$ merely satisfies $1 \leq s \leq t$. The matrices A and B will be called the row and column distortion matrices, and the system parameters s and t the row and column distortion ranks. There may be secret keys with different values of s and t, but the minimal values of s and t are determined by Z. Secret keys with t not minimal provide only partial decoders for the code with generator matrix Z.

Both s and t play a crucial role in the analysis of the PKC. In [4] Gabidulin suggested $s = 1$, and then, when the present author [7] gave an algorithm to break medium sized instances of the PKC, suggested in [6] to take $s = t$, which turns out to be an unmitigated disaster, since the algorithm of this paper will find a secret key to such an instance in polynomial time! However the algorithm does show how to choose s more appropriately.

1.4 The trapdoor attack of this paper

There are two distinct kinds of attack on any PKC, corresponding to two distinct problems. A **trapdoor attack** solves the **trapdoor problem** by obtaining the secret key (trapdoor) from the public key, whereas a **direct attack** addresses the **decryption problem** by showing that it is computationally feasible to decrypt individual messages. This paper presents a trapdoor attack, and does not tackle the question of whether the decryption problem might be easier than the trapdoor problem.

It was to improve security against a direct attack that Gabidulin introduced his PKC. What he showed was that for comparably sized codes a direct attack would be much harder to mount for his system than for the McEliece PKC, so much smaller codes could be chosen, resulting in a more practical system with a smaller public key. Unfortunately he chose the codes so small that his PKC became vulnerable to the trapdoor attack of this paper, and a program has been written using this attack which even on a personal computer will break instances that use codes of the size he suggested very quickly. The necessary increase in the size of the code used both destroys much of the advantage claimed for the Gabidulin system, and begs the question of whether it remains practical. The attack does show however that with careful choice of system parameters the codes can be chosen small enough to produce a public key which is smaller than that of the McEliece PKC.

A very interesting side feature of the attack is that it indicates that subject to some normalisation, trapdoors to the Gabidulin PKC, at least those of the kind being sought, are in most cases uniquely determined, and this may be one of the reasons they are easier to find than expected.

The attack consists of a polynomial time reduction of the trapdoor problem to a search problem that is easier to describe, and which with luck should be easier to analyse. The reduction is in the sense that under some mild assumptions any solution to an instance of the trapdoor problem provides a solution to the corresponding instance of a special form of the search problem. It is probable that these assumptions can be removed, and also probable that the special search problem is equivalent to a sub-problem of the trapdoor problem. "All" that is required therefore is to show that the special search problem is NP-complete and almost always hard, and then to show that decryption is at least as hard as finding a secret key. If that could be done it would certainly be worth finding a way of coping with any impracticalities of the Gabidulin PKC.

2 Summary of Results

2.1 On breaking the Gabidulin PKC

Consider an instance of the Gabidulin PKC of length m, dimension k, generating vector g with corresponding generator matrix G, row and column distortion matrices A and B, minimal row and column distortion ranks s and t, scramble matrix S, and public key $Z = S(G + AB)$. The breaking algorithm takes Z as input and returns the secret key (G, A, B, S) as output. In the ensuing discussion t is assumed given, but this is not in fact necessary. Without loss of generality B may be sought in row echelon form.

Write $n = k + t + 2$. It is necessary to assume the conditions $n \leq m$ and $t + 2 \leq k$, but note that if $n > m$ then the code P with generator matrix Z corrects no errors, and if $t + 2 > k$ then either P corrects no errors or $m \geq 3k$.

The cost of the algorithm depends on a quantity called the **deficiency** d of Z. In all cases $0 \leq d \leq t$, and computational evidence strongly suggests that $d \geq max(0, t - 2s)$, with equality almost always. It is defined with respect to a systematic form of a selection of n columns of Z, and does not appear to depend on which columns are selected. Suppose therefore that Z is in systematic form to start with.

Define the **partial column distortion matrix** C to be the first n columns of B. The bulk of the work of the breaking algorithm is to find C, and the main theorem of this paper is the one that shows how to reduce finding C to a search problem. It will be assumed throughout that C has rank t. Discussion is made more complicated when C does not have rank t, but it is then actually easier to find a trapdoor. The following notation is used:

1. For any integer k, I_k denotes a $k \times k$ identity matrix.
2. For any matrix X over $GF(2^m)$, $X^{(2)}$ denotes the result of squaring each element of X.
3. For any matrix X over $GF(2^m)$, $N(X)$ denotes a matrix whose columns form a basis of the null space of X, i.e., the set of column vectors v with $Xv = 0$.

Definition 2. Let $[I_k, U]$ be the first n columns of Z.
Write $V = U + U^{(2)}$, and let V have rank r.
The **deficiency** of Z is $d = t + 1 - r$.

Theorem 3 The Main Theorem.

Write $W = \begin{bmatrix} U \\ I_{t+2} \end{bmatrix} N(V)$, *so that* W *is an* $n \times (d+1)$ *matrix of rank* $d+1$.

Then under some mild assumptions, CW *has rank* d.

The search problem with parameters $(n, t, d), 0 \leq d \leq t \leq n/2 - 2$.

1. The general form.
   Given an $n \times (d+1)$ matrix X over $GF(2^m)$ of rank $d+1$.
   Find a $t \times n$ binary matrix D of rank t such that the rank of DX is d.
2. The special form.
   Given an $(n-t-2) \times (t+2)$ matrix X over $GF(2^m)$ such that $Y = X + X^{(2)}$ has rank $t + 1 - d$.
   Find a $t \times n$ binary matrix D of rank t such that $D \begin{bmatrix} X \\ I_{t+2} \end{bmatrix} N(Y)$ has rank d.

Brassard[1] shows that a proof that a problem is both NP-complete and in Co-NP is a proof that NP = Co-NP. However the search problem seems unlikely to be in Co-NP. A given instance of either form of the problem does not necessarily have a solution, and there seems no easy way of determining when it does not. The corresponding decision problem can just be: given an instance of the search problem, does it have a solution?

Theorem 4 The Breaking Theorem.

1. *Finding* C *can in most cases be reduced with* $O(k^3)$ *multiplications to an instance of the special search problem with parameters* (n, t, d).
   The reduction is in the sense that C *provides a solution to this instance.*
2. *This instance can be solved at a cost of* $O(nd2^{d(k+2)})$ *multiplications. For* $d = 1$ *and* $d = 2$, *the cost can be improved to* $O(n^d 2^{d(k+2)})$ *additions with storage for* $O(n^{d+1})$ *m-bit integers. For* $d = 0$ *the cost is* $O(n^2)$ *additions.*
3. *Once* C *is known, the remainder of the secret key can be found with* $O(k^3 + (m-k)t2^d)$ *multiplications.*

There is strong computational evidence that the row echelon form of B is uniquely determined, and indeed that when $d = max(0, t - 2s)$ the search problem has a unique solution in row echelon form. When it did not there were relatively few solutions, and just one of them enabled a full secret key to be found. All of them provided a partial secret key for the first n columns of Z, and since these columns are the input to the special search problem the indication is that the special search problem is equivalent to the trapdoor problem restricted to codes of length n.

In [6], Gabidulin took $s = t$, when for almost all instances the deficiency d will be 0, and the cost just $O(k^3)$ multiplications! He suggests $m = 20, k = 10, t = 3$, and $s = 3$. It takes just 2 seconds to break such an instance on a personal computer. When $d = 1$, the algorithm is still very fast. If in the example above s is chosen to be 1 as in the 1991 version of the PKC, then d will in most cases be 1, and the instance will still be broken in about 2 seconds.

2.2 On the minimum size of code needed for the Gabidulin PKC

Consider again an instance of the Gabidulin PKC with the parameters described in Section 2.1. It corrects $e = (m - k)$ div $2 - t$ errors, and the examples in [6] have $e = 2$, which seems a bit small to guard against a direct attack. In the example given below, the heuristic $2^e > k$ has been adopted, since this means that if a systematic generator matrix is chosen as public key information symbols in a codeword can then be hidden by distinct noise coordinates when performing encryption.

Theorem 5. *An instance with $m = 48, k = 24, s = 2$, and $t = 7$ will take about 2^{85} multiplications over $GF(2^{48})$ to break using the breaking algorithm for the modified PKC, and about 2^{112} multiplications using an extended version of the breaking algorithm for the original PKC given in [6].*

This example will have a public key of 56,000 bits, half that if given in systematic form, which compares with 500,000 bits for an instance of the McEliece PKC with the parameters suggested in [10]. It will have a deficiency of $d = 3$, and correct $e = 5$ errors. It should be regarded as having the absolute minimum size acceptable, and it would probably be better to choose $m = 64, k = 32, s = 2$, and $t = 7$, giving $d = 3, e = 9$, and a public key of 131,000 bits.

3 Some Technical Lemmas

At the heart of the main theorem is a technical lemma called the Matrix Update Lemma, whose proof seems to be difficult, and which has some interest in its own right. Proofs of the other two lemmas of this section are relatively easy and are omitted. The notations $X^{(2)}$ and $N(X)$ are those of Section 2.

Lemma 6. ***The Matrix Update Lemma***
Let K be a non singular $k \times k$ matrix over $GF(2^m)$, $J = K^{-1}$, and $L = J + J^{(2)}$.
Let B be a binary $k \times k$ matrix, and suppose $K^* = K + B$ is invertible.
Define corresponding J^* and L^* in the obvious way.
Suppose L and L^* have the same rank r, and that there is a permutation π of the columns of L and L^* for which the first r columns of $L\pi$ and $L^*\pi$ are independent.
Then there is an invertible matrix R such that $J^*N(L^*)R = JN(L)$, from which it follows that $N(L^*)R = (I_k + BJ)N(L)$.

Method of proof

The Sherman Morrison matrix update formula [2] provides an explicit formula for J^* in terms of J in the case when B has just one non-zero element, and can be used to prove the lemma for this case. To lift the result to the general case requires the assumption that K can be transformed to K^* with a succession of additions of 1 to one element while preserving the invertibility of K and the conditions on L and L^* at each stage. This is a long and unsatisfactory proof involving an additional assumption which is almost certainly unnecessary. Details can be found in [8].

Lemma 7. ***The rank 1 lemma***
Let G be a $k \times k$ Gabidulin matrix with generating vector g, let H be a $k \times f$ Gabidulin matrix with generating vector h, and suppose the vector $[g, h]$ has independent coordinates over $GF(2)$, so that G is non-singular. Let $X = G^{-1}H$. Then $X + X^{(2)}$ has rank 1, and has no zero elements.

Lemma 8. ***The null space lemma***
Let A and B be matrices over any field, each with the same number of columns. Then $rank(AN(B)) - rank(BN(A)) = rank(A) - rank(B)$.

4 The Breaking Algorithm

4.1 Overview

The object of this section is to prove the main theorem of Section 2, and to indicate how it is used to obtain the breaking theorem. There is a final paragraph on the solution of the search problem, but an efficient solution must form the subject of a separate paper. Details have been given in[8].

For the whole of this section the convention is adopted that matrix blocks are suffixed with the number of columns that they have. As in Section 2, $N(X)$ is a matrix whose columns form a basis of the null space of the matrix X, and $X^{(2)}$ is obtained by squaring each element of X.

Consider an instance of the Gabidulin PKC as described in Section 2. The breaking algorithm proceeds in three stages, but the story is told backwards, because that is the way the algorithm unfolds. In stage 3, the column distortion matrix B is assumed known, and the rest of the secret key is recovered. The method of doing so sets the framework on which stages 2 and 1 build. In stage 2, only the partial column distortion matrix C is known, and the method of stage 3 is extended using the rank 1 and null space lemmas to recover the rest of the column distortion matrix. Finally, in stage 1 only the public key is known, and the method of stage 2 is further extended using the matrix update lemma to dig out the partial column distortion matrix.

A number of assumptions have to be made, all of which are probably either provable or unnecessary. The first is probably unnecessary, but simplifies the discussion, and does in fact hold most of the time anyway.

Assumption 1 *Any selection of n columns of z are independent.*

4.2 Stage 3: The column distortion matrix is known

Stage 3 starts with the observation that since B is binary, the $m \times (m-t)$ matrix $N(B)$ can be taken to be binary, so that if $H = GN(B)$ then H is a $k \times (m-t)$ Gabidulin matrix whose generating vector h has linearly independent coordinates over $GF(2)$, and $ZN(B) = SH$. Summarising the relations between the matrices defined so far,

$$Z = S(G + AB), \quad H = GN(B), \quad ZN(B) = SH. \tag{1}$$

Assume from now on that Z is in systematic form, and that columns $k+1 \ldots k+t$ of B form an identity matrix. Since C has rank t, assumption 1 guarantees that this normalisation is possible. Write $f = m - k - t$, and partition Z, G, g, H, h, and B as follows :

$$\begin{array}{ll} Z = [I_k, Z_t, Z_f], & B = [B_k, I_t, B_f], \\ G = [G_k, G_t, G_f], & g = [g_k, g_t, g_f], \\ H = [H_k, H_f], & h = [h_k, h_f]. \end{array} \tag{2}$$

Take

$$N(B) = \begin{bmatrix} I_k, & 0 \\ B_k, & B_f \\ 0, & I_f \end{bmatrix} \begin{matrix} k \\ t \\ f. \end{matrix} \tag{3}$$

With this partitioning, (1) yields

$$H_f = H_k X, \tag{4}$$
$$[g_k, g_f] = h + g_t\,[B_k, B_f], \tag{5}$$
$$A = G_t + H_k U_t, \tag{6}$$
$$Q = SH_k, \tag{7}$$

where

$$\begin{aligned} Q &= I_k + Z_t B_k, \\ P &= Q^{-1}, \\ U &= P[Z_t, Z_f] = [U_t, U_f], \\ X &= U_f + U_t B_f. \end{aligned} \tag{8}$$

To solve (4) for h observe that g, and hence h, is only determined up to a scalar multiple, so assume that h has been normalised so that the first coordinate of h_f is 1. Let x_1 be the first column of X, and X_1 the $k \times k$ Gabidulin matrix whose generating vector is the 2^{m-k-1} th power of x_1, taken coordinatewise. Let e denote a k-vector of ones. Then after some manipulation, (4) implies $X_1 h_k = e$, which determines h_k and hence h, provided X_1 is non singular. The condition that X_1 is non singular is that the coordinates of x_1 are independent over $GF(2)$, and in view of (9) and (11) below, this requires

Assumption 2 *the rows of X are independent over $GF(2)$.*

Once h is known, (5) can be used to determine g, (6) to determine A, and (7) to determine S. In (5), g_t can be chosen randomly subject to ensuring that g has independent coordinates over $GF(2)$, and this flexibility of choice can be used to ensure A has its minimal rank s, which determines g uniquely when $d = max(0, t-2s)$. Note that (7) ensures that Q is invertible, since H_k and S are invertible.

4.3 Stage 2 : The partial column distortion matrix is known

In terms of the previous section, B_k and the first two columns of B_f are known, and the remaining columns of B_f have to be determined. From the definition of X in (8),

$$X^{(2)} + X = VY, \tag{9}$$

where

$$V = U + U^{(2)}, \quad Y = \begin{bmatrix} B_f \\ I_f \end{bmatrix} \begin{matrix} t \\ f \end{matrix}. \tag{10}$$

Equation (4) states that $H_f = H_k X$, so applying the rank 1 lemma gives

Lemma 9. ***The Stage 2 lemma***

$$V\,Y \text{ has rank 1, and has no zero elements.} \tag{11}$$

Suppose V has rank r, and let $d = t + 1 - r$. The columns of Y form a basis of the null space of $[I_t, B_f]$, so applying the null space lemma gives

Theorem 10 The Stage 2 Theorem.

$$[I_t, B_f]N(V) \text{ is a } t \times (d + f - 1) \text{ matrix of rank } d. \tag{12}$$

This theorem is used to determine B_f. The method requires

Assumption 3 *The first t columns of V span the column space of V, and no selection of d columns of $[I_t, B_f]N(V)$ are dependent.*

Assumption 3 means that the last $d + f - 1$ rows of $N(V)$ can be taken to be an identity matrix. Let b be the first column of B_f, and c be any other column. Then for a suitable known $r \times (d + 1)$ matrix W, equation (12) gives

$$[I_t, b, c] \begin{bmatrix} W \\ I_{d+1} \end{bmatrix} \begin{matrix} r \\ d+1 \end{matrix} \text{ has rank } d. \tag{13}$$

The vector b is known, and for $d < 2$ equation (13) determines c very quickly. For $d \geq 2$ it determines c after a search over the last $d-1$ coordinates of c. Thus when the first column of B_f is known, the Stage 2 theorem can be used to find each of the remaining columns of B_f in turn, at a total cost of $O(t(m-k)2^d)$ multiplications. Further details are given in [8].

It can be shown that due to the special form of Y the Stage 2 lemma implies

Lemma 11. ***The Stage 2 Corollary***

The first $t+1$ columns of V do span the column space of V.

This corollary will be used to show that under assumptions made in stage 3, the quantity d is the deficiency of Z as defined in Section 2. Note that the Stage 2 theorem implies that $1 \leq r \leq t+1$, so that $0 \leq d \leq t$.

4.4 Stage 1 : Only the public key is known

Stage 1 finds the first $n = k+t+2$ columns of B, and therefore restricts attention to the first n columns Z, so that the f of stages 2 and 3 is $f = 2$, but the symbol f will continue to be used to indicate the number of columns in matrix blocks. Write $p = t+2$ and $q = k-p$. The conditions $n \leq m$ and $t+2 \leq k$ ensure that there are n columns of Z to play with, and that $q \geq 0$.

In stage 1, the matrix V is not available since B is not known. The basic idea of stage 1 is to let $V0$ be the value of V obtained by setting $B = 0$, and to use the matrix update lemma to see how V and $V0$ are related. First some useful matrix blocks are defined. Note that since Z is in systematic form the block Z_q consists of q columns of Z. Define

$$D_k = \begin{bmatrix} B_k \\ 0 \end{bmatrix} \begin{matrix} t \\ k-t \end{matrix}, \quad E_k = \begin{bmatrix} B_k \\ 0 \end{bmatrix} \begin{matrix} t \\ 2 \end{matrix}, \quad Z_q = \begin{bmatrix} 0 \\ I_q \end{bmatrix} \begin{matrix} p \\ q \end{matrix}. \tag{14}$$

Write

$$E_k = [E_p, E_q]. \tag{15}$$

The first step is to define $V0$, and build it up to a square matrix so that the matrix update lemma can be applied. With the matrix P of equation (8), define

$$\begin{aligned} U0 &= [Z_t, Z_f], & U &= P\,U0, \\ V0 &= U0 + U0^{(2)}, & V &= U + U^{(2)}, \\ J0 &= [U0, Z_q], & J &= P\,J0, \\ K0 &= J0^{-1}, & K &= J^{-1}, \\ L0 &= J0 + J0^{(2)}, & L &= J + J^{(2)}. \end{aligned} \tag{16}$$

The matrices U and V defined here consist of the first $t+2$ columns of the U and V defined in (8) and (10). The matrices $U0$ and $V0$ are the U and V of section 2. Note that $J0$ is invertible by assumption 1, since it consists of k columns of Z. After some manipulation, (8) and (16) yield

$$K = K0 + D_k, \tag{17}$$

$$L0 = [\overset{p}{V0}, \overset{q}{0}]k, \qquad L = [\overset{p}{V}, \overset{q}{V\,E_q}]\,k. \tag{18}$$

The stage is now set for the matrix update lemma, but an assumption must be made to ensure it can be applied.

Assumption 4 *V and $V0$ have the same rank r, and there is a permutation π of the columns of V and $V0$ such the first r columns of $V\pi$ and $V0\pi$ are independent.*

Take

$$N(L0) = \begin{array}{c} \begin{matrix} p-r & q \end{matrix} \\ \begin{bmatrix} N(V0), & 0 \\ 0, & I_q \end{bmatrix} \end{array} \begin{matrix} p \\ q \end{matrix}, \quad N(L) = \begin{array}{c} \begin{matrix} p-r & q \end{matrix} \\ \begin{bmatrix} N(V), & E_q \\ 0, & I_q \end{bmatrix} \end{array} \begin{matrix} p \\ q \end{matrix}. \tag{19}$$

The matrix update lemma now says there is an invertible $k \times k$ matrix R with $N(L)R = (I_k + D_k\ J0)N(L0)$, and sorting out the matrix blocks in this expression shows that there is an invertible $p \times p$ matrix T with

$$N(V)T = (I_p + E_k\ U0)N(V0). \tag{20}$$

Now it is straightforward to see that

$$[I_t, B_f](I_p + E_k\ U0) = [B_k, I_t, B_f] \begin{bmatrix} U0 \\ I_p \end{bmatrix} \begin{matrix} k \\ p. \end{matrix} \tag{21}$$

The final step is to use the Stage 2 theorem, but this theorem was developed using all m columns of Z. However it remains true when only n columns are used, and states, with the Stage 1 definition of V and r, that $[I_t, B_f]N(V)$ has rank $d = t + 1 - r$. Further, the Stage 2 corollary together with assumption 4 ensures that the quantities d and r defined in Stages 1 and 2 are the same, and that d is the deficiency of Z as defined in section 2. The Stage 2 theorem, together with (20) and (21), gives

Theorem 12 The Stage 1 Theorem.

$$C \begin{bmatrix} U0 \\ I_p \end{bmatrix} N(V0) \textit{ has rank } d = t + 1 - r. \tag{22}$$

A closer examination reveals that provided C does have rank t this result remains true even when columns $k+1 \ldots k+t$ of C do not form an identity matrix, at least if assumption 1 holds, and with this observation the main theorem of Section 2 is proved.

4.5 Solving the general search problem

Given an $n \times (d+1)$ matrix X over $GF(2^m)$ of rank $d+1$, it is required to find a $t \times n$ binary matrix D of rank t such that the rank of DX is d, $0 \leq d \leq t \leq n/2-2$. The method of searching for D given in [8] requires an assumption which can be translated as one final assumption about the matrices C and $U0$ in (22).

Assumption 5 *The first d rows and columns of DX form an invertible matrix.*

D can be sought in row echelon form, and with assumption 5 it is enough to search over the first d rows and $n - t + d$ columns of D. Thus the search is over $d \times (n - t + d)$ binary row echelon matrices of rank d, and there are fewer than $3.5 * 2^{d(n-t)}$ of these. The work can be cut to $O(nd)$ multiplications per matrix tested by enumerating the matrices so that each differs from the previous one in just one element, and using the Sherman Morrison formula [2] as in the proof of the matrix update lemma. To finish on an aesthetically pleasing note, this enumeration is an adaptation of the following way of enumerating r-bit integers so that each differs from the previous one in just one bit position. Let $s = 2^r - 1$ and number the integers $a_0 \ldots a_s$, with any integer assigned to a_0. For $i = 0$ to $s - 1$ let j be minimal with bit j of i equal to zero, and obtain a_{i+1} by complementing bit j of a_i.

References

1. BRASSARD, G. "A Note on the Complexity of Cryptography." IEEE Transactions on Information Theory, Vol IT-25, no. 2, 1979.
2. BURDEN R.L., FAIRES J.D., and REYNOLDS A.C. "Numerical Analysis." 2nd. Ed., Prindle, Weber, and Schmidt, 1981. Page 458.
3. GABIDULIN E.M. "Theory of Codes with Maximum Rank Distance." Problems of Information Transmission, Vol 21 no. 1, 1985.
4. GABIDULIN E.M. "Ideals Over a Non-Commutative Ring and their Applications in Cryptography." Lecture Notes in Computer Science Vol 547, Proc. Eurocrypt 91, Springer Verlag, 1991.
5. GABIDULIN E.M. "A Fast Matrix Decoding Algorithm for Rank-Error-Correcting Codes." Lecture Notes in Computer Science Vol 573, Algebraic Coding, Springer Verlag, 1992.
6. GABIDULIN E.M. "On Public-Key Cryptosystems Based on Linear Codes : Efficiency and Weakness." Codes and Ciphers, Proc. 4th IMA Conference on Cryptography and Coding, 1993. IMA Press, 1995.
7. GIBSON J.K. "Severely Denting the Gabidulin Version of the McEliece Public Key Cryptosystem." Designs, Codes, and Cryptography, Vol 6, 1995.
8. GIBSON J.K. "Algebraic Coded Cryptosystems". PhD Thesis, Univ. of London, 1996.
9. GOLDREICH O., IMPAGLIAZZO R., LEVIN L., VENKATESAN R., and ZUCKERMAN D. "Security Preserving Amplification of Hardness." Proc. of the 31st Annual Symposium on the Foundations of Computer Science (FOCS), 1990.
10. McELIECE R.J. "A Public Key Cryptosystem Based on Algebraic Coding Theory". DSN Progress Report (Jan-Feb), Jet Propulsion Laboratory, California Institute of Technology, 1978.
11. NIEDERREITER H. "Knapsack-Type Cryptosystems and Algebraic Coding Theory." Problems of Control and Information Theory, Vol 15 no. 2, 1986.
12. SIDELNIKOV V.M. "A Public-Key Cryptosystem Based on Binary Reed-Muller Codes." Discrete Mathematics and Applications, Vol 4, no. 3, 1994.
13. SIDELNIKOV V.M. and SHESTAKOV S.O. "On Insecurity of Cryptosystems Based on Generalised Reed-Solomon Codes." Discrete Mathematics and Applications, Vol 2, no. 4, 1992.

Non-Linear Approximations in Linear Cryptanalysis

Lars R. Knudsen[1] and M.J.B. Robshaw[2]

[1] K.U. Leuven, ESAT, Kardinaal Mercierlaan 94, B-3001 Heverlee
email:knudsen@esat.kuleuven.ac.be

[2] RSA Laboratories, 100 Marine Parkway, Redwood City, CA 94065, USA
email:matt@rsa.com

Abstract. By considering the role of non-linear approximations in linear cryptanalysis we obtain a generalization of Matsui's linear cryptanalytic techniques. This approach allows the cryptanalyst greater flexibility in mounting a linear cryptanalytic attack and we demonstrate the effectiveness of our non-linear techniques with some simple attacks on LOKI91. These attacks potentially allow for the recovery of seven additional bits of key information with less than 1/4 of the plaintext that is required using current linear cryptanalytic methods.

1 Introduction

The technique of linear cryptanalysis [7] is now well known. Most dramatically it has provided the first experimental (though barely practical) compromise [8] of the Data Encryption Standard DES [9].

In addition to some theoretical and practical enhancements or extensions to linear cryptanalysis [4, 6, 11] it is natural to consider whether the linear approximations on which linear cryptanalysis relies can be replaced with non-linear approximations. Since there are far more non-linear approximations than linear approximations, it seems fair to say that by opening ourselves to their use, we might obtain a much improved attack on some cipher. As a motivational example, the best *linear* approximation to a DES S-box is to S5, and this approximation holds with an absolute valued bias of 20/64, yet there is a relatively simple *non-linear* approximation to S8 involving four input bits[3], which holds with absolute bias 28/64. While previous work [3] has already demonstrated insurmountable problems in the general use of non-linear approximations, we will show that they should not be abandoned and that non-linear approximations can offer effective additions to the basic techniques in use today.

In the following sections we describe the essential issues in linear cryptanalysis and the use of non-linear approximations within such an attack. We show that current linear cryptanalytic techniques are essentially special instances of

[3] Labeling the input bits to DES S-box S8 as $x_5 \dots x_0$ and the output bits as $y_3 \dots y_0$ the approximation $1 \oplus x_3 \oplus x_4 \oplus x_2x_3 \oplus x_3x_4 \oplus x_1x_2x_4 \oplus x_2x_3x_4 = y_0 \oplus y_1 \oplus y_2 \oplus y_3$ holds with probability 60/64.

Ueli Maurer (Ed.): EUROCRYPT '96 Proceedings, LNCS 1070

our more general approach and we demonstrate that our techniques have implications for both the design and cryptanalysis of block ciphers. In particular, our techniques pose a threat even when Matsui's advanced linear cryptanalytic attacks (in which the cryptanalyst guesses the key bits used to evaluate some S-box) are rendered impractical due to the use of large S-boxes. While we will motivate our discussion with examples that involve DES (since this is the cipher with which most people are familiar) we note that our current techniques do not seem to offer any significant advantage over existing attacks on DES. There are however some open questions in this regard and future research alone will determine if this is indeed the case. Instead, our techniques have been most useful in improving existing attacks [16] on LOKI91 [1] where it is straightforward to recover seven additional bits of the user-defined key while using less than 1/4 of the plaintext that is currently required. We also expect our techniques to be applicable to many other block ciphers.

2 Linear Cryptanalysis

In a linear cryptanalytic attack the cryptanalyst identifies a linear relation between some bits of the plaintext, some bits of the ciphertext and some bits of the user-provided key. While a relation between single bits of information which holds all the time (or none of the time) would be especially useful to a cryptanalyst, Matsui [7] showed that provided the relation does not hold exactly half the time, there are ways to extract key information by analyzing a large enough set of known plaintext and ciphertext pairs.

There are two basic approaches. The first is to use an approximation which relates bits of the user-defined key and the plaintext/ciphertext data in a linear way thereby providing one bit of key information when sufficient data is available. The second is to identify, by analysis of the block cipher, some bits of a linear approximation that depend for their value on a small subset of bits in the user-defined key. It is then assumed that only by making a correct guess for these key bits will the anticipated bias in certain bits of the plaintext/ciphertext data be detectable. Matsui showed how to use these key-bit guessing techniques in what are sometimes referred to as the *1R-* and *2R-methods*. The block ciphers we are concerned with are iterative and repeatedly use a round transformation during encryption. With the 1R-method the cryptanalyst guesses the value of part of the user-provided key in either the first or the last rounds, while in the 2R-method the guess is for part of the user-provided key from both the first and the last rounds simultaneously.

3 Linear and Non-Linear Approximations

Linear approximations are built up by analyzing individual rounds of the block cipher. For ease of exposition, we will consider a Feistel cipher [2] where at round i of the cipher we denote the partially encrypted data input to the round as C_h^{i-1} and C_l^{i-1}; the high-order half of the data and the low-order half of the data respectively. We shall denote the action of the round function with subkey k_i by $f(\cdot, k_i)$ and the output from the ith round of the cipher will be written as $C_h^i = C_l^{i-1}$ and $C_l^i = C_h^{i-1} \oplus f(C_l^{i-1}, k_i)$. Note that in this notation C_h^0, C_l^0 constitutes the plaintext and C_l^r, C_h^r constitutes the ciphertext produced by the r-round cipher (since there is no swap in the last round).

3.1 Joining Approximations

The notation $C_l^{i-1}[\alpha]$ (and later β, γ and δ) is used to denote a general and unspecified linear sum of bits of the data block C_l^{i-1}. An approximation to the action of a single round of the cipher might be written as

$$C_h^{i-1}[\alpha] \oplus C_l^{i-1}[\beta] = C_h^i[\gamma] \oplus C_l^i[\alpha] \oplus k_i[\delta] \qquad (1)$$

where $k_i[\delta]$ is a linear combination of subkey bits (the exact form of which will depend on the block cipher in question). By writing the approximation in this way, we are tacitly approximating the action of the round function by

$$\begin{aligned} C_l^{i-1}[\beta \oplus \gamma] \oplus k_i[\delta] &= C_h^{i-1}[\alpha] \oplus C_l^i[\alpha] \\ &= (C_h^{i-1} \oplus C_l^i)[\alpha]. \end{aligned} \qquad (2)$$

Suppose now that we have some partially encrypted data C_h^{i-1} and C_l^{i-1} and let us consider an approximation which involves a non-linear function of bits in C_h^{i-1}. We shall use the notation $C_h^{i-1}[p(\alpha)]$ where α is used to identify some set of bits and $p(\cdot)$ is, in this case, a non-linear polynomial involving these bits. Now forming a one round approximation as we had in (1) is difficult because, as we can see from (2), it requires that

$$(C_h^{i-1} \oplus C_l^i)[p(\alpha)] = C_h^{i-1}[p(\alpha)] \oplus C_l^i[p(\alpha)].$$

and for non-linear $p(\cdot)$ this will not, in general, hold. But while one-round approximations that are non-linear in the output bits from $f(C_l^{i-1}, k_i)$ cannot be joined together (when bitwise exclusive-or is used to combine this output with C_h^{i-1}) non-linear approximations can still be used in a variety of ways.

First note that the input to an approximation to the first and last rounds of some cipher need not be combined with any other approximations. Consequently approximations to these rounds can equally be linear or non-linear expressions in bits of the data input. Second, and more interestingly, we note that the 1R- and 2R-methods of linear cryptanalysis make certain bits of the input to the second (or penultimate) round available to the cryptanalysis. We can use this to our advantage and non-linear approximations can potentially be used in the *second* and the *penultimate* rounds of an attack on some block cipher. We will demonstrate this practically with an improved attack on LOKI91.

There is however one major problem that we have yet to overcome, and that is to identify and use non-linear approximations to a single round of a cipher.

3.2 Non-Linear Approximations to a Single Round

To illustrate our approach to using non-linear approximations in a single round of a cipher, we shall use as our example the round function used in DES. Consider the input to the ith round which we have denoted as C_h^{i-1} and C_l^{i-1}. The data C_l^{i-1} used as input to the round function $f(\cdot, k_i)$ is expanded from 32 to 48 bits and combined using exclusive-or with the subkey k_i for the round. The resultant 48 bits are then used as input to the non-linear transformation affected by eight S-boxes. The 32 bits produced as output are permuted and the result is combined using bitwise exclusive-or with C_h^{i-1}. The two data halves are then swapped.

Let us suppose that analysis of the S-boxes has revealed that an approximation consisting of a non-linear combination of some input bits to an S-box and a linear combination of the output bits is strongly biased. To exploit this in an attack, we need to transform the approximation across a DES S-box into an approximation across the entire round function. The output of the S-boxes can be easily related via the bit-wise permutation into an expression in the data bits output from the round function. For the non-linear combination of bits that are used as input to the S-boxes, it is harder to get an expression in terms of the bits that are used as input to the round function. This is because the key k_i is combined with the expanded C_l^{i-1} using bitwise exclusive-or. Denote the expansion of the data block C_l^{i-1} by $z_{47} \ldots z_0$. Combined with the key $k_{47} \ldots k_0$ this forms the input to the S-boxes $x_{47} \ldots x_0$ where $x_i = z_i \oplus k_i$ for $0 \leq i \leq 47$. Let us suppose, by way of illustration, that a non-linear approximation to the eighth S-box S8 involves $x_0 x_1$. Then depending on the actual values of k_0 and k_1 we can express $x_0 x_1$ in terms of z_0 and z_1. More explicitly, when $(k_0, k_1) = (0, 0)$ it is clear that $x_0 x_1 = z_0 z_1$ and when $(k_0, k_1) = (1, 1)$ we have $x_0 x_1 = z_0 z_1 \oplus z_0 \oplus z_1 \oplus 1$. For $(k_0, k_1) = (0, 1)$ we have that $x_0 x_1 = z_0 z_1 \oplus z_0$ and when $(k_0, k_1) = (1, 0)$ it follows that $x_0 x_1 = z_0 z_1 \oplus z_1$. Note that the key is *fixed* for all the data we collect. When a non-linear approximation is used in the first and/or last round of the cipher, the input to the round function can be directly observed in the plaintext or the ciphertext respectively. We might then assume that the value of the key bits involved in the non-linear terms of the approximation are fixed to some value and with a certain proportion of the keys, we will be correct in our analysis. We illustrate this phenomenon with a simple example using DES.

Example with DES. The following approximations to S-boxes S5 and S1 (`A`, `C` and `D` appear in [7, 8]) will be useful in attacking five-round DES. The input to an S-box will be denoted $x_5 \ldots x_0$ and the output $y_3 \ldots y_0$.

	box	*input*	*output*	*|bias|*
A	S5	x_4	$y_0 \oplus y_1 \oplus y_2 \oplus y_3$	20/64
D	S5	x_4	$y_1 \oplus y_2 \oplus y_3$	10/64
C	S1	x_2	y_2	2/64
A'	S5	$x_1 \oplus x_0 x_1 \oplus x_0 x_4 \oplus x_1 x_5 \oplus x_4 x_5 \oplus x_0 x_1 x_5 \oplus x_0 x_4 x_5$	$y_0 \oplus y_1 \oplus y_2 \oplus y_3$	24/64
D'	S5	$x_1 \oplus x_3 \oplus x_0 x_3 \oplus x_0 x_5 \oplus x_1 x_3 \oplus x_1 x_5 \oplus x_0 x_1 x_3 \oplus x_0 x_1 x_5$	$y_1 \oplus y_2 \oplus y_3$	18/64

Using the five-round linear approximation `DCA-A`, which holds with probability p where $(p-1/2)^{-2} = 68,720$, we can recover one bit of key information with the following success rates over 50 trials:

plaintexts	17,180	34,360	68,720
success rate	74%	88%	98%

Alternatively, one bit of key information can be recovered using the non-linear approximation `D'CA-A'` which holds with probability p' where $(p'-1/2)^{-2} = 14,728$. Note the reduced data requirements. Again, success rates are quoted for 50 trials.

plaintexts	3,682	7,364	14,728
success rate	86%	92%	100%

For this experiment, the key bits directly involved in the non-linear approximation in the outer rounds were fixed and known.

3.3 Recovering More Key Bits

In certain circumstances non-linear approximations can be used to give a mechanism which allows the recovery of more bits of key information with less plaintext. As might already be apparent, specific instances of our general approach are equivalent to Matsui's 1R- and 2R-methods.

So far we have dealt with the non-linearity in the input bits to some S-box by assuming that the key bits involved have a certain value and that for some proportion of the user-defined keys we are correct. There is however another approach. Whenever a product appears in a nonlinear approximation, the possible values for the key bits involved force us to consider alternative approximations. For instance, let us suppose that the product of the two least significant input bits x_0 and x_1 to S-box $S8$ in DES is equal to the linear sum of all the output bits from S-box $S8$ with some probability p. Define the absolute value of the bias of this approximation to be ϵ where $\epsilon = |p - 1/2|$. Suppose in our attack, that we know the corresponding bits z_0 and z_1 before transformation with the user-defined key k_0 and k_1 which gives $x_0 = z_0 \oplus k_0$ and $x_1 = z_1 \oplus k_1$. Since k_0 and k_1 are fixed, we can try each guess for k_0 and k_1 in turn with the data we have. When we make the correct key guess, we correctly reconstruct x_0 and x_1 the actual inputs to the S-box and hence the correct product x_0x_1. Suppose we guess incorrectly and choose $k_0 \oplus 1$ and k_1. Then we erroneously construct the values $x_0 \oplus 1$ and x_1 instead of x_0 and x_1. Now $(x_0 \oplus 1)x_1 = x_0x_1 \oplus x_1$ and this expression in the input bits will equal the sum of the output bits with probability p_1 say. Define $\epsilon_1 = |p_1 - 1/2|$. If $\epsilon_1 < \epsilon$ then by taking sufficient data the correct guess k_0, k_1 can be distinguished from $k_0 \oplus 1, k_1$. If $\epsilon_1 > \epsilon$ then the incorrect key guess will dominate, though in a practical attack we would use the approximation with the greater bias anyway (and in so doing we would recover the correct key guess). If $\epsilon_1 = \epsilon$ then the two guesses cannot be distinguished.

Example with DES. We can use the approximation `D'CA-A'` as defined previously to recover key bits used in the non-linear approximation. Denote the key bits used in S5 in round one as $k_5^1 \ldots k_0^1$ and the key bits used in S5 in round five as $k_5^5 \ldots k_0^5$. Analysis of `A'` and `D'` reveals that with `A'` we can reliably recover k_0^5, $k_1^5 \oplus k_4^5$ and k_5^5 and with `D'` we can recover k_0^1, k_1^1 and $k_3^1 \oplus k_5^1$. We obtained the following success rate over 50 trials when using the non-linear approximation `D'CA-A'` (which holds with probability p where $(p-1/2)^{-2} = 14,728$) to recover six bits of key material:

plaintexts	14,728	29,456	58,912	117,824
success rate	18%	38%	60%	82%

A Special Case. The 1R- and 2R-methods of Matsui, and even the basic technique of linear cryptanalysis which recovers one bit of key information, are all special instances of this more general technique.

With DES we might imagine using non-linear expressions of an S-box using all six input bits, see e.g. [15]. These 'approximations' would hold with probability 1 and we would expect to recover six bits of user-defined key. Of course, we could simply represent the action of these polynomials by means of the look-up table for the S-box. This gives us precisely the 1R- and 2R-methods. By choosing an incorrect key guess we are in effect deriving a different approximation to the S-box which holds with a reduced bias. With sufficient data the correct key guess can be distinguished. Note that when we have the polynomial expressions at our disposal we can actually evaluate which of the incorrect guesses are most likely to occur. In this way we can improve our basic attacks by allowing for certain, predicted incorrect answers and adjusting them accordingly. In experiments on DES this gives us an improvement in our attacks, but not by a significant margin.

4 Implications

4.1 Greater Cryptanalytic Flexibility

In practice, we recover key bits using non-linear techniques by first counting the number of plaintext/ciphertext pairs that fall into a variety of classes. These classes are defined according to the text involved in the nonlinear approximation (the *effective text* bits). We then process this data by guessing each possible value for the key bits involved in the non-linear approximation (the *effective key* bits) and combine this guess with the effective text. In this way scores can be kept for the number of times the bit identified by the linear approximation to the rest of the cipher is either 0 or 1. A guess can be made for the value of the effective key bits depending on these final scores. Thus the basic work effort in processing the data once it has been initially sorted is 2^{k+t} where k is the number of effective key bits and t is the number of effective text bits.

It is now clear that our more general approach to the use of non-linear approximations has numerous practical implications beyond the use of approximations with greater absolute biases. Using Matsui's 1R- and 2R-methods, the cryptanalyst is unnecessarily restricted to using a number of effective key and text bits that is a multiple of the number of bits involved in the input to some S-box. When larger S-boxes are used, and this is a common recommendation [13],

Matsui's 2R- and even the 1R-methods can become impractical just because the number of effective text and key bits becomes excessive. Existing examples of ciphers where the 2R-method is impractical include FEAL [14] and LOKI91 [16]. When the S-boxes are so large that the 1R-method itself becomes impractical then it might previously have been argued that the cryptanalyst would be reduced to recovering just a single bit of user-defined key. Instead the cryptanalyst can use non-linear approximations, in the fashion we have described here, to recover additional bits from the user-defined key. These techniques can be used to supplement the 2R-method, they can be used to supplement the 1R-method when the 2R-method is impractical and they can be used even if both the 2R- and 1R-methods are infeasible.

Example. In [12] "almost perfect non-linear functions" were studied. For ciphers constructed using these functions, linear approximations will have low absolute biases. Examples of such functions are $f(x) = x^{2^k+1}$ in $GF(2^n)$ for odd n [12]. The output bits of f are quadratic in the input bits and any linear approximation for f will have an absolute bias at most $2^{\frac{n+s}{2}-1}/2^n$, where $s = gcd(k,n)$ [10]. For a Feistel cipher with round function $F(x,k) = f(x \oplus k)$ with $n = 33$, $k = s = 1$ (given as an example in [12]) this yields a maximum bias for one round of 2^{-17}. Clearly, the 2R-method is impossible for this cipher, and the 1R-method requires many effective text and key bits. However the functions f are only quadratic, so non-linear approximations which involve only a few input bits might provide improved opportunities for attack. Experiments on the functions f defined above for small values of n confirm this. For $n = 7$, $k = s = 1$, the absolute value of the bias of a linear approximation is at most 8/128. With just two input bits, there exist non-linear approximations with absolute biases 16/128. For $n = 9$ and $k = s = 1$, the bias of a linear approximation is at most 16/512 yet with three input bits there exist non-linear approximations with biases 32/512. It is immediately clear that by using our non-linear techniques in the outer rounds of the cipher, the basic linear cryptanalytic attack can be readily improved.

4.2 The Non-Linear Approximation of Inner Rounds

While we might be familiar with the use of non-linear techniques in the outer rounds of a cipher it is interesting to observe that non-linear approximations can also be used in the second and penultimate round of a cipher. To illustrate this, suppose for some cipher that n bits from an S-box in round one are mapped to the same S-box in round two and that by using t effective text bits we can replicate the output from the S-box in round one. When this output is correct, n input bits to a single S-box in round two will be correct and we can use a non-linear function of these input bits in an approximation of the second round instead of the linear function that techniques currently demand. In practice we would increase the number of effective text bits to $t + n$ by additionally considering certain bits of C_h^0 to be effective. There would also be an increase in the number of effective key bits, to accommodate those used in the second round, but these might well be recoverable during the attack anyway. We provide experimental verification of this approach in our attack on LOKI91.

While it might appear that we are only able to improve attacks on a round by round basis, such improvements should not be overlooked. The plaintext requirements in a linear cryptanalytic attack are considered to be proportional to ϵ^{-2} where ϵ is the bias of the approximation [8] and increases in the bias of just two rounds of a cipher by a factor of $\sqrt{2}$ will give a reduction in plaintext requirements by a factor of 4.

5 LOKI91

LOKI91 is a DES-like block cipher that operates on 64-bit blocks and uses a 64-bit key [1]. The most interesting feature of LOKI91 for our purposes is that the cipher uses four identical S-boxes which map 12 bits to 8. Evidence for the resistance of LOKI91 to linear cryptanalysis was recently provided by Tokita et al. [16]. In this section we provide experimental verification of our new techniques. While we mounted our attacks on four-round LOKI91 (for reasons of practicality) the approximation we chose matched the outer rounds of the best linear approximation [16] that would be used to attack $(4 + 3r)$-round LOKI91 for $r > 0$. Clearly the plaintext requirements N for a linear cryptanalytic attack increase substantially as we add more rounds and we note that 16-round LOKI91 (when $r = 4$) remains immune to these attacks[4]. We will show that it is straightforward to use non-linear approximations in the first two rounds and in the last round of LOKI91 simultaneously, thereby improving the basic linear cryptanalytic attack. The polynomials we will use in our attack are given in Table 1, where we denote the input to the 12-bit S-box by $x_{11} \dots x_0$ and the output by $y_7 \dots y_0$.

Tokita et al. [16] point out that the S-boxes in LOKI91 are too large to allow the cryptanalyst to use the 2R-method and they restrict themselves to considering only the 1R-method as an alternative. This allows the recovery of 13 bits of user-defined key (with a work-effort proportional to 2^{24} operations). By reversing the role of the plaintext and ciphertext, potentially another 13 bits can be recovered leaving 38 bits to be discovered by exhaustive search (with a 2^{38} work effort).

With the non-linear approximations we have identified however, we can mount a range of attacks that are quite different from the typical approach of `?X-Y` where we use `?` to denote Matsui's 1R-method in the first round. These attacks have different work efforts and recover different numbers of key bits. By allowing for more work during the analysis of the data, more key bits might be recovered or alternatively less plaintext might be required for a successful attack.

The results of a series of experiments can be found in the attached Appendix. While we have obtained direct empirical evidence for the effectiveness of some

[4] For 4-, 7- and 10-round LOKI91 the known plaintext requirements are 2^{23}, 2^{40} and 2^{58} respectively. For 13- and 16-round LOKI91, linear cryptanalytic techniques are infeasible.

Table 1. Some linear and non-linear approximations for LOKI91.

	box	*input*	*output*	$\|bias\|$
X	S2	$x_2 \oplus x_6 \oplus x_{10}$	$y_4 \oplus y_5 \oplus y_6$	88/4096
Y	S2	$x_2 \oplus x_3 \oplus x_5 \oplus x_7 \oplus x_8$	$y_4 \oplus y_5 \oplus y_6$	108/4096
X'	S2	$x_2 \oplus x_{10} \oplus x_{10}x_6$	$y_4 \oplus y_5 \oplus y_6$	116/4096
Y.1	S2	$x_2 \oplus x_3 \oplus x_5 \oplus x_5x_7 \oplus x_3x_8 \oplus$ $x_5x_8 \oplus x_3x_5x_8 \oplus x_3x_7x_8 \oplus x_3x_5x_7$	$y_4 \oplus y_5 \oplus y_6$	136/4096
Y.2	S2	$x_2 \oplus x_3 \oplus x_5 \oplus x_8 \oplus x_5x_7 \oplus x_7x_8 \oplus$ $x_2x_3x_5 \oplus x_5x_7x_8 \oplus x_8x_5x_2$	$y_4 \oplus y_5 \oplus y_6$	130/4096
Y.3	S2	$x_2 \oplus x_3 \oplus x_5 \oplus x_7 \oplus x_3x_8 \oplus x_3x_7 \oplus$ $x_3x_5x_7 \oplus x_5x_7x_8 \oplus x_3x_5x_8$	$y_8 \oplus y_5 \oplus y_6$	110/4096

Table 2. The complexity of conventional and various new linear cryptanalytic attacks on LOKI91.

Attacks on $(4+3r)$-round LOKI91				
approximation	*# plaintexts*	*success rate*	*# key bits recovered*	*work effort*
?X-Y *current methods [16]*	$6,232,416\ (r=0)$ $N\ (r>0)$	94%	13	2^{24}
?X'-Y	$3,586,800\ (r=0)$ $0.58 \times N\ (r>0)$	90%	15	2^{29}
?X'-Y.1	$2,261,912\ (r=0)$ $0.36 \times N\ (r>0)$	84%*	15	2^{29}
?X'-Y.1	$2,261,912\ (r=0)$ $0.36 \times N\ (r>0)$	74%+	18	2^{37}
?X'-Y.1	$2,261,912\ (r=0)$ $0.36 \times N\ (r>0)$	68%+	19	2^{37}
?X'-Y.2 *and* ?X'-Y.3 *simultaneously*	$1,442,632\ (r=0)$ $0.23 \times N\ (r>0)$	86%+	20	2^{38}

* this applies to 1/16 keys but is an empirical result
+ a prediction derived from results presented in the Appendix

of our attacks, we have used experimental evidence to predict the success rate of others.

The results of our work have been summarized in Table 2. The number of key bits recovered refers to this single phase of the attack alone and further gains by reversing the role of plaintext and ciphertext have not been considered. When considering the work effort involved, recall that current methods already require a work effort proportional to 2^{38} encryptions in exhaustive search for the key bits not recovered via linear cryptanalysis.

We have also used multiple non-linear approximations in much the same way we might use multiple linear approximations [5]. The use of multiple non-linear approximations is much more complicated than the use of multiple linear approximations and considerable care has to be taken in deciding which non-linear approximations should be used together and exactly which bits of key information can be reliably recovered. Results given in the Appendix and in Table 2 demonstrate that additional substantial savings in the plaintext requirements can be expected in this way.

We see that numerous trade-offs are possible between the number of key bits recovered, the amount of plaintext required and the work effort the cryptanalyst might wish to invest in attacking some cipher. In short, the use of non-linear approximations offers greatly improved flexibility to the cryptanalyst.

6 Conclusions

We have presented a general approach to linear cryptanalysis which allows us to consider within the same framework all linear cryptanalytic techniques currently used. While this has opened numerous avenues for research it is already evident that there are several new developments.

When trying to accurately gauge the resistance of a block cipher to linear cryptanalysis, it is no longer sufficient to restrict attention to Matsui's 1R- and 2R-methods of linear cryptanalysis. There may well be circumstances where non-linear approximations, involving far fewer text and key bits than are required to describe an S-box, can be used to recover additional bits of the user-defined key with less plaintext than current linear techniques might suggest. Consequently our techniques offer the cryptanalyst much more flexibility in attacking a cipher than was previously appreciated. By adjusting the various requirements in an attack, the cryptanalyst can decide on the approach that is best suited to the resources available be they the amount of available data or the amount of computing power possessed by the cryptanalyst. These techniques will be a particular concern for ciphers that depend for their security on the fact that the 1R- and/or the 2R-methods are impractical due to reasons of work-effort rather than the amount of data required. We have also noted that some block cipher designs allow the use of non-linear approximations in the second and penultimate rounds of a cipher.

We have confirmed our techniques with attacks on reduced-round LOKI91 and we expect that seven additional bits of key information can be recovered with less than 1/4 of the plaintext than current techniques require. Further improvement may well be possible. In short, the additional flexibility available to a cryptanalyst has been demonstrated and linear cryptanalytic attacks on a wide variety of block ciphers may well be much improved with these new methods.

References

1. L. Brown and M. Kwan and J. Pieprzyk and J. Seberry. Improving resistance to differential cryptanalysis and the redesign of LOKI. In H. Imai and R.L. Rivest and

T. Matsumoto, editors, *Advances in Cryptology — AsiaCrypt '91*, Lecture Notes in Computer Science 453, Springer-Verlag (1993), 36–50.

2. H. Feistel. Cryptography and computer privacy. *Scientific American*, 228(5):15–23, 1973.
3. C. Harpes and G.G. Kramer and J.L. Massey. A generalization of linear cryptanalysis and the applicability of Matsui's piling-up lemma. In L.C. Guillou and J.J. Quisquater, editors, *Advances in Cryptology — Eurocrypt '95*, Lecture Notes in Computer Science 921, Springer-Verlag (1995), 24–38.
4. B.S. Kaliski and M.J.B. Robshaw. Linear cryptanalysis using multiple approximations. In Y.G. Desmedt, editor, *Advances in Cryptology — Crypto '94*, Lecture Notes in Computer Science 839, Springer-Verlag (1994), 26–39.
5. B.S. Kaliski and M.J.B. Robshaw. Linear cryptanalysis using multiple approximations and FEAL. In B. Preneel, editor, *Fast Software Encryption*, Lecture Notes in Computer Science 1008, Springer Verlag (1995), 249–264.
6. S.K. Langford and M.E. Hellman. Differential-linear cryptanalysis. In Y.G. Desmedt, editor, *Advances in Cryptology — Crypto '94*, Lecture Notes in Computer Science 839, Springer Verlag (1994), 17–25.
7. M. Matsui. Linear cryptanalysis method for DES cipher. In T. Helleseth, editor, *Advances in Cryptology — Eurocrypt '93*, Lecture Notes in Computer Science 765, Springer-Verlag (1994), 386–397.
8. M. Matsui. The first experimental cryptanalysis of the Data Encryption Standard. In Y.G. Desmedt, editor, *Advances in Cryptology — Crypto '94*, Lecture Notes in Computer Science 839, Springer-Verlag (1994), 1–11.
9. National Institute of Standards and Technology (NIST). *FIPS Publication 46-2: Data Encryption Standard.* December 30, 1993.
10. K. Nyberg. Differentially uniform mappings for cryptography. In T. Helleseth, editor, *Advances in Cryptology — Eurocrypt '93*, Lecture Notes in Computer Science 765, Springer-Verlag (1994), 55–64.
11. K. Nyberg. Linear approximation of block ciphers. In A. De Santis, editor, *Advances in Cryptology — Eurocrypt '94*, Lecture Notes in Computer Science 950, Springer-Verlag (1995), 439–444.
12. K. Nyberg and L.R. Knudsen. Provable security against a differential attack. *The Journal of Cryptology*, 8(1):27–38, 1995.
13. L. O'Connor. Properties of linear approximation tables. In B. Preneel, editor, *Fast Software Encryption*, Lecture Notes in Computer Science 1008, Springer Verlag (1995), 131–136.
14. K. Ohta and K. Aoki. Linear cryptanalysis of the Fast Data Encipherment Algorithm. In Y. Desmedt, editor, *Advances in Cryptology — Crypto '94*, Lecture Notes in Computer Science 839, Springer-Verlag (1994) 12–16.
15. I. Schaumüller-Bichl. Cryptanalysis of the Data Encryption Standard by a method of formal coding. In T. Beth, editor, *Cryptography, Proc. Burg Feuerstein 1982*, Springer-Verlag (1983), 235–255.
16. T. Tokita and T. Sorimachi and M. Matsui. Linear Cryptanalysis of LOKI and s^2DES. In J. Pieprzyk and R. Safavi-Naini, editors, *Advances in Cryptology — Asiacrypt '94*, Lecture Notes in Computer Science 917, Springer-Verlag (1995), 293–303.

Appendix

Experimental verification of the attack by Tokita et al. [16] on LOKI91 is provided in the following table with our experiments being carried out on a four-round version of the cipher. The results were obtained after 50 trials using Matsui's 1R-method and the approximation `?X-Y` as described previously. The approximation holds with probability p where $(p - 1/2)^{-2} = 779,052$ and 13 bits of key information can be recovered.

plaintexts	1,558,104	3,116,208	6,232,416
success rate	20%	64%	94%

By substituting the non-linear approximation `X'` for the linear approximation `X` used in round two of the approximation, we can obtain improved attacks. First we provide the success rate over 50 trials in recovering 15 bits of key information; we use Matsui's 1R-method and the approximation `?X'-Y` which holds with probability p where $(p - 1/2)^{-2} = 448,350$.

plaintexts	896,700	1,793,400	3,586,800
success rate	6%	38%	90%

To help in our later analysis, we will compare these success rates with those obtained over 50 trials when using the same approximation to recover just three bits of key information. Here we assume that the 12 bits of effective key used in S-box S2 in the first round remain fixed and known. This allows us to estimate how the success rate might degrade when we have to recover these additional 12 bits of key.

plaintexts	896,700	1,793,400	3,586,800
success rate	76%	92%	100%

Now consider using non-linear approximations in the last round by replacing `Y` with a non-linear approximation `Y.1` described previously. For one in 16 keys we obtain the following success rates over 50 trials when using Matsui's 1R-method and the approximation `?X'-Y.1` which holds with probability p where $(p - 1/2)^{-2} = 282,739$. For one in 16 keys, 15 bits of key information can be recovered with the following success rates:

plaintexts	565,478	1,130,956	2,261,912
success rate	8%	22%	84%

Instead of assuming the value of four key bits in the last round and being correct some proportion of the time we can recover these four key bits. To estimate the success rate of this approach, we will use Matsui's 1R-method with the correct guess to S2 in round one and the approximation `?X'-Y.1` (which holds with probability p where $(p - 1/2)^{-2} = 282,739$). In this way seven bits of key information can be recovered with the following success rates (over 50 trials):

plaintexts	565,478	1,130,956	2,261,912
success rate	40%	50%	76%

Alternatively, since recovery of one of the seven bits is somewhat unreliable we might recover just six bits. Then the success rates over 50 trials become:

plaintexts	565,478	1,130,956	2,261,912
success rate	55%	62%	82%

Using this information, we can now make predictions for the expected success rate in attacking LOKI91. We saw earlier that by deriving the 12 key bits of S-box 2 in the first round instead of fixing them as correct, our success rate with 3,586,800 plaintexts fell from 100% to 90%. From this we might estimate that by using `?X'-Y.1` we can recover 19 bits of key information (instead of 13) with a little more than one third the plaintext (2,261,912 instead of 6,232,416 plaintexts) with a slightly reduced success rate of 68% = 76% × 90% (from 94% previously). We could of course, suffice with recovering 18 bits of key information, in which case we might expect a success rate of 74%.

We might also consider the use of multiple non-linear approximations. Despite the additional complications of using multiple non-linear approximations, we note that more bits of user-defined key might be recovered with less plaintext. In the following table we give the success rates achieved in 50 trials with two non-linear approximations `?X'-Y.2` and `?X'-Y.3` defined previously. In these experiments we assume the correct key bits used in S2 in round one and we recover eight bits of key information.

plaintexts	360,658	721,316	1,442,632
success rate	26%	66%	96%

Using these results we might predict that we can use the two approximations `?X'-Y.1` and `?X'-Y.2` to recover 20 bits of key information instead of `?X-Y` to recover 13 bits of key information with essentially the same success rate (86% instead of 94%) but with much less than one quarter the plaintext (1,442,632 plaintexts instead of 6,232,416).

On the Difficulty of Software Key Escrow

Lars R. Knudsen[1] and Torben P. Pedersen[2]

[1] Katholieke Universiteit Leuven, Belgium, email: knudsen@esat.kuleuven.ac.be
[2] Cryptomathic, Denmark, email: tpp@cryptomathic.aau.dk

Abstract. At Eurocrypt'95, Desmedt suggested a scheme which allows individuals to encrypt in such a way that the receiver can be traced by an authority having additional information. This paper shows that the proposed scheme does not have the required properties, by devising three non-specified protocols misleading the authority. We also discuss how to repair Desmedt's scheme, such that our attacks are no longer possible. However, by allowing slightly more general, but absolutely realistic attacks also this improved system can be broken. In fact, we argue that software key escrow as proposed by Desmedt will be very hard to implement as it requires that the distributed public key can only be used in few, well-defined systems. Furthermore, even if this is achieved, most applications to key distribution can be broken.

1 Introduction

In key escrow systems, such as Clipper [5], it is necessary to be able to identify ciphertexts sent to a person whose messages are to be read by the authorities (given a court order, of course). The necessity of such identification is discussed in [4]. In Clipper the identification is enforced by adding a field, LEAF, to the ciphertext. If this field is missing the decryption device will refuse to decrypt. Thus this technique depends on the fact that this device is in a tamper resistant unit, such that decryption cannot be enforced.

At Eurocrypt'95, Desmedt suggested a key escrow scheme not depending on tamper resistant devices which allows individuals to encrypt information in such a way that the recipient (i.e. the person able to recover the clear text) can be traced by an authority having additional information [1]. According to [1] the investigation of such software key escrow systems has also been initiated by NIST.

Key escrow systems can only be argued secure in situations where the participants have not had the possibility to distribute other (secret) keys among themselves. This is a necessary assumption, because otherwise they could have used these keys instead of those distributed by the authority.

However, without physical protection such as that provided by tamper resistant smart cards no practical key escrow system can avoid that some users use a publicly described protocol different from that devised by the authority. We will say that such a *non-specified protocol* succeeds if, first, the users obtain the same level of security as in the specified protocol, and second, the receiver can

Ueli Maurer (Ed.): EUROCRYPT '96 Proceedings, LNCS 1070

decrypt the ciphertext correctly, but the authority cannot identify the receiver (either because the identification fails, or because a wrong user is identified).

In this paper we consider the system proposed in [1] and devise three non-specified protocols, by which users can communicate secretly and mislead the authority at the same time. By the first protocol it is possible to send a message to two or more collaborating receivers, either of who can then decipher the message. If the authority tries to identify the receiver an "innocent" individual (different from the collaborating receivers) may be identified. The success of this protocol depends on the ability of two collaborating receivers to communicate privately during key generation. Our second protocol does not require this, and enables any registered users to communicate secretly and at the same time mislead the authority. Our third and simpler protocol is applicable in the case where the escrow system is used for key distribution.

This paper is organised as follows. First, Section 2 discusses possible attacks on software key escrow. This is not a complete definition of such systems, but is meant to provide a general basis for our work. In Section 3 Desmedt's proposed software key escrow system is described briefly, and in Section 4 we give three attacks on Desmedt's scheme and suggest a redesign, which prevents the second and third attacks. However, the redesigned system can be broken by general attacks which additionally shows that a secure software key escrow system will in general be very hard to construct. This is discussed in Section 5.

2 Software Key Escrow

Software key escrow is only defined very informally in [1] by mentioning some of the properties, that such systems must have. It is out of the scope of this paper to give a complete definition (see [4] for a discussion of the properties of escrow systems), but before presenting our attacks the major components and properties of software key escrow are described.

A key escrow system involves a number of users, say $P_1, P_2, \ldots, P_n$, and an authority, A, which should be able to trace the recipient of encrypted messages (and subsequently decrypt the message, if applicable). The system consists of a protocol (or algorithm) for key generation, and algorithms for encrypting, decrypting and tracing as described below. All components must be efficient (i.e., run in polynomial time in a security parameter).

- Key generation: This is a protocol which results in each P_i getting a pair of public and secret keys (denoted (p_i, s_i)) and A obtaining some auxiliary information, aux.
- An encryption algorithm, E, which on input a message from a suitable defined message space, $\mathcal{M}$, and a public key produces a ciphertext.
- A decryption algorithm, D, which given a ciphertext and a secret key produces the corresponding clear text.
- An algorithm, ID, which on input a ciphertext, some public information and aux returns $i \in \{1, 2, \ldots, n\}$. Intuitively, i is the index of the person able to decrypt the ciphertext.

For this system to work properly, it must be required that if the keys are generated as prescribed, then

$$\forall i \in \{1, \dots, n\}, M \in \mathcal{M} :$$
$$D(E(M, p_i), s_i) = M \wedge ID(E(M, p_i), (p_1, \dots, p_n), aux) = i.$$

We next discuss some security aspects of such systems. In an attack, a sender S is trying to send an encrypted message which can be decrypted by a collusion of cooperating receivers, $R_1, \dots, R_k$ (note that Desmedt also allows receivers to conspire [1, Footnote 10]).

We make the restriction that S may not have sent or received any message over any private channels prior to the attack. This is quite restrictive, but as mentioned in the introduction, key escrow is only possible if S has not had any private communication with $R_1, \dots, R_k$. However, restricting the possible behaviour of the attacker does not make the attack weaker.

Let pub_inf_S denote all information which S has received prior to the attack and let pub_inf_i denote all the public information, which R_i has received for $i = 1, 2, \dots, k$. Finally, let pub_inf denote all information, which has been sent prior to the attack (by any participant) including the public keys. We assume that A has this maximal amount of information.

A generic attack runs as follows. Given a message, $M \in \mathcal{M}$, pub_inf_S and the public keys of $R_1, \dots, R_k$, S computes a number of ciphertexts $c_1, \dots, c_l$. Based on these, $(pub\_inf_i)_{i=1,2,\dots,k}$ and their secret keys, $R_1, \dots, R_k$ compute a message, $M' \in \mathcal{M}$. The attack is successful if

1. $M' = M$;
2. It is not easier to find M given $c_1, \dots, c_l$ and $(pub\_inf_j)_{j=1,\dots,k}$ than if M had just been encrypted as $E(M, p_j)$ (i.e., as in the specified protocol) for some j for which P_j is among $R_1, \dots, R_k$.
3. A is not able to identify any of the receivers. In other words, for all $i = 1, 2, \dots, l$ ID on input c_i, aux and the public string $(pub\_inf, c_1, \dots, c_l)$ either fails or outputs a number not identifying any of the receivers. In the first case A will discover the fraud, and in the second case A will be totally mislead.

A generic attack as described above can be executed in several ways. Some possibilities are:

- One receiver. This means that $k = 1$.
- Many receivers: A distinction can be made whether the receivers cooperate using a secret channel or only public discussions. Since, S is not allowed to use a private channel it could be argued that the same should hold for the receivers. However, in our opinion a strong key escrow system should also be able to cope with receivers using private communication internally, since we are looking at the transfer of a message from S to the group of receivers.
- Usage of public keys. We distinguish whether the public key is only used as input to the prescribed encryption algorithm (which may be possible) or it is used in other systems as well. In the latter case the attack can be prevented

using physically protected devices, whereas this may not help in the former. Note, however, that if a different encryption method is used A knows it as part of pub_inf.

As mentioned initially other attacks are conceivable, but in this paper we only consider attacks, which can be described in these terms.

3 The Proposed Solution

The scheme proposed in [1] is based on the ElGamal public key scheme (see [3]). First determine m such that at most $n \leq 2^m$ individuals can participate. Let $p, q_1, \ldots, q_m$ be large, different primes such that each q_i divides $p-1$, and let Q denote the product $\prod_{i=1}^{m} q_i$.[3] Furthermore, let g be an element in $\mathbb{Z}_p^*$ of order Q.

The authority selects these numbers together with a personal public number g_j for the j'th individual. If $\mathbf{e}_j = (e_1, \ldots, e_m) \in \{0,1\}^m \setminus \{0\}^m$ uniquely identifies the j'th participant, then

$$g_j = g^{\frac{Q}{\prod_{e_i=1} q_i}}.$$

Thus the order of g_j is $\prod_{e_i=1} q_i$, and this is different for different j's.

The j'th participant will have a secret key s_j and a public key (g_j, y_j) such that $y_j = g_j^{s_j}$. An encryption of $M \in \mathbb{Z}_p^*$ under this public key is a pair

$$(c_1, c_2) = (g_j^r, M \times y_j^r),$$

where $r \in \mathbb{Z}_{p-1}^*$ is chosen uniformly at random. A pair (c_1, c_2) can be decrypted as

$$M = c_2 / c_1^{s_j}.$$

The authority can trace the owner of the corresponding public key since c_1 has order $\prod_{e_i=1} q_i$, unless $\gcd(r, p-1) > 1$ in which case c_1 might be in a smaller subgroup. However, without knowing the factorisation of $p-1$ it seems hard to utilise this property in attacks against the system.

The scheme is used only to exchange a common session key, therefore the sender should choose a uniformly random $M \in \mathbb{Z}_p^*$. Once M has been obtained, both sender and receiver hash M to obtain a session key [1].

In [1] it has not been suggested how to generate the user identifier vectors $\mathbf{e}_j$. Desmedt does note, however, that first, there is no need for the authority to reveal the vectors or how they are computed, and second, it might be better to let the Hamming weight of all vectors $\mathbf{e}_j$ be identical.

[3] [1] suggests that each q_i is 320 bits long. Thus, as also noted by Desmedt, the scheme will be quite slow in practice for a moderate number of users.

4 Problems with the Solution

In the following we will first give a method, by which it is possible to send a message to two (or more) collaborating receivers, who can then decipher the message. If the authority tries to identify the receiver, a user different from the collaborating receivers may be identified or the identification fails (depending on the setup of the identity vectors). This attack requires that the two receivers select the same secret key. The second attack involves only one receiver, but requires two ciphertexts. The third attack requires only one receiver and one ciphertext, and works in the case where the escrow system is used for key distribution only.

4.1 Attack Involving Conspiring Receivers

Consider a scenario in which three participants cooperate, and denote these by S, P_i and P_j corresponding to one sender and two receivers. Let the public keys of P_i and P_j be (g_i, y_i) and (g_j, y_j), respectively.

Below it will be shown that S can send an encryption of a message in such a way that both P_i and P_j can decipher it, but if the authority tries to identify the recipient it will not obtain the identity of any of these three parties.

Protocol 1 *Using a private channel during key setup, P_i and P_j select $s_i = s_j = s$. P_i and P_j publish a message saying that they have chosen the same secret key. S encrypts $M \in \mathbb{Z}_p^*$ as*

$$(c_1, c_2) = ((g_i g_j)^r, M \times (y_i y_j)^r),$$

where $r \in \mathbb{Z}_{p-1}^*$ is chosen at random. This corresponds to encryption under the public key $(g_i g_j, y_i y_j)$. P_i (and P_j) can decipher the message as

$$M' = c_2 / c_1^{s_i}.$$

Here c_1 is in a subgroup identifying neither P_i nor P_j. Also, the protocol is easily extended to the cases where more than two receivers choose the same secret keys.

Whether c_1 identifies a registered user depends on how the user identifier vectors $\mathbf{e}_j$ are constructed. However, A will not be able to identify P_i or P_j. By choosing the identity vectors properly, it can, however, be ensured that c_1 will not encode a registered user.

Note, that the authority has no way to decide (let alone prove) whether two receivers select the same secret key (a publicly broadcast message does not serve as a proof).

4.2 Attacks Involving one Receiver

Consider a scenario in which a sender S and a receiver P_i try to attack the system using the following published protocol. Let (g_i, y_i) denote the public key of P_i and let (g_k, y_k) be the public key of some registered user $P_k \neq P_i$.

Protocol 2 *Initially P_i chooses a random element, $h \in \mathbb{Z}_p^*$ and publishes it. S encrypts $M \in \mathbb{Z}_p^*$ as follows. First, S sends to P_i*

$$C = (c_1, c_2) = (g_k^{r_1}, M \times y_i^r)$$

where $r, r_1 \in \mathbb{Z}_{p-1}^*$ are chosen at random. Next, S sends to P_i

$$C^* = (c_3, c_4) = (g_k^{r_2}, hg_i^r)$$

where r is as in c_2 and $r_2 \in \mathbb{Z}_{p-1}^*$ is chosen at random. Clearly, P_i (only) can decipher the message as

$$M' = c_2/(c_4/h)^{s_i}.$$

Here both c_1 and c_3 are in a subgroup identifying the registered user P_k. The purpose of h is to prevent that c_4 is in a small subgroup, which would identify P_i.

Note, that the authority even with the knowledge of the non-specified protocol has no way of deciding whether C and C^* contain two messages to P_k or one message to P_i.

For the application to key distribution, which is the typical situation [1], there is a simpler protocol.

Protocol 3 *Initially P_i chooses a random element, $h \in \mathbb{Z}_p^*$ and publishes it. S computes the session key, $M = g_k^{r_1}/y_i^r$, and sends to P_i*

$$C = (c_1', c_2') = (c_2, c_1) = (M \times y_i^r, hg_i^r)$$

where $r, r_1 \in \mathbb{Z}_{p-1}^*$ are chosen at random. P_i deciphers the message as

$$M' = c_2/(c_1/h)^{s_i}.$$

Again the purpose of h is to hide the attack. The authority has no way of deciding whether C contains a message to P_k using the specified protocol or contains a message to P_i using the non-specified Protocol 3, since the first component of the cipher text, $My_i^r = g_k^{r_1}$, identifies P_k as the recipient.

Note that the subgroup generated by g_i is by far large enough to encode all possible session keys (Desmedt suggests that g_i has order approximately 2^{320}, which should be compared with a, say, 128 bits session key).

The two attacks above exploit that the first and second part of the ciphertexts in the ElGamal system can be separated without destroying the ability for the receiver to decrypt, and the attacks can be prevented if both parts of the ciphertext are in the same subgroup. We do not know how to achieve this in general, but for the application to key distribution, it can be done by forcing M to be in the subgroup $<g_i>$ if the receiver is P_i. This can for example be done by choosing random $r_2 \in \mathbb{Z}_{p-1}^*$ and setting $M = g_i^{r_2}$. In that way both parts of the ciphertext belong to the same receiver dependent subgroup.

However, as discussed below, there are practical problems with this solution as well.

5 General Problems

In the attacks described above the public key was used only in the intended crypto systems. However, in the setup used in [1] it is possible to use the public keys in different crypto systems. One simple example is to use the Diffie-Hellman key exchange protocol [2]. Assume that a list of generators g_k has been broadcasted. Then any two users in the escrow system can use the generators and their own secret keys to exchange a new session key using the Diffie-Hellman protocol with a different generator each time.[4]

Another possibility is to replace c_1 by $g_i^r g_j$, where P_i publishes the index j. Here, the authority might discover the fraud (depending on the choice of user identity vectors).

Many such variations are possible, but the point we want to make is that ID must be able to cope with all of these and we expect it will be hard to come up with a method for doing that. The range of possible variations clearly depends on the public-key pairs and not on the specified encryption method. This is one problem with software key escrow.

Next, even if it was possible to construct a software key escrow system handling all variations of the prescribed encryption system, A may not be able to exploit this. If the system is used for key distribution, the authorities may not in practice be able to find the actual session key being used. Consider the case where two users, P_i and P_j, are going to use session keys $K_1, K_2, \ldots, K_m$ over a period of time. Using the escrowed public key system, they exchange a key k_l (which of course the authorities may be able to find). Then they compute the l'th session key as

$$\begin{aligned} K_1 &= \mathcal{H}(k_1) \\ K_l &= \mathcal{H}(K_{l-1}, k_l) \qquad l = 2, 3, \ldots \end{aligned}$$

where e.g. $\mathcal{H}$ is a public one-way hash function. Of course the method for doing this must be published (i.e., the authorities know it), but the authority will only be able to find K_l if it knows all previous keys. In other words, the authorities must tape all key exchanges!

6 Conclusion

In this paper we have shown that the scheme proposed by Desmedt does not have the required properties. We devised three non-specified protocols misleading the authority. We showed how to repair Desmedt's scheme, such that our attacks are no longer possible, but by allowing slightly more general attacks also this improved system was broken. We are convinced that the software key escrow as proposed by Desmedt will be very hard to implement as it requires that the

[4] Note, that a user, P_i, can raise any generator g_k to his secret key by choosing $c_2 \in \mathbb{Z}_p^*$ at random and asking his device to decrypt the cipher text (g_k, c_2). If this returns the message, M, then the required result can be obtained as $c_2/M \bmod p$.

distributed public keys can only be used in few, well-defined systems. In general, we showed how most key escrow applications to key distribution can be broken.

References

1. Y. Desmedt. Securing traceability of ciphertexts – towards a secure software key escrow system. In L.C. Guillou and J.-J. Quisquater, editors, *Advances in Cryptology - EUROCRYPT'95, LNCS 921*, pages 147–157. Springer Verlag, 1995.
2. W. Diffie and M. Hellman. New directions in cryptography. *IEEE Trans. on Information Theory*, IT-22(6):644–654, 1976.
3. T. ElGamal. A public key cryptosystem and a signature scheme based on discrete logarithms. *IEEE Trans. on Information Theory*, IT-31:469–472, 1985.
4. Y. Frankel and M. Yung. Escrow Encryption Systems Visited: Attacks, Analysis and Design. In *Advances in Cryptology - proceedings of CRYPTO 95*, volume 963 of *Lecture Notes in Computer Science*, pages 222–235. Springer-Verlag, 1995.
5. A proposed federal information processing standard for an escrowed encryption standard (EES). Federal register, July 30, 1993.

An Efficient Pseudo-Random Generator Provably as Secure as Syndrome Decoding

Jean-Bernard Fischer[1] and Jacques Stern[2]

[1]Thomson Consumer Electronics R&D France
Parc d'innovation n° 1, B.P. 120, 67403 Illkirch Cedex, France
fischerj@tce-rdf.fr

[2]Ecole Normale Supérieure, Laboratoire d'informatique
45, rue d'Ulm, 75230 Paris Cedex 05, France
Jacques.Stern@ens.fr

Abstract. We show a simple and efficient construction of a pseudo-random generator based on the intractability of an NP-complete problem from the area of error-correcting codes. The generator is proved as secure as a hard instance of the syndrome decoding problem. Each application of the scheme generates a linear amount of bits in only quadratic computing time.

1 Introduction

A pseudo-random generator is an algorithm producing strings of bits that look random. The concept of "randomly looking" has been formalized by Blum and Micali [4] within the framework of complexity theory. Yao [22] has shown that the existence of a one-way permutation is sufficient to construct a pseudo-random generator. Subsequently, a long series of deep articles led to the conclusion that the existence of a one-way function is equivalent to the hypothesis that a pseudo-random generator exists [15, 10, 14]. However, the theoretical constructions proposed in these articles are often impractical.

Several schemes have been proposed which have a "proven security", i.e. based on the difficulty of well known problems like factorization [21, 3, 1, 18] or the discrete logarithm [4, 16, 12]. But these propositions suffer from a relatively slow computing rate (i.e. they need much computation per generated bit). For example, outputting a single bit for the BBS generator takes quadratic time, and cubic time for the RSA based generators. This can be slightly enhanced to a $log_2(n)$ output.

Therefore, it is interesting to study new schemes based on difficult problems not related to number theory. In an early work [9], Goldreich, Krawczyk and Luby established that the existence of a pseudo-random generator could be based on hard problems from the theory of error-correcting codes. Unfortunately, their construction was a bit intricate. In the same vein, Impagliazzo and Naor [13] devised an elegant construction of a pseudo-random generator based on the subset-sum problem. Unfortunately, many researchers think that the underlying

Ueli Maurer (Ed.): EUROCRYPT '96 Proceedings, LNCS 1070

problem is computationnally rather weak. We present a new scheme based on the syndrome decoding problem, which is believed to be hard on most instances. Our scheme is extremely simple and achieves quadratic time with respect to the security parameters for producing a linear amount of random bits.

1.1 The Syndrome Decoding problem

In the field of error correcting codes, one of the basic open problems is to find efficient algorithms for the decoding of random linear codes. Codes with a constant information rate and correcting a constant fraction of bits are particularly interesting.

A (n, k, d) binary linear code is a subspace of $\{0, 1\}^n$ of size 2^k where every non zero word has weight at least d. It's information rate is k/n and it can correct up to $\lfloor \frac{d-1}{2} \rfloor$ errors. It can be defined by its parity check matrix which is a n-by-$(n-k)$ binary matrix with the property that, for each vector of the code, the product (mod 2) of the matrix by the vector is zero; this product can actually be computed for any vector and is called the syndrome. If the vector is not in the code, the syndrome is the sum of the columns of the matrix corresponding to positions where one bits are located and is non zero.

Random linear codes are defined by a random parity check matrix. For such codes, no efficient algorithm is known for finding the closest code word to a vector, given its syndrome. It is also difficult to find a word of given weight from his syndrome's value [2]. This is called the **syndrome decoding problem**.

These problems are NP-complete. For further information, we refer to the books by McWilliams and Sloane [17] for error correcting codes, and by Garey and Johnson [7] for NP-complete problems. The syndrome decoding problem is **NP-hard**; see Berlekamp, McEliece and van Tilborg [2] for a proof. It can be stated as follows [7]:

Instance: An $m \times n$ binary matrix $A = (a_{ij})$, a binary non-null vector $y = (y_1, \ldots, y_m)$, and a positive integer w.
Question: Is there a binary vector $x = (x_1, \ldots, x_n)$ with no more than w 1's such that, for $1 \leq j \leq m$, $\sum_{i=1}^{n} x_i \cdot a_{ij} \equiv y_j \pmod 2$?

Comment: The variant in which we ask for an x with *exactly* w 1's is NP-complete, even for $y = (0, 0, \ldots, 0)$. If we drop the word exactly, the question becomes open.

NP-hardness ensures that there is no polynomial-time algorithm for solving the problem in the worst case; however many NP-complete problems can be efficiently solved in the average case. So we have to study the hardness of a random instance. This leads to practical issues that have been extensively studied by various people, as reviewed by Chabaud [6, 19]. Algorithms known to solve the syndrome decoding problem are all probabilistic, so that we will speak about the probability of finding a word. They all have a computing complexity that grows exponentially in the size of n. They also give strong evidence that, in the case of random codes, the problem is the hardest for weights in the neighbourghood of the Gilbert-Warshamov bound corresponding to the dimensions of the code. The Gilbert-Warshamov bound λ of a (n, k, d) binary code is defined by the relation $1 - k/n = H_2(\lambda)$ where $H_2(x) = -x \log_2 x - (1-x)\log_2(1-x)$.

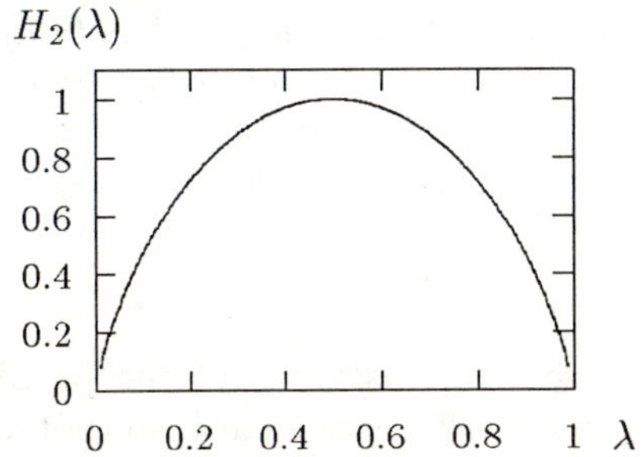

What comes out of the analysis is that it is relatively easy to find words of very low weight and given syndrome, but that the probability of finding one increases exponentially with the weight of the word (these algorithms are all probabilistic). However, the number of words having a given syndrome also grows exponentially with the weight; the point where there is an average of one word per syndrome value is the Gilbert-Warshamow bound. Finally, given a random vector with weight below the bound, the probability for it of having a pre-image is exponentially small in the weight.

We reach the following experimental conclusion: the difficulty of finding a word is a function of its weight that is growing until the Gilbert-Warshamov bound, and is then decreasing. So we can define a hard instance of syndrome decoding as an instance where the weight of the vectors is close to the Gilbert-Warshamov bound.

1.2 Formal version of the intractability assumption

In the sequel, we will only consider subsets D_n such that, for suitable functions $k(n)$ and $l(n)$, D_n is included in $\{0,1\}^{l(n)}$ and is the one-one image of $\{0,1\}^{k(n)}$ by a polynomial-time function. This is a particular case of what is called polynomially-samplable [8].

We now define what we mean by hard (this is essentially a simplified version of Goldreich [8]):

Definition 1 *A collection of functions* $\{f_n : D_n \mapsto \{0,1\}^{k(n)}\}$ *is called* ***strongly one-way*** *if the following two conditions hold:*

- *there exists a polynomial-time algorithm F that, on input* $x \in D_n$*, always outputs* $f_n(x)$.
- *for every probabilistic polynomial-time algorithm A, every* $c > 0$ *and all sufficiently large n's,*

$$\Pr(A(f_n(X_n)) \in f_n^{-1} f_n(X_n)) < \frac{1}{n^c}$$

where X_n is a random variable uniformely distributed over D_n.

We now consider a very general collection of functions related to the syndrome decoding problem.

Definition 2 *Let ρ be in $]0,1[$; let w and w' be two integer functions such that $w(n) \leq w'(n) < n$. The $SD(\rho, w, w')$ collection is the set of functions $\{f_n\}$ such that:*

$$D_n = \{(M,x), M \in \lfloor \rho n \rfloor \times n, x \in \{0,1\}^n / w(n) \leq |x| \leq w'(n)\}$$

$$\begin{aligned} f_n : \quad D_n &\longrightarrow \{0,1\}^{\lfloor \rho n \rfloor \cdot (n+1)} \\ (M,x) &\longmapsto \quad (M, M \cdot x) \end{aligned}$$

As we have seen in the previous section, instances of the problem where $w(n)$ and $w'(n)$ are very small or close to $n/2$ are not hard, so that we want to restrict the collection to the instances where the weight of x is near the Gilbert-Warshamov bound. Clearly, it is not known if such a collection is one-way, but we have seen that, despite extensive research, no efficient inversion algorithm has been found. So we make the assumption that the collection is one-way for weights slightly below the Gilbert-Warshamov bound.

Intractability assumption 1 *Let ρ be in $]0,1[$; let λ be defined by $\rho = H_2(\lambda)$ and $\lambda < 1/2$. Then, for any positive real ϵ, if we set $w(n) = \left\lfloor \frac{\lambda}{1+\epsilon} n \right\rfloor$ and $w'(n) = \lfloor \lambda n \rfloor$, the $SD(\rho, w, w')$ collection is strongly one-way.*

Note: D_n has to be polynomially-samplable. We will discuss this point later on.

Of particular interest to us is the case where the weight of x is fixed and is a constant fraction of n, i.e. $w(n) = w'(n) = \lfloor \delta n \rfloor$ for some δ in $]0,1[$. The corresponding intractability assumption reads as follows:

Intractability assumption 2 *Let ρ be in $]0,1[$. Then, for all δ in $]0,1/2[$ such that $H_2(\delta) < \rho$, the $SD(\rho, \delta, \delta)$ collection of functions is strongly one-way.*

We now write $SD(\rho, \delta)$ to refer to our second assumption with fixed parameters ρ and δ. We will occasionnally omit the parameters thus writing SD in place of $SD(\rho, \delta)$. The corresponding function will be denoted by $f_n^{\rho,\delta}$ or simply f_n and has domain $D_n^{\rho,\delta} = \{(M,x), M \in \lfloor \rho n \rfloor \times n, x \in \{0,1\}^n / |x| = \delta)\}$

Cryptographic applications of the syndrome decoding problem have appeared in an identification scheme devised by the second named author [20].

Note that if $H_2(\lambda) = \rho$ and $\delta < \frac{\lambda}{2}$, the intractability of $SD(\rho, \delta)$ is a particular case of the difficulty of decoding below half the minimum distance. Thus our assumption is stronger than the usual decoding assumptions (see [9]). The construction that appears in section 2 can equally be based on the hardness of decoding but, when we come to practical issues, codes of a larger dimension will be needed. This is why we chose to work with our SD assumption.

2 A pseudo-random generator based on the syndrome decoding problem

2.1 Construction of the generator

Our goal is to construct an efficient pseudo-random generator based on a hard problem, so that the generator inherits the hardness of the problem. We have defined a hard instance of the syndrome decoding problem and a collection of functions $SD(\rho, \delta)$ one-way under the second intractability assumption.

Let us first note that $f_n^{\rho,\delta}$ expands its input: the size of the input set is $2^{\lfloor \rho n \rfloor \cdot n} \cdot \binom{n}{\delta n}$, the size of the image set is $2^{\lfloor \rho n \rfloor \cdot n} \cdot 2^{\lfloor \rho n \rfloor}$; since $H_2(\delta) < \rho$, there exists a positive real ϵ such that $(1+\epsilon)\log_2 \binom{n}{\delta n} = \lfloor \rho n \rfloor$. That means that for a sufficiently large n, $f_n^{\rho,\delta}$ expands its input by some linear amount of bits. We note also that $f_n^{\rho,\delta}$ can be computed in time $O(n^2)$, since it is exactly the binary product of a $\lfloor \rho n \rfloor \times n$ matrix with a $\lfloor \rho n \rfloor$ column vector.

We construct the generator $G_{\rho,\delta}$ in the following way:

Input: $(M, x) \in D_n^{\rho,\delta}$
Output: $f_n^{\rho,\delta}(M, x) = (M, M \cdot x)$

Following a standard construction, we also consider an iterative generator $g_{\rho,\delta}$ that, on input (M, x), outputs as many bits as we like. To perform this iteration, we need an efficient algorithm that computes a vector of size n and weight δ from a $\log_2 \binom{n}{\delta n}$ bit number. For the time being, we consider such an algorithm A as granted and we will describe one in the next section. We get the following:

Input: $(M, x) \in D_n^{\rho,\delta}$

1. compute $y = M \cdot x$
2. separate y in two bit strings y_1 and y_2, y_1 being the first $\left\lceil \log_2 \binom{n}{\delta n} \right\rceil$ bits of y and y_2 the remaining bits.
3. **output** y_2
4. set $x \leftarrow A(y_1)$ and goto 1.

2.2 An algorithm for generating all words of given weight

The first and second intractability assumptions require a polynomial-time algorithm that samples the set of vectors of given weight. Such an algorithm is also needed in our scheme for the pseudo-random generator, but furthermore, it has to be computable in quadratic time to preserve the efficiency of the generator.

We will use an algorithm inspired by Guillot [11]. This algorithm is said quadratic, takes as input a word of exactly $\log_2 \binom{n}{w}$ bits and outputs a word of length n and weight $\lfloor \delta n \rfloor$.

However, in his paper, Guillot uses a heuristic approximation to justify the computing time $O(n^2)$. He assumes that multiplication and division of a large number (of size n) by a small number (of size $\log_2 n$) are linear because the small number has typically the size of a computer word. This argument is not enough for a more formal approach.

In the Turing machine model, the algorithm is "almost" quadratic since it has a of complexity $O(n^2 \log n)$. However the quadratic time bound holds in the model corresponding to random machines with logarithmic cost. See the appendix for a proof.

We now present the algorithm for generating words of given weight. It is based on an efficient way of outputting a word of length n and weight w given its index in the lexicographic ordering (see [11]).

We write the lexicographic enumeration algorithm in the following way:

Input: i, n, w

1. $c \leftarrow \binom{n}{w}$
2. while $n > 0$ do
   (a) $c' \leftarrow c \cdot \frac{n-w}{n}$
   (b) if $i \leq c'$
      - **output** 0
      - $c \leftarrow c'$
   (c) else
      - **output** 1
      - $i \leftarrow i - c'$
      - $c \leftarrow c \cdot \frac{w}{n}$
   (d) $n \leftarrow n - 1$

From the lemma, we note that the initial computation of $\binom{n}{w}$ takes quadratic time. The two cases in the while loop respectively take care of words where a zero (resp. a one) comes first: entering the loop with the initial values of the variables, we find $\binom{n-1}{w}$ words starting with 0, the remaining with 1. The same happens in subsequent iterations, mutatis mutandis.

2.3 Security of the scheme

Goldreich and Levin [10] have shown that the inner product is a hard bit for any one-way function. Recall that, if $x, r \in \{0,1\}^n$, the inner product $r \odot x$ is the parity of the number of positions where the bits of x and of r are both 1 ($r_i = x_i = 1$). The hardness result reads as follows:

Theorem 1 *[10] Let $f : D_n \subset \{0,1\}^{l(n)} \to \{0,1\}^{k(n)}$ be a one-way function. For every polynomial-time algorithm A, every polynomial p and all but finitely many n's,*

$$\Pr(A(f(x), r) = r \odot x) < \frac{1}{2} + \frac{1}{p(n)}$$

where the probability is taken over uniformly chosen $x \in D_n$ and $r \in \{0,1\}^{l(n)}$.

An algorithm is a pseudo-random generator if its output distribution is polynomial-time indistinguishable from a truly random distribution. Two distributions X and Y are indistinguishable in polynomial-time if, for every probabilistic polynomial-time algorithm D and every polynomial p, $|Prob(D(x) = 1) - Prob(D(y) = 1)| < \frac{1}{p(n)}$ where probabilities are taken over X and Y. We will prove that the generator $G_{\rho,\delta}$ is pseudo-random under intractability assumption 2.

Theorem 2 *If the $SD(\rho, \delta)$ collection is one-way, then $G_{\rho,\delta}$ is pseudo-random.*

Remark: By standard arguments, the same result extends to the iterative generator $g_{\rho,\delta}$.

Proof. This proof is inspired from Impagliazzo and Naor [13]. Let $G_{\rho,\delta}$ be the generator with matrix $M \in 2^{\lfloor \rho n \rfloor \times n}$ and weight $w = \lfloor \delta n \rfloor$ as defined in 2.1. If $G_{\rho,\delta}$ is not pseudo-random, we can build a distinguisher that accepts (i.e. outputs 1) with a different probability a string generated by $G_{\rho,\delta}$ and a random string. We can then use this distinguisher to predict the inner product of r and s with an advantage better then $\frac{1}{poly(n)}$ from given values of r and $G_{\rho,\delta}(s)$. Using the Goldreich-Levin theorem, we have a contradiction to the one-wayness of the corresponding $f_n^{\rho,\delta}$ function.

When we think of r and s as defining subsets of the matrix columns (the i-th column of the matrix is in the subset defined by r (resp. s) if the i-th bit of r (resp. s) is 1), we see that $r \odot s$ is the parity of the intersection. The idea is to use the distinguisher to predict this parity.

The distinguisher is fed with a matrix M and a binary word t of size $\lfloor \rho n \rfloor$. Without loss of generality, we can assume that, for infinitely many indices, the distinguisher

- outputs 1 with probability at least $\frac{1}{2} + \frac{1}{p(n)}$ if t is the product of the matrix with a word of weight w;
- outputs 1 with probability almost exactly $\frac{1}{2}$ if t is chosen uniformly in $\{0,1\}^{\lfloor \rho n \rfloor}$.

Let M in $\lfloor \rho n \rfloor \times n$ be a matrix, where c_i is the i-th column of M: $M = (c_i)_{1 \le i \le n}$. Given $r = (r_1, \ldots, r_n) \in \{0,1\}^n$ and $x \in \{0,1\}^{\lfloor \rho n \rfloor}$ both chosen at random, we construct a new matrix $M_x^r = (c_i')_{1 \le i < n}$ such that:

- if $r_i = 1$, the i-th column of M_x^r is the bitwise xor of c_i and x (i.e. $c_i' = c_i \oplus x$);
- if $r_i = 0$, the i-th column of M_x^r is c_i.

We let u denote a possible output of the pseudo-random generator, i.e $M \cdot s = u$ for some s. Let $k = |r \cap s|$ be the number of locations where the bits of r and s are both 1, and ϵ be the parity of k. As noted above, this is equivalent to saying that ϵ is the inner product of r and s. Let $\epsilon \cdot x = x$, if $\epsilon = 1$ and $0^{\lfloor \rho n \rfloor}$ otherwise. We observe that the result of $M_x^r.s$ is $u \oplus \epsilon \cdot x$, as established by the following computation:

$$\begin{aligned} M_x^r.s &= \bigoplus\nolimits_{c'_i \in s} c'_i \\ &= (\bigoplus\nolimits_{c_i \in s} c_i) \oplus (\bigoplus\nolimits_{c_i \in r \cap s} x) \\ &= u \oplus \epsilon \cdot x \end{aligned}$$

On input $(M_x^r, u \oplus \epsilon \cdot x)$, the distinguisher sees exactly the same distribution as on input (M, u). But then, the distinguisher outputs 1 on input $(M_x^r, u \oplus \epsilon \cdot x)$ with probability at least $\frac{1}{2} + \frac{1}{p(n)}$. On the other hand, if we replace ϵ by $\overline{\epsilon}$, then, due to the randomness of x, the distinguisher is fed with uniformly distributed inputs. The distinguisher outputs 1 with probability 1/2. This leads us to the following consruction:

Input: $M \in \{0,1\}^{\lfloor \rho n \rfloor \times n}, u \in \{0,1\}^{\lfloor \rho n \rfloor}, r \in \{0,1\}^n$

- choose a random $x \in \{0,1\}^{\lfloor \rho n \rfloor}$ and a random $\theta \in \{0,1\}$ (θ is our guess about the inner product)
- feed the distinguisher with $(M_x^r, u \oplus \theta \cdot x)$
- if the distinguisher answers 1, **output** θ, else **output** $\overline{\theta}$.

Theorem 3 *Our algorithm predicts the inner product with probability at least* $\frac{1}{2} + \frac{1}{2p(n)}$.

Proof. If we have guessed ϵ, our predictor is correct if the the distinguisher outputs 1. We have seen that this is the case with probability at least $\frac{1}{2} + \frac{1}{p(n)}$.

If we have not guessed ϵ correctly, the predictor sees the input as a totally random distribution. It then outputs 1 with probability almost $\frac{1}{2}$. Since both cases happen with probability $\frac{1}{2}$, the overall probability of the algorithm to predict the inner product is at least $\frac{1}{2} + \frac{1}{2p(n)}$. □

3 Performances

The computation of the product of the matrix by an vector is done solely by using logical operations like AND, XOR and PARITY, which leads to very fast implementations. The matrix can be either extensively described bit per bit, or defined as the output of a pseudo-random generator so that the matrix description remains small in size. This can be done very simply by using a congruential generator with different seeds for each line.

The main bottleneck in the algorithm comes from the sampling algorithm that computes a binary vector of given length and weight. We have to use multiplications and divisions, and that is costly in comparison with the previous operations. However, such computations can be greatly speeded up by doing some precomputations, like a table of the binomials that will be used. That leaves us with only substractions and comparisons, yelding a very fast computation.

Recent attacks on cryptosystems based on error-correcting codes [5] have shown that a $(512, 256)$ random linear code can be decoded up to half its minimum distance 58. That means that words of weight up to 30 can be found given their syndrome. So we can choose a weight between 50 and 57 with the assurance of a very good security.

The gain of the generator is $\rho n - \left\lceil \log_2 \binom{n}{\lfloor \delta n \rfloor} \right\rceil$. For a value of ρ fixed to 1/2, we have the following results:

n	512	512	512	728	728	1024	1024
$\lfloor \delta n \rfloor$	56	55	50	78	71	110	100
gain	5	8	23	11	32	12	43

As seen in the table, $n = 512$ and $\lfloor \delta n \rfloor = 55$ yields one byte per iteration, which looks very attractive.

The scheme as described in section 2 can be improved by precomputing the binomial coefficients. By thus constructing a table of binomials, we get rid of costly multiplications and divisions. The resulting scheme makes only use of comparisons, substractions of n-bit numbers and multiplications of a binary matrix with an n-bit vector. Note that those operations are very fast since they require only logical or fast instructions. The memory cost of a table of the binomial coefficients for the $(512, 256, 55)$ scheme is the following: we need 512×55 entries of size 256 bits, which makes a total of 880 kBytes of memory. This is clearly not an issue for todays computers.

On a SUN Sparc10 station, our implementation using a precomputed binomial table achieves an output rate of 3500 bits per second. RSA with a 512 bit modulus and small exponent is rated at about 0.005 sec per encryption using the chinese remainders. If we output $\log_2(n) = 9$ bits per application of the scheme, the output rate is about 1800 bits per second.

4 Conclusion

We have shown a construction for a pseudo-random generator with proven security. This generator is very efficient and simple, and its implementation is fairly straightforward. We hope that this work will encourage research of alternative solutions to number theory.

Acknowledgements

We thank Oded Goldreich and Mike Luby for discussions on the subject of this paper. Also, after this paper has been accepted for EUROCRYPT, we were informed that Ramarathnan Venkatesen had considered a similar construction. His work will appear elsewhere.

A Appendix

Lemma 1 *The product of an n-bit integer by an $\log_2 n$-bit integer is computable in linear time. The same property holds for the division.*

Remark: as will be seen from the proof, this actually holds in a model corresponding to random access machines with logarithmic cost. It is unclear that the result carries over in the Turing machine model.

Proof. Let x be a n-bit integer, y a $\log_2 n$-bit integer, and α a positive real smaller than $1/2$.

We write x and y in base $2^t = 2^{\lfloor \alpha \log_2 n \rfloor}$:

$$x = \sum_{i=0}^{\frac{n}{t}} x_i \cdot 2^{ti} \quad , \quad y = \sum_{j=0}^{\frac{\log_2 n}{t}} y_j \cdot 2^{tj}$$

Then $x \cdot y = \sum_{i,j} x_i \cdot y_j \cdot 2^{t(i+j)}$.

So the multiplication requires $\lceil \frac{n}{t} \rceil \times \left\lceil \frac{\log_2 n}{t} \right\rceil \simeq O(\frac{n}{\log_2 n})$:

- multiplications of two t-bit integers;
- shiftings of t-bit integers (the multiplication by $2^{t(i+j)}$);
- additions of two t-bit integers.

Addition and shifting are done in time linear in the length of the input, which is, in our case, in $O(\log_2 n)$.

It remains to prove that multiplication of two $log_2 n$-bit integers can be done within the same complexity bound. First, we construct once for all a table of all the possible products $x_i \cdot y_j$. Since x_i and y_j are in $\{0, .., 2^t\}$, the size of the table is at most $2^{\alpha \log_2 n} \times 2^{\alpha \log_2 n}$. Using the quadratic-time multiplication, the table can be computed in time $(2^{\alpha \log_2 n})^2 (\alpha \log_2 n)^2$; and since $\alpha < \frac{1}{2}$, this construction is done in time $O(n)$. Table look-up is performed in $O(\alpha \log_2 n + \alpha \log_2 n + \alpha \log_2 n) \simeq O(\log_2 n)$, so the complexity of our multiplication is also $O(\log_2 n)$.

Finally, the multiplication of an n-bit integer by an $\log_2 n$-bit integer requires the construction of a table done in $O(n)$ and $O(\frac{n}{\log_2 n})$ operations which are done in $O(\log_2 n)$, so that the whole scheme has a complexity of $O(n)$.. □

References

1. Alexi, W., Chor, B., Goldreich, O., Schnorr, C. P.: Rsa and rabin functions: certain parts are as hard as the whole. SIAM J. Computing **17** (1988) 194–209.
2. Berlekamp, E. R., McEliece, R. J., van Tilborg, H. C. A.:. On the inherent intractability of certain coding problems. In IEEE Trans. Information Theory (1978) IEEE pp. 384–386.
3. Blum, L., Blum, M., Shub, M.: A simple unpredictible pseudo-random number generator. SIAM J. Computing **15** (1986) 364–383.

4. Blum, M., Micali, S.: How to generate cryptographically strong sequences of pseudo-random bits. SIAM J. Computing **13** (1984) 850–863.
5. Canteaut, A., Chabaud, F.:. A general improvement of the previous attacks on McEliece's cryptosystem. Unpublished.
6. Chabaud, F.:. On the security of some cryptosystems based on error-correcting codes. In Advances in Cryptology: Proc. of EUROCRYPT'94 (1994) LNCS Springer-Verlag.
7. Garey, M. R., Johnson, D. S.:. Computers and intractability: a guide to the theory of NP-completeness. W. H. Freeman and Co 1979.
8. Goldreich, O.:. Foundations of cryptography (Fragments of a book). Weizmann Institut of Science 1995.
9. Goldreich, O., Krawczyk, H., Luby, M.:. On the existence of pseudo-random generators. In Proc. 29th Symp. on Foundations of Computing Science (1988) IEEE pp. 12–24.
10. Goldreich, O., Levin, L. A.:. Hard core predicate for any one-way function. In Proc. 21st Symp. on Theory of Computing (1989) ACM press pp. 25–32.
11. Guillot, P.:. Algorithmes pour le codage à poids constant. Unpublished.
12. Håstad, J., Schrift, A. W., Shamir, A.: The discrete logarithm modulo a composite hides $o(n)$ bits. J. of Computing and Systems Science **47** (1993) 376–404.
13. Impaggliazzo, R., Naor, M.:. Efficient cryptographic schemes provably as secure as subset sum. In Proc. 30th Symp. on Foundations of Computing Science (1989) IEEE pp. 236–241.
14. Impagliazzo, R., Levin, L. A., Luby, M.:. Pseudo-random generation from any one-way functions. In Proc. 21st Symp. on Theory of Computing (1989) ACM press pp. 12–24.
15. Levin, L. A.:. One-way functions and pseudo-random generators. In Proc. 21st Symp. on Theory of Computing (1985) ACM pp. 363–365.
16. Long, D. L., Wigderson, A.: The discrete log hides $o(\log n)$ bits. SIAM J. Computing **17** (1988) 363–372.
17. McWilliams, F. J., Sloane, N. J. A.:. The theory of error-correcting codes. North-Holland 1977.
18. Micali, S., Schnorr, C. P.:. Efficient, perfect random number generators. In Advances in Cryptology, Proc. of CRYPTO'88 (1988) vol. 576 of LNCS Springer Verlag.
19. Stern, J.:. A method for finding codewords of small weight. In Lecture Notes in Computer Science, Coding Theory and Applications vol. 388. Springer 1989 pp. 106–113.
20. Stern, J.:. A new identification scheme based on syndrome decoding. In Advances in Cryptology, Proc. of CRYPTO'93 (1993) vol. 773 of LNCS Springer-Verlag pp. 13–21.
21. Vazirani, U. V., Vazirani, V. V.:. Efficient and secure pseudo-random sequences from slightly-random sources. In Proc. 25th Symp. on Foundations of Computing Science (1984) IEEE pp. 458–463.
22. Yao, A. C.:. Theory and application of trapdoor functions. In Proc. 25th Symp. on Foundations of Computing Science (1982) IEEE pp. 80–91.

On the Existence of Secure Feedback Registers (Extended Abstract)

Andrew Klapper*

Department of Computer Science
763H Anderson Hall
University of Kentucky
Lexington KY 40506-0046.
Phone: (606) 257-6743; FAX: (606) 323-1971
E-mail: klapper@cs.engr.uky.edu
WWW: http://al.cs.engr.uky.edu/~klapper/andy.html

Abstract. Designers of stream ciphers have generally used ad hoc methods to build systems that are secure against known attacks. There is often a sense that this is the best that can be done, that any system will eventually fall to a practical attack. In this paper we show that there are families of keystream generators that resist all possible attacks of a very general type in which a small number of known bits of a keystream are used to synthesize a generator of the keystream (called a synthesizing algorithm). Such attacks are exemplified by the Berlekamp-Massey attack. We first formalize the notions of a family of feedback registers and of a synthesizing algorithm. We then show that for any function $h(n)$ that is in $\mathcal{O}(2^{n/d})$ for every $d > 0$, there is a secure family $\mathcal{B}$ of periodic sequences in the sense that any efficient synthesizing algorithm outputs a register of size $h(\log(\text{period}(B)))$ given the required number of bits of a sequence $B \in \mathcal{B}$ of large enough period. This result is tight in the sense it fails for any faster growing function $h(n)$. We also consider several variations on this scenario.

Index Terms – Binary sequences, nonlinear feedback registers, security, cryptography, stream ciphers.

1 Introduction

Historically, the design of stream ciphers has been largely a matter of finding ad hoc methods of foiling existing cryptanalytic attacks. Having their roots in Shannon's information theory, designers often feel that seeking a truly secure stream cipher is hopeless, that the best they can do is design a system that resists known attacks. The purpose of this paper is to explore the possibility that there exist families of stream ciphers that resist cryptanalysis by very large classes of attacks. We use asymptotic complexity rather than Shannon theory as

* This research funded in part by NSF grant #NCR-9400762.

Ueli Maurer (Ed.): EUROCRYPT '96 Proceedings, LNCS 1070

the basis for notions of security. A family of stream ciphers is secure against all attacks of a certain general type if all such attacks require asymptotically large numbers of bits of the keystream. Our approach to the construction of these families of stream ciphers, while recursive, gives no practical construction for such a family of stream ciphers.

The sort of attack we are concerned with uses a small number of known bits of a keystream to synthesize a fast generator for the keystream. Perhaps the best known example of such an attack is the Berlekamp-Massey algorithm [13]. If the keystream can be generated by a linear feedback shift register (or LFSR) of length n, then $2n$ bits of the sequence suffice for the Berlekamp-Massey algorithm to determine the LFSR that generates the keystream. The smallest such n is called the linear span of the keystream and is a well studied measure of security. The ingredients that make this attack of concern are as follows.

1. A class of fast devices (LFSRs) that generate all possible eventually periodic sequences.
2. A polynomial time algorithm A and a polynomial $p(n)$ such that if a sequence can be generated by a device of size n, then $p(n)$ bits of the sequence suffice for A to determine the device.

A great deal of energy has gone into the design of (nonlinear) feedback registers that resist the Berlekamp-Massey attack (see [4, 7, 8, 15, 16], to name but a few). Similar attacks exist in the literature. For example, the Berlekamp-Massey algorithm works in any odd characteristic, and a binary sequence can be treated as a sequence over any field [9]. Also, recently Klapper and Goresky have designed a class of devices called feedback with carry shift registers or FCSRs [10, 11], and an algorithm for synthesizing them based on 2-adic rational approximation theory [12]. Both these approaches have been used to cryptanalyze certain sequences that had previously been shown to resist the Berlekamp-Massey attack (in the first case, geometric sequences [4], in the second case summation combiners [15]).

In this paper we ask whether there is a family of efficiently generated sequences that resist all such attacks. The answer is affirmative. However, the techniques used to show their existence, while recursive, give no practical method for finding such a family. Even if we could give a reasonable description of such a family, it might not be possible to give a computationally effective description of its generators. This should not be seen as too much of a difficulty, however, as this is the case even for m-sequences. Finding generators for m-sequences amounts to finding primitive polynomials over $GF(2)$, and this is apparently a computationally hard problem unless one knows a factorization of $2^n - 1$ (although it is not hard for currently practical sizes). Yet m-sequences are commonly used in practice as the bases for keystream generators.

Related questions have been studied previously by Yao [18] and by Blum and Micali [2]. Their models and results were different, however, in a number of regards. First, their sequence generators were arbitrary polynomial time computable generators (in the size of the seed). We use a much more restrictive model based on the use of fast feedback registers for generation of bit streams.

Second, the attacks they were concerned with required the availability of all previously generated bits to predict the next bit (by a so-called next bit test). The attacks considered here require that only a small number (polynomially many in the size of the resulting generator) of bits be available to generate all remaining bits. Third, the attacks consider by Yao and Blum and Micali were probabilistic while those considered here are deterministic. Finally, the existence results they gave were based on unproved complexity theoretic assumptions, such as the intractability of the discrete logarithm problem. Our results hold independent of any such assumptions.

Maurer also considered the design of private key systems that resist all attacks [14]. His point of view differed from ours in that the system he designed required a globally accessible source of public randomness. Also, the notion of security was probabilistic – the probability that an enemy could obtain information was shown to be exceedingly small.

In Section 2 we abstract the notions of fast keystream generator and of efficient algorithms for synthesizing such generators given a small number of initial bits. In Section 3 we first show that there is a family of keystream generators that admits no such synthesizing algorithm. We then show that an efficient, secure family $\mathcal{B}$ of sequences exists. This family is secure in the sense that, for every family of keystream generators $\mathcal{F}$ that admits a synthesizing algorithm, the size of the smallest generator in $\mathcal{F}$ that outputs a given sequence B in $\mathcal{B}$ grows at a superpolynomial rate in the size of smallest efficient generator for B. In Section 4 we show that the bounds in Section 3 are optimal. In Sections 5 and 6 we consider two variants: the case where the cryptanalyst is only required to generate a fraction of the keystream; and the case where the number of bits the cryptanalyst has access to is linear in the size of the smallest generator.

2 Definitions

In this section we describe feedback registers, the basic objects of study of this paper, and notions of security for families of feedback registers.

Definition 1. A *feedback register* of length n is determined by a function $F : \{0,1\}^n \to \{0,1\}^n$, called the *feedback function.* The *state* of the register is an n-bit vector $\bar{x} = (x_0, \cdots, x_{n-1})$. The *output* from the state $\bar{x}$ is x_0, and the *next state* is $F(\bar{x})$.

Thus from a given state $\bar{x}$ a feedback register outputs an infinite eventually periodic binary sequence by iterating the output and next state operations. In algorithms dealing with descriptions of feedback functions, we assume that the functions are described by circuits using binary AND (denoted $\wedge$), binary XOR (denoted $\oplus$), and NOT (denoted $\neg$) gates. Binary OR gates could have been used instead of XOR gates, but for the functions described here we find XOR more convenient. Changing the types of gates only changes complexity measures by a constant multiple. The AND and XOR gates are assumed to have fan-in two.

Such circuits can be encoded as binary strings [1]. The *size* of a register F is the minimum number of gates in a circuit that computes the function F. The *depth* of a register F is the depth of the minimum depth circuit that computes F. In a software implementation, the time it takes to evaluate a circuit is proportional to its size. In a hardware implementation, evaluation time is proportional to depth.

Note that feedback registers are really a type of finite state machine *without input*. One can consider more general finite state machines without input, where the output is computed as a function of the state rather than as the rightmost bit of the state vector. However, any such machine can be easily converted into an equivalent machine (i.e., producing the same output sequence) of the type used here by increasing the length by one. This new bit is then updated by the composition of the original output and state change functions. The register has depth and size at most twice those of the original machine. Thus our results apply to the more general model as well. The simpler model is, however, easier to work with.

A *family of feedback registers*, $\mathcal{F}$, is an infinite collection of feedback registers such that every eventually periodic binary sequence can be output by at least one register in $\mathcal{F}$. We let $\mathcal{F}_n$ denote the set of feedback registers in $\mathcal{F}$ of length n. If B is an infinite eventually periodic binary sequence, then the $\mathcal{F}$-span of B, denoted $\lambda_{\mathcal{F}}(B)$, is the least integer n such that B can be output by a register in $\mathcal{F}_n$.

We are concerned with registers whose feedback functions can be computed quickly. Let $\delta(n)$ be the maximum over all F in $\mathcal{F}_n$ of the depth of F. We say $\mathcal{F}$ is *fast* if $\delta(n) \in \mathcal{O}(\log(n))$. Note that this implies that the sizes (numbers of gates) of the registers in $\mathcal{F}$ are polynomial in the lengths of the registers. In fact, in all but one case in this paper, the sizes of fast families of registers described are linear in the lengths of the registers.

Our basic concern is whether, given a small number of bits of a sequence B, we can efficiently synthesize the smallest register in $\mathcal{F}$ that outputs B.

Definition 2. Algorithm T is an *$\mathcal{F}$-synthesizing algorithm* if, when given the input $b_0, \cdots, b_{k-1}$,

1. T outputs the encoding of a circuit that computes a feedback function $F \in \mathcal{F}$; and
2. if n is the length of F, T also outputs an n-bit vector $\bar{a}$ such that the first k bits of the output of F with start state $\bar{a}$ are $b_0, \cdots, b_{k-1}$.

The algorithm may or may not be assumed to know the period of the sequence B. T is *effective* if:

1. It runs in polynomial time; and
2. There is a polynomial $p(n)$ such that if $n = \lambda_{\mathcal{F}}(B)$, on input $b_0, \cdots, b_{k-1}$ with $k \geq p(n)$, T outputs an $F \in \mathcal{F}$ of length n that generates B.

A family $\mathcal{F}$ of registers is *synthetic* if there is an effective $\mathcal{F}$-synthesizing algorithm.

Certain families of sequences that have played a significant role in cryptography are known to be synthetic.

Fact 3 *The family of LFSRs and the family of FCSRs are synthetic.*

We say that a family of sequences is secure with respect to a family of registers if there is either no way to synthesize the best register in the family for a given sequence, or the length of the best register grows quickly with period of the sequence.

Definition 4. Let $\mathcal{B} = B^1, B^2, \cdots$ be a sequence of binary sequences of increasing periods, and let $p_{\mathcal{B}}(n)$ be the period of B^n. Let $\Lambda_{\mathcal{F},\mathcal{B}}(n) = \lambda_{\mathcal{F}}(B^n)$. Then $\mathcal{B}$ is $\mathcal{F}$*-secure* if either

1. $\mathcal{F}$ is not synthetic; or
2. For every $k > 0$, we have

$$\Lambda_{\mathcal{F},\mathcal{B}}(n) \in \Omega(\log(p_{\mathcal{B}}(n))^k).$$

In either case, for large enough n a short register in $\mathcal{F}$ generating B^n cannot be found effectively. Our goal is to show the existence of a sequence of periodic binary sequences $\mathcal{B}$ such that

1. $\mathcal{B}$ is $\mathcal{F}$-secure for every family of feedback registers;
2. There is a family $\mathcal{F}$ of fast registers containing generators for the sequences in $\mathcal{B}$ whose lengths are logarithmic in the periods of the sequences.

In describing the growth rates of functions, we use the following terminology.

Definition 5. Let $f(n)$ be a function.

1. We say $f(n)$ is *subexponential* if for every $d > 0$, $f(n) \in \mathcal{O}(2^{n/d})$.
2. We say $f(n)$ is *superpolynomial* if for every $k > 0$, $f(n) \in \Omega(n^k)$.

Thus by our definition, a family is secure if it achieves superpolynomial security. In fact, we show that we can find families that achieve arbitrary subexponential security, not simply superpolynomial security. It is well known that there are subexponential superpolynomial functions.

3 Existence of Secure Feedback Registers

In this section we give theorems on the existence of feedback registers and sequences that resist all synthesis attacks in the sense that any such attack outputs inefficient generators.

Theorem 6. *Let $h(n)$ be any subexponential function. There exists a fast family $\mathcal{F}$ of registers such that for every synthetic family $\mathcal{F}'$, there are infinitely many registers F in $\mathcal{F}$ with output sequence S satisfying*

$$\lambda_{\mathcal{F}'}(S) \geq h(\lambda_{\mathcal{F}}(S)).$$

Proof: For each synthesis algorithm T, let $\mathcal{F}_T$ be the family of registers that is output by T. Let $\mathcal{F}^1, \mathcal{F}^2, \cdots$ be an enumeration of the synthetic families of registers such that each $\mathcal{F}_T$ occurs infinitely often. Let the corresponding synthesis algorithms be $T^1, T^2, \cdots$.

We construct $\mathcal{F}$ in stages by a kind of diagonalization argument. At the end of stage $i-1$ we will have constructed $\mathcal{F}$ for registers of lengths up to k_{i-1} so that the theorem holds for $\mathcal{F}^1, \cdots, \mathcal{F}^{i-1}$. We now show how to extend the construction to stage i.

Let $p(n)$ be a polynomial such that for every sequence B, T^i outputs a register that generates B given at least $p(\lambda_{\mathcal{F}^i}(B))$ bits of B. We may assume $p(n) = n^d$. Let r be larger than the period of any sequence generated by any register already in $\mathcal{F}$, and be large enough that for every $k \geq r$, we have

$$2^{k/d} > h(k+3).$$

Let n satisfy $2^r < p(n)$. Let k satisfy $2^k \leq p(n) < 2^{k+1}$. We construct a pair of registers F and G of length at most $k+3$ and depth at most $\lceil \log(k) \rceil + 1$, whose outputs agree on the first $2^{k+1} - 1$ terms, but not on the 2^{k+1}st term.

For F we choose a linear feedback shift register of length $k+1$ that outputs an m-sequence (of period $2^{k+1} - 1$). The feedback function of such a register is just a shift for k bits, and an XOR of at most $k+1$ bits. Thus it can be computed in depth $\lceil \log(k) \rceil$.

For G we take a length $k+3$ register with bits labeled x_{k+2} to x_0 from left to right. The leftmost $k+1$ bits are updated exactly as the $k+1$ bits of F. Bit x_1 changes only when the leftmost $k+1$ bits all equal 1. Bit x_0 (the output bit) always equals $x_1 \oplus x_2$. Suppose x_1 is initially 0, the leftmost $k+1$ bits of G are initially identical to the $k+1$ bits of F, and $x_0 = x_1 \oplus x_2$ initially. Then the output from G is strictly periodic with period $2(2^{k+1} - 1)$. The first half of one period equals a period of the output of F, while the second half equals the complement of a period of the output of F. The additional circuitry required for G has depth $\lceil \log(k) \rceil + 1$ since $x_1 = x_1 \oplus (x_2 \wedge \cdots \wedge x_{k+3})$, and $x_0 = (x_1 \oplus (x_2 \wedge \cdots \wedge x_{k+3})) \oplus x_3$ (remember: the new value of x_2 is the old value of x_3).

For initial values, we take $0, 1, 1, \cdots, 1$ for F, and $0, 1, 1, \cdots, 1, 0, 1$ for G. This gives the desired behavior. Let B^1 and B^2 be the resulting output sequences. Since $p(n) < 2^{k+1}$, T^i cannot distinguish these sequences with only $p(n)$ bits available. Thus at least one of the sequences, say B^m, has

$$\lambda_{\mathcal{F}^i}(B^m) > n \geq 2^{k/d} > h(k+3).$$

We put the corresponding register in $\mathcal{F}$ and let k_i be the length of that register. Thus

$$\lambda_{\mathcal{F}^i}(B^m) > h(k+3) \geq h(k_i) = h(\lambda_{\mathcal{F}}(B^m))$$

as desired. This concludes stage i.

To make $\mathcal{F}$ a family of registers (i.e., capable of generating every sequence), we add to $\mathcal{F}$ every linear feedback shift register with only a single tap in its feedback function. □

In particular, for the sequence $\mathcal{B}$ of registers constructed in the proof, there is no i such that $\Lambda_{\mathcal{F}^i,\mathcal{B}}(m)$ is in $\mathcal{O}(h(\Lambda_{\mathcal{F},\mathcal{B}}(m)))$, and $h(n)$ can be taken to be a superpolynomial function.

Corollary 7. *There exist (uncountably many) fast nonsynthetic families of registers.*

However, we want a stronger statement than that given by Theorem 6. All we know is that the above bound holds for infinitely many sequences in $\mathcal{B}$. We want it to hold for all sequences in $\mathcal{B}$ of sufficiently large period. That is, we want $\Lambda_{\mathcal{F}^i,\mathcal{B}}(m) \in \Omega(h(\Lambda_{\mathcal{F},\mathcal{B}}(m)))$. We can modify the above construction to achieve this, as follows.

Theorem 8. *Let $h(n)$ be any subexponential function. There exists a sequence of binary periodic sequences $\mathcal{B} = B^1, B^2, \cdots$ such that*

a. $\mathcal{B}$ can be generated by a fast family $\mathcal{F}$ of registers such that the length of the register generating B^m is at most twice the log of the period of B^m;
b. For every synthetic family $\mathcal{F}'$, if m is sufficiently large, then

$$\Lambda_{\mathcal{F}',\mathcal{B}}(m) \geq h(\log(\mathit{period}(B^m))).$$

In particular, if we let h be superpolynomial, then $\mathcal{B}$ satisfies the requirements at the end of Section 2.

Proof: We begin with an enumeration $\mathcal{F}^i$ of the synthetic families of registers and construct $\mathcal{B}$ by stages, as in the preceding proof. At the ith stage we construct B^i to have appropriate properties with respect to $\mathcal{F}^1, \cdots, \mathcal{F}^i$. Let $p(n) = n^d$ be so that for $1 \leq j \leq i$, T^j synthesizes a register in $\mathcal{F}^j$ that outputs any sequence S given $p(\lambda_{\mathcal{F}^j}(S))$ bits of S.

Let $t = \lceil \log(i) \rceil$. We construct B^i so that it has period $2^{k+1}+t-1$, and can be generated by a register of length $k+t+2$ and depth $\max(\lceil \log(k+1) \rceil, \lceil \log(t) \rceil)+3$ for some k.

Let r be

1. larger than the period of any previous B^j;
2. larger than t; and
3. large enough that, for every $k \geq r$, we have

$$2^{k/d} > h(\log(2^k + t)).$$

Choose n so that $n^d > 2^r$. Let k satisfy $2^k \leq n^d < 2^{k+1}$. We construct $i+1$ registers whose outputs are identical to one period of an m-sequence for $2^{k+1}-1$ bits. The jth register then outputs the binary expansion of the integer j. It is straightforward to check that this can be done within the stated bounds on length and depth.

There must be at least one of these sequences, which we denote B^i, that satisfies

$$\lambda_{\mathcal{F}^j}(B^i) > n \geq 2^{k/d} > h(\log(2^k + t)) = h(\log(\text{period}(B^i)))$$

for $1 \leq j \leq i$. This concludes stage i. □

The constructions in Theorems 6 and 8 can be made recursive. That is, there is an effective procedure which, given i, outputs a list of the registers in $\mathcal{F}_i$ in the first case or B^i (or a generator of B^i) in the second case. Such a procedure, however, is likely to be impractically slow.

4 Exponential Bounds Are Impossible

In this section we show that Theorem 8 is sharp in the sense that the function h cannot be replaced by an exponential function.

Theorem 9. *Let $h(n) = 2^{n/d}$ be an exponential function, and let $\mathcal{B} = B^1, B^2, \cdots$ be any sequence of periodic binary sequences. There exists a fast synthetic family of sequences $\mathcal{F}$ such that for every i,*

$$\lambda_{\mathcal{F}}(B^i) \leq h(\log(\textit{period}(B^i))).$$

The synthesis algorithm for $\mathcal{F}$ is assumed to know the period of the sequence.

Proof: We construct the family $\mathcal{F}$ by describing a register synthesis algorithm T. $\mathcal{F}$ is then the set of registers output by T.

A k bit register generated by T has the following form. The leftmost $k - 1$ bits operate independently of the rightmost bit. The rightmost bit is computed as a function of the leftmost $k-1$ bits. Thus the registers are, in effect, nonlinear feedback registers with nonlinear feedforward functions.

Algorithm T will produce a register of length $\lfloor p^{1/d} \rfloor$ when acting on a sequence of period p. Thus

$$\lambda_{\mathcal{F}}(B^i) = \left\lfloor \text{period}(B^i)^{1/d} \right\rfloor \leq h(\log(\text{period}(B^i))).$$

Since the number of bits the algorithm can have access to is polynomial in $\lambda_{\mathcal{F}}(B^i)$, we can assume T knows a complete period of period(B^i).

The first step is to construct a fast feedback register whose state sequence has period p. This can be done, for example, by constructing a maximal period LFSR of length k, with $2^{k-1} \leq p < 2^k$. Thus the period of this LFSR is $2^k - 1$. Such a LFSR can be found by an exhaustive search for a primitive polynomial of degree k. There are $2^k \leq 2p$ polynomials of degree k, and each can be checked for primitivity in time quasi-linear in p. Thus such a LFSR can be found in polynomial time. It can then be modified to switch back to its initial state after

p states by using a k-bit AND to check for the pth state. We call the resulting register G.

The construction is completed by finding a binary function on k bits that has the bits of the sequence as values on the p states of G. This can be written as an XOR of p terms, each an AND of k bits. Such an expression can be implemented as a circuit of depth $\lceil \log(p) \rceil + \lceil \log(k) \rceil$.

Finally, the resulting register is extended to length $\lfloor p^{1/d} \rfloor$ by padding it with $\lfloor p^{1/d} \rfloor - k$ dummy bits on the left. □

Theorem 9 is in fact true without knowledge of the period, but the polynomial bound on the number of bits available must be squared. This ensures that, for period p, p^2 bits are available. These are enough bits to determine the period unambiguously.

5 Partial Attacks

For many purposes the attacks considered in the preceding sections are too weak. A system is also vulnerable if an adversary can find a substantial number of bits of the keystream. This is especially true if there is enough context in the message to recover the remaining bits. If $\mathcal{F}$ is a family of registers, B is a sequence of (eventual) period m, and $0 < r \leq m$, then $\lambda_{\mathcal{F},r}(B)$ is the size of the smallest register F in $\mathcal{F}$ whose output agrees with B on at least r bits of each period[2] of B.

Definition 10. Let T be an $\mathcal{F}$-synthesizing algorithm and $0 < r(m) \leq m$. We say that T is *$r(m)$-effective for $\mathcal{F}$* if

1. It runs in polynomial time; and
2. There is a polynomial $p(n)$ such that if B is a sequence with (eventual) period m and $n = \lambda_{\mathcal{F},r(m)}(B)$, then on input $b_0, \cdots, b_{k-1}$ with $k \geq p(n)$, T outputs an $F \in \mathcal{F}$ of length n. If the sequence generated by F is B', then for any k,
$$|\{i, k \leq i \leq k+m-1 : b_i = b'_i\}| \geq r(m).$$

$\mathcal{F}$ is *$r(m)$-synthetic* if there is an $r(m)$-effective algorithm for $\mathcal{F}$.

Theorem 11. *Let $h(n)$ be subexponential and let $r(m) \in (m + \mathcal{O}(m^{1/2}))/2$. There exists a fast family $\mathcal{F}$ of registers such that for every $r(m)$-synthetic family $\mathcal{F}'$, there are infinitely many registers F in $\mathcal{F}$ with output sequence B of eventual period m satisfying*
$$\lambda_{\mathcal{F}',r(m)}(B) \geq h(\lambda_{\mathcal{F}}(B)).$$

[2] Some care must be taken here. The sequence B and the output sequence B' of F may have different periods, and in fact may not be strictly periodic, only eventually periodic. A reasonable interpretation is that $r/\text{period}(B)$ is less than or equal to the limit as n goes to ∞ of $|\{i, 1 \leq i \leq n : b_i = b'_i\}|/n$.

Proof Sketch: It is possible to construct a fast register such that one output period consists of an m-sequence followed by a degree one Reed-Muller code word. It is well known that the covering radius of the Reed-Muller code $RM(n, k)$ for fixed k is at most $(2^n - c2^{n/2})/2$, where c depends only on k [3]. The constant c can be made arbitrarily large by the choice of k. Taking complements, we see that there is a Reed-Muller codeword whose distance from any given sequence of length 2^n is at least $(2^n + c2^{n/2})/2$. $R(n, k)$ codewords can be generated by registers of length n and depth $\mathcal{O}(\log(n))$.

Let T be an $r(m)$-effective synthesis algorithm that is successful when given $p(\lambda_{\mathcal{F}',r(m)}(S))$ bits of any sequence S. We choose the sizes of the two parts of the above register so that the length $2^k - 1$ of the m-sequence is at least $p(h(\log(m)))$, where m is the period. We then choose the Reed-Muller codeword so that whatever sequence T outputs given $2^k - 1$ bits, the last 2^n bits disagree with the codeword on at least $(2^n + c2^{n/2})/2$ bits. It is possible to choose n and k so that this is more than $(m + \mathcal{O}(m^{1/2}))/2$. This is used to construct the family $\mathcal{F}$ in a manner similar to that in Theorem 6. □

This result will be improved if easily generated codes with small covering radii can be constructed. Coding theorists have studied covering radii for some years, but good asymptotic bounds are difficult to obtain and they seem to have not considered the question of fast generation of the codewords. It would also be desirable to find a sequence of sequences B^i so that B^i resists the first i $r(m)$-synthetic attacks. Using our techniques, such a construction would depend on finding easily generated codes with small *multicovering radii*, i.e., the smallest d such that every sequence is within distance d of at least i codewords. This concept appears to have not been studied by coding theorists.

6 Linear Synthesis Attacks

In this section we discuss the effect on our results of restricting the power of the synthesis algorithms.

As defined, synthesis algorithms depend on polynomial bounds. A synthesis algorithm for a family $\mathcal{F}$ of registers must work correctly if the number of bits available is at least a fixed polynomial in the $\mathcal{F}$-span, and the running time must be polynomially bounded in the number of bits available. If the degree of the polynomial is large, however, it is questionable whether such an attack should be considered strong enough to be of practical concern. By contrast, the Berlekamp-Massey and the 2-adic rational approximation algorithms work correctly if at least a linear number of bits are available. The former algorithm has quadratic running time, while the latter has quasi-quadratic running time. An algorithm is said to be a *linear synthesis algorithm* for a family $\mathcal{F}$ if it requires only a linear number of bits in $\lambda_{\mathcal{F}}(B)$ to synthesize a register in $\mathcal{F}$ that outputs B. Then $\mathcal{F}$ is said to be *linearly synthetic.* Theorems 6 and 8 can be improved if we restrict our attention to linear synthesis.

Theorem 12. *Let $h(n) \in o(2^n)$. There exists a sequence of binary periodic sequences $\mathcal{B} = B^1, B^2, \cdots$ such that* *a.* $\mathcal{B}$ *can be generated by a fast family* $\mathcal{F}$ *of registers such that the length of the register generating* B^i *is at most twice the log of the period of* B^i*;*

b. Let $\mathcal{F}'$ *be a linearly synthetic family. For every sufficiently large* i *we have*

$$\lambda_{\mathcal{F}'}(B^i) \geq h(\log(period(B^i))).$$

This result can then be shown to be tight.

Theorem 13. *Let* $h(n) = c2^n$*, for some constant* c*. Let* $\mathcal{B} = B^1, B^2, \cdots$ *be a sequence of periodic binary sequences. There exists a fast linearly synthetic family of sequences* $\mathcal{F}$ *such that for every* i*,*

$$\lambda_{\mathcal{F}}(B^i) \leq h(\log(period(B^i))).$$

The synthesis algorithm for $\mathcal{F}$ *is assumed to know the period of the sequence.*

7 Conclusions and Open Questions

We have described a general model for attacks on stream ciphers of a very general type. Using this model, we have proved the existence of families of sequence generators that resist all such attacks. The proof, however, does not give a practical construction. We hope to inspire researchers to search for such highly secure sequence generators with more natural descriptions. The basic open question we leave is whether practical constructions can be found for register and sequence families that satisfy the conclusions of Theorem 8 and 6.

We have also considered only one class of attack on stream ciphers. Other attacks are possible, for example probabilistic attacks such as correlation attacks [17], differential cryptanalysis [5], and linear cryptanalysis [6]. It is desirable to formalize such probabilistic attacks and (hopefully) prove the existence of classes of keystream generators that universally resist them.

We have concentrated on the depth of circuits as a measure of feasibility. This corresponds to time of evaluation. Size (number of gates) is also a concern as it impacts area and hence cost. In all our theorems except Theorem 9 the sizes of the resulting fast registers are linear in the lengths of the registers. In Theorem 9, the sizes of the fast registers are polynomial in their lengths. We leave open the question as to whether one can achieve smaller sizes than these.

References

1. J. Balcázar, J. Díaz, and J. Gabarró: Structural Complexity I. Berlin: Springer 1988.
2. M. Blum and S. Micali: How to generate cryptographically strong sequences of pseudorandom bits. SIAM Journal on Computing 13, 850-864 (1984).
3. G. Cohen and S. Litsyn: On the covering radius of Reed-Muller codes. Discrete Mathematics 106-107, 147-155 (1992).
4. A.H. Chan and R.A. Games: On the linear span of binary sequences from finite geometries, q odd. IEEE Transactions on Information Theory 36, 548-552 (1990).

5. C. Ding: The differential cryptanalysis and design of natural stream ciphers. In: R. Anderson (ed.): Fast Software Encryption: Proceedings of 1993 Cambridge Security Workshop. Lecture Notes in Computer Science 809. Berlin: Springer 1994, pp. 101-120.
6. J. Golić: Linear cryptanalyis of stream ciphers. In: B. Preneel (ed.): Fast Software Encryption: Proceedings of 1994 Leuven Security Workshop. Lecture Notes in Computer Science 1008. Berlin: Springer 1995, pp. 154-169.
7. E.J. Groth: Generation of binary sequences with controllable complexity. IEEE Transactions on Information Theory IT-17, 288-296 (1971).
8. E.L. Key: An Analysis of the structure and complexity of nonlinear binary sequence generators. IEEE Transactions on Information Theory IT-22, 732-736 (1976).
9. A. Klapper: The Vulnerability of Geometric Sequences Based on Fields of Odd Characteristic. Journal of Cryptology 7, 33-51 (1994).
10. A. Klapper and M. Goresky: 2-Adic Shift Registers. In : R. Anderson (ed.): Fast Software Encryption: Proceedings of 1993 Cambridge Security Workshop. Lecture Notes in Computer Science 809. Berlin: Springer 1994, pp. 174-178.
11. A. Klapper and M. Goresky: Feedback Shift Registers, Combiners with Memory, and 2-Adic Span, University of Kentucky, Deptartment of Computer Science Technical Report, 1995.
12. A. Klapper and M. Goresky: Cryptanalysis Based on 2-Adic Rational Approximation. In: D. Coppersmith (ed.) Advances in Cryptology – CRYPTO '95. Lecture Notes in Computer Science 963. Berlin: Springer 1994, pp. 262-273.
13. J.L. Massey: Shift register sequences and BCH decoding. IEEE Transactions on Information Theory IT-15, 122-127 (1969).
14. U. M. Maurer: A Provably-Secure Strongly-Randomized Cipher. In: S. Vanstone (ed.) Advances in Cryptology – CRYPTO '90. Lecture Notes in Computer Science 473. Berlin: Springer 1991, pp. 361-73.
15. R. Rueppel: Analysis and Design of Stream Ciphers. New York Springer, 1986.
16. R.A. Rueppel and O.J. Staffelbach: Products of linear recurring sequences sith maximum complexity, IEEE Transactions on Information Theory IT-33, 124-129 (1987).
17. T. Siegenthaler: Decrypting a class of stream ciphers using cipertext only. IEEE Transactions on Computing 34, 81-85 (1985).
18. A. Yao: Theory and applications of trapdoor functions. In: Proceedings, 23rd IEEE Symposium on Foundations of Computer Science, 1982, pp. 80-91.

Fast Low Order Approximation of Cryptographic Functions

Jovan Dj. Golić *

Information Security Research Centre, Queensland University of Technology
GPO Box 2434, Brisbane Q 4001, Australia
School of Electrical Engineering, University of Belgrade
Email: golic@fit.qut.edu.au

Abstract. A fast and efficient procedure for finding low order approximations to large boolean functions, if such approximations exist, is developed. The procedure uses iterative error-correction algorithms for fast correlation attacks on certain stream ciphers and is based on representing low order boolean functions by appropriate linear recurring sequences generated by binary filter generators. Applications and significance of the proposed method in the analysis and design of block and stream ciphers are also discussed.

1 Introduction

Encryption and decryption functions of binary block and stream ciphers in their various modes of operation are necessarily based on boolean functions. The boolean functions are secret key dependent in block ciphers and self-synchronizing stream ciphers and may be key independent in synchronous stream ciphers where the initial state is key dependent. Linear approximations of boolean functions in stream cipher applications have been studied in [22], [23], [21], [26], [16], [2] for memoryless combiners, in [24], [21], [2] for nonlinear filter generators, in [17], [6], [7] for combiners with memory, and in [7] for arbitrary keystream generators. These results are related to correlation attacks [23] or fast correlation attacks [15], [27] on shift register based keystream generators. On the other hand, a number of authors have investigated linear approximations of boolean and vectorial boolean functions in product block ciphers, and a breakthrough in this area was made by Matsui in his seminal work [13], initiating many follow-up papers on similar problems. Matsui developed an iterative (dynamic programming) method for finding linear approximations to encryption functions in product block ciphers and was the first to realize that even linear approximations with very small correlation coefficients can be used to reduce the uncertainty of the secret key. Maurer [14] has analyzed the security of self-synchronizing stream ciphers against the chosen-ciphertext attack and pointed out the importance of linear and other low order approximations to the key dependent feedback

* This research was supported in part by the Science Fund of Serbia, grant #0403, through the Institute of Mathematics, Serbian Academy of Arts and Sciences.

Ueli Maurer (Ed.): EUROCRYPT '96 Proceedings, LNCS 1070

function for approximate reconstruction of unknown plaintext from a given ciphertext which in turn may lead to the complete plaintext recovery by using the plaintext redundancy. The reason for this is that any boolean function of low algebraic/nonlinear order can be described and evaulated in terms of a relatively low number of coefficients in its algebraic normal form (ANF) even if the number of input variables is large. Of course, approximate decryption by means of low order approximations to decryption functions may also be possible for any block cipher as well [20].

The task of finding low order approximations to boolean functions necessarily involves computing or estimating the correlation coefficient between a given boolean function and a candidate boolean function of low algebraic order, where the correlation coefficient between any two boolean functions $f(X)$ and $g(X)$ of n variables $X = (x_1, \ldots, x_n)$ is as usual (e.g., see [21], [16]) defined as

$$c(f,g) \;=\; 2^{-n} \sum_X (-1)^{f(X)}(-1)^{g(X)} \;=\; \Pr\{f = g\} - \Pr\{f \neq g\}. \qquad (1)$$

The functions f and g are not correlated if $c(f,g) = 0$, and are strongly correlated if $c(f,g)$ is large in magnitude (i.e., close to ± 1). The objective of low order approximation of a given boolean function f is to find a boolean function g of low algebraic order such that the correlation coefficient $c(f,g)$ is relatively large. To compute $c(f,g)$ exactly for a candidate g, one has to examine all 2^n possible arguments, but to estimate it reliably only $O(1/c(f,g)^2)$ argument values are needed, under a reasonable probabilistic assumption that 2^n values of $g(X)$ are chosen independently at random so that $\Pr\{f = g\} = (1 + c(f,g))/2$. Accordingly, the correlation coefficient is considered to be large in magnitude if $|c(f,g)|$ is much bigger than $2^{-n/2}$. The exhaustive search over all $2^{\sum_{i=0}^{r}\binom{n}{i}}$ possible candidate functions g of order r or smaller is not feasible for moderately large n (e.g., $n \geq 64$) which is the case in cryptographic applications. It should be noted that for linear/affine approximations ($r = 1$) one may apply the fast Walsh transform algorithm for exact computation of the correlation coefficients between f and all the linear functions, with the computational complexity $O(n2^n)$ instead of 2^{2n} (e.g., see [21]). A similar algorithm for an arbitrary order r is not known. In any case, for 2^n very large the problem is how to find good candidate functions, if they exist. The problem is difficult and may even seem impossible to solve.

Maurer [14] pointed out that boolean functions of n variables and of order at most r can be regarded as codewords of a binary rth-order Reed-Muller code with parameters $(2^n, \sum_{i=0}^{r}\binom{n}{i}, 2^{n-r})$, see [25], where the information bits are the coefficients in the ANF of these functions. The considered problem can then be regarded as one of decoding such linear block codes, i.e., the minimum distance decoding of such codes is equivalent to finding a low order approximation to a given boolean function with the maximum correlation coefficient. Since the minimum distance is 2^{n-r}, one may correct any $2^{n-r-1} - 1$ or less errors by such codes which means that it is theoretically possible to determine uniquely the best rth-order approximation g to a given boolean function f if the correlation coefficient $c(f,g)$ is bigger than $1 - 2^{-r}$. However, as noted in [14], standard decoding procedures [25] for Reed-Muller codes (majority-logic decoding based on appropriate orthogonal parity-checks) are not feasible for large 2^n. Another important distinction is that in cryptographic applications the maximum magnitude of the correlation coefficients to rth-order boolean functions is expected to be much smaller than $1 - 2^{-r}$. Such approximations may no longer be useful for approximate decryption, but may be used in cryptanalytic attacks on the secret key. For example, Matsui [13] has shown that linear approximations to encryption functions in block ciphers with the correlation coefficients even close to $2^{-n/2}$ can be used to reduce the uncertainty of the secret key. Similar conclusions may hold for arbitrary low order approximations and for self-synchronizing and synchronous stream ciphers as well.

Maurer [14] has proposed two local decoding algorithms for Reed-Muller codes, one for affine approximations ($r = 1$) and the other for approximations of an arbitrary order r. Both are feasible for large 2^n and essentially consist in majority-logic decoding based on appropriate subsets of orthogonal parity-checks for the ANF coefficients of a boolean function g of order at most r (the information bits). The first algorithm is based on the parity-checks involving three bits only, whereas the second one is based on decoding short Reed-Muller codes derived from the long one and then on making a majority-logic decision over all the short codes for every coefficient of g. The short codes are obtained by setting some of the input variables to zero. Maurer suggested that with high probability the first algorithm can work even if the correlation coefficient is much smaller than 1/2 and that the second one may find the best rth-order approximation with the correlation coefficient bigger than $1 - 2^{-r}$.

Another, information set decoding (e.g., see [3]) approach to the low order approximation problem is taken in [20]. For approximations of order at most r, the information sets suggested are Hamming spheres of radius r. For an approximation with the correlation coefficient c, the expected number of sphere samples to be examined to find with high probability an error-free one can be estimated as $(2/(1+c))^{\sum_{i=0}^{r}\binom{n}{i}}$, which is feasible only for relatively large c.

The main objective of this paper is to develop a fast procedure for finding low order approximations to large boolean functions that can be successful even if the correlation coefficient of the best approximation is very small (e.g., much smaller than $1 - 2^{-r}$ for an rth-order approximation). Our solution is based on appropriate parity-checks, but unlike [14], the decision (majority-logic rule or maximum posterior probability rule) is not made on the ANF coefficients of the approximation function (information bits), but on all the codeword bits involved in the parity-checks. This implies that the observed set of the codeword bits should be closed with respect to all the parity-checks used. The decision process is then repeated iteratively, each time recomputing all the parity-checks, which greatly increases the error-correction capability, i.e., enables one to successfully deal with much smaller correlation coefficients of the best approximation. To the same end, it is also important that the parity-checks be chosen with as few terms as possible. After the iterative algorithm is completed, the number of remaining errors, i.e., the Hamming distance to the best low order approximation is considerably reduced. This then enables us to apply a simple information set decoding technique to reconstruct the codeword corresponding to the best approximation, if the correlation coefficient is not too small to be detected. Finally, the coefficients in its ANF are then obtained by an appropriate linear transform.

It remains to explain how to construct the codewords of the underlying linear code and how to find the required parity-checks. For a boolean function f of n variables to be analyzed, take a linear feedback shift register (LFSR) of length $m \geq n$ with a primitive feedback polynomial and a fixed initial state and select any consecutive n LFSR stages to form a filter generator. Then for each boolean function g of n variables and of order at most r with the zero constant term in its ANF, form a filter generator with g as a filter function and produce a sequence of length N. In view of an old result from [10], it follows that every such sequence satisfies a linear recurrence determined by a binary polynomial h_r of degree $m_r = \sum_{i=1}^{r} \binom{m}{i}$, provided that $N > m_r$. The sequences are different and constitute a linear code with $k_r = \sum_{i=1}^{r} \binom{n}{i}$ information bits (i.e., the coefficients in the ANF of g). The parity-checks are then constructed from low weight polynomial multiples of h_r where the weight of a binary polynomial is defined as the number of its nonzero terms. Note that m greater than n can make finding the low weight and low degree polynomial multiples of h_r easier (preferably, h_r itself should have a low weight).

Then, produce a sequence of length N by the filter generator with the given boolean function f as a filter function. This sequence is regarded as a received codeword at the output of a binary symmetric channel with the noise probability $(1 - c)/2$ corresponding to the assumed correlation coefficient c. Since c is assumed to be positive, we have to run the decoding procedure twice: once for the received codeword and second time for its binary complement. The iterative probabilistic or majority-logic decoding algorithm with information set decoding then yields a linear recurring sequence satisfying h_r that corresponds to an approximation to f of order at most r with the correlation coefficient close to c or bigger, if it exists. A condition for the minimum c that can be detected is pointed out. The solution need not be unique, especially if $r > 1$. Interestingly, it thus turns out that the low order approximation problem for boolean functions can essentially be reduced to the problem of fast correlation attacks on LFSR's with appropriate feedback polynomials. For $r = 1$ the feedback polynomials are primitive, but for $r > 1$ they are not. The basic iterative probabilistic decoding algorithm for fast correlation attacks was introduced in [15], while a similar iterative majority-logic decoding algorithm was independently proposed in [27]. Both the algorithms have origins in iterative error-correction decoding procedures given in [5], [11], and [3]. In a number of follow-up papers, these algorithms have been modified and further analyzed, e.g., see [4], [1], [18], [19], [28], [8]. The important difference that greatly facilitates the success of the low order approximation procedure is that the feedback polynomial, h_r, can be chosen so as to maximize the number of parity-checks associated with parity-check polynomials of low weight and not too large a degree, and finding such parity-checks can be done in precomputation time.

The rest of the paper is organized as follows. A more detailed description of the background work from [14] and [20] is presented in Section 2. The representation of low order boolean functions by filter generators is explained in Section 3, whereas the relation between low order approximation of boolean functions and fast correlation attacks is investigated in Section 4. Significance and potential applications of the proposed method in the design and analysis of block and stream ciphers are discussed in Section 5.

2 Background Work

Maurer [14] has proposed two local decoding algorithms for Reed-Muller codes that are feasible for large 2^n, one for affine approximations ($r = 1$) and the other for approximations of an arbitrary order r. Both essentially consist in majority-logic decoding based on appropriate subsets of orthogonal parity-checks for the ANF coefficients of a boolean function of order at most r (the information bits). Regarding the affine approximations, note that every $(2^n, n+1, 2^{n-1})$ first-order Reed-Muller code can be reduced to a $(2^n - 1, n, 2^{n-1})$ code being the dual of a binary Hamming code, by deleting the information/codeword bit corresponding to the constant term of an affine function. This means that linear boolean functions correspond to codewords of the dual of a binary Hamming code, see [25]. Majority-logic decoding of such codes is based on 2^{n-1} orthogonal parity-checks for each information bit, where each parity-check involves three bits only. The algorithm proposed in [14] for decoding long first-order Reed-Muller codes is then the same except that it uses subsets of the parity-checks, for the decoding to be feasible for large 2^n. The best linear/affine approximation with the correlation coefficient bigger than 1/2 is guaranteed to be found by this algorithm if all the parity-checks are used. Maurer suggested that this is with high probability true even if the correlation coefficient is much smaller than 1/2.

However, for an arbitrary r, the choice of a small subset of the parity-checks to be used in majority-logic decoding is not as simple as for $r = 1$. An interesting solution given in [14] is based on decoding short Reed-Muller codes derived from the long one and then on making a majority-logic decision over all the short codes for every information bit. The short codes of length 2^l are obtained by setting $n - l$ input variables to zero. It is recommended in [14] to choose sufficiently many subsets of l variables to cover every information bit of the long code if l is large, and to use all $\binom{n}{l}$ of them if l is relatively small. It is suggested that such an algorithm may with high probability find the best rth-order approximation with the correlation coefficient bigger than $1-2^{-r}$. As opposed to the case $r = 1$, Maurer did not discuss the situation when the correlation coefficient is smaller than $1 - 2^{-r}$. While it is intuitively clear that the proposed algorithm can work, the conditions for success are not quite clear (e.g., the choice of l).

Another, information set decoding (e.g., see [3]) approach to the low order approximation problem is suggested in [20]. It is well-known [25] that the ANF coefficients of a boolean function of order at most r can be uniquely determined from its values in the Hamming sphere of radius r around the all-zero vector by a linear transform. It is observed in [20] that the same holds for the Hamming sphere of radius r around any input vector as a center, where the corresponding linear transform incorporates the boolean derivatives of the function with respect to the center vector. In coding terms, the sets of codeword bits corresponding to these Hamming spheres represent particular examples of the information sets (there are many others), and the main point of information set decoding is to look for error-free information sets. Each Hamming sphere thus gives a candidate low order approximation to a given boolean function, and for each candidate the correlation coefficient is estimated on a set of $O(1/c^2)$ arguments, for an assumed value c. A candidate function with the maximum magnitude of the correlation coefficient estimate is then picked as a low order approximation. If an approximation with the correlation coefficient c exists, then the expected number of sphere samples to be examined to find with high probability an error-free one can be approximated as $(2/(1+c))^{\sum_{i=0}^{r}\binom{n}{i}}$. The computational complexity is thus prohibitively high, so that the method may work only for very large c, given that n is moderately large and r is not very small.

3 Low Order Functions and Filter Generators

In this section, it is defined how to construct the codewords of the underlying linear code used for low order approximation and how to find the desired parity-checks. For a boolean function of n variables to be analyzed, take a linear feedback shift register (LFSR) of length $m \geq n$ with a primitive feedback polynomial h. Choose and fix an arbitrary nonzero initial state and select arbitrary consecutive n out of m LFSR stages to form a filter generator. Recall [21] that a binary filter generator is a keystream generator consisting of a single binary LFSR and a boolean function whose inputs are taken from some shift register stages to produce the output. Such a generator realizes a linear/nonlinear feedforward transform of an LFSR sequence. More precisely, let $x = (x(t))_{t=-m}^{\infty}$ be a binary maximum-length sequence of period $2^m - 1$ generated from the assumed initial state $(x(t))_{t=-m}^{-1}$, let $f(x_1, \ldots, x_n)$ be a boolean function of n, $n \leq m$, input variables, and let the first n LFSR stages define the inputs to the filter function. Then the output sequence $y = (y(t))_{t=0}^{\infty}$ of the corresponding filter generator is defined by $y(t) = f(x(t-1), \ldots, x(t-n))$, $t \geq 0$.

For any $r \geq 1$ (for low order approximations r/n should be small), define a collection $\mathcal{G}_r$ of 2^{k_r}, $k_r = \sum_{i=1}^{r}\binom{n}{i}$, filter generators with the same initial state by using all possible boolean functions g of n variables and of order at most r, where the constant term in the ANF of g is assumed to be equal to zero. For simplicity, the parameters n and m are dropped from the notation. Recall that the algebraic normal form (ANF) of g is defined as $g(x_1, \ldots, x_n) = \sum_S a_S \prod_{i \in S} x_i$ where the sum is over all index sets $S \subseteq \{1, \ldots, n\}$ of cardinality at most r, and the coefficients a_S are binary. The output sequences produced by $\mathcal{G}_r$ are periodic with a period equal to $2^m - 1$ or to a factor of $2^m - 1$ and are all different since g are different and all 2^n possible arguments of g are used to produce the output bits. Furthermore, the set, $\mathcal{S}_r$, of 2^{k_r} different output sequences produced by $\mathcal{G}_r$ is a binary vector space of dimension k_r, because the ANF uniquely represents g and every g can be expressed as a sum of product boolean functions, whose ANF contains a single product term. The corresponding generating sequences for $\mathcal{S}_r$ are the k_r sequences produced by all k_r possible product boolean functions of n variables and of order at most r. This means that the output sequence produced by any g can be expressed as a linear combination of these generating sequences where the coefficients are exactly the ANF coefficients of g (see [21]).

Moreover, due to a well-known result from [10], the sequences from $\mathcal{S}_r$ all satisfy a linear recurrence defined by an appropriate binary polynomial h_r of degree $m_r = \sum_{i=1}^{r} \binom{m}{i}$. More precisely, if α is a root of h in a splitting field GF(2^m), then the roots of h_r in GF(2^m) are exactly all the powers α^e where e is an integer with an m-bit long binary expansion that contains at least one and at most r ones. Accordingly, h_r is the least common multiple of the minimum binary polynomials of all such powers. It can be obtained by standard algebraic techniques or, simply, by using the Berlekamp-Massey algorithm [12] over the binary field. Recall that the Berlekamp-Massey algorithm yields the shortest LFSR that generates a given finite field sequence of a finite length (its feedback polynomial is called the minimum feedback polynomial of the sequence, and is unique if its length is at most one half of the sequence length). It is shown in [21] that the minimum feedback polynomial of every sequence in $\mathcal{S}_r$ produced by any product boolean function g of i adjacent variables, $1 \leq i \leq r$, necessarily contains as roots all the powers α^e such that the binary expansion of e contains exactly i ones. For each $1 \leq i \leq r$, one may then take exactly one product boolean function of the first i variables, and h_r is then the least common multiple of the minimum feedback polynomials of the corresponding r binary sequences produced by these r product functions. To determine the individual feedback polynomials uniquely, it suffices to take the first $2m_r$ bits of these sequences and to apply the Berlekamp-Massey algorithm. The least common multiple can then be found efficiently by the Euclidean division algorithm. Alternatively, one may as well apply the multisequence Berlekamp-Massey algorithm [2] to these r product sequences of length $2m_r$ and thus directly obtain h_r.

Consequently, $\mathcal{S}_r$ is a set of 2^{k_r} binary sequences which can be generated by an LFSR of length m_r and the feedback polynomial h_r from 2^{k_r} different initial states. Each sequence in $\mathcal{S}_r$ is then uniquely determined by any m_r consecutive bits, by the forward and backward linear recurrences. Consider now a set of truncated output sequences of length $N > m_r$ produced by $\mathcal{G}_r$ by taking the first N output bits only. Since the sequences are different, this set is clearly a binary (N, k_r) linear code, denoted as $\mathcal{C}_r^N$, whose dimension is exactly k_r. The code $\mathcal{C}_r^N$ can be regarded as a subcode of a truncated cyclic code with the parity-check polynomial h_r. This cyclic code is a generalization of a cyclic representation of $(2^m - 1, \sum_{i=1}^{r} \binom{m}{i}, 2^{m-r})$ Reed-Muller codes associated with boolean functions of m variables with the zero constant term in the ANF and with the codeword bit corresponding to the all-zero vector omitted, see [9]. If $m = n$, then $m_r = k_r$ and $\mathcal{C}_r^N$ is a truncated cyclic code itself. The desired parity-checks correspond to low weight polynomial multiples of h_r.

It is allowed that m can be greater than n in order to make easier finding the low weight polynomial multiples of h_r whose degree is relatively small or moderately large, so that the length N need not be too large. For example, for $r = 1$ the parity-check polynomial h_r coincides with the LFSR polynomial h. It is therefore preferable that h be a trinomial, which may not exist for $m = n$ but exists for $m > n$. Of course, obtaining trinomial or low weight primitive polynomials of degree m by exhaustive search is relatively easy if the factorization of $2^m - 1$ is known. One may develop special methods for finding low weight polynomials h_r for any $r \geq 1$ as well. Starting from any determined low weight polynomial multiple of h_r, other low weight polynomial multiples can then be produced by the squaring technique proposed in [15]. In general, finding low weight polynomial multiples of h_r of not too large a degree can be performed by systematic search based on computing the residues of the single term (power) polynomials modulo h_r. For higher degrees, one may use the meet-in-the-meedle technique [15] or algorithms for computing discrete logarithms in fields of characteristic two, as suggested in [27]. In any case, finding an appropriate (optimal) primitive polynomial h and low weight polynomial multiples of not too large a degree for the corresponding polynomial h_r can be done in precomputation time. As usual [15], [1], any determined low weight polynomial multiple of weight W actually defines a set of W parity-checks corresponding to its different phase shifts. The parity-checks should be tested for orthogonality in which case some of them may be discarded. If N is large enough, the same set of the parity-checks (except for a phase shift) is used for most the codeword bits, and near the ends the set is reduced appropriately.

As noted above, since the dimension of the code $\mathcal{C}_r^N$ is k_r if $N > m_r$, every codeword in $\mathcal{C}_r^N$ uniquely determines a sequence in $\mathcal{S}_r$ and, hence, a boolean function g of order at most r as well. In turn, every codeword is uniquely determined by any m_r consecutive bits or by any other information set. Therefore, the ANF coefficients of g can be obtained from any m_r consecutive bits in the corresponding codeword. More precisely, each out of k_r ANF coefficients of g can be expressed as a linear function of any m_r consecutive bits from the associated codeword. To find these linear functions, it suffices to take the first m_r codeword bits (as variables) and to form a system of linear equations in the unknown ANF coefficients by expressing the sequence of m_r codeword bits as a linear combination, with unknown coefficients, of the k_r sequences of length m_r produced by all k_r possible product boolean functions of n variables and of order at most r. The corresponding system of m_r linear equations in k_r unknowns has rank k_r and, hence, has a unique solution for the unknown ANF coefficients given the first m_r codeword bits. The system is sparse and can be easily solved by standard techniques even if k_r and m_r are very large. This is executed in the precomputation time and as a result one thus obtains and stores a binary $k_r \times m_r$ matrix $\mathbf{A}_r$ defining a linear transform for the unknown ANF coefficients of g in terms of the first m_r bits of a given codeword in $\mathcal{C}_r^N$.

4 Low Order Approximations and Fast Correlation Attacks

In the previous section, a filter generator based representation of low order boolean functions as codewords in an appropriate binary linear code of essentially cyclic structure was defined. In this section, this representation is used to propose a solution to the low order approximation problem for large boolean functions in terms of iterative probabilistic or majority-logic decoding algorithms used in fast correlation attacks on certain stream ciphers. Assume that a boolean function f of n variables is given where n may be large. More precisely, we assume that f can be evaluated on a desired set of arguments of cardinality much smaller than 2^n.

Accordingly, as described in the previous section, choose an LFSR with an appropriate primitive feedback polynomial h of degree $m \geq n$, select and fix the LFSR initial state, and then, in terms of filter generators, define a binary (N, k_r) linear code $\mathcal{C}_r^N$, where $k_r = \sum_{i=1}^{r} \binom{n}{i}$ and $N > m_r$, $m_r = \sum_{i=1}^{r} \binom{m}{i}$. Its codewords satisfy a binary polynomial h_r of degree m_r and uniquely represent boolean functions g of n variables and of order at most r. Then compute a binary $k_r \times m_r$ matrix $\mathbf{A}_r$ defining a linear transform for the unknown ANF coefficients of g in terms of the first m_r bits of a given codeword in $\mathcal{C}_r^N$. The main precomputational effort is to determine a set, Λ_r, of low weight parity-check polynomials whose degrees should be as small as possible. Given n, a degree m and a primitive polynomial h should be optimized accordingly.

Then form a filter generator from the same LFSR by using the given function f as a filter function and produce a sequence of length N. This sequence is regarded as a received codeword for $\mathcal{C}_r^N$ at the output of a binary symmetric channel with the noise probability $p = (1 - c)/2$, corresponding to the assumed correlation coefficient c. So, the crucial point of our approach is to observe the values of f for the argument values corresponding to successive states of an LFSR with an appropriate primitive feedback polynomial. The objective of low order approximation of f is to find a boolean function g of order at most r such that the absolute value of the correlation coefficient $c(f, g)$ is c or larger, if such g exists. In coding terms, this problem then reduces to the minimum distance decoding of $\mathcal{C}_r^N$, i.e., to finding a codeword at the minimum Hamming distance (or close) to the received codeword. Since c is assumed to be positive, we have to run the decoding procedure twice: once for the received codeword and second time for its binary complement. Alternatively, one may incorporate the polynomial $1 + x$ as a factor of h_r to include the boolean functions g with the nonzero constant term in the ANF (then k_r is increased by one). As the codewords of $\mathcal{C}_r^N$ satisfy the linear recurrence defined by h_r, the minimum distance decoding of this code is then essentially similar to the problem of the LFSR initial state reconstruction from a noisy LFSR sequence which arises in correlation attacks [23] on certain stream ciphers based on memoryless combiners. In this case, the LFSR feedback polynomial is h_r, which is primitive only if $r = 1$. Since the number, 2^{k_r}, of possible LFSR initial states (i.e., the number of low order approximations g) is very large, only fast decoding procedures are of interest, which is essentially the situation dealt with in fast correlation attacks.

The solution is in iterative probabilistic or majority-logic decoding procedures with information set decoding. The basic iterative probabilistic decoding algorithm for fast correlation attacks was introduced in [15], while a similar iterative majority-logic decoding algorithm was independently proposed in [27]. Both the algorithms have origins in iterative error-correction decoding procedures given in [5], [11], and [3]. In a number of follow-up papers, these algorithms have been modified and further analyzed, e.g., see [4], [1], [18], [19], [28], [8]. The unknown codeword is assumed to have the form $\mathbf{z} + \mathbf{e}$, where $\mathbf{z} = (z_i)_{i=1}^N$ is the received codeword produced by f and $\mathbf{e} = (e_i)_{i=1}^N$ is the unknown error vector to be reconstructed. Iterative error-correction algorithms consist in making iterative decisions on all the bits in $\mathbf{e}$ based on the parity-check values being updated after every decision on $\mathbf{e}$. In majority-logic error-correction, the majority-logic decision rule is applied based on the number of satisfied (zero valued) parity-checks. The assumed value of the correlation coefficient c is not used, and the algorithm works well if c is not too small and, especially, if the parity-checks have the same weight. For smaller values of c and parity-checks of different weights, one should apply probabilistic error-correction, where the statistically optimal, maximum posterior probability decision rule is employed for each bit of $\mathbf{e}$ which minimizes the symbol error-rate in the first iteration step. A probabilistic model is used in which $\mathbf{e}$ is assumed to be a sequence of independent binary random variables (bits) in each iteration step. Initially, the error bits are assumed to be identically distributed with $\Pr\{e_i = 1\} = p = (1-c)/2$. Let in each iteration step, p_i and $\hat{p}_i$ denote the prior and posterior probabilities that $e_i = 1$, respectively, and let the corresponding correlation coefficient be defined as $c_i = 1 - 2p_i$. Let $\Lambda_{r,i}$ denote the set of the parity-checks used for e_i and let $s(\lambda)$ denote the binary value of a parity-check $\lambda \in \Lambda_{r,i}$. Let $c(\lambda)$ be the correlation coefficient associated with $\lambda \in \Lambda_{r,i}$ which is defined as the product of the correlation coefficients c_j for all the error bits e_j, $j \neq i$, involved in λ (since the error bits are assumed to be independent, $c(\lambda)$ is exactly the correlation coefficient of their modulo 2 sum [5]). If the parity-checks in $\Lambda_{r,i}$ are orthogonal, then their random values are independent when conditioned on the value of e_i, so that the posterior probability $\hat{p}_i$ is then for each $1 \leq i \leq N$ determined by

$$\frac{\hat{p}_i}{1-\hat{p}_i} = \frac{p_i}{1-p_i} \prod_{\lambda \in \Lambda_{r,i}} \left(\frac{1-c(\lambda)}{1+c(\lambda)} \right)^{1-2s(\lambda)} . \tag{2}$$

The same expression may be used for nonorthogonal parity-checks as well.

The main point of the iteration process is then to use the posterior probabilities computed in the current step as the prior probabilities for the next step. Equivalently (for orthogonal parity-checks [28], [18]), one may perform error-correction in each iteration step by using the maximum posterior probability decision rule: if $\hat{p}_i > 0.5$, then e_i is set to 1, the observed bit z_i is complemented, and $\hat{p}_i$ is set to $1 - \hat{p}_i$. With error-correction in each step, the experiments [15], [18], [19], [8] show that the posterior probabilities relatively quickly converge to the zero value for most positions i on a codeword length. This fact is a consequence of the fixed points of the mapping defined by (2) and does not necessarily mean that all or most the errors are thus corrected. But, hopefully, the number of errors (i.e., the Hamming distance to the best low order approximation) is reduced. One may then reset all the error probabilities to the initial value p [15] and repeat the iteration process for several times until all or most the errors are corrected. Experiments [8] show that some improvement is achieved with a fast resetting algorithm where resetting is performed according to the cumulative number of error-corrections, before the convergence point is reached. Alternatively, one may also use a modified equation (2) so that the first product term is always equal to $p/(1-p)$ or one, see [5], [28].

Let c_* denote the correlation coefficient $c(f, g)$ for the best low order approximation g to f. Experimental evidence reveals that most the errors are corrected if c_* is greater than an upper threshold value and if the assumed c is smaller than and relatively close to c_*. On the other hand, if c_* is smaller than or equal to a lower threshold value, then the number of errors can not be reduced, which means that the best low order approximation can not be found by using the assumed set of parity-checks. Between the two thresholds, the number of errors may be reduced, but remains relatively high on the average. According to a characterization of the lower threshold value obtained in [19], a necessary condition for a successful iterative error-correction can for relatively small c_* be approximated as

$$\sum_w \overline{M}_w c_*^{w-1} > 1 \qquad (3)$$

where $\overline{M}_w$ denotes the average number of the parity-checks of weight $w+1$ in $\Lambda_{r,i}$ over all positions $1 \leq i \leq N$. Experiments show that this condition is close to being sufficient as well. If c_* is smaller than the threshold implicit in (3), then the number of parity-checks must be increased. The significant gain obtained by iterative error-correction as compared with single-step error-correction can be seen in the case where all the parity-checks have the same weight (e.g., $w = 2$, see [14] for $r = 1$). Then the condition (3) becomes $\overline{M}_w c_*^{w-1} > 1$, whereas for single-step error-correction for any m_r consecutive codeword bits the condition for success can be expressed as $m_r \overline{M}_w c_*^{2w} > 1$. So, by iterative error-correction algorithms one may find low order approximations with very small correlation coefficients, much smaller than $1 - 2^{-r}$, if they exist.

After a number of iteration rounds, the iterative error-correction is completed, and an estimate $\hat{\mathbf{z}}$ of the closest codeword is obtained. In general, it may contain a number of residual errors, which are then corrected by the information set decoding procedure. One may use simple information sets of m_r consecutive bits in $\hat{\mathbf{z}}$ ($N - m_r + 1$ of them) in search of an error-free one. For each assumed information set one then computes the remaining codeword bits by the forward and backward linear recurrence, and then the correlation coefficient between each such candidate codeword and the received one is estimated by using $O(1/c^2)$ codeword bits. Unlike [20], this can be done without computing the ANF coefficients of a low order boolean function g corresponding to the assumed information set. A candidate codeword is accepted if the computed correlation coefficient estimate is consistent with the assumed value c or bigger. If an accepted codeword is found, then the ANF coefficients of the corresponding low order approximation g are computed from the first m_r codeword bits by the matrix $\mathbf{A}_r$.

We have thus shown that the problem of finding a low order approximation to a large boolean function f can be solved by iterative probabilistic decoding algorithms combined with information set decoding both applied to a sequence of values of f for the argument values taken from successive states of an LFSR with an appropriate primitive feedback polynomial, h. However, there is a number of important differences from standard fast correlation attacks. The main advantage is that the feedback polynomial, h_r, of the underlying LFSR can be chosen in precomputation time so as to optimize the success of iterative probabilistic decoding. If $r = 1$, then $h_r = h$ is a primitive polynomial and the situation is very much similar to the one in fast correlation attacks on memoryless combiners. More precisely, this is the case if the best affine approximation to f is unique and if its correlation coefficient, c_*, to f is 'considerably' bigger than for other affine functions. Since the number, n, of input variables of f is large, this is very likely to be true if c_* is much bigger than $2^{-n/2}$. If there exists a number of affine functions with mutually close correlation coefficients to f much bigger than $2^{-n/2}$ (the case of multiple affine/linear approximations), then the situation is more similar to the one in fast correlation attacks on nonlinear filter generators, see [4]. The problem in this case is that different affine functions are mutually uncorrelated, which may confuse the iterative error-correction algorithms. On the other hand, unlike [4], [24], we are here satisfied with any found affine approximation, not all of them. The problem may be resolved by using more complicated information sets, e.g., chosen from a number of the most significant probabilities (the smallest ones after the complementation) in the error probability vector after one or just a few iteration steps.

If $r > 1$, then h_r is not a primitive polynomial and its degree m_r is large if n is large. Fortunately, the influence of large m_r on the success of iterative error-correction is insignificant, see (3). Only the final, information set decoding stage is slightly affected. Also, the precomputational effort to find the low weight parity-checks and to compute the matrix $\mathbf{A}_r$ is increased. In addition, for $r > 1$, due to the minimum distance property of rth-order boolean functions, it should be expected that the best rth-order approximation to f with a correlation coefficient much bigger than $2^{-n/2}$, if it exists, is essentially not unique. Namely, for any rth-order function with the correlation coefficient c_* to f, it is very likely that there exist a number of rth-order functions with the correlation coefficients to f of the order of $(1 - 2^{-(r-1)})\,c_*$, which may be considered 'close' to c_*. However, due to the same effect, these multiple rth-order approximations are mutually correlated with the correlation coefficients close to $1 - 2^{-(r-1)}$, which is less confusing for the iterative error-correction algorithms.

There is another potential advantage to be used for any $r \geq 1$. For any chosen primitive polynomial h, one may use different LFSR initial states to form a set of filter generators giving rise to a set of the corresponding codes to which iterative probabilistic decoding algorithms can be applied simultaneously. Moreover, one may also deal with different polynomials h. Suppose that none of the codeword estimates has yielded the desired low order approximation. It is now possible to combine individual codeword estimates by an appropriate procedure, e.g., by a majority-logic decision on the corresponding ANF coefficients obtained by applying the matrix $\mathbf{A}_r$ to the first m_r bits of each of the codeword estimates. This can be useful especially in the case of multiple low order approximations.

5 Conclusions

A solution to a difficult, low order approximation problem for large boolean functions is developed by establishing a connection between binary filter generators and iterative error-correction algorithms used in fast correlation attacks on certain stream ciphers. A boolean function f to be approximated has to be evaluated on a set of arguments corresponding to successive states of an LFSR with an appropriate primitive feedback polynomial. The proposed procedure is fast and can with high probability find low order approximations with very small correlation coefficients to f, if such approximations exist. The correlation coefficient can be much smaller than $1 - 2^{-r}$, which is the lower bound for the best rth-order approximation to be unique necessarily. Its magnitude is practically limited only by the computational power available.

The proposed method may have wide cryptographic applications. First, if f is a secret key dependent decryption function, then in the chosen-ciphertext scenario, the method can be used for approximate decryption of self-synchronizing stream ciphers [14] or block ciphers [20], provided the correlation coefficient of the found low order approximation is big enough with respect to the plaintext redundancy. More importantly, the method can generally be used for the analysis of any large boolean functions in various cryptographic applications. In this case, f is known and can be evaluated on an arbitrary set of arguments. In block ciphers, f can be an encryption boolean function of both the secret key and plaintext input variables. Low order approximations even with very small correlation coefficients may then be used for the secret key reconstruction from a sufficient number of known (possibly chosen) plaintext-ciphertext pairs, as is demonstrated in [13] for linear approximations. Alternatively, apart from the black-box approach, in a structure-based approach, one may find low order approximations to large boolean functions employed in one-round functions of product block ciphers and then combine them to obtain an overall approximation for the whole cipher, see [13] for $r = 1$. Of course, rth-order boolean functions are not closed under composition for $r > 1$, but any resulting approximation, of not necessarily low order, may be a basis for the secret key reconstruction as long as the number of nonzero terms in its ANF is not too large.

In binary self-synchronizing stream ciphers, low order approximations to the feedback function, as a boolean function of both the secret key and ciphertext, can also be used for the secret key reconstruction from known or chosen ciphertext. In binary synchronous stream ciphers, every keystream bit is a boolean function of the secret key and possibly of known message key as well. Low order approximations to such boolean functions, for a suitable set of keystream bits, can be a basis for the secret key reconstruction from known keystream sequence and known or chosen message key. Another interesting objective would be to approximate every keystream bit as a low order boolean function of a number (close to the memory size of the keystream generator) of previous keystream bits, where the secret key is fixed and unknown. The resulting linear [7] (for $r = 1$) or nonlinear models of the keystream generator may then be used for the plaintext reconstruction from known ciphertext or, even, for the secret key reconstruction as well. In a structure-based approach, one may determine and use linear approximations to the next-state and output boolean functions to obtain linear sequential circuit approximations of the whole keystream generator [6], [7], which in turn can be exploited for finding linear models and for correlation attacks as well.

References

1. V. Chepyzhov and B. Smeets, "On a fast correlation attack on stream ciphers," Advances in Cryptology – EUROCRYPT '91, *Lecture Notes in Computer Science*, vol. 547, D. W. Davies ed., Springer-Verlag, pp. 176-185, 1991.
2. C. Ding, G. Xiao, and W. Shan, *The Stability Theory of Stream Ciphers. Lecture Notes in Computer Science*, vol. 561, Springer-Verlag, 1991.
3. G. C. Clark, Jr. and J. B. Cain, *Error-Correcting Coding for Digital Communications.* New York: Plenum Press, 1982.
4. R. Forré, "A fast correlation attack on nonlinearly feedforward filtered shift-register sequences," Advances in Cryptology – EUROCRYPT '89, *Lecture Notes in Computer Science*, vol. 434, J.-J. Quisquater and J. Vandewalle eds., Springer-Verlag, pp. 586-595, 1990.
5. R. G. Gallager, "Low-density parity-check codes," *IRE Trans. Inform. Theory*, vol. IT-8, pp. 21-28, Jan. 1962.
6. J. Dj. Golić, "Correlation via linear sequential circuit approximation of combiners with memory," Advances in Cryptology – EUROCRYPT '92, *Lecture Notes in Computer Science*, vol. 658, R. A. Rueppel ed., Springer-Verlag, pp. 113-123, 1993.
7. J. Dj. Golić, "Linear cryptanalysis of stream ciphers," Fast Software Encryption – Leuven '94, *Lecture Notes in Computer Science*, vol. 1008, B. Preneel ed., Springer-Verlag, pp. 154-169, 1995.
8. J. Dj. Golić, M. Salmasizadeh, A. Clark, A. Khodkar, and E. Dawson, "Discrete optimisation and fast correlation attacks," Cryptographic Policy and Algorithms – Brisbane '95, *Lecture Notes in Computer Science*, vol. 1029, E. Dawson and J. Golić eds., Springer-Verlag, pp. 186-200, 1996.
9. T. Kasami, S. Lin, and W. W. Peterson, "New generalizations of the Reed-Muller codes, part I: primitive codes," *IEEE Trans. Inform. Theory*, vol. IT-14, pp. 189-199, Mar. 1968.
10. E. L. Key, "An analysis of the structure and complexity of nonlinear binary sequence generators," *IEEE Trans. Inform. Theory*, vol. IT-22, pp. 732-736, Nov. 1976.
11. J. L. Massey, *Threshold Decoding.* Cambridge, MA: MIT Press, 1963.

12. J. L. Massey, "Shift-register synthesis and BCH decoding," *IEEE Trans. Inform. Theory*, vol. IT-15, pp. 122-127, Jan. 1969.
13. M. Matsui, "Linear cryptanalysis method for DES cipher," Advances in Cryptology – EUROCRYPT '93, *Lecture Notes in Computer Science*, vol. 765, T. Helleseth ed., Springer-Verlag, pp. 386-397, 1994.
14. U. M. Maurer, "New approaches to the design of self-synchronizing stream ciphers," Advances in Cryptology – EUROCRYPT '91, *Lecture Notes in Computer Science*, vol. 547, D. W. Davies ed., Springer-Verlag, pp. 458-471, 1991.
15. W. Meier and O. Staffelbach, "Fast correlation attacks on certain stream ciphers," *Journal of Cryptology*, vol. 1(3), pp. 159-176, 1989.
16. W. Meier and O. Staffelbach, "Nonlinearity criteria for cryptographic functions," Advances in Cryptology – EUROCRYPT '89, *Lecture Notes in Computer Science*, vol. 434, J.-J. Quisquater and J. Vandewalle eds., Springer-Verlag, pp. 549-562, 1990.
17. W. Meier and O. Staffelbach, "Correlation properties of combiners with memory in stream ciphers," *Journal of Cryptology*, vol. 5(1), pp. 67-86, 1992.
18. M. J. Mihaljević and J. Dj. Golić, "A comparison of cryptanalytic principles based on iterative error-correction," Advances in Cryptology – EUROCRYPT '91, *Lecture Notes in Computer Science*, vol. 547, D. W. Davies ed., Springer-Verlag, pp. 527-531, 1991.
19. M. J. Mihaljević and J. Dj. Golić, "Convergence of a Bayesian iterative error-correction procedure on a noisy shift register sequence," Advances in Cryptology – EUROCRYPT '92, *Lecture Notes in Computer Science*, vol. 658, R. A. Rueppel ed., Springer-Verlag, pp. 124-137, 1993.
20. W. Millan, "Low order approximation of cipher functions," Cryptographic Policy and Algorithms – Brisbane '95, *Lecture Notes in Computer Science*, vol. 1029, E. Dawson and J. Golić eds., Springer-Verlag, pp. 144-155, 1996.
21. R. A. Rueppel, *Analysis and Design of Stream Ciphers.* Berlin: Springer-Verlag, 1986.
22. T. Siegenthaler, "Correlation immunity of nonlinear combining functions for cryptographic applications," *IEEE Trans. Inform. Theory*, vol. IT-30, pp. 776-780, Sept. 1984.
23. T. Siegenthaler, "Decrypting a class of stream ciphers using ciphertext only," *IEEE Trans. Comput.*, vol. C-34, pp. 81-85, Jan. 1985.
24. T. Siegenthaler, "Cryptanalyst's representation of nonlinearly filtered ML-sequences," Advances in Cryptology – EUROCRYPT '85, *Lecture Notes in Computer Science*, vol. 219, F. Pichler ed., Springer-Verlag, pp. 103-110, 1986.
25. F. J. Williams and N. J. Sloane, *The Theory of Error-Correcting Codes.* Amsterdam: North-Holland, 1988.
26. G. Z. Xiao and J. L. Massey, "A spectral characterization of correlation-immune combining functions," *IEEE Trans. Inform. Theory*, vol. IT-34, pp. 569-571, May 1988.
27. K. Zeng and M. Huang, "On the linear syndrome method in cryptanalysis," Advances in Cryptology – CRYPTO '88, *Lecture Notes in Computer Science*, vol. 403, S. Goldwasser ed., Springer-Verlag, pp. 469-478, 1990.
28. M. V. Živković, "On two probabilistic decoding algorithms for binary linear codes," *IEEE Trans. Inform. Theory*, vol. IT-37, pp. 1707-1716, Nov. 1991.

Construction of *t*-Resilient Functions over a Finite Alphabet

Paul Camion * and Anne Canteaut **

INRIA Projet Codes
Domaine de Voluceau
78153 Le Chesnay Cedex, FRANCE
email: {Paul.Camion, Anne.Canteaut}@inria.fr

Abstract. We extend the notions of correlation-immune functions and resilient functions to functions over any finite alphabet endowed with the structure of an Abelian group. Thus we generalize the results of Gopalakrishnan and Stinson as we give an orthogonal array characterization and a Fourier transform characterization for resilient functions over any finite alphabet. This leads to a generalization of some related cryptographic objects as perfect local randomizers. It also enables us to construct new resilient functions by composition of resilient functions of smaller order.

1 Introduction

Resilient functions were introduced independently by Chor *et al.* [4] and Bennett, Brassard and Robert [1] and were originally applied respectively to the generation of random strings in presence of faulty processors and to key distribution especially for quantum cryptography. Several other applications afterwards emerged and the theory of resilient functions (or the equivalent combinatorial structure of orthogonal arrays) is now almost omnipresent in cryptography.

These functions are first of all used for designing running-keys for stream ciphers; in the common case, the running-key generator is composed of several linear feedback shift registers combined by a non-linear function f; f should then be a correlation-immune function in order to resist Siegenthaler's correlation attack [12]. A resilient function is usually chosen. The output digits are then uniformly distributed. In a more general view, Maurer and Massey [9] showed that an additive stream cipher can be provably-secure under the restriction that the number of plaintext digits that the enemy can obtain is limited: the running-key generator thus should be a perfect local randomizer, what is equivalent to the structure of an orthogonal array.

A second application consists in designing "conventional" cryptographic primitives, *i.e.* primitives based on a network with some gates. Such a network

* Centre National de la Recherche Scientifique

** Grant-holder from the DRET, also with École Nationale Supérieure de Techniques Avancées, 32 boulevard Victor, F-75015 Paris.

Ueli Maurer (Ed.): EUROCRYPT '96 Proceedings, LNCS 1070

contains both confusion boxes for hiding any structure and diffusion boxes for merging several inputs. Schnorr and Vaudenay [11] recommend that the diffusion boxes should be functions realizing perfect diffusion in order to avoid some cryptanalysis, especially collision attacks. These functions are called multipermutations and they can be deduced from perfect local randomizers of maximal order. These objects are also used in threshold schemes for secret sharing.

In this paper we extend the notions of correlation-immune functions and resilient functions to functions over any finite alphabet endowed with an Abelian group structure. We generalize the characterizations of q-ary resilient functions given by Gopalakrishnan and Stinson [6]: we give in section 2 an orthogonal array characterization and in section 3 a characterization by means of characters (similar to a Fourier transform characterization). Section 4 applies this generalization to perfect local randomizers and it establishes the link with coding theory. These generalizations also enable us to construct new resilient functions by composition of resilient functions of smaller order. This construction can immediately be applied to the combination of linear feedback shift registers.

2 Correlation immune functions and orthogonal arrays

Let $\mathcal{F}$ denote a finite alphabet with q elements ($q \geq 2$). Let $f : \mathcal{F}^n \to \mathcal{F}^\ell$ be a function and let $\{X_1, X_2, ..., X_n\}$ be a set of random input variables assuming values from $\mathcal{F}$ with independent equiprobable distributions (*i.e.* every input vector occurs with probability $\frac{1}{q^n}$).

The function f may satisfy the following properties:

- f is *balanced* if each possible output vector occurs with equal probability $\frac{1}{q^\ell}$.
- f is *correlation-immune with respect to the subset* $T \subset \{1, 2, \ldots, n\}$ if the probability distribution of the output vector is unaltered when $\{X_i, i \in T\}$ is fixed and $\{X_i, i \notin T\}$ is a set of independent equiprobable random variables.
- f is *t-th order correlation-immune* if for every T of cardinality at most t, f is correlation-immune with respect to T.
- f is *t-resilient* if f is t-th order correlation-immune and balanced.

Correlation-immune functions are closely related to the combinatorial structures introduced by Rao as orthogonal arrays [10].

Definition 1. An orthogonal array A of size m, n constraints, strength t and index λ over the alphabet $\mathcal{F}$ (or with q levels) is an $m \times n$ array of which rows are the vectors from a subset M of $\mathcal{F}^n$ such that $|M| = m$ which has the property that in any subset of t columns of A, each of the q^t vectors of $\mathcal{F}^t$ appears exactly λ times as a row. Such an array is denoted by (m, n, q, t). Clearly $m = \lambda q^t$.

In [3] it was observed that the characterization by Xiao and Massey [15] of a t-th order correlation immune function $f : \{0,1\}^n \to \{0,1\}$ is equivalent to the following property: the array of which rows are the vectors of $f^{-1}(1)$ is an orthogonal array of strength t. In [6] K. Gopalakrishnan and D.R. Stinson show directly that $f : GF(q)^n \to GF(q)^\ell$ is t-th order correlation immune if and only if $\forall y \in GF(q)^\ell$, $f^{-1}(y)$ consists in the rows of an orthogonal array A_y of strength t.

In fact characterizing the t-th order correlation immune functions in terms of orthogonal arrays is merely translating the probability definition into an enumeration definition. Then this characterization holds for any finite alphabet $\mathcal{F}$. We sum up what is needed as follows:

Proposition 2. *If the independent equiprobable random variables $X_1, \ldots, X_n$ are defined on a finite alphabet $\mathcal{F}$, then $f(X_1, \ldots, X_n)$, which has its values in a finite set E, is a t-order correlation immune function with respect to the alphabet $\mathcal{F}$ if and only if $\forall y \in E$, $f^{-1}(y)$ consists in the rows of an orthogonal array of strength t over $\mathcal{F}$.*

Additionally, f is t-resilient if

$$\forall y, y' \in E, |f^{-1}(y)| = |f^{-1}(y')|$$

3 Characterization by means of characters

In [6] K. Gopalakrishnan and D.R. Stinson give a characterization of correlation immune functions in terms of Fourier transform when the alphabet $\mathcal{F}$ is $GF(q)$. We here give statements which are valid for any finite alphabet $\mathcal{F}$ of order q, $q \geq 2$ endowed with the structure of an Abelian group.

We know that the homomorphisms from the Abelian group $\mathcal{F}$ into the multiplicative group of $\mathbf{C}$ form an Abelian group $\mathcal{F}'$, called the characters group, which is isomorphic with $\mathcal{F}$. For $x \in \mathcal{F}$ and $y \in \mathcal{F}'$ we denote by $< x, y >$ the complex image of x under the character y.

For example if $\mathcal{F}$ is the additive group $(GF(q), +)$ of the Galois field $GF(q)$ where $q = p^s$, p a prime, then $< x, y >= \theta^{Tr_{GF(q)/GF(p)}(xy)}$ where θ is a primitive p-th root of unity in $\mathbf{C}$.

If $\mathcal{F}$ is the additive group $(\mathbf{Z}_q, +)$, *i.e.* a cyclic group of order q, then $< x, y >= \theta^{xy}$ where θ is a primitive q-th root of unity in $\mathbf{C}$ and where the product xy is performed in the ring $\mathbf{Z}_q$. We will need the following classical lemma:

Lemma 3. *Let F and G be two Abelian groups with respective characters groups F' and G'. Then the characters group of $H = F \times G$ is $F' \times G'$.*
For $h = (f, g) \in F \times G$ and $h' = (f', g') \in F' \times G'$, we have $< h, h' >=< f, f' >< g, g' >$.

We now show how the Fourier transform characterization of K. Gopalakrishnan and D.R. Stinson can be stated for a general Abelian group and is then a straightforward corollary of theorem 4.4 of Delsarte ([5] page 43).

Let $\mathcal{F}$ be an Abelian group. The n-th Cartesian power $G = \mathcal{F}^n$ is then an Abelian group in its turn. The Hamming weight of an element x of G is the number $w_H(x)$ of components of x in $\mathcal{F}$ which are distinct from zero. Theorem 4.4 of Delsarte can be written as follows.

Theorem 4. *The array consisting of a set $M \subset G$ of λq^t rows is orthogonal with n constraints, q levels, strength t and index λ if and only if*

$$\forall y \in G', 1 \leq w_H(y) \leq t, \sum_{x \in M} < x, y >= 0$$

We now deduce a general characterization of correlation immune functions in terms of Fourier transform.

Theorem 5. *The function $f : \mathcal{F}^n \to \mathcal{F}^\ell$ is t-th order correlation immune if and only if:*

$$\forall v \in \mathcal{F}^\ell, \forall u \in \mathcal{F}^n, 1 \leq w_H(u) \leq t, \sum_{x \in \mathcal{F}^n} < x, u >< f(x), v >= 0$$

Proof. This condition is sufficient: we write $\hat{a}_{y,u}$ for $\sum_{x \in f^{-1}(y)} < x, u >$, with the convention $\hat{a}_{y,u} = 0$ when $f^{-1}(y) = \emptyset$.
Then the above relations can be written as:

$$\forall v \in \mathcal{F}^\ell, \forall u \in \mathcal{F}^n, 1 \leq w_H(u) \leq t, \sum_{y \in \mathcal{F}^\ell} \hat{a}_{y,u} < y, v >= 0$$

Since the matrix of group characters of the Abelian group $\mathcal{F}^\ell$ is invertible then we have: $\forall u \in \mathcal{F}^n, 1 \leq w_H(u) \leq t, \hat{a}_{y,u} = 0$.
Then Theorem 4 applies: $\forall y \in \mathcal{F}^\ell$, $f^{-1}(y)$ is a $(|f^{-1}(y)|, n, q, t)$ orthogonal array over $\mathcal{F}$.
The converse also results from Theorem 4.

4 Perfect local randomizers over any finite alphabet

As pointed out by Maurer and Massey [9] one of the most important cryptographic applications of orthogonal arrays consists in designing running-key generators for additive stream ciphers. The problem is then to transform a k-component secret sequence into a longer one of n components which will be added to the plaintext. Since such a running-key can obviously not be completely random, the associate stream cipher can not be provably secure. However the running-key generator can be designed such that if the k input components are uniformly random, then any subset of t or less components of the output sequence is a set of uniformly random digits. Such a generator is called a (k, n) *perfect local randomizer of order t*. The use of a perfect local randomizer then leads to a provably-secure stream cipher under the assumption that the enemy is able to obtain only a limited number of plaintext digits.

This concept exactly corresponds to the combinatorial structure of orthogonal arrays. Furthermore Massey showed in [8] that it can be relied, even in non-linear case, to the dual distance of a code, *i.e.* the smallest positive weight of the MacWilliams' transform of the distance distribution of the code, as defined by Delsarte [5].

We can now generalize the concept of perfect local randomizer over any finite alphabet $\mathcal{F}$ of size q since Delsarte proved the previous property about the dual distance for a code over a finite alphabet endowed with the structure of an Abelian group.

Proposition 6. *An injective function $f : \mathcal{F}^k \to \mathcal{F}^n$, where $k < n$, is a (k,n) perfect local randomizer of order t*
if and only if the $q^k \times n$ array whose rows are the vectors of $f(\mathcal{F}^k)$ is a (q^k, n, q, t) orthogonal array
if and only if f is the encoder for an (n,k) systematic code $\mathcal{C}$ over $\mathcal{F}$ (not necessarily linear) with dual distance $d^\perp < t$.
$d^\perp$ is here the smallest index $i > 0$ such that $b_i > 0$ where $(b_0, \ldots, b_n)$ is given by the generalized MacWilliams' identity :

$$\sum_{i=0}^{n} b_i X^{n-i} Y^i = H_{\mathcal{C}}^{\perp}(X,Y) = \frac{1}{|\mathcal{C}|} H_{\mathcal{C}}(X+qY, X-Y)$$

if $H_{\mathcal{C}}(X,Y) = \sum_{i=0}^{n} a_i X^{n-i} Y^i$ is the Hamming-weight enumerator of $\mathcal{C}$.

[9] and [2] give some bounds stemming from coding theory on the order of binary (k,n) perfect local randomizers. But we can now wonder whether, for fixed k and n, there exists (k,n) perfect local randomizers over some other alphabets whose order exceeds these bounds. In the following example, we use a construction suggested in [14] and we obtain $(2,4)$ perfect local randomizers of order 2 over some cyclic groups whereas they do not exist in binary case.

Example 1. Let $\mathcal{F}$ be the cyclic group $(\mathbf{Z}_q, +)$ and $\mathcal{A}$ be the orthogonal array whose rows are the 4-tuples $(x_1, x_2, x_1 + ax_2, x_1 + bx_2)$ where $a, b \in \mathbf{Z}_q$.
Theorem 4 says that $\mathcal{A}$ is an orthogonal array of strength t over $\mathbf{Z}_q$ if and only if its dual in the characters group contains no element of Hamming weight less than or equal to t.
In this case it means that

$$\forall x \in \mathcal{A}, \forall y, 1 \le w_H(y) \le t, \sum_{i=1}^{n} x_i y_i \neq 0$$

where the product $x_i y_i$ is performed in the ring $\mathbf{Z}_q$, because $< x, y >= \theta^{xy}$ where θ is a primitive q-th root of unity.
If we write this condition for all y of weight 2, we clearly obtain, as a corollary of Theorem 4, that $\mathcal{A}$ is an orthogonal array of strength 2 if and only if a, b and $(a-b)$ are not zero divisors.
For instance the array formed by the 4-tuples $(x_1, x_2, x_1 + 4x_2, x_1 + 11x_2)$ is an orthogonal array of strength 2 over $\mathbf{Z}_{15}$.
Then, as pointed out in [14], $\mathcal{A}$ cannot be an orthogonal array of strength 2 when q is even.

Perfect local randomizers of maximal order can also be used for designing conventional cryptographic primitives because they realize perfect diffusion. Schnorr and Vaudenay [11] formalized this idea through the equivalent concept of multipermutation:

Definition 7. A (r, n) multipermutation over a finite alphabet $\mathcal{F}$ is a function f from $\mathcal{F}^r$ to $\mathcal{F}^n$ such that 2 different $(r+n)$-tuples of the form $(x, f(x))$ cannot collide in any r positions
$\Leftrightarrow f$ is a $(r, r+n)$ perfect local randomizer of order r over $\mathcal{F}$.

They claim that all diffusion boxes of the network representing a cryptographic primitive should be multipermutations: if the network contains a gate which does not realize perfect diffusion, it is then possible to find some values such that both inputs and outputs of the gate are close according to the Hamming distance. For example S. Vaudenay constructed some collisions on the first 2 rounds of MD4 using the fact that the diffusion boxes in these rounds are not multipermutations [13].

The design of cryptographic primitives then leads to the search of multipermutations over a given alphabet $\mathcal{F}$. Proposition 6 enables us to construct such functions from codes over $\mathcal{F}$. In particular MDS codes provide multipermutations [13].

5 Construction of new correlation immune functions by composition

The characterizations given in sections 2 and 3 are now used for constructing t-th order correlation immune functions over a finite alphabet by composition of correlation immune functions of smaller order. As above $\mathcal{F}$ is a finite alphabet of size q endowed with the structure of some Abelian group.

Definition 8. Let $(g_i)_{1 \leq i \leq k}$ be a family of functions:

$$g_i : \mathcal{F}^m \to \mathcal{F}^d = \mathcal{A}, \text{ where } d \leq m$$

We define the function g from $\mathcal{F}^{mk}$ to $\mathcal{A}^k$ by $g(x_1, \ldots, x_k) = (g_1(x_1), \ldots, g_k(x_k))$. Let h be a function:

$$h : (\mathcal{A})^k \to \mathcal{F}^\ell, \text{ where } \ell \leq kd$$

The composed function $f = h \circ g$ is defined by:

$$\begin{array}{rccc} f: & \mathcal{F}^{mk} & \to & \mathcal{F}^\ell \\ & (x_1, \ldots, x_k) & \mapsto & h(g_1(x_1), \ldots, g_k(x_k)) \end{array}$$

Proposition 9. *If every g_i is balanced and if h is r-th order correlation immune with respect to $\mathcal{A}$, then $h \circ g$ is r-th order correlation immune with respect to $\mathcal{F}^m$.*

Proof. Let $v \in \mathcal{F}^\ell$ and let $R = \{i_1, \ldots, i_r\}$ be a r-element subset of $\{1, \ldots, k\}$ and $\bar{R} = \{j_1, \ldots, j_{k-r}\}$ be the complementary set.
Since h is r-th order correlation immune with respect to $\mathcal{A}$, $h^{-1}(v)$ is an orthogonal array with k constraints, strength r and index λ_v over the alphabet $\mathcal{A}$. Given a vector $a = (a_{i_1}, \ldots, a_{i_r}) \in \mathcal{A}^r$, the number of elements $z = (z_1, \ldots, z_k) \in \mathcal{A}^k$ in $h^{-1}(v)$ such that $(z_{i_1}, \ldots, z_{i_r}) = a$ is then equal to λ_v.
We denote by g_R the function $(x_{i_1}, \ldots, x_{i_r}) \mapsto (g_{i_1}(x_{i_1}), \ldots, g_{i_r}(x_{i_r})$ and by $g_{\bar{R}}$ the function $(x_{j_1}, \ldots, x_{j_r}) \mapsto (g_{j_1}(x_{j_1}), \ldots, g_{j_{k-r}}(x_{j_{k-r}}))$.
By assumption, every g_i is balanced; this entails that $|g_i^{-1}(a_i)| = |\mathcal{F}|^{m-d}$. Then $\forall b = (b_{j_1}, \ldots, b_{j_{k-r}})$, $g_{\bar{R}}^{-1}(b)$ is a subset of $\mathcal{F}^{m(k-r)}$ of size $|\mathcal{F}|^{(m-d)(k-r)}$. In the same way $|g_R^{-1}(a)| = |\mathcal{F}|^{(m-d)r}$ and $(g_R^{-1}(a))_{a \in \mathcal{A}^r}$ is a partition of $(\mathcal{F}^m)^r$.

Hence every r-tuple of $(\mathcal{F}^m)^r$ appears as the projection on R of exactly $\lambda_v|\mathcal{F}|^{(m-d)(k-r)}$ elements in $(h \circ g)^{-1}(v)$. It means that$(h \circ g)^{-1}(v)$ is an orthogonal array with k constraints, strength r, index $\lambda_v q^{(m-d)(k-r)}$ over the alphabet $\mathcal{F}^m$.

Proposition 10. *If $f = h \circ g$ is r-th order correlation immune with respect to $\mathcal{F}^m$ and if $\forall 1 \leq i \leq k$, g_i is t-th order correlation immune with respect to $\mathcal{F}$, then f is t'-th order correlation immune with respect to $\mathcal{F}$ where $t' = (t+1)(r+1) - 1$.*

Proof. Let $\mathcal{B} = \mathcal{F}^m$ and $u \in \mathcal{B}^k$. We write $u = (u_1, \ldots, u_k)$, $u_i \in \mathcal{B}$. The Hamming weight of u in $\mathcal{B}^k$, *i.e.* $|\{i/u_i \neq 0\}|$, is denoted by $W_H(u)$ while the Hamming weight of u in $\mathcal{F}^{mk}$, *i.e.* the number of non-zero components of u in $\mathcal{F}$ is denoted by $w_H(u)$.
The function f is r-th order correlation immune with respect to $\mathcal{B}$ means that $\forall v \in \mathcal{F}^\ell$, $f^{-1}(v)$ is an orthogonal array of strength r over $\mathcal{B}$. By theorem 4 we have

$$\forall u \in \mathcal{B}^k,\ 1 \leq W_H(u) \leq r, \qquad \sum_{x \in f^{-1}(v), x \in \mathcal{B}^k} < x, u >= 0$$

Now if $W_H(u) > r$ and $w_H(u) < (r+1)(t+1)$, then there is an index $i \in \{1, \ldots, k\}$ such that $1 \leq w_H(u_i) \leq t$. Then we get by lemma 3:

$$\sum_{x \in f^{-1}(v), x \in \mathcal{F}^{mk}} < x, u >= \sum_{y \in h^{-1}(v)} \sum_{x \in g^{-1}(y)} < x, u >$$

$$= \sum_{y \in h^{-1}(v)} \prod_{i=1}^{k} \sum_{x_i \in g_i^{-1}(y_i)} < x_i, u_i >$$

Since g_i is t-th order correlation immune, at least one of the factors $\sum_{x_i \in g_i^{-1}(y_i)} < x_i, u_i >$ is zero. Thus we obtain:

$$\forall u \in \mathcal{F}^{mk},\ 1 \leq w_H(u) \leq t', \qquad \sum_{x \in f^{-1}(v), x \in \mathcal{F}^{mk}} < x, u >= 0$$

As a consequence of these two propositions we obtain the following theorem.

Theorem 11. *If every g_i is t-resilient with respect to $\mathcal{F}$ and if h is r-th order correlation immune with respect to $\mathcal{A}$, then $h \circ g$ is t'-th order correlation immune with respect to $\mathcal{F}$, where $t' = (t+1)(r+1) - 1$.*

Corollary 12. *If every g_i is t-resilient with respect to $\mathcal{F}$ and if h is r-resilient with respect to $\mathcal{A}$, then $h \circ g$ is t'-resilient with respect to $\mathcal{F}$, where $t' = (t+1)(r+1) - 1$.*

The parameters of the orthogonal arrays $g_i^{-1}(z), z \in \mathcal{A}$ are (q^{m-d}, m, q, t), $\lambda_g = q^{m-d-t}$. Those of $h^{-1}(z), z \in \mathcal{F}^\ell$ are $(q^{dk-\ell}, k, q^d, r)$, $\lambda_h = q^{dk-\ell-r}$. This results in orthogonal arrays $f^{-1}(z), z \in \mathcal{F}^\ell$ with parameters $(q^{km-\ell}, km, q, (t+1)(r+1)-1)$, $\lambda_f = q^{km-\ell-tr-t-r}$.

Zhang and Zheng presented at Eurocrypt'95 some results about the construction of new binary resilient functions from old ones by addition (section 3 in [16]) and by composition with a permutation (section 4 in [16]). These results are immediate corollaries of the previous theorem and they can be generalized for functions over any finite alphabet.

Corollary 13. *Let $g_i : \mathcal{F}^m \to \mathcal{F}^d$, $i = 1, \ldots, k$ be k t-resilient functions with respect to $\mathcal{F}$ and $h : (\mathcal{F}^d)^k \to \mathcal{F}^d$ be the addition over $\mathcal{F}^d$. Then the composed function f is a t'-resilient function with respect to $\mathcal{F}$ where $t' = k(t+1) - 1$.*

$$\begin{array}{rccc} f: & \mathcal{F}^{mk} & \to & \mathcal{F}^d \\ & (x_1, \ldots, x_k) & \mapsto & g_1(x_1) + \ldots + g_k(x_k) \end{array}$$

Corollary 14. *Let $g : \mathcal{F}^m \to \mathcal{F}^d$ be a t-resilient function with respect to $\mathcal{F}$ and h be a permutation of $\mathcal{F}^d$. Then $h \circ g$ is still a t-resilient function with respect to $\mathcal{F}$.*

6 Combining LFSRs for designing running-key generators

A common type of running-key generator used in stream ciphers consists of several binary Linear Feedback Shift Registers (LFSRs) whose outputs are combined by a boolean function f. This function has to be nonlinear in order to avoid an attack by the Berlekamp-Massey shift register synthesis algorithm. Furthermore Siegenthaler [12] has shown that f has to be correlation-immune, otherwise the generator structure is not resistant to a correlation attack. The problem is now to find some nonlinear and correlation-immune combining functions. The previous study enables us to construct such functions and in particular to combine a great number of different LFSRs.

Thanks to Theorem 11 we obtain the order of correlation-immunity of f without writing its truth table which is usually very large. In the following examples we construct a 3-resilient boolean function of degree 2 and a 5-resilient boolean function of degree 4 for combining respectively 6 and 12 LFSRs. We here denote $GF(q)$ by $\mathbf{F}_q$.

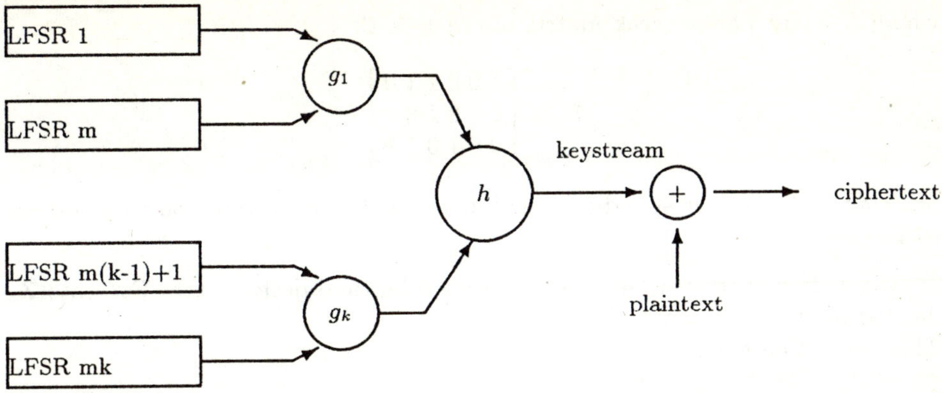

Fig. 1. Combining LFSRs with a composed function $f = h \circ g$

Example 2.
Let $g_1 = g_2 : \quad \mathbf{F}_2^3 \quad \to \quad \mathbf{F}_2^2$
$(x_1; x_2; x_3) \mapsto (x_1 + x_2; x_1 + x_3)$
This function is 1-resilient with respect to $\mathbf{F}_2$.
Let $h : (\mathbf{F}_2^2)^2 \to \mathbf{F}_2$. The transposed of its truth table T_h is given by:

$$T_h^t = \left[\begin{array}{c} 0\,0\,0\,0\,1\,1\,1\,1 \\ 0\,0\,1\,1\,1\,1\,0\,0 \\ \hline 0\,1\,1\,1\,0\,0\,0\,1 \\ 1\,1\,1\,0\,0\,1\,0\,0 \end{array}\right] \begin{array}{c} x_1 \\ x_2 \\ x_3 \\ x_4 \end{array}$$

h is 1-resilient with respect to $\mathbf{F}_2^2$ and it is nonlinear as a function from $(\mathbf{F}_2)^4$ onto $\mathbf{F}_2$ since $h(x_1; x_2; x_3; x_4) = x_1 + x_4 + x_2x_3 + x_2x_4$.
The composed function $f : \mathbf{F}_2^6 \to \mathbf{F}_2$
$f(x_1; x_2; x_3; x_4; x_5; x_6) = x_1 + x_2 + x_4 + x_6 + x_1x_5 + x_1x_6 + x_3x_5 + x_3x_6$ is then 3-resilient with respect to $\mathbf{F}_2$.

Its truth table T_f is then a binary orthogonal array of size 32, 6 constraints, index 4 and strength 3:

$$\left[\begin{array}{c} 0\,0\,0\,0\,1\,1\,1\,1\,0\,0\,0\,0\,1\,1\,1\,1\,1\,1\,1\,1\,0\,0\,0\,0\,0\,0\,0\,0\,1\,1\,1\,1 \\ 0\,0\,0\,0\,1\,1\,1\,1\,0\,0\,0\,0\,1\,1\,1\,1\,0\,0\,0\,0\,1\,1\,1\,1\,1\,1\,1\,1\,0\,0\,0\,0 \\ 0\,0\,0\,0\,1\,1\,1\,1\,1\,1\,1\,1\,0\,0\,0\,0\,0\,0\,0\,0\,1\,1\,1\,1\,0\,0\,0\,0\,1\,1\,1\,1 \\ 0\,1\,1\,0\,0\,1\,1\,0\,1\,0\,0\,1\,1\,0\,0\,1\,0\,1\,0\,1\,0\,1\,0\,1\,0\,1\,0\,1\,0\,1\,0\,1 \\ 0\,1\,0\,1\,0\,1\,0\,1\,0\,1\,1\,0\,0\,1\,1\,0\,0\,1\,0\,1\,0\,1\,0\,1\,0\,1\,1\,0\,0\,1\,1\,0 \\ 1\,0\,0\,1\,1\,0\,0\,1\,0\,1\,0\,1\,0\,1\,0\,1\,0\,1\,1\,0\,0\,1\,1\,0\,0\,1\,0\,1\,0\,1\,0\,1 \end{array}\right] \begin{array}{c} x_1 \\ x_2 \\ x_3 \\ x_4 \\ x_5 \\ x_6 \end{array}$$

Example 3.
Let $g_1 = g_2 : \mathbf{F}_2^6 \to \mathbf{F}_2^3$
$x \mapsto xH^t$

where H is the parity-check matrix of the code $\mathcal{C}$,

$$H = \begin{bmatrix} 1\,0\,0\,1\,1\,0 \\ 0\,1\,0\,1\,0\,1 \\ 0\,0\,1\,0\,1\,1 \end{bmatrix}$$

Since $d^{\perp} = 3$, the corresponding function g_1 is a 2-resilient function with respect to $\mathbf{F}_2$.

Let α be a root of $X^3 + X + 1$ and let ϕ be the bijection from $\mathbf{F}_{2^3}$ onto $\mathbf{Z}_8$ defined by $\forall i,\ \phi(\alpha^i) = i$ and $\phi(0) = 0$.
Then we define h as:

$$\begin{array}{llll} h: & \mathbf{F}_{2^3} \times \mathbf{F}_{2^3} & \rightarrow & \mathbf{F}_2 \\ & (x, y) & \mapsto & \phi_0^{-1}(\phi(x) + \phi(y)) \end{array}$$

where the addition is performed in $\mathbf{Z}_8$ and $\phi_0^{-1}(x)$ denotes the low-weight bit of $\phi^{-1}(x)$.
By construction, h is 1-resilient with respect to $\mathbf{F}_2^3$. If h is considered as a function over $(\mathbf{F}_2)^6$, we obtain the boolean form:
$h(x_1; x_2; x_3; y_1; y_2; y_3) = x_1 + y_1 + x_1y_1 + x_1y_2 + x_1y_3 + x_2y_1 + x_2y_3 + x_3y_1 + x_3y_2 + x_1x_3y_1 + x_1y_1y_3 + x_1x_2y_1y_3 + x_1x_2y_2y_3 + x_1x_3y_1y_2 + x_1x_3y_1y_3 + x_2x_3y_1y_2$
Since h is a boolean function of degree 4, the composed function $f = h \circ g$ is a boolean function with 12 variables of degree 4 and 5-resilient.

One of the advantages of using a composed combining function is that the computation can be parallelized in a natural way.

In some applications, the combining function is used as a secret key. This function is then transmitted as the sequence of its outputs, *i.e.* $\ell 2^m$ bits for $f: \mathbf{F}_2^m \rightarrow \mathbf{F}_2^\ell$. If a composed function is used, we only have to send the small functions (g_i) and h, *i.e.* $k2^m d + 2^{kd}$ bits, while transmitting any function for combining km LFSRs requires 2^{km} bits.

References

1. C.H. Bennett, G. Brassard, and J.-M. Robert. Privacy amplification by public discussion. *SIAM J. Computing*, 17(2):210–229, april 1988.
2. J. Bierbrauer, K. Gopalakrishnan, and D.R. Stinson. Bounds for resilient functions and orthogonal arrays. In Y.G. Desmedt, editor, *Advances in Cryptology - CRYPTO'94*, number 839 in Lecture Notes in Computer Science, pages 247–256, 1994.
3. P. Camion, C. Carlet, P. Charpin, and N. Sendrier. On correlation-immune functions. In J. Feigenbaum, editor, *Advances in Cryptology - CRYPTO'91*, number 576 in Lecture Notes in Computer Science, pages 86–100. Springer-Verlag, 1992.
4. B. Chor, O. Goldreich, J. Hastad, J. Freidmann, S. Rudich, and R. Smolensky. The bit extraction problem or t-resilient functions. In *Proc. 26th IEEE Symposium on Foundations of Computer Science*, pages 396–407, 1985.
5. P. Delsarte. An algebraic approach to the association schemes of coding theory. Thesis, Université catholique de Louvain, 1973.

6. K. Gopalakrishnan and D.R. Stinson. Three characterizations of non-binary correlation-immune and resilient functions. *Designs, Codes and Cryptography*, 5:241–251, 1995.
7. F.J. MacWilliams and N.J.A. Sloane. The Theory of Error-correcting Codes. North-Holland, 1983.
8. J.L. Massey. Some applications of coding theory in cryptography. In *IMA Conference Proceedings on Cryptography and Coding IV*, 1993.
9. U.M. Maurer and J.L. Massey. Perfect local randomness in pseudo-random sequences. In G. Brassard, editor, *Advances in Cryptology - CRYPTO'89*, number 435 in Lecture Notes in Computer Science, pages 100–112. Springer-Verlag, 1990.
10. C.R. Rao. Factorial experiments derivable from combinatorial arrangements of arrays. *J. Roy. Statist.*, 9:128–139, 1947.
11. C.-P. Schnorr and S. Vaudenay. Black box cryptanalysis of hash networks based on multipermutations. In A. De Santis, editor, *Advances in Cryptology - EUROCRYPT'94*, number 950 in Lecture Notes in Computer Science, pages 47–57. Springer-Verlag, 1995.
12. T. Siegenthaler. Correlation-immunity of nonlinear combining functions for cryptographic applications. *IEEE Trans. Inform. Theory*, IT-30(5):776–780, 1984.
13. S. Vaudenay. On the need for multipermutations: cryptanalysis of MD4 and SAFER. In *Fast Software Encryption*, Lecture Notes in Computer Science. Springer-Verlag. to appear.
14. S. Vaudenay. *La sécurité des primitives cryptographiques*. PhD thesis, Université Paris 7, 1995. in french.
15. G. Xiao and J.L. Massey. A spectral characterization of correlation-immune combining functions. *IEEE Trans. Inform. Theory*, IT-34(3):569–571, 1988.
16. X. Zhang and Y. Zheng. On nonlinear resilient functions. In L. Guillou and J.J. Quisquater, editors, *Advances in Cryptology - EUROCRYPT'95*, number 921 in Lecture Notes in Computer Science, pages 274–288. Springer-Verlag, 1995.

Auto-Correlations and New Bounds on the Nonlinearity of Boolean Functions

Xian-Mo Zhang[1] and Yuliang Zheng[2]

[1] The University of Wollongong, Wollongong, NSW 2522, Australia
xianmo@cs.uow.edu.au
[2] Monash University, Frankston, Melbourne, VIC 3199, Australia
yzheng@fcit.monash.edu.au

Abstract. It is a well known fact that the nonlinearity of a function f on the n-dimensional vector space V_n is bounded from above by $2^{n-1} - 2^{\frac{1}{2}n-1}$. In cryptographic practice, nonlinear functions are usually constructively obtained in such a way that they support certain mathematical or cryptographic requirements. Hence an important question is how to calculate the nonlinearity of a function when extra information is available. In this paper we address this question in the context of auto-correlations, and derive four (two upper and two lower) bounds on the nonlinearity of a function (see Table 1). Strengths and weaknesses of each bound are also examined. In addition, a few examples are given to demonstrate the usefulness of the bounds in practical applications. We anticipate that these four bounds will be very useful in calculating the nonlinearity of a cryptographic function when certain extra information on the auto-correlations of the function is available.

1 Introduction

The significance of nonlinear functions in cryptology is best illustrated by the success of linear cryptanalytic attacks recently discovered by Matsui in [6]. Realizing its importance, cryptographers often wish to find out the nonlinearity of a cryptographic function, or when the exact value is not easily obtainable, a lower and/or an upper bound on the nonlinearity.

A well-known fact about the upper bound on nonlinearity is $N_f \leq 2^{n-1} - 2^{\frac{1}{2}n-1}$, where N_f denotes the nonlinearity of f and f is a function from V_n (the n-dimensional vector space on $GF(2)$) to $GF(2)$. In contrast, less is known about the lower bound on nonlinearity, other than (to the authors knowledge) some progress made in [11, 13], as well as such trivial facts as $N_f > 0$ if and only if f is nonlinear.

In cryptographic practice, such as the design of a substitution-box employed by a private key encryption algorithm or a one-way hashing algorithm, or a nonlinear feedback function used in a pseudorandom sequence generator, one usually generates a nonlinear function in such a way that the function would satisfy certain mathematical or cryptographic requirements. A question one would face is how to calculate the nonlinearity of the function using extra information available on the function. If the exact value of the nonlinearity cannot be easily obtained,

Ueli Maurer (Ed.): EUROCRYPT '96 Proceedings, LNCS 1070

the next question is how to estimate the nonlinearity using extra information on the function.

This paper addresses the two questions mentioned above. In particular, we derive four formulas for estimating the nonlinearity of a function, among which two are about upper bound while the other are about lower bounds. Table 1 summarizes the four bounds on nonlinearity. We hope that these bounds will be particularly helpful in estimating the nonlinearity of a cryptographic function when extra information on the auto-correlations of the function is available.

The rest of the paper is organized as follows: Section 2 introduces the basic notions and notations used in this paper. Section 3 proves two upper bounds on nonlinearity, while Section 4 provides details on two lower bounds on nonlinearity. A few example applications are provided in Section 5, which show the usefulness of the bounds in practice.

2 Definitions

We consider Boolean functions from V_n to $GF(2)$ (or simply functions on V_n), where V_n is the vector space of n tuples of elements from $GF(2)$. The *truth table* of a function f on V_n is a $(0,1)$-sequence defined by $(f(\alpha_0), f(\alpha_1), \ldots, f(\alpha_{2^n-1}))$, and the *sequence* of f is a $(1,-1)$-sequence defined by $((-1)^{f(\alpha_0)}, (-1)^{f(\alpha_1)}, \ldots, (-1)^{f(\alpha_{2^n-1})})$, where $\alpha_0 = (0,\ldots,0,0)$, $\alpha_1 = (0,\ldots,0,1)$, $\ldots$, $\alpha_{2^{n-1}-1} = (1,\ldots,1,1)$. The *matrix* of f is a $(1,-1)$-matrix of order 2^n defined by $M = ((-1)^{f(\alpha_i \oplus \alpha_j)})$. f is said to be *balanced* if its truth table contains an equal number of ones and zeros.

An *affine* function f on V_n is a function that takes the form of $f(x_1,\ldots,x_n) = a_1x_1 \oplus \cdots \oplus a_nx_n \oplus c$, where $a_j, c \in GF(2)$, $j = 1,2,\ldots,n$. Furthermore f is called a *linear* function if $c = 0$.

Definition 1. The *Hamming weight* of a $(0,1)$-sequence s, denoted by $W(s)$, is the number of ones in the sequence. Given two functions f and g on V_n, the *Hamming distance* $d(f,g)$ between them is defined as the Hamming weight of the truth table of $f(x) \oplus g(x)$, where $x = (x_1,\ldots,x_n)$. The *nonlinearity* of f, denoted by N_f, is the minimum Hamming distance between f and all affine functions on V_n, i.e., $N_f = \min_{i=0,1,\ldots,2^{n+1}-1} d(f,\varphi_i)$ where $\varphi_0, \varphi_1, \ldots, \varphi_{2^{n+1}-1}$ are all the affine functions on V_n.

Note that the maximum nonlinearity of functions on V_n coincides with the covering radius of the first order binary Reed-Muller code $RM(1,n)$ of length 2^n, which is bounded from above by $2^{n-1} - 2^{\frac{1}{2}n-1}$ (see for instance [3]). Hence $N_f \leq 2^{n-1} - 2^{\frac{1}{2}n-1}$ for any function on V_n.

Next we introduce the definition of propagation criterion from [8].

Definition 2. Let f be a function on V_n. We say that f satisfies

1. the *propagation criterion with respect to* α if $f(x) \oplus f(x \oplus \alpha)$ is a balanced function, where $x = (x_1,\ldots,x_n)$ and α is a vector in V_n.

2. the *propagation criterion of degree k* if it satisfies the propagation criterion with respect to all $\alpha \in V_n$ with $1 \leq W(\alpha) \leq k$.

$f(x) \oplus f(x \oplus \alpha)$ is also called the *directional derivative* of f in the direction α. Further work on the topic can be found in [7].

Given two sequences $a = (a_1, \ldots, a_m)$ and $b = (b_1, \ldots, b_m)$, their component-wise product is defined by $a * b = (a_1 b_1, \ldots, a_m b_m)$. The scalar product $\langle a, b\rangle$ of a and b is defined as the sum of the components in $a * b$. Note that depending on where the components of a and b are drawn from, the meaning of a "sum" operation may vary.

Definition 3. Let f be a function on V_n. For a vector $\alpha \in V_n$, denote by $\xi(\alpha)$ the sequence of $f(x \oplus \alpha)$. Thus $\xi(0)$ is the sequence of f itself and $\xi(0) * \xi(\alpha)$ is the sequence of $f(x) \oplus f(x \oplus \alpha)$. The *auto-correlation* of f with a shift α is defined as

$$\Delta(\alpha) = \langle \xi(0), \xi(\alpha)\rangle.$$

A $(1, -1)$-matrix H of order m is called a *Hadamard* matrix if $HH^t = mI_m$, where H^t is the transpose of H and I_m is the identity matrix of order m. A Sylvester-Hadamard matrix of order 2^n, denoted by H_n, is generated by the following recursive relation

$$H_0 = 1,\ H_n = \begin{bmatrix} H_{n-1} & H_{n-1} \\ H_{n-1} & -H_{n-1} \end{bmatrix},\ n = 1, 2, \ldots. \tag{1}$$

Let ℓ_i, $0 \leq i \leq 2^n - 1$, be the i row (column) of H_n. By Lemma 1 of [10], ℓ_i is the sequence of a linear function $\varphi_i(x)$ defined by the scalar product $\varphi_i(x) = \langle \alpha_i, x\rangle$, where α_i is the ith vector in V_n according to the ascending lexicographic order.

Definition 4. Let f be a function on V_n. The Walsh-Hadamard transform of f is defined as

$$\hat{f}(\alpha) = 2^{-\frac{n}{2}} \sum_{x \in V_n} (-1)^{f(x) \oplus \langle \alpha, x\rangle}$$

where $\alpha = (a_1, \ldots, a_n) \in V_n$, $x = (x_1, \ldots, x_n)$, $\langle \alpha, x\rangle$ is the scalar product of α and x, namely, $\langle \alpha, x\rangle = \bigoplus_{i=1}^{n} a_i x_i$, and $f(x) \oplus \langle \alpha, x\rangle$ is regarded as a real-valued function.

The Walsh-Hadamard transform, also called the discrete Fourier transform, has numerous applications in areas ranging from physical science to communications engineering. It appears in several slightly different forms [9, 5, 4]. The above definition follows the line in [9]. It can be equivalently written as

$$(\hat{f}(\alpha_0), \hat{f}(\alpha_1), \ldots, \hat{f}(\alpha_{2^n-1})) = 2^{-\frac{n}{2}} \xi H_n$$

where α_i is the ith vector in V_n according to the ascending order, ξ is the sequence of f and H_n is the Sylvester-Hadamard matrix of order 2^n.

Definition 5. A function f on V_n is called a *bent* function if its Walsh-Hadamard transform satisfies

$$\hat{f}(\alpha) = \pm 1$$

for all $\alpha \in V_n$.

Bent functions on V_n exist only when n is even [9]. They achieve the highest possible nonlinearity $2^{n-1} - 2^{\frac{1}{2}n-1}$.

The following lemma will be used in this paper (For a proof see for instance Lemma 6 of [10].)

Lemma 6. *The nonlinearity of a function f on V_n can be calculated by*

$$N_f = 2^{n-1} - \frac{1}{2}\max\{|\langle \xi, \ell_i \rangle|, 0 \leq i \leq 2^n - 1\}$$

where ξ is the sequence of f and ℓ_0, ..., ℓ_{2^n-1} are the rows of H_n, namely, the sequences of the linear functions on V_n.

As the number of linear functions on V_n is exponential in n, it is impractical to calculate N_f for a large n by examining all linear functions against the formula in Lemma 6.

3 Two Upper Bounds on Nonlinearity

Let f be a function on V_n and ξ be the sequence of f. The following is a special form of the Wiener-Khintchine Theorem [1]:

$$(\Delta(\alpha_0), \Delta(\alpha_1), \ldots, \Delta(\alpha_{2^n-1}))H_n = (\langle \xi, \ell_0 \rangle^2, \ldots, \langle \xi, \ell_{2^n-1} \rangle^2). \tag{2}$$

By exploring (2) in different ways, we will obtain two upper bounds on the nonlinearity of functions.

3.1 The First Upper Bound

Our first upper bound can be regarded as a straightforward application of (2). For simplicity, write

$$\eta^* = (\Delta(\alpha_0), \Delta(\alpha_1), \ldots, \Delta(\alpha_{2^n-1}))$$

and

$$\xi^* = (\langle \xi, \ell_0 \rangle^2, \ldots, \langle \xi, \ell_{2^n-1} \rangle^2).$$

Then (2) is simplified to $\eta^* H_n = \xi^*$. This causes $(\eta^* H_n)(\eta^* H_n)^T = \xi^* \xi^{*T}$, i.e.,

$$2^n \sum_{j=0}^{2^n-1} \Delta^2(\alpha_j) = \sum_{j=0}^{2^n-1} \langle \xi, \ell_j \rangle^4.$$

Thus there exists a j_0, $0 \leq j_0 \leq 2^n - 1$, such that

$$\langle \xi, \ell_{j_0} \rangle^4 \geq \sum_{j=0}^{2^n-1} \Delta^2(\alpha_j).$$

Note that $\Delta(\alpha_0) = \Delta(0) = 2^n$. Hence from Lemma 6, we have

Theorem 7. *For any function f on V_n, the nonlinearity of f satisfies*

$$N_f \leq 2^{n-1} - \frac{1}{2}\sqrt[4]{2^{2n} + \sum_{j=1}^{2^n-1} \Delta^2(\alpha_j)}.$$

It is easy to verify that the bound in Theorem 7 does not exceed the well-known bound $2^{n-1} - 2^{\frac{1}{2}n-1}$. In addition, as the equality holds if f is bent, the bound is tight.

3.2 The Second Upper Bound

In order to derive the second upper bound on nonlinearity, we generalize (2) in the following direction. For any integer t, $0 \leq t \leq n$, rewrite (2) as

$$(\Delta(\alpha_0), \Delta(\alpha_1), \ldots, \Delta(\alpha_{2^n-1}))(H_{n-t} \times H_t) = (\langle \xi, \ell_0 \rangle^2, \ldots, \langle \xi, \ell_{2^n-1} \rangle^2)$$

where $\times$ denotes the Kronecker product (see P.421, [5]).

Now set

$$\sigma_j = \sum_{k=0}^{2^t-1} \langle \xi, \ell_{j2^t+k} \rangle^2,$$

where $j = 0, 1, \ldots, 2^{n-t} - 1$, Let $e = (1, \ldots, 1)$ be the all-one sequence of length 2^t and I denote the identity matrix of order 2^{n-t}. Then

$$(\Delta(\alpha_0), \Delta(\alpha_1), \ldots, \Delta(\alpha_{2^n-1}))(H_{n-t} \times H_t)(I \times e^T) = (\langle \xi, \ell_0 \rangle^2, \ldots, \langle \xi, \ell_{2^n-1} \rangle^2)(I \times e^T).$$

Note that $(H_{n-t} \times H_t)(I \times e^T) = (H_{n-t}I) \times (H_t e^T)$ and $H_t e^T = (2^t, 0, \ldots, 0)^T$. Hence

$$(\Delta(\alpha_0), \Delta(\alpha_1), \ldots, \Delta(\alpha_{2^n-1}))(H_{n-t} \times (2^t, 0, \ldots, 0)^T) = (\sigma_0, \sigma_1, \ldots, \sigma_{2^{n-t}-1})$$

and

$$2^t(\Delta(\alpha_0), \Delta(\alpha_{2^t}), \Delta(\alpha_{2\cdot 2^t}), \ldots, \Delta(\alpha_{(2^{n-t}-1)2^t}))H_{n-t} = (\sigma_0, \sigma_1, \ldots, \sigma_{2^{n-t}-1}).$$

Thus we have proved the following result:

Lemma 8. *Let f be a function on V_n and ξ be the sequence of f. For any integer t, $0 \leq t \leq n$, set $\sigma_j = \sum_{k=0}^{2^t-1} \langle \xi, \ell_{j2^t+k} \rangle^2$, where $j = 0, 1, \ldots, 2^{n-t} - 1$. Then*

$$2^t(\Delta(\alpha_0), \Delta(\alpha_{2^t}), \Delta(\alpha_{2\cdot 2^t}), \ldots, \Delta(\alpha_{(2^{n-t}-1)2^t}))H_{n-t} = (\sigma_0, \sigma_1, \ldots, \sigma_{2^{n-t}-1}) \quad (3)$$

We can see that (3) is more general than (2), by noting the fact that the two equations become identical when $t = 0$.

Now compare the jth components in the two sides of (3), we have

$$2^t \sum_{k=0}^{2^{n-t}-1} a_k \Delta(\alpha_{k\cdot 2^t}) = \sigma_j, \quad (4)$$

where $j = 0, 1, \ldots, 2^{n-t} - 1$ and $(a_0, a_1, \ldots, a_{2^{n-t}-1})$ denotes the jth row (column) of H_{n-t}. Since we also have $\sigma_j = \sum_{k=0}^{2^t-1} \langle \xi, \ell_{j2^t+k} \rangle^2$, for any fixed j there is a k_0, $0 \leq k_0 \leq 2^t - 1$, such that $|\langle \xi, \ell_{j2^t+k_0} \rangle| \geq \sqrt{\sum_{k=0}^{2^{n-t}-1} a_k \Delta(\alpha_{k \cdot 2^t})}$. As $\Delta(\alpha_0) = 2^n$, by using Lemma 6, we have

$$N_f \leq 2^{n-1} - \frac{1}{2}\sqrt{2^n + \sum_{k=1}^{2^{n-t}-1} a_k \Delta(\alpha_{k \cdot 2^t})}.$$

Now note that $\alpha_0, \alpha_{2^t}, \alpha_{2 \cdot 2^t}, \ldots, \alpha_{(2^{n-t}-1)2^t}$ form a $(n-t)$-dimensional linear subspace of V_n with $\{\alpha_{2^t}, \alpha_{2^{t+1}}, \ldots, \alpha_{2^{n-1}}\}$ as its basis, and that the nonlinearity of a function is invariant under a nondegenerate linear transformation on the input coordinates. Set $r = n - t$. By using a nondegenerate linear transformation on the input coordinates, we have proved the following lemma:

Lemma 9. *For any integer r, $0 \leq r \leq n$, let $\beta_1, \ldots, \beta_r$ be r linearly independent vectors in V_n. Write $\gamma_j = c_1\beta_1 \oplus \cdots \oplus c_r\beta_r$, where $j = 0, 1, \ldots, 2^r - 1$ and $(c_1, \ldots, c_r)$ is the binary representation of integer j. Then*

$$N_f \leq 2^{n-1} - \frac{1}{2}\sqrt{2^n + \sum_{j=1}^{2^r-1} a_j \Delta(\gamma_j)}$$

holds for every row (column), denoted by $(a_0, a_1, \ldots, a_{2^r-1})$, of H_r, where $a_0 = 1$ due to the structure of a Sylvester-Hadamard matrix.

In practice, simpler forms than that in Lemma 9 would be preferred. This can be achieved by letting $r = 1$ in Lemma 9. This results in

$$N_f \leq 2^{n-1} - \frac{1}{2}\sqrt{2^n \pm \Delta(\beta)},$$

for any nonzero vector $\beta \in V_n$. Thus we have derived a simple formula for the upper bound on nonlinearity:

Theorem 10. *For any function f on V_n, the nonlinearity of f satisfies*

$$N_f \leq 2^{n-1} - \frac{1}{2}\sqrt{2^n + \Delta_{max}},$$

where $\Delta_{max} = \max\{|\Delta(\alpha)| | \alpha \in V_n, \alpha \neq 0\}$.

In situations where a more accurate estimate of nonlinearity is required, slightly more involved forms can be used. In particular, by substituting r with 2 in Lemma 9, we have

(i) $N_f \leq 2^{n-1} - \frac{1}{2}\sqrt{2^n + \Delta(\beta) + \Delta(\gamma) + \Delta(\beta \oplus \gamma)}$,
(ii) $N_f \leq 2^{n-1} - \frac{1}{2}\sqrt{2^n + \Delta(\beta) - \Delta(\gamma) - \Delta(\beta \oplus \gamma)}$,
(iii) $N_f \leq 2^{n-1} - \frac{1}{2}\sqrt{2^n - \Delta(\beta) + \Delta(\gamma) - \Delta(\beta \oplus \gamma)}$,

(iv) $N_f \le 2^{n-1} - \frac{1}{2}\sqrt{2^n - \Delta(\beta) - \Delta(\gamma) + \Delta(\beta \oplus \gamma)}$.

where β and γ are nonzero vectors in V_n with $\beta \neq \gamma$. These four formulas are subsumed in the following corollary:

Corollary 11. *Let f be a function on V_n. Then*

1. *for any nonzero vectors $\beta, \gamma \in V_n$ with $\beta \neq \gamma$, the nonlinearity f satisfies*

$$N_f \le 2^{n-1} - \frac{1}{2}\sqrt{2^n + |\Delta(\beta)| + |\Delta(\gamma)| - |\Delta(\beta \oplus \gamma)|};$$

2. *for $|\Delta(\alpha_{j_1})| \ge |\Delta(\alpha_{j_2})| \ge \cdots \ge |\Delta(\alpha_{j_{2^n-1}})|$ where $(j_1, \ldots, j_{2^n-1})$ is a permutation of $(1, \ldots, 2^n - 1)$, the nonlinearity f satisfies*

$$N_f \le 2^{n-1} - \frac{1}{2}\sqrt{2^n + |\Delta(\alpha_{j_1})| + |\Delta(\alpha_{j_2})| - |\Delta(\alpha_{j_3})|}.$$

None of the bounds in Lemma 9, Theorem 10 and Corollary 11 goes beyond the well-known bound $2^{n-1} - 2^{\frac{1}{2}n-1}$. The equalities in these bounds hold if f is bent, which indicates that all the bounds are tight.

4 Two Lower Bounds on Nonlinearity

In comparison with upper bounds, far less is known about lower bounds on nonlinearity, although some progress in this direction has been made in [11, 13]. This section proves two lower bounds on nonlinearity, of which the first lower bound has an extremely simple form while the second reveals an intimate relationship between the lower bound on nonlinearity and the propagation characteristic.

4.1 The First Lower Bound

Let $\xi = (a_0, a_1, \ldots, a_{2^n-1}) = (\overline{b_0}, \overline{b_1}, \ldots, \overline{b_{2^{n-1}-1}})$ be the sequence of a function on V_n where each $\overline{b_j} = (a_{2j}, a_{2j+1})$ is called a *basis*. A basis, say $\overline{b_j}$, is called a $(++)$-*basis* if $\overline{b_j} = \pm(1,1)$ and is called a $(+-)$-*basis* if $\overline{b_j} = \pm(1,-1)$. A fact is that any $(1,-1)$-sequence of length 2^n ($n \ge 2$) is a concatenation of $(++)$-bases and $(+-)$-bases.

In the following discussion, the number of $(++)$-bases in a sequence under consideration will be denoted by $\tau(++)$ and the number of $(+-)$-bases by $\tau(+-)$.

Lemma 12. *Let ξ be the sequence of a function f on V_n. Then $\tau(++) = 2^{n-2} + \frac{1}{4}\Delta(\alpha_1)$ and $\tau(+-) = 2^{n-2} - \frac{1}{4}\Delta(\alpha_1)$, where $\alpha_1 = (0, \ldots, 0, 1)$, the binary representation of integer 1.*

Proof. Write $\xi = a_0, a_1, a_2, a_3, \ldots, a_{2^n-2}, a_{2^n-1}$. Thus $\xi(\alpha_1) = a_1, a_0, a_3, a_2, \ldots, a_{2^n-1}, a_{2^n-2}$ and

$$\Delta(\alpha_1) = \langle \xi, \xi(\alpha_1) \rangle = \sum_{j=0}^{2^{n-1}-1} (a_{2j}a_{2j+1} + a_{2j+1}a_{2j}).$$

Note that

$$a_{2j}a_{2j+1} + a_{2j+1}a_{2j} = \begin{cases} 2 & \text{if } (a_{2j}a_{2j+1}) \text{ is a } (++)\text{-basis} \\ -2 & \text{if } (a_{2j}a_{2j+1}) \text{ is a } (+-)\text{-basis} \end{cases}$$

Thus $\Delta(\alpha_1) = 2(\tau(++) - \tau(+-))$. On the other hand, $2(\tau(++) + \tau(+-)) = 2^n$. Hence $\tau(++) = 2^{n-2} + \frac{1}{4}\Delta(\alpha_1)$ and $\tau(+-) = 2^{n-2} - \frac{1}{4}\Delta(\alpha_1)$. □

Lemma 13. *For any function f on V_n, the nonlinearity of f satisfies*

$$N_f \geq 2^{n-2} - \frac{1}{4}|\Delta(\alpha_1)|.$$

Proof. Obviously, $W(f) \geq \tau(+-)$. By using Lemma 12, $W(f) \geq 2^{n-2} - \frac{1}{4}\Delta(\alpha_1)$, where $W(f)$ is the Hamming weight of f i.e. the number of ones f assumes.

Set $g_j(x) = f(x) \oplus \varphi_j(x)$, where φ_j is the linear function on V_n, whose sequence is ℓ_i, $j = 0, 1, \ldots, 2^n - 1$.

Similarly to $\Delta(\alpha)$ for f, we can write $\Delta^{(j)}$ to denote the auto-correlation of g_j. It is easy to verify that

$$\Delta^{(j)}(\alpha_1) = \begin{cases} \Delta(\alpha_1) & \text{if } \varphi_j(\alpha_1) = 0 \\ -\Delta(\alpha_1) & \text{if } \varphi_j(\alpha_1) = 1 \end{cases}$$

By the same reasoning for $W(f)$, we have

$$W(f \oplus \varphi_j) \geq \begin{cases} 2^{n-2} - \frac{1}{4}\Delta(\alpha_1) & \text{if } \varphi_j(\alpha_1) = 0 \\ 2^{n-2} + \frac{1}{4}\Delta(\alpha_1) & \text{if } \varphi_j(\alpha_1) = 1 \end{cases}$$

Finally, note that $d(f, \varphi_j) = W(f \oplus \varphi_j)$. Hence we have $N_f \geq 2^{n-2} - \frac{1}{4}|\Delta(\alpha_1)|$. □

Now we introduce the first lower bound on nonlinearity:

Theorem 14. *For any function f on V_n, the nonlinearity of f satisfies*

$$N_f \geq 2^{n-2} - \frac{1}{4}\Delta_{min},$$

where $\Delta_{min} = \min\{|\Delta(\alpha)| | \alpha \in V_n, \alpha \neq 0\}$.

Proof. For any fixed s, $0 \leq s \leq 2^n - 1$, let A be a nondegenerate matrix of order n, over $GF(2)$, such that $\alpha_1 A = \alpha_s$. Define $g(x) = f(xA)$. Set $xA = u$. Hence $g(x) = f(u)$ where $xA = u$. Note that

$$g(x) \oplus g(x \oplus \alpha_1) = f(xA) \oplus f(xA \oplus \alpha_1 A) = f(u) \oplus f(u \oplus \alpha_s). \quad (5)$$

Similarly to $\Delta(\alpha)$ defined for f, we can write $\Delta'(\alpha)$ as the auto-correlation of g.

From (5), $\Delta'(\alpha_1) = \Delta(\alpha_s)$. By using Lemma 13, $N_g \geq 2^{n-2} - \frac{1}{4}|\Delta'(\alpha_1)|$. Since A is nondegenerate, $N_g = N_f$. Hence $N_f \geq 2^{n-2} - \frac{1}{4}|\Delta(\alpha_s)|$. As s is arbitrary, $N_f \geq 2^{n-2} - \frac{1}{4}\Delta_{min}$. □

Theorem 14 is tight. This can be seen from the following fact. Let $f(x) = x_1\varphi(y) \oplus \psi(y)$ be a function on V_n, where $x = (x_1, \ldots, x_n)$, $y = (x_3, \ldots, x_n)$, φ and ψ are linear functions on V_{n-2} and $\varphi \neq \psi$. Note that f is quadratic. Using the truth table of f, we can verify that the nonlinearity of f is $N_f = 2^{n-2}$. Obviously, $\Delta(\alpha_{2^{n-1}}) = 0$, where $\alpha_{2^{n-1}} = (1, 0, \ldots, 0)$ is the binary representation of integer 2^{n-1}. This means that the equality in Theorem 14 holds for such a function $f(y) = x_1\varphi(y) \oplus \psi(y)$.

4.2 The Second Lower Bound

By using a result in [2], the authors pointed out in [13] that if f, a function on V_n, satisfies the propagation criterion with respect to all but a subset $\Re$ of vectors in V_n, then the nonlinearity of f satisfies

$$N_f \geq 2^{n-1} - 2^{\frac{n}{2}-1}|\Re|^{\frac{1}{2}}. \tag{6}$$

More recently, a further improvement has been made in [11]:

$$N_f \geq 2^{n-1} - 2^{n-\frac{1}{2}\rho-1} \tag{7}$$

where ρ is the maximum dimension of the linear sub-spaces in $\{0\} \cup \Re^c$ and $\Re^c = V_n - \Re$. (see Theorem 11, [11]).

A shortcoming with (6) and (7) is that when $|\Re|$ is large, estimates provided by (6) or (7) are too far from the real value. For example, let g be a bent function on V_n (n must be even). Suppose $n \geq 4$. Now we construct a function f on V_n: $f(x) = g(x)$ if $x \neq 0$ and $f(0) = 1 \oplus g(0)$. Since $W(g)$ is even, $W(f)$ must be odd. Hence f does not satisfy the propagation characteristics with respect to any vectors and hence $|\Re| = 2^n$. In this case both (6) and (7) give the trivial inequality $N_f \geq 0$. This problem is addressed in the rest of this section.

Let f, a function on V_n, satisfy the propagation criterion with respect to all but a subset $\Re$ of vectors in V_n. For any integer t, $0 \leq t \leq n$, set

$$\Omega = \{\alpha_0, \alpha_{2^t}, \alpha_{2\cdot 2^t}, \ldots, \alpha_{(2^{n-t}-1)2^t}\}.$$

Recall $\alpha_0, \alpha_{2^t}, \alpha_{2\cdot 2^t}, \ldots, \alpha_{(2^{n-t}-1)2^t}$ form a $(n-t)$-dimensional linear subspace of V_n, and $\{\alpha_{2^t}, \alpha_{2^{t+1}}, \ldots, \alpha_{2^{n-1}}\}$ is a basis of this subspace.

From (4),

$$\sigma_j \leq 2^t(\Delta(\alpha_0) + (|\Re \cap \Omega| - 1)\Delta_{max}),$$

where $\Delta_{max} = \max\{|\Delta(\alpha)| |\alpha \in V_n, \alpha \neq 0\}$ and $\sigma_j = \sum_{k=0}^{2^t-1}\langle\xi, \ell_{j2^t+k}\rangle^2$, $j = 0, 1, \ldots, 2^{n-t}-1$. Hence

$$\langle\xi, \ell_{j2^t+k}\rangle^2 \leq 2^t(\Delta(\alpha_0) + (|\Re \cap \Omega| - 1)\Delta_{max}),$$

$j = 0, 1, \ldots, 2^{n-t}-1$, $k = 0, 1, \ldots, 2^t-1$.

Note that $\Delta(\alpha_0) = 2^n$. By using Lemma 6, the nonlinearity of f satisfies

$$N_f \geq 2^{n-1} - 2^{\frac{1}{2}t-1}\sqrt{2^n + (|\Re \cap \Omega| - 1)\Delta_{max}}.$$

Set $r = n - t$. By using a nondegenerate linear transformation on the variables, we have the second lower bound:

Theorem 15. *Let f, a function on V_n, satisfy the propagation criterion with respect to all but a subset $\Re$ of vectors in V_n. Let W be any r-dimensional linear subspace of V_n, $r = 0, 1, \ldots, n$. Then the nonlinearity of f satisfies*

$$N_f \geq 2^{n-1} - 2^{\frac{1}{2}(n-r)-1}\sqrt{2^n + (|\Re \cap W| - 1)\Delta_{max}},$$

where $\Delta_{max} = \max\{|\Delta(\alpha)||\alpha \in V_n, \alpha \neq 0\}$.

Since $|\Delta(\alpha)| \leq 2^n$ for each $\alpha \in V_n$, from Theorem 15, we have

Corollary 16. *Let f, a function on V_n, satisfy the propagation criterion with respect to all but a subset $\Re$ of vectors in V_n. Let W be any r-dimensional linear subspace of V_n, $r = 0, 1, \ldots, n$. Then the nonlinearity of f satisfies*

$$N_f \geq 2^{n-1} - 2^{n-\frac{1}{2}r-1}\sqrt{|\Re \cap W|}.$$

Theorem 15 is more general and gives a better estimate of lower bound than all other known lower bounds. To see this, let $W = V_n$ i.e. $r = n$. Hence we have $N_f \geq 2^{n-1} - \frac{1}{2}\sqrt{2^n + (|\Re| - 1)\Delta_{max}}$. As $\Delta_{max} \leq 2^n$, this estimate is clearly better than (6). On the other hand, if $\Re \cap W = \{\alpha_0 = 0\}$ then $N_f \geq 2^{n-1} - 2^{n-\frac{1}{2}r-1}$, which is exactly (7).

Corollary 16 shows a subtle relationship between the nonlinearity and the propagation characteristic: the nonlinearity is not only influenced by the size of $\Re$ but also by the distribution of $\Re$. This is expressed in a different way in the following corollary:

Corollary 17. *Let f, a function on V_n, satisfy the propagation criterion with respect to all but a subset $\Re$ of vectors in V_n. If the nonlinearity of f satisfies*

$$N_f \leq 2^{n-1} - 2^{n-\frac{1}{2}r-1}p,$$

where r is an integer, $0 \leq r \leq n$, and $p > 0$, then there is a r-dimensional linear subspace of V_n, say W, such that $|\Re \cap W| \geq p^2$.

Table 1 summarizes the main results obtained in this paper, namely two upper and two lower bounds on the nonlinearity of cryptographic functions.

5 Examples and Applications

5.1 For the Two Upper Bounds

The upper bounds stated in Theorems 7 and 10, as well as those in Corollary 11, all represent an improvement on the well-known upper bound $N_f \leq 2^{n-1} - 2^{\frac{1}{2}n-1}$. We found that the two upper bounds described in Theorems 7 and 10, however, have different strengths and weaknesses. This is illustrated by examining the following two different cases.

In the first case, we consider a function f on V_n satisfying the propagation criterion with respect to all but a small subset $\Re$ of vectors in V_n. In particular,

Table 1. Upper and Lower Bounds on Nonlinearity

Upper Bounds	Theorem 7: $N_f \le 2^{n-1} - \frac{1}{2}\sqrt[4]{2^{2n} + \sum_{j=1}^{2^n-1} \Delta^2(\alpha_j)}$
	Theorem 10: $N_f \le 2^{n-1} - \frac{1}{2}\sqrt{2^n + \Delta_{max}}$
Lower Bounds	Theorem 14: $N_f \ge 2^{n-2} - \frac{1}{4}\lvert\Delta_{min}\rvert$
	Theorem 15: $N_f \ge 2^{n-1} - 2^{\frac{1}{2}(n-r)-1}\sqrt{2^n + (\lvert\Re \cap W\rvert - 1)\Delta_{max}}$

where
$\Delta(\alpha) = \langle \xi(0), \xi(\alpha)\rangle$ is the auto-correlation of f with a shift α,
$\Delta_{max} = \max\{|\Delta(\alpha)| | \alpha \in V_n, \alpha \neq 0\}$,
$\Delta_{min} = \min\{|\Delta(\alpha)| | \alpha \in V_n, \alpha \neq 0\}$,
$\Re$ is the set of vectors where the propagation criterion is not fulfilled by f, and W is any r-dimensional linear subspace of V_n, $r = 0, 1, \ldots, n$.

when $|\Re| = 2$, by Corollary 2 of [13], there exists a nondegenerate matrix A of order n over $GF(2)$ such that

$$f(xA) = c_1 x_1 \oplus g(y)$$

where $g(y)$ is a bent function on V_{n-1} and $x = (x_1, y) \in V_n$. In the same paper it was also proved that the two vectors in $\Re$, say $\beta_0 = 0$ and $\beta_1 \neq 0$, satisfy $\Delta(\beta_j) = \pm 2^n$, $j = 0, 1$.

Using Theorem 7,

$$N_f \le 2^{n-1} - \frac{1}{2}\sqrt[4]{2^{2n} + 2^{2n}} = 2^{n-1} - \frac{1}{2}\sqrt[4]{2} \cdot 2^{\frac{1}{2}n}, \tag{8}$$

while using Theorem 10,

$$N_f \le 2^{n-1} - \frac{1}{2}\sqrt{2^n + 2^n} = 2^{n-1} - \frac{1}{2}\sqrt{2} \cdot 2^{\frac{1}{2}n}. \tag{9}$$

For this particular example, the right hand side of (9) is clearly less than that of (8). Consequently, Theorem 10 provides a better estimate than Theorem 7 does.

In the second case, we consider a function g on V_n that is defined as $g(x) = 0$ if $x \neq 0$ and $g(0) = 1$. It is easy to check that for such a function g, $\Delta(\alpha) = \pm(2^n - 4)$ if $\alpha \neq 0$, namely $\Re = V_n$.

Applying Theorem 7,

$$N_f \le 2^{n-1} - \frac{1}{2}\sqrt[4]{2^{2n} + (2^n - 1)(2^n - 4)^2}, \tag{10}$$

while applying Theorem 10,

$$N_f \le 2^{n-1} - \frac{1}{2}\sqrt{2^n + (2^n - 4)} = 2^{n-1} - \frac{1}{2}\sqrt{2^{n+1} - 4}. \tag{11}$$

One can check that the right hand side of (10) is less than that of (11). Hence for such a function g Theorem 7 provides more accurate information than Theorem 10 does.

Theorem 7 generally provides a more accurate estimate on the upper bound of nonlinearity than Theorem 10 when $\Re$ is large, but less so when $\Re$ is small.

Let f, a function on V_n, satisfy the propagation criterion with respect to all but a subset $\Re$ of vectors in V_n. From Theorem 7,

$$N_f \leq 2^{n-1} - \frac{1}{2}\sqrt[4]{2^{2n} + |\Re|\Delta_{min}^2},$$

where $\Delta_{min} = \min\{|\Delta(\alpha)| | \alpha \in V_n, \alpha \neq 0\}$.

It is easy to verify that $|\Delta(\alpha)|$ is divisible by four. Thus $\Delta(\alpha) \neq 0$ implies $|\Delta(\alpha)| \geq 4$. From Theorem 7,

$$N_f \leq 2^{n-1} - \frac{1}{2}\sqrt[4]{2^{2n} + 16|\Re|}.$$

Now we consider another example. From Theorem 3 of [12], if f is a non-bent cubic function then $\Delta_{max} \geq 2^{\frac{1}{2}(n+1)}$, where $\Delta_{max} = \max\{|\Delta(\alpha)| | \alpha \in V_n, \alpha \neq 0\}$. Applying Theorem 10 in this paper, we have

$$N_f \leq 2^{n-1} - \frac{1}{2}\sqrt{2^n + 2^{\frac{1}{2}(n+1)}}.$$

On the other hand, from Theorem 14 in this paper, we obtain Theorem 12 of [11]: if a function f on V_n satisfies the propagation criterion with respect to a vector then the nonlinearity of f satisfies $N_f \geq 2^{n-2}$. In other words, if the nonlinearity of f is less than 2^{n-2} then f does not satisfy the propagation criterion with respect to any vector.

5.2 For the Two Lower Bounds

First, we consider an arbitrary function f on V_n, f. f can always be written as $f(x) = p(y)x_t \oplus q(y)$, for a fixed t, $1 \leq t \leq n$, where $x = (x_1, \ldots, x_n)$, $y = (x_1, \ldots, x_{t-1}, x_{t+1}, \ldots, x_n)$, p and q are functions on V_{n-1}. We can conclude that the nonlinearity of f, N_f, satisfies $N_f \geq 2^{n-2}$ if p is balanced. This follows from the fact that f satisfies the propagation criterion with respect to $\alpha_{2^{n-t}} = (0, \ldots, 0, 1, 0, \ldots, 0)$, whose tth component is the only nonzero bit. Hence according to Theorem 14, we have $N_f \geq 2^{n-2}$.

Now we consider another example that is related to Theorem 15. Let f be a function on V_n, whose nonlinearity N_f satisfies $N_f = 2^{n-2}$. The function $f(x) = x_1\varphi(y) \oplus \psi(y)$ presented at the end of Subsection 4.1 is an example of such a function. For any function f with $N_f = 2^{n-2}$, the equality in Corollary 17 which is derived from Theorem 15, holds when $p = 2^{\frac{1}{2}r-1}$, where r is an arbitrary integer, $2 \leq r \leq n$. Using the same corollary, one can see that there is a r-dimensional linear subspace of V_n, say W, such that $|\Re \cap W| \geq 2^{r-2}$. In particular, when $r = n$, i.e. $W = V_n$, we have $|\Re| \geq 2^{n-2}$.

6 Conclusion

Two upper and two lower bounds on the nonlinearity of a Boolean function have been established. These bounds could be particularly useful when certain structural information on a Boolean function is available. All the bounds have been primarily based on the auto-correlation of a function under consideration. This opens up a possible new avenue for future research, that is to extend the results so that they take into account other factors such as linear structures, algebraic degree and global avalanche characteristics (GAC) introduced in [12].

Acknowledgments: We would like to thank the anonymous referees for Eurocrypt'96 whose comments helped in improving the presentation of this paper.

References

1. Beauchamp, K. G.: Applications of Walsh and Related Functions with an Introduction to Sequency Functions. Academic Press London, New York, Tokyo 1984.
2. Carlet, C.: Partially-bent functions. Designs, Codes and Cryptography **3** (1993) 135–145.
3. Cohen, G. D., Karpovsky, M. G., H. F. Mattson, J., Schatz, J. R.: Covering radius — survey and recent results. IEEE Transactions on Information Theory **IT-31** (1985) 328–343.
4. Dillon, J. F.: A survey of bent functions. The NSA Technical Journal (1972) 191–215. (unclassified)
5. MacWilliams, F. J., Sloane, N. J. A.: The Theory of Error-Correcting Codes. North-Holland Amsterdam, New York, Oxford 1978.
6. Matsui, M.: Linear cryptanalysis method for DES cipher. In Advances in Cryptology - EUROCRYPT'93 (1994) vol. 765, LNCS Springer-Verlag, Berlin, New York pp. 386–397.
7. Preneel, B., Govaerts, R., Vandewalle, J.: Boolean functions satisfying higher order propagation criteria. In Advances in Cryptology - EUROCRYPT'91 (1991) vol. 547, LNCS Springer-Verlag, Berlin, New York pp. 141–152.
8. Preneel, B., Leekwijck, W. V., Linden, L. V., Govaerts, R., Vandewalle, J.: Propagation characteristics of boolean functions. In Advances in Cryptology - EUROCRYPT'90 (1991) vol. 437, LNCS Springer-Verlag, Berlin, New York pp. 155–165.
9. Rothaus, O. S.: On "bent" functions. Journal of Combinatorial Theory **Ser. A, 20** (1976) 300–305.
10. Seberry, J., Zhang, X. M., Zheng, Y.: Nonlinearity and propagation characteristics of balanced boolean functions. Information and Computation **119** (1995) 1–13.
11. Seberry, J., Zhang, X. M., Zheng, Y.: The relationship between propagation characteristics and nonlinearity of cryptographic functions. Journal of Universal Computer Science **1** (1995) 136–150. (available at `http://hgiicm.tu-graz.ac.at/`)
12. Zhang, X. M., Zheng, Y.: GAC — the criterion for global avalanche characteristics of cryptographic functions. Journal of Universal Computer Science **1** (1995) 316–333. (available at `http://hgiicm.tu-graz.ac.at/`)
13. Zhang, X. M., Zheng, Y.: Characterizing the structures of cryptographic functions satisfying the propagation criterion for almost all vectors. Design, Codes and Cryptography **7** (1996) 111–134.

Foiling Birthday Attacks in Length-Doubling Transformations

Benes: a non-reversible alternative to Feistel

William Aiello and Ramarathnam Venkatesan

Math and Cryptography Research Group, Bell Communications Research, 445 South Street, Morristown NJ 07960. {venkie,aiello}@bellcore.com

Abstract. For many cryptographic primitives, e.g., hashing and pseudorandom functions & generators, doubling the output length is useful even if the doubling transformation is not reversible. For these cases, we present a non-reversible construction based on a Benes network, as an alternative to the traditional Feistel construction (which is the basis of DES).

Assuming that a given primitive behaves like an n-bit to n-bit random function, we present a length-doubling scheme that yields a $2n$-bit to $2n$-bit function that provably requires $\Omega(2^n)$ queries to distinguish with $\Theta(1)$ probability from a truly random function of that length. This is true even if the adversary is of unlimited computing power and is allowed to query the function adaptively. Our construction is minimal in the sense that omitting any operation makes the resulting network susceptible to birthday attacks using $O(2^{n/2})$ queries.

Feistel networks also use truly random n-bit functions to achieve $2n$-bit functions. Luby and Rackoff [16] showed that 3 and 4 round Feistel networks require $\Omega(2^{n/2})$ queries to distinguish with $\Theta(1)$ probability from truly random. We show that these bounds are tight by showing that these networks are susceptible various types of birthday attacks using $O(2^{n/2})$ queries.

1 Introduction

Many cryptographic primitives in practice are believed to behave like "random functions" or at least this turns out be a good empirical approximation. Using the random function model, several works have made a rigorous analysis of some standard and new cryptographic schemes [1, 2, 20, 22].

In fact, most designs of primitives (e.g., MD5,SHA) involve *rounds* of "mixing" the input, creating an "avalanche effect," and making the result look "random." In the case of DES, one starts with a 32-bit valued primitive which is iterated 16 rounds to get a 64-bit valued "random permutation." In the case of, say, 128-bit cryptographic hash function constructions based on 64-bit block cyphers, meticulous care must be exerted to ensure that the resultant function behaves like a 128-bit random function. Otherwise, it may yield to 2^{32} step birthday attacks as a 64-bit random function would. In fact our work originated in the process of

Ueli Maurer (Ed.): EUROCRYPT '96 Proceedings, LNCS 1070

looking for a practical scheme that avoids these problems and admits an analysis in a random function model. Recent attacks on some of these cryptographic primitives are practical [10] or bordering on feasibility [21]. Hence constructions using old smaller-length primitives to get new longer-length primitives—with a provable increase in security—would be desirable.

The Feistel transformation (See Fig. 1) is an obvious candidate for such a construction, and indeed, its security properties have been well studied. Luby and Rackoff [16] study three and four rounds of the Feistel transformation. They show that using pseudo-random functions (introduced in [11]) as n-bit primitives yields a $2n$-bit pseudo-random permutation. In a crucial step in their proof, they analyze the case when the primitives are n-bit truly random functions. They show that the three-round Feistel network requires $\Omega(2^{n/2})$ queries to distinguish with $\Theta(1)$ probability from a truly random $2n$ bit function. (Later, Maurer [17] simplified their proof.) However, they show that the same network can be distinguished in a constant number of queries if the adversary is allowed to ask for inverses of points chosen in the range. They then show that the four-round Feistel network requires $\Omega(2^{n/2})$ queries to distinguish with $\Theta(1)$ probability from a truly random $2n$ bit function even when inverse queries are allowed.

Luby and Rackoff were concerned with the polynomial time invariant model where the difference between the security of 2^n and $2^{n/2}$ is not important. However, in practice this difference can be crucial. For example, using a construction with security $2^{n/2}$ to design a 64-bit function from 32-bit random primitives would yield a function which could be distinguished in approximately 2^{16} queries whereas using a construction with 2^n security would require approximately 2^{32} queries. Hence, an important goal is to resolve the query security of the three-and-four-round Feistel constructions. In this paper we show that the Luby-Rackoff bounds are tight by showing that these networks are susceptible to various types of birthday attacks using $O(2^{n/2})$ queries.

Given the limited security provided by using just a few rounds of Feistel it is natural to ask if there is an alternative construction which admits analysis and provides greater security. In this paper we provide such an alternative which we call the Benes network construction (two back-to-back butterflies, see Fig. 1). The Benes construction has the following properties. First, it is formally provable that our functions cannot be distinguished with $\Theta(1)$ probability, in an information theroretic sense, from truly random ones, unless it is queried $\Omega(2^n)$ times. Second, it is minimal in the sense that deleting any one of the operations reduces the security. Third, it yields constructions and variations that are efficient.

We introduce a formal notion of (query) security in Section 2. Generalizing birthday and other statistical attacks, we introduce the notion of a *dependency graph* on a (query) sample of size q. The nodes of this graph are pairs of strings which are internal variables of the construction that are not directly observable from the input-output relations. Two types of dependencies are identified for these variables which are signified by edges of two colors between corresponding nodes. We show that the output random variables are k-wise independent if and only if there are no alternatingly colored l-cycles in the graph, for $l \leq k \leq q$. We then show that with very high probability the dependency graph has no such q cycles.

Our construction has many applications including authentication, random number generation, stream or packet encypherment, and reducing correlations in key exchange protocols. We also suggest a way to double hash code lengths which admits some parallelism and eludes attacks like [21, 10]. (See Section 3.)

2 Definitions and Main Results

Let $\mathbf{F}_n$ be the set of all functions $f : \{0,1\}^n \rightarrow \{0,1\}^n$. We would like to construct a family of functions from $2n$ bits to $2n$ bits using functions from $\mathbf{F}_n$ such that the functions drawn randomly from this new family behave very much like randomly chosen functions from $\mathbf{F}_{2n}$. To formalize this we make the following definitions.

Adaptive Adversaries: Let A be an information theoretic adversary (i.e., of unbounded computing power) which can make queries to a function as an oracle. We limit our adversaries (only) by the number of query points. A can *adaptively* make queries and obtain function values at the query points. Then, over this sample he could perform *any* test. We say A distinguishes $\mathbf{G}_n \subset \mathbf{F}_n$ from $\mathbf{H}_n \subset \mathbf{F}_n$ with advantage

$$|\Pr[A^g(1^n)=1|g \in_R \mathbf{G}_n] - \Pr[A^g(1^n)=1|g \in_R \mathbf{H}_n]|.$$

When $\mathbf{G}_n$ and $\mathbf{H}_n$ are understood from context let $q_A(n)$ be the number of queries made by $A(1^n)$.

Definition 1 (Query Security) *A function family $\mathbf{G}_n \subset \mathbf{F}_n$ has query security at least $s(n)$ if there is an constant $\alpha > 0$ such that all information theoretic adversaries A can distinguish $\mathbf{G}_n$ from $\mathbf{F}_n$ with advantage at most $(q_A(n)/s(n))^\alpha$. For the purposes of this paper α will always be 2.*

For example, suppose that $\mathbf{G}_n$ can be distinguished from $\mathbf{F}_n$ in q queries with advantage at most $q^2/2^n$. Then the query security of $\mathbf{G}_n$ is at least $2^{n/2}$. When it is clear from context that we are using the information theoretic model we will simply denote query security by security.

The Feistel transformation is a well-known function family from $2n$ bits to $2n$ bits and it is natural to ask whether it achieves sufficient security. Let us first review the construction.

For any $f \in \mathbf{F}_n$ define the $2n$ bit to $2n$ bit Feistel transformation G_f as $G_f(l,r) = (r, l \oplus f(r))$. Given a collection of k functions $\mathcal{A} = (f_1, f_2, \ldots, f_k)$ from n bit to n bit define $G_{\mathcal{A}} \in \mathbf{F}_{2n}$ as the composition of $G_{f_1}, G_{f_2}, \ldots, G_{f_k}$. More explicity, if the input to $G_{\mathcal{A}}$ is denoted l_0, r_0 then the output l_k, r_k can be computed by the recurrence $l_i = r_{i-1}$, $r_i = f_i(r_{i-1}) \oplus l_{i-1}$. We say that l_i, r_i are the output of the ith round. DES may be described by $G_{\mathcal{A}}$ where there are $k = 16$ functions (rounds) and the functions f_i are given by the DES key and the s-boxes. For now we will consider functions which are truly random functions.

Denote the set of all $G_{\mathcal{A}}$ (where each of the k functions in $\mathcal{A}$ range over all the functions in $\mathbf{F}_n$) as $\mathbf{G}_{2n}^k$.

As is well known, the Feistel transformation is a permutation. For permutations the definition of security must be modified since a random permutation on n bits can be distiguished from a random function from n bits to n bits in $\theta(2^{n/2})$ queries (a random function will repeat with constant probability whereas a permutation obviously will not). When discussing a permutation family we implicitly assume that the adversary is trying to distinguish it from a random permutation, and the definition of security is adjusted accordingly.

Not only is the Feistel transformation a permutation, it is also invertible (even without inverting the underlying n bit to n bit random functions). Following [16], define super query security, or super security, identically to query security except that the adversary is allowed to query both the function and its inverse.

Luby and Rackoff [16] studied the security and super security of Feistel transformations (with random functions) with a small number of rounds. They broke two round Feistel in a constant number of function queries, and they broke three round Feistel in a constant number of function and inverse queries. To complement these results they derived lower bounds, summarized below, for the security and super-security of the three and four round Feistel transformations, respectively.

THEOREM 1 *(Luby, Rackoff) The security of $\mathbf{G}_{2n}^3$ is $\Omega(2^{n/2})$ and the super security of $\mathbf{G}_{2n}^4$ is also $\Omega(2^{n/2})$.*

The proof of this theorem, and the others cited in this section, will be given in subsequent sections.

For DES $n = 32$ and so the above suggests that three (four) rounds of DES may have (super) query security of 2^{16} or more. In practice, this is very little security and so a natural question is whether the lower bound of Luby and Rackoff can be improved. We show that it cannot by providing the following matching upper bound.

THEOREM 2 *The security of $\mathbf{G}_{2n}^3$ and $\mathbf{G}_{2n}^4$ is $O(2^{n/2})$. Moreover, the adversary need not make any inverse queries.*

In [27] three generalizations of the Feistel transformation are described. These transformations map kn bit to kn bits using functions from $\mathbf{F}_n$. Zheng, et. al. show that if they are run for sufficiently many rounds (i.e., $2k-1$, $2k$, and $k+1$ depending on the variation) then they have security $\Omega(2^{n/2})$. Using arguments similar to those for the Feistel transformation, we can show that this is tight. We omit the details for now.

Given the limited security of the three and four round Feistel transformations, a natural problem is to construct a $2n$-to-$2n$ bit transformation which achieves security $\Omega(2^n)$ using n-to-n bit random functions and just a few rounds. The emphasis here is on security and not on invertibility so that non-invertible transformations are acceptable.

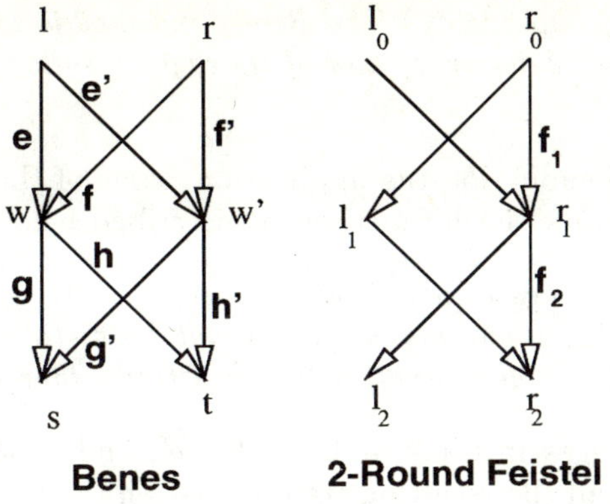

Fig. 1. Benes and Feistel (2-round) transformations from $2n$-bits to $2n$-bits. Edge labels denote random functions from n-bits to n-bits. Unlabelled edges are identities . Node values are bitwise xor of values of incoming edges.

In this paper we describe one solution to this problem. (See Fig. 1) Given four functions e, f, e', f' from n bits to n bits, we use them to define the butterfly transformation from $2n$ bits to $2n$ bits. On input l, r, the output w, w' is given by

$$w = e(l) \oplus f(r); \quad w' = e'(l) \oplus f'(r).$$

Let $\mathbf{B}_{2n}$ be the set of all butterfly transformations where e, f, e', f' range over $\mathbf{F}_n$. Given eight functions from n bits to n bits, e, f, e', f', g, g', h, h', define the Benes transformation (back-to-back butterfly) as the composition of two butterfly transformations. The first stage is as above. Then, the second transformation maps w, w' into s, t as follows:

$$s = g(w) \oplus g'(w'); \quad t = h(w) \oplus h'(w').$$

Let $\mathbf{B}_{2n}^2$ be the set of all Benes transformations where each of the eight functions range over $\mathbf{F}_n$.

Clearly, functions drawn randomly from $\mathbf{B}_{2n}^2$ are information theoretically distinguishable from functions drawn randomly from $\mathbf{F}_{2n}$. However, as we state formally below, even an information theoretic adversary requires a large number of queries to the randomly drawn functions in order to distinguish $\mathbf{B}_{2n}^2$ from $\mathbf{F}_{2n}$ with noticeable advantage.

THEOREM 3 *The Benes family $\mathbf{B}_{2n}^2$ has security $\Theta(2^n)$.*

Corollary 1 *The Benes transformation using n-bit pseudo-random functions in place of n-bit random functions yields a $2n$-bit pseudo-random function.*

The proof of this corollary follows the proof in [16] and is omitted.

In a natural sense the Benes construction is optimal. In fact, we next show that its security drops to $O(2^{n/2})$ queries, if any edge is *deleted*.

THEOREM 4 (Edge Optimality) *The Benes and modified Benes transformations are minimal: i.e., deletion of any of its edges results in a function which has security* $O(2^{n/2})$.

Simplifications: Depending on the application, some of the random functions can be replaced by simpler hash functions as described below.

THEOREM 5 *The Benes transformation using k-universal hash functions in the top butterfly produces outputs which cannot be distinguished from k-wise independent outputs in q queries with advantage better than* $q^2/2^{2n}$.

If the two cross edges in the first butterfly, e', and f, are replaced by the identity function we call the resulting transformation the modified Benes transformation. All of the results above hold for the modified Benes transformation as well.

Finally, we would like to mention another candidate method for producing a $2n$ bit to $2n$ function family from a n bit to n bit function family. Suppose that the functions in the function family $\mathbf{H}_n \subset \mathbf{F}_n$ can be indexed by a key of length n. Then a function family from $2n$ to $2n$ bits with a key of length $2n$ can be constructed as follows. Given k_1, k_2 as the $2n$-bit key and w, x as the $2n$-bit input, compute the output y, z as follows. First compute $k_1' = f_{k_1}(w)$ and $k_2' = f_{k_2}(w)$. Then compute $y = f_{k_1'}(x)$ and $z = f_{k_2'}(x)$. This construction is similar to the construction of Goldwasser, Goldreich, and Micali [11]. Using analysis similar to that in [11] it can be shown that if $\mathbf{H}_n$ is pseudo-random (as defined in [11]) then the new family is pseudo-random [24, 1]; however, a simple birthday attack on k_1' or k_2' upper bounds the query security by $O(2^{n/2})$ [24].

3 Applications to Hashing

Our construction gives a hueristic for doubling the output length of keyed hash functions (See for example [23]). Let H be a one-way hash function that behaves as a random function to n bits when keyed by a random string K. Define $\tilde{H}_K(x) \equiv H(K, x)$. MD5 is a candidate for such a hash function with $n = 128$. Let $\bar{K} = K_1, \ldots, K_8$ and let $B^2_{\bar{K}}$ be the modified Benes transformation where the random functions are instantiated by the keyed hash functions H_{K_i}, $i := 1, \ldots, 8$. Now to hash a document D, devide the text in some well-defined way into two equal parts D_0 and D_1, and compute $B^2_{\bar{K}}(D_0, D_1)$. The output length of $B^2_{\bar{K}}$ is twice that of $H(K, D)$. Surprisingly, the running times have approximately the same ratio. This is because the four hash functions computed in the top butterfly of the Benes transformation each operate on only half the document. The hash computations in the bottom butterfly are all on inputs of size n independent of the length of the document. Note that the Benes transformation admits some parallelism: two independent processes would run in approximately half the time of one sequential process.

To avoid attacks such as those in [5, 7, 10, 21], $\bar{K}$ may itself need to be seeded in such a way as to not allow the adversary to vary one of the eight keys while leaving the others fixed. In practice this can be instantiated by letting $K_1, \ldots, K_8$ be the output of a cryptographically secure random generator on a random seed [6, 26]. Such a transformation is one-way and almost surely one-to-one.

4 Security of Feistel Transformations

Proof of theorem 2

3-round case: The adversary evaluates the given function on $q+2$ inputs. The first q distinct inputs are $(l_0, r_0^{(1)}), \ldots, (l_0, r_0^{(q)})$. For notational simplicity let $r_1^{(m)} = \alpha_m$, and $r_2^{(m)} = \beta_m$, and $r_3^{(m)} = \gamma_m$, $m := 1, \ldots, q$. Using this notation, the corresponding outputs are labelled by $(\beta_1, \gamma_1), \ldots, (\beta_q, \gamma_q)$. (See Fig. 2)

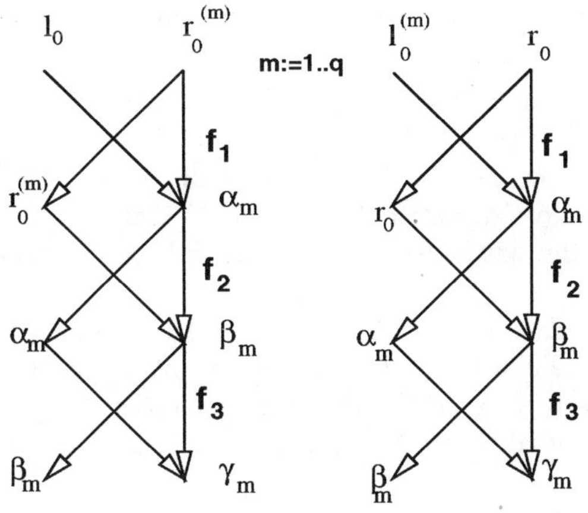

Fig. 2. Distinguishing Three Round Feistel Tranformations from Random Ones:Attacks matching the lower bounds on Luby-Rackoff pseudo-random functions

The adversary computes $\beta_m \bigoplus r_0^{(m)}$, $m := 1, \ldots, q$, and checks for collisions. If he finds a collision at $m = i$ and $m = j$ he queries at $l_0', r_0^{(m)}$, and obtains outputs β_m', γ_m', for $m := i, j$. If now $\beta_i' \bigoplus r_0^i = \beta_j' \bigoplus r_0^j$, the adversary rejects the function as non-random.

Now let us analyze how G_{f_1,f_2,f_3} fares under this adversary. With probability $\Omega(q^2/2^n)$, (for $q^2/2^n < \delta < 1$) there exist an i and a j such that $f_1(r_0^{(i)}) = f_1(r_0^{(j)})$. Since l_0 is held constant and $\alpha_m = l_0 \bigoplus f_1(r_0^{(m)})$, we have $\alpha_i = \alpha_j$ and $f_2(\alpha_i) = f_2(\alpha_j)$. Since $\beta_m = r_0^{(m)} \bigoplus f_2(\alpha_m)$ one gets the collision $\beta_i \bigoplus r_0^{(i)} = \beta_j \bigoplus r_0^{(j)}$. It is easy to check that $\beta_i' \bigoplus r_0^{(i)} = \beta_j' \bigoplus r_0^{(j)}$ as well. Hence with probability $\Omega(q^2/2^n)$ the adversary will reject $G_{\mathcal{A}}$. It is easy to show that the adversary will reject truly random permutation with probability $O(q^2/2^{2n})$. We omit the details here.

We have a second attack on 3-round Feistel but due to lack of space we omit it. We can also upper bound the security of the generalized Feistel transformations described by Zheng, et. al. [27]. The two $k+1$ round transformations are broken using attacks similar to the attack above and the $2k-1$ round transformation is broken using an attack similar to our second attack on the three rounds. The complete description of these attacks will be given in the full paper.

4-round Case: In addition to the notation above let $r_4^{(m)} = \delta_m$ Adversary evaluates the function on q distinct inputs $(l_0^{(m)}, r_0)$ and gets outputs γ_m, δ_m, and checks whether there exists i, j so that $l_i \bigoplus \gamma_i = l_j \bigoplus \gamma_j$. It can be checked that the probability this occurs for the 4-round Feistel is approximately twice the probability this occurs for a truly random permutation.

5 Analysis of Benes Transformation

Recall that we do not insist on invertible transformations. As a starting point for understanding the implications of this assumption we first analyze the K transformation which we now define. As we will see, the Benes transformation is simply the bitwise xor of two independent K transformations. While the K transformation has the same security as 3-round Feistel transformations, it is easier to analyze.

Given e, f, g, and h in $\mathbf{F}_n$ and input l, r, $K_{e,f,g,h}(l,r)$ is computed as follows. Let $w = e(l) \bigoplus f(r)$. Then the output s, t is simply $g(w), h(w)$. To visualize the K transformation simply delete all the edges incident to the intermediate node w' in the Benes transformation (See Figure 3).

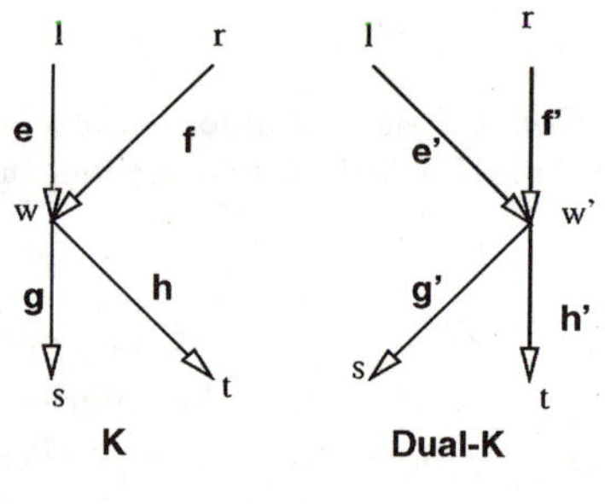

Fig. 3. The K and Dual-K transformations, which jointly yield a 2x2 double butterfly

Lemma 1 *If e, f, g, and h are truly random functions then $K_{e,f,g,h}$ has security* $\Theta(2^{n/2})$.

Proof: To show that the security is $\Omega(2^{n/2})$ note that if the $w_1, \ldots, w_q$ are all distinct then all the bits of the output s_i, t_i, $i = 1, \ldots, q$, are uniform and independent. Hence, following [16] and [17], the distinguishing advantage is at most the probability that the w_i are not all distinct. For any two distinct inputs, l_i, r_i and l_j, r_j, the probability that $w_i = w_j$ is $1/2^n$, since e and f are truly random. It follows that the distinguishing advantage is at most $q^2/2^{n+1}$.

This security bound is tight. In $\Theta(2^{n/2})$ queries of K there exists i, j such that $w_i = w_j$, and hence $s_i, t_i = s_j, t_j$, with constant probability, . But the probability that the entire output collides for a random function in this many queries is $\Theta(2^{-n})$.

Simplifications: If e is a 2-universal hash function and f is the identity function (or visa versa) one gets the same security. Call this the modified K transformation. To achieve a lower bound on security the analysis is the same as above except that there are two cases when analyzing the probability that $w_i = w_j$. If $l_i = l_j$ then r_i must be distinct from r_j (since queries are distinct), hence w_i is distinct from w_j and the probability is zero. If $l_i \neq l_j$ then the probability that $w_i = w_j$ is 2^{-n} since the hash function is 2-universal. We omit the simple upper bound of the security.

Having analyzed K, we define $B^2(l, r)$ as the bitwise exclusive-or of the outputs of $K_{e,f,g,h}(l, r)$ and $K_{e',f',g',h'}(l, r)$. We will show that this exclusive-or at least *squares* the security. For a quick review of our notation, see Figure 1. We will now prove Theorem 3.

Proof of Theorem 3:

Before analyzing the double butterfly transformation we will first show that a single butterfly produces random and independent output except when the inputs have a special form. Given a set of q pairs $(w_1, w_1'), \ldots, (w_q, w_q')$, the **dependency graph** on these pairs is defined as follows. Consider the pairs as nodes in a graph. If any two nodes in the graph are equal in the left-hand coordinate put an edge between them and color it with the label "left." Edges so colored will be called "left edges." If any two nodes in the graph are equal in the right-hand coordinate put a "right edge" between them.

Note that the edge relation is transitive. For example, if there is a right edge between node u and v and another right edge between v and w, then there is a right edge between u and w.

Define a *bichromatic path or cycle* to be a path or cycle, respectively, which contains both left and right edges if it is of length greater than one. (For notational convenience we will consider every path of length one to be bichromatic). Define an *alternating path or cycle* to be a path or cycle, respectively, in which the edges stricly alternate color as the path or cycle is traversed. Clearly, an alternating path (cycle) is a bichromatic path (cycle). The following is also true.

Claim 1 *If there is a bichromatic cycle then there is an alternating cycle.*

Proof: Omitted.

We can now state our main lemma.

Lemma 2 *The outputs of a butterfly transformation are random and independent iff the dependency graph of the inputs has no alternating cycles.*

Proof:

For reasons that will be clear below we will use the notation of the second butterfly in the double butterfly transformation. That is, the inputs and outputs are denoted $(w_1, w'_1), \ldots, (w_q, w'_q)$ and $(s_1, t_1), \ldots, (s_q, t_q)$, respectively, where $s_i = g(w_i) \oplus g'(w'_i)$ and $t_i = h(w_i) \oplus h'(w'_i)$.

To start let us describe a simple relationship for alternating paths. Without loss of generality let $(w_1, w'_1), (w_2, w'_2), \ldots, (w_{l+1}, w'_{l+1})$ be an alternating path with l edges. Let $(s_1, t_1), \ldots, (s_{l+1}, t_{l+1})$ be the associated outputs. The following claim can be easily verified by induction.

Claim 2 *If an alternating path begins with a right-edge and ends with a left-edge, then*

$$\bigoplus_{m=1}^{l+1} s_m = g(w_1) \bigoplus g'(w'_{l+1})$$

If the path begins with a left-edge rather than a right-edge, $g'(w'_1)$ is substituted for $g(w_1)$ in the above. If the path ends with a right-edge rather than a left-edge, $g(w_{l+1})$ is substituted for $g'(w'_{l+1})$ in the above.

The expressions for $\bigoplus_{m=1}^{l+1} t_m$ in terms of h and h' are analogous.

Demonstrating the correlation due to an alternating cycle is easy. An alternating cycle is simply an alternating path with an even number of edges where the node 1 and node $l+1$ are identified. (i.e., $w_{l+1} = w_1$ and $w'_{l+1} = w'_1$). Using the expression above for even length paths, the sum of the output values around the cycle is given by $\left(\bigoplus_{m=1}^{l} s_m\right) \bigoplus s_{l+1} = g(w_1) \bigoplus g'(w'_{l+1})$. Since $s_{l+1} = g(w_{l+1}) \bigoplus g'(w'_{l+1})$ and $g(w_{l+1}) = g(w_1)$, it follows that $\bigoplus_{m=1}^{l} s_m = 0$ for an alternating cycle.

Now suppose that there is no alternating cycle. We will show that all of the outputs are random and independent. We will first show that $s_1, \ldots, s_q$ are uniform and independent. A similar argument shows that the $t_1, \ldots, t_q$ are uniform and independent. That the two sequences are independent of each other follows from the fact that g and g' are indpendent of h and h'.

We will use the following claim which follows from the transitivity of the edges and the lack of alternating cycles.

Claim 3 *If there is a bichromatic path between two nodes, then there is a unique alternating path between those two nodes which is also the shortest path.*

Assume that the dependency graph is connected. (If not, repeat the analysis below on each component.) We start by finding a node which has only right edges or only left edges incident. It is easy to check that such a node must exist since the dependency graph has no alternating cycles. Without loss of generality, assume that this node has only right edges. Relabel this node to (w_1, w'_1).

Now create a breadth-first search tree with (w_1, w_1') as the root and label the nodes according to the breadth-first order. As is well known, the tree paths are the shortest paths between the root and the other nodes. By Claim 3 all shortest paths are alternating paths. Hence, the color of the edges of the tree alternate with the level. For example, the first level edges (between the root and the depth 1 nodes) are colored "right," and the second level edges are colored "left," etc. We will use the following claim about this tree.

Claim 4 *(i) Suppose a node v has breadth-first order i and depth $d > 0$ which is even. Let the right coordinate of v be w_i'. No other node with breadth-first order less than i has right coordinate equal to w_i'. In fact, all other nodes with right coordinate w_i' are children of v.*

(ii) Suppose a node v has breadth-first order i and depth $d \geq 1$ which is odd. Let the left coordinate of v be w_i. No other node with breadth-first order less than i has left coordinate equal to w_i. In fact, all other nodes with left coordinate equal to w_i are children of v.

Proof: (i) Due to the fact that the levels of the tree alternate color, v is connected to its parent by a left edge and connected to all of its children by right edges. If v were connected by a right edge to another node in the discrepancy graph besides its children in the breadth-first search tree, then there would be a bichromatic cycle in the discrepancy graph. (ii) Similar. ■

For fixed but arbitrary values of $\sigma_1, \ldots, \sigma_q$, define $E(i)$ for $i > 0$ to be the event that $(s_1 = \sigma_1) \wedge \cdots \wedge (s_i = \sigma_i)$ and $E(0)$ to be the null event where, as before, $s_i = g(w_i) \oplus g'(w_i')$. We must show that $\Pr[E(q)] = 2^{-qn}$. We start as follows:

$$\Pr[E(q)] = \sum_{\bar{g}_1} \Pr[g(w_1) = \bar{g}_1] \; \Pr[E(q) \mid g(w_1) = \bar{g}_1].$$

Since $\Pr[g(w_1) = \bar{g}_1] = 2^{-n}$ for all $\bar{g}_1 \in \{0,1\}$, it is enough to show that $\Pr[E(q) \mid g(w_1) = \bar{g}_1] = 2^{-qn}$ for all $\bar{g}_1$. Fix an arbitrary value of $\bar{g}_1$. As can be easily verified, it is enough to show that $\Pr[s_i = \sigma_i \mid E(i-1) \wedge g(w_1) = \bar{g}_1] = 2^{-n}$ for all $i := 1, \ldots, q$.

First consider $i := 1$. In this case, $\Pr[g(w_1) \oplus g'(w_1') = \sigma_1 \mid g(w_1) = \bar{g}_1]$ which is clearly equal to 2^{-n}.

Now consider the case when $i \geq 1$. Let $1 < \alpha < \beta < \gamma < \cdots < i$ be the breadth-first order of the nodes on the path from the root to (w_i, w_i'). That is, this path is given by $(w_1, w_1'), (w_\alpha, w_\alpha'), (w_\beta, w_\beta'), \ldots, (w_i, w_i')$. Suppose (w_i, w_i') has odd depth. Using the path formula in Claim 2 the following holds,

$$\begin{aligned} &\Pr[g(w_i) \oplus g'(w_i') = \sigma_i \mid E(i-1) \wedge g(w_1) = \bar{g}_1] \\ &= \Pr[g(w_i) \oplus \bar{g}_1 = \sigma_1 \oplus \sigma_\alpha \oplus \sigma_\beta \oplus \cdots \oplus \sigma_i \mid E(i-1) \wedge g(w_1) = \bar{g}_1]. \end{aligned}$$

By Claim 4, w_i is not a left coordinate for any node with breadth-first order less than i. Hence, the event $g(w_i) \oplus \bar{g}_1 = \sigma_1 \oplus \sigma_\alpha \oplus \cdots \oplus \sigma_i$ is independent of the event $E(i-1) \wedge g(w_1) = \bar{g}_1$ and thus the above probability is 2^{-n}.

The analysis is similar in the case that (w_i, w_i') has even depth.

■

Before completing the main theorem, let us state the following corollary of Lemma 2.

Corollary 2 *The outputs of a butterfly transformation are k-wise independent iff the dependency graph of the inputs contains no alternating cycles of length k.*

Proof: If there is an alternating cycle of length k in the inputs then the corresponding outputs sum to zero as before. To show the converse consider any k outputs and their corresponding inputs. Apply Lemma 2 to dependency graph induced by these input nodes. There is no alternating cycle in this dependency graph by hypothesis, and hence all k outputs are independent. ■

Let us now return to the proof of the main theorem. By Lemma 2, if the dependency graph of the outputs of the first butterfly $(w_1, w_1'), \ldots, (w_q, w_q')$ does not contain an alternating cycle, then the outputs of the second butterfly are uniform and independent. Hence, the advantage of an adversary is bounded from above by the probability that the dependency graph of $(w_1, w_1'), \ldots, (w_q, w_q')$ contains an alternating cycle.

The number of possible alternating cycles of length $2j$ on q nodes is $q!/(q-2j)!j$. Hence the probability that there is an alternating cycle is

$$\leq \sum_j \frac{q!}{(q-2j)!j} 2^{-2nj} \leq \sum_j \left(\frac{q^2}{2^{2n}}\right)^j \leq \frac{q^2}{2^{2n}}.$$

assuming $q^2/2^{2n} < 1$.

This concludes the proof that the security of the Benes transformation is $\Omega(2^n)$. The proof that the security is $O(2^n)$ is easy and omitted due to lack of space.

Lemma 3 *The modified Benes transformation has security $\Omega(2^n)$.*

Proof Sketch: It can be shown that the probability that the top butterfly produces an alternating cycle of length $2j$ is $\leq 2^{-2jn}$. But we omit the details. ■

Finally, let us sketich the proof of the minimality of the modified Benes transformation.

Proof Sketch of Theorem 4. When one of the edges of the top butterfly is deleted it is easy to create a sequence of q inputs which yields an alternating cycle of length two in the intermediate variables with probability $\Theta(q^2/2^n)$.

When one of the edges of the bottom butterfly is deleted it is easy to show that either the left or right hand output repeats with probability approximately twice as large as for a random function. ■

6 Open Questions

A natural open problem is bounding the query security for the five-round Feistel transformation. A related problem is determining the number of rounds needed to achieve query security 2^n.

Unfortunately, n-bit truly random primitives are not available for values of n of interest. In such a case the actual security of the Benes or Feistel construction depends a great deal on the quality of the underlying primitive. For example, with $n = 32$, the four-round Feistel transformation with truly random functions requires approximately 2^{16} queries to distinguish from a truly random 64-bit function. However, when the truly random functions are instantiated by S-boxes, differential cryptanalysis [4] needs only 16 chosen plaintext queries (or 2^{33} known plaintext queries) for the independent key case. (See also, [13, 18].) However, additional rounds appear to add increasing amounts of security. Shedding light on how additional rounds of the Feistel or Benes transformation may improve security in the complexity-theoretic setting is an important open problem.

References

1. M. Bellare, R. Canetti, and H. Krawcyk, "Keying MD5 – Message Authentication via Iterated Pseudorandomness," manuscript.
2. M. Bellare, J. Kilian, and P. Rogaway, "The Security of Cipher Block Chaining," *Advances in Cryptology–Crypto '94*, Springer Verlag (1994).
3. E. Biham and A. Shamir, *Differential Cryptanalysis of the Data Encryption Standard,* Springer Verlag (1993).
4. E. Biham and A. Shamir, "Differential Cryptanalysis of Snefru, Khafre, REDOC II, LOKI, Lucifer," *Advances in Cryptology–Crypto '91,* Springer Verlag (1992).
5. E. Biham and A. Shamir, "Differential Cryptanalysis of Feal and N-hash", *Advances in Cryptology–Eurocrypt '91,* Springer Verlag (1991).
6. M. Blum and S. Micali, "How to Generate Cryptographically Strong Sequences of Pseudorandom Bits," *SIAM Journal on Computing,* **13** pp. 850-864 (1984).
7. D. Coppersmith, "Another Birthday Attack," *Advances in Cryptology–Crypto '85,* Springer Verlag (1986).
8. I. Damgard, "A Design Principle for Hash Functions," *Advances in Cryptology–Crypto '89,* Springer Verlag (1989).
9. D. Davies and W. Price, *Security for Computer Networks (2e),* John Wiley (1989).
10. H. Dobbertin, "Cryptanalysis of MD4," To appear at the Fast Software Encryption Workshop, February, 1996.
11. O. Goldreich, S. Goldwasser, and S. Micali, "How To Construct Random Functions," *JACM,* **33**, 4, pp. 792-807 (1986).
12. J. Hastad, R. Impagliazzo, L. Levin, and M. Luby, "Pseudorandom Generation From One-Way Functions," *Proc. ACM Symp. on Theory of Computing,* (1989); "Pseudorandom Generators Under Uniform Assumptions," *Proc. of the ACM Symp. on Theory of Computing* (1990)
13. S. Langford and M. Hellman, "Differential-Linear Cryptanalysis," *Advances in Cryptology–Crypto '94,* Springer Verlag (1994).

14. L. Levin, "One-Way Functions and Pseudo-Random Generators," *Proc. of the ACM Symp. on Theory of Computing* (1985).
15. M. Luby, *Pseudorandomness And Its Cryptographic Applications,* Princeton Univ. Press, to appear.
16. M. Luby and C. Rackoff, "How to Construct Pseudorandom Permutations from Pseudorandom Functions," *SIAM Journal on Computing,* **17**, 373-386 (1988).
17. U. Maurer, "A Simplified and Generalized Treatment of Luby-Rackoff Pseudo-Random Permutation Generators," *Advances in Cryptology–Eurocrypt '92,* Springer Verlag (1992).
18. M. Matsui, "The First Experimental Cryptanalysis of the Data Encryption Standard," *Advances in Cryptology–Crypto '94,* Springer Verlag (1994).
19. R. Merkle, "A Fast in Software One-Way Hash Function," *Journal of Cryptology,* **3**, 1, pp. 43-58 (1990).
20. R. Merkle, "One-Way Hash Functions and DES," *Advances in Cryptology–Crypto '89,* Springer Verlag (1989).
21. P. van Oorschot and M. Wiener, "Parallel Collision Search with Application to Hash Functions and Discrete Logarithms," *Proc. of the 2nd ACM Conf. on Computer and Communications Security,* (1994).
22. B. Preneel, *Analysis and Design of Cryptographic Hash Functions,* Ph.D Thesis, Katholieke Universiteit Leuven (1993).
23. B. Preneel, and P. van Oorschot, "MDx-MAC and Building Fast MACs from Hash Functions," *Advances in Cryptology–Crypto '95,* Springer Verlag (1995).
24. V. Shoup, personal communication (1995).
25. A. Wyner, "The Wire-Tap Channel," *Bell System Technical Journal,* **54** (1975).
26. A. Yao, "Theory and Applications of Trapdoor Functions," *Proc. of the IEEE Symp. on Foundations of Computer Science,* (1982).
27. Y. Zheng, T. Matsumoto, and H. Imai, "On the Construction of Block Ciphers Provably Secure and Not Relying on Any Unproved Hypotheses," *Advances in Cryptology–Crypto '89* (1989).

Session Key Distribution Using Smart Cards

Victor Shoup and Avi Rubin

Bellcore, 445 South St., Morristown, NJ 07960
{shoup,rubin}@bellcore.com

Abstract. In this paper, we investigate a method by which smart cards can be used to enhance the security of session key distribution in the third-party setting of Needham & Schroeder. We extend the security model of Bellare & Rogaway to take into account both the strengths and weaknesses of smart card technology, we propose a session key distribution protocol, and we prove that it is secure assuming pseudo-random functions exist.

1 Introduction

Let us recall the basic session key distribution problem in the third-party setting of Needham & Schroeder [4]. We have a *server* and a set of *hosts*, all of which contain secret keys. During the course of the protocol, on each host several *processes* attempt to establish session keys with processes on other hosts. The processes communicate with each other and with the server. We assume that an *adversary* has complete control over the communications network: it may deliver messages out of order, delete or modify messages, and create new messages or even initiate new processes. We also assume that the adversary can obtain session keys that have already been established, and can even corrupt a host, obtaining its long-term secret key.

Faced with such a powerful adversary, the goal of a session key distribution protocol is basically to prevent the adversary from obtaining any information about session keys that it should not "obviously" have.

In the important paper of Bellare & Rogaway [1], these notions were for the first time properly formalized, and a protocol was presented and proved secure, assuming the existence of pseudo-random functions (PRFs) [2]. Many papers have addressed the session key distribution problem, and we refer the reader to [1] for more references and a discussion of its history.

One source of insecurity in this setting is the storage of the long-term secret keys on the hosts. If *ever* an adversary can corrupt a host and obtain its secret key, then for that host *all* is lost: all conversations past and future encrypted using session keys established by processes on that host can be decrypted by the adversary. Faced with the reality of known (and unknown) security holes in operating systems and other software, this is a serious problem.

One way to address this problem is to store the secret keys on a "smart card," or other kind of secure, tamper-resistant chip, instead of on the host. However, there has been little formal analysis of exactly what security gains this approach might offer.

Ueli Maurer (Ed.): EUROCRYPT '96 Proceedings, LNCS 1070

If we are going to place the secret key in a special computing device, requiring all access to the key to go through this device, it seems both useful and natural to make this device as simple and computationally limited as possible. This leads to the following point of view:

- we shall use a smart card only to generate session keys, which are then stored in the private memory of a process on the host which performs encryption or other cryptographic functions itself;
- we shall use a smart card only as a *stateless* probabilistic device, or probabilistic oracle: on input x, the card outputs a function whose value is determined by x, its secret key, and some random bits; in particular, the output does not depend on previous inputs.

The first assumption is justified by the very limited computational power of smart card chips, as well as their very low I/O bandwidth. The second assumption is justified by the very limited amount of memory available on smart cards, and allows an unbounded number of processes on a given host to be simultaneously executing the protocol with minimal interference with one another, and minimal overhead and bookkeeping on the smart card.

Given this setting, we extend the notion of security. As before, the adversary has complete control over the communications network, and we allow the adversary to obtain the session key from a process upon demand; more generally, the process will give the adversary all of the information it obtained through its interaction with the smart card.

Under normal circumstances, only a process on the host will be able to directly access the smart card. However, the adversary may occasionally be able to directly access the smart card. Note that this type of attack actually encompasses many possibilities: a network break-in or virus, the replacement of the host's software by rogue software, and physically stealing or borrowing the smart card. Obviously, while an adversary has access to a host's smart card, it can mimic a process on that host. In our formal definition of security, we shall require that this is essentially all the adversary can do; in particular, the adversary gains no knowledge of session keys generated at any other time, past or future.

Also, if an adversary physically steals the card, then with some effort and expense, it may be able to break the hardware security defenses of the card, and obtain its secret key. We of course allow this as a possibility, but require that session keys unrelated to this host are still secure.

We shall formalize the above security model, and present a protocol that is secure in this model. We build on the work of Leighton & Micali [3], designing a protocol in which the server is essentially just another smart card, and in which access to the server is required only the first time a process on one host talks to a process on another host. Also, both the server and the host smart cards need only compute a few pseudo-random functions, which might be very efficiently implemented using DES or a keyed version of a hash function such as SHA or MD5.

The rest of this paper is organized as follows. In §2, we show how to modify and extend the Leighton-Micali protocol to obtain a provably secure session key distribution protocol in the original Bellare-Rogaway model. We include this, since to obtain our main result, we need to make very similar arguments, and the result itself may be of independent interest. Then in §3 we present our formal definition of security in the smart card setting, and we describe and analyze our new protocol.

2 Session Key Distribution Without Smart Cards Revisited

2.1 The Bellare-Rogaway Model

We first recall the formal model and definition of security for a session key distribution given in Bellare & Rogaway [1], which we paraphrase and simplify somewhat.

At system initialization, a security parameter k is specified, along with some number n of hosts. For simplicity, we assume the hosts are named $1, \ldots, n$, although our definitions and results easily extend to host names chosen dynamically by an adversary. Some random bits are generated, and keys $K, K_1, \ldots, K_n$ are generated, K is stored in the server S and each K_i is stored in each host i.

For each pair i, j of hosts, and each $u \geq 1$, there is a process $\Pi(i; j, u)$ which is attached to host i and is (attempting) to establish a session with a process on host j. As there may be more than one such process, we index them by u, as indicated.

The adversary is a polynomial-time, probabilistic algorithm. On input 1^k, it chooses n, bounded by a polynomial in k, and then runs the system initialization routine. The adversary then interacts with the processes and the server. This interaction is simply a sequence of time-ordered question/answer pairs: the adversary asks a question addressed to a process, a host, or the server and gets an answer. The time-ordered list of questions and answers is called the *transcript*, and this together with the adversary's coin tosses is its *view*.

The simplest type of question and answer corresponds to the delivery of a message to a process or the server and a response. Note that a process carries state, so that the answer to one question may depend on previous questions sent to that process. As the interaction proceeds, a process may output a special message indicating *acceptance*, which implies that that process has established a session key. Note that in all of our protocols, the server carries no state, so we do not introduce the notion of multiple instances of the server.

There are two other types of questions the adversary can ask. First, the adversary can request that a process $\Pi(i; j, u)$ that has accepted reveal its session key; in this case, we say $\Pi(i; j, u)$ has been *opened*. Second, the adversary can request a host i to reveal its secret key K_i; in this case, we say that host i has been *opened*.

The session key distribution protocol specifies how any process will answer a sequence of questions, and how the server answers its questions. The protocol should also specify a *partner function*. This is a function that maps a process $\Pi(i;j,u)$ to a process $\Pi(j;i,v)$, or indicates no partner, and which can be computed efficiently from the adversary's transcript.

A process $\Pi(i;j,u)$ is said to hold a *fresh* session key if the following conditions hold: it has accepted, it is unopened, its partner (if it has one) is unopened, and hosts i and j are unopened.

Note that freshness can easily be determined from the transcript.

At the very end of the interaction, the adversary either simply stops, or *selects* a process holding a fresh session key; in the former case, the adversary scores 0; in the latter case, the adversary is given a random string and the session key of that process, in a random order, and must guess which is which; it scores 1 if correct and -1 if incorrect. The *advantage* of the adversary is defined as the absolute value of the expected value (over the entire experiment) of its score.

Finally, a session key distribution protocol is called *secure* if the following hold:

S1 for any adversary, for any pair of processes $\Pi(i;j,u)$ and $\Pi(j;i,v)$, if the adversary faithfully transmits messages between the two processes and the server, the two processes accept and share the same session key;

S2 for every adversary, its advantage is negligible (as a function of the security parameter k).

2.2 Protocol SK1

We now describe a new protocol, which we call *SK1*, for session key distribution in the third-party model, and prove its security in the Bellare-Rogaway security model. This protocol is a modification and extension of one proposed by Leighton & Micali [3] before the Bellare-Rogaway security model was proposed, and indeed, no formal statements about security are claimed or proved in that paper. We found that several modifications to the protocol were necessary to obtain our proof of security, even though it is not clear that without these modifications the protocol is insecure.

We assume that we have a PRF generator f that for security parameter k takes a k-bit secret key, produces a k-bit output, and allows inputs of up to $2k+1$ bits. For a key K and input x, we write $f_K(x)$ for the value of the PRF.

We assume that we have n hosts. At system initialization time, three random keys K, K', and K'' of length k are chosen as the secret keys of the server S.

We introduce some notation. For $1 \leq i,j \leq n$, let $K(i) = f_K(i)$ and $K(i,j) = f_{K(i)}(j)$. Similar notations are introduced for K' and K''. We define $P(i,j) = K(j,i) \oplus K'(i,j)$ and $A(i,j) = f_{K''(i)}(j \cdot P(i,j))$. Finally, we write $r \leftarrow R_k$ to denote assignment of a random k-bit string to r.

The secret key stored in host i consists of the triple $(K(i), K'(i), K''(i))$.

The protocol for a process A on host i to establish a session key with process B on host j runs as follows. We assume A initiates the protocol, calling A the *initiator* and B the *responder*. When a process accepts, it assigns the value of the session key to the variable ω.

Step 1a A sends (i, j) to S.
Step 1b A sets $r \leftarrow R_k$ and sends r to B.
Step 2a S receives (i, j) from A and sends $\pi = P(i, j), \alpha = A(i, j)$ to A.
Step 2b B receives r from A, sets $s \leftarrow R_k$, accepts setting $\omega = f_{K(j,i)}(0 \cdot s)$, and sends $s, f_{K(j,i)}(1 \cdot r \cdot s)$ to A.
Step 3a A receives π, α from S, rejects if $\alpha \neq f_{K''(i)}(j \cdot \pi)$, and otherwise computes $\kappa = \pi \oplus K'(i, j)$.
Step 3b A receives s, β from B, rejects if $\beta \neq f_\kappa(1 \cdot r \cdot s)$, and otherwise accepts setting $\omega = f_\kappa(0 \cdot s)$.

Finally, to complete the description of the protocol, we specify a partner function. An initiator $\Pi(i; j, u)$ has as its partner $\Pi(j; i, v)$ if $\Pi(i; j, u)$ received a message s, β in step 3b, and $P(j; i, v)$ is the unique responder of the form $P(j; i, \cdot)$ that sent a message s, β' in step 2b; otherwise, $\Pi(i; j, u)$ has no partner. A responder $P(j; i, v)$ has as its partner $\Pi(i; j, u)$ if $P(j; i, v)$ received the message r in step 2b and $\Pi(i; j, u)$ is the unique initiator of the form $\Pi(i; j, \cdot)$ that sent the message r in step 1b.

Before discussing security, we note that this scheme has a couple of practical advantages over the Bellare-Rogaway protocol. First, although the number of flows in both protocols is 4, this protocol requires only 2 parallel rounds of flows, while the Bellare-Rogaway protocol requires 3. Second, and more importantly, the server need only be contacted the first time a process on host i initiates the protocol with a process on host j: the $P(i, j)$, $A(i, j)$ values can be cached on host i; moreover, this cache can be held in insecure memory, since we can can view this cache as being maintained by the adversary, and the proof of security applies without changing the model or the protocol. If process A finds what it needs in the cache, only 2 flows and 1 round are required.

We also note that the random strings r and s could each be replaced by counters, which is actually more secure.

2.3 Security of Protocol SK1

We now prove:

Theorem 1. *If f is a secure PRF generator, then protocol* SK1 *is secure.*

Condition S1 in the definition of security is clear, so we concentrate on S2. To prove Theorem 1, we show that if the protocol is insecure, then a simple 2-process protocol is insecure, and conclude by showing that this protocol is secure.

We now define a session key distribution protocol *SK2* involving two hosts H_1 and H_2 who share a random k-bit key L. The protocol allows a process A on H_1 to establish a session key with process B on H_2. Here A is always the initiator. The protocol runs as follows.

Step 1 A sets $r \leftarrow R_k$ and sends r to B.

Step 2 B receives r from A, sets $s \leftarrow R_k$, computes the session key as $f_L(0 \cdot s)$, accepts and sends $s, f_L(1 \cdot r \cdot s)$ to A.

Step 3 A receives s, β from B, rejects if $\beta \neq f_L(1 \cdot r \cdot s)$, and otherwise accepts and computes its session key as $f_L(0 \cdot s)$.

The partner function for protocol *SK2* is defined just as for *SK1*.

Lemma 1. *Assume f is a secure PRF generator. If* SK1 *is insecure, then* SK2 *is insecure.*

Proof. Suppose we are given an adversary that has a nonnegligible advantage over *SK1*. We view the entire interaction of the adversary, the processes, and the server as a single algorithm, and we transform this algorithm in several stages into an adversary that has a nonnegligible advantage over *SK2*.

Stage 1. First, we modify the algorithm so that at the beginning of execution a pair (i_0, j_0) of hosts is chosen at random. Now the algorithm runs as before, except that we insist that the adversary select a process of the form $\Pi(i_0; j_0, \cdot)$ or $\Pi(j_0; i_0, \cdot)$, making it stop without a selection otherwise. This decreases the adversary's advantage by a factor of $n(n-1)/2$, and so it is still nonnegligible.

We make two further modifications. We stop the entire algorithm if the adversary ever opens host i_0 or j_0. This does not change the adversary's advantage at all. We also stop the algorithm if the adversary does not select an initiator on i_0 or a responder on j_0. This decreases the adversary's advantage by a factor of 2, and so it is still nonnegligible.

Stage 2. We now replace all the keys $K(i), K'(i), K''(i)$ for $1 \leq i \leq n$ by random k-bit strings. The adversary's advantage must still be nonnegligible; otherwise, we would have a statistical test for the PRF collection $\{f_K(\cdot), f_{K'}(\cdot), f_{K''}(\cdot)\}$, which is impossible by assumption.

Stage 3. Next, we modify the algorithm so that any initiator $\Pi(i_0; j, u)$ rejects if it receives a message π, α in step 3a that was not previously output by the server on input (i_0, j). The adversary's advantage must still be nonnegligible, since otherwise we would have a statistical test for the PRF $f_{K''(i_0)}(\cdot)$.

Stage 4. We now replace $K(j_0, i)$ for all i and $K'(i_0, j)$ for all j by random k-bit strings. Again, the adversary must still have a nonnegligible advantage, since otherwise we would have a statistical test for $\{f_{K(j_0)}(\cdot), f_{K'(i_0)}(\cdot)\}$.

Stage 5. We next replace $P(i_0, j_0)$ by a random k-bit string. This change does not affect the probability distribution of the adversary's view, since $P(i_0, j_0) = K(j_0, i_0) \oplus K'(i_0, j_0)$, and $K'(i_0, j_0)$ does not affect the value of any other strings seen by the adversary, except through its affect on $P(i_0, j_0)$.

Stage 6. Now, given two hosts H_1 and H_2 taking part in protocol *SK2*, using the unknown but randomly chosen key L, we let the processes on H_1 play the role of initiator processes on host i_0, and the processes on H_2 play the role of responders on j_0. The key L takes the place of the key $K(j_0, i_0)$. The algorithm as it now stands can be executed without actually using the value of L, except indirectly through the responses of the processes on H_1 and H_2. Thus, the algorithm is an adversary with nonnegligible advantage over *SK2*. □

Lemma 2. *If f is a secure PRF generator, then protocol* SK2 *is secure.*

Proof. We argue by replacing $f_L(\cdot)$ by a truly random function F in the protocol, showing that this modified protocol is secure. If the original protocol were insecure, this would give us a statistical test for $f_L(\cdot)$.

It is straightforward to see that with overwhelming probability, the following events occur:

(i) all r-outputs by H_1-processes are distinct,
(ii) all s-outputs by H_2-processes are distinct, and
(iii) if any process A on H_1 accepts, and A output r and received s, then there is a process B on H_2 that received r and output s.

Conditioning on these events, it is easy to see that the adversary's advantage is 0. To see this, suppose the adversary were to select a process B on H_2 that holds $F(0 \cdot s)$. Then, by (ii), no other H_2-process holds $F(0 \cdot s)$, and by (i) and (iii), any H_1-process that holds $F(0 \cdot s)$ must be B's partner. Likewise, if the adversary were to select a process A on H_1 that holds $F(0 \cdot s)$, then by (i), (ii), and (iii), there are no other H_1-processes that hold $F(0 \cdot s)$, and by (ii) there is exactly one H_2-process that holds $F(0 \cdot s)$, which is A's partner. Thus, the adversary did not open any process holding $F(0 \cdot s)$, and hence has advantage 0. □

One final remark about the security of Protocol SK1 is in order. Note that process B essentially accepts unconditionally, without challenging A at all. Thus, an adversary could make B accept without any legitimate process A being involved at all. However, if the adversary does this, the adversary will have no idea what B's session key is, and so it is not clear why an adversary would do this. This point illustrates a difference between session-key distribution and entity authentication: usually, two parties engaging a session key protocol are not so much interested in verifying that they are really talking to each other *at that moment*, but rather, they want to be able to authenticate and/or encrypt messages that are sent after the protocol has terminated. Recognizing these two security goals as distinct is one of the contributions of the Bellare-Rogaway model. Of course, Protocol SK1 could easily be modified to provide mutual authentication as well, if that were desired.

3 Using Smart Cards

3.1 A New Security Model

We now define what we mean by security for a smart card based protocol. Our starting point is the model in §2.1, and we focus on the differences. As indicated in the introduction, secret keys will be stored in the smart cards, and the smart cards will then be used in a stateless fashion, as probabilistic oracles, to compute session keys which are then stored in the private memory of a process on its host.

System initialization is as before, except that the secret keys are stored in the smart cards, not the hosts.

The adversary may obtain question/answer pairs as before. However, the two *open* operations are defined differently, and there is a new operation: *access*.

First, the adversary may *open* any process at any time, even if it has not accepted; upon receiving an *open* request, the process must reveal a complete description of the conversation it has carried out with its smart card, (and the outcomes of its coin-tosses if the process is probabilistic). This type of attack is at least as powerful as reading the private memory of a process (which is presumably normally protected by operating system security defenses), including its session key, as well as obtaining the session key via cryptanalysis or other means.

Second, the adversary may *open* a host's smart card at any time. When this happens, the adversary is given the secret keys stored on the corresponding smart card. In practice, this type of attack will presumably be difficult to mount, as it entails physically obtaining the smart card, and somehow breaking the card's physical security defenses.

Third, the adversary may *access* a host's smart card at any time. That is, the adversary may ask any question of the smart card that conforms to the smart card's functional interface, and receive the corresponding answer. This type of attack subsumes several others, including a network break-in or virus, replacement of the host's software by rogue software, or physically stealing the card.

The transcript, view, and partner function are defined as before, except that the exact forms of the questions and answers are defined as above.

We now define the freshness of session keys to capture the intuition outlined in §1. A process $\Pi(i; j, u)$ holds a *fresh* session key if the following conditions hold: it has accepted, it is unopened, its partner (if it has one) is unopened, the smart cards on hosts i and j are unopened, and j's smart card has not been accessed between the times of $\Pi(i; j, u)$'s first and last questions.

Again, note that freshness can be determined from the transcript.

The protocol is said to be *secure* if condition S1 and S2 hold, exactly as before.

3.2 Protocol SK3

We now describe our smart card based protocol, *SK3*. This protocol is derived from protocol *SK1*.

Secret keys are generated just as for SK1, except that the keys are stored in the smart cards. Also, the smart card of host i is given a random k-bit string $T(i)$. We adopt all of the notation from §2.2, i.e., $K(i)$, $A(i, j)$, etc.

There are really three protocols here: a server interface, a smart card interface, and a process-to-process protocol.

The server interface is exactly as in *SK1*.

There are four types of queries that can be made of all smart cards, where we write $C_i(\cdot)$ for a query to i's smart card. For clarity, we sometime use host i and sometimes j.

- $C_i(1) = (r, f_{T(i)}(r))$, where $r \leftarrow R_k$.
- $C_j(2, i, r) = (s, \beta, \omega)$, where $s \leftarrow R_k$, $\beta = f_{K(j,i)}(1 \cdot r \cdot s)$, and $\omega = f_{K(j,i)}(00 \cdot s)$.
- $C_i(3, j, r, s, \pi, \alpha, \beta, \gamma) = ()$ or (δ, ω). This is computed as follows. Check if $f_{T(i)}(r) = \gamma$ and $f_{K''(i)}(j \cdot \pi) = \alpha$. If not, output $()$. Otherwise, set $\kappa = \pi \oplus K'(i, j)$. Check if $f_\kappa(1 \cdot r \cdot s) = \beta$. If not, output $()$. Otherwise, set $\delta = f_\kappa(01 \cdot s)$ and $\omega = f_\kappa(00 \cdot s)$ and output (δ, ω).
- $C_j(4, i, s, \delta) = 1$ if $f_{K(j,i)}(01 \cdot s) = \delta$, and 0 otherwise.

Finally, the process-to-process protocol is as follows. We assume process A is an initiator on host i, and process B is a responder on host j. Upon acceptance, a process assigns the session key to the variable ω.

Step 1a A sends (i, j) to S.
Step 1b A sets $(r, \gamma) = C_i(1)$ and sends r to B.
Step 2a S receives (i, j) from A and sends $P(i, j), A(i, j)$ to A.
Step 2b B receives r from A, sets $(s, \beta, \omega) = C_j(2, i, r)$, and sends s, β to A.
Step 3 A receives π, α from S and s, β from B. A computes $C_i(3, j, r, s, \pi, \alpha, \beta, \gamma)$. If this is $()$, A rejects, otherwise A accepts, assigns this value to (δ, ω), and sends δ to B.
Step 4 B receives δ from A, and accepts if $C_j(4, i, s, \delta) = 1$, and rejects otherwise.

The partner function for this protocol is defined exactly as in protocol *SK1*.

Before proving the security of Protocol SK3, we discuss its practicality. Although this protocol may at first look complicated, the smart card itself must do relatively little computation or bookkeeping. In fact, we are currently working on a prototype implementation, using a very typical, inexpensive smart card, and we comment on our preliminary design.

First, we note that as in Protocol SK1, we can replace the random strings r and s by counters. This violates our "stateless" requirement, but in practice one usually needs to maintain state anyway to generate pseudo-random numbers. On a smart card, there is usually some writable, non-volatile memory, and we only need a single, say 8 byte, counter per smart card.

Second, we can assume that host names are actually hash values, so we can assume all host names are 16 bytes if, say, MD5 is used as the hash function.

Third, we might use keyed MD5 or SHA for the pseudo-random function, perhaps truncating its output to 8 bytes, and using 8-byte secret keys. SHA implementations are already available on many inexpensive smart cards.

The most complicated query that the smart card must process is the type 3 query. The bulk of the time will be spent performing the pseudo-random function evaluations, and moving data in and out of the card. The card must perform 6 pseudo-random function evaluations, input about 64 bytes of data, and output about 16 bytes of data. This is well within the capabilities of many commonly available, inexpensive smart cards.

3.3 Security of Protocol SK3

We now prove:

Theorem 2. *Assuming f is a secure PRF generator, then protocol* SK3 *is secure.*

Our proof of this theorem follows the same strategy as that of Theorem 1: we show that if SK3 were insecure, then a certain two-host smart card based protocol, *SK4*, would also be insecure. Then we prove that *SK4* is secure.

Protocol *SK4* involves two hosts, H_1 and H_2. Host H_1 has a smart card C_1 with secret keys L and T. Host H_2 has a smart card C_2 with the same secret key L. Card C_1 responds to two types of queries (1 and 3) and C_2 responds to two types of queries (2 and 4), as follows.

- $C_1(1) = (r, f_T(r))$, where $r \leftarrow R_k$.
- $C_2(2, r) = (s, \beta, \omega)$, where $s \leftarrow R_k$, $\beta = f_L(1 \cdot r \cdot s)$, and $\omega = f_L(00 \cdot s)$.
- $C_1(3, r, s, \beta, \gamma) = ()$ or (δ, ω). This is computed as follows. Check if $f_T(r) = \gamma$ and $f_L(1 \cdot r \cdot s) = \beta$. If not, output $()$. Otherwise, set $\delta = f_L(01 \cdot s)$ and $\omega = f_L(00 \cdot s)$ and output (δ, ω).
- $C_2(4, i, s, \delta) = 1$ if $f_L(01 \cdot s) = \delta$, and 0 otherwise.

The process-to-process protocol for *SK4* is as follows. We let A denote a process on H_1, which is always an initiator, and B denote a process on H_2, which is always a responder. Upon acceptance, the session key is stored in ω.

Step 1 A sets $(r, \gamma) = C_1(1)$ and sends r to B.
Step 2 B receives r from A, sets $(s, \beta, \omega) = C_2(2, i, r)$, and sends s, β to A.
Step 3 A receives s, β from B. A computes $C_1(3, r, s, \beta, \gamma)$. If this is $()$, A rejects, otherwise A accepts, assigns this value to (δ, ω), and sends δ to B.
Step 4 B receives δ from A, and accepts if $C_2(4, s, \delta) = 1$, and rejects otherwise.

The definition of the partner function is the same as above.

Lemma 3. *Assume f is secure PRF generator. Then if* SK3 *is insecure, then* SK4 *is also insecure.*

Proof. The proof of this is almost identical to that of Lemma 1, and so we omit it. □

Lemma 4. *Assume f is a secure PRF generator. Then protocol* SK4 *is secure.*

Proof. Again, we prove this by replacing f_L by a random function F and f_T by a random function G.

Now, an adversary can access a smart card directly, or indirectly via a process. Regardless of how these accesses occur, it is straightforward (if tedious) to see that with overwhelming probability, the following events occur:

(i) all r-outputs from type 1 queries are distinct,
(ii) all s-outputs from type 2 queries are distinct,
(iii) for any type 3 query that accepts with inputs r, s at time τ_3, r was output by a type 1 query at time τ_1 and s was output by a type 2 query with input r at time τ_2, where $\tau_1 < \tau_2 < \tau_3$,
(iv) for any type 4 query that accepts with input s at time τ_4, there is a type 3 query that accepted with inputs r, s for some r at time $\tau_3 < \tau_4$, and
(v) for any type accepting type 3 query with inputs r, s made by an unopened process, there is no other accepting type 3 query with inputs r', s for any r'.

Conditioning on these events, the adversary's advantage is 0. To see this, suppose an adversary were to select a process B on H_2 holding the fresh session key $F(00 \cdot s)$. Then B made a type 4 query at some time τ_4, and by (iii) and (iv), certain type 1, 2, and 3 queries were made, as described above, at times $\tau_1 < \tau_2 < \tau_3 < \tau_4$. By the freshness of B's key, the type 3 query was made by some process A on H_1, and was not made directly by the adversary. By (i), the type 1 query was also made by A, and by (ii), the type 2 query was made by B. It follows that A is B's partner, and hence could not have been opened. From (ii) and (v), it then follows that $F(00 \cdot s)$ was never revealed to the adversary.

Suppose the adversary were to select a process A on H_1 holding the fresh session key $F(00 \cdot s)$. Then A made a type 3 query at some time τ_3, and by (iii), certain type 1 and 2 queries were made at times $\tau_1 < \tau_2 < \tau_3$. By the freshness of A's key, the type 2 query was made by some process B on H_2, and not directly by the adversary. By (ii), B is A's partner, and so could not have been opened. From (ii) and (v), it follows that $F(00 \cdot s)$ was never revealed to the adversary. □

We remark that in Protocol SK3, unlike Protocol SK1, B must challenge A in order to meet our definition of security in the smart card setting. To see why this is so, suppose an adversary can access host i's smart card twice over some long period of time. Then at any time in between, the adversary could get B to accept a session key and encrypt some files, and with the second access, the adversary could get the session key, and decrypt the files. This is precisely the kind of attack we wish to foil.

References

1. M. Bellare and P. Rogaway. Provably secure session key distribution—the three party case. In *27th Annual ACM Symposium on Theory of Computing*, pages 57–66, 1995.
2. O. Goldreich, S. Goldwasser, and S. Micali. How to construct random functions. *Journal of the ACM*, 33:210–217, 1986.
3. T. Leighton and S. Micali. Secret-key agreement without public-key cryptography. In *Advances in Cryptology–Crypto '93*, pages 456–479, 1993.
4. R. Needham and M. Schroeder. Using encryption for authentication in large networks of computers. *Communications of the ACM*, 21:993–999, 1978.

On Diffie-Hellman Key Agreement with Short Exponents

Paul C. van Oorschot • Michael J. Wiener

Bell-Northern Research, Box 3511 Station C
Ottawa, Ontario K1Y 4H7, Canada
{paulv,wiener}@bnr.ca

Abstract. The difficulty of computing discrete logarithms known to be "short" is examined, motivated by recent practical interest in using Diffie-Hellman key agreement with short exponents (e.g. over Z_p with 160-bit exponents and 1024-bit primes p). A new divide-and-conquer algorithm for discrete logarithms is presented, combining Pollard's lambda method with a partial Pohlig-Hellman decomposition. For random Diffie-Hellman primes p, examination reveals this partial decomposition itself allows recovery of short exponents in many cases, while the new technique dramatically extends the range. Use of subgroups of large prime order precludes the attack at essentially no cost, and is the recommended solution. Using safe primes also precludes this particular attack and allows improved exponentiation performance, although parameter generation costs are dramatically higher.

1 Introduction

Diffie-Hellman key agreement [3] allows two parties A and B to derive a common secret by communications over an unsecured channel, while sharing no user-specific keying material a priori. A prime p and element $g \in Z_p^*$ of large multiplicative order are fixed. A chooses a random integer x, $1 \leq x \leq p-2$, and sends to B the value $g^x \bmod p$ (hereafter, reduction mod p is not explicitly noted). B responds by choosing a random y, $1 \leq y \leq p-2$, and sending to A the value g^y. A and B may then respectively compute a common secret key K as $K = (g^y)^x$ and $K = (g^x)^y$. Due to the intractability of the discrete logarithm problem [10] for appropriate p, an eavesdropper is unable to compute x or y from observation of g^x and g^y, and thus unable to compute K in the same manner as A or B. It is widely believed that computing discrete logs is required for any party other than A or B to compute K, although this remains an open question [12]. For protection from active adversaries, the technique must be augmented; various authenticated key agreement protocols are available [17].

Regarding appropriate choice of the prime p, two issues are size and structure. Regarding bitsize, taking current algorithms into account and depending on the security requirement, 512 bits is typically specified as a minimum, and 1024 bits (or more) is commonly recommended and generally considered safe for most applications. Regarding structure, it is well-known that p must be such that $p-1$

Ueli Maurer (Ed.): EUROCRYPT '96 Proceedings, LNCS 1070

contains a large prime factor, to preclude feasibility of the discrete log algorithm of Pohlig and Hellman [14].

Efficient implementation of Diffie-Hellman key agreement entails efficient modular exponentiation, which requires efficient modular multiplication. For a modulus p of bitlength m, mod p exponentiation with m-bit exponents using the basic square-and-multiply method [7] requires about m modular squarings and $c \cdot m$ (m-bit) modular multiplies, where naively, $c = 0.5$ (on average); improvements are possible. Standard techniques [2] for each of (m-bit) multiplication mod p and modular reduction require $O(m^2)$ bit operations.

Diffie-Hellman is a preferred mechanism for generating ephemeral keys. Performance issues arise as security considerations demand moduli well beyond 512 bits in some applications. Since the cost of computing g^x depends linearly on the bitlength of x, ensuing real-time costs have motivated use of exponents x of less than full (m-bit) length, e.g. for $\lg x$ as small as 128 or 160. This is somewhat analogous to the widespread use of short public exponents such as $e = 2^{16} + 1$ in the RSA [16] public-key operation. Care is necessary to ensure such optimizations do not introduce security weaknesses. For example, precautions are necessary in some applications when using $e = 3$ in RSA [4], and using a short RSA private exponent is known to be insecure [21].

This paper examines the security implications of using short Diffie-Hellman exponents. The major conclusions are that use of random primes p combined with short exponents is generally insecure, and that the use of large prime-order subgroups is highly recommended. §2 reviews standard techniques for computing discrete logs in cyclic groups, including the case of short exponents. §3 presents a new method combining Pollard's lambda method with partial recovery of a secret exponent by a (partial) Pohlig-Hellman decomposition, allowing an alarmingly effective attack when short exponents are used and the group in question has order n of arbitrary factorization (e.g. $n = p - 1$ for random prime moduli p). §4 examines the use of short exponents with safe primes, while §5 examines use of short exponents when computations are restricted to large subgroups of prime order. Both techniques, when used appropriately, preclude the known attacks; each offers different advantages. Safe primes may allow further computational savings during exponentiation if a generator such as $g = 2$ is used, while use of prime-order subgroups are dramatically (e.g. more than an order of magnitude) less costly with respect to parameter generation (namely p). Much of the discussion applies to exponentiation-based systems beyond Diffie-Hellman, i.e. more general discrete logarithm problems.

2 Background on Discrete Logarithm Techniques

In this section, the basic methods for computing discrete logs in cyclic groups are reviewed: Shanks' method, and Pollard's more practical rho and lambda methods. The Pohlig-Hellman decomposition technique, of use in conjunction with any of these, is also reviewed. Advanced readers may omit this section.

The discrete logarithm problem for cyclic groups is as follows: given a cyclic group G of order n (i.e. having n elements), generator $g \in G$, and element $y \in G$, find x such that $y = g^x$. One such group is the multiplicative group Z_p^* of integers modulo a prime p; this group has order $n = p - 1$.

Shanks' method. Aside from exhaustive search, the simplest idea for solving this problem is Shanks' "baby-step giant-step" method [8] (p.9 and 575-576). It requires $O(n^{1/2})$ steps and the same order of space, where a step is one group operation. Define $t = \lceil n^{1/2} \rceil$. Compute $(g^t)^i$ for $1 \leq i \leq t$, and store the ordered pair $((g^t)^i, i)$ in a table, sorted by first component (in constant time using conventional hashing). To find the logarithm x, compute $y \cdot g^j (= g^{x+j})$ for $j \geq 0$. Stop when finding a j yielding a value stored in the table; this is guaranteed for some $j \leq t - 1$. At this point, $g^{ti} = g^{x+j}$, implying $ti \equiv x + j \pmod{n}$. Then $x = ti - j \bmod n$ is the desired log. The running time is $O(t)$ steps where $t = n^r$ and $r = 1/2$. The algorithm may be generalized using $0 \leq r \leq 1$, requiring a one-time precomputation of $O(n^r)$ time and space, and a per-logarithm computation of $O(n^{1-r})$ time; $r = 0$ is exhaustive search, while $r = 1$ is table lookup. For example, $r = 1/3$ uses less space and more time. As overall time cannot be reduced below $n^{1/2}$ and space is typically more expensive, $r > 1/2$ is not interesting unless computing a very large number of logarithms.

Pollard rho. In practice, Pollard's *rho method* for discrete logarithms [15] is preferable to Shanks. It has similar square-root running time (heuristic, whereas Shanks is deterministic), but entirely avoids the large space requirement. While further details are omitted here (as the main focus is the lambda method), it is noted that this memoryless rho method can be parallelized with perfect linear speedup [20]; that is, essentially an r-fold speedup is possible using r processors.

Pollard lambda. A lesser-known algorithm due to Pollard, the *lambda method* [15], more affectionately called the *method for catching kangaroos*, can be used when the pursued logarithm x is known to lie within a restricted interval of width w. Given a group G of order n and known integers b and w, it finds the logarithm x of an element $y = g^x \in G$ in time $O(w^{1/2})$ and space for $O(\log w)$ group elements, provided it is guaranteed that $b < x < b + w$. If x is not found on the first iteration, the probability of which can be controlled, subsequent iterations may be run as required. The technique is as follows.

The method involves computing two sequences (trails) of points T and W (representing paths travelled by tame and wild kangaroos). T computes the sequence $y'_0, y'_1, \ldots, y'_N$, where $y'_{i+1} = y'_i \cdot g^{f(y'_i)}$ using the "random" function $f(y'_i)$ whose output takes values from a set R. At the point y'_N, T halts and "sets a trap" hoping to catch W should W land at this point during its own trail $y = y_0, y_1, \ldots, y_N$; this will occur if W's trail hits any point y'_i. The tame trail begins at $y'_0 = g^{b+w}$, and proceeds to y'_N. Note $\log_g(y'_N) = \log_g(y'_0) + d'_N$, where $d'_N = \sum_{i=0}^{N'-1} f(y'_i) \bmod n$. The wild trail begins at $y_0 = y$, and concludes when $y_M = y'_N$ for some point y_M in W's trail, at which point the logarithm x of y is computed as $x = b + w + d'_N - d_M \bmod n$. If no collision $y_M = y'_N$ occurs before d_M exceeds $w + d'_N$, the hunt is terminated with failure (W has travelled beyond the trap). The failure probability for a single iteration is controlled by parameter θ (see below), which should be set to minimize the expected overall work (balancing expected number of iterations and work per iteration).

The sequences y'_i and y_i can be viewed as deterministic paths which are stepped by random values from an integer set R of mean m; by rough analysis, each of the N points in T's trail provides an independent chance with probability $1/m$ of catching W. For $\theta = N/m$ and m large, the probability of success is $p_S = 1-(1-m^{-1})^{\theta m} \approx 1-e^{-\theta}$. For optimum performance, set $m = \alpha \cdot w^{1/2}$ for α as optimized below. Then for example, for $\theta = 4$, $p_S = 0.98$ ($\theta = 1$ gives $p_S = 0.63$) and the total expected work, $N + M$, minimized by $\alpha = 1/4$, is $O(w^{1/2})$ steps. More generally, $2\sqrt{\theta w}$ is the expected work given θ, when minimized using $\alpha = 1/(2\sqrt{\theta})$ [15]. Pollard suggests computing and storing g^s for all $s \in R$ used. and therefore choosing $|R| \ll w^{1/2}$. $R = \{2^0, 2^1, 2^2, \ldots, 2^{L-1}\}$ is one suggestion (for an appropriate bound L), with $f(y_i) = 2^j$ where $j = y_i \bmod L$.

Pohlig-Hellman decomposition. Given the prime power factorization of n (with q_v the largest prime divisor), a divide-and-conquer technique known as *Pohlig-Hellman decomposition* [14] can be used to reduce the running time for each of the Shanks, rho and lambda methods, by decomposing the original large discrete log problem into a number of smaller such sub-problems. For Shanks, the reduction results in overall time and space $O(\sqrt{q_v})$; for rho and lambda, the reduction is to such time and negligible space. The original problem is to find x, given a group G of order n (e.g. $G = Z_p^*$, $n = p-1$), g, and y where $y = g^x$. This is reduced to one of finding c_i discrete logs in a subgroup of order q_i for each prime power $q_i^{c_i}$ dividing n. Let $n = \prod_{i=1}^{v} q_i^{c_i}$ where $q_i < q_{i+1}$, q_i prime. For simplicity, consider the case $c_i = 1$ for all i (distinct prime factors); the technique is easily generalized. For a fixed i, compute $y^{n/q_i} = (g^{n/q_i})^x$. The result takes on one of q_i values, defining the simpler sub-problem of finding the discrete logarithm x_i ($= x \bmod q_i$) in a group of q_i elements generated by g^{n/q_i}. Once x_i is found for all i, the Chinese Remainder Theorem allows solution of the simultaneous congruences $x \equiv x_i \bmod q_i$, yielding $x \bmod \prod q_i$, which is $x \bmod n$ as originally desired. The overall complexity is dominated by the cost of finding x_v, the logarithm for the largest prime factor q_v.

Computing Discrete Logs of Restricted Form. While sub-exponential time index-calculus techniques (see [9]) for computing discrete logarithms in groups with additional structure are in general more powerful than those of Shanks and Pollard, the latter are typically more effective when the order n of the group factors such that a Pohlig-Hellman decomposition is possible, or when the exponent is small. This paper restricts attention to methods applicable to arbitrary cyclic groups. For a cyclic group G of order n (e.g. $n = p-1$ for Z_p^*), it follows from the discussion above that:

(i) discrete logs can be found in $O(n^{1/2})$ time and negligible space; and
(ii) time can be reduced to $O(q^{1/2})$ if q is the largest prime divisor of n.

For an appropriate bound B, call a prime factor q_i of n *small* if $q_i < B$, and call n *smooth* (more specifically: B-smooth) if all of its prime factors are small in this sense. To be of interest, B is chosen depending on the computational resources available, and for the present purposes, defined such that when n is B-smooth, discrete logarithms may feasibly be computed using Pohlig-Hellman decomposition. For non-smooth n, finding x (given y where $y = g^x$) appears difficult for random x of approximate bitlength $\lg p$.[1] In the sections listed below, the following approaches for constraining the size of exponents are examined:

§3: restricting exponents to random integers x in the range $[1, w]$;
§4: using a safe prime $p = 2q + 1$ (q prime) along with the first option; and
§5: restricting computations to a subgroup of prime order q where $q \approx w$.

3 Restricting Exponents to the Range $[1, w]$

Pollard's lambda method allows extraction of logs with running time about the square-root of the size of the interval in question. The requirement of a fixed level of security, say 2^t (i.e. t bits), defines a (not necessarily greatest) lower bound on the size of Diffie-Hellman exponents. More specifically, if exponents are limited to random integers x of bitlength w, this imposes the constraint $w \geq 2^{2t}$. However, if attacks better than the basic square-root methods exist, this bound on w fails to provide t bits of security. Indeed, Lemma 2 implies a greater lower bound, resulting from such an improved attack.

To explore the security impact of short exponents, consider the amount of information which may be obtained from a Pohlig-Hellman decomposition in this case of short exponents, for a group G of order n (e.g. $n = p - 1$ for $G = Z_p^*$). As previously, assume $n = \prod_{i=1}^{v} q_i$ where $q_i < q_{i+1}$. The task is to find x given y ($= g^x$). For each B-smooth prime factor q_i, it is feasible to compute $x_i = x \bmod q_i$. Suppose there are $r \leq v$ such small q_i. Combine these x_i using the Chinese Remainder Theorem to recover $x \bmod B_r$ where $B_r = \prod_{i=1}^{r} q_i$. If $B_r > x$, this yields x itself, while for $B_r \leq x$ it yields $k = \lg(B_r)$ bits of information about x. The bitlength of the product of all small prime factors of n is k, and each q_i essentially leaks $\lg q_i$ bits of x. This raises two important questions. Let $\lg x = u$.

Q1: For a random prime p, what is the expected number of bits k of x leaked?
Q2: Is there an attack finding the remaining $u - k$ bits of x in $O(\sqrt{2^{u-k}})$ time? (If p leaks k bits of x, t bits of security would then require $\lg x \geq 2t + k$.)

Related to Q1 and of more direct practical interest is the question: for a random prime p, with what probability is x fully revealed ($B_r > x$)? Both this and Q1 depend on the size of x relative to the smoothness bound B. The expectation

[1] "lg" is used to denote base-2 logarithms; "ln" denotes natural logarithms.

is that $k \approx \lg B$ (see §3.1), and thus one may expect full compromise when $\lg x \approx \lg B$, although there is considerable variation. Perhaps more significant is the affirmative answer to Q2, using a new technique (see §3.2).

3.1 Expected Size of Product of Short Factors of $p - 1$

Again let B be an upper bound such that computing discrete logs is computationally feasible in groups of prime order $q \leq B$. Consider first, for a random prime modulus p, the expected bitlength of the product B_r of all "small" primes $p_i < B$ which divide $p - 1$. (More generally, the question relates to divisors of a group order n.) Each such prime contributes $\lg p_i$ bits to $k = \lg B_r$, and p_i divides a random number with probability $1/p_i$ (refined further below). The expected bitlength of B_r can thus be approximated as:

$$k \approx \sum_{p_i \leq B} \frac{\lg p_i}{p_i} .$$

This sum may be further approximated by summing, rather than over all primes p_i, over all integers $i \geq 2$ weighted by the probability i is prime (estimated as $1/\ln i$ by the Prime Number Theorem). Then, since $\sum_{i=2}^{B} i^{-1} \approx \ln B$,

$$k \approx \sum_{i=2}^{B} \frac{\lg i}{i} \cdot \frac{1}{\ln i} = \sum_{i=2}^{B} \frac{1}{i} \frac{1}{\ln 2} \approx \lg B .$$

A slightly more precise estimate results by replacing $1/p_i$ by $1/(p_i - 1)$, justified as follows. Of interest is whether $p_i | p - 1$. Since p_i does not divide p, $p \bmod p_i \neq 0$ and thus $p - 1 \bmod p_i \neq -1$, leaving only $p_i - 1$ (not p_i) possible residue classes. Moreover, $1/(p_i - 1)$ may itself be refined to $p_i/(p_i - 1)^2$, to account for divisors p_i of higher multiplicity. Numerical summation of this refinement, given in Lemma 1, supports the estimate above. (While such a result is known, and may be derived rigourously using advanced number theory, a heuristic derivation from first principles as given above is considered appealing.)

Lemma 1. *For a random prime p and a fixed bound B (see above), the expected bitlength $k = \lg(B_r)$ of the product of all prime divisors $p_i \leq B$ of $p - 1$ is*

$$k \approx \sum_{p_i \leq B} \lg p_i \left(\frac{p_i}{(p_i - 1)^2} \right) \approx \lg B + C_1$$

where $C_1 \approx 0.94$, and $C_1 < 1.0$ for $B > 2^{10}$.

This answers Q1 (but see also Table 2); note that k is independent of $\lg p$. Table 1 provides supporting results for a small sample of random primes p, indicating the average, minimum, and maximum bitlengths of the product of all B-smooth prime divisors of $p - 1$. Note the large deviation from the mean, and that values B in Table 1 are relatively small.

The cryptographic significance of Lemma 1 is as follows. An adversary with sufficient computational resources to compute discrete logs in cyclic groups of order up to 2^s implies $B \approx 2^s$. One then expects about $k = s$ bits of an exponent x are leaked by a "random" prime modulus p (revealing x entirely if $\lg x < s$).

B	$\lg(B_r)$ for 100 primes $p \approx 2^{1024}$		
	mean	min	max
2^{16}	16.4	1.0	47.2
2^{32}	31.3	1.0	112.2
2^{48}	52.1	2.6	194.4
2^{64}	65.0	2.6	243.1

Table 1. Smoothness of $p-1$ relative to B. $B_r = \prod q_i^{c_i}$ where $q_i \leq B$, $q_i^{c_i} | p-1$.

3.2 Lambda Method Restricted to a Strategic Interval

A new technique for computing discrete logs is now presented, which is computationally feasible when exponents x are bounded to $x \approx 2^u$ for (in)appropriate u. The technique first recovers what information about x may be obtained from a partial Pohlig-Hellman decomposition (say k bits), and then employs the lambda method to recover the remaining bits. The combined technique runs in time $O(2^{(u-k)/2})$. This answers Q2 in the affirmative.

Let $y = g^x$ be an element of a group G of order n, with the usual task to determine x. Isolate the smooth factors of n and write $n = zQ$ where $z = B_r$ (see §3) is the product of smooth factors, and has bitlength approximately k. Compute V where $V = x \bmod z$, by a partial Pohlig-Hellman decomposition (see §2). Write $x = Az + V$, where $0 \leq V < z$ with A as yet unknown. Then $y = g^x = g^{Az+V}$. Now $A \leq x/z$ implies $A \in [0, 2^c]$, where $c \approx u - k$ bits of x remain unknown after finding V. Compute g^V and $y^* = y/g^V = g^{Az} = h^A$ where $h = g^z$ is known. Consider the new problem of finding the discrete logarithm A (relative to h) of y^*, given y^* and the base h (in place of g). Use the lambda algorithm (see §2) to find A. Using h in place of g here restricts the trail points to a subset of cardinality about 2^c. As required in the lambda method, the log to be found (here A in place of x) is known to lie in a restricted range $[b, b+w] = [0, 2^c]$ of width $w = 2^c$. The expected running time to find A is thus $O(\sqrt{2^c})$. Knowing z and V, this allows computation of $x = Az + V$.

An example with concrete parameters is given for clarity. Let $G = Z_p^*$ and $n = p - 1$ with a 1024-bit prime p and 160-bit x (so $u = 160$). Suppose $k = 100$ bits of x are recovered using Pohlig-Hellman (so $\lg z \approx 100$). Then $\lg A \approx 60$ ($c = 60$), and although h generates a subgroup of order $\approx 2^{1024-100}$, recovery of A by the lambda method is feasible, in $O(2^{30})$ steps, because A is known to lie in the interval $A \in [0, 2^{60}]$ of width $w = 2^{60}$. Note that while the Shanks method is also easily adapted to restricted intervals, it is much more costly than the lambda due to memory requirements. Furthermore, the rho method is not feasible – direct use results in running time which is square-root but in a group of cardinality 2^{924}, and adaptations remain far inferior to the lambda method.

In summary, the technique allows an attack on Diffie-Hellman (and similar exponentiation-based systems) which has running time (in number of group operations) significantly better than square root of the exponent space size (e.g.

$\sqrt{2^{160}} = 2^{80}$). Instead, it is the larger of the square root after this is first reduced to account for leaked bits recoverable by partial Pohlig-Hellman decomposition (e.g. $\sqrt{2^{160-100}} = 2^{30}$), and the square root of the largest prime factor of n used in this decomposition. This establishes the following result.

Lemma 2. *The security of discrete exponentiation in a group of order n using exponents $x \approx 2^u$ is at most $\frac{1}{2} \cdot \max(u-k, \lg(q_r))$ bits, where k is the number of bits of x feasibly recoverable by a partial Pohlig-Hellman decomposition (using a partial factorization of n), and q_r is the largest prime factor of n used therein.*

In other words, the running time is $O(\max(\sqrt{2^{u-k}}, \sqrt{q_r}))$. By Lemma 1, for $G = Z_p^*$ with random primes p, one expects $k \approx \lg B$ for a smoothness bound B.

At present, it seems dangerous to assume other than that an analogous general result holds, when the exponent space is restricted to any arbitrary set S of cardinality 2^u. Related to this, the rho algorithm is adaptable to the case where exponents x are constrained by bounding their Hamming weight. For example, Heiman [5] describes how to do so using Shanks' method (the rho method would furthermore remove memory requirements). We are aware of no "faster than square-root" method on S in this case; the above combined method does not appear to apply directly. Of related interest, Yacobi [22] has sketched a technique for improving exponentiation performance (saving multiplications but not squarings) based on use of exponents which are compressible in the Ziv-Lempel sense.

Table 2 provides insight into the practical implications of Lemma 2. It was constructed by generating 100 random 1024-bit primes p (as per Table 1), and partially factoring each using an implementation of the elliptic curve factorization method, specifically tuned and run to find prime factors up to 85 bits in length (thus with high probability extracting all 80-bit factors). This allowed determination of k for use in the attack of Lemma 2.

Table 2 gives empirical values for the percentage of cases this attack succeeds for exponents $x \approx 2^u$, assuming attackers capable of 2^c total modular multiplications (roughly corresponding to an ability to take logs in groups of order $\approx 2^{2c}$). For example, for 32% of these 1024-bit primes, an adversary capable of 2^{40} multiplications mod p would find a 160-bit logarithm x. An ideal method accelerating exponentiation via short exponents would have, in Table 2, for the best attack, the entry "100%" only for (roughly) $u \leq 2c$, and "0%" for all $u > 2c$: this appears to be the case for safe primes (§4) and prime-order subgroups (§5).

adversary	exponent bitlength u						
power 2^c	64	96	128	160	192	224	256
2^{24}	81%	45%	18%	10%	1%	0%	0%
2^{32}	100%	68%	38%	25%	12%	2%	1%
2^{40}	100%	84%	55%	32%	22%	7%	2%

Table 2. Sample success rate of discrete log attack in 2^c steps, for 1024-bit primes.

Prior to this result, it has been suggested that using a 160-bit exponent x provides 80 bits of security, for primes p which are not "Pohlig-Hellman weak". It is now seen that even "partial" Pohlig-Hellman weakness may significantly reduce attack times. Note the power of the divide-and-conquer nature of the attack: if $n = p-1$ contains, for example, divisors whose bitlengths sum to $u/2$, a u-bit logarithm can be recovered by determining $u/2$ bits through a partial Pohlig-Hellman decomposition in $O(2^{u/4})$ (and typically less than $2^{u/4}$) steps, and $u/2$ bits through subsequent use of the lambda method on the appropriate subproblem in a further $O(2^{u/4})$ steps, giving an overall cost of $O(2^{u/4})$ steps. Previously, the best attack would require the minimum of the time to run either Pohlig-Hellman or a square-root method on the entire problem, i.e. $O(2^{u/2})$.

4 Use of Short Exponents with Safe Primes

Prior uncertainty about the security implications of using arbitrary prime moduli p with short exponents x has motivated (e.g. [6, 1]) the use of *safe primes* p, of the form $p = 2q + 1$ where q is also prime. This precludes the attack of Lemma 2 because a partial Pohlig-Hellman decomposition yields only a single bit of information about an exponent x. Against this attack, it appears safe to use exponents $x \approx 2^u$, with $u = 2t$ determined such that $O(2^t)$ operations are computationally infeasible (perhaps $t = 80$ for commercial security).

It should be emphasized, however, that when using short exponents, *it is not the single very large prime q that provides protection against Lemma 2*, but rather that the total bitlength of smooth factors is $k = 1$; this differs significantly from the situation for an ordinary Pohlig-Hellman attack against a full-length exponent. For example, $p = Rq + 1$ with q very large and R relatively small, e.g. $\lg R = r = 20$ bits, nonetheless leaks 20 bits of information about an exponent x (of bitlength $2t$ say). This reduces security from t to $t - (r/2)$ bits, which for short exponents (t small) may bring an attack per Lemma 2 within range.

An advantage of using safe primes $p = 2q+1$ is that all group elements of Z_p^* other than ± 1 are then known to have order either q or $2q$. Consequently $g = 2$ is known to be a generator for the full group of $2q$ elements if 2 is a quadratic non-residue mod p (in this case one bit of a logarithm x is available by a partial Pohlig-Hellman decomposition), and a generator for the subgroup of q elements when 2 is a quadratic residue (in this case, $g = 2$ does not leak even one bit).[2] In modular exponentiation using base $g = 2$, the cost of the modular multiplies (but not squarings) effectively disappears. Ordinarily, multiplies are more costly than squarings, although the number of multiplies is substantially less. In efficient implementations, this number is reduced further. All points considered, one may expect use of $g = 2$ to result in modular exponentiation performance improved by 20% overall, vs. an arbitrary generator g. As the main motivation for use of short exponents is improved performance, this is significant.

[2] A more important point is that use of a generator for the subgroup of order q corresponds to a prime-order subgroup as per §5 (albeit the maximal proper subgroup), which avoids the attack detailed in the last paragraph of §4.

One drawback, however, is the computational cost of finding safe primes. An obvious (but inefficient) method to find an m-bit safe prime p is to generate and search some space of candidate primes $q = q_i$ of $m-1$ bits, verify that q is prime, and then verify the candidate $p_i = 2q_i + 1$ is also prime. While the density of primes in search sequences $2q_i + 1$ differs somewhat from that of the density of primes among all integers, the latter is $1/\ln p$ (e.g. 1 in $710 \approx \ln 2^{1024}$ for 1024-bit integers). A standard optimization is to filter candidate primes using small-prime sieve techniques. But even advanced techniques require some form of double search, generating many primes q_i before a safe prime p emerges. In contrast, the cost of parameter generation in the alternative of using prime-order subgroups (§5) is essentially that of generating a single candidate 1024-bit prime. Use of safe primes thus appears to introduce a substantial penalty, with parameter generation time increased by a factor roughly equal to the number of trials required to generate an $m-1$ bit prime q_i.

A drawback of more general concern for basic forms of Diffie-Hellman key agreement is a potentially fatal protocol attack (rather than an algorithmic attack on exponentiation itself) which, although observed by others (including S. Vanstone), appears to not yet be widely recognized. The attack applies also for safe primes, except when the large prime-order subgroup thereof is used (as noted above). Note that if α generates Z_p^* where $p = 2q + 1$, then $\beta = \alpha^q = \alpha^{(p-1)/2} = -1$ is an element of order 2. If A and B respectively send each other unauthenticated ephemeral exponentials α^x and α^y (as in §1), an active intruder may substitute $(\alpha^x)^q$ for the first, and $(\alpha^y)^q$ for the second. The shared key computed by both parties is then $K = \alpha^{xyq} = \beta^{xy}$, which is $+1$ or -1 depending on the parity of xy. (The attack generalizes directly for $p = Rq+1$, in which case K takes on one of R values from the group of order R generated by $\beta = \alpha^q$; for appropriately small R, K may thus be easily found by the intruder by exhaustive trial.) This again motivates the use of prime-order subgroups (§5).

5 Restricting Computations to Prime-order Subgroups

To meet the objective of improved running time through use of short exponents, the recommended alternative is to employ an idea used in Schnorr's signature scheme [18] and in DSA [19], to guarantee that computations are carried out in a large subgroup of cardinality $q \approx 2^u$ where q is prime (a prime-order subgroup). For t bits of security, set $u = 2t$ (e.g. $u = 160$ is used in DSA). If $g \in Z_p^*$ is a generator, and q divides $p-1$, then $\beta = g^{(p-1)/q}$ generates a subgroup of order q. Using β in place of g as a base for exponentiation, all exponents x may be reduced modulo q. Such an element β of order q may be found as follows. Select a random element $h \in Z_p^*$ and compute $\beta = h^{(p-1)/q}$; repeat until $\beta \neq 1$. (While it suffices to first find a generator g and then use $g = h$ with guaranteed success, finding such a g is not mandatory, and moreover requires knowledge of the factorization of $p-1$.)

The expected number of repetitions to find $\beta \neq 1$ is $q/(q-1) \approx 1$, established as follows. A trial fails if the order of h divides $Q = (p-1)/q$; otherwise $h^{(p-1)/q}$

has order q (success). Since exactly Q elements have order which divides Q, the proportion of elements h which fails is $Q/(p-1) = 1/q$.

The use of prime-order subgroups is by far preferable to using random primes (§3) and attempting to increase the exponent bitlength from $2t$ to $2t + t'$ to compensate for divisors of $p - 1$. The latter not only increases exponentiation time, but an appropriate value of t' varies with p, can only be determined with certainty by factoring $p - 1$, and with small probability may be quite large. The use of prime-order subgroups has the advantage over safe primes that prime generation does not require guaranteeing a large prime divisor $q = (p-1)/2$; only a prime divisor $q \approx 2^{2t}$ is required. Since typically $2t \ll \lg p$ (e.g. 160 vs. 1024), the cost of constructing, by well-known techniques [13], a prime p such that $p-1$ has a $2t$-bit prime divisor q is little more than for finding a random prime p. In addition, the use of prime-order subgroups precludes the attack discussed in the last paragraph of §4.

6 Concluding Remarks

Although the details differ, Pollard's lambda method can be parallelized analogously to the rho method [20]. Thus all aspects of the short-exponent discrete log attack of Lemma 2 can be parallelized, and the task can be distributed over large collections of computing platforms [11], with small memory requirements.

For a security requirement of t bits when using secret exponents x in Diffie-Hellman exponentiation (mod p) and similar systems, use of random primes p together with $\lg x \approx u$ is clearly insecure for $u = 2t$ (and even larger). Susceptibility to attacks based on a partial Pohlig-Hellman decomposition (stemming from divisors of $p - 1$) is significant when using short exponents x. In this case, random primes p should not be used.

The results herein firmly establish that some measure must be taken to ensure security is preserved when using short exponents for Diffie-Hellman exponentiation. Aside from precluding strict Pohlig-Hellman attacks, this requirement was hitherto folklore, which has nonetheless apparently helped motivate the use of safe primes in practical protocols such as Photuris [6] and SKIP [1]. We are aware of no effective attacks against the combined use of (appropriately) short exponents with computations restricted to (sufficiently) large prime-order subgroups. Use of prime-order subgroups allows more efficient generation of ephemeral Diffie-Hellman parameters. In contrast, finding safe primes p introduces considerable expense, although pre-computing a safe prime off-line and using $g = 2$ as a base allows improved real-time performance. However, in this case, it is recommended that the safe prime be one for which $g = 2$ generates a large prime-order subgroup as well.

References

1. A. Aziz, "Simple Key Management for Internet Protocols (SKIP)", Internet Draft (work in progress), draft-ietf-ipsec-skip-04.txt, November 1995.

2. A. Bosselaers, R. Govaerts, J. Vandewalle, "Comparison of three modular reduction functions", *Crypto'93*, Springer-Verlag LNCS 773, pp.175-176.
3. W. Diffie, M. Hellman, "New directions in cryptography", *IEEE IT-22* (1976) pp.644-654.
4. J. Hastad, "On using RSA with low exponent in a public-key network". *Crypto'85*, Springer-Verlag LNCS 218, pp.403–408.
5. R. Heiman, "A note on discrete logarithms with special structure", *Eurocrypt'92*, Springer-Verlag LNCS 658, pp.454-457.
6. P. Karn, W.A. Simpson, "The Photuris session key management protocol". Internet Draft (work in progress), draft-ietf-ipsec-photuris-06.txt, October 1995.
7. D.E. Knuth, *The Art of Computer Programming, vol.2: Seminumerical Algorithms*, 2nd edition, Addison-Wesley, 1981.
8. D.E. Knuth, *The Art of Computer Programming, vol.3: Sorting and Searching*, Addison-Wesley, 1973.
9. B.A. LaMacchia, A.M. Odlyzko, "Computation of discrete logarithms in prime fields", *Designs, Codes and Cryptography*, vol.1 no.1 (May 1991), pp.47-62.
10. K.S. McCurley, "The discrete logarithm problem", pp.49-74 in: *Cryptology and Computational Number Theory – Proc. Symp. Applied Math.*, vol. 42 (1990). AMS.
11. A.K. Lenstra, M.S. Manasse, "Factoring by electronic mail", *Eurocrypt'89*, Springer-Verlag LNCS 434, pp.355-371.
12. U.M. Maurer, "Towards the equivalence of breaking the Diffie-Hellman protocol and computing discrete logarithms". *Crypto'94*, Springer-Verlag LNCS 839, pp.271-281.
13. U.M. Maurer, "Fast Generation of Prime Numbers and Secure Public-Key Cryptographic Parameters", *J. Cryptology*, vol.8 no.3 (1995), 123-156.
14. S.C. Pohlig, M.E. Hellman, "An improved algorithm for computing logarithms over $GF(p)$ and its cryptographic significance", *IEEE Trans. Information Theory*, vol. IT-24, no.1 (Jan. 1978), pp.106-110.
15. J.M. Pollard, "Monte Carlo methods for index computation (mod p)", *Math. Comp.*, vol.32 no.143 (July 1978) pp.918-924.
16. R.L. Rivest, A. Shamir, L. Adleman, "A method for obtaining digital signatures and public key cryptosystems", *C.ACM*, vol.21 no.2 (Feb. 1978), pp.120–126.
17. R. Rueppel, P.C. van Oorschot, "Modern key agreement techniques", *Computer Communications*, vol.17 no.7 (July 1994), pp.458-465.
18. C.P. Schnorr, "Efficient signature generation by smart cards", *J. Cryptology* vol.4 (1991), pp.161-174.
19. U.S. Department of Commerce / N.I.S.T., *Digital Signature Standard*, FIPS 186, National Technical Information Service, Springfield, Virginia, May 1994.
20. P.C. van Oorschot, M.J. Wiener, "Parallel collision search with application to hash functions and discrete logarithms", *Proc. 2nd ACM Conference on Computer and Communications Security* (Nov. 1994), Fairfax, VA, pp.210-218.
21. M.J. Wiener, "Cryptanalysis of short RSA secret exponents", *IEEE Trans. on Info. Theory*, vol.36 no.3 (May 1990), pp.553–558.
22. Y. Yacobi, "Discrete-log with compressible exponents", *Crypto'90*, Springer-Verlag LNCS 537, pp.639-643.

On the Security of a Practical Identification Scheme

Victor Shoup

Bellcore, 445 South St., Morristown, NJ 07960
shoup@bellcore.com

Abstract. We analyze the security of an interactive identification scheme. The scheme is the obvious extension of the original square root scheme of Goldwasser, Micali and Rackoff to 2^mth roots. This scheme is quite practical, especially in terms of storage and communication complexity. Although this scheme is certainly not new, its security was apparently not fully understood. We prove that this scheme is secure if factoring integers is hard, even against active attacks where the adversary is first allowed to pose as a verifier before attempting impersonation.

1 Introduction

An *identification scheme* is an interactive protocol in which one party, P (the prover), tries to convince another party, V (the verifier), of its identity. The prover P has a secret key that allows it, and no one else, to convince the verifier of its identity.

There are several types of attacks that an adversary, trying to impersonate P, may attempt, which we categorize as follows. In a *passive attack*, before the adversary tries to impersonate P, he tries to learn something about P's secret key by interacting with P; however, the adversary is not allowed to deviate from V's protocol (this attack includes eavesdropping). Clearly, security against only passive attacks is not very satisfactory, as P must trust V to follow the protocol.

In an *active attack*, the adversary interacts with P, perhaps several times, posing as V, but not necessarily following V's protocol. Security against active attacks is obviously preferable to security against only passive attacks.

There are stronger types of attacks that one may consider, such as those discussed in the paper of Bellare and Rogaway [1]. However, security against active attacks is sufficient in most practical situations where identification is the only goal, such as when a smart card proves its identity to an untrusted verification device in order to gain acces to some resource.

In this paper, we analyze the security of an identification scheme. The scheme is the obvious extension of the original square root scheme of Goldwasser, Micali and Rackoff [4] to 2^mth roots. This scheme is quite practical, especially in terms of storage and communication complexity. Although this scheme is certainly not new, its security was apparently not fully understood. We prove that—like the square root scheme—this scheme is secure against active attacks if factoring integers is hard.

Ueli Maurer (Ed.): EUROCRYPT '96 Proceedings, LNCS 1070

The square root and 2^mth root schemes

Let us first recall the square root scheme. For a given security parameter k, a secret/public key pair is generated as follows. A modulus n is constructed by multiplying two distinct, randomly selected primes, both of binary length k; also, an element $a \in \mathbf{Z}_n^*$ is chosen at random, and we set $b = a^2$. The public key is (b, n), and the secret key is a.

Let m be a parameter such that 2^m grows faster than any polynomial in k. The protocol then repeats the following m times:

1. P chooses $r \in \mathbf{Z}_n^*$ at random, computes $x = r^2$, and sends x to V.
2. V chooses $e \in \{0, 1\}$ at random, and sends e to P.
3. P computes $y = r \cdot a^e$ and sends y to V; V accepts if $y^2 = x \cdot b^e$, and rejects otherwise.

Upon termination, V accepts if it accepted at every iteration, and otherwise rejects.

The results of Goldwasser, Micali, and Rackoff imply that the square root scheme is secure against active attacks if factoring is hard.

We consider the following variant, which might be called the 2^mth root scheme. For security parameter k, a secret/public key pair is generated as follows. A modulus n is constructed by multiplying two distinct, randomly selected primes, both of binary length k, and both congruent to 3 mod 4; also, an element $a \in \mathbf{Z}_n^*$ is chosen at random, and we set $b = a^q$, where $q = 2^m$, and m is a parameter such that 2^m grows faster than any polynomial in k. The public key is (b, n), and the secret key is a.

The protocol then executes the following—just once:

1. P chooses $r \in \mathbf{Z}_n^*$ at random, computes $x = r^q$, and sends x to V.
2. V chooses $e \in \{0, \ldots, q-1\}$ at random, and sends e to P.
3. P computes $y = r \cdot a^e$ and sends y to V; V accepts if $y^q = x \cdot b^e$, and rejects otherwise.

Clearly, the 2^mth root is scheme fairly efficient, and is vastly superior to the square root scheme in terms of communication complexity.

Our proof of security does not show that this protocol is zero-knowledge (in the sense of [4]). Moreover, this scheme is not a proof of knowledge (in the sense of [2]). Indeed, observe that a prover P' that somehow knows a^2 can make V accept with probability 1/2, since P' can respond correctly to all even challenges e; however, given a^2 and a^{2^m}, we cannot efficiently compute c such that $c^{2^m} = a^{2^m}$ (unless factoring is easy). As we shall see, this apparent lack of "soundness" is not really a problem at all, and is in fact crucial to our proof of security, which utilizes what might be called a partial zero-knowledge simulation technique.

Other identification schemes

There are many identification schemes in the literature; we mention just a few.

There are several other variants of the square root scheme, but the only other one in the literature that is secure against active attacks if factoring is hard is the Fiat/Shamir (FS) scheme [3]. While the time complexities of the FS and the 2^mth root schemes are similar, the 2^mth root scheme has much smaller space and communication complexities.

The Guillou/Quisquarter (GQ) scheme [6, 7] is the same as the 2^mth root scheme, except that 2^m is replaced by an m-bit prime number. It is only known to be secure against *passive* attacks, provided that RSA-inversion is hard (a possibly stronger assumption than the hardness of factoring). It is mentioned in [6] that using a power of two would be possible, but no indication of the security of such a scheme is given.

Ong and Schnorr [10] propose a scheme that generalizes the FS and 2^mth root schemes, but only analyze its security against passive attacks. Ohta and Okamoto [8] discuss other generalizations of the FS scheme.

Other identification schemes are based on the hardness of the discrete logarithm problem. The scheme of Schnorr [11] is only known to be secure against *passive* attacks, provided the discrete logarithm problem in (a subgroup of) $\mathbf{Z}_p^*$, where p is prime, is hard. The communication, space, and time complexities for the 2^mth root scheme and the Schnorr schemes are similar; however, the "on-line" time complexity for the prover in the Schnorr scheme is significantly smaller.

Okamoto [9] gives modifications of the GQ and Schnorr schemes which are proved secure, even against active attacks, under the same intractability assumptions of the corresponding original schemes.[1] These schemes are slightly less efficient than the corresponding original schemes.

Overview

The rest of the paper is organized as follows: in §2, we formally state our definition of security; in §3, we give a proof of security for the 2^mth root scheme; in §4, we prove that the generalization proposed by Ong and Schnorr is also secure against active attacks; we make some concluding remarks in §5.

2 Definition of Security

For conciseness and clarity, we adopt the notation of [5] for expressing the probability of various events. If S is a probability space, then $[S]$ denotes the set of elements in this space that occur with nonzero probability. For probability spaces $S_1, S_2, \ldots$, the notation

$$\Pr[p(x_1, x_2, \ldots) \mid x_1 \leftarrow S_1; x_2 \leftarrow S_2; \ldots]$$

denotes the probability that the relation $p(x_1, x_2, \ldots)$ holds when each x_i is chosen, in the given order, from the corresponding probability space S_i.

[1] That paper also suggests a scheme (Scheme 3) whose security is supposedly based on factoring, but the claims of security made in that paper are evidently false.

A probabilistic algorithm A on a specific input x produces an output string according to some probability distribution. We denote by $A(x)$ the probability space of output strings.

Generally, an *identification scheme* (G, P, V) consists of a probabilistic, polynomial-time algorithm G, and two probabilistic, polynomial-time, interactive algorithms P and V with the following properties.

1. The algorithm G is a *key-generation algorithm.* It takes as input a string of the form 1^k (i.e., k written in unary), and outputs a pair of strings (S, I). k is called the *security parameter*, S is called a *secret key*, and I is called a *public key.*
2. P receives as input the pair (S, I) and V receives as input I. After an interactive execution of P and V, V outputs a 1 (indicating "accept") or a 0 (indicating "reject"). For a given S and I, the output of V at the end of this interaction is of course a probability space and is denoted by $(P(S, I), V(I))$.
3. A legitimate prover should always be able to succeed in making the verifier accept. Formally, for all k and for all $(S, I) \in [G(1^k)]$, $(P(S, I), V(I)) = 1$ with probability 1.

An *adversary* (P', V') is a pair of probabilistic, polynomial-time, interactive algorithms. For a given secret/public key pair (S, I), we denote by $(P(S, I), V'(I))$ the string h output by V' (on input I) after interacting with P (on input (S, I)) some number of times. Note that these interactions are performed sequentially. Again, for a given S and I, $(P(S, I), V'(I))$ is a probability space. The string h (a "help string") is used as input to P', which attempts to make V (on input I) accept.

Definition 1. *An identification scheme* (G, P, V) *is* secure against active attacks *if for all adversaries* (P', V'), *for all constants* $c > 0$, *and for all sufficiently large* k,

$$\Pr[s = 1 \mid (S, I) \leftarrow G(1^k);\ h \leftarrow (P(S, I), V'(I));\ s \leftarrow (P'(h), V(I))] < k^{-c}.$$

3 Security of the 2^mth root scheme

Our proof of security is based on the assumption that factoring is hard. We make this assumption precise.

For $k \geq 5$, let H_k be the probability space consisting the uniform distribution over all integers n of the form $n = p_1 \cdot p_2$, where p_1 and p_2 are distinct primes of binary length k, and $p_1 \equiv p_2 \equiv 3 \pmod 4$.

The **Factoring Intractability Assumption (FIA)** is the following assertion:

for all probabilistic, polynomial-time algorithms A, *for all* $c > 0$, *and for all sufficiently large* k,

$$\Pr[x \text{ is a nontrivial factor of } n \mid n \leftarrow H_k;\ x \leftarrow A(n)] < k^{-c}.$$

We shall prove:

Theorem 1. *Under the FIA, the 2^mth root scheme is secure against active attacks.*

To prove this theorem, we show that any adversary that succeeds in an impersonation attempt with non-negligible probability can be converted into a probabilistic, polynomial-time factoring algorithm that succeeds with non-negligible probability. This is Lemma 1 below.

Let (P', V') be such an adversary. Then there are polynomials $T_i(k)$, $N_i(k)$, $T_{ol}(k)$, and $T_p(k)$ as follows.

- $T_i(k)$ is a bound on the time required for V' to run the protocol once with P, and includes the computation time of P. This computation is done "on-line," and thus will typically have to be fast.
- $N_i(k)$ is a bound on the number of times V' runs the protocol with P. This will typically be small.
- $T_{ol}(k)$ is a bound on the "off-line" time for V'; i.e., all time spent by V' other than running the protocol with P.
- $T_p(k)$ is a bound on the running-time of P' and V. This computation is also "on-line," and thus will also typically have to be fast.

For a given public key (b, n) and "help string" h, let

$$\epsilon(h, b, n) = \Pr[(P'(h), V(b, n)) = 1].$$

Then there exist polynomials $Q_1(k)$ and $Q_2(k)$ and an infinite set $K \subset \mathbf{Z}_{>0}$ such that for all $k \in K$, the probability

$$\Pr[\epsilon(h, b, n) \geq Q_2(k)^{-1} \mid (a, (b, n)) \leftarrow G(1^k);\ h \leftarrow (P(a, (b, n)), V'(b, n))]$$

is at least $Q_1(k)^{-1}$.

Lemma 1. *Assume an adversary as above. Then there is a probabilistic factoring algorithm A that runs in time*

$$O((N_i(k)T_i(k) + T_p(k))Q_2(k) + T_{ol}(k))$$

such that for all sufficiently large $k \in K$,

$$\Pr[x \text{ is a nontrivial factor of } n \mid n \leftarrow H_k;\ x \leftarrow A(n)] \geq Q_1(k)^{-1}/8.$$

The special form of integers $n \in [H_k]$ implies that the operation of squaring on $\mathbf{Z}_n^*$ acts as a permutation on the subgroup $(\mathbf{Z}_n^*)^2$ of squares. Also, every square z in $\mathbf{Z}_n^*$ has precisely 4 square roots, exactly one of which is also a square. For convenience, and quite arbitrarily, for $w \in \mathbf{Z}_n^*$ we define $C(w) \in \{1, \ldots, 4\}$ to be the relative position of w among the 4 square roots of w^2 when viewed as integers between 0 and $n - 1$.

We now describe and at the same time analyze our factoring algorithm. In all statements concerning probabilities, the underlying probability space consists of the random choice of the input n and the coin tosses of the algorithm.

On input $n \in [H_k]$, the algorithm begins by computing l as the smallest nonnegative integer with $2^l \geq Q_2(k)$. We require that $0 \leq l \leq m-1$, which will hold for all sufficiently large k, since we are assuming that 2^m grows faster than any polynomial in k.

The algorithm runs in three stages, as follows.

Stage 1. *This stage takes as input n, runs in time $O(N_i(k)T_i(k)Q_2(k)+T_{ol}(k))$, and outputs (v, b, h) where $v, b \in \mathbf{Z}_n^*$ with $v^{2^{m-l}} = b$ and h is a "help string." Moreover, we have:*

(i) if $k \in K$, then $\Pr[\epsilon(h, b, n) \geq Q_2(k)^{-1}] \geq Q_1(k)^{-1}/2$;
(ii) the distribution of $C(v)$ is uniform and independent of that of (h, b, n).

This stage runs as follows. We choose $v \in \mathbf{Z}_n^*$ at random and compute $b = v^{2^{m-l}}$. Note that the distribution of (b, n) is independent of $C(v)$, and is the same as that of an ordinary public key—this is because squaring permutes $(\mathbf{Z}_n^*)^2$, and so b should be, and is, just a random square. We then simulate the interaction $(P(\cdot, b, n), V'(b, n))$. This is complicated by the fact that we do not have at hand a value a such that $a^{2^m} = b$, but rather v with $v^{2^{m-l}} = b$.

We employ a variation of a zero-knowledge simulation technique introduced by Goldwasser, Micali, and Rackoff [4], which might be called partial zero-knowledge simulation. We replace the identification protocol with the following:

1′. P chooses $e_0' \in \{0, \ldots, 2^l - 1\}$ at random, chooses $r \in \mathbf{Z}_n^*$ at random, computes $x = r^{2^m} \cdot b^{-e_0'}$, and sends x to V'.
2′. V' computes a challenge $e \in \{0, \ldots, 2^m - 1\}$ and sends e to P.
3′. P writes $e = e_1 2^l + e_0$. If $e_0 \neq e_0'$, we go back to step 1′ ("undoing" the computation of V'). Otherwise, P computes $y = r \cdot v^{e_1}$ and sends y to V'.

An easy calculation shows that if $e_0 = e_0'$, then $y^{2^m} = x \cdot b^e$; moreover, it is easily seen that the distribution of (x, y) is precisely the same as it would be in the original protocol, and is independent of $C(v)$.

The expected number of loop iterations until $e_0 = e_0'$ is 2^l. Over the course of the entire interaction between P and V', the expected total number of challenges is at most $2^l N_i(k)$. If the total number of challenges ever exceeds twice this amount, we quit and output an arbitrary h; otherwise, we output the h that V' outputs. We also output v and b.

That completes the description of Stage 1. All of the claims made above about this stage are easily verified.

Stage 2. *This stage takes as input h, b, and n from above, and runs in time $O(T_p(k)Q_2(k))$. It reports failure or success, and upon success outputs $z \in \mathbf{Z}_n^*$ and $f \in \{0, \ldots, 2^m - 1\}$ such that $z^{2^m} = b^f$ and $f \not\equiv 0 \pmod{2^{l+1}}$. The probability of success, given that $\epsilon(h, b, n) \geq Q_2(k)^{-1}$, is at least $1/2$.*

Let $\epsilon = \epsilon(h, b, n)$, and assume $\epsilon \geq Q_2(k)^{-1}$.

We use a slight variation of an argument in Feige, Fiat, and Shamir [2]. Consider the Boolean matrix M whose rows are indexed by the coin toss string ω of P' and whose columns are indexed by the challenges e of V. $M(\omega, e) = 1$ if and only if this choice of ω and e causes V to accept.

Call a row ω in M heavy if the fraction of 1's in the row is at least $3\epsilon/4$. Observe that the fraction of 1's in the matrix that lie in heavy rows is at least $1/4$. Now consider a heavy row ω, and a challenge e such that $M(\omega, e) = 1$. Consider the fraction of challenges e' with the property that $M(\omega, e') = 1$ and $e' \not\equiv e \pmod{2^{l+1}}$. This fraction is at least

$$3\epsilon/4 - 2^{-l-1} \geq 2^{-l-2} > Q_2(k)^{-1}/8.$$

Stage 2 runs as follows. Run $(P'(h), V(b, n))$ up to $O(Q_2(k))$ times, or until V accepts. If V accepts, we have a relation $y^{2^m} = xb^e$. Fixing the coin tosses of P', run the interaction again up to $O(Q_2(k))$ times, or until V accepts again with a challenge $e' \not\equiv e \pmod{2^{l+1}}$. If V accepts with such a challenge, then we have another relation $(y')^{2^m} = xb^{e'}$.

The above can be repeated some constant number of times to raise the probability of finding two such relations to at least $1/2$. Upon finding two such relations, and ordering them so that $e > e'$, we output $z = y/y'$ and $f = e - e'$.

That completes the description and analysis of Stage 2.

Stage 3 of our factoring algorithm is executed only if Stage 2 succeeds.

Stage 3. *This stage takes as input n, the value v from Stage 1, and the values z and f from Stage 2. It runs in time $O(k^3)$. The probability that it outputs a nontrivial factor of n, given that Stage 2 succeeded, is $1/2$.*

This stage runs as follows. We write $f = u2^t$, where u is odd and $0 \leq t \leq l$. Set $w = z^{2^{l-t}}$. We claim that with probability $1/2$, $\gcd(v^u - w, n)$ is a nontrivial factor of n.

To see this, first note that $w^{2^{m-l+t}} = b^{u2^t}$, and hence $w^{2^{m-l}} = b^u$ (as squaring permutes $(\mathbf{Z}_n^*)^2$). We have $(v^u)^{2^{m-l}} = b^u$ and hence $(v^u)^2 = w^2$ (again, squaring permutes $(\mathbf{Z}_n^*)^2$). But since u is odd, and by the independence of $C(v)$ and w, $C(v^u)$ has a uniform distribution independent from $C(w)$, and so with probability $1/2$, $v^u \neq \pm w$. In this case, $\gcd(v^u - w, n)$ is a nontrivial factor of n.

That completes the description and analysis of Stage 3.

It follows that for sufficiently large $k \in K$, the overall success probability of our factoring algorithm is at least

$$Q_1(k)^{-1}/2 \times 1/2 \times 1/2 = Q_1(k)^{-1}/8.$$

That completes the description and analysis of our factoring algorithm, and the proof of Lemma 1.

4 The Ong and Schnorr Generalization

In this section, we consider a generalization of the 2^mth root scheme that was proposed by Ong and Schnorr [10], and prove that it is secure against active attacks if factoring is hard.

In this scheme, the modulus n is chosen precisely as before. There are two parameters s and m, chosen so that 2^{sm} grows faster than any polynomial in k. Set $q = 2^m$. A private key consists of a list $a_1, \ldots, a_s$ of randomly chosen elements of $\mathbf{Z}_n^*$; the corresponding public key consists of $b_1, \ldots, b_s \in \mathbf{Z}_n^*$, where $b_i = a_i^q$ for $1 \leq i \leq s$.

The protocol then runs as follows:

1. P chooses $r \in \mathbf{Z}_n^*$ at random, computes $x = r^q$, and sends x to V.
2. V chooses $e_1, \ldots, e_s \in \{0, \ldots, q-1\}$ at random, and sends $e_1, \ldots, e_s$ to P.
3. P computes $y = r a_1^{e_1} \cdots a_s^{e_s}$ and sends y to V; V accepts if $y^q = x b_1^{e_1} \cdots b_s^{e_s}$, and otherwise rejects.

By setting $s = 1$, this scheme degenerates to the 2^mth root scheme. This scheme allows one to somewhat reduce the time complexity at the expense of increasing the key size.

Theorem 2. *Under the FIA, the general Ong and Schnorr scheme is secure against active attacks.*

The proof is similar to that of Theorem 1; we sketch the differences. In the factoring algorithm, the value l is chosen to be the least nonnegative integer such that $2^{s(l+1)} \geq 2Q_2(k)$. As before, we require that $0 \leq l \leq m-1$, but this will hold for all sufficiently large k.

In Stage 1, for $1 \leq i \leq s$, we choose $v_i \in \mathbf{Z}_n^*$ at random, and compute $b_i = v_i^{2^{m-l}}$. Then we perform the same simulation as in Stage 1, except this time, we have to guess the low-order l bits of each of the s challenges.

Stage 2 is easily modified so as to obtain $z \in \mathbf{Z}_n^*$ and integers $f_1, \ldots, f_s$ such that $z^{2^m} = \prod_i b_i^{f_i}$ and not all f_i are divisible by 2^{l+1}.

In Stage 3, for $1 \leq i \leq s$, write $f_i = u_i 2^{t_i}$, and let $t = \min\{t_i\} \leq l$. Then it is easy to see that with probability 1/2,

$$\gcd(z^{2^{l-t}} - \prod_{i=1}^{s} v_i^{u_i 2^{t_i - t}}, n)$$

is a nontrivial factor of n.

5 Conclusion

5.1 Constructiveness and efficiency of the reduction

Although our proof of security is valid, it is open to a couple of criticisms. First, it is not entirely constructive, since to build our factoring algorithm, we need not only descriptions of the adversary's algorithms, but also the polynomials $Q_2(k)$ and $N_i(k)$. By allowing our factoring algorithm to have just an expected running time bound, we could do without $N_i(k)$. However, it is not clear if we can do without $Q_2(k)$. Second, in comparison, say, with the reduction from factoring to impersonating one obtains with the FS scheme, ours is less efficient, since our factoring algorithm has to repeat computations of V' many times. Compensating for this is the fact that the computations that need to be repeated are all "on-line," and so presumably fast.

5.2 Multi-user environment

We have stated the protocols and definition of security from the point of view a single user. Consider a a system consisting of many (but polynomial in k) users. Before attempting an impersonation, we allow an adversary to interact arbitrarily with all users in the system in an arbitrary fashion, interleaving communications arbitrarily. We also allow an adversary to corrupt any users it wants, obtaining their private keys upon demand. After this interaction, the adversary tries to impersonate a non-corrupted user of its choice. Note that the adversary makes this choice dynamically; if the choice were static, the analysis of the multi-user case would trivially reduce to the single-user case.

To reduce factoring to impersonating in this case, we can use the obvious technique of first picking a user at random and giving them the number we want to factor, and generating ordinary key pairs for all other users. We then hope that the adversary picks the user with our number.

As with the FS scheme, all users can share the same modulus n in the 2^mth root scheme. However, to reduce factoring to impersonating in this case, we still have to pick a user at random, and give this user $v, b \in \mathbf{Z}_n^*$ with $v^{2^{m-l}} = b$. Again, the other users get ordinary key pairs, and we have to hope that the adversary chooses to impersonate our user. This is unlike the FS scheme, where every user gets ordinary key pairs, and the impersonation of any user factors n with high probability.

5.3 Using general moduli

Our proofs of Theorems 1 and 2 relied on the fact that the prime factors of n were both congruent to 3 mod 4. However, this is not a serious restriction, and it is not hard to prove that these theorems hold for random primes. It is not clear if this is of any theoretical or practical value, and from a security perspective, it seems advisable to stick with the special moduli.

References

1. M. Bellare, J. Kilian, and P. Rogaway. Entity authentication and key distribution. In *Advances in Cryptology—Crypto '93*, pages 232–233, 1993.

2. U. Feige, A. Fiat, and A. Shamir. Zero-knowledge proofs of identity. *J. Cryptology*, 1:77–94, 1988.
3. A. Fiat and A. Shamir. How to prove yourself: practical solutions to identification and signature problems. In *Advances in Cryptology—Crypto '86*, pages 186–194, 1986.
4. S. Goldwasser, S. Micali, and C. Rackoff. The knowledge complexity of interactive proof systems. *SIAM J. Comput.*, 18:186–208, 1989.
5. S. Goldwasser, S. Micali, and R. Rivest. A digital signature scheme secure against adaptive chosen-message attacks. *SIAM J. Comput.*, 17:281–308, 1988.
6. L. Guillou and J. Quisquater. A "paradoxical" identity-based signature scheme resulting from zero-knowledge. In *Advances in Cryptology–Crypto '88*, pages 216–231, 1988.
7. L. Guillou and J. Quisquater. A practical zero-knowledge protocol fitted to security microprocesors minimizing both transmission and memory. In *Advances in Cryptology–Eurocrypt '88*, pages 123–128, 1988.
8. K. Ohta and T. Okamoto. A modification of the Fiat-Shamir Scheme. In *Advances in Cryptology–Crypto '88*, pages 232–243, 1988.
9. T. Okamoto. Provably secure and practical identification schemes and corresponding signature schemes. In *Advances in Cryptology–Crypto '92*, pages 31–53, 1992.
10. H. Ong and C. Schnorr. Fast signature generation with a Fiat Shamir-like scheme. In *Eurocrypt*, pages 432–440, 1990.
11. C. Schnorr. Efficient signature generation by smart cards. *J. Cryptology*, 4:161–174, 1991.

Robust Threshold DSS Signatures

Rosario Gennaro*, Stanisław Jarecki*, Hugo Krawczyk** and Tal Rabin*

Abstract. We present threshold DSS (Digital Signature Standard) signatures where the power to sign is shared by n players such that for a given parameter $t < n/2$ any subset of $2t + 1$ signers can collaborate to produce a valid DSS signature on any given message, but no subset of t corrupted players can forge a signature (in particular, cannot learn the signature key). In addition, we present a robust threshold DSS scheme that can also tolerate $n/3$ players who refuse to participate in the signature protocol. We can also endure $n/4$ maliciously faulty players that generate incorrect partial signatures at the time of signature computation. This results in a highly secure and resilient DSS signature system applicable to the protection of the secret signature key, the prevention of forgery, and increased system availability.

Our results significantly improve over a recent result by Langford from CRYPTO'95 that presents threshold DSS signatures which can stand much smaller subsets of corrupted players, namely, $t \approx \sqrt{n}$, and do not enjoy the robustness property. As in the case of Langford's result, our schemes require no trusted party. Our techniques apply to other threshold ElGamal-like signatures as well. We prove the security of our schemes solely based on the hardness of forging a regular DSS signature.

1 Introduction

Using a threshold signature scheme, digital signatures can be produced by a group of players rather than by one party. In contrast to the regular signature schemes where the signer is a single entity which holds the secret key, in threshold signature schemes the secret key is shared by a group of n players. In order to produce a valid signature on a given message m, individual players produce their *partial signatures* on that message, and then combine them into a full signature on m. A distributed signature scheme achieves threshold $t < n$, if no coalition of t (or less) players can produce a new valid signature, even after the system has produced many signatures on different messages. A signature resulting from a threshold signature scheme is the same as if it was produced by a single signer possessing the full secret signature key. In particular, the validity of this signature can be verified by anyone who has the corresponding unique public verification key. In other words, the fact that the signature was produced in a distributed fashion is transparent to the recipient of the signature.

---

* MIT Laboratory for Computer Science, 545 Tech Square, Cambridge, MA 02139, USA. Email: `{rosario,stasio,talr}@theory.lcs.mit.edu`

** IBM T.J.Watson Research Center, PO Box 704, Yorktown Heights, New York 10598, USA. Email: `hugo@watson.ibm.com`

Ueli Maurer (Ed.): EUROCRYPT '96 Proceedings, LNCS 1070

Threshold signatures are motivated both by the need that arises in some organizations to have a group of employees agree on a given message (or a document) before signing it, as well as by the need to protect signature keys from the attack of internal and external adversaries. The latter becomes increasingly important with the actual deployment of public key systems in practice. The signing power of some entities, (e.g., a government agency, a bank, a certification authority) inevitably invites attackers to try and "steal" this power. The goal of a threshold signature scheme is twofold: To increase the availability of the signing agency, and at the same time to increase the protection against forgery by making it harder for the adversary to learn the secret signature key. Notice that in particular, the threshold approach rules out the naive solution based on traditional secret sharing, where the secret key is shared in a group but reconstructed by a *single* player each time that a signature is to be produced. Such protocol would contradict the requirement that no t (or less) players can ever produce a new valid signature. In threshold schemes, multiple signatures are produced without an exposure or an explicit reconstruction of the secret key.

Threshold signatures are part of a general approach known as *threshold cryptography* which was introduced by the works of Boyd [Boy86], Desmedt [Des88], and Desmedt and Frankel [DF90]. This approach has received considerable attention in the literature; we refer the reader to [Des94] for a survey of the work in this area. Particular examples of solutions to threshold signatures can be found in [DF92, DDFY94] for the case of RSA signatures, and [Har94, Lan95] for ElGamal-type of signatures.

In this work we present a threshold signature system for DSS, the Digital Signature Standard [fST91]. The importance of providing threshold solutions for signatures schemes used in practice, is that those systems are the ones that will be deployed in the real world and hence they are the ones that require real protection. Threshold DSS signatures schemes were recently studied by Langford [Lan95]. DSS signatures turn out to be less amenable to sharing techniques than RSA or even other ElGamal-type of signatures, e.g., see [Har94]. Langford has overcome some of these difficulties in the case of DSS, exhibiting a solution which requires a group of $n = t^2 - t + 1$ players in order to tolerate up to t players that might refuse to participate in the signature protocol. [1] Thus, for n given servers this solution can resist up to $\sqrt{n}$ corrupted parties.

In general, one would like to have higher thresholds, because they achieve increased security at a given system cost (i.e., a given number of servers). In our work we present threshold DSS signature schemes, where in order to achieve a security threshold t we need $2t + 1$ active signers during signature computation; hence, achieving thresholds of up to $\frac{n-1}{2}$. In addition, we improve on [Lan95] by providing a *robust threshold signature scheme* for DSS which can withstand the participation of dishonest signers during the signature computation operation. Namely, we provide a mechanism that succeeds in constructing a valid signature even if the partial signatures contributed by some of the signers are incorrect. The solution in [Lan95] for DSS does not enjoy this property. In fact, without a "correction" capability as in our solution, or at least a

[1] Langford presents some additional schemes but of more limited applicability: a 2-out-of-n scheme that withstands up to one faulty party, and a general t-out-of-n scheme that uses precomputed tables of one-time shares and that requires a higher level of trust for the generation of these tables. See [Lan95] for details.

detection mechanism for wrong partial signatures, one may need to try an (exponential in t) number $\binom{n}{2t+1}$ of subsets of signers before finding a subset that generates a valid DSS signature. In our case, we achieve a robust threshold solution to DSS signatures tolerating t faults: that is, t or less corrupted players will not be able to forge signatures, and neither will they be able to prevent the system from computing correct signatures by either refusing to cooperate ($t \leq n/3$ in this case) or by behaving in any arbitrary malicious way (in this case $t \leq n/4$.)[2]

Moreover, our schemes do not require trusting any particular party at any time, including the initial secret key generation. This is an important property achieved by some other ElGamal based threshold signature schemes (including the DSS solution in [Lan95]), but not known for threshold RSA signatures. In the complete version of the paper we will present some additional results, including the application of our techniques to solving threshold signatures for other discrete–log based signatures [ElG85, NR94, HPM94].

Remarkably, our solutions for robust threshold DSS signatures can be *proactivized* using the recent techniques of [HJJ+95] (based on proactive secret sharing of the signature key [HJKY95]). In this way, one can keep the DSS signature key fixed for a long time while its shares can be refreshed periodically. An adversary that tries to break the threshold signature scheme needs then to corrupt t servers *in one single period of time* (which may be as short as one day, one week, etc.), as opposed to having the whole lifetime of the key (e.g., 2 years) to do so.

Technical Overview. The threshold DSS signatures schemes need to deal with two technical difficulties. Combining shares of two secrets, a and b, into shares of the product of these secrets, ab; and producing shares for a secret a given the shares of its reciprocal a^{-1} (computations are over a field Z_q). Langford [Lan95] solves both problems by presenting a multiplicative version of secret sharing that results in polynomials of degree $O(t^2)$; this requires a high number of active signers for signature computation and allows for only a small threshold. In our case, we solve the first problem (sharing of a product of secrets) using a single product of polynomials (with combined degree $2t$ resulting in the need for only $2t + 1$ active signers). For the second problem, the sharing of a reciprocal, we introduce a simple and novel solution, which does not incur any additional increase in the number of signers. The solution to this problem is of independent interest and has applications to other threshold ElGamal-like signatures. In addition to these techniques we use many tools from other works, such as verifiable secret sharing (both computational and information-theoretic versions), shared generation/distribution of secrets, re-randomization of secret shares, and more. For achieving the robustness of our schemes we apply error correcting techniques due to Berlekamp and Welch [BW] that achieve a very high rate of error correction, which in our scenario translates into supporting higher thresholds. We prove the security of our schemes assuming the infeasibility of forging a regular DSS signature. That is, our schemes are secure if and only if DSS is unforgeable.

[2] The robustness property has been known for some other shared signature schemes, e.g., Harn's solution [Har94] for threshold AMV-signatures enjoys this property. As for threshold RSA, robust solutions have been only recently found (see [FGY96, GJKR96]).

2 The Digital Signature Standard (DSS)

The Digital Signature Standard (DSS) [fST91] is a signature scheme based on the El-Gamal [ElG85] and Schnorr's [Sch91] signature schemes, which was adopted as the US standard digital signature algorithm. In our description of the DSS protocol we follow the notation introduced in [Lan95], which differs from the original presentation of [fST91] by switching k and k^{-1}. This change will allow a clearer presentation of our threshold DSS signature protocols.

Key Generation. A DSS key is composed of public information p, q, g, a public key y and a secret key x, where:
1. p is a prime number of length l where l is a multiple of 64 and $512 \leq l \leq 1024$.
2. q is a 160-bit prime divisor of $p-1$.
3. g is an element of order q in Z_p^*. The triple (p, q, g) is public.
4. x is the secret key of the signer, a random number $1 \leq x < q$.
5. $y = g^x \mod p$ is the public verification key.

Signature Algorithm. Let m be a hash of the message to be signed. The signer picks a random number k such that $1 \leq k < q$, calculates $k^{-1} \mod q$, and sets

$$r = (g^{k^{-1}} \mod p) \mod q$$
$$s = k(m + xr) \mod q$$

The pair (r, s) is a signature of m.

Verification Algorithm. A signature (r, s) of a message m can be publicly verified by checking that $r = (g^{ms^{-1}} y^{rs^{-1}} \mod p) \mod q$ where s^{-1} is computed modulo q.

3 Model and Definitions

In this section we introduce our communication model and provide definitions of secure threshold signature schemes.

Communication Model. We assume that our computation model is composed of a set of n *players* $\{P_1, \ldots, P_n\}$ who can be modeled by polynomial-time randomized Turing machines. They are connected by a complete network of private (i.e. untappable) point-to-point channels. In addition, the players have access to a dedicated broadcast channel; by dedicated we mean that if player P_i broadcasts a message, it will be recognized by the other players as coming from P_i. These assumptions (privacy of the communication channels and dedication of the broadcast channel) allow us to focus on a high-level description of the protocols. However, it is worth noting that these abstractions can be substituted with standard cryptographic techniques for privacy, commitment and authentication.

The Adversary. We assume that an adversary, $\mathcal{A}$, can corrupt up to t of the n players in the network. We distinguish between three kinds of (increasingly powerful) adversaries:

- An *Eavesdropping Adversary* learns all the information stored at the corrupted nodes and hears all the broadcasted messages.

– A *Halting Adversary* is an eavesdropping adversary that may *also* cause corrupted players to stop sending messages during the execution of the protocol (e.g., by crashing or disconnecting a machine).
– A *Malicious Adversary* is an eavesdropping adversary that may *also* cause corrupted players to divert from the specified protocol in *any* (possibly malicious) way.

We assume that the computational power of the adversary is adequately modeled by a probabilistic polynomial time Turing machine. (In fact, it suffices for our results to assume that the adversary cannot forge regular DSS signatures, which, in turn, implies the infeasibility of computing discrete logarithms.)

Given a protocol $\mathcal{P}$ the *view* of the adversary, denoted by $\mathcal{VIEW}_{\mathcal{A}}(\mathcal{P})$, is defined as the probability distribution (induced by the random coins of the players) on the knowledge of the adversary, namely, the computational history of all the corrupted players, and the public communications and output of the protocol.

Signature Scheme. A signature scheme $\mathcal{S}$ is a triple of efficient randomized algorithms (Key-Gen, Sig, Ver). Key-Gen is the *key generator* algorithm. It outputs a pair (y, x), such that y is the *public key* and x is the *secret key* of the signature scheme. Sig is the *signing* algorithm: on input a message m and the secret key x, it outputs *sig*, a signature of the message m. Ver is the *verification* algorithm. On input a message m, the public key y, and a string sig, it checks whether *sig* is a proper signature of m.

Threshold secret sharing. Given a secret value s we say that the values $(s_1, \ldots, s_n)$ constitute a (t, n)-threshold secret sharing of s if t (or less) of these values reveal no information about s, and if there is an efficient algorithm that outputs s having $t + 1$ of the values s_i as inputs.

Threshold signature schemes. Let $\mathcal{S}$=(Key-Gen, Sig, Ver) be a signature scheme. A (t, n)-threshold signature scheme $\mathcal{TS}$ for $\mathcal{S}$ is a pair of protocols (Thresh-Key-Gen, Thresh-Sig) for the set of players $\{P_1, \ldots, P_n\}$.

Thresh-Key-Gen is a distributed key generation protocol used by the players to jointly generate a pair (y, x) of public/private keys. At the end of the protocol the private output of player P_i is a value x_i such that the values $(x_1, \ldots, x_n)$ form a (t, n)-threshold secret sharing of x. The public output of the protocol contains the public key y. The pairs (y, x) of public/secret key pairs are produced by Thresh-Key-Gen with the same probability distribution as if they were generated by Key-Gen protocol of the regular signature scheme S.

Thresh-Sig is the distributed signature protocol. The private input of P_i is the value x_i. The public inputs consist of a message m and the public key y. The output of the protocol is the value $sig = \mathsf{Sig}(m, x)$. (The verification algorithm is, therefore, the same as in the regular signature scheme $\mathcal{S}$.)

Secure Threshold Signature Schemes. Our definition of security includes both *unforgeability* and *robustness*.

Definition 1. We say that a (t, n)-threshold signature scheme $\mathcal{TS}$ =(Thresh-Key-Gen,Thresh-Sig) is *unforgeable*, if no malicious adversary who corrupts at most t players can produce the signature on any new (i.e., previously unsigned) message m, given the view of the protocol Thresh-Key-Gen and of the protocol Thresh-Sig on input messages $m_1, \ldots, m_k$ which the adversary adaptively chose.

This is the analogous to the notion of existential unforgeability under chosen message attack as defined by Goldwasser, Micali, and Rivest [GMR88]. Following [GMR88] one can also define weaker notions of unforgeability.

In order to prove unforgeability we use the concept of *simulatable adversary view* [GMR89, MR92]. Intuitively, this means that the adversary who sees all the information of the corrupted players and the signature of m, could generate by itself all the other public information produced by the protocol Thresh-Sig. In other words, the run of the protocol provides no useful information to the adversary other than the final signature on m.

Definition 2. A threshold signature scheme $\mathcal{TS}$ =(Thresh-Key-Gen,Thresh-Sig) is *simulatable* if the following properties hold:

1. The protocol Thresh-Key-Gen is simulatable. That is, there exists a simulator SIM_1 that, on input the public key y and the public output generated by an execution of Thresh-Key-Gen, can simulate the view of the adversary on that execution.
2. The protocol Thresh-Sig is simulatable. That is, there exists a simulator SIM_2 that, on input the public input of Thresh-Sig (in particular y and m), t shares $x_{i_1}, \ldots, x_{i_t}$ and the signature s of m, can simulate the view of the adversary on an execution of Thresh-Sig that generates s as an output.

This is actually a stronger property than what we need. Indeed it would be enough for us to say that the executions of the protocols Thresh-Key-Gen and Thresh-Sig give the adversary no advantage in forging signatures for the scheme $\mathcal{S}$. In other words, we could allow the adversary to gain knowledge provided that such knowledge is useless for forging. However our stronger definition subsumes this specific goal and provides a proof of security for any of the "flavors" of signature security as listed in [GMR88]. Indeed one can prove that if the underlying signature scheme $\mathcal{S}$ is unforgeable (in any of the flavors of [GMR88]) and $\mathcal{TS}$ is simulatable then $\mathcal{TS}$ is unforgeable (with the same flavor of $\mathcal{S}$)

Robustness means that the protocol will compute a correct output even in the presence of halting or malicious faults. We will talk about (h, c, n)*-robustness* to indicate that the adversary is allowed to halt up to h players and corrupt maliciously up to c players ($h + c \leq t$ where t is total number of corrupted players).

Definition 3. A threshold signature scheme $\mathcal{TS}$ =(Thresh-Key-Gen,Thresh-Sig) is (h, c, n)*-robust* if even in the presence of an adversary who halts h players and corrupts c players ($h + c \leq t$), both Thresh-Key-Gen and Thresh-Sig complete successfully.

A complete formalization of the definition of secure threshold signature schemes can be found in [Gen96].

4 Existing Tools

Here we briefly recall a few known techniques that we use in our solutions.

Shamir's Secret Sharing. [Sha79]
Given a secret σ, choose at random a polynomial $f(x)$ of degree t, such that $f(0) = \sigma$. Give to player P_i a share $\sigma_i \triangleq f(i) \bmod q$ where q is a prime (We use the interpolation values $i = 1, 2, \ldots, n$ for simplicity; any values in Z_q can be used as well.) We will write $(\sigma_1, \ldots, \sigma_n) \xleftrightarrow{(t,n)} \sigma \bmod q$ to denote such a sharing. This protocol generates no public output. It can tolerate t eavesdropping faults if $n \geq t + 1$ and, additionally, t halting faults if $n \geq 2t + 1$. By using error-correcting techniques (as first suggested in [MS81]) the protocol can also tolerate f malicious faults (among the players, excluding the dealer) if $n \geq t + 2f + 1$. In the following we will refer to this protocol by Shamir-SS.

Feldman's Verifiable Secret Sharing. [Fel87].
This protocol can tolerate up to $\frac{n-1}{2}$ malicious faults *including the dealer*. Like Shamir's scheme, it generates for each player P_i a share σ_i, such that $(\sigma_1, \ldots, \sigma_n) \xleftrightarrow{(t,n)} \sigma \bmod q$. If $f(x) = \sum_j a_j x^j$ then the dealer broadcasts the values $\alpha_j = g^{a_j} \bmod p$. This will allow the players to check that the values σ_i really define a secret by checking that $g^{\sigma_i} = \prod \alpha_j^{i^j}$. It will also allow detection of incorrect shares σ_i' at reconstruction time. Notice that the value of the secret is only computationally secure, e.g., the value $g^{a_0} = g^{\sigma} \bmod p$ is leaked. In the following we will refer to this protocol by Feldman-VSS.

Unconditionally Secure Verifiable Secret Sharing. [FM88, Ped91b].
In contrast to Feldman's VSS protocol, this protocol provides information theoretic secrecy for the shared secret. This is required by some of our techniques in order to achieve provable security. There are two possible implementation of this primitive. One is by Feldman and Micali [FM88] and is based on a bivariate polynomial sharing. Each player receives a share as in Shamir's case plus some extra information that will allow him to check (by exchanging messages with the other players) that the shares do define a polynomial. This implementation tolerates $\frac{n-1}{3}$ malicious faults. Another possible implementation is the one by Pedersen [Ped91b]. In this implementation the private information of player P_i is the value σ_i such that $(\sigma_1, \ldots, \sigma_n) \xleftrightarrow{(t,n)} \sigma \bmod p$. The dealer then commits to each share using an unconditionally secure commitment scheme based on the hardness of discrete log (that is the secrecy of the committed value is unconditional, but it is possible to open the commitment in a different way if one is able to solve discrete log.) The commitment has homomorphic properties that allow the players to check that the shares define a secret as in Feldman's VSS. If one assumes that players are not able to open the commitment in different ways, then at reconstruction time bad shares are detected. The scheme tolerates $\frac{n-1}{2}$ malicious faults. Both implementations can be used in our main protocol. In the following we will refer to this protocol as Uncond-Secure-VSS.

Joint Random Secret Sharing. [Ped91a, Ped91b].
In a Joint Random Secret Sharing scheme the players *collectively* choose shares corresponding to a (t, n)-secret sharing of a random value. At the end of such a protocol each

player P_i has a share σ_i, where $(\sigma_1, \ldots, \sigma_n) \stackrel{(t,n)}{\longleftrightarrow} \sigma$, and σ is uniformly distributed over the interpolation field. As with a regular (t, n)-secret sharing scheme the value σ is kept secret from every player, and even from any coalition of t players. To realize such a protocol, all players act as dealers of a random local secret that they choose. The final share σ_i $(i = 1, \ldots, n)$ is computed as the sum of the shares dealt to P_i by each player (consequently, the joint secret equals the sum of all dealt secrets). It can be shown that as long as all players correctly share their local secrets and (at least) one of these secrets is chosen randomly then the resultant shares interpolate to a random secret σ. In the cases where active corrupted players, that may deviate from the protocol, are considered, one needs to perform the dealing by each player using a verifiable secret sharing protocol. The basic properties of this protocol, namely, the kind of public information it generates, and its fault tolerance are inherited from the underlying secret sharing scheme. In the following we will refer to these protocols as Joint-Shamir-RSS, Joint-Feldman-RSS or Joint-Uncond-Secure-RSS depending which of the secret sharing schemes is used.

Joint Zero Secret Sharing. [BGW88]
This protocol generates a *collective* sharing of a "secret" whose value is zero. Such a protocol is similar to the above joint random secret sharing protocol but instead of local random secrets each player deals a sharing of the value zero. When verifiability is required each player deals its shares using Feldman-VSS. The correct dealing of the value zero is verified by checking that the free coefficient p_0 of each dealing polynomials is 0 (i.e., by checking that $g^{p_0} = 1$). We will refer to this protocol as Joint-Zero-SS. Notice that by adding such "zero-shares" to existent shares of a secret σ, one obtains a randomization of the shares of σ without changing the secret. This is the way we will typically use the Joint-Zero-SS protocol.

5 DSS Threshold Key-generation without a Trusted Party

An instance (p, q, g) of DSS can be generated using a public procedure (e.g., as specified in [fST91]), or using randomness which is jointly provided by the trustees. To generate a pair of public and private keys in a distributed setting *without a trusted party*, we use a *joint verifiable secret sharing* protocol, following the protocol of Pedersen [Ped91a]. That is the players run an execution of Joint-Feldman-RSS (Section 4). The output of such a protocol is a secret sharing $(x_1, \ldots, x_n) \stackrel{(t,n)}{\longleftrightarrow} x \bmod q$ of a random value x which in addition reveals $y = g^x \bmod p$. The pair (y, x) is taken to be the public/private key pair.

6 Basic Modules of our Solution

We start by introducing two building blocks which are central to our solution for threshold DSS signatures. The first is an elegant and simple procedure for the shared computation of reciprocals. This procedure is used in our protocols in the following way: the players first produce a joint sharing of a random k, and then compute from these shares a sharing of the reciprocal k^{-1}; the latter in turn are used to compute $r = g^{k^{-1}}$

(it is essential for the security of our application that information on k is not revealed during this process).

Problem 1: Computing reciprocals
Given a secret k mod q which is shared among players $P_1, ...P_n$, generate a sharing of the value k^{-1} mod q, without revealing information on k and k^{-1}.

Each player P_i holds a share k_i corresponding to a (t, n) secret sharing of k, namely, $(k_1, \ldots, k_n) \stackrel{(t,n)}{\longleftrightarrow} k$. The computation of shares for k^{-1} is accomplished as follows.

1. The players jointly generate a (t, n) sharing of a *random* element $a \in Z_q$ using any Joint-RSS protocol (Section 4). We denote the resulting shares by $a_1, a_2, \ldots, a_n$, i.e., $(a_1, \ldots, a_n) \stackrel{(t,n)}{\longleftrightarrow} a$.
2. The players execute a $(2t, n)$ Joint-Zero-SS protocol (Section 4) after which each player P_i holds a share b_i of the "secret" 0. (The implicit interpolation polynomial is of degree $2t$.)
3. The players reconstruct the value $\mu = ka$ by broadcasting the values $k_i a_i + b_i$, and interpolating the corresponding $2t$-degree polynomial.
4. Each player computes his share u_i of k^{-1} by setting $u_i \triangleq \mu^{-1} a_i \bmod q$.

We refer to the above protocol as the Reciprocal Protocol. The following lemmas can be proven concerning this protocol.

Lemma 4. *It holds that* $(u_1, \ldots, u_n) \stackrel{(t,n)}{\longleftrightarrow} k^{-1}$.

Intuitively, the value μ revealed in the protocol gives no information on k since μ is the product of k with a random element a. This property is stated in the following lemma.

Lemma 5. *(Informal) There exists a simulator* $\mathcal{SIM}$ *such that for any adversary* $\mathcal{A}$ *with access to t shares* $k_{i_1}, \ldots, k_{i_t}$ *of k,* $\mathcal{VIEW}_{\mathcal{A}}$*(Reciprocal-Protocol*$(k_1, ..., k_n)$*) is computationally indistinguishable from* $\mathcal{SIM}(k_{i_1}, ..., k_{i_t})$.

The proofs of the above lemmas are omitted here as they are implicit in the proofs of our protocols.

Problem 2: Multiplication of two secrets.
Given two secrets u and v, which are both shared among the players, compute the product uv, while maintaining both of the original values secret (aside from the obvious information which is revealed from the result).

Given that u and v are each shared by a polynomial of degree t, each player can locally multiply his shares of u and v, and the result will be a share of uv on a polynomial of degree $2t$. Consequently, the value uv can still be reconstructed from a set of $2t + 1$ correct shares. An additional re-randomization procedure (using the Joint-zero-SS protocol of Section 4) is required to protect the secrecy of the multiplied secret; this randomization is essential because a polynomial of degree $2t$ which is the product of two polynomials of degree t is not a random polynomial, and would expose information about u and v.

We note that this solution to the problem of secret multiplication is a simplified version of the the protocols for the same problem presented in [BGW88, CCD88]. (In contrast to those works, in our case secrets are multiplied only once, thus saving most of the complexity of the solutions in the above works which mainly deal with the problem of repetitive multiplication. Even the simplified version of Rabin [Rab95] for repetitive multiplication involves non-trivial zero-knowledge proofs for verifiability.)

7 DSS-Thresh-Sig-1: Eavesdropping & Halting Adversary

In this section we present our basic protocol for generating a distributed DSS signature.

- It is a secure DSS threshold signature scheme in the presence of an Eavesdropping Adversary (Section 3) when the number of players is $n \geq 2t+1$ where t is the number of faults.
- It is a secure DSS threshold signature scheme in the presence of a Halting Adversary (Section 3) when the number of players is $n \geq 3t+1$ where t is the number of faults.

In other words, this protocol preserves security (secrecy and unforgeability) in the presence of less than a half eavesdropping faults. On other hand, this protocol is robust in the presence of an adversary that in addition to eavesdropping can halt the operation of up to a third of the players by, for example, crashing servers, or disconnecting them from the communication lines.

Outline. Initially every player P_i has a share x_i of the secret key x, shared through a polynomial $F(\cdot)$ of degree t, i.e. $(x_1, \ldots, x_n) \stackrel{(t,n)}{\longleftrightarrow} x \bmod q$. First the players generate distributively a random k (through a random t-degree polynomial $G(\cdot)$) by running the Joint Random Secret Sharing protocol Joint-Shamir-RSS (Section 4). To compute $r = g^{k^{-1}} \bmod p$ without revealing k, the players use a variation of the Reciprocal Protocol (Section 6) where the value $g^{k^{-1}}$ is reconstructed rather than the value k^{-1}. For the generation of the signature's value s, we note that $s = k(m + xr) \bmod q$ corresponds to the constant term of the multiplication polynomial $G(\cdot)(m + rF(\cdot))$. Since the players have shares of both $G(\cdot)$ and $m + rF(\cdot)$, they can compute s by performing the Multiplication Protocol (Section 6). The full description of protocol DSS-Thresh-Sig-1 is presented in Figure 1. It incorporates the multiplication and reciprocal protocols from Section 6.

Notation. In the description of DSS-Thresh-Sig-1 we use the following notation for two share interpolation operations:

- $v =$ Interpolate$(v_1, \ldots, v_n)$. If $\{v_1, \ldots, v_n\}$ $(n \geq 2t+1)$ is a set of values, such that at most t are *null* and all the remaining ones lie on some t-degree polynomial $F(\cdot)$, then $v \stackrel{\Delta}{=} F(0)$. The polynomial can be computed by standard polynomial interpolation.
- $\beta =$ Exp-Interpolate$(w_1, \ldots, w_n)$. If $\{w_1, \ldots, w_n\}$ $(n \geq 2t+1)$ is a set of values such that at most t are *null* and the remaining ones are of the form $g^{a_i} \bmod p$

where the a_i's lie on some t-degree polynomial $G(\cdot)$, then $\beta \triangleq g^{G(0)}$. This can be computed by $\beta = \prod_{i \in V'} w_i^{\lambda_{i,V'}} = \prod_{i \in V'} (g^{G(i)})^{\lambda_{i,V'}}$, where V' is a $(t+1)$-subset of the correct w_i's and $\lambda_{i,V'}$'s are the corresponding Lagrange interpolation coefficients.

Lemma 6. *DSS*-Thresh-Sig-*1 is a simulatable (in particular unforgeable) threshold DSS signature generation protocol in the presence of up to t eavesdropping faults, where the total number of players is* $n \geq 2t+1$.

Lemma 7. *DSS*-Thresh-Sig-*1 is a* $(t, 0, n = 3t+1)$*-robust threshold DSS signature generation protocol, namely it tolerates up to t eavesdropping and halting faults if the total number of players is* $n \geq 3t+1$.

The proofs of these lemmas follow the same lines of the proof of Theorem 9 in Section 8. From the above lemmas we derive the following:

Theorem 8. *DSS*-Thresh-Sig-*1 is a secure, i.e. robust and unforgeable, threshold DSS signature in the presence of t eavesdropping (halting) faults if the total number of players is* $n \geq 2t+1$ *(*$n \geq 3t+1$*)*

8 Robust Threshold DSS Protocols

In this section we present a robust version of protocol DSS-Thresh-Sig-1 which remains secure even in the presence of a fully *malicious adversary*. The protocol, DSS-Thresh-Sig-2, relies on no assumptions beyond the unforgeability of regular DSS signatures, and can tolerate $\frac{n-1}{4}$ malicious faults.

Outline. The protocol is very similar to DSS-Thresh-Sig-1. The only difference is that here we need verifiable sharing of secrets since we assume a Malicious Adversary. The random value k is jointly generated by the players using an *unconditionally* secure VSS (Section 4). This guarantees that absolutely no information is leaked on the values k or k^{-1}. Then the players compute r as in DSS-Thresh-Sig-1, with the only difference that now the random value a is jointly generated using Feldman's VSS protocol. As before s is computed from the appropriate shares. Whenever we reconstruct a secret, in order to detect bad shares contributed by malicious players we perform error-correcting using the Berlekamp and Welch decoder [BW]. As before randomization of polynomials (through the joint zero secret sharing protocols) is added in various places in order to hide possible partial information. The full protocol is exhibited in Figure 2

Notation. In the protocol, we use the following notation:

$$v = \text{EC-Interpolate}(v_1, \ldots, v_n)$$

If $\{v_1, \ldots, v_n\}$ $(n = 4t+1)$ is a set of values, such that at least $3t$ of the values lie on some $2t$-degree polynomial $F(\cdot)$, then $v \triangleq F(0)$. The polynomial can be computed by using the Berlekamp-Welch decoder [BW].

An important technical contribution of our paper is the simulation and the proof of the security of this protocol. We prove the following theorem:

DSS Signature Generation – Protocol DSS-Thresh-Sig-1

1. **Generate k**
   The trustees generate a secret random value k, uniformly distributed in Z_q, with a polynomial of degree t, using Joint-Shamir-RSS (Section 4), which creates shares $(k_1, \ldots, k_n) \stackrel{(t,n)}{\longleftrightarrow} k \bmod q$.

   Secret information of T_i : share k_i of k

2. **Generate random polynomials with constant term 0**
   Execute two instances of Joint-Zero-SS with polynomials of degree $2t$. Denote the shares created in these protocols as $\{b_i\}_{i\in\{1\ldots n\}}$ and $\{c_i\}_{i\in\{1\ldots n\}}$.

   Secret information of T_i : shares b_i, c_i

3. **Compute $r = g^{k^{-1}} \bmod p \bmod q$**
   (a) The trustees generate a random value a, uniformly distributed in Z_q^*, with a polynomial of degree t, using Joint-Shamir-RSS, which creates shares $(a_1, \ldots, a_n) \stackrel{(t,n)}{\longleftrightarrow} a \bmod q$.

   Secret information of T_i : share a_i of a

   (b) Trustee T_i broadcasts $v_i = k_i a_i + b_i \bmod q$ and $w_i = g^{a_i} \bmod p$. If T_i does not participate his values are set to $null$. Notice that $(v_1, \ldots, v_n) \stackrel{(2t,n)}{\longleftrightarrow} ka \bmod q$.

   Public information: $\{v_i\}_{i\in\{1\ldots n\}}, \{g^{a_i}\}_{i\in\{1\ldots n\}}$

   (c) Trustee T_i locally computes
   - $\mu \stackrel{\triangle}{=}$ Interpolate$(v_1, \ldots, v_n) \bmod q$ $\quad [= ka \bmod q]$
   - $\beta \stackrel{\triangle}{=}$ Exp-Interpolate$(w_1, \ldots, w_n) \bmod p$ $\quad [= g^a \bmod p]$
   - $r \stackrel{\triangle}{=} \beta^{\mu^{-1}} \bmod p \bmod q$ $\quad [= (g^a)^{\mu^{-1}} = g^{k^{-1}} \bmod p \bmod q]$

   Public information: r

4. **Generate $s = k(m + xr) \bmod q$**
   (a) Trustee T_i broadcasts $s_i = k_i(m + x_i r) + c_i \bmod q$. If T_i does not participate, his value s_i is set to $null$. Notice that $(s_1, \ldots, s_n) \stackrel{(2t,n)}{\longleftrightarrow} k(m + xr) \bmod q$.

   Public information: $\{s_i\}_{i\in\{1\ldots n\}}$

   (b) Each trustee computes $s \stackrel{\triangle}{=}$ Interpolate$(s_1, \ldots, s_n) \bmod q$.

   Public information: s

5. **Output** (r, s) as the signature for m.

Fig. 1. DSS-Thresh-Sig-1 – Halting ($n \geq 3t + 1$) or Eavesdropping ($n \geq 2t + 1$) Adversary

Theorem 9. *Protocol DSS-*Thresh-Sig*-2 is a secure (unforgeable and robust) threshold signature protocol for DSS resistant to t faults against a Malicious Adversary, when the number of players is* $n \geq 4t + 1$.

It is important to note that unforgeability is obtained for $n \geq 2t + 1$ (see Lemma 11), while $n \geq 4t + 1$ is needed only for robustness (see Lemma 10.)

Lemma 10. *DSS-*Thresh-Sig*-2 is a (h, c, n)-robust threshold DSS signature generation protocol, if $h + c \leq t$ and $n \geq 4t + 1$, that is DSS-*Thresh-Sig*-2 can tolerate up to $\frac{n-1}{4}$ malicious faults*

Proof. The correctness of the protocol is due to the error correcting capabilities of polynomial interpolation. Since we are interpolating a polynomial of degree $deg = 2t$ and we have $faults = t$ possible errors, using the Berlekamp–Welch bound we get that the number of points needed in order to correctly interpolate is $deg + 2faults + 1 = 4t + 1$. Hence, we set $n \geq 4t + 1$.

In order to prove the unforgeability of our protocol, we shall generate a simulator $\mathcal{SIM}$-2 which on input the public key $y \triangleq g^x$, a message m and its signature (r, s), the secret values of t players (without loss of generality) $x_1, ..., x_t$, can generate for the adversary a view of the protocol which is computationally indistinguishable from the actual view of the execution of the protocol. Note that when we say "without loss of generality", there are two issues which are addressed here: *i*) that we are taking the *first t* shares, *ii*) that $\mathcal{SIM}$ can not do better if it receives less than t shares. Both these points are easily argued.
The simulator $\mathcal{SIM}$-2 is a two phase protocol. The first one computes all the necessary information, and in the second phase it carries out the communication with the adversary $\mathcal{A}$ in accordance with protocol DSS-Thresh-Sig. The input to the second protocol is the output of the first one. $\mathcal{SIM}$-2 is described in Figure 3.

Lemma 11. *Fix a Malicious adversary $\mathcal{A}$. where t is the number of faults. $\mathcal{VIEW}_{\mathcal{A}}$(DSS-*Thresh-Sig*-2 $(x_1, ..., x_n, (m, y)) = (r, s))$ is computationally indistinguishable from $\mathcal{SIM}(m, (r, s), y, x_1, ..., x_t)$.*

Proof. We shall exhibit the proof by analyzing the information generated by the protocol and the simulator in each step (the numbering of steps corresponds to the procedure described as $\mathcal{SIM}$–Conversation in Figure 3 and to the steps in protocol DSS-Thresh-Sig-2).

1. Both the protocol and the simulator execute a sharing of a random secret. As the sharing is information theoretically secure all subsets of t shares have the same probability. Thus, the sharings of two (possibly) different secrets, generate the same distribution for the sets of size t. As $\mathcal{A}$ sees t shares in the protocol, and receives t shares from the simulator, this step is secure.
2. The reasoning is similar to the previous step, but here the sharing is of a zero value, and the attached verifiability procedure is computationally secure. The simulatability of this step follows from the simulatability of Joint-Feldman-RSS.

DSS Signature Generation – Protocol DSS-Thresh-Sig-2

1. **Generate k**
   The trustees generate a secret value k, uniformly distributed in Z_q, by running Joint-Uncond-Secure-RSS with a polynomial of degree t. Notice that this generates $(k_1, \ldots, k_n) \overset{(t,n)}{\longleftrightarrow} k \bmod q$.

Secret information of T_i : a share k_i of k

2. **Generate random polynomials with constant term 0**
   Execute two instances of Joint-Zero-SS with polynomials of degree $2t$ as underlying scheme. Denote the shares created in these protocols as $\{b_i\}_{i \in \{1 \ldots n\}}$ and $\{c_i\}_{i \in \{1 \ldots n\}}$.

Secret information of T_i : shares b_i, c_i Public information: $g^0 = 1,\ g^{b_i},\ g^0 = 1,\ g^{c_i},\ 1 \le i \le n$

3. **Generate $r = g^{k^{-1}} \bmod p \bmod q$**
   (a) Generate a random value a, uniformly distributed in Z_q^*, with a polynomial of degree t, using Joint-Feldman-RSS.

Secret information of T_i : a share a_i of a Public information: $g^a,\ g^{a_i},\ 1 \le i \le n$

   (b) Trustee T_i broadcasts $v_i = k_i a_i + b_i \bmod q$. If T_i doesn't broadcast a value set v_i to *null*.

Public information: $v_1, \ldots, v_n$ where for at least $n - t$ values j it holds that $v_j = k_j a_j + b_j \bmod q$

   (c) Trustee T_i computes locally
   - $\mu \triangleq$ EC-Interpolate$(v_1, \ldots, v_n) \bmod q$ $\quad [= ka \bmod q]$
   - $\mu^{-1} \bmod q$ $\quad [= k^{-1}a^{-1} \bmod q]$
   - $r \triangleq (g^a)^{\mu^{-1}} \bmod p \bmod q$ $\quad [= g^{k^{-1}} \bmod p \bmod q]$

   Note: Even though the above computations are local, as they are done on public information we can assume that:

Public information: r

4. **Generate $s = k(m + xr) \bmod q$**
   Trustee T_i broadcasts $s_i = k_i(m + x_i r) + c_i \bmod q$.

Public information: $s_1, \ldots, s_n$ where for at least $n - t$ values j it holds that $s_j = k_j(m + x_j r) + c_j \bmod q$

   Set $s \triangleq$ EC-Interpolate$(s_1, \ldots, s_n)$.
5. **Output** the pair (r, s) as the signature for m

Fig. 2. DSS - Distributed signature generation - Malicious Adversary, $n \ge 4t + 1$

$\mathcal{SIM}$

Input: public key y, message m, signature (r, s), shares $x_1, \ldots, x_t$

$\mathcal{SIM}$–Computation

1. Pick random value $\hat{k}$ uniformly distributed in $[0..q-1]$. Generate sharing using unconditionally secure VSS for $\hat{k}$, denote the output of the sharing by $\hat{k}_1, \ldots, \hat{k}_n$.
2. Execute two instances of Joint-Zero-SS with polynomials of degree $2t$. Set $\hat{b}_i$, $\hat{c}_i$ $g^{\hat{b}_i}$ and $g^{\hat{c}_i}$ for $1 \leq i \leq n$ to the output of these invocations.
3. Choose a random value $\hat{\mu}$ uniformly distributed in $[0..q-1]$. Denote $r^{\hat{\mu}}$ by $g^{\hat{a}}$. (We stress that $g^{\hat{a}}$ is only a notation for $r^{\hat{\mu}}$; the value $\hat{a}$ is never explicitly computed in the simulation).
4. Choose t random values $\hat{a}_1, \ldots, \hat{a}_t$ uniformly distributed in $[0..q-1]$. Compute $g^{\hat{a}_i}$ for $1 \leq i \leq t$. From the values $g^{\hat{a}}$ and $\hat{a}_1, \ldots, \hat{a}_t$, generate $g^{\hat{a}_i}$ for $t+1 \leq i \leq n$. Note that $g^{\hat{a}_j} = g^{\lambda_{j,0}\hat{a} + \sum_{i=1}^{t} \lambda_{j,i}\hat{a}_i} = (g^{\hat{a}})^{\lambda_{j,0}} g^{\sum_{i=1}^{t} \lambda_{j,i}\hat{a}_i}$ for known values $\lambda_{j,i}$.
5. Compute $\hat{v}_i \triangleq \hat{a}_i \hat{k}_i + \hat{b}_i$ for $1 \leq i \leq t$. Compute share $\hat{v}_i$ for $t+1 \leq i \leq 2t$, such that $\hat{v}_i$ for $1 \leq i \leq 2t$ define a polynomial $f(x)$ of degree $2t$, such that $f(0) = \hat{\mu}$. Complete the shares $\hat{v}_i$ for $2t+1 \leq i \leq n$ so that $\hat{v}_i \triangleq f(i)$.
6. Compute $\hat{s}_i \triangleq \hat{k}_i(m + x_i r) + \hat{c}_i$ for $1 \leq i \leq t$. Compute share $\hat{s}_i$ for $t+1 \leq i \leq 2t$, such that $\hat{s}_1, \ldots, \hat{s}_{2t}$ define a polynomial $g(x)$ of degree $2t$, such that $g(0) = s$. Complete the shares $\hat{s}_i$ for $2t+1 \leq i \leq n$ so that $\hat{s}_i \triangleq g(i)$.

$\mathcal{SIM}$–Conversation

Comment: In each of the following steps we describe the information which $\mathcal{SIM}$ gives to $\mathcal{A}$. Each of these steps relates to the same numbered step in protocol DSS-Thresh-Sig-2.

1. shares $\hat{k}_1, \ldots, \hat{k}_t$
2. shares $\hat{b}_i$, $\hat{c}_i$ for $1 \leq i \leq t$
   public values $g^0 = 1$, $g^{\hat{b}_i}$, $1 \leq i \leq n$
   $g^0 = 1$, $g^{\hat{c}_i}$, $1 \leq i \leq n$
3. (a) shares $\hat{a}_1, \ldots, \hat{a}_t$
   public values $g^{\hat{a}}$ and $g^{\hat{a}_i}$ for $1 \leq i \leq n$
   (b) public values $\hat{v}_1, \ldots, \hat{v}_n$
   (c) twiddles his thumbs
4. public values: $\hat{s}_1, \ldots, \hat{s}_n$

Fig. 3. Simulation Protocol for DSS-Thresh-Sig-2

3. (a) In the protocol $\mathcal{A}$ receives t shares $a_1, ..., a_t$ of a proper sharing including g^a and g^{a_i} for $1 \leq i \leq n$. As before a_i for $1 \leq i \leq t$ is uniformly distributed in $[0..q-1]$. The values $\hat{a}_i$ for $1 \leq i \leq t$ were choosen by $\mathcal{SIM}$, under the exact same distribution (Step 4), hence the two distributions are the same. The value $g^{\hat{a}}$ was generated by choosing a random value $\hat{\mu}$ uniformly distributed in $[1..q-1]$ and computing $r^{\hat{\mu}}$ which is equal to $g^{k^{-1}\hat{\mu}}$. The value $k^{-1}\hat{\mu}$ is uniformly distributed in $[1..q-1]$ hence the distribution of g^a and $g^{\hat{a}}$ are computationally indistiguishable. The rest of the values $g^{\hat{a}_i}$ for $t+1 \leq i \leq n$, are obtained through a deterministic computation from $g^{\hat{a}}$ and $g^{\hat{a}_i}$ for $1 \leq i \leq t$, hence they too are compuationally indistinguishable from g^{a_i} for $1 \leq i \leq t$.
   (b) The public values $v_1, ..., v_n$ interpolate to some random uniformly distributed value in $[1..q-1]$. The shares $\hat{v}_1, ..., \hat{v}_n$ interpolate the value $\hat{\mu}$ which is random and uniformly distributed in $[1..q-1]$. In addition, the share v_i, for $1 \leq i \leq t$, satisfies that $v_i = k_i a_i + b_i$. The share $\hat{v}_i$, for $1 \leq i \leq t$ was generated in this manner ($\mathcal{SIM}$-Computation Step 5).
4. Same argument as above noting that the shares interpolate the secret s, and that they were properly generated in $\mathcal{SIM}$-Computation Step 6

This completes the proof of Lemma 11.

9 Malicious Adversary, $n \geq 3t + 1$

We have also devised a DSS distributed signature generation protocol which is secure in the presence of a Malicious Adversary when $n \geq 3t + 1$ where t is the number of faults. In other words, it is secure against an adversary who can corrupt at most a third of the players and can make them deviate arbitrarily from their prescribed instructions. For lack of space we present only an outline of the protocol. The details will appear in the complete version of the paper.

However, this algorithm is provably secure only under the following assumption: let p be a prime of the form $p = kq + 1$ where q is another large prime and g an element of order q in Z_p^*. Let G be the subgroup generated by g.

Conjecture 1 *Choose u, v at random, uniformly and independently in Z_q. The following probability distributions on $G \times G$, $(g^u \bmod p,\ g^v \bmod p)$ and $(g^u \bmod p,\ g^{u^{-1}} \bmod p)$ are computationally indistinguishable.*

In other words, we assume that for random u, the value g^u reveals no computational information on the value $g^{u^{-1}}$.

Outline. This protocol differs from the DSS-Thresh-Sig-2 by more extensive use of Feldman-type verifiability instead of using unconditioanlly secure VSS and error-correcting codes. This shift allows for achieving robustness in the presence of larger number of malicious faults (a third instead of one fourth). The random value k is distributively generated using Feldman's VSS. Notice that this expose the value g^k which is extra information that the adversary would not receive from a regular DSS signature. However if Conjecture 1 holds we can claim that this knowledge would not help an adversary in forging signatures (indeed if it did, such an adversary could be used to distinguish between "reciprocals in the exponent" – where k replaces the value u in the conjecture.) A difficulty arises when in the protocol we need to reveal the product of two secrets (i.e., when using the Multiplication Protocol of section 6). In this case, the public information of Feldman's VSS is not enough to detect faulty players who reveal incorrect multiplication shares. In order to overcome this difficulty we require the players to perform Chaum's zero–knowledge proof of equality of discrete-logs [Cha90] (originally designed in the context of undeniable signatures). The basic idea is that if two secrets a and b are shared with Feldman's VSS, then each player has a share $c_i = a_i b_i$ of $c = ab$. However if we want to reconstruct c, we cannot sieve out bad shares as in Feldman, since we do not have the values g^{c_i} but only g^{a_i} and g^{b_i}. So we require each player to publish $g^{a_i b_i}$ and prove using Chaum's proof that $DL_g(g^{a_i}) = DL_{g^{b_i}}(g^{a_i b_i})$. As before, randomization of polynomials is added when needed in order to protect partial information.

10 Efficiency Considerations

As in the case of the generation of regular DSS signatures the most expensive part of our protocols is the computation of r, as it includes all the modular exponentiations and the interactive exchange of messages between players. However (as in the case of regular DSS signatures) such computation can be performed off-line. In this case the signature generation becomes extremely efficient and non-interactive.

References

[BGW88] M. Ben-Or, S. Goldwasser, and A. Wigderson. Completeness Theorems for Non-cryptographic Fault-Tolerant Distributed Computations. In *Proc. 20th ACM Symp. on Theory of Computing*, pages 1–10, 1988.

[Boy86] C. Boyd. Digital Multisignatures. In H. Baker and F. Piper, editors, *Cryptography and Coding*, pages 241–246. Claredon Press, 1986.

[BW] E. Berlekamp and L. Welch. Error correction of algebraic block codes. US Patent 4,633,470.

[CCD88] D. Chaum, C. Crepeau, and I. Damgard. Multiparty Unconditionally Secure Protocols. In *Proc. 20th ACM Symp. on Theory of Computing*, pages 11–19, 1988.

[Cha90] D. Chaum. Zero–knowledge undeniable signatures. In *Proc. EUROCRYPT 90*, pages 458–464. Springer-Verlag, 1990. Lecture Notes in Computer Science No. 473.

[DDFY94] Alredo De Santis, Yvo Desmedt, Yair Frankel, and Moti Yung. How to share a function securely. In *Proc. 26th ACM Symp. on Theory of Computing*, pages 522–533, Santa Fe, 1994.

[Des88] Yvo Desmedt. Society and group oriented cryptography: A new concept. In Carl Pomerance, editor, *Proc. CRYPTO 87*, pages 120–127. Springer-Verlag, 1988. Lecture Notes in Computer Science No. 293.

[Des94] Yvo G. Desmedt. Threshold cryptography. *European Transactions on Telecommunications*, 5(4):449–457, July 1994.

[DF90] Yvo Desmedt and Yair Frankel. Threshold cryptosystems. In G. Brassard, editor, *Proc. CRYPTO 89*, pages 307–315. Springer-Verlag, 1990. Lecture Notes in Computer Science No. 435.

[DF92] Y. Desmedt and Y. Frankel. Shared generation of authenticators and signatures. In J. Feigenbaum, editor, *Proc. CRYPTO 91*, pages 457–469. Springer-Verlag, 1992. Lecture Notes in Computer Science No. 576.

[ElG85] T. ElGamal. A public key cryptosystem and a signature scheme based on discrete logarithms. *IEEE Trans. Info. Theory*, IT 31, 1985.

[Fel87] P. Feldman. A Practical Scheme for Non-Interactive Verifiable Secret Sharing. In *Proc. 28th IEEE Symp. on Foundations of Comp. Science*, pages 427–437, 1987.

[FGY96] Y. Frankel, P. Gemmel, and M. Yung. Witness-based cryptographic program checking and robust function sharing. To appear in proceedings of STOC96, 1996.

[FM88] P. Feldman and S. Micali. An Optimal Algorithm for Synchronous Byzantine Agreement. In *Proc. 20th ACM Symp. on Theory of Computing*, pages 148–161, 1988.

[fST91] National Institute for Standards and Technology. Digital Signature Standard (DSS). Technical Report 169, August 30 1991.

[Gen96] Rosario Gennaro. Theory and practice of verifiable secret sharing. Ph.D. thesis, Massachusetts Institute of Technology, to appear, 1996.

[GJKR96] Rosario Gennaro, Stanislaw Jarecki, Hugo Krawczyk, and Tal Rabin. Robust and efficient sharing of rsa functions. manuscript, 1996.

[GMR88] Shafi Goldwasser, Silvio Micali, and Ronald L. Rivest. A digital signature scheme secure against adaptive chosen-message attacks. *SIAM J. Computing*, 17(2):281–308, April 1988.

[GMR89] S. Goldwasser, S. Micali, and C. Rackoff. The knowledge complexity of interactive proof-systems. *SIAM. J. Computing*, 18(1):186–208, February 1989.

[Har94] L. Harn. Group oriented (t,n) digital signature scheme. *IEEE Proc.-Comput.Digit.Tech*, 141(5), Sept 1994.

[HJJ+95] Amir Herzberg, Markus Jakobson, Stanislaw Jarecki, Hugo Krawczyk, and Moti Yung. Proactive proactive public key and signature systems. manuscript, 1995.

[HJKY95] Amir Herzberg, Stanislaw Jarecki, Hugo Krawczyk, and Moti Yung. Proactive secret sharing, or: How to cope with perpetual leakage. In *Proc. CRYPTO 95*. Springer-Verlag, August 1995. Lecture Notes in Computer Science No. 963.

[HPM94] P. Horster, H. Petersen, and M. Michels. Meta-elgamal signatures schemes. In *2nd ACM Conference on Computer and Communications Security*, pages 96–107, 1994.

[Lan95] S. Langford. Threshold dss signatures without a trusted party. In *Crypto '95*, pages 397–409. Springer-Verlag, 1995. Lecture Notes in Computer Science No. 963.

[MR92] S. Micali and P. Rogaway. Secure computation. In J. Feigenbaum, editor, *Proc. CRYPTO 91*, pages 392–404. Springer-Verlag, 1992. Lecture Notes in Computer Science No. 576.

[MS81] R. McEliece and D. Sarwate. On sharing secrets and reed-solomon codes. *Communications of the ACM*, 24(9):583–584, September 1981.

[NR94] K. Nyberg and R. Rueppel. Message recovery for signature schemes based on the discrete logarithm problem. In *Proc. EUROCRYPT 94*, pages 175–190, 1994.

[Ped91a] T. Pedersen. Distributed provers with applications to undeniable signatures. In *Proc. EUROCRYPT 91*, 1991.

[Ped91b] T. Pedersen. Non-interactive and information-theoretic secure verifiable secret sharing. In *Proc. CRYPTO 91*, pages 129–140, 1991.

[Rab95] M. Rabin. A Simplification Approach to Distributed Multiparty Computations. personal communication, 1995.

[Sch91] C. P. Schnorr. Efficient signature generation by smart cards. *Journal of Cryptology*, 4:161–174, 1991.

[Sha79] A. Shamir. How to Share a Secret. *Communications of the ACM*, 22:612–613, 1979.

New Convertible Undeniable Signature Schemes

Ivan Damgård
Aarhus University, Computer Science Department, BRICS,
Ny Munkegade, DK-8000 Århus C
and
Torben Pedersen
Cryptomathic,
Århus Science Park, Gustav Wieds Vej 10, DK-8000 Århus C

Abstract. Undeniable signatures are like ordinary digital signatures, except that testing validity of a signature requires interaction with the signer. This gives the signer additional control over who will benefit from being convinced by a signature, and is particularly relevant when signing sensitive, non-public data. Convertible undeniable signatures offer additional flexibility in that there is a separate verification key that can be used to verify a signature (without interaction). This allows the signer to delegate the ability to verify signatures to one or more participants, and ultimately to convert all signatures to ordinary ones by making the verification key public. While provably secure theoretical solutions exist for convertible schemes, earlier practical schemes proposed have either been broken or their status as far as security is concerned is very unclear. In this paper, we present two new convertible schemes, in which forging signatures is provably equivalent to forging El Gamal signatures. The difficulty of verifying signatures without interacting with the signer is based on the factoring problem for one of the schemes and on the Diffie-Hellman problem for the other scheme.

1 Introduction and Related Work

Undeniable signatures are like ordinary digital signatures, except that testing validity of a signature requires interaction with the signer. There must be an interactive protocol, both for verifying and disavowing a signature. This gives the signer additional control over who will benefit from being convinced by a signature, and is particularly relevant when signing sensitive, non-public data: Two parties entering into a confidential business agreement will of course want each other to be committed to the deal, but will certainly not want the contents of the agreement to become public, together with a signature anyone can verify. Undeniable signatures are clearly more suitable for this situation than classical ones, since the signer then has the option of saying "no comments" if the data and signature is published e.g. by the press. But note that in case of a legal dispute, he can still be required to confirm or deny the signature and could be considered bound to the signature if he refuses to cooperate.

Ueli Maurer (Ed.): EUROCRYPT '96 Proceedings, LNCS 1070

Undeniable signatures were first introduced by Chaum and van Antwerpen [CvA90], who proposed a scheme based on discrete logarithms. The existence of undeniable signatures was proved to be equivalent to existence of one-way functions by Micali [Mic90].

In [DY91], Desmedt and Yung point out that a group of mutually distrusting verifiers could all get convinced about a signature while only executing one verification protocol with the signer. In general this requires that the verifiers do a multiparty computation. Since such computations are often feasibly only in theory, this may not be a very realistic attack. Nevertheless, it can be prevented completely using a technique known as designated verifier protocols suggested by Jakobson et al.[JKR96] (based partly on ideas by Chaum). In such a protocol, only the verfier whose public key is used in the proof will be convinced. The protocols we present in this paper can all be turned into designated verifier protocols.

Convertible undeniable signatures offer additional flexibility in that there is a separate verification key that can be used to verify a signature (without interaction). This allows the signer to delegate the ability to verify signatures to one or more participants, and ultimately to convert all signatures to ordinary ones by making the verification key public. As an application of this, consider the problem of keeping digital records of confidential political decisions. Authenticating such records with standard signatures is hardly acceptable: if the data leak to the press, anyone can verify the signatures. Undeniable signatures are clearly more suitable in this respect. However, such records usually become publicly accessible after some years, and should therefore also become publicly *verifiable*. However, the signer who generated the undeniable signatures may at this point be unable to handle the verification requests that may now be submitted to him: it may be infeasible because of the number of requests to handle, or the signer may not even be present. This can be solved using a convertible scheme: the signer could make the verification key public after a certain period, or give it initially to a trusted third party, who would release it later.

Even if signatures are never converted in the above sense, convertible schemes can still be useful: in many applications, signatures are generated once, but verified many times. If there is a separate verification key, it can be distributed to a large number of locations. This facilitates handling many verifications without compromising security of the secret key needed to generate signatures.

Convertible undeniable signatures were introduced by Boyar, Chaum, Damgård and Pedersen [BCDP91], who proved that such schemes exist if and only if one-way functions exist. They also proposed a practical scheme based on the discrete logarithm problem. This scheme, however, has recently been broken by Markus Michels [Mic95]. He also proposed a modification that seems secure against this attack, but the modified scheme does not seem to have a provable relation to any well established intractability assumption.

In this paper, we present two new convertible schemes, in which forging signatures is provably equivalent to forging El Gamal signatures. The difficulty of verifying signatures without interacting with the signer is based on the factoring problem for one of the schemes and on the Diffie-Hellman problem for the other scheme. The schemes are provably secure under appropriate intractability assumptions for the underlying signature and encryption schemes.

2 Definitions and Notation

In this section we define the concept of a (convertible) undeniable signature scheme. We use the standard concepts of interactive Turing machines, interactive proof systems and zero-knowledge without further explanation. The reader is referred to [GMR89] for details.

An undeniable signature scheme consists of the following 6 components:

- A *Key generator algorithm* GEN. This is a probabilistic polynomial time algorithm, which receives 1^k as input, where k is a security parameter, and generates as output a triple of keys (K_S, K_V, K_P), called the *secret, verification* and *public* key, respectively. The secret key K_S is used by the signer to create undeniable signatures, while the keys K_V and K_P are used by the signer and verifier, respectively, in the confirmation and disavowal protocols. The scheme defines a set of *legal public keys* called $\mathcal{L}$. Any K_P generated by GEN must be in $\mathcal{L}$.
  For some schemes, it will be the case that $K_V = K_S$. For others, including the convertible ones, they will be different. To apply the scheme, the signer will run GEN and publish K_P, while keeping K_S and K_V for himself. For convertible schemes, he may publish K_V at some later time, or distribute it to a limited set of parties.
- A *Signature algorithm* SIGN. This is a probabilistic polynomial time algorithm, which receives a secret key K_S and a message m, and outputs a signature s. The message, resp. the signature are in $\mathcal{M}$ resp. $\mathcal{S}$, which are sets of binary strings called the *message space* resp. the *signature space*. We note that since SIGN is allowed to be probabilistic, s may not be uniquely determined from m and K_S.
- A mapping VALID which given a public key $K_P \in \mathcal{L}$ and a message $m \in \mathcal{M}$ uniquely identifies a subset of the possible signatures. The intuition is that VALID(m, K_P) is the set of signatures valid w.r.t. a given public key and message.
- A *Verification protocol* (C, V_C). This is a pair of interactive polynomial time Turing machines called the *Confirmer* and the *Verifier*. The common input consists of a message $m \in \mathcal{M}$, a string $z \in \mathcal{S}$, and a public key K_P. The confirmer receives as private input a verification key K_V. Intuitively, z is a signature, which the confirmer claims is valid w.r.t. m and K_P. The protocol is designed to convince V_C about this.
- A *Disavowal protocol* (D, V_D). This is a pair of interactive polynomial time Turing machines called the *Denier* and the *Verifier*. The common input consists of a message $m \in M$, a string $z \in Z$ and public key K_P. The denier receives as private input a verification key K_V. Intuitively, z is a signature,

which the denier claims is invalid w.r.t. m and K_P. The protocol is designed to convince V_D about this.
- A *Signature simulator* SIGN_{Sim}. This is a probabilistic polynomial time algorithm which receives a message m and a public key K_P as input and outputs an element in S called a *simulated signature*. The intuition is that a simulated signature should look like a real signature to anyone who knows only public information. Therefore someone who receives a message and a purported signature from an untrusted source cannot tell on his own if the signature is valid, since it might as well be a simulated one.

In order for the scheme to make sense, the following basic properties are required from its components:

- The signature algorithm always produces valid signatures. More formally: Let the triple (K_S, K_V, K_P) be a possible output from GEN. Then, on input (m, K_S), SIGN always produces an output in $\text{VALID}(m, K_P)$.
- The signer can always confirm a correct signature without revealing any side information, but cannot convince the verifier that an incorrect signature is valid. As a part of this proof, he may need to also convince the verifier that the public key was correctly generated. More formally:
  The confirmation protocol is a zero-knowledge interactive proof system for the language $\{(m, z, K_P) |\ K_P \in \mathcal{L} \text{ and } z \in \text{VALID}(m, K_P)\}$, where we require completeness with probability 1.
- The signer can always disavow an invalid signature (no matter how it was produced) without revealing any side information, but cannot convince the verifier that a valid signature is incorrect. As a part of this proof, he may need to also convince the verifier that the public key was correctly generated. More formally:
  The disavowal protocol is a zero-knowledge interactive proof system for the language $\{(m, z, K_P) |\ K_P \in \mathcal{L} \text{ and } z \notin \text{VALID}(m, K_P)\}$, where we require completeness with probability 1.

We have required that both protocols, in addition to the statement on z, convince the verifier that $K_P \in \mathcal{L}$. Formally, this is necessary since $\text{VALID}(m, K_P)$ is undefined if $K_P \notin \mathcal{L}$. There may be a very real problem behind this, since for some schemes the signer could cheat in the verification or disavowal if $K_P \notin \mathcal{L}$.

For some schemes, including the ones we present here, $\mathcal{L}$ is polynomial time recognisable, in which case there is nothing extra to prove, the verifier can check himself that $K_P \in \mathcal{L}$.

In the following, an *undeniable signature scheme* should be taken to mean a 6-tuple $(\text{GEN}, \text{SIGN}, (C, V_C), (D, V_D), \text{VALID}, \text{SIGN}_{\text{Sim}})$ with the above description and properties. So far, we have only covered part of the security we want (by requiring (C, V_C) and (D, V_D) to be zero-knowledge interactive proofs). The rest of the security comes in two parts, one dealing with security against verifying signatures without knowing, K_V, and one dealing with security against forgeries.

For the first part we need to introduce a *distinguisher enemy* which is trying to verify a signature.

Definition 1. A *distinguisher enemy* E_D is a probabilistic polynomial time algorithm, which can be used in the following type of experiment:

1. GEN is executed on input 1^k, let the output be K_S, K_V, K_P. As input, E_D gets K_P and 1^k.
2. E_D may now make any number of ***status requests*** and ***signature requests.*** In a status request, E_D produces a pair (m, z), and receives a 1-bit answer which is 1, iff $z \in \text{VALID}(m, K_P)$. In a signature request, E_D produces a message m and receives the result of running SIGN on input m, K_S.
3. Let M be the set of messages occurring in status or signature requests done in step 2. Now E_D outputs a message $m_0 \notin M$, and receives a string z_0, which is either the result of running SIGN on m, K_S, or the result of running SIGN_{Sim} on m, K_P. We refer to these two cases as *the real case* and *the simulated case*, resp.
4. E_D may now make any number of status or signature requests, provided that m_0 does not occur as the message in any request, and z_0 does not occur in any status request.
5. Finally E_D outputs 1 bit.

We must now define what it means that E_D is capable of distinguishing the simulated and the real case:

Definition 2. Let $p_{\text{real}}(k)$, resp. $p_{\text{sim}}(k)$ be the probability that E_D outputs 1 in the real, resp. the simulated case above. These probabilities are taken over the random choices made by E_D, GEN and SIGN.

E_D is *successful* against the scheme defined by the 6-tuple

$$(\text{GEN}, \text{SIGN}, (C, V_C), (D, V_D), \text{VALID}, \text{SIGN}_{\text{Sim}}),$$

if there is a polynomial P such that for infinitely many k,

$$|p_{\text{real}}(k) - p_{\text{sim}}(k)| \geq 1/P(k).$$

The reader may notice that the verify and disavowal protocols do not enter explicitly into the definition of a distinguisher enemy. We could have included them by saying that the enemy at each status request, in addition to the status of z, also gets to execute the appropriate protocol playing the role of V_C or V_D. However, the success of such an enemy would imply the success of an enemy of our kind: we have demanded that the protocols be zero-knowledge, and so the executions could be replaced by simulations without affecting significantly the final output.

We also remark that we have not considered parallel executions of the verify and/or disavowal protocols. In theory, this can always be justified, if the signer simply refuses to execute more than one protocol at a time. Even if this is not done in practice, it does not seem to lead to problems for the concrete schemes we present: although zero-knowledge is generally not closed under parallel composition, the concrete protocols involved here can reasonably be conjectured to be secure, even when executed in parallel.

We can now finally state:

Definition 3. An undeniable signature scheme is said to be *signature indistinguishable* if no distinguisher enemy has success against it.

We now come to the other part of security. For this, we need a new kind of enemy:

Definition 4. A *signature enemy* E_S is a probabilistic polynomial time algorithm, which can be used in the following type of experiment:

1. GEN is executed on input 1^k, let the output be K_S, K_V, K_P. As input, E_S gets K_P and 1^k.
2. E_S may now make any number of *status requests* and *signature requests* (see Definition 1).
3. Let M be the set of messages occurring in status or signature requests done in step 2. Now E_S outputs a message $m_0 \notin M$, and a string z_0.

We must now define what it means that E_S has success:

Definition 5. Let $p_{\text{sig}}(k)$ be the probability that E_S outputs (m_0, z_0) such that $z_0 \in \text{VALID}(m_0, K_P)$. This probability is taken over the random choices made by E_D, GEN and SIGN.

E_S is *successful* against the scheme

$$(\text{GEN}, \text{SIGN}, (C, V_C), (D, V_D), \text{VALID}, \text{SIGN}_{\text{Sim}}),$$

if there is a polynomial P such that for infinitely many k,

$$p_{\text{sig}}(k) \geq 1/P(k).$$

Definition 6. An undeniable signature scheme is said to be *unforgeable* if no signature enemy has success against it.

Finally, we need to define the additional property that a convertible scheme should have. From an undeniable signature scheme **S** described by the 6-tuple $(\text{GEN}, \text{SIGN}, (C, V_C), (D, V_D), \text{VALID}, \text{SIGN}_{\text{Sim}})$, we can always build an ordinary signature scheme with secret key K_S and public key (K_V, K_P). Signatures are generated by running SIGN and can be verified by simulating the verification protocol. This requires no interaction, when K_V is known (although for practical schemes there may be more efficient ways to verify). We call this the *derived signature scheme* of **S**. In cases where $K_V = K_S$, the derived scheme is of course totally insecure. But for convertible schemes, we would like it to be secure in the standard sense of Goldwasser, Micali and Rivest (refer to [GMR88] for details):

Definition 7. An undeniable signature scheme is said to be *convertible*, if its derived signature scheme is not existentially forgeable under an adaptive chosen message attack.

To build a convertible scheme, it seems like a natural idea to generate an ordinary signature and encrypt it under some public-key probabilistic encryption scheme. Indeed, this idea can be quite easily proved to work, if the signature and encryption schemes are secure in a strong enough sense. However, even if those schemes were practical, the combined result will not be practical in general. This is because the only general way to build verification and disavowal protocols is by secure circuit evaluation, which will be polynomial time, but usually horrible in practice. Thus, to preserve efficiency in a practical sense a more careful way of doing the combination is needed. We show two examples of this in the following sections.

3 Two Schemes

This section presents two convertible undeniable signature schemes obtained from the El Gamal signature scheme [EG85]. In El Gamal signatures the public key is a triple (p, t, g, h), where p is a prime, t divides $p-1$ and g generates the subgroup, G, of Z_p^* of order t. Finally, $h = g^x \bmod p$, where $x \in \{0, 1, \ldots, t-1\}$ is the secret key. The signature on a message $m \in \{0, 1, \ldots, t-1\}$ is a pair $(r, s) \in G \times Z_t$ satisfying $g^m = h^r r^s \bmod p$ (when r is in the exponent, the binary representation of r is interpreted as a number in Z_t). A signature is made by choosing $b \in Z_t^*$ at random, computing $r = g^b \bmod p$ and finding s as the solution to the equation $m = rx + bs \bmod t$.

For security and efficiency reasons, a hash value of the message and not the message itself is usually signed. In the following it will therefore implicitly be assumed that m is the result of hashing the actual message using an agreed hash function. This also means that the message space of the two schemes presented below is $\{0,1\}^*$.

Both convertible undeniable signature schemes below are obtained by encrypting the second part of the signature (s). One scheme uses Rabin encryption [Rab79] and the other uses Diffie-Hellman encryption [DH76, EG85].

Some common notation will be used in addition to that already introduced. If a is an element of a well defined group, $\mathrm{ord}(a)$ denotes the order of a, $<a>$ denotes the subgroup generated by a, and $\log_a b$ denotes the discrete logarithm of $b \in <a>$ with respect to a.

Both schemes require that $p = \omega t + 1$, where t is of a special form and $\omega \in N$. One way to achieve this is to first generate t as required and then $p = \omega t + 1$ as small as possible. In [Wag79] it is argued that given a random t, p can be expected to be less than $t \log_2^2 t$.

3.1 Rabin Encryption of s

This scheme assumes that t is selected as a product of two large primes q_1 and q_2. Knowing the factorisation of t allows verification of signatures. Thus the scheme can be described as follows:

- The key generator, generates p and t, where t is the product of two k-bits primes q_1 and q_2. Next, using the factorisation of $p-1$, g of order t and $x \in Z_t^*$ are chosen, and $h = g^x \bmod p$ is computed. The public key is $K_P = (p, t, g, h)$, the secret key is $K_S = x$ and the verification key is $K_V = (q_1, q_2)$.
  The language, $\mathcal{L}$, of legal public keys depends on a parameter k_{min} and is defined as the set of tuples (p, t, g, h) such that $g^t = h^t = 1 \bmod p$ and all divisors of t have binary length at least k_{min}.
  Remark Membership of $\mathcal{L}$ can be verified in polynomial time, whenever k_{min} is logarithmic in k. $\mathcal{L}$ allows keys for which g and h have order less than t, and t is the product of several small primes.
- A signature on a message m is pair $(r, E(s))$ computed by making an El Gamal signature (r, s) on m and computing $E(s) = s^2 \bmod t$.
- Given a signature (r, E) on m, let u denote $g^m h^{-r} \bmod p$. Then the set of valid signatures on m is defined as follows:

$$\text{VALID}(m, K_P) = \left\{(r, E) \in G \times Z_t^* \mid \exists s \in Z_t^* : u = r^s \wedge r^E = u^s\right\}.$$

  Remark Clearly, $\text{SIGN}(m, x) \in \text{VALID}(m, K_P)$. On the other hand, if $(r, E) \in \text{VALID}(m, K_P)$, then $E = s^2 \bmod \text{ord}(r)$ for some s such that (r, s) is a signature on m. If the signature is constructed using SIGN then $\text{ord}(r)$ equals t, but in general they may be different. This will, however, not cause any security problems.
- The signature simulator selects $r \in G$ at random and $E(s)$ as a random quadratic residue modulo t.

To complete the description of the schemes, protocols for verifying and disavowing signatures must be given. The definition of $\text{VALID}(m, K_P)$ shows that these can be based on zero-knowledge proofs of equality and inequality of discrete logarithms.

For verification, the variant of Schnorr [Sch91] presented in [CP93] can be used to obtain a zero-knowledge proof for $\text{VALID}(m, K_P)$. If the challenge is selected from a suitable set (e.g. among 2^{20} possibilities) only two or three iterations are needed making the verification protocol practical, and the protocol can still be simulated efficiently. Another possibility is the cut-and-choose protocol of [CEG87]. However, the zero-knowledge protocol of [Cha91] does not work immediately, since the signer may cheat if u and r are in different subgroups.

The protocol for disavowal can be obtained by techniques similar to those used for denying signatures in [BCDP91].

3.2 Diffie-Hellman Encryption of s

This scheme assumes that t is a prime. The number s is then encrypted using Diffie-Hellman encryption modulo t. The scheme is defined as follows:

- The key generator, generates a k-bits prime t and a prime p of the form $p = \omega t + 1$. Next, g of order t and $x \in Z_t^*$ are chosen and $h = g^x \bmod$

p is computed. Furthermore, a generator α of Z_t^* and $v \in \{0, 1, \ldots, t - 1\}$ are selected and β is computed as $\alpha^v \bmod t$. The public key is $K_P = (p, t, g, h, \alpha, \beta)$, the secret key is $K_S = x$ and the verification key is $K_V = v$. The language, $\mathcal{L}$, of legal public keys, is defined as the following set of tuples $(p, t, g, h, \alpha, \beta)$ such that t is a prime, $g^t = h^t = 1 \bmod p$ and both α and β generate Z_t^*. The owner must publish the factorisation of $t - 1$ allowing other parties to verify that α and β generate Z_t^*.
Remark Unlike the previous scheme, this one allows several persons to use the same p, t, g and α. If these numbers are published a priori as system parameters, the key generator just has to select x and v and compute h and β.

- A signature on a message m is a pair $(r, E(s, \rho))$ computed by making an El Gamal signature (r, s) on m, selecting $\rho \in Z_{t-1}$ at random and computing $E(s, \rho) = (\alpha^\rho, s\beta^\rho)$ modulo t.
- Given a signature (r, E) on m, let u denote $g^m h^{-r} \bmod p$ and let $E = (E_1, E_2)$. Then the set of valid signatures on m is defined as follows:

$$\textsc{Valid}(m, K_P) =$$

$$\{(r, E) \in G \times Z_t^* \times Z_t^* \mid \exists s \in Z_t : \log_\alpha \beta = \log_{E_1}(E_2 s^{-1}) \wedge u = r^s\}.$$

Clearly, $\textsc{Sign}(m, x) \in \textsc{Valid}(m, K_P)$.

- The signature simulator selects $r \in G$ at random and E as a pair of random elements of Z_t^*.

Next protocols for verifying and disavowing signatures are described. Given a possibly false signature (r, E) on m, let $E = (z_1, z_2)$ and let $u = g^m h^{-r} \bmod p$ as above. For verification the verifier must show that (z_1, z_2) encrypts a number, s such that $u = r^s \bmod p$ and for disavowal the denier must show that (z_1, z_2) encrypts a number s such that $u \neq r^s \bmod p$. An interactive bi-proof for this is depicted in Figure 1. A bi-proof system uses the same protocol for verification and disavowal. The verifier will accept the verification or the disavowal depending on the outcome of the protocol (see [FOO91]) for details).

This protocol requires a proof that E' is an encryption of ss' (see Figure 1 for the notation). Such a proof can for example be obtained using the efficient zero-knowledge proof in [Cha91]. However, in the case of verification the prover can do even better, by sending $\rho + \rho' \bmod t$. This is possible if the prover knows ρ (e.g., as a consequence of choosing ρ using a function from a family of pseudo random functions [GGM84]). In both cases the following holds:

Proposition 8. *If the protocol in Figure 1 is repeated $l = \Omega(k)$ times it is a perfectly zero-knowledge proof system for* $\textsc{Valid}(m, K_P)$. *In general a cheating prover can convince a verifier with probability at most 2^{-l}.*

Proof
Completeness and Soundness
Completeness is clear by inspection of the protocol.

The verifier first checks that $(r, E) \in G \times Z_t^* \times Z_t^*$. In particular this implies that r must have order t. If this fails the verifier will reject in case of verification and accept in case of disavowal.
Using v, the prover next computes s such that (z_1, z_2) is an encryption of s. Then the following is repeated l times:

1. The prover chooses $\rho' \in Z_{t-1}$ and $s' \in Z_t^*$ at random and sends $E' = \left(z_1\alpha^{\rho'}, z_2 s'\beta^{\rho'}\right)$ and $w = u^{s'} \bmod p$ to the verifier.
2. The verifier chooses $b \in \{0, 1\}$ at random and sends b to the prover.
3. If $b = 0$ the prover sends back the pair (s', ρ'). Otherwise, if $b = 1$ the prover sends back $ss' \bmod t$ and proves (possibly interactively) that E' is an encryption of ss'.
4. If $b = 0$ the verifier checks that E' and w are computed as in Step 1. If $b = 1$ the verifier checks the proof of the decryption of E'. If this fails the verifier rejects the proof. Otherwise, if the prover is verifying a signature, the verifier accepts if

$$r^{ss'} = w \bmod p$$

and if the prover is disavowing a signature the verifier accepts if $r^{ss'} \neq w \bmod p$

Fig. 1. Bi-proof system for $\text{VALID}(m, K_P)$ (if $l = k$). The common input is (K_P, r, u, z_1, z_2) and the private input of the prover is v such that $\beta = \alpha^v \bmod t$.

For soundness first observe that we may assume that r has order t, since otherwise the verifier would immediately reject. We now show that if for at least one of the iterations, the prover is capable of satisfying the verifier for both $b = 0$ and $b = 1$, then the input signature is valid. This immediately implies that the prover can cheat with probability at most 2^{-l}. In the initial message of the round the prover sends an encryption (E_1', E_2') and a number w. A correct answer to $b = 0$ is a pair of numbers s', ρ' such that

$$(E_1', E_2') = (z_1\alpha^{\rho'}, z_2 s'\beta^{\rho'}) \text{ and } w = u^{s'}.$$

A correct answer to $b = 1$ is a number d for which $r^d = w$ for verification and $r^d \neq w$ for disavowal. Moreover we know that (E_1', E_2') encrypts d (since the prover decrypts it directly in the verification case), i.e. that for some γ

$$(E_1', E_2') = (\alpha^\gamma, d\beta^\gamma).$$

By putting the two equations on (E_1, E_2) together, we can obtain that $(z_1, z_2) = (\alpha^{\gamma-\rho'}, s'^{-1}d\beta^{\gamma-\rho'})$ where s'^{-1} denotes the multiplicative inverse modulo t. Since t is also the order of r, the fact that for verification $u^{s'} = w = r^d$ implies that $u = r^{s'^{-1}d}$. Thus we have shown that for verification, (z_1, z_2) encrypts the discrete log base r of u, which is the condition specified in the definition of $\text{VALID}(m, K_P)$.

Zero-Knowledge

We exhibit a simulator for one round of the verification case:

1. Choose c to be 0 or 1 at random.
2. If $c = 0$, follow the prover's algorithm for computing E' and $w = u^{s'}$ and send them to the verifier.
   If $c = 1$, choose $d \in Z_t^*$ at random and compute E' as an encryption of d. Compute $w = r^d$ and send E' and w to the verifier.
3. Receive b from the verifier.
4. If $c \neq b$, rewind the verifier and go to step 1.
   If $c = b = 0$, send s', ρ' to the verifier.
   If $c = b = 1$, send d to the verifier and convince him that E' encrypts d (following the prover's procedure for doing this).

To simulate l rounds, just repeat this simulation.

Observe that the prover's first message is always an encryption of a random number d, and a w such that $w = r^d$. Hence the simulators first message has the same distribution as the prover's and is in particular independent of c. Hence the expected number of rewinds is 2 and the complete simulation runs in expected linear time. It is easy to check that the answers generated by the simulator in step 4 have the same distribution as the prover's responses. Thus the simulation is perfect. □

When the protocol is used to deny signatures, it is only computationally zero-knowledge. The problem is that the for the case $b = 1$ it does not seem possible to come up with both the product ss' and $u^{s'}$ since $u^{1/s}$ is not known. Instead, this case is simulated by choosing ss' at random, making a random encryption of ss' and instead of $u^{s'}$ a random number in <g> is selected. To show that this simulation works, the following assumption is necessary:

Assumption EDL If p, t, α and β are selected as described by GEN, then given a pair (a, b) of elements of Z_t^* it is not feasible to say if (a, b) is chosen at random or as a random pair satisfying $\log_\alpha \beta = \log_a b$.

This assumption has previously been used in [CvA90, BCDP91].

Proposition 9. *Under Assumption EDL, the protocol in Figure 1 is a computationally zero-knowledge proof system for the complement of* VALID(m, K_P).

Proof

Completeness and soundness

Again completeness is clear. For soundness first observe that we may assume that r has order t, since otherwise the verifier would immediately accept. As in the proof of Proposition 8 correct answers to both $b = 0$ and $b = 1$ allows us to write $(z_1, z_2) = (\alpha^{\gamma-\rho'}, s'^{-1}d\beta^{\gamma-\rho'})$ where s'^{-1} denotes the multiplicative inverse modulo t. We know that $u^{s'} = w \neq r^d$, whence $u \neq r^{s'^{-1}d}$. Since we still have that $s'^{-1}d$ is the number encrypted in (z_1, z_2), the condition for being in VALID(m, K_P) is not satisfied.

This shows that given that the prover cannot cheat in any of the proofs that (E_1', E_2') encrypts d, his chance of cheating is at most 2^{-l}. Let ϵ be the probability with which the prover can cheat in one such proof. Then the probability that he can cheat in any of the l proofs is at most $l\epsilon$. We may assume that ϵ is exponentially small in k - it may even be 0, if the prover can decrypt the pair directly. Therefore also $l\epsilon$ is exponentially small. This clearly implies that his overall chance is exponentially small in k (if we use $l = k$), and is in fact 2^{-l} if $\epsilon = 0$.

Zero-knowledge

The simulation works as follows:

1. Choose c to be 0 or 1 at random.
2. If $c = 0$, follow the prover's algorithm for computing E' and $w = u^{s'}$ and send them to the verifier.
   If $c = 1$, choose $d \in Z_t^*$ at random and compute E' as an encryption of d. Choose w at random and send E' and w to the verifier.
3. Receive b from the verifier.
4. If $c \neq b$, rewind the verifier and go to step 1.
   If $c = b = 0$, send s', ρ' to the verifier.
   If $c = b = 1$, send d to the verifier and convince him that E' encrypts d (following the prover's procedure for doing this).

To simulate l rounds, just repeat this simulation.

Let the simulators first message be the encryption (E_1', E_2') and the number w. Let s' be the number encrypted by the pair $(E_1' z_1^{-1}, E' z_2^{-1})$. Now, if $c = 0$, $w = u^{s'}$ while if $c = 1$, w is independent of s'. Distinguishing the two cases is at least as hard as deciding if $\log_\alpha(E_1' z_1^{-1}) = \log_\beta(s'^{-1} E_2' z_2^{-1})$. Hence if the probability that $b = c$ is significantly different from 1/2, the verifier could be used to construct an algorithm contradicting assumption EDL. Hence, under EDL, the simulation runs in expected polynomial time.

This also shows that the cases $b = 1$ and $b = 0$ occur in the simulation with probabilities as in the real conversation except for a superpolynomially small error. Now note that the distribution of the simulation given that $b = 0$ is the same as for the conversation, whereas the distribution given that $b = 1$ is different from the conversation. However, by the same argument as before the two cannot be distinguished in polynomial time under assumption EDL. □

Remark The verification protocol is not as efficient as the one for the scheme based on Rabin encryption, however this scheme offers additional flexibility, such as

- The signer can convert single signatures (selective conversion as described in [BCDP91]) by releasing ρ.
- If the signer chooses a list of β-values, different β's can be used for different classes of signatures. All signatures in one class can then be converted by publishing the corresponding $\log_\alpha \beta$.

4 Security of the Schemes

This section analyses the security of the two schemes, with respect to forgeries and recognising signatures.

4.1 Forging Signatures

For both schemes it is sufficient (and necessary, if the signatures are converted) to show that the they are secure if the verification key is published.

Proposition 10. *The schemes using Rabin respectively Diffie-Hellman encryption are unforgeable, if the El Gamal scheme combined with the chosen hash function is secure against adaptively chosen message attacks for primes of the form $\omega t + 1$ where t is the product of two large known primes respectively t is a large known prime.*

Proof sketch
Given a method for forging signatures in one of the two schemes, signatures can be forged in the corresponding El Gamal scheme using the following adaptively chosen message attack:

1. Generate the verification key, and the corresponding part of the public key in the undeniable signature scheme.
2. Execute the attack against the undeniable scheme with the resulting public key. Whenever, an undeniable signature on a message, m, is requested in this attack, ask for an El Gamal signature on m and encrypt s to obtain the required undeniable signature. Whenever, the attacker asks if $z \in \text{VALID}(m, K_P)$ for some message m, this is answered by decrypting z and verifying the signature.
3. Finally, the attack outputs an undeniable signature on a new message, m_0. This signature can be made into an ordinary El Gamal signature by decrypting s.

□

Corollary 11. *Both schemes are convertible if the El Gamal schemes they are based on are secure against adaptively chosen message attacks.*

5 Signature Indistinguishability

Recall the definition of signature indistinguishability from Section 2. First, note that for both schemes, it is enough to argue indistinguishability in the case where the enemy knows K_S, as this can only make his task easier. In this case, being able to get signatures on chosen messages is of no additional help. In the following, an active, resp. passive attack is one where the enemy uses, resp. does not use the oracle for testing validity of signatures of his choice.

5.1 The Scheme using Rabin Encryption

When the enemy is given a purported signature (r, E) on m, all he knows is that if the signature is valid then the s determined by the equation $m - xr = bs \bmod t$ (where b is the discrete log of r base g) equals the s' determined by the equation

$s'^2 = E \bmod t$. If the enemy neither knows b nor the factorisation of t this seems to be difficult to decide.

In an active attack, the enemy may try to manipulate the equations in order to get the oracle to solve his problem. For example, if m' satisfies that $m - xr = m' - xr^{\rho^{-1}}$ for some ρ, then $(r^{\rho^{-1}}, E\rho^2) \in \text{VALID}(m', K_P)$ iff $(r, E) \in \text{VALID}(m, K_P)$. Recall, however, that m is actually a hash value, so that this attack is useless, unless the hash function can be inverted on m'.

We therefore conjecture that if discrete log mod p, factorisation of t, and inversion of the hash function are hard problems, then this scheme is signature indistinguishable.

5.2 The Scheme using Diffie-Hellman Encryption

In this scheme, the enemy must decide, given $m, r, (E_1, E_2)$ whether the s determined by the equation $m - xr = bs \bmod t$ (where b is the discrete log of r base g), is also the value encrypted by the pair (E_1, E_2). Even if the enemy knows b, and hence s, he is left with the problem of deciding whether $\log_\alpha \beta = \log_{E_1}(E_2 s^{-1})$. Hence, in a passive attack, the enemy's problem is at least as hard as deciding equality of discrete logs (assumption EDL).

In an active attack, the enemy may try as above to exploit the multiplicative properties of the encryption. Indeed, manipulations similar to the example above are possible. Once again, however, this seems useless, unless the hash function can be inverted. We therefore conjecture that if assumption EDL holds, and the hash function used is one-way, this scheme is signature indistinguishable. We remark that exactly the same assumptions were used for the scheme from [CvA90], the oldest surviving undeniable signature scheme.

References

[BCDP91] J. Boyar, D. Chaum, I. Damgård, and T. Pedersen. Convertible Undeniable Signatures. In *Advances in Cryptology - proceedings of CRYPTO 90*, Lecture Notes in Computer Science, pages 189 – 205. Springer-Verlag, 1991.

[CEG87] D. Chaum, J.-H. Evertse, and J. van de Graaf. An Improved Protocol for Demonstrating Possession of a Discrete Logarithm and some Generalizations. In *Advances in Cryptology - proceedings of EUROCRYPT 87*, Lecture Notes in Computer Science, pages 127–141, 1987.

[Cha91] D. Chaum. Zero-Knowledge Undeniable Signatures. In *Advances in Cryptology - proceedings of EUROCRYPT 90*, Lecture Notes in Computer Science, pages 458 – 464. Springer Verlag, 1991.

[CP93] D. Chaum and T.P. Pedersen. Wallet Databases with Observers. In *Advances in Cryptology - proceedings of CRYPTO 92*, Lecture Notes in Computer Science, pages 89–105. Springer-Verlag, 1993.

[CvA90] D. Chaum and H. van Antwerpen. Undeniable Signatures. In *Advances in Cryptology - proceedings of CRYPTO 89*, Lecture Notes in Computer Science, pages 212–216. Springer Verlag, 1990.

[DH76] W. Diffie and M. E. Hellman. New Directions in Cryptography. *IEEE Trans. Inform. Theory*, IT–22(6):644–654, November 1976.

[DY91] Y. Desmedt and M. Yung. Weaknesses of Undeniable Signature Schemes. In *Advances in Cryptology - proceedings of EUROCRYPT 91*, volume 547 of *Lecture Notes in Computer Science*, pages 205–220. Springer-Verlag, 1991.

[EG85] T. El Gamal. A Public Key Cryptosystem and a Signature Scheme Based on Discrete Logarithms. In *Advances in Cryptology - proceedings of CRYPTO 84*, Lecture Notes in Computer Science, pages 10 –18. Springer-Verlag, 1985.

[FOO91] A. Fujioka, T. Okamoto and K. Ohta. Interactive Bi-Proof Systems and Undeniable Signature Schemes. In *Advances in Cryptology - proceedings of EUROCRYPT 91*, volume 547 of *Lecture Notes in Computer Science*, pages 243–256. Springer-Verlag, 1991.

[GGM84] O. Goldreich, S. Goldwasser, and S. Micali. How to Construct Random Functions. In *Proceedings of the 25th IEEE Symposium on the Foundations of Computer Science*, 1984.

[GMR88] S. Goldwasser, S. Micali, and R. L. Rivest. A Digital Signature Scheme Secure against Adaptive Chosen Message Attack. *SIAM Journal on Computing*, 17(2):281 – 308, April 1988.

[GMR89] S. Goldwasser, S. Micali, and C. Rackoff. The Knowledge Complexity of Interactive Proof-Systems. *SIAM Journal of Computation*, 18(1):186–208, 1989.

[JKR96] M. Jakobsson, K. Sako and R. Impagliazzo: Designated Verifier Proofs and Their Applications, 1996. These proceedings.

[Mic90] S. Micali, August 1990. Personal communication.

[Mic95] M. Michels. Breaking and Repairing a Convertible Undeniable Signature Scheme. Technical Report TR-95-10-D, University of Technology, Chemnitz-Zwickau, June 1995. To appear at ACM Security, March 1996.

[Rab79] M. O. Rabin. Digitalized Signatures and Public-Key Functions as Intractable as factorization. Technical Report MIT/LCS/TR-212, Laboratory for Computer Science, MIT, January 1979.

[Sch91] C. P. Schnorr. Efficient Signature Generation by Smart Cards. *Journal of Cryptology*, 4(3):161–174, 1991.

[Wag79] S. S. Wagstaff Jr. Greatest of the Least Primes in Arithmetic Progression Having a Given Modulus. *Mathematics of Computation*, 33(147):1073 – 1080, July 1979.

Security Proofs for Signature Schemes

David Pointcheval
David.Pointcheval@ens.fr

Jacques Stern
Jacques.Stern@ens.fr

École Normale Supérieure
Laboratoire d'informatique
45, rue d'Ulm
75230 Paris Cedex 05

Abstract. In this paper, we address the question of providing security proofs for signature schemes in the so-called random oracle model [1]. In particular, we establish the generality of this technique against adaptively chosen message attacks. Our main application achieves such a security proof for a slight variant of the El Gamal signature scheme [4] where committed values are hashed together with the message. This is a rather surprising result since the original El Gamal is, as RSA [11], subject to existential forgery.

1 Introduction

Since the appearance of the public key cryptography, in the famous Diffie-Hellman paper [2], a significant line of research has tried to provide "provable" security for cryptographic protocols. In the area of computational security, proofs have been given in the asymptotic framework of complexity theory. Still, these are not absolute proofs since cryptography ultimately relies on the existence of one-way functions and the $\mathcal{P}$ vs. $\mathcal{NP}$ question. Rather, they are computational reductions to and from well established problems from number theory such as factoring, the discrete logarithm problem or the root extraction problem, on which RSA relies [11].

In the present paper we will exclusively focus on signatures. As shown in the Diffie-Hellman paper [2], the trapdoor function paradigm allows to create signatures in the public key setting. Nevertheless, both the RSA scheme and the El Gamal scheme are not provably secure since they are subject to existential forgery. In other words, it is easy to create a new valid message-signature pair. In many cases, this is not really dangerous because the message is not intelligible or does not have the proper redundancy. Still an RSA signature does not prove by itself the identity of the sender.

The first signature scheme proven secure against a very general attack, the so-called adaptively chosen-message attack which will be defined later in this paper, has been proposed by Goldwasser-Micali-Rivest [6] in 1984. It uses the notion of claw-free permutations. We refer to [6] for details.

In 1986, a new paradigm for signature schemes was introduced. It is derived from zero-knowledge identification protocols involving a prover and a verifier [5],

Ueli Maurer (Ed.): EUROCRYPT '96 Proceedings, LNCS 1070

and uses hash functions in order to create a kind of virtual verifier. In [3], Fiat and Shamir proposed a zero-knowledge identification protocol based on the hardness of extracting square roots. They also described the corresponding signature scheme and outlined its security. Similar results for other signature schemes like Schnorr's [12] are considered as folklore results but have never appeared in the literature.

In this paper, we review the basic method for proving security of signature schemes in the random oracle model [1] and surprisingly, we prove the security of a very close variant of the El Gamal signature scheme.

2 Framework

2.1 Generic Signature Schemes

In a signature scheme, each user publishes a public key while keeping for himself a secret key. A user's signature on a message m is a value which depends on m and on the user's public and secret keys in such a way that anyone can check validity just by using the public key. However, it is hard to forge a user's signature without knowing his secret key. In this section, we will give a more precise definition of a signature scheme and of the possible attacks against such schemes. These definitions are based on [6].

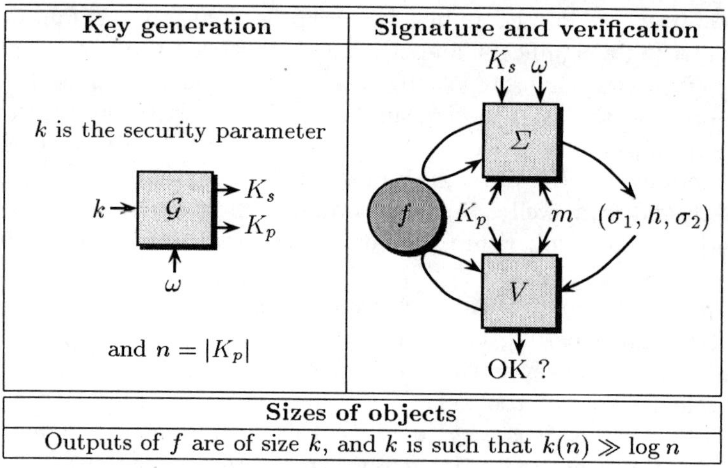

Fig. 1. Signature schemes

Definition 1. A signature scheme is defined by the following (see figure 1):

- the *key generation algorithm* $\mathcal{G}$ which, on input 1^k, where k is the security parameter, produces a pair (K_p, K_s) of matching public and secret keys. It is clear that $\mathcal{G}$ must be a probabilistic algorithm.

- the *signing algorithm* Σ which, given a message m and a pair of matching public and secret keys (K_p, K_s), produces a signature. The signing algorithm might be probabilistic, and in some schemes it might receive other inputs as well.
- the *verification algorithm* V which, given a signature σ, a message m and a public key K_p, tests whether σ is a valid signature of m with respect to K_p. In general, the verification algorithm need not be probabilistic.

Signature schemes often use a hash function f. In this paper, we will only consider signature schemes which, on the input message m, produce triplets (σ_1, h, σ_2) independent of previous signature. In those triplets (σ_1, h, σ_2), h is the hash value of (m, σ_1) and σ_2 just depends on σ_1, the message m, and h. This covers the case of Fiat-Shamir [3], Schnorr [12] and many others. In some cases, σ_1 or h can be omitted, but we will keep them for more generality.

2.2 Attacks

We will only consider two different scenarios involving probabilistic polynomial time Turing machines, the no-message attack and the adaptively chosen message attack (see figure 2).

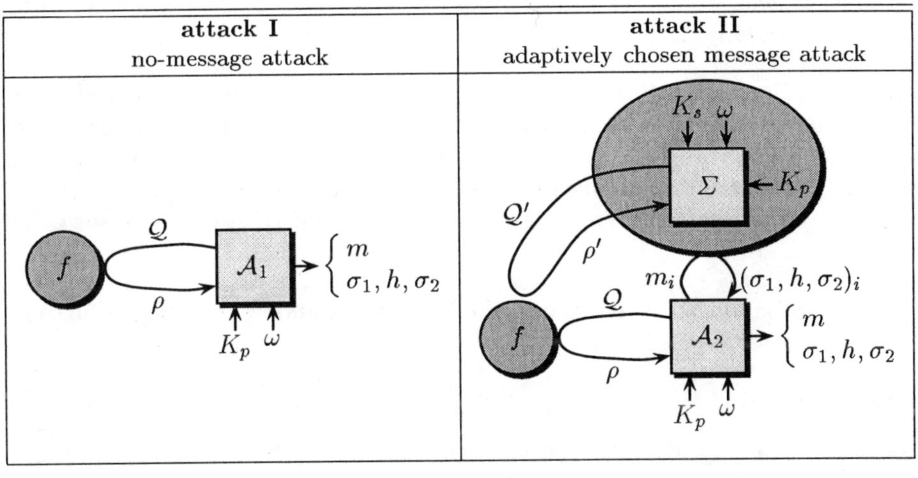

Fig. 2. Attacks

In the former, the attacker only knows the signer's public key. In the latter, he can dynamically ask the legitimate user to sign any message, using him as a kind of oracle. For the resistance against adaptively chosen message attacks, which is a stronger requirement, we will use the possible simulation of the legitimate signer, which relies on the honest verifier zero-knowledge property of the identification scheme.

2.3 The Random Oracle Model

As we already pointed out, signature schemes often use a hash function f (e.g. MD5 [10] or SHS [8]). This use of hash functions may have been motivated by the wish to sign long messages with a single signature. Accordingly, the requirement of the function was collision freeness. It was later realized that hash functions were an essential ingredient for the security of the signature schemes. Still, in order to actually provide such a security proof, stronger assumptions seem to be needed and several authors (e.g. [3] and [1]) have suggested to use to hypothesis that f is actually a random function. We follow this suggestion by using the corresponding model, called the "random oracle model". In this model, the hash function can be seen as an oracle which produces a random value for each new query. Of course, if the same query is asked twice, identical answers are obtained. Proofs in this model ensure security of the overall design of a signature scheme provided the hash function has no weakness.

3 The Oracle Replay Attack

In this section, we will prove a key lemma, which we call the forking lemma and which will be repeatedly used in the sequel. This lemma uses the "oracle replay attack": by a polynomial replay of the attack with the same random tape and a different oracle, we obtain two signatures of a specific form which open a way to solve the underlying hard problem.

Lemma 2 (the forking lemma). *Let $\mathcal{A}$ be a Probabilistic Polynomial Time Turing machine, given only the public data as input. If $\mathcal{A}$ can find, with non-negligible probability, a valid signature $(m, \sigma_1, h, \sigma_2)$, then, with non-negligible probability, a replay of this machine, with the same random tape and a different oracle, outputs two valid signatures $(m, \sigma_1, h, \sigma_2)$ and $(m, \sigma_1, h', \sigma_2')$ such that $h \neq h'$.*

Remark. Probabilities are taken over random tapes, random oracles, and in some cases, over messages and keys.

Before we prove this result, we state a well-known probabilistic lemma:

Lemma 3. *Let $A \subset X \times Y$, such that $\Pr[A(x, y)] \geq \epsilon$, then there exists $\Omega \subset X$ such that*
i) $\Pr[x \in \Omega] \geq \epsilon/2$
ii) whenever $a \in \Omega$, $\Pr[A(a, y)] \geq \epsilon/2$

With this lemma, we can split X in two subsets, a subset Ω consisting of "good" x's which provide a non-negligible probability of success over y, and its complement. We now return to the forking lemma.

Proof. We assume that we have a no-message attacker $\mathcal{A}$, which is a probabilistic polynomial time Turing machine with a random tape ω. During the attack, this machine asks a polynomial number of questions to the random oracle f. We may assume that these questions are distinct, for instance, $\mathcal{A}$ can store questions and answers in a table. Let $\mathcal{Q}_1, \ldots, \mathcal{Q}_Q$ be the Q distinct questions, where Q is a polynomial, and let $\rho_1, \ldots, \rho_Q$ be the Q answers of f. It is clear that a random choice of f exactly corresponds to a random choice of $\rho_1, \ldots, \rho_Q$. For a random choice of $\omega, \rho_1, \ldots, \rho_Q$, with non-negligible probability, $\mathcal{A}$ outputs a valid signature $(m, \sigma_1, h, \sigma_2)$. It is easy to see that the probability for the precise query (m, σ_1) not to be asked is negligible, because of the randomness of $f(m, \sigma_1)$. So, the probability that the query (m, σ_1) is one of the $\mathcal{Q}_i$'s, e.g. $\mathcal{Q}_\beta$, is non-negligible. Since β is between 1 and $Q(n)$, there exist a β and a polynomial P such that the probability of success, over $\omega, \rho_1, \ldots, \rho_Q$, with $\mathcal{Q}_\beta = (m, \sigma_1)$ is greater than $1/P(n)$ (see figure 3).

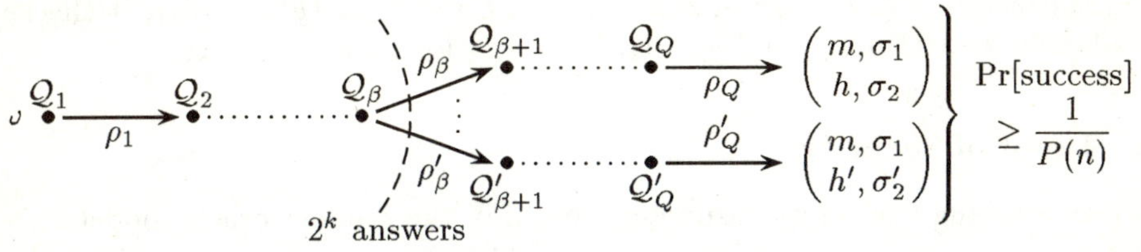

Fig. 3. The forking lemma

With such a β, using lemma 3, we get the existence of a non-negligible subset Ω_β of "good" ω's. For such a "good" ω, the probability of success, over $\rho_1, \ldots, \rho_Q$, with $\mathcal{Q}_\beta = (m, \sigma_1)$, is greater than $1/2P(n)$. With such β and ω, using lemma 3 again, we obtain the existence of a non-negligible subset $R_{\beta,\omega}$ of "good" $(\rho_1, \ldots, \rho_{\beta-1})$'s. For such a "good" $(\rho_1, \ldots, \rho_{\beta-1})$, the probability of success of the attacker, over $\rho_\beta, \ldots, \rho_Q$, with $\mathcal{Q}_\beta = (m, \sigma_1)$, is greater than $1/4P(n)$. Then, with such β, ω and $(\rho_1, \ldots, \rho_{\beta-1})$, if we randomly chose $\rho_\beta, \ldots, \rho_Q$ and $\rho'_\beta, \ldots, \rho'_Q$, with a non-negligible probability, we obtain two valid signatures $(m, \sigma_1, h, \sigma_2)$ and $(m, \sigma_1, h', \sigma'_2)$ such that $h \neq h'$; this uses the fact that $k(n) \gg \log n$.

Finally, with a random choice of $\beta, \omega, \rho_1, \ldots, \rho_{\beta-1}, \rho_\beta, \ldots, \rho_Q$ and $\rho'_\beta, \ldots, \rho'_Q$, we obtain, with a non-negligible probability, two valid signatures $(m, \sigma_1, h, \sigma_2)$ and $(m, \sigma_1, h', \sigma'_2)$ such that $h \neq h'$.

4 The Fiat-Shamir Signature Scheme

We will now apply the lemma to the Fiat-Shamir signature scheme in order to prove its security against no-message attacks. This result is outlined in [3] and we include it for the reader's convenience.

4.1 Description

Firstly, we describe the single key Fiat-Shamir signature scheme [3]:

- the key generation algorithm: for a security parameter k, it chooses two large primes p and q which are kept secret and computes their product N and defines a random hash function f with a k-bit output. Then, it chooses a random $s \in \mathbb{Z}/N\mathbb{Z}$ and publishes its square $v = s^2 \bmod N$. N and f are public and s is the secret key.
- the signature algorithm: in order to sign a message m, one generates k random numbers, $r_i \in \mathbb{Z}/N\mathbb{Z}$ for $i = 1, \ldots, k$, computes their respective squares $x_i = r_i^2 \bmod N$ as well as the challenge $h = (e_1 \ldots e_k) = f(m, x_1, \ldots, x_k)$. From these data, one sets $y_i = r_i s^{e_i} \bmod N$ and outputs $\sigma_1 = (x_1, \ldots, x_k)$ and $\sigma_2 = (y_1, \ldots, y_k)$. The signature is (σ_1, h, σ_2).
- the verification algorithm is as follows: for a given message m and a given signature $\sigma_1 = (x_1, \ldots, x_k)$, $h = (e_1 \ldots e_k)$ and $\sigma_2 = (y_1, \ldots, y_k)$, it checks whether $h = f(m, \sigma_1)$ and $y_i = r_i s^{e_i} \bmod N$ for all i.

4.2 Proof of Security

From the forking lemma we easily get a proof in the random oracle model.

Theorem 4. *Consider a no-message attack in the random oracle model. If an existential forgery of the Fiat-Shamir signature scheme is possible with non-negligible probability, then factorization of RSA moduli can be performed in polynomial time.*

Proof. Let $N \in \mathbb{N}$ be the integer to factor. Let us choose $s \in_R \mathbb{Z}/N\mathbb{Z}$, and let $v = s^2 \bmod N$. If an attacker $\mathcal{A}_1$ can break the Fiat-Shamir signature scheme, then by using the forking lemma, he can obtain two valid signatures $(m, \sigma_1, h, \sigma_2)$ and $(m, \sigma_1, h', \sigma_2')$, such that $h \neq h'$. From this, we get i such that $h_i \neq h_i'$, say $h_i = 0$ and $h_i' = 1$. We get $y_i^2 = x_i \bmod N$ and $y_i'^2 = x_i v \bmod N$. If we let $z = y_i' y_i^{-1} \bmod N$, then $z^2 = v = s^2 \bmod N$.

Since the algorithm cannot distinguish s from other roots, we conclude that, with a probability 1/2, $\gcd(z - s, N)$ provides a factor of N.

Remark. Because of the easy simulation of the communication with an honest verifier, even in the context of the parallel version of Fiat-Shamir, the proof of security against adaptively chosen message attacks is straightforward.

5 The Modified El Gamal Signature Scheme

The original El Gamal signature scheme [4] was proposed in 1985 but its security was never proved equivalent to the discrete logarithm problem nor to the Diffie-Hellman problem. Using the forking lemma, we will prove the security of a slight variant of this scheme.

5.1 Description of the Original Scheme

Let us begin with a description of the original scheme [4]:

- the key generation algorithm: it chooses a random large prime p of size n and a generator g of $(\mathbb{Z}/p\mathbb{Z})^\star$, both public. Then, for a random secret key $x \in \mathbb{Z}/(p-1)\mathbb{Z}$, it computes the public key $y = g^x \bmod p$.
- the signature algorithm: in order to sign a signature of a message m, one generates a pair (r, s) such that $g^m = y^r r^s \bmod p$. To achieve this aim, one has to choose a random $K \in (\mathbb{Z}/(p-1)\mathbb{Z})^\star$, compute the exponentiation $r = g^K \bmod p$ and solve the linear equation $m = xr + Ks \bmod (p-1)$. The algorithm finally outputs (r, s).
- the verification algorithm checks the equation $g^m = y^r r^s \bmod p$.

5.2 Security

As already seen in the original paper, one cannot show that the scheme is fully secure because it is subject to existential forgery.

Theorem 5. *The original El Gamal signature scheme is existentially forgeable.*

Proof. This is a well-known result, but we describe two level of forgeries:

1. the one parameter forgery: let $e \in_R \mathbb{Z}/(p-1)\mathbb{Z}$, if we let $r = g^e y \bmod p$ and $s = -r \bmod p-1$, it is easy to see that (r, s) is a valid signature for the message $m = es \bmod p-1$.
2. the two parameter forgery: let $e \in_R \mathbb{Z}/(p-1)\mathbb{Z}$ and $v \in_R (\mathbb{Z}/(p-1)\mathbb{Z})^\star$, if we let $r = g^e y^v \bmod p$ and $s = -rv^{-1} \bmod p-1$, then (r, s) is a valid signature for the message $m = es \bmod p-1$.

We now modify this scheme by using a hash function.

5.3 Description of the modified El Gamal scheme

In this variant, we replace m by the hash value of the entire part of the computation bound not to change, namely $f(m, r)$.

- the key generation algorithm: unchanged.
- the signature algorithm: in order to sign a message m, one generates a pair (r, s) such that $g^{f(m,r)} = y^r r^s \bmod p$. In order to achieve this aim, one generates K and r the same way as before and solves the linear equation $f(m, r) = xr + Ks \bmod (p-1)$. The algorithm outputs $(r, f(m, r), s)$.
- the verification algorithm checks the signature equation with the obvious changes due to the hash function.

5.4 Proofs of security

In this section, we will see that the modification allows to prove the security of the scheme even against an adaptively chosen message attack, at least for a large variety of moduli. We let $|p|$ denote the length of an integer p.

Definition 6. Let α be a fixed real. An α-hard prime number p is such that the factorization of $p-1$ yields $p-1 = QR$ with Q prime and $R \leq |p|^\alpha$.

Remark. Those prime moduli are precisely those used for cryptographic applications of the discrete logarithm problem.

Security against a no-message attack. Firstly, we study the resistance of the modified El Gamal Signature scheme against no-message attacks.

Theorem 7. *Consider a no-message attack in the random oracle model against schemes using α-hard prime moduli. Probabilities are taken over random tapes, random oracles and public keys. If an existential forgery of this scheme has non-negligible probability of success, then the discrete logarithm problem with α-hard prime moduli can be solved in polynomial time.*

Proof. Using the forking lemma, we get two valid signatures (m, r, h, s) and (m, r, h', s') such that $g^h = r^s y^r \bmod p$ and $g^{h'} = r^{s'} y^r \bmod p$. Hence, we get $g^{hs'-h's} = y^{r(s'-s)} \bmod p$ and $g^{h'-h} = r^{s-s'} \bmod p$. Since g is a generator of $(\mathbb{Z}/p\mathbb{Z})^\star$, there exist t and x such that $g^t = r \bmod p$ and $g^x = y \bmod p$. Therefore,

$$hs' - h's = xr(s' - s) \bmod p - 1 \quad (1)$$
$$h' - h = t(s - s') \bmod p - 1 \quad (2)$$

Since h and h' come from "oracle replay", we may further assume $h - h'$ is prime to Q, so that $\gcd(s - s', Q) = 1$. Nevertheless, we cannot make any further assumption for r, and accordingly, two cases appear:

case 1: r is prime to Q. In this case, equation (1) provides the Q modular part of x, $x = (hs' - h's)(r(s - s'))^{-1} \bmod Q$. With an exhaustive search over the R modular part of x, we can find an x which satisfies $y = g^x \bmod p$.

case 2 otherwise, $r = bQ$ with b small. In this case, equation (2) provides the Q modular part of t, $t = (h - h')(s - s')^{-1} \bmod Q$. With an exhaustive search over the R modular part of t, we can find a t which satisfies $bQ = g^t \bmod p$. We note that t is prime to Q.

At this point, we have a probabilistic polynomial time Turing machine $\mathcal{M}$ which, on input (g, y), outputs, with non-negligible probability, $x \in \mathbb{Z}/(p-1)\mathbb{Z}$ such that $y = g^x \bmod p$ (case 1) or $b \in \mathbb{Z}/R\mathbb{Z}$ and $t \in \mathbb{Z}/(p-1)\mathbb{Z}$ such that $bQ = g^t \bmod p$ (case 2). Probabilities are taken over g, y, and the random tapes of $\mathcal{M}$. Using lemma 3, let $\mathcal{G}$ be a non-negligible set of g's such that whenever $g \in \mathcal{G}$, the set of y's which provides the above witnesses is non-negligible. To make things precise, we consider both probabilities to be greater than ε, where ε is the inverse of some polynomial. Let G_{good} be the set of $g \in \mathcal{G}$ which lead to the first case with probability greater than $\varepsilon/2$. Let G_{bad} be the set of $g \in \mathcal{G}$ which lead to the second case with probability greater than $\varepsilon/2$. We know that $\mathcal{G}$ is the union $G_{good} \cup G_{bad}$.

If G_{good} has probability greater than $\varepsilon/2$, then we have a probabilistic polynomial time Turing machine which can compute, for a non-negligible part of (g, y), the discrete logarithm of y relatively to g.

Otherwise, bad g's are in proportion greater than $\varepsilon/2$. Since the set of possible b's is polynomial, we get a fixed b and a non-negligible subset $G_{bad}(b)$ of bad g's such that, with non-negligible probability, $\mathcal{M}(g, y)$ outputs integers b and t such that $bQ = g^t \bmod p$. Let $g \in G_{bad}(b)$ and y be any number. Running $\mathcal{M}(g, z)$, for random z, we get, with non-negligible probability, some t such that $g^t = bQ \bmod p$. Running $\mathcal{M}(yg^\ell, z')$, for random ℓ and z', we get, with non-negligible probability, $yg^\ell \in G_{bad}(b)$ and some t' such that $(yg^\ell)^{t'} = bQ = g^t \bmod p$. Hence, $xt' = t - \ell t' \bmod (p-1)$. Since t' is prime to Q, we get $x \bmod Q$. After polynomially many trials over the R modular part of x, we find the logarithm of y. Then we have another probabilistic polynomial time Turing machine $\mathcal{M}'$ which can compute for a non-negligible part of (g, y), the discrete logarithm of y relatively to g.

Now, let fix g and y. Running the machine on (g^u, yg^v) with random u and v, we obtain, with non-negligible probability, an x such that $yg^v = g^{ux} \bmod p$, hence we get $y = g^{ux-v} \bmod p$. This finally contradicts the intractability assumption.

Security against an adaptively chosen message attack. We now prove a more surprising theorem about the security against adaptively chosen message attacks. In the adaptively chosen message scenario, the attacker uses the signer as a kind of oracle. If it is possible to simulate the signer Σ by a simulator $\mathcal{S}$ who does not know the secret key (see figure 4), then we can make the attacker and the simulator collude in order to break the signature scheme, and, the same way as before, we can solve the discrete logarithm.

Lemma 8. For α-hard prime numbers, the signer can be simulated with an indistinguishable distribution.

Proof. A key ingredient of the proof is as follows: values returned by the random oracle can be freely computed and have no correlation with messages whose signature is requested.

In this proof, we identify the output set H of random oracles with the set $\{0, \ldots, 2^k - 1\}$ and we assume that $2^k \geq Q$.

Using the two parameter forgery for the Q modular part, and an exhaustive search for the other part, we can obtain an indistinguishable simulation: we first randomly choose $u \in \mathbb{Z}/Q\mathbb{Z}$, $t \in (\mathbb{Z}/Q\mathbb{Z})^\star$ and $\ell \in (\mathbb{Z}/R\mathbb{Z})^\star$. Then, we let $e = uR \bmod (p-1)$, $v = tR \bmod (p-1)$ and $r = (g^e y^v) g^{Q\ell} \bmod p$. We start the simulation again in the (unlikely) situation where r is not a generator of

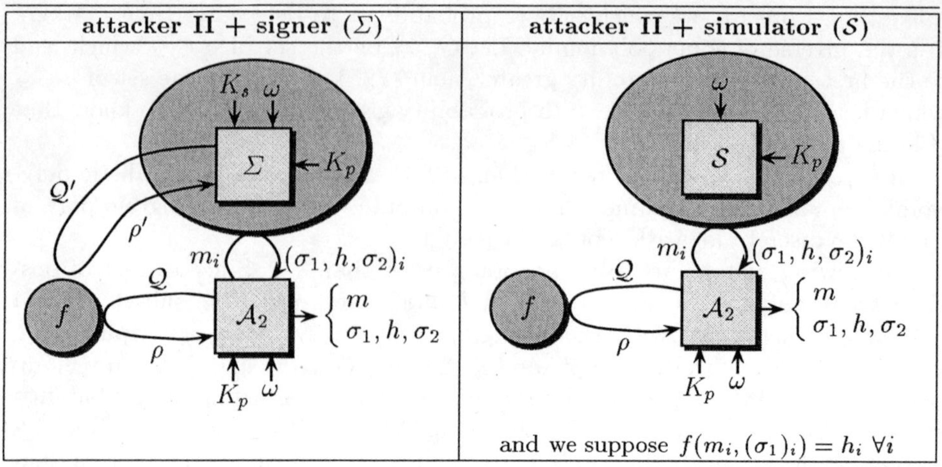

Fig. 4. Adaptively chosen message scenario

$(\mathbb{Z}/p\mathbb{Z})^\star$. This corresponds to separately dealing with the forgery in the two subgroups respectively generated by g^R and g^Q. Mimicking the two parameter forgery in the subgroup generated by g^R, we need to set $s = -rv^{-1} \bmod Q$ and $h = -erv^{-1} \bmod Q$. For the R modular part, we randomly choose $h \bmod R$ until $h \in H$, and we exhaustively search for an s which satisfies $g^h = y^r r^s \bmod p$: taking logarithms, this reads as $h = rx + Q\ell s \bmod R$, so that the number of trials is only polynomial. We can easily check that the triplet (r, h, s) is a valid signature of a message m as soon as $h = f(m, r)$.

Let $(r, h, s) \in (\mathbb{Z}/p\mathbb{Z})^\star \times H \times \mathbb{Z}/(p-1)\mathbb{Z}$ such that $g^h = r^s y^r \bmod p$ and r is a generator of $(\mathbb{Z}/p\mathbb{Z})^\star$. Trying to output this signature through our simulation yields the system of equations

$$\begin{cases} hv + re = 0 & \bmod Q \\ xv + e = \log_g r & \bmod Q \end{cases}$$

If $h \neq xr \bmod Q$, then there is exactly one solution and therefore one way for $\mathcal{S}$ to generate such a signature. If $h = xr \bmod Q$, then $\mathcal{S}$ can generate such a signature only if $r = h = s = 0 \bmod Q$, and $Q-1$ different ways.

Both types of exceptions contribute to the overall distance by some term bounded by $\frac{2R}{(Q-1)\varphi(R)}$ which is less than $4\alpha n^{\alpha+1} \times 2^{-n}$, a negligible value, where $n = |p|$

Theorem 9. *Consider an adaptively chosen message attack in the random oracle model against schemes using α-hard prime moduli. Probabilities are taken over random tapes, random oracles and public keys. If an existential forgery of this scheme has non-negligible probability of success, then the discrete logarithm problem with α-hard prime moduli can be solved in polynomial time.*

Proof. For each simulated signature of m_i, (r_i, h_i, s_i), $\mathcal{S}$ is assumed to have asked $f(m_i, r_i)$ and obtained h_i, a new random value. We observe that collisions of queries happen with negligible probability, therefore, the attacker cannot distinguish the simulator from the legitimate signer. And then, like in theorem 7, a collusion of the attacker and the simulator enables to compute discrete logarithms.

6 Further Results

In this section, we mention several additional results: the first is the extension of theorem 4 to the adaptively chosen message attack. Furthermore, because of the possible simulation of the Schnorr scheme, we can prove the following theorem in the random oracle model:

Theorem 10. *If an existential forgery of the Schnorr signature scheme, under an adaptively chosen message attack, has non-negligible probability of success, then the discrete logarithm in subgroups can be solved in polynomial time.*

The same results are true for every signature scheme which comes from the transformation of a honest verifier zero-knowledge identification protocol (Guillou-Quisquater [7], the Permuted Kernel Problem [13], the Syndrome Decoding problem [14], the Constrained Linear Equations [15], the Permuted Perceptrons Problem [9], etc.). For each of them, existential forgery under an adaptively chosen-message attack in the random oracle model is equivalent to the problem on which the identification scheme relies .

References

1. M. Bellare and P. Rogaway. Random Oracles are Practical: a paradigm for designing efficient protocols. In *Proceedings of the 1st ACM Conference on Computer and Communications Security*, pages 62–73, 1993.
2. W. Diffie and M.E. Hellman. New Directions in Cryptography. In *IEEE Transactions on Information Theory*, volume IT–22, no. 6, pages 644–654, november 1976.
3. A. Fiat and A. Shamir. How to Prove Yourself: practical solutions of identification and signature problems. In A. M. Odlyzko, editor, *Advances in Cryptology – Proceedings of CRYPTO '86*, volume 263 of *Lecture Notes in Computer Science*, pages 186–194. Springer-Verlag, 1987.
4. T. El Gamal. A Public Key Cryptosystem and a Signature Scheme Based on Discrete Logarithms. In *IEEE Transactions on Information Theory*, volume IT–31, no. 4, pages 469–472, july 1985.
5. S. Goldwasser, S. Micali, and C. Rackoff. Knowledge Complexity of Interactive Proof Systems. In *Proceedings of the 17th ACM Symposium on the Theory of Computing STOC*, pages 291–304. ACM, 1985.
6. S. Goldwasser, S. Micali, and R. Rivest. A Digital Signature Scheme Secure Against Adaptative Chosen-Message Attacks. *SIAM journal of computing*, 17(2):281–308, april 1988.

7. L.C. Guillou and J.-J. Quisquater. A Practical Zero-Knowledge Protocol Fitted to Security Microprocessor Minimizing Both Transmission and Memory. In C. G. Günter, editor, *Advances in Cryptology – Proceedings of EUROCRYPT '88*, volume 330 of *Lecture Notes in Computer Science*, pages 123–128. Springer-Verlag, 1988.
8. NIST. Secure Hash Standard (SHS). Federal Information Processing Standards PUBlication 180–1, April 1995.
9. D. Pointcheval. A New Identification Scheme Based on The Perceptrons Problem. In L.C. Guillou and J.-J. Quisquater, editors, *Advances in Cryptology – Proceedings of EUROCRYPT '95*, volume 921 of *Lecture Notes in Computer Science*, pages 319–328. Springer-Verlag, 1995.
10. R. Rivest. The MD5 Message-Digest Algorithm. RFC 1321, April 1992.
11. R. Rivest, A. Shamir, and L. Adleman. A Method for Obtaining Digital Signatures and Public Key Cryptosystems. *Communications of the ACM*, 21(2):120–126, february 1978.
12. C.P. Schnorr. Efficient Identification and Signatures for Smart Cards. In G. Brassard, editor, *Advances in Cryptology – Proceedings of CRYPTO '89*, volume 435 of *Lecture Notes in Computer Science*, pages 235–251. Springer-Verlag, 1990.
13. A. Shamir. An Efficient Identification Scheme Based on Permuted Kernels. In G. Brassard, editor, *Advances in Cryptology – Proceedings of CRYPTO '89*, volume 435 of *Lecture Notes in Computer Science*, pages 606–609. Springer-Verlag, 1990.
14. J. Stern. A New Identification Scheme Based on Syndrome Decoding. In D. R. Stinson, editor, *Advances in Cryptology – proceedings of CRYPTO '93*, volume 773 of *Lecture Notes in Computer Science*, pages 13–21. Springer-Verlag, 1994.
15. J. Stern. Designing Identification Schemes with Keys of Short Size. In Y. G. Desmedt, editor, *Advances in Cryptology – proceedings of CRYPTO '94*, volume 839 of *Lecture Notes in Computer Science*, pages 164–173. Springer-Verlag, 1994.

The Exact Security of Digital Signatures–How to Sign with RSA and Rabin

Mihir Bellare[1] and Phillip Rogaway[2]

[1] Department of Computer Science and Engineering, Mail Code 0114, University of California at San Diego, 9500 Gilman Drive, La Jolla, CA 92093, USA. E-mail: mihir@cs.ucsd.edu ; Web page: http://www-cse.ucsd.edu/users/mihir

[2] Department of Computer Science, University of California at Davis, Davis, CA 95616, USA. E-mail: rogaway@cs.ucdavis.edu

Abstract. We describe an RSA-based signing scheme which combines essentially optimal efficiency with attractive security properties. Signing takes one RSA decryption plus some hashing, verification takes one RSA encryption plus some hashing, and the size of the signature is the size of the modulus. Assuming the underlying hash functions are ideal, our schemes are not only provably secure, but are so in a *tight* way—an ability to forge signatures with a certain amount of computational resources implies the ability to invert RSA (on the same size modulus) with about the same computational effort. Furthermore, we provide a second scheme which maintains all of the above features and in addition provides message recovery. These ideas extend to provide schemes for Rabin signatures with analogous properties; in particular their security can be tightly related to the hardness of factoring.

1 Introduction

A widely employed paradigm for signing with RSA is to first "hash" the message into a domain point of RSA and then decrypt (ie. exponentiate with the RSA decryption exponent). In particular, this is the basis of several existing standards. Unfortunately, the security of the standardized schemes cannot be justified under standard assumptions about RSA, even assuming the underlying hash functions are ideal.

We propose new schemes, both for signing and for signing with message recovery. They are as simple and efficient as the standardized ones. (In particular, signing takes one RSA decryption plus some hashing, verification takes one RSA encryption plus some hashing, and the size of the signature is the size of the modulus.) But, assuming the underlying hash function is ideal, our methods are not only provably secure, but provably secure in a strong sense: the security of our schemes can be *tightly* related to the security of the RSA function.

Besides providing concrete new schemes for signing with RSA, this work highlights the importance, for practical applications of provable security, of consideration of the tightness of the security reduction, and also provides a rare example of modifying one provably-good scheme in order to obtain another which has a better security bound.

Ueli Maurer (Ed.): EUROCRYPT '96 Proceedings, LNCS 1070

Let us now expand on all of the above. We begin by looking at current practice. Then we consider the full domain hash scheme of [3] which is provable, and discuss its exact security. Finally we come to our new schemes, PSS and PSS-R, and their exact security.

1.1 Signing with RSA– Current practice

THE RSA SYSTEM. In the RSA public key system [15] a party has public key (N, e) and secret key (N, d), where N is a k-bit modulus, the product of two $(k/2)$-bit primes, and $e, d \in \mathsf{Z}^*_{\phi(N)}$ satisfy $ed \equiv 1 \bmod \varphi(N)$. (Think of $k = 1024$, a recommended modulus size these days.) Recall that the RSA function $f\colon \mathsf{Z}^*_N \to \mathsf{Z}^*_N$ is defined by $f(x) = x^e \bmod N$ and its inverse $f^{-1}\colon \mathsf{Z}^*_N \to \mathsf{Z}^*_N$ is defined by $f^{-1}(y) = y^d \bmod N$ $(x, y \in \mathsf{Z}^*_N)$. The generally-made assumption is that f is trapdoor one-way— roughly, if you don't know d (or the prime factors of N) then it is hard to compute $x = f^{-1}(y)$ for a y drawn randomly from Z^*_N.

HASH-THEN-DECRYPT SCHEMES. A widely employed paradigm to sign a document M is to first compute some "hash" $y = \mathit{Hash}(M)$ and then set the signature to $x = f^{-1}(y) = y^d \bmod N$. (To verify that x is a signature of M, compute $f(x) = x^e \bmod N$ and check this equals $\mathit{Hash}(M)$.) In particular, this is the basis for several existing standards. A necessary requirement on *Hash* in such a scheme is that it be collision-intractable and produce a k-bit output in Z^*_N. Accordingly, *Hash* is most often implemented via a cryptographic hash function like $H = \mathsf{MD5}$ (which yields a 128 bit output and is assumed to be collision-intractable) and some padding. A concrete example of such a scheme is [16, 17], where the hash is

$$\mathit{Hash}_{\mathrm{PKCS}}(M) = \mathtt{0x\,00\,01\,FF\,FF}\ \cdots\ \mathtt{FF\,FF\,00} \parallel H(M) .$$

Here $\parallel$ denotes concatenation, and enough 0xFF-bytes are used so as to make the length of $\mathit{Hash}_{\mathrm{PKCS}}(M)$ equal to k bits.

SECURITY. We draw attention to the fact that the security of a hash-then-decrypt signature depends very much on how exactly one implements *Hash*. In particular, it is important to recognize that the security of a signature scheme like $\mathit{Sign}_{\mathrm{PKCS}}(M) = f^{-1}(\mathit{Hash}_{\mathrm{PKCS}}(M))$ can't be justified given (only) that RSA is trapdoor one-way, even under the assumption that hash function H is ideal. (The reason is that the set of points $\{\, \mathit{Hash}_{\mathrm{PKCS}}(M) : M \in \{0,1\}^* \,\}$ has size at most 2^{128} and hence is a very sparse, and a very structured, subset of Z^*_N.) We consider this to be a disadvantage. We stress that we don't know of any *attack* on this scheme. But we prefer, for such important primitives, to have some proof of security rather than just an absence of known attacks.

The same situation holds for other standards, including ISO 9796 [10]. (There the function *Hash* involves no cryptographic hashing, and the message M is easily recovered from $\mathit{Hash}(M)$. This doesn't effect the points we've just made.)

The above discussion highlights that *collision-intractability is not enough.* The function $\mathit{Hash}_{\mathrm{PKCS}}$ is guaranteed to be collision-intractable if we use a collision-intractable H. But this won't suffice to get a proof of security.

1.2 FDH and its exact security

THE FDH SCHEME. In earlier work [3] we suggested to hash M onto the full domain Z_N^* of the RSA function before decrypting. That is, $Hash_{\mathrm{FDH}}$: $\{0,1\}^* \to Z_N^*$ is understood to hash strings "uniformly" into Z_N^*, and the signature of M is $Sign_{\mathrm{FDH}}(M) = f^{-1}(Hash_{\mathrm{FDH}}(M))$. (Candidates for suitable functions $Hash_{\mathrm{FDH}}$ can easily be constructed out of MD5 or similar hash functions, as described in [3].) We call this the Full-Domain-Hash scheme (FDH).

PROVABLE SECURITY OF FDH. Assuming *Hash* is ideal (ie. it behaves like a random function of the specified domain and range) the security of FDH can be proven assuming only that RSA is a trapdoor permutation. (This is a special case of [3, Section 4], which considers this construction with an arbitrary trapdoor permutation.) This makes the security guarantee of the FDH scheme superior to those of the schemes we discussed in Section 1.1.

Now we want to go further. We will explain how, within the class of provable schemes, quality depends on the quantifiable notion of *exact security.* In this paper we compute the exact security of the FDH scheme, and then we offer a new scheme which has better exact security.

EXACT SECURITY. We quantify the security of RSA as a trapdoor permutation. We say it is (t', ϵ')-secure if an attacker, given y drawn randomly from Z_N^* and limited to running in time $t'(k)$, succeeds in finding $f^{-1}(y)$ with probability at most $\epsilon(k)$. Values of t', ϵ' for which it is safe to assume RSA is (t', ϵ')-secure can be provided based on the perceived cryptanalytic strength of RSA.

Next we quantify the security of a signature scheme. A signature scheme is said to be $(t, q_{\mathrm{sig}}, q_{\mathrm{hash}}, \epsilon)$-secure if an attacker, provided the public key, allowed to run for time $t(k)$, allowed a chosen-message attack in which she can see up to $q_{\mathrm{sig}}(k)$ legitimate message-signature pairs, and allowed q_{hash} invocations of the (ideal) hash function, is successful in forging the signature of a new message with probability at most $\epsilon(k)$.

EXACT SECURITY OF FDH. The "exact security" of the reduction of [3] used to prove the security of the FDH signature scheme is analyzed in Theorem 1. It says that if RSA is (t', ϵ')-secure and $q_{\mathrm{sig}}, q_{\mathrm{hash}}$ are given then the FDH signature scheme is $(t, q_{\mathrm{sig}}, q_{\mathrm{hash}}, \epsilon)$-secure for $t = t' - \mathrm{poly}(q_{\mathrm{sig}}, q_{\mathrm{hash}}, k)$ and $\epsilon = (q_{\mathrm{sig}} + q_{\mathrm{hash}}) \cdot \epsilon'$. Here poly is some some small polynomial explicitly specified in Theorem 1.

We note that ϵ could thus be considerably larger than ϵ'. This means that even if RSA is quite strong, the guarantee on the signature scheme could be quite weak. To see this, say we would like to allow the forger to see at least $q_{\mathrm{sig}}(k) = 2^{30}$ example signatures and compute hashes on, say, $q_{\mathrm{hash}} = 2^{60}$ strings. Then even if the RSA inversion probability was originally as low as 2^{-61}, all we can say is that the forging probability is now at most $1/2$, which is not good enough. To compensate, we will have to be able to assume that $\epsilon'(k)$ is very, very low, like 2^{-100}. This means that we must have a fairly large value of k, ie. a larger modulus. But this affects the efficiency of the scheme, because the time to do the underlying modular exponentiation grows (and rather quickly) as the modulus size increases. We prefer to avoid this.

We reiterate the crucial point: if the reduction proving security is "loose," like the one above, the efficiency of the scheme is impacted, because we must move to a larger security parameter. Thus, it would be nice to have "tighter" reductions, meaning ones in which ϵ is almost the same as ϵ', with the relations amongst the other parameters staying about the same as they are now.

One might suggest that it is possible to prove a better security bound for FDH than that outlined above. Perhaps, but we don't know how. Instead, we will strengthen the scheme so that a better security bound can be proven.

CLARIFICATION. Before going on, let us clarify our assessments of scheme quality. We are *not* saying the FDH scheme is bad. Indeed, since it is provable, it is ahead of schemes discussed in Section 1.1, and a viable alternative to them. What we are saying is that it is possible to do *even better* than FDH. That is, it is possible to get a scheme which is not only proven secure, but has strong exact security. This successor to FDH is the scheme we discuss next.

1.3 New schemes: PSS and PSS-R

PSS. We introduce a new scheme which we call the *probabilistic signature scheme* (PSS). It is fully specified in Section 4.

The idea is to strengthen the FDH scheme by making the hashing probabilistic. In order to sign message M, the signer first picks a random seed r of length k_0, where $k_0 < k$ is a parameter of the scheme. Then using some hashing, in a specific way we specify, the signer produces from M and r an image point $y = \mathit{Hash}_{\mathsf{PSS}}(M, r) \in \mathsf{Z}_N^*$. As usual, the signature is $x = f^{-1}(y) = y^d \bmod N$. (Verification is a bit more tricky than usual, since one cannot simple "re-compute" this probabilistic hash, but still takes only one RSA encryption and some hashing. See Section 4.) In particular, our scheme is as efficient as the schemes discussed above. But Theorem 2 shows that the security can be *tightly* related to that of RSA. Roughly, it says that if RSA is (t', ϵ')-secure then, given $q_{\mathrm{sig}}, q_{\mathrm{hash}}$, scheme PSS is $(t, q_{\mathrm{sig}}, q_{\mathrm{hash}}, \epsilon)$-secure for $t = t' - \mathrm{poly}(q_{\mathrm{sig}}, q_{\mathrm{hash}}, k)$ and $\epsilon = \epsilon' - o(1)$. Here $o(1)$ denotes a function exponentially small in k_0 and k_1 (another parameter of the scheme) and poly denotes a specific polynomial, both of these explicitly specified in the theorem.

Continuing the above example, if the RSA inversion probability was originally as low as 2^{-61}, the probability of forgery for the signature scheme is almost equally low, regardless of the number of sign and hash queries the adversary makes!

PSS WITH RECOVERY. We also have a variant of PSS, called PSS-R, which provides message recovery. The goal is to save on bandwidth. Rather than transmit the message M and its signature x, a single "enhanced signature" τ, of length less than $|M| + |x|$, is transmitted. The verifier will be able to recover M from τ and simultaneously check the authenticity. With security parameter $k = 1024$, our scheme enables one to authenticate a message of up to $n = 767$ bits by transmitting only a total of k bits. PSS-R accomplishes this by appropriately "folding" the message into the signature in such a way that the verifier can recover it. The efficiency and security are the same as for PSS. See Section 5.

RABIN SIGNATURES. The same ideas apply for the Rabin function, and, in particular, we have both a basic Rabin scheme and a variant which provides for message recovery, with security tightly related to the hardness of factoring. See Section 6.

1.4 Discussion

The above illustrates that to fairly compare the efficiency of two provably-secure schemes one needs to look at more than just computation time for a k-bit key. Schemes FDH and PSS have essentially the same computation time when k is fixed. But since PSS has tighter provable security one can safely use a smaller modulus size and thus, ultimately, get greater efficiency.

A numerical example may help to make this clear. Let us again assume that the forger F can compute the hash of at most 2^{60} strings and that she can obtain the signatures of at most 2^{30} messages. Assume that it takes time $Ce^{1.923(\log N)^{1/3}(\log\log N)^{2/3}}$ to invert RSA [12]. Then, our theorems imply that if you use FDH then you must select a modulus of 3447 bits in order to get the same degree of guaranteed-security as you would have gotten had you selected a modulus of 1024 bits and used PSS.

1.5 Related work

We have already discussed the PKCS standards [16, 17] and the ISO standard [10] and seen that their security cannot be justified based on the assumption that RSA is trapdoor one-way. Other standards, such as [1], are similar to [16], and the same statement applies.

The schemes we discuss in the remainder of this section do not use the hash-then-decrypt paradigm.

Signature schemes whose security can be provably based on the RSA assumption include [9, 2, 11, 20, 6]. The major plus of these works is that they do not use an ideal hash function (random oracle) model— the provable security is in the standard sense. On the other hand, the security reductions are quite loose for each of those schemes. On the efficiency front, the efficiency of the schemes of [9, 2, 11, 20] is too poor to seriously consider them for practice. The Dwork-Naor scheme [6], on the other hand, is computationally quite efficient, taking two to six RSA computations, although there is some storage overhead and the signatures are longer than a single RSA modulus. This scheme is the best current choice if one is willing to allow some extra computation and storage, and one wants well-justified security *without* assuming an ideal hash function.

Back among signature schemes which assume an ideal hash, a great many have been proposed, based on RSA, the hardness of factoring, or other assumptions. Most of these schemes are derived from identification schemes, as was first done by [8]. Some of these methods are provable (in the ideal hash model), some not. In some of the proven schemes exact security is analyzed; usually it is not. In no case that we know of is the security tight. The efficiency varies. The computational requirements are often lower than a hash-then-decrypt RSA signature, although key sizes are typically larger.

The paradigm of protocol design with ideal hash functions (aka random oracles) is developed in [3] and continued in [4]. The current paper is in some ways the analogue, for digital signatures, of our earlier work on encryption [4]. Further work on signing in the random oracle model includes Pointcheval and Stern [13]. (They do not consider exact security, and it may be helpful to do so in their context.)

2 Definitions

We provide definitions for an exact security treatment of RSA, basic signature schemes, and signing with recovery.

2.1 An exact treatment of RSA

THE RSA FAMILY. RSA is a family of *trapdoor permutations.* It is specified by the RSA generator, $\mathcal{RSA}$, which, on input 1^k, picks a pair of random distinct $(k/2)$-bit primes and multiplies them to produce a modulus N. It also picks, at random, an encryption exponent $e \in \mathsf{Z}^*_{\varphi(N)}$ and computes the corresponding decryption exponent d so that $ed \equiv 1 \bmod \varphi(N)$. The generator returns N, e, d, these specifying $f\colon \mathsf{Z}^*_N \to \mathsf{Z}^*_N$ and $f^{-1}\colon \mathsf{Z}^*_N \to \mathsf{Z}^*_N$, which are defined by $f(x) = x^e \bmod N$ and $f^{-1}(y) = y^d \bmod N$. Recall that both functions are permutations, and, as the notation indicates, inverses of each other.

The trapdoor permutation generator $\mathcal{RSA}$–3 is identical to $\mathcal{RSA}$ except that the encryption exponent e is fixed to be 3. More generally, $\mathcal{RSA}$–e provides an encryption exponent of the specified constant. Other variants of $\mathcal{RSA}$ use a somewhat different distribution on the modulus N. Our results, though stated for $\mathcal{RSA}$, also hold for these other variants.

EXACT SECURITY OF THE RSA FAMILY. An *inverting algorithm* for $\mathcal{RSA}$, I, gets input N, e, y and tries to find $f^{-1}(y)$. Its success probability is the probability it outputs $f^{-1}(y)$ when N, e, d are obtained by running $\mathcal{RSA}(1^k)$ and y is set to $f(x)$ for an x chosen at random from Z^*_N. The standard asymptotic definition of security asks that the success probability of any PPT (probabilistic, polynomial time) algorithm be a negligible function of k. We want to go further. We are interested in exactly how much time an inverting algorithm uses and what success probability it achieves in this time. Formally an inverting algorithms is said to be a t-inverter, where $t\colon \mathsf{N} \to \mathsf{N}$, if its running time plus the size of its description is bounded by $t(k)$, in some fixed standard model of computation. We say that I (t, ϵ)-breaks $\mathcal{RSA}$, where $\epsilon\colon \mathsf{N} \to [0, 1]$, if I is a t-inverter and for each k the success probability of I is at least $\epsilon(k)$. Finally, we say that $\mathcal{RSA}$ is (t, ϵ)-secure if there is no inverter which (t, ϵ)-breaks $\mathcal{RSA}$.

EXAMPLE. The asymptotically best factoring algorithm known (NFS) takes time which seems to be about $e^{1.9k^{1/3}(\log k)^{2/3}}$ to factor a k-bit modulus. So one might be willing to assume that the trapdoor permutation family $\mathcal{RSA}$ is (t,ϵ)-secure for any (t,ϵ) satisfying $t(k)/\epsilon(k) \le Ce^{k^{1/4}}$, for some particular constant C.

2.2 Signature schemes and their exact security

SIGNATURE SCHEMES. A *digital signature scheme* $\Pi = (\mathit{Gen}, \mathit{Sign}, \mathit{Verify})$ is specified by a key generation algorithm, *Gen*, a signing algorithm, *Sign*, and a verifying algorithm, *Verify*. The first two are probabilistic, and all three should run in expected polynomial time. Given 1^k, the key generation algorithm outputs a pair of matching public and secret keys, (pk, sk). The signing algorithm takes the message M to be signed and the secret key sk, and it returns a signature $x = \mathit{Sign}_{sk}(M)$. The verifying algorithm takes a message M, a candidate signature x', and the public key pk, and it returns a bit $\mathit{Verify}_{pk}(M, x')$, with 1 signifying "accept" and 0 signifying "reject." We demand that if x was produced via $x \leftarrow \mathit{Sign}_{sk}(M)$ then $\mathit{Verify}_{pk}(M, x) = 1$.

One or more strong hash functions will usually be available to the algorithms *Sign* and *Verify*, their domain and range depending on the scheme. We model them as ideal, meaning that if hash function h is invoked on some input, the output is a uniformly distributed point of the range. (But if invoked twice on the same input, the same thing is returned both times.) Formally, h is a random oracle. It is called a hash oracle and it is accessed via oracle queries: an algorithm can write a string z and get back $h(z)$ in time $|z|$.

SECURITY OF SIGNATURE SCHEMES. Definitions for the security of signatures in the asymptotic setting were provided by Goldwasser, Micali and Rivest [9], and enhanced to take into account the presence of an ideal hash function in [3]. Here we provide an exact version of these definitions.

A forger takes as input a public key pk, where $(pk, sk) \stackrel{R}{\leftarrow} \mathit{Gen}(1^k)$, and tries to forge signatures with respect to pk. The forger is allowed a chosen message attack in which it can request, and obtain, signatures of messages of its choice. This is modeled by allowing the forger oracle access to the signing algorithm. The forger is deemed *successful* if it outputs a *valid forgery*—namely, a message/signature pair (M, x) such that $\mathit{Verify}_{pk}(M, x) = 1$ but M was not a message of which a signature was requested earlier of the signer. The forger is said to be a $(t, q_{\text{sig}}, q_{\text{hash}})$-forger if its running time plus description size is bounded by $t(k)$; it makes at most $q_{\text{sig}}(k)$ queries of its signing oracle; and it makes a total of at most $q_{\text{hash}}(k)$ queries of its various hash oracles. As a convention, the time $t(k)$ includes the time to answer the signing queries. Such a forger F is said to $(t, q_{\text{sig}}, q_{\text{hash}}, \epsilon)$-break the signature scheme if, for every k, the probability that F outputs a valid forgery is at least $\epsilon(k)$. Finally we say that the signature scheme $(\mathit{Gen}, \mathit{Sign}, \mathit{Verify})$ is $(t, q_{\text{sig}}, q_{\text{hash}}, \epsilon)$-secure if there is no forger who $(t, q_{\text{sig}}, q_{\text{hash}}, \epsilon)$-breaks the scheme.

For simplicity we will assume that a forger does any necessary book-keeping so that it never repeats a hash query. (It might repeat a signing query. If the scheme is probabilistic, this might help it.)

2.3 Quantifying the quality of reductions

Our theorems will have the form: If $\mathcal{RSA}$ is (t', ϵ')-secure, then some signature scheme $\Pi = (Gen, Sign, Verify)$ is $(t, q_{\mathrm{sig}}, q_{\mathrm{hash}}, \epsilon)$-secure. The proof will take a forger F who $(t, q_{\mathrm{sig}}, q_{\mathrm{hash}}, \epsilon)$-breaks Π and produce from F an inverter I who (t', ϵ')-breaks $\mathcal{RSA}$. The quality of the reduction is in how the primed variables depend on the unprimed ones. We will typically view $q_{\mathrm{sig}}, q_{\mathrm{hash}}$ as given, these being query bounds we are willing to allow. (For example, $q_{\mathrm{sig}} = 2^{30}$ and $q_{\mathrm{hash}} = 2^{60}$ are reasonable possibilities.) Obviously we want t' to be as large as possible and we want ϵ' to be as small as possible. We are usually satisfied when $t' = t - \mathrm{poly}(q_{\mathrm{hash}}, q_{\mathrm{sig}}, k)$ and $\epsilon' \approx \epsilon$.

3 The Full-Domain-Hash Scheme – FDH

THE SCHEME. Signature scheme FDH $= (GenFDH, SignFDH, VerifyFDH)$ is defined as follows [3]. The key generation algorithm, on input 1^k, runs $\mathcal{RSA}(1^k)$ to obtain (N, e, d). It outputs (pk, sk), where $pk = (N, e)$ and $sk = (N, d)$. The signing and verifying algorithms have oracle access to a hash function $H_{\mathrm{FDH}}\colon \{0,1\}^* \to \mathsf{Z}_N^*$. (In the security analysis it is assumed to be ideal. In practice it can be implemented on top of a cryptographic hash function such as SHA-1.) Signature generation and verification are as follows:

$SignFDH_{N,d}(M)$
  $y \leftarrow H_{\mathrm{FDH}}(M)$
  return $y^d \bmod N$

$VerifyFDH_{N,e}(M, x)$
  $y \leftarrow x^e \bmod N$; $y' \leftarrow H_{\mathrm{FDH}}(M)$
  if $y = y'$ **then return** 1 **else return** 0

SECURITY. The following theorem summarizes the exact security of the FDH scheme as provided by the reduction of [3]. The proof is straightforward, but it is instructive all the same, so we include it. The disadvantage of the result, from our point of view, is that ϵ' could be much smaller than ϵ.

Theorem 1. *Suppose $\mathcal{RSA}$ is a (t', ϵ')-secure. Then, for any $q_{\mathrm{sig}}, q_{\mathrm{hash}}$, signature scheme* FDH *is $(t, q_{\mathrm{sig}}, q_{\mathrm{hash}}, \epsilon)$-secure, where*

$$t(k) = t'(k) - [q_{\mathrm{hash}}(k) + q_{\mathrm{sig}}(k) + 1] \cdot \Theta(k^3) \quad \text{and}$$
$$\epsilon(k) = [q_{\mathrm{sig}}(k) + q_{\mathrm{hash}}(k)] \cdot \epsilon'(k) .$$

Proof. Let F be a forger which $(t, q_{\mathrm{sig}}, q_{\mathrm{hash}}, \epsilon)$-breaks FDH. We present an inverter I which (t', ϵ')-breaks $\mathcal{RSA}$.

Inverting algorithm I is given as input (N, e, y) where N, e, d were obtained by running the generator $\mathcal{RSA}(1^k)$, and y was chosen at random from Z_N^*. It is trying to find $x = f^{-1}(y)$, where f is the RSA function described by N, e. It forms the public key N, e of the Full-Domain-Hash signature scheme, and starts running F on input of this key. Forger F will make two kinds of oracle queries: hash oracle queries and signing queries. Inverter I must answer these queries itself. For simplicity we assume that if F makes sign query M then it has already made hash oracle query M. (We will argue later that this is wlog.) Let $q = q_{\text{sig}} + q_{\text{hash}}$. Inverter I picks at random an integer j from $\{1, \ldots, q\}$. Now we describe how I answers oracle queries. Here i is a counter, initially 0.

Suppose F makes hash oracle query M. Inverter I increments i and sets $M_i = M$. If $i = j$ then it sets $y_i = y$ and returns y_i. Else it picks r_i at random in Z_N^*, sets $y_i = f(r_i)$, and returns y_i.

Alternatively, suppose F makes signing query M. By assumption, there was already a hash query of M, so $M = M_i$ for some i. Let I return the corresponding r_i as the signature.

Eventually, F halts, outputting some (attempted forgery) (M, x). Let inverting algorithm I output x. Without loss of generality (see below) we may assume that $M = M_i$ for some i. In that case, if (M, x) is a valid forgery, then, with probability at least $1/q$, we have $i = j$ and $x = f^{-1}(y_i) = f^{-1}(y)$ was the correct inverse for f.

The running time of I is that of F plus the time to choose the y_i-values. The main thing here is one RSA computation for each y_i, which is cubic time (or better). This explains the formula for t.

It remains to justify the assumptions. Recall that I is running F. So if the latter makes a sign query without having made the corresponding hash query, I at once goes ahead and makes the hash query itself. Similarly for the output forgery. All this means that the effective number of hash queries is at most $q_{\text{hash}} + q_{\text{sig}} + 1$, which is the number we used in the time bound above. □

Is there a different proof which would achieve a translation in which t is like the above but ϵ is $\Omega(\epsilon')$? We don't believe so. Instead we will modify the scheme to get the security we want. We do this by making the hashing probabilistic.

4 The Probabilistic Signature Scheme – PSS

Here we propose a new scheme—a probabilistic generalization of FDH. It preserves the efficiency and provable security of FDH but achieves the latter with a much better security bound.

4.1 Description of the PSS

Signature scheme $\mathsf{PSS}[k_0, k_1] = (\mathit{GenPSS}, \mathit{SignPSS}, \mathit{VerifyPSS})$ is parameterized by k_0 and k_1, which are numbers between 1 and k satisfying $k_0 + k_1 \leq k - 1$. To be concrete, the reader may like to imagine $k = 1024$, $k_0 = k_1 = 128$.

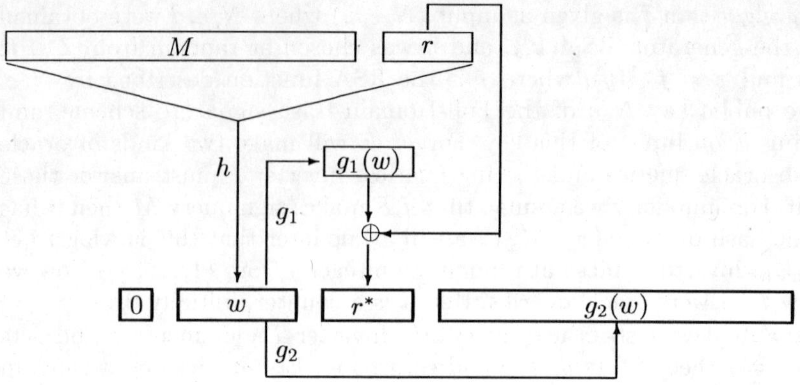

Fig. 1. PSS: Components of image $y = 0 \parallel w \parallel r^* \parallel g_2(w)$ are darkened. The signature of M is $y^d \bmod N$.

The key generation algorithm *GenPSS* is identical to *GenFDH*: on input 1^k, run $\mathcal{RSA}(1^k)$ to obtain (N, e, d), and output (pk, sk), where $pk = (N, e)$ and $sk = (N, d)$.

The signing and verifying algorithms make use of two hash functions. The first, h, called the compressor, maps as h: $\{0,1\}^* \to \{0,1\}^{k_1}$ and the second, g, called the generator, maps as g: $\{0,1\}^{k_0} \to \{0,1\}^{k-k_1-1}$. (The analysis assumes these to be ideal. In practice they can be implemented in simple ways out of cryptographic hash functions like MD5, as discussed in Appendix A.) Let g_1 be the function which on input $w \in \{0,1\}^{k_0}$ returns the first k_0 bits of $g(w)$, and let g_2 be the function which on input $w \in \{0,1\}^{k_0}$ returns the remaining $k - k_0 - k_1 - 1$ bits of $g(w)$. We now describe how to sign and verify. Refer to Figure 1 for a picture.

SignPSS (M)
  $r \stackrel{R}{\leftarrow} \{0,1\}^{k_0}$; $w \leftarrow h(M \parallel r)$; $r^* \leftarrow g_1(w) \oplus r$
  $y \leftarrow 0 \parallel w \parallel r^* \parallel g_2(w)$
  return $y^d \bmod N$

VerifyPSS (M, x)
  $y \leftarrow x^e \bmod N$
  Break up y as $b \parallel w \parallel r^* \parallel \gamma$. (That is, let b be the first bit of y, w the next k_1 bits, r^* the next k_0 bits, and γ the remaining bits.)
  $r \leftarrow r^* \oplus g_1(w)$
  if ($h(M \parallel r) = w$ and $g_2(w) = \gamma$ and $b = 0$) **then return** 1
  else return 0

The step $r \stackrel{R}{\leftarrow} \{0,1\}^{k_0}$ indicates that the signer picks at random a seed r of k_0 bits. He then concatenates this seed to the message M, effectively "randomizing" the message, and hashes this down, via the "compressing" function, to a k_1 bit string w. Then the generator g is applied to w to yield a k_0 bit string $r^* = g_1(w)$ and a $k - k_0 - k_1 - 1$ bit string $g_2(w)$. The first is used to "mask" the seed r, resulting in the masked seed r^*. Now $w \| r^*$ is pre-pended with a 0 bit and appended with $g_2(w)$ to create the image point y which is decrypted under the RSA function to define the signature. (The 0-bit is to guarantee that y is in Z_N^*.) Notice that a new seed is chosen for each message. In particular, a given message has many possible signatures, depending on the value of r chosen by the signer.

Given (M, x), the verifier first computes $y = x^e \bmod N$ and recovers r^*, w, r. These are used to check that y was correctly constructed, and the verifier only accepts if all the checks succeed.

Note the efficiency of the scheme is as claimed. Signing takes one application of h, one application of g, and one RSA decryption, while verification takes one application of h, one application of g, and one RSA encryption.

4.2 Security of the PSS

The following theorem proves the security of the PSS based on the security of RSA, but with a relation between the two securities that is much tighter than the one we saw for the FDH scheme. The key difference is that $\epsilon(k)$ is within an additive, rather than multiplicative, factor of $\epsilon'(k)$, and this additive factor decreases exponentially with k_0, k_1. The relation between t and t' is about the same as in Theorem 1.

Theorem 2. *Suppose that $\mathcal{RSA}$ is (t', ϵ')-secure. Then for any $q_{\text{sig}}, q_{\text{hash}}$ the signature scheme* PSS$[k_0, k_1]$ *is $(t, q_{\text{sig}}, q_{\text{hash}}, \epsilon)$-secure, where*

$$t(k) = t'(k) - [q_{\text{sig}}(k) + q_{\text{hash}}(k) + 1] \cdot k_0 \cdot \Theta(k^3), \quad \textit{and}$$

$$\epsilon(k) = \epsilon'(k) + [2(q_{\text{sig}}(k) + q_{\text{hash}}(k))^2 + 1] \cdot (2^{-k_0} + 2^{-k_1}) \,.$$

The rest of this section is devoted to a sketch of the proof of this theorem.

Proof Sketch. Let F be a forger which $(t, q_{\text{sig}}, q_{\text{hash}}, \epsilon)$-breaks the PSS. We present an inverter I which (t', ϵ')-breaks the trapdoor permutation family $\mathcal{RSA}$.

The input to I is N, e and η where η was chosen at random from Z_N^*, and N, e, d were chosen by running the generator $\mathcal{RSA}(1^k)$. (But d is not provided to I!) We let $f\colon Z_N^* \to Z_N^*$ be $f(x) = x^e \bmod N$. I wants to compute $f^{-1}(\eta) = \eta^d \bmod N$. It forms the public key N, e, and starts running F on input this key. F will make oracle queries (signing queries, h-oracle queries, and g-oracle queries), which I must answer itself. We assume no hash query (h or g) is repeated (but a signing query might be repeated). We let $Q_1, \ldots, Q_{q_{\text{sig}}+q_{\text{hash}}}$ denote the sequence of oracle queries that F makes. (This is a sequence of random variables.) This list includes all queries, and we implicitly assume that along with each Q_i is an indication of whether it is a signing oracle query, an h-oracle query or a g-oracle query. In the process of answering these queries, I will "build" or "define" the functions h, g.

I maintains a counter i, initially 0, which is incremented for each query. We now indicate how the queries are answered. It depends on the type of query.

Answering signing queries. First, suppose $Q_i = M$ is a signing query. Let us first try to give some intuition, and then the precise instructions for I to answer the query.

The problem is that I cannot answer a signing query as the signer would since it doesn't know f^{-1}. So, it first picks a point $x \in Z_N^*$, and then arranges that $y = f(x)$ be the image point of a signature of M. (It does this by viewing y as $0 \parallel w \parallel r^* \parallel \gamma$, and then defining $h(M \parallel r) = w$ and $g(w) = r^* \oplus r \parallel \gamma$, for some random r.) At this point, x can be returned as a legitimate signature of M. Some technicalities include making sure there are no conflicts (re-defining h or g on points where their values were already assigned) and making sure y has first bit 0. These are attended to in the following full description of the instructions for I to answer signing query Q_i:

(1) Increment i and let $M_i = Q_i$.
(2) Pick $r_i \stackrel{R}{\leftarrow} \{0,1\}^{k_0}$. (Recall this notation means r_i is chosen at random from $\{0,1\}^{k_0}$.)
(3) If $\exists\, j : j < i : r_j = r_i$ then `abort`.
(4) `Repeat` $x_i \stackrel{R}{\leftarrow} \mathsf{Z}_N^*$; $y_i \leftarrow f(x_i)$ `until` the first bit of y_i is 0.
(5) Break up y_i to write it as $0 \parallel w_i \parallel r_i^* \parallel \gamma_i$. (That is, let w_i be the k_0 bits following the 0, let r_i^* be the next k_1 bits, and let γ_i be the last $k - k_0 - k_1 - 1$ bits.)
(6) Set $h(M_i \parallel r_i) = w_i$.
(7) If $\exists\, j : j < i : w_j = w_i$ then `abort`.
(8) Set $g_1(w_i) = r_i^* \oplus r_i$; Set $g_2(w_i) = \gamma_i$; Set $g(w_i) = g_1(w_i) \parallel g_2(w_i)$.
(9) Return x_i to F as the answer to signing query $Q_i = M_i$.

Answering h-oracle queries. Next, suppose Q_i is an h-oracle query. We may assume it has length at least k_0 since otherwise it doesn't help the adversary to make this query. Again, before the precise instructions, here is the intuition. The query looks like $M \parallel r$. We want to arrange that, if F later forges a signature of M using seed r then[3] we invert f at η. To arrange this, we will associate to query $M \parallel r$ an image of the form ηx_i^e, where x_i is random. (Thus if F later comes up with an $f^{-1}(\eta x_i^e) = x_i \eta^d$, then I can divide out x_i and recover $\eta^d = f^{-1}(\eta)$.) This is done by choosing a random x_i, viewing ηx_i^e as $0 \parallel w \parallel r^* \parallel \gamma$, and, as before, defining $h(M \parallel r) = w$ and $g(w) = r^* \oplus r \parallel \gamma$. The detailed instructions for I to answer h-oracle query Q_i (taking into account technicalities similar to the above) are:

(1) Increment i and break up Q_i as $M_i \parallel r_i$. (That is, let r_i be the last k_0 bits of Q_i and let M_i be the rest).
(2) Say Q_i is *old* if $\exists\, j : j < i : M_j \parallel r_j = M_i \parallel r_i$, and *new* otherwise. (Since h-queries are not repeated, Q_i is old iff M_i was signing query M_j and in the

[3] F might forge a signature of M with a seed r' such that h-query $M \parallel r'$ was never made. But the probability of this is very low.

process of answering it above we picked $r_j = r_i$.) Now if Q_i is old then set $(w_i, r_i^*, \gamma_i) = (w_j, r_j^*, \gamma_j)$ and return w_j (which is $h(M_j \| r_j)$); Else go on to next step.

(3) Repeat $x_i \stackrel{R}{\leftarrow} \mathsf{Z}_N^*$; $z_i \leftarrow f(x_i)$; $y_i \leftarrow \eta z_i \bmod N$ until the first bit of y_i is 0.

(4) Break up y_i to write it as $0 \| w_i \| r_i^* \| \gamma_i$.

(5) Set $h(M_i \| r_i) = w_i$.

(6) If $\exists j : j < i : w_j = w_i$ then abort.

(7) Set $g_1(w_i) = r_i^* \oplus r_i$; Set $g_2(w_i) = \gamma_i$; Set $g(w_i) = g_1(w_i) \| g_2(w_i)$.

(8) Return w_i to F as the answer to h-oracle query $Q_i = M_i \| r_i$.

Answering g-oracle queries. Last, suppose Q_i is a g-oracle query. We may assume it has length k_1 since otherwise it doesn't help the adversary to make this query. This time, there is not much to do:

(1) Increment i and let $w_i = Q_i$.

(2) If $\exists j : j < i : w_j = w_i$ then return $g(w_j)$. Else pick a string $\alpha \stackrel{R}{\leftarrow} \{0,1\}^{k-k_0-1}$, set $g(w_i) = \alpha$, and return α.

Analysis. Let Distinct be the event that we never abort in Steps (3) or (7) in answering signing queries or Step (6) in answering h-oracle queries. The reader can verify that $\Pr[\neg\text{Distinct}] \leq p$ where $p = 2(q_{\text{sig}} + q_{\text{hash}})^2 \cdot (2^{-k_0} + 2^{-k_1})$. So with probability $\epsilon - p$, Distinct holds and F halts and outputs a valid forgery (M, x). Assume we are in this situation, and let $y = f(x) = x^e \bmod N$. If the first bit of y is not 0 then the forgery is invalid, so assume this bit is 0. So we can break y up to view it as $0 \| w \| r^* \| \gamma$. Let $r = r^* \oplus g_1(w)$. We now claim that with probability at least $\epsilon - p - 2^{-k_1}$, there is an i such that: $(M, r, w, r^*, \gamma) = (M_i, r_i, w_i, r_i^*, \gamma_i)$; h-oracle query $Q_i = M_i \| r_i$ was made; and this query was new when it was made. Assuming this claim we have $y = y_i = \eta z_i^e \bmod N$. Now I outputs $x/z_i \bmod N$. Note $(x/z_i)^e = y^e/z_i^e = \eta$ so x/z_i is indeed $f^{-1}(\eta)$ as desired.

Now let us justify the claim. If $M \| r \neq M_i \| r_i$ for all i then the probability that $h(M \| r) = w$ is at most 2^{-k_1}. So now assume there is such an i. Since (M, x) is a valid forgery we know that M was never a signing query, so it must be that $M \| r$ was a h-oracle query. Furthermore, for the same reason, it must have been new.

Finally, note that the time for Step (4) in answering signing queries and Step (3) in answering h-oracle queries can't be bounded. But the expected time is two executions of the loop. So we just stop the loop after $1 + k_0$ steps. This adds at most 2^{-k_0} to the error, completing our proof sketch. □

We stress how this proof differs from that of Theorem 1. There, we had to "guess" the value of $i \in \{1, \ldots, q_{\text{sig}} + q_{\text{hash}}\}$ for which F would forge a message, and we were only successful if we guessed right. Here we are successful (except with very small probability) no matter what is the value of i for which the forgery occurs.

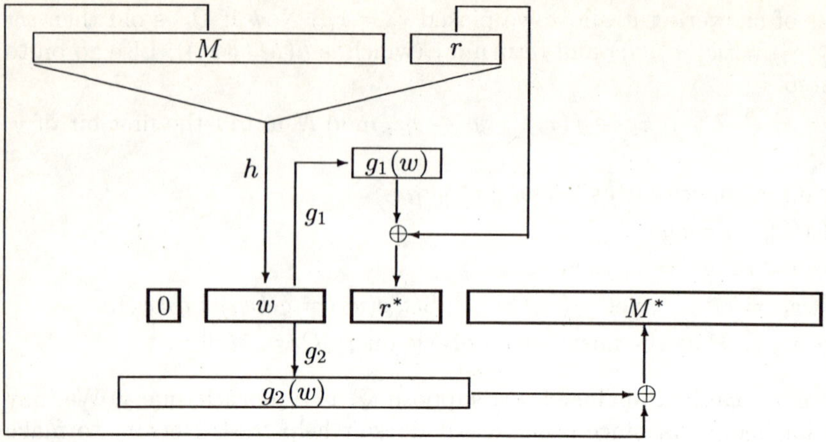

Fig. 2. PSS-R: Components of image $y = 0 \,||\, w \,||\, r^* \,||\, M^*$ are darkened.

5 Signing with Message Recovery – PSS-R

MESSAGE RECOVERY. In a standard signature scheme the signer transmits the message M in the clear, attaching to it the signature x. In a scheme which provides message recovery, only an "enhanced signature" is transmitted. The goal is to save on the bandwidth for a signed message: we want the length of this enhanced signature to be smaller than $|M| + |x|$. (In particular, when M is short, we would like the length of τ to be k, the signature length.) The verifier recovers the message M from the enhanced signature and checks authenticity at the same time.

We accomplish this by "folding" part of the message into the signature in such a way that it is "recoverable" by the verifier. When the length n of M is small, we can in fact fold the entire message into the signature, so that only a k bit quantity is transmitted. In the scheme below, if the security parameter is $k = 1024$, we can fold up to 767 message bits into the signature.

DEFINITION. Formally, the key generation and signing algorithms are as before, but *Verify* is replaced by *Recover*, which takes pk and x and returns $Recover_{pk}(x) \in \{0,1\}^* \cup \{\mathsf{REJECT}\}$. The distinguished point REJECT is used to indicate that the recipient rejected the signature; a return value of $M \in \{0,1\}^*$ indicates that the verifier accepts the message M as authentic. The formulation of security is the same except for what it means for the forger to be *successful*: it should provide an x such that $Recover_{pk}(x) = M \in \{0,1\}^*$, where M was not a previous signing query. We demand that if x is produced via $x \leftarrow Sign_{sk}(M)$ then $Recover_{pk}(x) = M$.

A simple variant of PSS achieves message recovery. We now describe that scheme and its security.

THE SCHEME. The scheme $\mathsf{PSS\text{-}R}[k_0, k_1] = (\mathit{GenPSSR}, \mathit{SignPSSR}, \mathit{RecPSSR})$ is parameterized by k_0 and k_1, as before. The key generation algorithm is *GenPSS*, the same as before. As with PSS, the signing and verifying algorithms depend on hash functions $h\colon \{0,1\}^* \to \{0,1\}^{k_1}$ and $g\colon \{0,1\}^{k_0} \to \{0,1\}^{k-k_1-1}$, and we use the same g_1 and g_2 notation. For simplicity of explication, we assume that the messages to be signed have length $n = k - k_0 - k_1 - 1$. (Suggested choices of parameters are $k = 1024$, $k_0 = k_1 = 128$ and $n = 767$.) In this case, we produce "enhanced signatures" of only k bits from which the verifier can recover the n-bit message and simultaneously check authenticity. Signature generation and verification proceed as follows. Refer to Figure 2 for a picture.

SignPSSR (M)
  $r \stackrel{R}{\leftarrow} \{0,1\}^{k_0}$; $w \leftarrow h(M \parallel r)$; $r^* \leftarrow g_1(w) \oplus r$
  $M^* \leftarrow g_2(w) \oplus M$
  $y \leftarrow 0 \parallel w \parallel r^* \parallel M^*$
  return $y^d \bmod N$

RecPSSR (x)
  $y \leftarrow x^e \bmod N$
  Break up y as $b \parallel w \parallel r^* \parallel M^*$. (That is, let b be the first bit of y, w the next k_1 bits, r^* the next k_0 bits, and M^* the remaining bits.)
  $r \leftarrow r^* \oplus g_1(w)$
  $M \leftarrow M^* \oplus g_2(w)$
  if ($h(M \parallel r) = w$ and $b = 0$) **then return** M **else return** REJECT

The difference in *SignPSSR* with respect to *SignPSS* is that the last part of y is not $g_2(w)$. Instead, $g_2(w)$ is used to "mask" the message, and the masked message M^* is the last part of the image point y.

The above is easily adapted to handle messages of arbitrary length. A fully-specified scheme would use about $\min\{k,\, n + k_0 + k_1 + 16\}$ bits.

SECURITY. The security of PSS-R is the same as for PSS.

Theorem 3. *Suppose that* $\mathcal{RSA}$ *is* (t', ϵ')*-secure. Then for any* $q_{\rm sig}, q_{\rm hash}$ *the signing-with-recovery scheme* $\mathsf{PSS\text{-}R}[k_0, k_1]$ *is* $(t, q_{\rm sig}, q_{\rm hash}, \epsilon)$*-secure, where*

$$t(k) = t'(k) - [q_{\rm sig}(k) + q_{\rm hash}(k) + 1] \cdot k_0 \cdot \Theta(k^3), \quad \textit{and}$$
$$\epsilon(k) = \epsilon'(k) + [2(q_{\rm sig}(k) + q_{\rm hash}(k))^2 + 1] \cdot (2^{-k_0} + 2^{-k_1})\,.$$

The proof of this theorem is very similar to that of Theorem 2 and hence is omitted.

6 Rabin signatures – PRab and PRab-R

The ideas of this paper extend to Rabin signatures [18, 19], yielding a signature scheme and a signing with recovery scheme whose security can be tightly related to the hardness of factoring.

THE SCHEME. Scheme $\mathsf{PRab}[k_0, k_1] = (GenPRab, SignPRab, VerifyPRab)$, the probabilistic Rabin scheme, depends on parameters k_0, k_1, where $k_0 + k_1 \leq k$. Algorithm *GenPRab*, on input 1^k, picks a pair of random distinct $(k/2)$-bit primes p, q and multiplies them to produce the k-bit modulus N. It outputs (pk, sk), where $pk = N$ and $sk = (N, p, q)$.

The signing and verifying algorithms of PRab use hash functions h, g, where $h\colon \{0,1\}^* \to \{0,1\}^{k_1}$ and $g\colon \{0,1\}^{k_0} \to \{0,1\}^{k-k_1}$. We let g_1 be the function which on input $w \in \{0,1\}^{k_0}$ returns the first k_0 bits of $g(w)$, and let g_2 be the function which on input $w \in \{0,1\}^{k_0}$ returns the remaining $k - k_0 - k_1$ bits of $g(w)$.

The signing procedure, *SignPRab*, is similar to the corresponding *SignPSS*, but it returns a random square root of the image y, as opposed to $y^d \bmod N$. We stress that a random root is chosen; a fixed one won't do. The verification procedure checks if the square of the signature has the correct image. Thus verification is particularly fast. Here, in full, are *SignPRab* and *VerifyPRab*:

SignPRab (M)
  repeat
    $r \stackrel{R}{\leftarrow} \{0,1\}^{k_0}$; $w \leftarrow h(M \,\|\, r)$; $r^* \leftarrow g_1(w) \oplus r$
    $y \leftarrow w \,\|\, r^* \,\|\, g_2(w)$
  until y is a quadratic residue mod$N$.
  Let $\{x_1, x_2, x_3, x_4\}$ be the four distinct square roots of y in Z_N^*.
  Let $x \stackrel{R}{\leftarrow} \{x_1, x_2, x_3, x_4\}$.
  return x

VerifyPRab (M, x)
  $y \leftarrow x^2 \bmod N$
  Break up y as $w \,\|\, r^* \,\|\, \gamma$. (That is, let w be the first k_1 bits of y,
    r^* the next k_0 bits, and γ the remaining bits.)
  $r \leftarrow r^* \oplus g_1(w)$
  if ($h(M \,\|\, r) = w$ and $g_2(w) = \gamma$) **then return** 1 **else return** 0

EXACT SECURITY OF FACTORING. This scheme is based on the hardness of factoring, so we need an exact security formulation of the hardness of factoring assumption.

A factoring algorithm takes a k-bit number and tries to factor it. It is a t-factoring algorithm if the size of its description plus its running time is at most $t(k)$ for every k. We say that A (t, ϵ)-factors if, given a number which is the product of two random distinct $(k/2)$-bit primes, A produces the correct factorization with probability at least $\epsilon(k)$. We say that factoring is (t, ϵ)-hard if there is no algorithm which (t, ϵ)-factors. A reasonable assumption would be that factoring is (t, ϵ)-hard for any t, ϵ satisfying $t(k)/\epsilon(k) = e^{k^{1/4}(\log k)^{3/4}}$.

SECURITY OF THE PRab. The following theorem says that the security of PRab is similar to that of PSS.

Theorem 4. *Suppose that factoring is (t', ϵ')-hard. Then for any $q_{\rm sig}, q_{\rm hash}$ the signature scheme* $\mathsf{PRab}[k_0, k_1]$ *is $(t, q_{\rm sig}, q_{\rm hash}, \epsilon)$-secure, where*

$$t(k) = t'(k) - [q_{\rm sig}(k) + q_{\rm hash}(k) + 1] \cdot k_0 \cdot \Theta(k^2), \quad \textit{and}$$
$$\epsilon(k) = 2\epsilon'(k) + [4(q_{\rm sig}(k) + q_{\rm hash}(k))^2 + 2] \cdot (2^{-k_0} + 2^{-k_1}) .$$

The proof of this theorem is analogous to that of Theorem 2. Given a forger F who $(t, q_{\rm sig}, q_{\rm hash}, \epsilon)$-breaks PRab we construct an algorithm which (t', ϵ')-factors. We begin by picking an element $\alpha \in \mathsf{Z}_N^*$ at random and setting $\eta = \alpha^2 \bmod N$. Then we proceed as in the proof of Theorem 2, with e set to 2 rather than to the RSA encryption exponent. We thereby recover a square root of η with probability $\epsilon(k) - \delta(k)$ where $\delta(k) = [2(q_{\rm sig}(k) + q_{\rm hash}(k))^2 + 1] \cdot (2^{-k_0} + 2^{-k_1})$. But with probability $\epsilon(k)/2 - \delta(k)$ this square root is different from α and hence we factor N. Thus we have a factor of two deterioration in the success probability. On the other hand, there is an improvement in the time complexity, since our algorithm has to raise numbers to the power two rather than to an arbitrary RSA exponent e, thereby bringing the $\Theta(k^3)$ time to $\Theta(k^2)$. Also, it is a potentially weaker assumption to say that factoring is (t', e') hard.

RECOVERY. As with PSS, we can add message recovery to the PRab scheme in the same way, resulting in the PRab-R signing-with-recovery scheme. Its security is the same as that of PRab.

References

1. D. BALENSON, "Privacy Enhancement for Internet Electronic Mail: Part III: Algorithms, Modes, and Identifiers," IETF RFC 1423, February 1993.
2. M. BELLARE AND S. MICALI, "How to sign given any trapdoor permutation," *JACM* Vol. 39, No. 1, 214-233, January 1992.
3. M. BELLARE AND P. ROGAWAY, "Random oracles are practical: a paradigm for designing efficient protocols," *Proceedings of the First Annual Conference on Computer and Communications Security*, ACM, 1993.
4. M. BELLARE AND P. ROGAWAY, "Optimal Asymmetric Encryption," *Advances in Cryptology – Eurocrypt* 94 *Proceedings*, Lecture Notes in Computer Science Vol. 950, A. De Santis ed., Springer-Verlag, 1994.
5. W. DIFFIE AND M. E. HELLMAN, "New directions in cryptography," *IEEE Trans. Info. Theory* IT-22, 644-654, November 1976.
6. C. DWORK AND M. NAOR. An efficient existentially unforgeable signature scheme and its applications. *Advances in Cryptology – Crypto* 94 *Proceedings*, Lecture Notes in Computer Science Vol. 839, Y. Desmedt ed., Springer-Verlag, 1994.
7. T. EL GAMAL, "A public key cryptosystem and a signature scheme based on discrete logarithms," *IEEE Transactions on Information Theory*, Vol. 31, No. 4, July 1985.
8. A. FIAT AND A. SHAMIR, "How to prove yourself: practical solutions to identification and signature problems," *Advances in Cryptology – Crypto* 86 *Proceedings*, Lecture Notes in Computer Science Vol. 263, A. Odlyzko ed., Springer-Verlag, 1986.

9. S. Goldwasser, S. Micali and R. Rivest, "A digital signature scheme secure against adaptive chosen-message attacks," *SIAM Journal of Computing,* 17(2):281–308, April 1988.
10. ISO/IEC 9796, "Information Technology Security Techniques – Digital Signature Scheme Giving Message Recovery," International Organization for Standards, 1991.
11. M. Naor and M. Yung, "Universal one-way hash functions and their cryptographic applications," *Proceedings of the* 21st *Annual Symposium on Theory of Computing*, ACM, 1989.
12. A. Lenstra and H. Lenstra (eds.), "The development of the number field sieve," Lecture Notes in Mathematics, vol 1554, Springer-Verlag, 1993.
13. D. Pointcheval and J. Stern, "Security proofs for signatures," *Advances in cryptology – Eurocrypt 96 Proceedings,* Lecture Notes in Computer Science, U. Maurer ed., Springer-Verlag, 1996.
14. R. Rivest, "The MD5 Message-Digest Algorithm," IETF RFC 1321, April 1992.
15. R. Rivest, A. Shamir and L. Adleman, "A method for obtaining digital signatures and public key cryptosystems," CACM 21 (1978).
16. RSA Data Security, Inc., "PKCS #1: RSA Encryption Standard (Version 1.4)." June 1991.
17. RSA Data Security, Inc., "PKCS #7: Cryptographic Message Syntax Standard (version 1.4)." June 1991.
18. M. Rabin, "Digital signatures," in *Foundations of secure computation,* R. A. Millo et. al. eds, Academic Press, 1978.
19. M. Rabin., "Digital signatures and public key functions as intractable as factorization," MIT Laboratory for Computer Science Report TR-212, January 1979.
20. J. Rompel, "One-Way Functions are Necessary and Sufficient for Secure Signatures," *Proceedings of the* 22nd *Annual Symposium on Theory of Computing*, ACM, 1990.
21. H. Williams, "A modification of the RSA public key encryption procedure," *IEEE Transactions on Information Theory*, Vol. IT-26, No. 6, November 1980.

A How to implement the hash functions h, g

In the PSS we need a concrete hash function h with output length some given number k_1. Typically we will construct h from some cryptographic hash function H such as $H =$ MD5 or $H =$ SHA-1. Ways to do this have been discussed before in [3, 4]. For completeness we quickly summarize some of these possibilities. The simplest is to define $h(x)$ as the appropriate-length prefix of

$$H(\texttt{const}.\langle 0\rangle.x) \parallel H(\texttt{const}.\langle 1\rangle.x) \parallel H(\texttt{const}.\langle 2\rangle.x) \parallel \cdots .$$

The constant const should be unique to h; to make another hash function, g, simply select a different constant.

Author Index

Aiello, William 307
Beaver, Donald 119
Bellare, Mihir 399
Blackburn, Simon R. 107
Bleichenbacher, Daniel 10
Boyar, Joan 131
Burmester, Mike 96, 107
Camion, Paul 283
Canteaut, Anne 283
Coppersmith, Don 1, 155, 178
Cramer, Ronald 72
Damgård, Ivan 372
Desmedt, Yvo 107
Eisfeld, Jörg 60
Fischer, Jean-Bernard 245
Franklin, Matthew 1, 72
Gennaro, Rosario 354
Gibson, Keith 212
Golić, Jovan Dj. 268
Hong, Seong-Min 166
Impagliazzo, Russell 143
Jakobsson, Markus 143
Jarecki, Stanislaw 354
Klapper, Andrew 256
Knudsen, Lars R. 224, 237
Krawczyk, Hugo 354
Kurosawa, Kaoru 200
Meyer, Bernd 49
Müller, Volker 49
Ogata, Wakaha 200
Oh, Sang-Yeop 166
Patarin, Jacques 1, 33
Pedersen, Torben P. 237, 372
Peralta, René 131
Pfitzmann, Birgit 84
Pointcheval, David 387
Preneel, Bart 19
Rabin, Tal 354
Reiter, Michael 1
Robshaw, Matthew J. B. 224
Rogaway, Phillip 399
Rubin, Avi 321
Sako, Kazue 143
Schoenmakers, Berry 72
Schunter, Matthias 84
Schwenk, Jörg 60
Shoup, Victor 321, 344
Stadler, Markus 190
Stern, Jacques 245, 387
van Oorschot, Paul C. 19, 332
Venkatesan, Ramarathnam 307
Wiener, Michael J. 332
Wild, Peter R. 107
Yoon, Hyunsoo 166
Yung, Moti 72
Zhang, Xian-Mo 294
Zheng, Yuliang 294

Lecture Notes in Computer Science

For information about Vols. 1–996

please contact your bookseller or Springer-Verlag

Vol. 997: K.P. Jantke, T. Shinohara, T. Zeugmann (Eds.), Algorithmic Learning Theory. Proceedings, 1995. XV, 319 pages. 1995.

Vol. 998: A. Clarke, M. Campolargo, N. Karatzas (Eds.), Bringing Telecommunication Services to the People – IS&N '95. Proceedings, 1995. XII, 510 pages. 1995.

Vol. 999: P. Antsaklis, W. Kohn, A. Nerode, S. Sastry (Eds.), Hybrid Systems II. VIII, 569 pages. 1995.

Vol. 1000: J. van Leeuwen (Ed.), Computer Science Today. XIV, 643 pages. 1995.

Vol. 1001: M. Sudan, Efficient Checking of Polynomials and Proofs and the Hardness of Approximation Problems. XIV, 87 pages. 1995.

Vol. 1002: J.J. Kistler, Disconnected Operation in a Distributed File System. XIX, 249 pages. 1995.

VOL. 1003: P. Pandurang Nayak, Automated Modeling of Physical Systems. XXI, 232 pages. 1995. (Subseries LNAI).

Vol. 1004: J. Staples, P. Eades, N. Katoh, A. Moffat (Eds.), Algorithms and Computation. Proceedings, 1995. XV, 440 pages. 1995.

Vol. 1005: J. Estublier (Ed.), Software Configuration Management. Proceedings, 1995. IX, 311 pages. 1995.

Vol. 1006: S. Bhalla (Ed.), Information Systems and Data Management. Proceedings, 1995. IX, 321 pages. 1995.

Vol. 1007: A. Bosselaers, B. Preneel (Eds.), Integrity Primitives for Secure Information Systems. VII, 239 pages. 1995.

Vol. 1008: B. Preneel (Ed.), Fast Software Encryption. Proceedings, 1994. VIII, 367 pages. 1995.

Vol. 1009: M. Broy, S. Jähnichen (Eds.), KORSO: Methods, Languages, and Tools for the Construction of Correct Software. X, 449 pages. 1995. Vol.

Vol. 1010: M. Veloso, A. Aamodt (Eds.), Case-Based Reasoning Research and Development. Proceedings, 1995. X, 576 pages. 1995. (Subseries LNAI).

Vol. 1011: T. Furuhashi (Ed.), Advances in Fuzzy Logic, Neural Networks and Genetic Algorithms. Proceedings, 1994. (Subseries LNAI).

Vol. 1012: M. Bartošek, J. Staudek, J. Wiedermann (Eds.), SOFSEM '95: Theory and Practice of Informatics. Proceedings, 1995. XI, 499 pages. 1995.

Vol. 1013: T.W. Ling, A.O. Mendelzon, L. Vieille (Eds.), Deductive and Object-Oriented Databases. Proceedings, 1995. XIV, 557 pages. 1995.

Vol. 1014: A.P. del Pobil, M.A. Serna, Spatial Representation and Motion Planning. XII, 242 pages. 1995.

Vol. 1015: B. Blumenthal, J. Gornostaev, C. Unger (Eds.), Human-Computer Interaction. Proceedings, 1995. VIII, 203 pages. 1995.

VOL. 1016: R. Cipolla, Active Visual Inference of Surface Shape. XII, 194 pages. 1995.

Vol. 1017: M. Nagl (Ed.), Graph-Theoretic Concepts in Computer Science. Proceedings, 1995. XI, 406 pages. 1995.

Vol. 1018: T.D.C. Little, R. Gusella (Eds.), Network and Operating Systems Support for Digital Audio and Video. Proceedings, 1995. XI, 357 pages. 1995.

Vol. 1019: E. Brinksma, W.R. Cleaveland, K.G. Larsen, T. Margaria, B. Steffen (Eds.), Tools and Algorithms for the Construction and Analysis of Systems. Selected Papers, 1995. VII, 291 pages. 1995.

Vol. 1020: I.D. Watson (Ed.), Progress in Case-Based Reasoning. Proceedings, 1995. VIII, 209 pages. 1995. (Subseries LNAI).

Vol. 1021: M.P. Papazoglou (Ed.), OOER '95: Object-Oriented and Entity-Relationship Modeling. Proceedings, 1995. XVII, 451 pages. 1995.

Vol. 1022: P.H. Hartel, R. Plasmeijer (Eds.), Functional Programming Languages in Education. Proceedings, 1995. X, 309 pages. 1995.

Vol. 1023: K. Kanchanasut, J.-J. Lévy (Eds.), Algorithms, Concurrency and Knowlwdge. Proceedings, 1995. X, 410 pages. 1995.

Vol. 1024: R.T. Chin, H.H.S. Ip, A.C. Naiman, T.-C. Pong (Eds.), Image Analysis Applications and Computer Graphics. Proceedings, 1995. XVI, 533 pages. 1995.

Vol. 1025: C. Boyd (Ed.), Cryptography and Coding. Proceedings, 1995. IX, 291 pages. 1995.

Vol. 1026: P.S. Thiagarajan (Ed.), Foundations of Software Technology and Theoretical Computer Science. Proceedings, 1995. XII, 515 pages. 1995.

Vol. 1027: F.J. Brandenburg (Ed.), Graph Drawing. Proceedings, 1995. XII, 526 pages. 1996.

Vol. 1028: N.R. Adam, Y. Yesha (Eds.), Electronic Commerce. X, 155 pages. 1996.

Vol. 1029: E. Dawson, J. Golić (Eds.), Cryptography: Policy and Algorithms. Proceedings, 1995. XI, 327 pages. 1996.

Vol. 1030: F. Pichler, R. Moreno-Díaz, R. Albrecht (Eds.), Computer Aided Systems Theory - EUROCAST '95. Proceedings, 1995. XII, 539 pages. 1996.

Vol. 1031: M. Toussaint (Ed.), Ada in Europe. Proceedings, 1995. XI, 455 pages. 1996.

Vol. 1032: P. Godefroid, Partial-Order Methods for the Verification of Concurrent Systems. IV, 143 pages. 1996.

Vol. 1033: C.-H. Huang, P. Sadayappan, U. Banerjee, D. Gelernter, A. Nicolau, D. Padua (Eds.), Languages and Compilers for Parallel Computing. Proceedings, 1995. XIII, 597 pages. 1996.

Vol. 1034: G. Kuper, M. Wallace (Eds.), Constraint Databases and Applications. Proceedings, 1995. VII, 185 pages. 1996.

Vol. 1035: S.Z. Li, D.P. Mital, E.K. Teoh, H. Wang (Eds.), Recent Developments in Computer Vision. Proceedings, 1995. XI, 604 pages. 1996.

Vol. 1036: G. Adorni, M. Zock (Eds.), Trends in Natural Language Generation - An Artificial Intelligence Perspective. Proceedings, 1993. IX, 382 pages. 1996. (Subseries LNAI).

Vol. 1037: M. Wooldridge, J.P. Müller, M. Tambe (Eds.), Intelligent Agents II. Proceedings, 1995. XVI, 437 pages. 1996. (Subseries LNAI).

Vol. 1038: W: Van de Velde, J.W. Perram (Eds.), Agents Breaking Away. Proceedings, 1996. XIV, 232 pages. 1996. (Subseries LNAI).

Vol. 1039: D. Gollmann (Ed.), Fast Software Encryption. Proceedings, 1996. X, 219 pages. 1996.

Vol. 1040: S. Wermter, E. Riloff, G. Scheler (Eds.), Connectionist, Statistical, and Symbolic Approaches to Learning for Natural Language Processing. IX, 468 pages. 1996. (Subseries LNAI).

Vol. 1041: J. Dongarra, K. Madsen, J. Waśniewski (Eds.), Applied Parallel Computing. Proceedings, 1995. XII, 562 pages. 1996.

Vol. 1042: G. Weiß, S. Sen (Eds.), Adaption and Learning in Multi-Agent Systems. Proceedings, 1995. X, 238 pages. 1996. (Subseries LNAI).

Vol. 1043: F. Moller, G. Birtwistle (Eds.), Logics for Concurrency. XI, 266 pages. 1996.

Vol. 1044: B. Plattner (Ed.), Broadband Communications. Proceedings, 1996. XIV, 359 pages. 1996.

Vol. 1045: B. Butscher, E. Moeller, H. Pusch (Eds.), Interactive Distributed Multimedia Systems and Services. Proceedings, 1996. XI, 333 pages. 1996.

Vol. 1046: C. Puech, R. Reischuk (Eds.), STACS 96. Proceedings, 1996. XII, 690 pages. 1996.

Vol. 1047: E. Hajnicz, Time Structures. IX, 244 pages. 1996. (Subseries LNAI).

Vol. 1048: M. Proietti (Ed.), Logic Program Syynthesis and Transformation. Proceedings, 1995. X, 267 pages. 1996.

Vol. 1049: K. Futatsugi, S. Matsuoka (Eds.), Object Technologies for Advanced Software. Proceedings, 1996. X, 309 pages. 1996.

Vol. 1050: R. Dyckhoff, H. Herre, P. Schroeder-Heister (Eds.), Extensions of Logic Programming. Proceedings, 1996. VII, 318 pages. 1996. (Subseries LNAI).

Vol. 1051: M.-C. Gaudel, J. Woodcock (Eds.), FME'96: Industrial Benefit and Advances in Formal Methods. Proceedings, 1996. XII, 704 pages. 1996.

Vol. 1052: D. Hutchison, H. Christiansen, G. Coulson, A. Danthine (Eds.), Teleservices and Multimedia Communications. Proceedings, 1995. XII, 277 pages. 1996.

Vol. 1053: P. Graf, Term Indexing. XVI, 284 pages. 1996. (Subseries LNAI).

Vol. 1054: A. Ferreira, P. Pardalos (Eds.), Solving Combinatorial Optimization Problems in Parallel. VII, 274 pages. 1996.

Vol. 1055: T. Margaria, B. Steffen (Eds.), Tools and Algorithms for the Construction and Analysis of Systems. Proceedings, 1996. XI, 435 pages. 1996.

Vol. 1056: A. Haddadi, Communication and Cooperation in Agent Systems. XIII, 148 pages. 1996. (Subseries LNAI).

Vol. 1057: P. Apers, M. Bouzeghoub, G. Gardarin (Eds.), Advances in Database Technology — EDBT '96. Proceedings, 1996. XII, 636 pages. 1996.

Vol. 1058: H. R. Nielson (Ed.), Programming Languages and Systems – ESOP '96. Proceedings, 1996. X, 405 pages. 1996.

Vol. 1059: H. Kirchner (Ed.), Trees in Algebra and Programming – CAAP '96. Proceedings, 1996. VIII, 331 pages. 1996.

Vol. 1060: T. Gyimóthy (Ed.), Compiler Construction. Proceedings, 1996. X, 355 pages. 1996.

Vol. 1061: P. Ciancarini, C. Hankin (Eds.), Coordination Languages and Models. Proceedings, 1996. XI, 443 pages. 1996.

Vol. 1062: E. Sanchez, M. Tomassini (Eds.), Towards Evolvable Hardware. IX, 265 pages. 1996.

Vol. 1063: J.-M. Alliot, E. Lutton, E. Ronald, M. Schoenauer, D. Snyers (Eds.), Artificial Evolution. Proceedings, 1995. XIII, 396 pages. 1996.

Vol. 1064: B. Buxton, R. Cipolla (Eds.), Computer Vision – ECCV '96. Volume I. Proceedings, 1996. XXI, 725 pages. 1996.

Vol. 1065: B. Buxton, R. Cipolla (Eds.), Computer Vision – ECCV '96. Volume II. Proceedings, 1996. XXI, 723 pages. 1996.

Vol. 1066: R. Alur, T.A. Henzinger, E.D. Sontag (Eds.), Hybrid Systems III. IX, 618 pages. 1996.

Vol. 1067: H. Liddell, A. Colbrook, B. Hertzberger, P. Sloot (Eds.), High-Performance Computing and Networking. Proceedings, 1996. XXV, 1040 pages. 1996.

Vol. 1068: T. Ito, R.H. Halstead, Jr., C. Queinnec (Eds.), Parallel Symbolic Languages and Systems. Proceedings, 1995. X, 363 pages. 1996.

Vol. 1069: J.W. Perram, J.-P. Müller (Eds.), Distributed Software Agents and Applications. Proceedings, 1994. VIII, 219 pages. 1996. (Subseries LNAI).

Vol. 1070: U. Maurer (Ed.), Advances in Cryptology – EUROCRYPT '96. Proceedings, 1996. XII, 417 pages. 1996.

Vol. 1071: P. Miglioli, U. Moscato, D. Mundici, M. Ornaghi (Eds.), Theorem Proving with Analytic Tableaux and Related Methods. Proceedings, 1996. X, 330 pages. 1996. (Subseries LNAI).